Pseudodoxia Epidemica:

Or

Enquiries into
Commonly Presumed Truths

1672

Sir Thomas Browne

CONTENTS

The First Book: Containing the General Part

The Second Book:
Of sundry popular Tenents concerning Minerall, and
vegetable bodies, generally held for trueth, which examined,
prove either false, or dubious

The Third Book:
Of divers popular and received Tenents concerning Animals, which examined, prove either false or dubious

The Fourth Book:
Of many popular and received Tenents concerning Man.

The Fifth Book:
Of many things questionable as they are commonly described in Pictures

1. Sundry divinations vulgarly raised upon spots in our nails.
2. That Children would naturally speak Hebrew.
3. Of refraining to kill Swallows.
4. Of lights burning dimme at the apparition of spirits.
5. Of the wearing of Corall.
6. Of Moses his rod in the discovery of Mines.
7. Of discovering of doubtfull matters by booke or staffe.
8. Of the nominall observation of the severall daies of the week.
9. Of many other.

The Sixth Book:
Concerning Sundry Tenents Geographicall and Historicall.

The Seventh Book:
Concerning many Historicall Tenents generally received, and some deduced from the History of Holy Scripture.

1. Of the woman that conceived in a Bathe.

2. Of Crassus that never laughed but once.

3. That our Saviour never laughed.

4. Of Sergius the second, or Bocca *de Porco*.

5. That Tamerlane was a Scythian shepheard.

TO THE READER

Would truth dispense, we could be content, with Plato, that knowledge were but remembrance; that intellectual acquisition were but reminiscential evocation, and new Impressions but the colouring of old stamps which stood pale in the soul before. For what is worse, knowledge is made by oblivion, and to purchase a clear and warrantable body of Truth, we must forget and part with much we know. Our tender Enquiries taking up Learning at large, and together with true and assured notions, receiving many, wherein our reviewing judgments do find no satisfaction. And therefore in this *Encyclopædie* and round of Knowledge, like the great and exemplary Wheels of Heaven, we must observe two Circles: that while we are daily carried about, and whirled on by the swindge and rapt of the one, we may maintain a natural and proper course, in the slow and sober wheel of the other. And this we shall more readily perform, if we timely survey our knowledge; impartially singling out those encroachments, which junior compliance and popular credulity hath admitted. Whereof at present we have endeavoured a long and serious *Adviso*; proposing not only a large and copious List, but from experience and reason attempting their decisions.

And first we crave exceeding pardon in the audacity of the Attempt, humbly acknowledging a work of such concernment unto truth, and difficulty in it self, did well deserve the conjunction of many heads. And surely more advantageous had it been unto Truth, to have fallen into the endeavors of some co-operating advancers, that might have performed it to the life, and added authority thereto; which the privacy of our condition, and unequal abilities cannot expect. Whereby notwithstanding we have not been diverted; nor have our solitary attempts been so discouraged, as to despair the favourable look of Learning upon our single and unsupported endeavours.

Nor have we let fall our Pen, upon discouragement of Contradiction, Unbelief and Difficulty of disswasion from radicated beliefs, and points of high prescription, although we are very sensible, how hardly teaching years do learn, what roots old age contracteth unto errors, and how such as are but acorns in our younger brows, grow Oaks in our elder heads, and become inflexible unto the powerfullest arm of reason. Although we have also beheld, what cold requitals others have found in their several redemptions of Truth; and how their ingenuous Enquiries have been dismissed with censure, and obloquie of singularities.

Some consideration we hope from the course of our Profession, which though it leadeth us into many truths that pass undiscerned by others, yet doth it disturb their Communications, and much interrupt the office of our Pens in their well intended Transmissions. And therefore surely in this work attempts will exceed performances; it being composed by snatches of time, as medical vacations, and the fruitless importunity of *Uroscopy* would permit us. And therefore also, perhaps it hath not found that regular and constant stile, those infallible experiments and those assured determinations, which the subject sometime requireth, and might be expected from others, whose quiet doors and unmolested hours afford no such distractions. Although whoever shall indifferently perpend the exceeding difficulty, which either the obscurity of the subject, or unavoidable paradoxology must often put upon the Attemptor, he will easily discern, a work of this nature is not to be performed upon one legg; and should smel of oyl, if duly and deservedly handled.

Our first intentions considering the common interest of Truth, resolved to propose it unto the Latine republique and equal Judges of *Europe*, but owing in the first place this service unto our Country, and therein especially unto its ingenuous Gentry, we have declared our self in a language best conceived. Although I confess the quality of the Subject will sometimes carry us into expressions beyond meer English apprehensions. And indeed, if elegancy still proceedeth, and English Pens maintain that stream, we have of late observed to flow from many; we shall within few years be fain to learn Latine to understand English, and a work will prove of equal facility in either. Nor have we addressed our Pen or Stile unto the people, (whom Books do not redress, and are this way incapable of reduction) but unto the knowing and leading part of Learning. As well understanding (at least probably hoping) except they be watered from higher regions, and fructifying meteors of Knowledge, these weeds must lose their alimental sap, and wither of themselves. Whose conserving influence, could our endeavours prevent, we should trust the rest unto the sythe of *Time*, and hopefull dominion of Truth.

We hope it would not be unconsidered, that we find no open tract, or constant manuduction in this Labyrinth; but are oft-times fain to wander in the *America* and untravelled parts of Truth. For though not many years past, Dr. *Primrose* hath made a learned Discourse of vulgar Errors in Physick, yet have we discussed but two or three thereof. *Scipio Mercurii* hath also left an excellent tract in *Italian*, concerning popular Errors; but confining himself only unto those in Physick, he hath little conduced unto the generality of our doctrine. *Laurentius Joubertus*, by the same Title led our expectation into thoughts of great relief; whereby notwithstanding we reaped no advantage; it answering scarce at all the promise of the inscription. Nor perhaps (if it were yet extant) should we find any farther Assistance from that ancient piece of *Andreas*, pretending the same Title. And therefore we are often constrained to stand alone against the strength of opinion, and to meet the *Goliah* and Giant of Authority, with contemptible pibbles, and feeble arguments, drawn from the scrip and slender stock of our selves. Nor have we indeed scarce named any Author whose name we do not honour; and if detraction could invite us, discretion surely would contain us from any derogatory intention, where highest Pens and friendliest eloquence must fail in commendation.

And therefore also we cannot but hope the equitable considerations, and candour of reasonable minds. We cannot expect the frown of *Theology* herein; nor can they which behold the present state of things, and controversie of points so long received in Divinity, condemn our sober Enquiries in the doubtfull appertinancies of Arts, and Receptaries of Philosophy. Surely Philologers and Critical Discoursers, who look beyond the shell and obvious exteriors of things, will not be angry with our narrower explorations. And we cannot doubt, our Brothers in Physick (whose knowledge in Naturals will lead them into a nearer apprehension of many things delivered) will friendly accept, if not countenance our endeavours. Nor can we conceive it may be unwelcome unto those honoured Worthies, who endeavour the advancement of Learning: as being likely to find a clearer progression, when so many rubs are levelled, and many untruths taken off, which passing as principles with common beliefs, disturb the tranquility of Axioms, which otherwise might be raised. And wise men cannot but know, that arts and learning want this expurgation: and if the course of truth be permitted unto its self, like that of time and uncorrected computations, it cannot escape many errors, which duration still enlargeth.

Lastly, we are not Magisterial in opinions, nor have we Dictator-like obtruded our conceptions; but in the humility of Enquiries or disquisitions, have only proposed them unto more ocular discerners. And therefore opinions are free, and open it is for any to think or declare the contrary. And we shall so far encourage contradiction, as to promise no disturbance, or re-oppose any Pen, that shall Fallaciously or captiously refute us; that shall only lay hold of our lapses, single out Digressions, Corollaries, or Ornamental conceptions, to evidence his own in as indifferent truths. And shall only take notice of such, whose experimental and judicious knowledge shall solemnly look upon it; not only to destroy of ours, but to establish of his own; not to traduce or extenuate, but to explain and dilucidate, to add and ampliate, according to the laudable custom of the Ancients in their sober promotions of Learning. Unto whom notwithstanding, we shall not contentiously rejoin, or only to justifie our own, but to applaud or confirm his maturer assertions; and shall confer what is in us unto his name and honour; Ready to be swallowed in any worthy enlarger: as having acquired our end, if any way, or under any name we may obtain a work, so much desired, and yet desiderated of Truth.

Thomas Browne.

The Postscript

Readers,

To enform you of the Advantages of the present Impreßion, and disabuse your expectations of any future Enlargements; these are to advertise thee, that this Edition comes forth with very many Explanations, Additions, and Alterations throughout, besides that of one entire Chapter: But that now this Work is compleat and perfect, expect no further Additions.

THE
FIRST BOOK:
OR
GENERAL PART

CHAPTER I

Of the Causes of Common Errors

The first and Father-cause of common Error, is, The common infirmity of Human Nature; of whose deceptible condition, although perhaps there should not need any other eviction, than the frequent Errors we shall our selves commit, even in the express declarement hereof: yet shall we illustrate the same from more infallible constitutions, and persons presumed as far from us in condition, as time, that is, our first and ingenerated forefathers. From whom as we derive our Being, and the several wounds of constitution; so, may we in some manner excuse our infirmities in the depravity of those parts, whose Traductions were pure in them, and their Originals but once removed from God. Who notwithstanding (if posterity may take leave to judg of the fact, as they are assured to suffer in the punishment) were grosly deceived, in their perfection; and so weakly deluded in the clarity of their understanding, that it hath left no small obscurity in ours, How error should gain upon them.

For first, They were deceived by Satan; and that not in an invisible insinuation, but an open and discoverable apparition, that is, in the form of a Serpent; whereby although there were many occasions of suspition, and such as could not easily escape a weaker circumspection, yet did the unwary apprehension of *Eve* take no advantage thereof. It hath therefore seemed strange unto some, she should be deluded by a Serpent, or subject her reason to a beast, which God had subjected unto hers. It hath empuzzled the enquiries of others to apprehend, and enforced them unto strange conceptions, to make out, how without fear or doubt she could discourse with such a creature, or hear a Serpent speak, without suspition of Imposture. The wits of others have been so bold, as to accuse her simplicity, in receiving his Temptation so coldly; and when such specious effects of the fruit were Promised, as to make them like God; not to desire, at least not to wonder he pursued not that benefit himself. And had it been their own case, would perhaps have replied. If the tast of this Fruit maketh the eaters like *Gods*, why remainest thou a Beast? If it maketh us but *like Gods*, we are so already. If thereby our eyes shall be opened hereafter, they are at present quick enough, to discover thy deceit; and we desire them no opener, to behold our own shame. If to know good and evil be our advantage, although we have Free-will unto both, we desire to perform but one; We know 'tis good to obey the commandment of God, but evil if we transgress it.

They were deceived by one another, and in the greatest disadvantage of Delusion, that is, the stronger by the weaker: For *Eve* presented the Fruit, and *Adam* received it from her. Thus the *Serpent* was cunning enough, to begin the deceit in the weaker, and the weaker of strength, sufficient to consummate the fraud in the stronger. Art and fallacy was used unto her; a naked offer proved sufficient unto him: So his superstruction was his Ruine, and the fertility of his Sleep an issue of Death unto him. And although the condition of Sex, and posteriority of Creation, might somewhat extenuate the Error of the Woman: Yet was it very strange and inexcusable in the Man; especially, if as some affirm, he was the wisest of all men since; or if, as others have conceived, he was not ignorant of the Fall of the Angels, and had thereby Example and punishment to deterr him.

They were deceived from themselves, and their own apprehensions; For *Eve* either mistook, or traduced the commandment of God: *Of every Tree of the Garden thou mayest freely eat, but of the Tree of knowledg of good and evil thou shalt not eat: for in the day thou eatest thereof, thou shalt surely die.* Now *Eve* upon the question of the *Serpent*, returned the Precept in different terms: *You shall not eat of it, neither shall you touch it, lest perhaps you die.* In which delivery, there were no less than two mistakes, or rather additional mendacities; for the Commandment forbad not the touch of the Fruit; and positively said, *Ye shall surely die*: but she extenuating, replied, *ne fortè moriamini, lest perhaps ye die.* For so in the vulgar translation it runneth, and so it is expressed in the *Thargum* or paraphrase of *Jonathan.* And therefore although it be said, and that very truely, *that the Devil was a lyer from the beginning*, yet was the Woman herein the

4

first express beginner: and falsified twice, before the reply of *Satan*. And therefore also, to speak strictly, the sin of the Fruit was not the first Offence: They first transgressed the Rule of their own Reason; and after the Commandment of God.

They were deceived through the Conduct of their Senses, and by Temptations from the Object it self; whereby although their intellectuals had not failed in the Theory of truth, yet did the inservient and brutal Faculties controll the suggestion of Reason: Pleasure and Profit already overswaying the instructions of Honesty, and Sensuality perturbing the reasonable commands of Vertue. For so it is delivered in the Text: That when the Woman saw, *that the Tree was good for food*, and *that it was pleasant unto the eye*, and *a Tree to be desired to make one wise, she took of the fruit thereof and did eat.* Now hereby it appeareth, that *Eve*, before the Fall, was by the same and beaten way of allurements inveigled, whereby her posterity hath been deluded ever since; that is, those three delivered by St. *John, The lust of the flesh, the lust of the eye, and the pride of life*: Wherein indeed they seemed as weakly to fail, as their debilitated posterity, ever after. Whereof notwithstanding, some in their imperfection, have resisted more powerful temptations; and in many moralities condemned the facility of their seductions.

Again, they might, for ought we know, be still deceived in the unbelief of their Mortality, even after they had eat of the Fruit: For, *Eve* observing no immediate execution of the Curse, she delivered the Fruit unto *Adam*: who, after the tast thereof, perceiving himself still to live, might yet remain in doubt, whether he had incurred Death; which perhaps he did not indubitably believe, until he was after convicted in the visible example of *Abel*. For he that would not believe the Menace of God at first, it may be doubted whether, before an ocular example, he believed the Curse at last. And therefore they are not without all reason, who have disputed the Fact of *Cain*: that is, although he purposed to do mischief, whether he intended to kill his Brother; or designed that, whereof he had not beheld an example in his own kind. There might be somewhat in it, that he would not have done, or desired undone, when he brake forth as desperately, as before he had done uncivilly, *My iniquity is greater than can be forgiven me.*

Some nicities I confess there are which extenuate, but many more that aggravate this Delusion; which exceeding the bounds of this

Discourse, and perhaps our Satisfaction, we shall at present pass over. And therefore whether the Sin of our First Parents were the greatest of any since; whether the transgression of *Eve* seducing, did not exceed that of *Adam* seduced; or whether the resistibility of His Reason, did not equivalence the facility of her Seduction; we shall refer it to the *Schoolman*; Whether there was not in *Eve* as great injustice in deceiving her husband, as imprudence in being deceived her self; especially, if foretasting the Fruit, her eyes were opened before his, and she knew the effect of it, before he tasted of it; we leave it unto the *Moralist*. Whether the whole relation be not Allegorical, that is, whether the temptation of the Man by the Woman, be not the seduction of the rational and higher parts by the inferiour and feminine faculties: or whether the Tree in the midst of the Garden, were not that part in the Center of the body, in which was afterward the appointment of Circumcision in Males, we leave it unto the *Thalmudist*. Whether there were any Policy in the Devil to tempt them before the Conjunction, or whether the Issue before tentation, might in justice have suffered with those after, we leave it unto the *Lawyer*. Whether *Adam* foreknew the advent of Christ, or the reparation of his Error by his Saviour; how the execution of the Curse should have been ordered, if, after *Eve* had eaten, *Adam* had yet refused. Whether if they had tasted the Tree of life, before that of Good and Evil, they had yet suffered the curse of Mortality: or whether the efficacy of the one had not over-powred the penalty of the other, we leave it unto GOD. For he alone can truly determine these, and all things else; Who as he hath proposed the World unto our disputation, so hath he reserved many things unto his own resolution; whose determination we cannot hope from flesh, but must with reverence suspend unto that great Day, whose justice shall either condemn our curiosities, or resolve our disquisitions.

Lastly, Man was not only deceivable in his Integrity, but the Angels of light in all their Clarity. He that said, He would be like the highest did Erre, if in some way he conceived himself so already: but in attempting so high an effect from himself, he mis-understood the nature of God, and held a false apprehension of his own; whereby vainly attempting not only insolencies, but impossibilities, he deceived himself as low as Hell. In brief, there is nothing infallible but GOD, who cannot possibly Erre. For things are really true as they correspond unto His conception; and have so much verity as they hold of conformity unto that Intellect, in whose *Idea* they had their first determinations. And therefore being the Rule, he cannot be Irregular;

nor, being Truth it self, conceavably admit the impossible society of Error. .

CHAPTER II

A further Illustration of the same

Being thus deluded before the Fall, it is no wonder if their conceptions were deceitful, and could scarce speak without an Error after. For, what is very remarkable (and no man that I know hath yet observed) in the relations of Scripture before the Flood, there is but one speech delivered by Man, wherein there is not an erroneous conception; and, strictly examined, most hainously injurious unto truth. The pen of *Moses* is brief in the account before the Flood, and the speeches recorded are but six. The first is that of *Adam*, when upon the expostulation of God, he replied; *I heard thy voice in the Garden, and because I was naked I hid my self.* In which reply, there was included a very gross Mistake, and, if with pertinacity maintained, a high and capital Error. For thinking by this retirement to obscure himself from God, he infringed the omnisciency and essential Ubiquity of his Maker. Who as he created all things, so is he beyond and in them all, not only in power, as under his subjection, or in his presence, as being in his cognition; but in his very Essence, as being the soul of their causalities, and the essential cause of their existencies. Certainly, his posterity at this distance and after so perpetuated an impairment, cannot but condemn the poverty of his conception, that thought to obscure himself from his Creator in the shade of the Garden, who had beheld him before in the darkness of his Chaos, and the great obscurity of Nothing; that thought to fly from God, which could not fly himself; or imagined that one tree should conceal his nakedness from Gods eye, as another had revealed it unto his own. Those tormented Spirits that wish the mountains to cover them, have fallen upon desires of minor absurdity, and chosen ways of less improbable concealment. Though this be also as ridiculous unto reason, as fruitless unto their desires; for he that laid the foundations of the Earth, cannot be excluded the secrecy of the Mountains; nor can there any thing escape the perspicacity of those eyes which were before light, and in whose opticks there is no opacity. This is the consolation of all good men, unto whom his Ubiquity affordeth continual comfort and security: And this is the affliction of Hell, unto whom it affordeth despair, and remediless calamity. For those restless Spirits that fly the face of the Almighty, being deprived the fruition of his eye, would also avoid the extent of his hand; which being impossible, their sufferings are desperate, and their afflictions without evasion; until they can get out of *Trismegistus* his Circle, that is, to extend their wings above the Universe, and pitch beyond Ubiquity.

The Second is that speech of *Adam* unto God: *The woman whom thou gavest me to be with me, she gave me of the Tree, and I did eat.* This indeed was an unsatisfactory reply, and therein was involved a very impious Error, as implying God the Author of sin, and accusing his Maker of his transgression. As if he had said, If thou hadst not given me a woman, I had not been deceived: Thou promisedst to make her a help, but she hath proved a destruction unto me: Had I remained alone, I had not sinned; but thou gavest me a Consort, and so I became seduced. This was a bold and open accusation of God, making the fountain of good, the contriver of evil, and the forbidder of the crime an abettor of the fact prohibited. Surely, his mercy was great that did not revenge the impeachment of his justice; And his goodness to be admired, that it refuted not his argument in the punishment of his excusation, and only pursued the first transgression without a penalty of this the second.

The third was that of *Eve*; *The Serpent beguiled me, and I did eat.* In which reply, there was not only a very feeble excuse, but an erroneous translating her own offence upon another; Extenuating her sin from that which was an aggravation, that is, to excuse the Fact at all, much more upon the suggestion of a beast, which was before in the strictest terms prohibited by her God. For although we now do hope the mercies of God, will consider our degenerated integrities unto some minoration of our offences; yet had not the sincerity of our first parents so colourable expectations, unto whom the commandment was but single, and their integrities best able to resist the motions of its transgression. And therefore so heinous conceptions have risen hereof, that some have seemed more angry there-with, than God himself: Being so exasperated with the offence, as to call in question their salvation, and to dispute the eternal punishment of their Maker. Assuredly with better reason may posterity accuse them than they the Serpent or one another; and the displeasure of the *Pelagians* must needs be irreconcilable, who peremptorily maintaining they can fulfil the whole Law, will insatisfactorily condemn the non-observation of one.

The fourth, was that speech of *Cain* upon the demand of God, *Where is thy brother?* and he said, *I know not.* In which Negation, beside the open impudence, there was implied a notable Error; for returning a lie unto his Maker, and presuming in this manner to put off the Searcher of hearts, he denied the omnisciency of God, whereunto there is nothing concealable. The answer of Satan in the case of *Job*, had more of truth, wisdom, and Reverence, than this; *Whence comest thou Satan?* and he said, *From compassing of the Earth.* For though an enemy of God, and hater of all Truth, his wisdom will hardly permit him to falsifie with the All-mighty. For well understanding the Omniscience of his nature, he is not so ready to deceive himself, as to falsifie unto him whose cognition is no way deludable. And therefore when in the tentation of Christ he played upon the fallacy, and thought to deceive the Author of Truth, the Method of this proceeding arose from the uncertainty of his Divinity; whereof had he remained assured, he had continued silent; nor would his discretion attempt so unsucceedable a temptation. And so again at the last day, when our offences shall be drawn into accompt, the subtility of that Inquisitor shall not present unto God a bundle of calumnies or confutable accusations, but will discreetly offer up unto his Omnisciency, a true and undeniable list of our transgressions.

The fifth is another reply of *Cain* upon the denouncement of his curse, *My iniquity is greater than can be forgiven:* For so it is expressed in some Translations. The assertion was not only desperate, but the conceit erroneous, overthrowing that glorious Attribute of God, his Mercy, and conceiving the sin of murder unpardonable. Which how great soever, is not above the repentance of man, but far below the mercies of God, and was (as some conceive) expiated in that punishment he suffered temporally for it. There are but two examples of this error in holy Scripture, and they both for Murder, and both as it were of the same person; for Christ was mystically slain in *Abel*, and therefore *Cain* had some influence on his death as well as *Judas*; but the sin had a different effect on *Cain*, from that it had on *Judas*; and

10

most that since have fallen into it. For they like *Judas* desire death, and not unfrequently pursue it: *Cain* on the contrary grew afraid thereof, and obtained a securement from it. Assuredly, if his dispair continued, there was punishment enough in life, and Justice sufficient in the mercy of his protection. For the life of the desperate equalls the anxieties of death; who in uncessant inquietudes but act the life of the damned, and anticipate the desolations of Hell. 'Tis indeed a sin in man, but a punishment only in Devils, who offend not God but afflict themselves, in the appointed despair of his mercies. And as to be without hope is the affliction of the damned, so is it the happiness of the blessed; who having all their expectations present, are not distracted with futurities: So is it also their felicity to have no Faith; for enjoying the beatifical vision, there is nothing unto them inevident; and in the fruition of the object of Faith, they have received the full evacuation of it.

The last speech was that of *Lamech, I have slain a man to my wound, and a young man to my hurt*: If *Cain* be avenged seven fold, truly *Lamech* seventy and seven fold. Now herein there seems to be a very erroneous Illation: from the Indulgence of God unto *Cain*, concluding an immunity unto himself; that is, a regular protection from a single example, and an exemption from punishment in a fact that naturally deserved it. The Error of this offender was contrary to that of *Cain*, whom the *Rabbins* conceive that *Lamech* at this time killed. He despaired in Gods mercy in the same Fact, where this presumed of it; he by a decollation of all hope annihilated his mercy, this by an immoderancy thereof destroyed his Justice. Though the sin were less, the Error was as great; For as it is untrue, that his mercy will not forgive offenders, or his benignity co-operate to their conversions; So is it also of no less falsity to affirm His justice will not exact account of sinners, or punish such as continue in their transgressions.

Thus may we perceive, how weakly our Fathers did Erre before the Floud, how continually and upon common discourse they fell upon Errors after; it is therefore no wonder we have been erroneous ever since. And being now at greatest distance from the beginning of Error, are almost lost in its dissemination, whose waies are boundless, and confess no circumscription.

CHAPTER III

Of the second cause of Popular Errors; the erroneous disposition of the People.

Having thus declared the fallible nature of Man even from his first production, we have beheld the general cause of Error. But as for popular Errors, they are more neerly founded upon an erroneous inclination of the people; as being the most deceptable part of Mankind and ready with open armes to receive the encroachments of Error. Which condition of theirs although deducible from many Grounds, yet shall we evidence it but from a few, and such as most neerly and undeniably declare their natures.

How unequal discerners of truth they are, and openly exposed unto Error, will first appear from their unqualified intellectuals, unable to umpire the difficulty of its dissensions. For Error, to speak largely, is a false judgment of things, or an essent unto falsity. Now whether the object whereunto they deliver up their assent be true or false, they are incompetent judges.

For the assured truth of things is derived from the principles of knowledg, and causes which determine their verities. Whereof their uncultivated understandings, scarce holding any theory, they are but bad discerners of verity; and in the numerous track of Error, but casually do hit the point and unity of truth.

Their understanding is so feeble in the discernment of falsities, and averting the Errors of reason, that it submitteth unto the fallacies of sense, and is unable to rectifie the Error of its sensations. Thus the greater part of Mankind having but one eye of Sense and Reason, conceive the Earth far bigger than the Sun, the fixed Stars lesser than the Moon, their figures plain, and their spaces from Earth equidistant. For thus their Sense informeth them, and herein their reason cannot Rectifie them; and therefore hopelessly continuing in mistakes, they live and die in their absurdities; passing their days in perverted apprehensions, and conceptions of the World, derogatory unto God, and the wisdom of the Creation.

Again, being so illiterate in the point of intellect, and their sense so incorrected, they are farther indisposed ever to attain unto truth; as commonly proceeding in those wayes, which have most reference unto sense, and wherein there lyeth most notable and popular delusion.

For being unable to wield the intellectuall arms of reason, they are fain to betake themselves unto wasters, and the blunter weapons of truth: affecting the gross and sensible ways of Doctrin, and such as will not consist with strict and subtile Reason. Thus unto them a piece of Rhetorick is a sufficient argument of Logick; an Apologue of *Esop*, beyond a Syllogism in *Barbara*; parables than propositions, and proverbs more powerful than demonstrations. And therefore are they led rather by Example, than Precept; receiving perswasions from visible inducements, before intellectual instructions. And therefore also they judg of human actions by the event; for being uncapable of operable circumstances, or rightly to judg the prudentiality of affairs, they only gaze upon the visible success, and thereafter condemn or cry up the whole progression. And so from this ground in the Lecture of holy Scripture, their apprehensions are commonly confined unto the literal sense of the Text; from whence have ensued the gross and duller sort of Heresies. For not attaining the deuteroscopy, and second intention of the words, they are fain to omit their Superconsequencies, Coherencies, Figures, or Tropologies; and are not sometime perswaded by fire beyond their literalities. And therefore also things invisible, but unto intellectual discernments, to humour the grosness of their comprehensions, have been degraded from their proper forms, and God himself dishonoured into manual expressions. And so likewise being unprovided, or unsufficient for higher speculations, they will alwayes betake themselves unto sensible representations, and can hardly be restrained the dulness of Idolatry. A sin or folly not only derogatory unto God but men; overthrowing their Reason, as well as his Divinity. In brief, a reciprocation, or rather, an inversion of the Creation, making God one way, as he made us another; that is, after our Image, as he made us after His own.

Moreover, their understanding thus weak in it self, and perverted by sensible delusions, is yet farther impaired by the dominion of their appetite; that is, the irrational and brutal part of the soul, which lording it over the soveraign faculty, interrupts the actions of that noble part, and choaks those tender sparks, which *Adam* hath left them of reason. And therefore they do not only swarm with Errors, but vices depending thereon. Thus they commonly affect no man any further than he deserts his reason, or complies with their aberrancies. Hence they imbrace not vertue for it self, but its reward; and the argument from pleasure or Utility is far more powerful, than that from vertuous Honesty: which *Mahomet* and his contrivers well understood, when he set out the felicity of his Heaven, by the contentments of flesh, and the delights of sense, slightly passing over the accomplishment of the Soul, and the beatitude of that part which Earth and visibilities too weakly affect. But the wisdom of our Saviour, and the simplicity of his truth proceeded another way; defying the popular provisions of happiness from sensible expectations; placing his felicity in things removed from sense, and the intellectual enjoyment of God. And therefore the doctrine of the one was never affraid of Universities, or endeavoured the banishment of learning, like the other. And though *Galen* doth sometimes nibble at *Moses*, and, beside the Apostate Christian, some *Heathens* have questioned his Philosophical part, or treaty of the Creation: Yet is there surely no reasonable *Pagan*, that will not admire the rational and well grounded precepts of Christ; whose life, as it was conformable unto his Doctrine, so was that unto the highest rules of Reason; and must therefore flourish in the advancement of learning, and the perfection of parts best able to comprehend it.

Again, Their individual imperfections being great, they are moreover enlarged by their aggregation; and being erroneous in their single numbers, once hudled together, they will be Error it self. For being a confusion of knaves and fools, and a farraginous concurrence of all conditions, tempers, sexes, and ages; it is but natural if their determinations be monstrous, and many waies inconsistent with Truth. And therefore wise men have alwaies applauded their own judgment, in the contradiction of that of the People; and their soberest adversaries, have ever afforded them the stile of fools and mad men; and, to speak impartially, their actions have made good these *Epithets*. Had

Orestes been Judge, he would not have acquitted that *Lystrian* rabble of madness, who, upon a visible miracle, falling into so high a conceit of *Paul* and *Barnabas*, that they termed the one *Jupiter*, the other *Mercurius*; that they brought Oxen and Garlands, and were hardly restrained from sacrificing unto them; did notwithstanding suddenly after fall upon *Paul*, and having stoned him drew him for dead out of the City. It might have hazzarded the sides of *Democritus*, had he been present at that tumult of *Demetrius*; when the people flocking together in great numbers, some crying one thing, and some another, and the assembly was confused, and the most part knew not wherefore they were come together; notwithstanding, all with one voice for the space of two hours cried out, Great is *Diana* of the *Ephesians*. It had overcome the patience of *Job*, as it did the meekness of *Moses*, and would surely have mastered any, but the longanimity, and lasting sufferance of God; had they beheld the Mutiny in the wilderness, when, after ten great Miracles in *Egypt*, and some in the same place, they melted down their stoln ear-rings into a Calf, and monstrously cryed out; *These are thy Gods*, O Israel, *that brought thee out of the land of* Egypt. It much accuseth the impatience of *Peter*, who could not endure the staves of the multitude, and is the greatest example of lenity in our Saviour, when he desired of God forgiveness unto those, who having one day brought him into the City in triumph, did presently after, act all dishonour upon him, and nothing could be heard but, *Crucifige*, in their Courts. Certainly he that considereth these things in Gods peculiar people, will easily discern how little of truth there is in the waies of the Multitude; and though sometimes they are flattered with that *Aphorism*, will hardly believe, The voice of the people to be the voice of God.

Lastly, being thus divided from truth in themselves, they are yet farther removed by advenient deception. For true it is (and I hope I shall not offend their vulgarities,) if I say, they are daily mocked into Error by subtler devisors, and have been expressly deluded by all professions and ages. Thus the *Priests* of Elder time, have put upon them many incredible conceits, not only deluding their apprehensions with Ariolation, South-saying, and such oblick Idolatries, but winning their credulities unto the literal and down-right adorement of Cats, Lizzards, and Beetles. And thus also in some Christian Churches, wherein is presumed an irreprovable truth, if all be true that is suspected, or half what is related; there have not wanted many strange deceptions, and some thereof are still confessed by the name of Pious Frauds. Thus

Theudas an Impostor was able to lead away Four thousand into the Wilderness, and the delusions of *Mahomet* almost the fourth part of Mankind. Thus all Heresies, how gross soever, have found a welcome with the people. For thus, many of the Jews were wrought into belief that *Herod* was the *Messias*; and *David George* of *Leyden and Arden*, were not without a party amongst the people, who maintained the same opinion of themselves almost in our days.

Physitians (many at least that make profession thereof) beside divers less discoverable wayes of fraud, have made them believe, there is the book of fate, or the power of *Aarons* brest plate, in Urins. And therefore hereunto they have recourse, as unto the Oracle of life, the great determinator of Virginity, Conception, Fertility, and the Inscrutable infirmities of the whole Body. For as though there were a seminality in Urine, or that, like the Seed, it carried with it the *Idea* of every part, they foolishly conceive, we visibly behold therein the Anatomy of every particle, and can thereby indigitate their Diseases: And running into any demands, expect from us a sudden resolution in things, whereon the Devil of *Delphos* would demurr; and we know hath taken respite of some dayes to answer easier questions.

Saltimbancoes, *Quacksalvers*, and *Charlatans*, deceive them in lower degrees. Were *Esop* alive, the *Piazza* and *Pont-Neuf* could not speak their fallacies; mean while there are too many, whose cries cannot conceal their mischief. For their Impostures are full of cruelty, and worse than any other; deluding not only unto pecuniary defraudations, but the irreparable deceit of death.

Astrologers, which pretend to be of *Cabala* with the Starrs (such I mean as abuse that worthy Enquiry) have not been wanting in their deceptions; who having won their belief unto principles whereof they make great doubt themselves, have made them believe that arbitrary events below, have necessary causes, above; whereupon their credulities assent unto any Prognosticks, and daily swallow the Predictions of men, which, considering the independency of their causes, and contingency in their Events, are only in the prescience of God.

Fortune-tellers, Juglers, Geomancers, and the like incantory Impostors, though commonly men of Inferiour rank, and from whom without Illumination they can expect no more than from themselves, do daily and professedly delude them. Unto whom (what is deplorable in Men and Christians) too many applying themselves; betwixt jest and earnest, betray the cause of Truth, and sensibly make up the legionary body of Error.

Statists and Politicians, unto whom Ragione di Stato, is the first Considerable, as though it were their business to deceive the people, as a Maxim, do hold, that truth is to be concealed from them; unto whom although they reveal the visible design, yet do they commonly conceal the capital intention. And therefore have they ever been the instruments of great designes, yet seldom understood the true intention of any, accomplishing the drifts of wiser heads, as inanimate and ignorant Agents, the general design of the World; who though in some Latitude of sense, and in a natural cognition perform their proper actions, yet do they unknowingly concurr unto higher ends, and blindly advance the great intention of Nature. Now how far they may be kept in ignorance a greater example there is in the people of Rome; who never knew the true and proper name of their own City. For, beside that common appellation received by the Citizens, it had a proper and secret name concealed from them: Cujus alterum nomen discere secretis Ceremoniarum nefas habetur, saith Plinie; lest the name thereof being discovered unto their enemies, their Penates and Patronal Gods might be called forth by charms and incantations. For according unto the tradition of Magitians, the tutelary Spirits will not remove at common appellations, but at the proper names of things whereunto they are Protectors.

Thus having been deceived by themselves, and continually deluded by others, they must needs be stuffed with Errors, and even over-run with these inferiour falsities; whereunto whosoever shall resign their reasons, either from the Root of deceit in themselves, or inability to resist such trivial deceptions from others, although their condition and fortunes may place them many Spheres above the multitude, yet are they still within the line of Vulgarity, and Democratical enemies of truth.

CHAPTER IV

Of the nearer and more Immediate Causes of popular Errors, both in the wiser and common sort, Misapprehension, Fallacy, or false deduction, Credulity, Supinity, adherence unto Antiquity, Tradition and Authority.

The first is a mistake, or a misconception of things, either in their first apprehensions, or secondary relations. So *Eve* mistook the Commandment, either from the immediate injunction of God, or from the secondary narration of her Husband. So might the Disciples mistake our Saviour, in his answer unto *Peter* concerning the death of *John*, as is delivered, *John* 21: Peter *seeing* John *said unto* Jesus, *Lord, and what shall this man do?* Jesus *saith, If I will, that he tarry till I come, what is that unto thee? Then went this saying abroad among the brethren, that that Disciple should not die.* Thus began the conceit and opinion of the *Centaures*: that is, in the mistake of the first beholders, as is declared by *Servius*; when some young *Thessalians* on horseback were beheld afar off, while their horses watered, that is, while their heads, were depressed, they were conceived by the first Spectators, to be but one animal; and answerable hereunto have their pictures been drawn ever since.

And, as simple mistakes commonly beget fallacies, so men rest not in false apprehensions, without absurd and inconsequent deductions; from fallacious foundations and misapprehended *mediums,* erecting conclusions no way inferrible from their premises. Now the fallacys whereby men deceive others, and are deceived themselves, the

Ancients have divided into Verbal and Real. Of the Verbal, and such as conclude from mistakes of the Word, although there be no less than six, yet are there but two thereof worthy our notation, and unto which the rest may be referred; that is the fallacy of Equivocation and Amphibology which conclude from the ambiguity of some one word, or the ambiguous Syntaxis of many put together. From this fallacy arose that calamitous Error of the Jews, misapprehending the Prophesies of their *Messias*, and expounding them always unto literal and temporal expectations. By this way many Errors crept in and perverted the Doctrin of *Pythagoras*, whilst men received his Precepts in a different sense from his intention; converting Metaphors into proprieties, and receiving as literal expressions, obscure and involved truths. Thus when he enjoyned his Disciples an abstinence from Beans, many conceived they were with severity debarred the use of that pulse; which notwithstanding could not be his meaning; for as *Aristoxenus*, who wrote his life averreth, he delighted much in that kind of food himself. But herein, as *Plutarch* observeth, he had no other intention than to dissuade men from Magistracy, or undertaking the publick offices of state; for by beans was the Magistrate elected in some parts of *Greece*; and, after his daies, we read in *Thucydides*, of the Councel of the bean in *Athens*. The same word also in Greek doth signifie a Testicle, and hath been thought by some an injunction only of Continency, as *Aul. Gellius* hath expounded, and as *Empedocles* may also be interpreted: that is, *Testiculis miseri dextras subducite*; and might be the original intention of *Pythagoras*; as having a notable hint hereof in Beans, from the natural signature of the venereal organs of both Sexes. Again, his injunction is, not to harbour Swallows in our Houses: Whose advice notwithstanding we do not contemn, who daily admit and cherish them: For herein a caution is only implied, not to entertain ungrateful and thankless persons, which like the Swallow are no way commodious unto us; but having made use of our habitations, and served their own turns, forsake us. So he commands to deface the Print of a Cauldron in the ashes, after it hath boiled. Which strictly to observe were condemnable superstition: But hereby he covertly adviseth us not to persevere in anger; but after our choler hath boiled, to retain no impression thereof. In the like sense are to be received, when he adviseth his Disciples to give the right hand but to few, to put no viands in a Chamber-pot, not to pass over a Balance, not to rake up fire with a Sword, or piss against the Sun. Which ænigmatical deliveries comprehend useful verities, but being mistaken by literal Expositors at the

19

first, they have been mis-understood by most since, and may be occasion of Error to Verbal capacities for ever.

This fallacy in the first delusion Satan put upon *Eve*, and his whole tentation might be the same continued; so when he said, *Ye shall not die*, that was, in his equivocation, ye shall not incurr a present death, or a destruction immediately ensuing your transgression. *Your eyes shall be opened*; that is, not to the enlargement of your knowledg, but discovery of your shame and proper confusion; *You shall know good and evil*; that is, you shall have knowledge of good by its privation, but cognisance of evil by sense and visible experience. And the same fallacy or way of deceit, so well succeeding in Paradise, he continued in his Oracles through all the World. Which had not men more warily understood, they might have performed many acts inconsistent with his intention. *Brutus* might have made haste with *Tarquine* to have kissed his own Mother. The *Athenians* might have built them woodden walls, or doubled the Altar at *Delphos*.

The circle of this fallacy is very large; and herein may be comprised all Ironical mistakes, for intended expressions receiving inverted significations; all deductions from Metaphors, Parables, Allegories, unto real and rigid interpretations. Whereby have risen not only popular Errors in Philosophy, but vulgar and senseless Heresies in Divinity; as will be evident unto any that shall examine their foundations, as they stand related by *Epiphanius*, *Austin*, or *Prateolus*.

Other waies there are of deceit; which consist not in false apprehensions of Words, that is, Verbal expressions or sentential significations, but fraudulent deductions, or inconsequent illations, from a false conception of things. Of these extradictionary and real fallacies, *Aristotle* and *Logicians* make in number six, but we observe that men are most commonly deceived by four thereof: those are *Petitio principii*, *A dicto secundum quid ad dictum simpliciter*, *A non causa pro causa*; And, *fallacia consequentis*.

The first is, *Petitio principii*. Which fallacy is committed, when a question is made a *medium*, or we assume a *medium* as granted, whereof we remain as unsatisfied as of the question. Briefly, where that is assumed as a Principle to prove another thing, which is not conceded as true it self. By this fallacy was *Eve* deceived, when she took for granted, a false assertion of the Devil; *Ye shall not surely die; for God doth know that in the day ye shall eat thereof, your eyes shall be opened, and you shall be as Gods.* Which was but a bare affirmation of Satan, without proof or probable inducement, contrary unto the command of God, and former belief of her self. And this was the Logick of the *Jews* when they accused our *Saviour* unto *Pilate*; who demanding a reasonable impeachment, or the allegation of some crime worthy of Condemnation, they only replied, *If he had not been worthy of Death, we would not have brought Him before thee.* Wherein there was neither accusation of the person, nor satisfaction of the Judg; who well understood, a bare accusation was not presumption of guilt, and the clamours of the people no accusation at all. The same Fallacy is sometime used in the dispute, between *Job* and his friends; they often taking that for granted which afterward he disproveth.

The second is, *A dicto secundum quid ad dictum simpliciter*, when from that which is but true in a qualified sense, an inconditional and absolute verity is inferred; transferring the special consideration of things unto their general acceptions, or concluding from their strict acception, unto that without all limitation. This fallacy men commit when they argue from a particular to a general; as when we conclude the vices or qualities of a few, upon a whole Nation. Or from a part unto the whole. Thus the Devil argues with our Saviour: and by this, he would perswade Him he might be secure, if he cast himself from the Pinnacle: For, said he, it is written, *He shall give his Angels charge concerning thee, and in their hands they shall bear thee up, lest at any time thou dash thy foot against a stone.* But this illation was fallacious, leaving one part of the Text, *He shall keep thee in all thy wayes*; that is, in the wayes of righteousness, and not of rash attempts: so he urged a part for the whole, and inferred more in the conclusion, than was contained in the premises. By the same fallacy we proceed, when we conclude from the sign unto the thing signified. By this incroachment, Idolatry first crept in, men converting the symbolical use of Idols into their proper Worship, and receiving the representation of things as the substance and thing it self. So the Statue of *Belus* at first erected in his memory, was in after-times adored as a Divinity. And so also in the Sacrament of the *Eucharist*, the Bread and Wine which were but the signals or visible signs, were made the things signified, and worshipped as the Body of Christ. And hereby generally men are deceived that take things spoken in some Latitude without any at all. Hereby the *Jews* were deceived concerning the commandment of the Sabbath, ac-

21

cusing our Saviour *for healing the sick*, and his Disciples *for plucking the ears of Corn upon that day*. And by this deplorable mistake they were deceived unto destruction, upon the assault of *Pompey* the great, made upon that day; by whose superstitious observations they could not defend themselves, or perform any labour whatever.

The third is, *A non causa pro causa*, when that is pretended for a cause which is not, or not in that sense which is inferred. Upon this consequence the law of *Mahomet* forbids the use of Wine; and his Successors abolished Universities. By this also manny Christians have condemned literature, misunderstanding the councel of Saint *Paul*, who adviseth no further than to beware of Philosophy. On this Foundation were built the conclusions of Southsayers in their Augurial, and Tripudiary divinations; collecting presages from voice or food of Birds, and conjoyning Events unto causes of no connection. Hereupon also are grounded the gross mistakes, in the cure of many diseases; not only from the last medicine, and sympathetical Receipts, but Amulets, Charms, and all incantatory applications; deriving effects not only from inconcurring causes, but things devoid of all efficiency whatever.

The fourth is, the Fallacy of the Consequent; which if strictly taken, may be a fallacious illation in reference unto antecedency, or consequency; as to conclude from the position of the antecedent to the position of the consequent, or from the remotion of the consequent to the remotion of the antecedent. This is usually committed, when in connexed Propositions the Terms adhere contingently. This is frequent in Oratory illations; and thus the *Pharisees*, because He conversed with Publicans and Sinners, accused the holiness of Christ. But if this Fallacy be largely taken, it is committed in any vicious illation, offending the rules of good consequence: and so it may be very large, and comprehend all false illations against the setled Laws of Logick: But the most usual inconsequencies are from particulars, from negatives, and from affirmative conclusions in the second figure, wherein indeed offences are most frequent, and their discoveries not difficult.

CHAPTER V

Of Credulity and Supinity

A third cause of common Errors is the Credulity of men, that is, an easie assent to what is obtruded, or a believing at first ear, what is delivered by others. This is a weakness in the understanding, without examination assenting unto things, which from their Natures and Causes do carry no perswasion; whereby men often swallow falsities for truths, dubiosities for certainties, feasibilities for possibilities, and things impossible as possibilities themselves. Which, though the weakness of the Intellect, and most discoverable in vulgar heads; yet hath it sometime fallen upon wiser brains, and great advancers of Truth. Thus many wise *Athenians* so far forgot their Philosophy, and the nature of humane production, that they descended unto belief, that the original of their Nation was from the Earth, and had no other beginning then the seminality and womb of their great Mother. Thus is it not without wonder, how those learned *Arabicks* so tamely delivered up their belief unto the absurdities of the *Alcoran*. How the noble *Geber*, *Avicenna*, and *Almanzor*, should rest satisfied in the nature and causes of Earthquakes, delivered from the doctrine of their *Prophet*; that is, from the motion of a great Bull, upon whose horns all earth is poised. How their faiths could decline so low, as to concede their generations in Heaven, to be made by the smell of a Citron, or that the felicity of their Paradise should consist in a Jubile of copulation, that is, a coition of one act prolonged unto fifty years. Thus is it almost beyond wonder, how the belief of reasonable creatures, should ever submit unto Idolatry: and the credulity of those men scarce credible (without presumption of a second Fall) who could believe a Deity in the work of their own hands. For although in that ancient and diffused adoration of Idols, unto the *Priests* and subtiler heads, the worship perhaps might be symbolical, and as those Images some way related unto their Deities; yet was the Idolatry direct and down-right in the people; whose credulity is illimitable, who may be made believe that any thing is God; and may be made believe there is no God at all.

And as credulity is the cause of Error, so Incredulity oftentimes of not enjoying truth: and that not only an obstinate incredulity, whereby we will not acknowledge assent unto what is reasonably inferred, but any Academical reservation in matters of easie truth, or rather sceptical infidelity against the evidence of reason and sense. For these are conceptions befalling wise men, as absurd as the apprehensions of fools, and the credulity of the people which promiscuously swallow any thing. For this is not only derogatory unto the wisdom of God, who hath proposed the World unto our knowledge, and thereby the notion of Himself; but also detractory unto the intellect, and sense of man expressedly disposed for that inquisition. And therefore, *hoc tantum scio, quod nihil scio*, is not to be received in an absolute sense, but is comparatively expressed unto the number of things whereof our knowledg is ignorant. Nor will it acquit the insatisfaction of those which quarrel with all things, or dispute of matters, concerning whose verities we have conviction from reason, or decision from the inerrable and requisite conditions of sense. And therefore if any affirm, the earth doth move, and will not believe with us, it standeth still; because he hath probable reasons for it, and I no infallible sense, nor reason against it, I will not quarrel with his assertion. But if, like *Zeno*, he shall walk about, and yet deny there is any motion in Nature, surely that man was constituted for *Anticera*, and were a fit companion for those, who having a conceit they are dead, cannot be convicted into the society of the living.

The fourth is a Supinity, or neglect of Enquiry, even of matters whereof we doubt; rather believing, than going to see; or doubting with ease and *gratìs*, than believing with difficulty or purchase. Whereby, either from a temperamental inactivity, we are unready to put in execution the suggestions or dictates of reason; or by a content and acquiescence in every species of truth, we embrace the shadow thereof, or so much as may palliate its just and substantial requirements. Had our fore-Fathers sat down in these resolutions, or had their curiosities been sedentary, who pursued the knowledge of things through all the corners of nature, the face of truth had been obscure unto us, whose lustre in some part their industries have revealed.

24

Certainly the sweat of their labours was not salt unto them, and they took delight in the dust of their endeavours. For questionless, in Knowledg there is no slender difficulty; and Truth, which wise men say doth lye in a Well, is not recoverable but by exantlation. It were some extenuation of the Curse, if *In sudore vultus tui* were confinable unto corporal exercitations, and there still remained a Paradise, or unthorny place of knowledg. But now our understandings being eclipsed, as well as our tempers infirmed, we must betake ourselves to wayes of reparation, and depend upon the illumination of our endeavours. For, thus we may in some measure repair our primary ruines, and build our selves Men again. And though the attempts of some have been precipitous, and their Enquiries so audacious, as to come within command of the flaming swords, and lost themselves in attempts above humanity; yet have the Enquiries of most defected by the way, and tired within the sober circumference of Knowledg.

And this is the reason, why some have transcribed any thing; and although they cannot but doubt thereof, yet neither make Experiment by sense, or Enquiry by reason; but live in doubts of things, whose satisfaction is in their own power; which is indeed the inexcusable part of our ignorance, and may perhaps fill up the charge of the last day. For, not obeying the dictates of Reason, and neglecting the cries of Truth, we fail not only in the trust of our undertakings, but in the intention of man it self. Which although more venial in ordinary constitutions, and such as are not framed beyond the capacity of beaten notions, yet will it inexcusably condemn some men, who having received excellent endowments, have yet sate down by the way, and frustrated the intention of their habilities. For certainly, as some men have sinned in the principles of humanity, and must answer, for not being men, so others offend, if they be not more. *Magis extra vitia, quam cum virtutibus*, would commend those: These are not excusable without an Excellency. For, great constitutions, and such as are constellated unto knowledge, do nothing till they out-do all; they come short of themselves, if they go not beyond others; and must not sit down under the degree of Worthies. God expects no lustre from the minor Stars; but if the Sun should not illuminate all, it were a sin in Nature. *Ultimus bonorum*, will not excuse every man, nor is it sufficient for all to hold the common level: Mens names should not only distinguish them: A man should be something, that men are not, and individual in somewhat beside his proper Name. Thus while it exceeds not the bounds of reason and modesty, we cannot condemn singularity.

Nos numerus sumus, is the Motto of the multitude, and for that reason are they Fools. For things as they recede from unity, the more they approach to imperfection, and Deformity; for they hold their perfection in their Simplicities, and as they nearest approach to God.

Now as there are many great Wits to be condemned, who have neglected the increment of Arts, and the sedulous pursuit of knowledge; so are there not a few very much to be pitied, whose industry being not attended with natural parts, they have sweat to little purpose, and rolled the stone in vain. Which chiefly proceedeth from natural incapacity, and genial indisposition, at least, to those particulars whereunto they apply their endeavours. And this is one reason why, though Universities be ful of men, they are oftentimes empty of learning: Why, as there are some men do much without learning, so others but little with it, and few that attain to any measure of it. For many heads that undertake it, were never squared, nor timber'd for it. There are not only particular men, but whole Nations indisposed for learning; whereunto is required, not only education, but a Pregnant *Minerva*, and teeming Constitution. For the Wisdom of God hath divided the *Genius* of men according to the different affairs of the World: and varied their inclination according to the variety of Actions to be performed therein. Which they who consider not, rudely rushing upon professions and ways of life, unequal to their natures; dishonour, not only themselves and their Functions, but pervert the harmony of the whole World. For, if the World went on as God hath ordained it, and were every one imployed in points concordant to their Natures, Professions: Arts and Commonwealths would rise up of themselves; nor needed we a Lanthorn to find a man in *Athens*.

CHAPTER VI

Of adherence unto Antiquity

But the mortallest enemy unto Knowledge, and that which hath done the greatest execution upon truth, hath been a peremptory adhesion unto Authority, and more especially, the establishing of our belief upon the dictates of Antiquity. For (as every capacity may observe) most men of Ages present, so superstitiously do look on Ages past, that the Authorities of the one, exceed the reasons of the other: Whose persons indeed being far removed from our times, their works, which seldom with us pass uncontrouled, either by contemporaries, or immediate successors, are now become out of the distance of Envies; and the farther removed from present times, are conceived to approach the nearer unto truth it self. Now hereby methinks we manifestly delude our selves, and widely walk out of the track of Truth.

For first, Men hereby impose a Thraldom on their Times, which the ingenuity of no Age should endure, or indeed, the presumption of any did ever yet enjoyn. Thus *Hippocrates* about 2000 years ago, conceived it no injustice, either to examine or refute the Doctrines of his Predecessors: *Galen* the like, and *Aristotle* the most of any. Yet did not any of these conceive themselves infallible, or set down their dictates as verities irrefragable, but when they deliver their own Inventions, or reject other men's Opinions, they proceed with Judgment and Ingenuity; establishing their assertion, not only with great solidity, but submitting them also unto the correction of future discovery.

Secondly, Men that adore times past, consider not that those times were once present; that is, as our own are at this instant, and we our selves unto those to come, as they unto us at present, as we relye on them, even so will those on us, and magnifie us hereafter, who at present condemn our selves. Which very absurdity is daily committed amongst us, even in the esteem and censure of our own times. And to speak impartially, old Men, from whom we should expect the greatest example of Wisdom, do most exceed in this point of folly; commending the days of their youth, which they scarce remember, at least well understood not; extolling those times their younger years have heard their Fathers condemn, and condemning those times the gray heads of their posterity shall commend. And thus is it the humour of many heads, to extol the days of their Fore-fathers, and declaim against the wickedness of times present. Which notwithstanding they cannot handsomly do, without the borrowed help and Satyrs of times past; condemning the vices of their own times, by the expressions of vices in times which they commend; which cannot but argue the community of vice in both. *Horace* therefore, and *Juvenal*, and *Persius* were no Prophets, although their lines did seem to indigitate and point at our times. There is a certain list of vices committed in all Ages, and declaimed against by all Authors, which will last as long as human nature; which digested into common places, may serve for any Theme, and never be out of date until Dooms-day.

Thirdly, The Testimonies of Antiquity, and such as pass oraculously amongst us, were not, if we consider them, always so exact, as to examine the doctrine they delivered. For some, and those the acutest of them, have left unto us many things of falsity; controlable, not only by critical and collective reason, but common and Country observation.

Hereof there want not many examples in *Aristotle*, through all his Book of Animals; we shall instance onely in three of his Problems, and all contained under one Section. The first enquireth, why a Man doth cough, but not an Oxe or Cow; whereas, notwithstanding the contrary is often observed by Husbandmen, and stands confirmed by those who have expresly treated *De Re Rustica*, and have also delivered divers remedies for it. Why Juments, as Horses, Oxen, and Asses, have no eructation or belching, whereas indeed the contrary is often observed, and also delivered by *Columella*. And thirdly, Why Man alone hath gray hairs? whereas it cannot escape the eyes, and ordinary observation of all men, as Horses, Dogs, and Foxes, wax gray with age in our Countries; and in the colder Regions, many other Animals without it. And though favourable constructions may somewhat extenuate the rigour of these concessions, yet will scarce any palliate that in the

28

fourth of his Meteors, that Salt is easiest dissolvable in cold water: Nor that of *Diascorides*, that Quicksilver is best preserved in Vessels of Tin and Lead.

Other Authors write often dubiously, even in matters wherein is expected a strict and definitive truth; extenuating their affirmations, with *aiunt, ferunt, fortasse*: as *Diascorides, Galen, Aristotle*, and many more. Others by hear-say; taking upon trust most they have delivered, whose Volumes are meer Collections, drawn from the mouths or leaves of other Authors; as may be observed in *Plinie, Elian, Athenæus*, and many more. Not a few transcriptively, subscribing their Names unto other mens endeavours, and meerly transcribing almost all they have written. The *Latines* transcribing the *Greeks*, the *Greeks* and *Latines*, each other.

Thus hath *Justine* borrowed all from *Trogus Pompeius*, and *Julius Solinus*, in a manner transcribed *Plinie*. Thus have *Lucian* and *Apuleius* served *Lucius Pratensis* ; men both living in the same time, and both transcribing the same Author, in those famous Books, Entituled *Lucius* by the one, and *Aureus Asinus* by the other. In the same measure hath *Simocrates* in his Tract *De Nilo*, dealt with *Diodorus Siculus*, as may be observed in that work annexed unto *Herodotus*, and translated by *Jungermannus*. Thus *Eratosthenes* wholly translated *Timotheus de Insulis*, not reserving the very Preface. The same doth *Strabo* report of *Eudorus*, and *Ariston*, in a Treatise entituled *De Nilo*. *Clemens Alexandrinus* hath observed many examples hereof among the *Greeks*; and *Pliny* speaketh very plainly in his Preface, that conferring his Authors, and comparing their works together, he generally found those that went before *verbatim* transcribed, by those that followed after, and their Originals never so much as mentioned. To omit how much of the wittiest piece of *Ovid* is beholden unto *Parthenius Chius*; even the magnified *Virgil* hath borrowed, almost in all his Works; his *Eclogues* from *Theocritus*, his *Georgicks* from *Hesiod* and *Aratus*, his *Aeneads* from *Homer*, the second Book whereof containing the exploits of *Sinon* and the *Trojan* Horse (as *Macrobius* observeth) he hath *verbatim* derived from *Pisander*. Our own Profession is not excusable herein. Thus *Oribasius, Ætius*, and *Ægineta*, have in a manner transcribed *Galen*. But *Marcellus Empericus*, who hath left a famous Work *De Medicamentis*, hath word for word transcribed all *Scribonius Largus, De Compositione Medicamentorum*, and not left out his very Peroration. Thus may we perceive the Ancients were but men, even like our selves. The practice of transcription in our days, was no Monster in theirs: *Plagiarie* had not its Nativity with Printing, but began in times when thefts were difficult, and the paucity of Books scarce wanted that Invention.

Nor did they only make large use of other Authors, but often without mention of their names. *Aristotle*, who seems to have borrowed many things from *Hippocrates*, in the most favourable construction, makes mention but once of him, and that by the by, and without reference unto his present Doctrine. *Virgil*, so much beholding unto *Homer*, hath not his name in all his Works: and *Plinie*, who seems to borrow many Authors out of *Dioscorides*, hath taken no notice of him. I wish men were not still content to plume themselves with others Feathers. Fear of discovery, not single ingenuity affords Quotations rather than Transcriptions; wherein notwithstanding the Plagiarisme of many makes little consideration, whereof though great Authors may complain, small ones cannot but take notice.

Fourthly, While we so eagerly adhere unto Antiquity, and the accounts of elder times, we are to consider the fabulous condition thereof. And that we shall not deny, if we call to mind the Mendacity of *Greece*, from whom we have received most relations, and that a considerable part of ancient Times, was by the *Greeks* themselves termed μύθικον, that is, made up or stuffed out with Fables. And surely the fabulous inclination of those days, was greater then any since; which swarmed so with Fables, and from such slender grounds, took hints for fictions, poysoning the World ever after; wherein how far they exceeded, may be exemplified from *Palephatus*, in his Book of *Fabulous Narrations*. That Fable of *Orpheus*, who, by the melody of his Musick, made Woods and Trees to follow him, was raised upon a slender foundation; for there were a crew of mad women, retired unto a Mountain from whence being pacified by his Musick, they descended with boughs in their hands, which unto the fabulosity of those times proved a sufficient ground to celebrate unto all posterity the Magick of *Orpheus* Harp, and its power to attract the sensless Trees about it. That *Medea* the famous Sorceress could renew youth, and make old men young again, was nothing else, but that from the knowledge of Simples she had a Receit to make white hair black, and reduce old heads, into the tincture of youth again. The Fable of *Gerion* and *Cerberus* with three heads, was this: *Gerion* was of the City of *Tricarinia*, that is, of three heads, and *Cerberus* of the same place was one of his Dogs, which running into a Cave upon pursuit of his Masters Oxen, *Hercules* perforce drew him out of that place, from whence the conceits of those days affirmed no less, then that *Hercules* descended into Hell, and brought up *Cerberus* into the habitation of the living. Upon the like grounds was raised the figment of *Briareus*, who dwelling in a City called *Hecatonchiria*, the fansies of those times assigned him an hundred hands. 'Twas ground enough to fansie wings unto *Dædalus*, in that he stole out of a Window from *Minos*, and sailed away with his son *Icarus*: who steering his course wisely, escaped; but his son carrying too high a sail was drowned. That *Niobe* weeping over her children, was turned into a Stone, was nothing else, but that during her life she erected over their Sepultures a Marble Tomb of her own. When *Acteon* had undone himself with Dogs, and the prodigal attendants of hunting, they made a solemn story how he was devoured by his Hounds. And upon the like grounds was raised the Anthropophagie of *Diomedes* his horses. Upon as slender foundation was built the Fable of the *Minotaure*; for one *Taurus* a servant of *Minos* gat his Mistris *Pasiphae* with child, from whence the Infant was named *Minotaurus*. Now this unto the fabulosity of those times was thought sufficient to accuse *Pasiphae* of Beastiality, or admitting conjunction with a Bull; and in succeeding ages gave a hint of depravity unto *Domitian* to act the Fable into reality. In like manner, as *Diodorus* plainly delivereth, the famous Fable of *Charon* had its Nativity; who being no other but the common Ferry-man of *Egypt*, that wafted over the dead bodies from *Memphis*, was made by the *Greeks* to be the Ferry-man of Hell, and solemn stories raised after of him. Lastly, we shall not need to enlarge, if that be true which grounded the generation of *Castor* and *Helen* out of an Egg, because they were born and brought up in an upper room, according unto the word ὦον, which with the *Lacædemonians* had also that signification.

Fifthly, We applaud many things delivered by the Ancients, which are in themselves but ordinary, and come short of our own Conceptions. Thus we usually extol, and our Orations cannot escape the sayings of the wise men of *Greece*. *Nosce teipsum*, of *Thales*: *Nosce tempus*, of *Pittacus*: *Nihil nimis*, of *Cleobulus*; which notwithstanding to speak indifferently, are but vulgar precepts in Morality, carrying with them nothing above the line, or beyond the extemporary sententiosity of common conceits with us. Thus we magnifie the Apothegms or reputed replies of Wisdom, whereof many are to be seen in *Laertius*, more in *Lycosthenes*, not a few in the second Book of *Macrobius*, in the sals of *Cicero*, *Augustus*, and the Comical wits of those times: in most whereof there is not much to admire, and are methinks exceeded, not only in the replies of wise men, but the passages of society, and urbanities of our times. And thus we extol their Adages, or Proverbs; and *Erasmus* hath taken great pains to make collections of them, whereof notwithstanding, the greater part will, I believe, unto indifferent Judges be esteemed no extraordinaries; and may be parallel'd, if not exceeded, by those of more unlearned Nations, and many of our own.

Sixthly, We urge Authorities in points that need not, and introduce the testimony of ancient Writers, to confirm things evidently believed, and whereto no reasonable hearer but would assent without them; such as are, *Nemo mortalium omnibus horis sapit. Virtute nil præstantius, nil pulchrius. Omnia vincit amor. Præclarum quiddam veritas.* All which, although things known and vulgar, are frequently urged by many men, and though trivial verities in our mouths, yet, noted from *Plato*, *Ovid*, or *Cicero*, they become reputed elegancies. For many hundred to instance but in one we meet with while we are writing. *Antonius Guevera* that elegant *Spaniard*, in his Book entituled, *The Dial of Princes*, beginneth his Epistle thus. *Apolonius Thyaneus*, disputing with the Scholars of *Hiarchas*, said, that among all the affections of nature, nothing was more natural, then the desire all have to preserve life. Which being a confessed Truth, and a verity acknowledged by all, it was a superfluous affectation to derive its Authority from *Apolonius*, or seek a confirmation thereof as far as *India*, and the learned Scholars of *Hiarchas*. Which whether it be not all one to strengthen common Dignities and Principles known by themselves, with the Authority of Mathematicians; or think a man should believe, the whole is greater then its parts, rather upon the Authority of *Euclide*, then if it were propounded alone; I leave unto the second and wiser cogitations of all men. 'Tis sure a Practice that savours much of Pedantry; a reserve of Puerility we have not shaken off from School; where being seasoned with Minor sentences, by a neglect of higher Enquiries, they prescribe upon our riper ears, and are never worn but with our memories.

Lastly, While we so devoutly adhere unto Antiquity in some things, we do not consider we have deserted them in several others. For they indeed have not onely been imperfect, in the conceit of some things, but either ignorant or erroneous in many more. They understood not the motion of the eighth sphear from West to East, and so conceived the longitude of the Stars invariable. They conceived the torrid Zone unhabitable, and so made frustrate the goodliest part of the Earth. But we now know 'tis very well empeopled, and the habitation thereof esteemed so happy, that some have made it the proper seat of Paradise; and been so far from judging it unhabitable, that they have made it the first habitation of all. Many of the Ancients denied the *Antipodes*, and some unto the penalty of contrary affirmations; but the experience of our enlarged navigations, can now assert them beyond all dubitation. Having thus totally relinquisht them in some things, it may not be presumptuous, to examine them in others: but surely most unreasonable to adhere to them in all, as though they were infallible, or could not err in any.

CHAPTER VII

Of Authority.

Nor is onely a resolved prostration unto Antiquity a powerful enemy unto knowledge, but any confident adherence unto Authority, or resignation of our judgements upon the testimony of any Age or Author whatsoever.

For first, to speak generally, an argument from Authority to wiser examinations, is but a weaker kind of proof; it being a topical probation, and as we term it, an inartificial argument, depending upon a naked asseveration: wherein neither declaring the causes, affections or adjuncts of what we believe, it carrieth not with it the reasonable inducements of knowledge. And therefore *Contra negantem principia, Ipse dixit,* or *Oportet discentem credere,* although Postulates very accommodable unto *Junior* indoctrinations; yet are their Authorities but temporary, and not to be imbraced beyond the minority of our intellectuals. For our advanced beliefs are not to be built upon dictates, but having received the probable inducements of truth, we become emancipated from testimonial engagements, and are to erect upon the surer base of reason.

Secondly, Unto reasonable perpensions it hath no place in some Sciences, small in others, and suffereth many restrictions, even where it is most admitted. It is of no validity in the Mathematicks, especially the mother part thereof, Arithmetick and Geometry. For these Sciences concluding from dignities and principles known by themselves: receive not satisfaction from probable reasons, much less from bare and peremptory asseverations. And therefore if all *Athens* should decree, that in every Triangle, two sides, which soever be taken, are greater then the side remaining, or that in rectangle triangles the square which is made of the side that subtendeth the right angle, is equal to the squares which are made of the sides containing the right angle: although there be a certain truth therein, Geometricians notwithstanding would not receive satisfaction without demonstration thereof. 'Tis true, by the vulgarity of Philosophers, there are many points believed without probation; nor if a man affirm from *Ptolomy*, that the Sun is bigger then the Earth, shall he probably meet with any contradiction: whereunto notwithstanding Astronomers will not assent without some convincing argument or demonstrative proof thereof. And therefore certainly of all men a Philosopher should be no swearer; for an oath which is the end of controversies in Law, cannot determine any here; nor are the deepest Sacraments or desperate imprecations of any force to perswade, where reason only, and necessary *mediums* must induce.

In Natural Philosophy more generally pursued amongst us, it carrieth but slender consideration; for that also proceeding from setled Principles, therein is expected a satisfaction from scientifical progressions, and such as beget a sure rational belief. For if Authority might have made out the assertions of Philosophy, we might have held that Snow was black, that the Sea was but the sweat of the Earth, and many of the like absurdities. Then was *Aristotle* injurious to fall upon *Melissus*, to reject the assertions of *Anaxagoras*, *Anaximander*, and *Empedocles*; then were we also ungrateful unto himself, from whom our *Junior* endeavours embracing many things on his authority, our mature and secondary enquiries, are forced to quit those receptions, and to adhere unto the nearer account of Reason. And although it be not unusual, even in Philosophical Tractates to make enumeration of Authors, yet are there reasons usually introduced, and to ingenious Readers do carry the stroke in the perswasion. And surely if we account it reasonable among our selves, and not injurious unto rational Authors, no farther to abet their Opinions then as they are supported by solid Reasons: certainly with more excusable reservation may we shrink at their bare testimonies; whose argument is but precarious, and subsists upon the charity of our assentments.

In Morality, Rhetorick, Law and History, there is I confess a frequent and allowable use of testimony; and yet herein I perceive, it is not unlimitable, but admitteth many restrictions. Thus in Law both Civil and Divine: that is onely esteemed a legal testimony, which receives comprobation from the mouths of at least two witnesses; and that not only for prevention of calumny, but assurance against mistake; whereas notwithstanding the solid reason of one man, is as sufficient as the clamor of a whole Nation; and with imprejudicate apprehensions begets as firm a belief as the authority or aggregated testimony of many hundreds. For reason being the very root of our natures, and the principles thereof common unto all, what is against the Laws of true reason, or the unerring understanding of any one, if rightly apprehended; must be disclaimed by all Nations, and rejected even by mankind.

Again, A testimony is of small validity if deduced from men out of their own profession; so if *Lactantius* affirm the Figure of the Earth is plain, or *Austin* deny there are *Antipodes*; though venerable Fathers of the Church, and ever to be honoured, yet will not their Authorities prove sufficient to ground a belief thereon. Whereas notwithstanding the solid reason or confirmed experience of any man, is very approvable in what profession soever. So *Raymund Sebund* a Physitian of *Tholouze*, besides his learned Dialogues *De Natura humana*, hath written a natural Theologie; demonstrating therein the Attributes of God, and attempting the like in most points of Religion. So *Hugo Grotius* a Civilian, did write an excellent Tract of the verity of Christian Religion. Wherein most rationally delivering themselves, their works will be embraced by most that understand them, and their reasons enforce belief even from prejudicate Readers. Neither indeed have the Authorities of men been ever so awful, but that by some they have been rejected, even in their own professions. Thus *Aristotle* affirming the birth of the Infant or time of its gestation, extendeth sometimes unto the eleventh Month, but *Hippocrates*, averring that it exceedeth not the tenth: *Adrian* the Emperour in a solemn process, determined for *Aristotle*; but *Justinian* many years after, took in with *Hippocrates* and reversed the Decree of the other. Thus have Councils, not only condemned private men, but the Decrees and Acts of one another. So *Galen* after all his veneration of *Hippocrates*, in some things hath fallen from him. *Avicen* in many from *Galen*; and others succeeding from him. And although the singularity of *Paracelsus* be intolerable, who sparing onely *Hippocrates*, hath reviled not onely the Authors, but almost all the learning that went before him; yet is it not much less injurious unto knowledge obstinately and inconvincibly to side with any one. Which humour unhappily possessing many, they have by prejudice withdrawn themselves into parties, and contemning

36

the soveraignty of truth, seditiously abetted the private divisions of error.

Moreover a testimony in points Historical, and where it is of unavoidable use, is of no illation in the negative, nor is it of consequence that *Herodotus* writing nothing of Rome, *there* was therefore no such City in his time; or because *Dioscorides* hath made no mention of Unicorns horn, there is therefore no such thing in Nature. Indeed, intending an accurate enumeration of Medical materials, the omission hereof affords some probability, it was not used by the Ancients, but will not conclude the non-existence thereof. For so may we annihilate many Simples unknown to his enquiries, as *Senna, Rhubarb, Bezoar, Ambregris*, and divers others. Whereas indeed the reason of man hath not such restraint; concluding not onely affirmatively but negatively; not onely affirming there is no magnitude beyond the last heavens, but also denying there is any vacuity within them. Although it be confessed, the affirmative hath the prerogative illation, and *Barbara* engrosseth the powerful demonstration.

Lastly, The strange relations made by Authors, may sufficiently discourage our adherence unto Authority, and which if we believe we must be apt to swallow any thing. Thus *Basil* will tell us, the Serpent went erect like Man, and that that Beast could speak before the Fall. *Tostatus* would make us believe that *Nilus* encreaseth every new Moon. *Leonardo Fioravanti* an Italian Physitian, beside many other secrets, assumeth unto himself the discovery of one concerning Pellitory of the Wall; that is, that it never groweth in the sight of the *North* star. *Dove si possa vedere la stella Tramontana*, wherein how wide he is from truth, is easily discoverable unto every one, who hath but Astronomy enough to know that Star. *Franciscus Sanctius* in a laudable Comment upon *Alciats* Emblems, affirmeth, and that from experience, a Nightingale hath no tongue. *Avem Philomelam lingua carere pro certo affirmare possum, nisi me oculi fallunt.* Which if any man for a while shall believe upon his experience, he may at his leisure refute it by his own. What fool almost would believe, at least, what wise man would relie upon that Antidote delivered by *Pierius* in his Hieroglyphicks against the sting of a Scorpion? that is, to sit upon an Ass with one's face toward his tail; for so the pain leaveth the Man, and passeth into the Beast. It were methinks but an uncomfortable receit for a Quartane Ague (and yet as good perhaps as many others used) to have recourse unto the *Recipe* of *Sammonicus*; that is, to lay the fourth Book of *Homers* Iliads under ones head, according to the precept of that Physitian and Poet, *Moeoniæ Iliados quartum suppone trementi.* There are surely few that have belief to swallow, or hope enough to experiment the Collyrium of *Albertus*; which promiseth a strange effect, and such as Thieves would count inestimable, that is, to make one see in the dark: yet thus much, according unto his receit, will the right eye of an Hedge-hog boiled in oyl, and preserved in a brazen vessel effect. As strange it is, and unto vicious inclinations were worth a night's lodging with *Lais*, what is delivered in *Kiranides*; that the left stone of a Weesel, wrapt up in the skin of a she Mule, is able to secure incontinency from conception.

These with swarms of others have men delivered in their Writings, whose verities are onely supported by their authorities: But being neither consonant unto reason, nor correspondent unto experiment, their affirmations are unto us no axioms: We esteem thereof as things unsaid, and account them but in the list of nothing. I wish herein the *Chymists* had been more sparing: who over-magnifying their preparations, inveigle the curiosity of many, and delude the security of most. For if experiments would answer their encomiums, the Stone and Quartane Agues were not opprobrious unto Physitians: we might contemn that first and most uncomfortable Aphorism of *Hippocrates*, for surely that Art were soon attained, that hath so general remedies; and life could not be short, were there such to prolong it.

CHAPTER VIII

A brief enumeration of Authors.

NOW for as much as we have discoursed of Authority, and there is scarce any tradition or popular error but stands also delivered by some good Author; we shall endeavour a short discovery of such, as for the major part have given authority hereto: who though excellent and useful Authors, yet being either transcriptive, or following common relations, their accounts are not to be swallowed at large, or entertained without all circumspection. In whom the *ipse dixit*, although it be no powerful argument in any, is yet less authentick then in many other, because they deliver not their own experiences, but others affirmations, and write from others, as later pens from them.

1. The first in order, as also in time shall be *Herodotus* of *Halicarnassus*. An excellent and very elegant Historian; whose Books of History were so well received in his own days, and at their rehearsal in the Olympick games, they obtained the names of the nine Muses; and continued in such esteem unto descending ages, that *Cicero* termed him, *Historiarum parens*. And *Dionysius* his Countryman, in an Epistle to *Pompey*, after an express comparison, affords him the better of *Thucydides*; all which notwithstanding, he hath received from some, the stile of *Mendaciorum pater*. His authority was much infringed by *Plutarch*, who being offended with him, as *Polybius* had been with *Philarcus* for speaking too coldly of his Countrymen, hath left a particular Tract, *De malignitate Herodoti*. But in this latter Century, *Camerarius* and *Stephanus* have stepped in, and by their witty Apologies, effectually endeavoured to frustrate the Arguments of *Plu-*

tarch, or any other. Now in this Author, as may be observed in our ensuing discourse, and is better discernable in the perusal of himself, there are many things fabulously delivered, and not to be accepted as truths: whereby nevertheless if any man be deceived, the Author is not so culpable as the Believer. For he indeed imitating the Father Poet, whose life he hath also written, and as *Thucydides* observeth, as well intending the delight as benefit of his Reader, hath besprinkled his work with many fabulosities; whereby if any man be led into error, he mistaketh the intention of the Author, who plainly confesseth he writeth many things by hear-say, and forgetteth a very considerable caution of his; that is, *Ego quæ fando cognovi, exponere narratione mea debeo omnia: credere autem esse vera omnia, non debeo.*

2. In the second place is *Ctesias* the Cnidian, Physitian unto *Artaxerxes* King of *Persia*, his Books are often recited by ancient Writers, and by the industry of *Stephanus* and *Rhodomanus*, there are extant some fragments thereof in our days; he wrote the History of *Persia*, and many narrations of *India*. In the first, as having a fair opportunity to know the truth, and as *Diodorus* affirmeth the perusal of *Persian* Records, his testimony is acceptable. In his *Indian* Relations, wherein are contained strange and incredible accounts, he is surely to be read with suspension. These were they which weakned his authority with former ages; for as we may observe, he is seldom mentioned, without a derogatory Parenthesis in any Author. *Aristotle* besides the frequent undervaluing of his authority, in his Books of Animals gives him the lie no less then twice, concerning the seed of Elephants. *Strabo* in his eleventh Book hath left a harder censure of him. *Equidem facilius Hesiodo & Homero, aliquis fidem adhibuerit, itémque Tragicis Poetis, quam Ctesiæ, Herodoto, Hellanico & eorum similibus.* But *Lucian* hath spoken more plainly then any. *Scripsit Ctesias de Indorum regione, deque iis quæ apud illos sunt, ea quæ nec ipse vidit, neque ex ullius sermone audivit.* Yet were his relations taken up by some succeeding Writers, and many thereof revived by our Countryman, Sir *John Mandevil*, Knight and Doctor in Physick; who after thirty years peregrination died at *Liege*, and was there honourably interred. He left a Book of his Travels, which hath been honoured with translation of many Languages, and now continued above three hundred years; herein he often attesteth the fabulous relations of *Ctesias*, and seems to confirm the refuted accounts of Antiquity. All which may still be received in some acceptions of morality, and to a pregnant invention, may afford commendable mythologie; but in a natural and proper ex-

position, it containeth impossibilities, and things inconsistent with truth.

3. There is a Book *De mirandis auditionbus*, ascribed unto *Aristotle*; another *De mirabilibus narrationibus*, written long after by *Antigonus*, another also of the same title by *Phlegon Trallianus*, translated by *Xilander*, and with the Annotations of *Meursius*, all whereof make good the promise of their titles, and may be read with caution. Which if any man shall likewise observe in the Lecture of *Philostratus*, concerning the life of *Apollonius*, and even in some passages of the sober and learned *Plutarchus*; or not only in ancient Writers, but shall carry a wary eye on *Paulus Venetus, Jovius, Olaus Magnus, Nierembergius*, and many other: I think his circumspection is laudable, and he may thereby decline occasion of Error.

4. *Dioscorides Anazarbeus*, he wrote many Books in Physick, but six thereof *De Materia Medica*, have found the greatest esteem: he is an Author of good antiquity and use, preferred by *Galen* before *Cratevas, Pamphilus*, and all that attempted the like description before him; yet all he delivereth therein is not to be conceived Oraculous. For beside that, following the wars under *Anthony*, the course of his life would not permit a punctual *Examen* in all; there are many things concerning the nature of Simples, traditionally delivered, and to which I believe he gave no assent himself. It had been an excellent Receit, and in his time when Saddles were scarce in fashion of very great use, if that were true which he delivers, that *Vitex*, or *Agnus Castus* held only in the hand, preserveth the rider from galling. It were a strange effect, and Whores would forsake the experiment of *Savine*, if that were a truth which he delivereth of Brake or female Fearn, that onely treading over it, it causeth a sudden abortion. It were to be wished true, and women would idolize him, could that be made out which he recordeth of *Phyllon, Mercury*, and other vegetables, that the juice of the male Plant drunk, or the leaves but applied unto the genitals, determines their conceptions unto males. In these relations although he be more sparing, his predecessors were very numerous; and *Galen* hereof most sharply accuseth *Pamphilus*. Many of the like nature we meet sometimes in *Oribasius, Ætius, Trallianus, Serapion, Evax*, and *Marcellus*, whereof some containing no colour of verity, we may at first sight reject them: others which seem to carry some face of truth, we may reduce unto experiment. And herein we shall rather perform good offices unto truth, then any disservice unto their relators, who have well

41

deserved of succeeding Ages; from whom having received the conceptions of former Times, we have the readier hint of their conformity with ours, and may accordingly explore and sift their verities.

5. *Plinius Secundus* of *Verona*; a man of great Eloquence, and industry indefatigable, as may appear by his writings, especially those now extant, and which are never like to perish, but even with learning it self; that is, his Natural History. He was the greatest Collector or Rhapsodist of the Latines, and as *Suetonius* observeth, he collected this piece out of two thousand Latine and Greek Authors. Now what is very strange, there is scarce a popular error passant in our days, which is not either directly expressed, or diductively contained in this Work; which being in the hands of most men, hath proved a powerful occasion of their propagation. Wherein notwithstanding the credulity of the Reader is more condemnable then the curiosity of the Author: for commonly he nameth the Authors from whom he received those accounts, and writes but as he reads, as in his Preface to *Vespasian* he acknowledgeth.

6. *Claudius Ælianus*, who flourished not long after in the reign of *Trajan*, unto whom he dedicated his Tacticks; an elegant and miscellaneous Author, he hath left two Books which are in the hands of every one, his History of Animals, and his *Varia Historia*. Wherein are contained many things suspicious, not a few false, some impossible; he is much beholding unto *Ctesias*, and in many uncertainties writes more confidently then *Pliny*.

7. *Julius Solinus*, who lived also about this time: He left a Work entitled *Polyhistor*, containing great variety of matter, and is with most in good request at this day. But to speak freely what cannot be concealed, it is but *Pliny* varied, or a transcription of his Natural History; nor is it without all wonder it hath continued so long, but is now likely, and deserves indeed to live for ever; not onely for the elegancy of the Text, but the excellency of the Comment, lately performed by *Salmasius*, under the name of *Plinian*-Exercitations.

8. *Athenæus*, a delectable Author, very various, and justly stiled by *Casaubon*, *Græcorum Plinius*. There is extant of his, a famous Piece, under the name of *Deipnosophista*, or *Coena Sapientum*, containing the Discourse of many learned men, at a Feast provided by

Laurentius. It is a laborious Collection out of many Authors, and some whereof are mentioned no where else. It containeth strange and singular relations, not without some spice or sprinkling of all Learning. The Author was probably a better Grammarian then Philosopher, dealing but hardly with *Aristotle* and *Plato*, and betrayeth himself much in his Chapter *De Curiositate Aristotelis*. In brief, he is an Author of excellent use, and may with discretion be read unto great advantage: and hath therefore well deserved the Comments of *Casaubon* and *Dalecampius*. But being miscellaneous in many things, he is to be received with suspition; for such as amass all relations, must erre in some, and may without offence be unbelieved in many.

9. We will not omit the works of *Nicander*, a Poet of good antiquity: that is, is *Theriaca*, and *Alexipharmaca*, Translated and Commented by *Gorræus*: for therein are contained several Traditions, and popular Conceits of venemous Beasts; which only deducted, the Work is to be embraced, as containing the first description of poysons and their antidotes, whereof *Dioscorides*, *Pliny*, and *Galen*, have made especial use in elder times; and *Ardoynus*, *Grevinus*, and others, in times more near our own. We might perhaps let pass *Oppianus*, that famous Cilician Poet. There are extant of his in Greek, four Books of Cynegeticks or Venation, five of Halieuticks or Piscation, commented and published by *Ritterhusius*; wherein describing Beasts of venery and Fishes, he hath indeed but sparingly inserted the vulgar conceptions thereof. So that abating the annual mutation of Sexes in the *Hyæna*, the single Sex of the *Rhinoceros*, the Antipathy between two Drums, of a Lamb and a Wolfes skin, the informity of Cubs, the venation of *Centaures*, the copulation of the *Murena* and the Viper, with some few others, he may be read with great delight and profit. It is not without some wonder his Elegant Lines are so neglected. Surely hereby we reject one of the best Epick Poets, and much condemn the Judgement of *Antoninus*, whose apprehensions so honoured his Poems, that as some report, for every verse, he assigned him a Stater of Gold.

10. More warily are we to receive the relations of *Philes*, who in *Greek Iambicks* delivered the proprieties of Animals, for herein he hath amassed the vulgar accounts recorded by the Ancients, and hath therein especially followed *Ælian*. And likewise *Johannes Tzetzes*, a Grammarian, who besides a Comment upon *Hesiod* and *Homer*, hath left us *Chiliads de Varia Historia*; wherein delivering the accounts of

Ctesias, Herodotus, and most of the Ancients, he is to be embraced with caution, and as a transcriptive Relator.

11. We cannot without partiality omit all caution even of holy Writers, and such whose names are venerable unto all posterity: not to meddle at all with miraculous Authors, or any Legendary relators, we are not without circumspection to receive some Books even of authentick and renowned Fathers. So are we to read the leaves of *Basil* and *Ambrose,* in their Books entituled *Hexameron,* or *The Description of the Creation*; Wherein delivering particular accounts of all the Creatures, they have left us relations sutable to those of *Ælian, Plinie,* and other Natural Writers; whose authorities herein they followed, and from whom most probably they desumed their Narrations. And the like hath been committed by *Epiphanius,* in his *Physiologie*: that is, a Book he hath left concerning the Nature of Animals. With no less caution must we look on *Isidor* Bishop of *Sevil*; who having left in twenty Books, an acurate work *De Originibus,* hath to the Etymologie of Words, superadded their received Natures; wherein most generally he consents with common Opinions and Authors which have delivered them.

12. *Albertus* Bishop of *Ratisbone,* for his great Learning and latitude of Knowledge, sirnamed *Magnus.* Besides Divinity, he hath written many Tracts in Philosophy; what we are chiefly to receive with caution, are his Natural Tractates, more especially those of Minerals, Vegetables, and Animals, which are indeed chiefly Collections out of *Aristotle, Ælian,* and *Pliny,* and respectively contain many of our popular Errors. A man who hath much advanced these Opinions by the authority of his Name, and delivered most Conceits, with strict Enquiry into few. In the same *Classis* may well be placed *Vincentius Belluacensis,* or rather he from whom he collected his *Speculum naturale,* that is, *Guilielmus de Conchis*; and also *Hortus Sanitatis,* and *Bartholomeus Glanvil,* sirnamed *Anglicus,* who writ *De proprietatibus Rerum.* Hither also may be referred *Kiranides,* which is a Collection out of *Harpocration* the Greek, and sundry Arabick Writers; delivering not onely the Natural but Magical propriety of things; a Work as full of Vanity as Variety; containing many relations, whose Invention is as difficult as their Beliefs, and their Experiments sometime as hard as either.

13. We had almost forgot *Jeronimus Cardanus* that famous Physician of *Milan*, a great Enquirer of Truth, but too greedy a Receiver of it. He hath left many excellent Discourses, Medical, Natural, and Astrological; the most suspicious are those two he wrote by admonition in a dream, that is *De Subtilitate & Varietate Rerum*. Assuredly this learned man hath taken many things upon trust, and although examined some, hath let slip many others. He is of singular use unto a prudent Reader; but unto him that onely desireth Hoties, or to replenish his head with varieties; like many others before related, either in the Original or confirmation, he may become no small occasion of Error.

14. Lastly, Authors are also suspicious, not greedily to be swallowed, who pretend to write of Secrets, to deliver Antipathies, Sympathies, and the occult abstrusities of things; in the list whereof may be accounted, *Alex. Pedimontanus*, *Antonius Mizaldus*, *Trinum Magicum*, and many others. Not omitting that famous Philosopher of *Naples*, *Baptista Porta*; in whose Works, although there be contained many excellent things, and verified upon his own Experience; yet are there many also receptary, and such as will not endure the test. Who although he hath delivered many strange Relations in his Phytognomonica, and his Villa; yet hath he more remarkably expressed himself in his Natural Magick, and the miraculous effects of Nature. Which containing various and delectable subjects, withall promising wondrous and easie effects, they are entertained by Readers at all hands; whereof the major part sit down in his authority, and thereby omit not onely the certainty of Truth, but the pleasure of its Experiment.

Thus have we made a brief Enumeration of these Learned Men; not willing to decline their Works (without which it is not easie to attain any measure of general Knowledge,) but to apply themselves with caution thereunto. And seeing the lapses of these worthy Pens, to cast a wary eye on those diminutive, and pamphlet Treaties daily published amongst us. Pieces maintaining rather Typography then Verity, Authors presumably writing by Common Places, wherein for many years promiscuously amassing all that makes for their subject, they break forth at last in trite and fruitless Rhapsodies; doing thereby not onely open injury unto Learning, but committing a secret treachery upon truth. For their relations falling upon credulous Readers, they meet with prepared beliefs; whose supinities had rather assent unto all, then adventure the trial of any.

Thus, I say, must these Authors be read, and thus must we be read our selves; for discoursing of matters dubious, and many controvertible truths; we cannot without arrogancy entreat a credulity, or implore any farther assent, then the probability of our Reasons, and verity of experiments induce.

CHAPTER IX

Of the same

There are beside these Authors and such as have positively promoted errors, divers others which are in some way accessory; whose verities although they do not directly assert, yet do they obliquely concur unto their beliefs. In which account are many holy Writers, Preachers, Moralists, Rhetoricians, Orators and Poets; for they depending upon Invention, deduce their mediums from all things whatsoever; and playing much upon the simile, or illustrative argumentation: to induce their Enthymemes unto the people, they took up popular conceits, and from traditions unjustifiable or really false, illustrate matters of undeniable truth. Wherein although their intention be sincere, and that course not much condemnable; yet doth it notoriously strengthen common Errors, and authorise Opinions injurious unto truth.

Thus have some Divines drawn into argument the Fable of the *Phoenix*, made use of that of the *Salamander, Pelican, Basilisk*, and divers relations of *Plinie*; deducing from thence most worthy morals, and even upon our Saviour. Now although this be not prejudicial unto wiser Judgments, who are but weakly moved with such arguments, yet it is oft times occasion of Error unto vulgar heads, who expect in the Fable as equal a truth as in the Moral, and conceive that infallible Philosophy, which is in any sense delivered by Divinity. But wiser discerners do well understand, that every Art hath its own circle; that the effects of things are best examined, by sciences wherein are delivered their causes; that strict and definitive expressions, are alway required in Philosophy, but a loose and popular delivery will serve oftentimes in Divinity. As may be observed even in holy Scripture, which often omitteth the exact account of things; describing them rather to our apprehensions, then leaving doubts in vulgar minds, upon their unknown and Philosophical descriptions. Thus it termeth the Sun and the Moon the two great lights of Heaven. Now if any shall from hence conclude, the Moon is second in magnitude unto the Sun, he must excuse my belief; and it cannot be strange, if herein I rather adhere unto the demonstration of *Ptolomy*, then the popular description of *Moses*. Thus is it said, *Chron.* 2. 4, That *Solomon* made a molten Sea of ten Cubits from brim to brim round in compass, and five Cubits the height thereof, and a line of thirty Cubits did compass it round about. Now in this description, the circumference is made just treble unto the Diameter; that is, as 10. to 30. or 7. to 21. But *Archimedes* demonstrates, that the proportion of the Diameter unto the circumference, is as 7. unto almost 22. which will occasion a sensible difference, that is almost a Cubit. Now if herein I adhere unto *Archimedes* who speaketh exactly, rather then the sacred Text which speaketh largely; I hope I shall not offend Divinity: I am sure I shall have reason and experience of every circle to support me.

Thus Moral Writers, Rhetoricians and Orators make use of several relations which will not consist with verity. *Aristotle* in his Ethicks takes up the conceit of the *Bever*, and the divulsion of his Testicles. The tradition of the Bear, the Viper, and divers others are frequent amongst Orators. All which although unto the illiterate and undiscerning hearers may seem a confirmation of their realities; yet is this no reasonable establishment unto others, who will not depend hereon otherwise then common Apologues: which being of impossible falsities, do notwithstanding include wholsome moralities, and such as expiate the trespass of their absurdities.

The Hieroglyphical doctrine of the Ægyptians (which in their four hundred years cohabitation some conjecture they learned from the Hebrews) hath much advanced many popular conceits. For using an Alphabet of things, and not of words, through the image and pictures thereof, they endeavoured to speak their hidden conceits in the letters and language of Nature. In pursuit whereof, although in many things, they exceeded not their true and real apprehensions; yet in some other they either framing the story, or taking up the tradition, conducible unto their intentions, obliquely confirmed many falsities; which as authentick and conceded truths did after pass unto the Greeks, from them unto other Nations, and are still retained by symbolical Writers, Emblematists, Heralds, and others. Whereof some are strictly maintained for truths, as naturally making good their artificial representations; others symbolically intended, are literally received, and swallowed in the first sense, without all gust of the second. Whereby we pervert the profound and mysterious knowledge of Ægypt; containing the Arcana's of Greek Antiquities, the Key of many obscurities and ancient learning extant. Famous herein in former Ages were *Heraiscus, Cheremon, Epius,* especially *Orus Apollo Niliacus*: who lived in the reign of *Theodosius,* and in Ægyptian language left two Books of Hieroglyphicks, translated into Greek by *Philippus,* and a large collection of all made after by *Pierius.* But no man is likely to profound the Ocean of that Doctrine, beyond that eminent example of industrious Learning, *Kircherus.*

Painters who are the visible representers of things, and such as by the learned sense of the eye endeavour to inform the understanding, are not inculpable herein, who either describing Naturals as they are, or actions as they have been, have oftentimes erred in their delineations. Which being the Books that all can read, are fruitful advancers of these conceptions, especially in common and popular apprehensions: who being unable for farther enquiry, must rest in the draught and letter of their descriptions.

Lastly, Poets and Poetical Writers have in this point exceeded others, trimly advancing the Ægyptian notions of *Harpies, Phoenix, Gryphins,* and many more. Now however to make use of Fictions, Apologues, and Fables, be not unwarrantable, and the intent of these inventions might point at laudable ends; yet do they afford our junior capacities a frequent occasion of error, setling impressions in our tender memories, which our advanced judgments generally neglect to expunge. This way the vain and idle fictions of the Gentiles did first insinuate into the heads of Christians; and thus are they continued even unto our days. Our first and literary apprehensions being commonly instructed in Authors which handle nothing else; wherewith our memories being stuffed, our inventions become pedantick, and cannot avoid their allusions; driving at these as at the highest elegancies, which are but the frigidities of wit, and become not the genius of manly ingenuities. It were therefore no loss like that of *Galens* Library, if these had found the same fate; and would in some way requite the neglect of solid Authors, if they were less pursued. For were a pregnant wit educated in ignorance hereof, receiving only impressions from realities; upon such solid foundations, it must surely raise more substantial superstructions, and fall upon very many excellent strains, which have been jusled off by their intrusions.

CHAPTER X

Of the last and common Promoter of false Opinions, the endeavours of Satan

But beside the infirmities of humane Nature, the seed of Error within our selves, and the several ways of delusion from each other, there is an invisible Agent, and secret promoter without us, whose activity is undiscerned, and plays in the dark upon us; and that is the first contriver of Error, and professed opposer of Truth, the Devil. For though permitted unto his proper principles, *Adam* perhaps would have sinned without the suggestion of Satan: and from the transgressive infirmitives of himself might have erred alone, as well as the Angels before him: And although also there were no Devil at all, yet there is now in our Natures a confessed sufficiency unto corruption, and the frailty of our own Oeconomie, were able to betray us out of Truth, yet wants there not another Agent, who taking advantage hereof proceedeth to obscure the diviner part, and efface all tract of its traduction. To attempt a particular of all his wiles, is too bold an Arithmetick for man: what most considerably concerneth his popular and practised ways of delusions, he first deceiveth mankind in five main points concerning God and himself.

And first his endeavours have ever been, and they cease not yet to instill a belief in the mind of Man, there is no God at all. And this he principally endeavours to establish in a direct and literal apprehension; that is, that there is no such reality existent, that the necessity of his entity dependeth upon ours, and is but a Political Chymera; that the natural truth of God is an artificial erection of Man, and the Creator himself but a subtile invention of the Creature. Where he succeeds not thus high, he labours to introduce a secondary and deductive Atheism; that although men concede there is a God, yet should they deny his providence. And therefore assertions have flown about, that he intendeth only the care of the species or common natures, but letteth loose the guard of individuals, and single existencies therein: that he looks not below the Moon, but hath designed the regiment of sublunary affairs unto inferiour deputations. To promote which apprehensions, or empuzzel their due conceptions, he casteth in the notions of fate, destiny, fortune, chance, and necessity; terms commonly misconceived by vulgar heads, and their propriety sometime perverted by the wisest. Whereby extinguishing in minds the compensation of vertue and vice, the hope and fear of Heaven or Hell; they comply in their actions unto the drift of his delusions, and live like creatures without the capacity of either.

Now hereby he not onely undermineth the Base of Religion, and destroyeth the principle preambulous unto all belief; but puts upon us the remotest Error from Truth. For Atheism is the greatest falsity, and to affirm there is no God, the highest lie in Nature. And therefore strictly taken, some men will say his labour is in vain; For many there are, who cannot conceive there was ever any absolute *Atheist*; or such as could determine there was no God, without all check from himself, or contradiction from his other opinions. And therefore those few so called by elder times, might be the best of *Pagans*; suffering that name rather in relation to the gods of the Gentiles, then the true Creator of all. A conceit that cannot befal his greatest enemy, or him that would induce the same in us; who hath a sensible apprehension hereof, for he believeth with trembling. To speak yet more strictly and conformably unto some Opinions, no creature can wish thus much; nor can the Will which hath a power to run into velleities, and wishes of impossibilities, have any *utinam* of this. For to desire there were no God, were plainly to unwish their own being; which must needs be annihilated in the substraction of that essence which substantially supporteth them, and restrains them from regression into nothing. And if as some contend, no creature can desire his own annihilation, that Nothing is not appetible, and not to be at all, is worse then to be in the miserablest condition of something; the Devil himself could not embrace that motion, nor would the enemy of God be freed by such a Redemption.

But coldly thriving in this design, as being repulsed by the principles of humanity, and the dictates of that production, which cannot deny its original, he fetcheth a wider circle; and when he cannot make men conceive there is no God at all, he endeavours to make them believe there is not one, but many: wherein he hath been so successful with common heads, that he hath led their belief thorow all the Works of Nature.

Now in this latter attempt, the subtilty of his circumvention, hath indirectly obtained the former. For although to opinion there be many gods, may seem an excess in Religion, and such as cannot at all consist with Atheism, yet doth it deductively and upon inference include the same, for Unity is the inseparable and essential attribute of Deity; and if there be more then one God, it is no Atheism to say there is no God at all. And herein though *Socrates* only suffered, yet were *Plato* and *Aristotle* guilty of the same Truth; who demonstratively understanding the simplicity of perfection, and the indivisible condition of the first causator, it was not in the power of Earth, or Areopagy of Hell to work them from it. For holding an Apodictical knowledge, and assured science of its verity, to perswade their apprehensions unto a plurality of gods in the world, were to make *Euclide* believe there were more then one Center in a Circle, or one right Angle in a Triangle; which were indeed a fruitless attempt, and inferreth absurdities beyond the evasion of Hell. For though Mechanick and vulgar heads ascend not unto such comprehensions, who live not commonly unto half the advantage of their principles; yet did they not escape the eye of wiser *Minerva's*, and such as made good the genealogie of *Jupiters* brains; who although they had divers stiles for God, yet under many appellations acknowledged one divinity: rather conceiving thereby the evidence or acts of his power in several ways and places, then a multiplication of Essence, or real distraction of unity in any one.

Again, To render our errors more monstrous (and what unto miracle sets forth the patience of God,) he hath endeavoured to make the world believe, that he was God himself; and failing of his first attempt to be but like the highest in Heaven, he hath obtained with men to be the same on Earth. And hath accordingly assumed the annexes of Divinity, and the prerogatives of the Creator, drawing into practice the operation of miracles, and the prescience of things to come. Thus hath he in a specious way wrought cures upon the sick: played over the wondrous acts of Prophets, and counterfeited many miracles of Christ and his Apostles. Thus hath he openly contended with God, and to this effect his insolency was not ashamed to play a solemn prize with *Moses*; wherein although his performance were very specious, and beyond the common apprehension of any power below a Deity; yet was it not such as could make good his Omnipotency. For he was wholly confounded in the conversion of dust into lice. An act Philosophy can scarce deny to be above the Power of Nature, nor upon a requisite predisposition beyond the efficacy of the Sun. Wherein notwithstanding the head of the old Serpent was confessedly too weak for *Moses* hand, and the arm of his Magicians too short for the finger of God.

Thus hath he also made men believe that he can raise the dead, that he hath the key of life and death, and a prerogative above that principle which makes no regression from privations. The Stoicks that opinioned the souls of wise men dwelt about the Moon, and those of fools wandred about the Earth, advantaged the conceit of this effect; wherein the Epicureans, who held that death was nothing, nor nothing after death, must contradict their principles to be deceived. Nor could the Pythagorian or such as maintained the transmigration of souls give easie admittance hereto: for holding that separated souls successively supplied other bodies, they could hardly allow the raising of souls from other worlds, which at the same time, they conceived conjoyned unto bodies in this. More inconsistent with these Opinions, is the Error of Christians, who holding the dead do rest in the Lord, do yet believe they are at the lure of the Devil: that he who is in bonds himself commandeth the fetters of the dead, and dwelling in the bottomless lake, the blessed from *Abrahams* bosome, that can believe the real resurrection of *Samuel*: or that there is any thing but delusion in the practice of Necromancy and popular raising of Ghosts.

He hath moreover endeavoured the opinion of Deity, by the delusion of Dreams, and the discovery of things to come in sleep, above the prescience of our waked senses. In this expectation he perswaded the credulity of elder times to take up their lodging before his temple, in skins of their own sacrifices: till his reservedness had contrived answers, whose accomplishments were in his power, or not beyond his presagement. Which way, although it hath pleased Almighty God, sometimes to reveal himself, yet was the proceeding very different. For the revelations of Heaven are conveyed by new impressions, and the immediate illumination of the soul, whereas the deceiving spirit, by concitation of humours, produceth his conceited phantasms, or by compounding the species already residing, doth make up words which mentally speak his intentions.

But above all he most advanced his Deity in the solemn practice of Oracles, wherein in several parts of the World, he publikely professed his Divinity; but how short they flew of that spirit, whose omniscience, they would resemble, their weakness sufficiently declared. What jugling there was therein, the Orator plainly confessed, who being good at the same game himself, could say that *Pythia* Philippised. Who can but laugh at the carriage of *Ammon* unto *Alexander*, who addressing unto him as a god, was made to believe, he was a god himself? How openly did he betray his Indivinity unto *Crœus*, who being ruined by his Amphibology, and expostulating with him for so ungrateful a deceit, received no higher answer then the excuse of his impotency upon the contradiction of fate, and the setled law of powers beyond his power to controle! What more then sublunary directions, or such as might proceed from the Oracle of humane Reason, was in his advice unto the Spartans in the time of a great Plague; when for the cessation thereof, he wisht them to have recourse unto a Fawn, that is in open terms, unto one *Nebrus*, a good Physitian of those days? From no diviner a spirit came his reply unto *Caracalla*, who requiring a remedy for his Gout, received no other counsel then to refrain cold drink; which was but a dietetical caution, and such as without a journey unto *Æsculapius*, culinary prescription and kitchin Aphorisms might have afforded at home. Nor surely if any truth there were therein, of more then natural activity was his counsel unto *Democratus*; when for the Falling-sickness he commended the Maggot in a Goats head. For many things secret are true: sympathies and antipathies are safely authentick unto us, who ignorant of their causes may yet acknowledge their effects. Beside, being a natural Magician he may perform many acts in ways above our knowledge, though not transcending our natural power, when our knowledge shall direct it. Part hereof hath been discovered by himself, and some by humane indagation: which though magnified as fresh inventions unto us, are stale unto his cognition. I hardly believe he hath from elder times unknown the verticity of the Loadstone; surely his perspicacity discerned it to respect the North, when ours beheld it indeterminately. Many secrets there are in Nature of difficult discovery unto man, of easie knowledge unto Satan; whereof some his vain glory cannot conceal, others his envy will not discover.

Again, Such is the mysterie of his delusion, that although he labour to make us believe that he is God, and supremest nature whatsoever, yet would he also perswade our beliefs, that he is less then Angels or men; and his condition not onely subjected unto rational powers, but the actions of things which have no efficacy on our selves. Thus hath he inveigled no small part of the world into a credulity of artificial Magick: That there is an Art, which without compact commandeth the powers of Hell; whence some have delivered the polity of spirits, and left an account even to their Provincial Dominions: that they stand in awe of Charms, Spels, and Conjurations; that he is afraid of letters and characters, of notes and dashes, which set together do signifie nothing, not only in the dictionary of man, but the subtiler vocabulary of Satan. That there is any power in *Bitumen*, Pitch, or Brimstone, to purifie the air from his uncleanness; that any vertue there is in *Hipericon* to make good the name of *fuga Dœmonis*, any such Magick as is ascribed unto the Root *Baaras* by *Josephus*, or *Cynospastus* by *Ælianus*, it is not easie to believe; nor is it naturally made out what is delivered of *Tobias*, that by the fume of a Fishes liver, he put to flight *Asmodeus*. That they are afraid of the pentangle of *Solomon*, though so set forth with the body of man, as to touch and point out the five places wherein our Saviour was wounded, I know not how to assent. If perhaps he hath fled from holy Water, if he cares not to hear the sound of *Tetragrammaton*, if his eye delight not in the sign of the Cross; and that sometimes he will seem to be charmed with words of holy Scripture, and to flie from the letter and dead verbality, who must onely start at the life and animated interiours thereof: It may be feared they are but *Parthian* flights, *Ambuscado* retreats, and elusory tergiversations: Whereby to confirm our credulities, he will comply with the opinion of such powers, which in themselves have no activities. Whereof having once begot in our minds an assured dependance, he makes us relie on powers which he but precariously obeys; and to desert those true and only charms which Hell cannot withstand.

Lastly, To lead us farther into darkness, and quite to lose us in this maze of Error, he would make men believe there is no such creature as himself: and that he is not only subject unto inferiour creatures, but in the rank of nothing. Insinuating into mens minds there is no Devil at all, and contriveth accordingly, many ways to conceal or indubitate his existency. Wherein beside that, he annihilates the blessed Angels and Spirits in the rank of his Creation; he begets a security of himself, and a careless eye unto the last remunerations. And therefore

56

hereto he inveigleth, not only *Sadduces* and such as retain unto the Church of God: but is also content that *Epicurus, Democritus*, or any Heathen should hold the same. And to this effect he maketh men believe that apparitions, and such as confirm his existence are either deceptions of sight, or melancholly depravements of phansie. Thus when he had not onely appeared but spake unto *Brutus*; *Cassius* the Epicurian was ready at hand to perswade him, it was but a mistake in his weary imagination, and that indeed there were no such realities in nature. Thus he endeavours to propagate the unbelief of Witches, whose concession infers his co-existency; by this means also he advanceth the opinion of total death, and staggereth the immortality of the soul; for, such as deny there are spirits subsistent without bodies, will with more difficulty affirm the separated existence of their own.

Now to induce and bring about these falsities, he hath laboured to destroy the evidence of Truth, that is the revealed verity and written Word of God. To which intent he hath obtained with some to repudiate the Books of *Moses*, others those of the Prophets, and some both: to deny the Gospel and authentick Histories of Christ; to reject that of *John*, and to receive that of *Judas*; to disallow all, and erect another of *Thomas*. And when neither their corruption by *Valentinus* and *Arrius*, their mutilation by *Marcion, Manes*, and *Ebion* could satisfie his design, he attempted the ruine and total destruction thereof; as he sedulously endeavoured, by the power and subtilty of *Julian, Maximinus*, and *Dioclesian*.

But the longevity of that piece, which hath so long escaped the common fate, and the providence of that Spirit, which ever waketh over it, may at last discourage such attempts; and if not make doubtful its Mortality, at least indubitably declare; this is a stone too big for *Saturns* mouth, and a bit indeed Oblivion cannot swallow.

And thus how strangely he possesseth us with Errors may clearly be observed, deluding us into contradictory and inconsistent falsities; whilest he would make us believe, That there is no God. That there are many. That he himself is God. That he is less then angels or Men. That he is nothing at all.

Nor hath he only by those wiles depraved the conception of the Creator, but with such Riddles hath also entangled the Nature of our Redeemer. Some denying his Humanity, and that he was one of the Angels, as *Ebion*; that the Father and Son were but one person, as *Sabellius*. That his body was phantastical, as *Manes*, *Basilides*, *Priscillian*, *Jovinianus*; that he only passed through *Mary*, as *Utyches* and *Valentinus*. Some denying his Divinity; that he was begotten of humane principles, and the seminal son of *Joseph*; as *Carpocras*, *Symmachus*, *Photinus*: that he was *Seth* the Son of *Adam*, as the *Sethians*: that he was less then Angels, as *Cherinthus*: that he was inferiour unto *Melchisedec*, as *Theodotus*: that he was not God, but God dwelt in him, as *Nicholaus*: and some embroyled them both. So did they which converted the Trinity into a Quaternity, and affirmed two persons in Christ, as *Paulus Samosatenus*: that held he was Man without a Soul, and that the Word performed that office in him, as *Apollinaris*: that he was both Son and Father, as *Montanus*: that *Jesus* suffered, but Christ remained impatible, as *Cherinthus*. Thus he endeavours to entangle Truths: And when he cannot possibly destroy its substance, he cunningly confounds its apprehensions; that from the inconsistent and contrary determinations thereof, consectary impieties, and hopeful conclusions may arise, there's no such thing at all.

CHAPTER XI.

A further Illustration

Now although these ways of delusions most Christians have escaped, yet are there many other whereunto we are daily betrayed, and these we meet with in obvious occurrents of the world, wherein he induceth us, to ascribe effects unto causes of no cognation; and distorting the order and theory of causes perpendicular to their effects, he draws them aside unto things whereto they run parallel, and in their proper motions would never meet together.

Thus doth he sometime delude us in the conceits of Stars and Meteors, beside their allowable actions ascribing effects thereunto of independent causations. Thus hath he also made the ignorant sort believe that natural effects immediately and commonly proceed from supernatural powers: and these he usually drives from Heaven, his own principality the Air, and Meteors therein; which being of themselves the effects of natural and created causes, and such as upon a due conjunction of actives and passives, without a miracle must arise unto what they appear; are always looked on by ignorant spectators as supernatural spectacles, and made the causes or signs of most succeeding contingencies. To behold a Rainbow in the night, is no prodigy unto a Philosopher. Then Eclipses of Sun or Moon, nothing is more natural. Yet with what superstition they have been beheld since the Tragedy of *Nicias* and his Army, many examples declare.

True it is, and we will not deny, that although these being natural productions from second and setled causes, we need not alway look upon them as the immediate hand of God, or of his ministring Spirits; yet do they sometimes admit a respect therein; and even in their naturals, the indifferency of their existencies contemporised unto our actions, admits a farther consideration.

That two or three Suns or Moons appear in any mans life or reign, it is not worth the wonder. But that the same should fall out at a remarkable time, or point of some decisive action; that the contingency of the appearance should be confined unto that time; that those two should make but one line in the Book of Fate, and stand together in the great Ephemerides of God; beside the Philosophical assignment of the cause, it may admit a Christian apprehension in the signality.

But above all he deceiveth us, when we ascribe the effects of things unto evident and seeming causalities, which arise from the secret and undiscerned action of himself. Thus hath he deluded many Nations in his Augurial and Extispicious inventions, from casual and uncontrived contingencies divining events succeeding. Which *Tuscan* superstition seizing upon *Rome*, hath since possessed all *Europe*. When *Augustus* found two galls in his sacrifice, the credulity of the City concluded a hope of peace with *Anthony*; and the conjunction of persons in choler with each other. Because *Brutus* and *Cassius* met a Blackmore, and *Pompey* had on a dark or sad coloured garment at *Pharsalia*; these were presages of their overthrow. Which notwithstanding are scarce Rhetorical sequels; concluding Metaphors from realities, and from conceptions metaphorical inferring realities again.

Now these divinations concerning events, being in his power to force, contrive, prevent, or further, they must generally fall out conformably unto his predictions. When *Graceus* was slain, the same day the Chickens refused to come out of the Coop: and *Claudius Pulcher* underwent the like success, when he contemned the Tripudiary Augurations: They died not because the Pullets would not feed: but because the Devil foresaw their death, he contrived that abstinence in them. So was there no natural dependence of the event. An unexpected way of delusion, and whereby he more easily led away the incircumspection of their belief. Which fallacy he might excellently have acted before the death of *Saul*; for that being within his power to foretell, was not beyond his ability to foreshew: and might have contrived signs thereof through all the creatures, which visibly confirmed by the event, had proved authentick unto those times, and advanced the Art ever after.

He deludeth us also by Philters, Ligatures, Charms, ungrounded Amulets, Characters, and many superstitious ways in the cure of common diseases: seconding herein the expectation of men with events of his own contriving. Which while some unwilling to fall directly upon Magick, impute unto the power of imagination, or the efficacy of hidden causes, he obtains a bloody advantage: for thereby he begets not only a false opinion, but such as leadeth the open way of destruction. In maladies admitting natural reliefs, making men rely on remedies, neither of real operation in themselves, nor more then seeming efficacy in his concurrence. Which whensoever he pleaseth to withdraw, they stand naked unto the mischief of their diseases; and revenge the contempt of the medicines of the Earth which God hath created for them. And therefore when neither miracle is expected, nor connection of cause unto effect from natural grounds concluded; however it be sometime successful, it cannot be safe to rely on such practises, and desert the known and authentick provisions of God. In which rank of remedies, if nothing in our knowledge or their proper power be able to relieve us, we must with patience submit unto that restraint, and expect the will of the Restrainer.

Now in these effects although he seems oft-times to imitate, yet doth he concur unto their productions in a different way from that spirit which sometime in natural means produceth effects above Nature. For whether he worketh by causes which have relation or none unto the effect, he maketh it out by secret and undiscerned ways of Nature. So when *Caius* the blind, in the reign of *Antoninus*, was commanded to pass from the right side of the Altar unto the left, to lay five fingers of one hand thereon, and five of the other upon his eyes; although the cure succeeded and all the people wondered, there was not any thing in the action which did produce it, nor any thing in his power that could enable it thereunto. So for the same infirmity, when *Aper* was counselled by him to make a Collyrium or ocular medicine with the blood of a white Cock and Honey, and apply it to his eyes for three days: When *Julian* for his spitting of blood, was cured by Honey and Pine nuts taken from his Altar: When *Lucius* for the pain in his side, applied thereto the ashes from his Altar with wine; although the remedies were somewhat rational, and not without a natural vertue unto such intentions, yet need we not believe that by their proper faculties they produced these effects.

But the effects of powers Divine flow from another operation; who either proceeding by visible means or not, unto visible effects, is able to conjoin them by his co-operation. And therefore those sensible ways which seem of indifferent natures, are not idle ceremonies, but may be causes by his command, and arise unto productions beyond their regular activities. If *Nahaman* the Syrian had washed in *Jordan* without the command of the prophet, I believe he had been cleansed by them no more then by the waters of *Damascus*. I doubt if any beside *Elisha* had cast in salt, the waters of *Jericho* had not been made wholsome. I know that a decoction of wild gourd or Colocynthis (though somewhat qualified) will not from every hand be dulcified unto aliment by an addition of flower or meal. There was some natural vertue in the Plaister of figs applied unto *Ezechias*; we find that gall is very mundificative, and was a proper medicine to clear the eyes of *Tobit*: which carrying in themselves some action of their own, they were additionally promoted by that power, which can extend their natures unto the production of effects beyond their created efficiencies And thus may he operate also from causes of no power unto their visible effects; for he that hath determined their actions unto certain effects, hath not so emptied his own, but that he can make them effectual unto any other.

Again, Although his delusions run highest in points of practice, whose errors draw on offensive or penal enormities, yet doth he also deal in points of speculation, and things whose knowledge terminates in themselves. Whose cognition although it seems indifferent, and therefore its aberration directly to condemn no man; yet doth he hereby preparatively dispose us unto errors, and deductively deject us into destructive conclusions.

That the Sun, Moon, and Stars are living creatures, endued with soul and life, seems an innocent Error, and an harmless digression from truth; yet hereby he confirmed their Idolatry, and made it more plausibly embraced. For wisely mistrusting that reasonable spirits would never firmly be lost in the adorement of things inanimate, and in the lowest form of Nature; he begat an opinion that they were living creatures, and could not decay for ever.

That spirits are corporeal, seems at first view a conceit derogative unto himself, and such as he should rather labour to overthrow;

yet hereby he establisheth the Doctrine of Lustrations, Amulets and Charms, as we have declared before.

That there are two principles of all things, one good, and another evil; from the one proceeding vertue, love, light, and unity; from the other, division, discord, darkness, and deformity, was the speculation of *Pythagoras, Empedocles*, and many ancient Philosophers, and was no more then *Oromasdes* and *Arimanius* of *Zoroaster*. Yet hereby he obtained the advantage of Adoration, and as the terrible principle became more dreadful then his Maker; and therefore not willing to let it fall, he furthered the conceit in succeeding Ages, and raised the faction of *Manes* to maintain it.

That the feminine sex have no generative emission, affording no seminal Principles of conception, was *Aristotles* Opinion of old, maintained still by some, and will be countenanced by him forever. For hereby he disparageth the fruit of the Virgin, frustrateth the fundamental Prophesie, nor can the seed of the Woman then break the head of the Serpent.

Nor doth he only sport in speculative Errors, which are of consequent impieties; but the unquietness of his malice hunts after simple lapses, and such whose falsities do only condemn our understandings. Thus if *Xenophanes* will say there is another world in the Moon; If *Heraclitus* with his adherents will hold the Sun is no bigger then it appeareth; If *Anaxagoras* affirm that Snow is black; If any other opinion there are no *Antipodes*, or that Stars do fall, he shall not want herein the applause or advocacy of Satan. For maligning the tranquility of truth, he delighteth to trouble its streams; and being a professed enemy unto God (who is truth it self) he promoteth any Error as derogatory to his nature; and revengeth himself in every deformity from truth. If therefore at any time he speak or practise truth it is upon design, and a subtile inversion of the precept of God, to do good that evil may come of it. And therefore sometime we meet with wholsome doctrines from Hell; *Nosce teipsum*, the Motto of *Delphos*, was a good precept in morality: That a just man is beloved of the gods, an uncontrolable verity. 'Twas a good deed, though not well done, which he wrought by *Vespasian*, when by the touch of his foot he restored a lame man, and by the stroak of his hand another that was blind, but the intention hereof drived at his own advantage; for hereby he not only confirmed the opinion of his power with the people, but his integrity with Princes; in whose power he knew it lay to overthrow his Oracles, and silence the practice of his delusions.

But of such a diffused nature, and so large is the Empire of Truth, that it hath place within the walls of Hell, and the Devils themselves are daily forced to practise it; not onely as being true themselves in a Metaphysical verity, that is, as having their essence conformable unto the Intellect of their Maker, but making use of Moral and Logical verities; that is, whether in the conformity of words unto things, or things unto their own conceptions, they practise truth in common among themselves. For although without speech they intuitively conceive each other, yet do their apprehensions proceed through realities; and they conceive each other by species, which carry the true and proper notions of things conceived. And so also in Moral verities, although they deceive us, they lie not unto each other; as well understanding that all community is continued by Truth, and that of Hell cannot consist without it.

To come yet nearer the point, and draw into a sharper angle; They do not only speak and practise truth, but may be said wellwishers hereunto, and in some sense do really desire its enlargement. For many things which in themselves are false, they do desire were true; He cannot but wish he were as he professeth, that he had the knowledge of future events; were it in his power, the Jews should be in the right, and the *Messias* yet to come. Could his desires effect it, the opinion of *Aristotle* should be true, the world should have no end, but be as immortal as himself. For thereby he might evade the accomplishment of those afflictions, he now but gradually endureth; for comparatively unto those flames, he is but yet in *Balneo*, then begins his *Ignis Rotæ*, and terrible fire, which will determine his disputed subtilty, and even hazard his immortality.

But to speak strictly, he is in these wishes no promoter of verity, but if considered some ways injurious unto truth; for (besides that if things were true, which now are false, it were but an exchange of their natures, and things must then be false, which now are true) the setled and determined order of the world would be perverted, and that course of things disturbed, which seemed best unto the immutable contriver. For whilest they murmur against the present disposure of things, regulating determined realities unto their private optations, they rest not in their established natures; but unwishing their unalterable verities, do tacitely desire in them a difformity from the primitive Rule, and the Idea of that mind that formed all things best. And thus he offendeth truth even in his first attempt: For not content with his created nature, and thinking it too low, to be the highest creature of God, he offended the Ordainer, not only in the attempt, but in the wish and simple volition thereof.

End of Book I

THE SECOND
BOOK

Of sundry popular Tenets concerning Mineral, and vegetable bodies, generally held for truth: which examined, prove either false, or dubious.

CHAPTER I

Of Crystal

Hereof the common Opinion hath been, and still remaineth amongst us, that Crystal is nothing else but Ice or Snow concreted, and by duration of time, congealed beyond liquation. Of which assertion, if prescription of time, and numerosity of Assertors, were a sufficient demonstration, we might sit down herein, as an unquestionable truth; nor should there need *ulterior* disquisition. For few Opinions there are which have found so many friends, or been so popularly received, through all Professions and Ages. *Pliny* is positive in this Opinion: *Crystallus fit gelu vehementius concreto:* the same is followed by *Seneca*, Elegantly described by *Claudian*, not denied by *Scaliger*, some way affirmed by *Albertus*, *Brasavolus*, and directly by many others. The venerable Fathers of the Church have also assented hereto; As *Basil* in his *Hexameron*, *Isidore* in his Etymologies, and not only *Austin* a Latine Father, but *Gregory* the Great, and *Jerome* upon occasion of that term expressed in the first of *Ezekiel*.

All which notwithstanding, upon a strict enquiry, we find the matter controvertible, and with much more reason denied then is as yet affirmed. For though many have passed it over with easie affirmatives, yet are there also many Authors that deny it, and the exactest Mineralogists have rejected it. *Diodorus* in his eleventh Book denieth it, (if Crystal be there taken in its proper acception, as *Rhodiginus* hath used it, and not for a Diamond, as *Salmatius* hath expounded it) for in that place he affirmeth; *Crystallum esse lapidem ex aqua pura concretum, non tamen frigore sed divini caloris vi. Solinus* who transcribed *Pliny*, and therefore in almost all subscribed unto him, hath in this point dissented from him. *Putant quidam glaciem coire, & in Crystallum corporari, sed frustra. Mathiolus* in his Comment upon *Dioscorides*, hath with confidence rejected it. The same hath been performed by *Agricola de natura fossilium*; by *Cardan, Bœtius de Boot, Cæsius Bernardus, Sennertus*, and many more.

Now besides Authority against it, there may be many reasons deduced from their several differences which seem to overthrow it. And first, a difference is probable in their concretion. For if Crystal be a stone (as in the number thereof it is confessedly received,) it is not immediately concreted by the efficacy of cold, but rather by a Mineral spirit, and lapidifical principles of its own, and therefore while it lay *in solutis principiis*, and remained in a fluid Body, it was a subject very unapt for proper conglaciation; for Mineral spirits do generally resist and scarce submit thereto. So we observe that many waters and springs will never freeze, and many parts in Rivers and Lakes, where there are Mineral eruptions, will still persist without congelations, as we also observe in *Aqua fortis*, or any Mineral solution, either of Vitriol, Alum, Salt-petre, Ammoniac, or Tartar, which although to some degree exhaled, and placed in cold Conservatories, will Crystallize and shoot into white and glacious bodies; yet is not this a congelation primarily effected by cold, but an intrinsecal induration from themselves; and a retreat into their proper solidities, which were absorbed by the liquor, and lost in a full imbibition thereof before. And so also when wood and many other bodies do putrifie, either by the Sea, other waters, or earths abounding in such spirits; we do not usually ascribe their induration to cold, but rather unto salinous spirits, concretive juices, and causes circumjacent, which do assimilate all bodies not indisposed for their impressions.

But Ice is water congealed by the frigidity of the air, whereby it acquireth no new form, but rather a consistence or determination of its diffluency, and amitteth not its essence, but condition of fluidity. Neither doth there any thing properly conglaciate but water, or watery humidity; for the determination of quick-silver is properly fixation, that of milk coagulation, and that of oyl and unctious bodies, only incrassation; And therefore *Aristotle* makes a trial of the fertility of humane seed, from the experiment of congelation; for that (saith he) which is not watery and improlifical will not conglaciate; which perhaps must not be taken strictly, but in the germ and spirited particles: for Eggs I observe will freeze, in the albuginous part thereof. And upon this ground *Paracelsus* in his Archidoxis, extracteth the magistery of wine; after four moneths digestion in horse-dung, exposing it unto the extremity of cold; whereby the aqueous parts will freeze, but the Spirit retire and be found congealed in the Center.

But whether this congelation be simply made by cold, or also by co-operation of any nitrous coagulum, or spirit of Salt the principle of concretion; whereby we observe that Ice may be made with Salt and Snow by the fire side; as is also observable from Ice made by Saltpetre and water, duly mixed and strongly agitated at any time of the year, were a very considerable enquiry. For thereby we might clear the generation of Snow, Hail, and hoary Frosts, the piercing qualities of some winds, the coldness of Caverns, and some Cells. We might more sensibly conceive how Salt-petre fixeth the flying spirits of Minerals in Chymical Preparations, and how by this congealing quality it becomes an useful medicine in Fevers.

Again, The difference of their concretion is collectible from their dissolution; which being many ways performable in Ices, is few ways effected in Crystal. Now the causes of liquation are contrary to those of concretion; and as the Atoms and indivisible parcels are united, so are they in an opposite way disjoyned. That which is concreted by exsiccation or expression of humidity, will be resolved by humectation, as Earth, Dirt, and Clay; that which is coagulated by a fiery siccity, will suffer colliquation from an aqueous humidity, as Salt and Sugar, which are easily dissoluble in water, but not without difficulty in oyl, and well rectified spirits of Wine. That which is concreted by cold, will dissolve by a moist heat, if it consist of watery parts, as Gums, Arabick, Tragacanth, Ammoniac and others; in an airy heat or oyl, as all resinous bodies, Turpentine, Pitch, and Frankincense; in both, as gummy resinous bodies, Mastick, Camphire and Storax; in neither, as neutrals and bodies anomalous hereto, as Bdellium, Myrrhe, and others. Some by a violent dry heat, as Metals; which although corrodible by waters, yet will they not suffer a liquation from the powerfullest heat, communicable unto that element. Some will dissolve by this heat although their ingredients be earthy, as Glass, whose materials are fine Sand, and the ashes of Chali or Fearn; and so will Salt run with fire, although it be concreted by heat. And this way may be effected a liquation in Crystal, but not without some difficulty; that is, calcination or reducing it by Art into a subtle powder; by which way and a vitreous commixture, Glasses are sometime made hereof, and it becomes the chiefest ground for artificial and factitious gemms. But the same way of solution is common also unto many Stones; and not onely Beryls and Cornelians, but Flints and Pebbles, are subject unto fusion, and will run like Glass in fire.

But Ice will dissolve in any way of heat, for it will dissolve with fire, it will colliquate in water, or warm oyl; nor doth it only submit unto an actual heat, but not endure the potential calidity of many waters. For it will presently dissolve in cold *Aqua fortis*, sp. of Vitriol, Salt, or Tartar, nor will it long continue its fixation in spirits of Wine, as may be observed in Ice injected therein.

Again, The concretion of Ice will not endure a dry attrition without liquation; for if it be rubbed long with a cloth, it melteth. But Crystal will calefie unto electricity, that is, a power to attract straws or light bodies, and convert the needle freely placed. Which is a declarement of very different parts, wherein we shall not inlarge, as having discoursed concerning such bodies in the Chap. of Electricks.

They are differenced by supernatation or floating upon water; for Crystal will sink in water, as carrying in its own bulk a greater ponderosity then the space in any water it doth occupy; and will therefore only swim in molten Metal and Quicksilver. But Ice will swim in water of what thinness soever; and though it sink in oyl, will float in spirits of Wine or *Aqua vitæ*. And therefore it may swim in water, not only as being water it self, and in its proper place, but perhaps as weighing somewhat less then the water it possesseth. And therefore as it will not sink unto the bottom, so will it neither float above like lighter bodies, but being near in weight, lie superficially or almost horizontally unto it. And therefore also an Ice or congelation of Salt or Sugar, although it descend not unto the bottom, yet will it abate, and decline below the surface in thin water, but very sensibly in spirits of Wine. For Ice although it seemeth as transparent and compact as Crystal, yet is it short in either; for its atoms are not concreted into continuity, which doth diminish its translucency; it is also full of spumes and bubbles, which may abate its gravity. And therefore waters frozen in Pans, and open Glasses, after their dissolution do commonly leave a froth and spume upon them, which are caused by the airy parts diffused in the congealable mixture which uniting themselves and finding no passage at the surface, do elevate the mass, and make the liquor take up a greater place then before: as may be observed in Glasses filled with water, which being frozen, will seem to swell above the brim. So that if in this condensation any one affirmeth there is also some rarefaction, experience may assert it.

They are distinguished in substance of parts and the accidents thereof, that is, in colour and figure; for Ice is a similary body, and homogeneous concretion, whose material is properly water, and but accidentally exceeding the simplicity of that element. But the body of Crystal is mixed; its ingredients many, and sensibly containeth those principles into which mixt bodies are reduced. For beside the spirit and mercurial principle it containeth a sulphur or inflamable part, and that in no small quantity; for besides its Electrick attraction, which is made by a sulphureous effluvium, it will strike fire upon percussion like many other stones, and upon collision with Steel actively send forth its sparks, not much inferiourly unto a flint. Now such bodies as strike fire have sulphureous or ignitible parts within them, and those strike best, which abound most in them. For these scintillations are not the accension of the air, upon the collision of two hard bodies, but rather the inflamable effluencies or vitrified sparks discharged from the bodies collided. For Diamonds, Marbles, Heliotropes and Agaths, though hard bodies, will not readily strike fire with a Steel, much less with one another: Nor a Flint so readily with a Steel, if they both be very wet, for then the sparks are sometimes quenched in their eruption.

It containeth also a salt, and that in some plenty, which may occasion its fragility, as is also observable in Coral. This by the Art of Chymistry is separable, unto the operations whereof it is liable, with other concretions, as calcination, reverberation, sublimation, distillation: And in the preparation of Crystal, *Paracelsus* hath made a rule for that of Gemms. Briefly, it consisteth of parts so far from an Icie dissolution, that powerful menstruums are made for its emollition; whereby it may receive the tincture of Minerals, and so resemble Gemms, as *Boetius* hath declared in the distillation of Urine, spirits of Wine, and Turpentine; and is not only triturable, and reducible into powder, by contrition, but will subsist in a violent fire, and endure a vitrification. Whereby are testified its earthly and fixed parts. For vitrification is the last work of fire, and a fusion of the Salt and Earth, which are the fixed elements of the composition, wherein the fusible Salt draws the Earth and infusible part into one continuum, and therefore ashes will not run from whence the Salt is drawn, as bone ashes prepared for the Test of Metals. Common fusion in Metals is also made by a violent heat, acting upon the volatile and fixed, the dry and humid parts of those bodies; which notwithstanding are so united, that upon attenuation from heat, the humid parts will not fly away, but draw the fixed ones into fluor with them. Ordinary liquation in wax and oily bodies is made by a gentler heat, where the oyl and salt, the fixed and fluid principles will not easily separate. All which, whether by vitrification, fusion or liquation, being forced into fluent consistencies, do naturally regress into their former solidities. Whereas the melting of Ice is a simple resolution, or return from solid to fluid parts, wherein it naturally resteth.

As for colour, although Crystal in his pellucid body seems to have none at all, yet in its reduction into powder, it hath a vail and shadow of blew; and in its courser pieces, is of a sadder hue then the powder of Venice glass; and this complexion it will maintain although it long endure the fire. Which notwithstanding needs not move us unto wonder; for vitrified and pellucid bodies, are of a clearer complexion in their continuities, then in their powders and Atomical divisions. So *Stibium* or glass of *Antimony*, appears somewhat red in glass, but in its powder yellow; so painted glass of a sanguine red will not ascend in powder above a murrey.

As for the figure of Crystal (which is very strange, and forced *Pliny* to despair of resolution) it is for the most part hexagonal or six cornered; being built upon a confused matter, from whence as it were from a root angular figures arise, even as in the Amethyst and Basaltes. Which regular figuration hath made some opinion, it hath not its determination from circumscription, or as conforming unto contiguities, but rather from a seminal root, and formative principle of its own, even as we observe in several other concretions. So the stones which are sometime found in the gall of a man, are most triangular and pyramidal, although the figure of that part seems not to cooperate thereto. So the *Asteria* or *lapis stellaris*, hath on it the figure of a Star, so *Lapis Judaicus* hath circular lines in length all down its body, and equidistant, as though they had been turned by Art. So that we call a Fayrie stone, and is often found in *gravel pits* amongst us, being of an hemispherical figure, hath five double lines arising from the center of its basis, which if no accretion distract them, do commonly concur, and meet in the pole thereof. The figures are regular in many other stones, as in the Belemnites, *Lapis Anguinus*, *Cornu Ammonis*, and many more; as by those which have not the experience hereof may be observed in their figures expressed by Mineralogists. But Ice receiveth its figure according unto the surface wherein it concreteth, or the circum-ambiency which conformeth it. So it is plain upon the surface of water, but round in Hayl (which is also a glaciation,) and figured in its guttulous descent from the air, and so growing greater or lesser according unto the accretion or pluvious aggelation about the mother and fundamental Atomes thereof; which seems to be some feathery particle of Snow; although Snow it self be sexangular, or at least of a starry and many-pointed figure.

They are also differenced in the places of their generation; for though Crystal be found in cold countries, and where Ice remaineth long, and the air exceedeth in cold, yet is it also found in regions, where Ice is seldom seen or soon dissolved; as *Pliny* and *Agricola* relate of *Cyprus*, *Caramania* and an Island in the Red sea; It hath been also found in the veins of Minerals, sometimes agglutinated unto lead, sometimes in Rocks, opacous stones, and the marble face of *Octavius* Duke of *Parma*. It hath also constant veins; as beside others, that of mount *Salvino* about the Territory of *Bergamo*; from whence if part be taken, in no long tract of time out of the same place, as from its mineral matrix, others are observed to arise. Which made the learned *Cerautus* to conclude, *Fideant hi an sit glacies, an vero corpus fossile.* It is also found in the veins of Minerals, in rocks, and sometime in common earth. But as for Ice, it will not readily concrete but in the approachment of the air, as we have made trial in glasses of water, covered an inch with oyl, which will not easily freeze in hard frosts of our climate. For water commonly concreteth first in its surface, and so conglaciates downward; and so will it do although it be exposed in the coldest metal of lead, which well accordeth with that expression of *Job*, *The waters are hid as with a stone, and the face of the deep is frozen.* But whether water which hath been boiled or heated, doth sooner receive this congelation, as commonly is delivered, we rest in the experiment of *Cabeus*, who hath rejected the same in his excellent discourse of Meteors.

They have contrary qualities elemental, and uses medicinal; for Ice is cold and moist, of the quality of water; but Crystal is cold and dry, according to the condition of the earth. The use of Ice is condemned by most Physicians, that of crystal commended by many. For although *Dioscorides* and *Galen* have left no mention thereof, yet hath *Mathiolus*, *Agricola*, and many commended it in dysenteries and fluxes; all for the increase of milk, most Chymists for the Stone, and some, as *Brassavolus* and *Boetius*, as an antidote against poyson. Which occult and specifical operations are not expectable from Ice; for being but water congealed, it can never make good such qualities; nor will it reasonably admit of secret proprieties, which are the affections of forms, and compositions at distance from their elements.

Having thus declared what Crystal is not, it may afford some satisfaction to manifest what it is. To deliver therefore what with the judgement of approved Authors, and best reason consisteth, It is a Mineral body in the difference of stones, and reduced by some unto that subdivision, which comprehendeth gemms, transparent and resembling Glass or Ice, made of a lentous percolation of earth, drawn from the most pure and limpid juice thereof, owing unto the coldness of the earth some concurrence or coadjuvancy, but not immediate determination and efficiency, which are wrought by the hand of its concretive spirit, the seeds of petrification and Gorgon within it self. As sensible Philosophers conceive of the generation of Diamonds, Iris, Berils. Not making them of frozen icecles, or from meer aqueous and glaciable substances, condensing them by frosts into solidities, vainly to be expected even from Polary congelations: but from thin and finest earths, so well contempered and resolved, that transparency is not hindred; and containing lapidifical spirits, able to make good their solidities against the opposition and activity of outward contraries, and so leave a sensible difference between the bonds of glaciation, which in the mountains of Ice about the Northern Seas, are easily dissolved by ordinary heat of the Sun, and between the finer legatures of petrification, whereby not only the harder concretions of Diamonds and Saphirs, but the softer veins of Crystal remain indissolvable in scorching Territories, and the *Negro* land of Congor.

And therefore I fear we commonly consider subterranities, not in contemplations sufficiently respective unto the Creation. For though *Moses* have left no mention of Minerals, nor made any other description then sutes unto the apparent and visible Creation, yet is there unquestionably, a very large Classis of Creatures in the Earth, far above the condition of the elementarity. And although not in a distinct and indisputable way of vivency, or answering in all points the properties or affections of Plants, yet in inferiour and descending constitutions, they do like these contain specifical distinctions, and are determined by seminalities, that is, created and defined seeds committed unto the Earth from the beginning. Wherein although they attain

76

not the indubitable requisites of Animation, yet have they a near affinity thereto. And though we want a proper name and expressive appellation, yet are they not to be closed up in the general name of concretions; or lightly passed over as only Elementary and Subterraneous mixtions.

The principle and most gemmary affection is its Tralucency: as for irradiancy or sparking which is found in many gemms, it is not discoverable in this, for it cometh short of their compactness and durity; and therefore requireth not the Emery, as the Saphir, Granate, and Topaz, but will receive impression from Steel, in a manner like the Turchois. As for its diaphanity or perspicuity, it enjoyeth that most eminently; and the reason thereof is its continuity; as having its earthy and salinous parts so exactly resolved, that its body is left imporous and not discreted by atomical terminations. For, that continuity of parts is the cause of perspicuity, it is made perspicuous by two ways of experiment. That is, either in effecting transparency in those bodies which were not so before, or at least far short of the additional degree: So Snow becomes transparent upon liquation, so Horns and Bodies resolvable into continued parts or gelly. The like is observable in oyled paper, wherein the interstitial divisions being continuated by the accession of oyl, it becometh more transparent, and admits the visible rayes with less umbrosity. Or else the same is effected by rendering those bodies opaceous, which were before pellucid and perspicuous.

So Glass which was before diaphanous, being by powder reduced into multiplicity of superficies, becomes an opacous body, and will not transmit the light. So it is in Crystal powdered, and so it is also before; for if it be made hot in a crucible, and presently projected upon water, it will grow dim, and abate its diaphanity; for the water entering the body, begets a division of parts, and a termination of Atoms united before unto continuity.

The ground of this Opinion might be, first the conclusions of some men from experience; for as much as Crystal is found sometimes in rocks, and in some places not much unlike the stirrious or stillicidious dependencies of Ice. Which notwithstanding may happen either in places which have been forsaken or left bare by the earth, or may be petrifications, or Mineral indurations, like other gemms, proceeding from percolations of the earth disposed unto such concretions.

The second and most common ground is from the name *Crystallus*, whereby in Greek both Ice and Crystal are expressed; which many not duly considering, have from their community of name, conceived a community of nature; and what was ascribed unto the one, not unfitly appliable unto the other. But this is a fallacy of Æquivocation, from a society in name inferring an Identity in nature. By this fallacy was he deceived that drank *Aqua fortis* for strong water: By this are they deluded, who conceive *sperma Coeti* which is found about the head, to be the spawn of the Whale: Or take *sanguis draconis* (which is the gumme of a tree,) to be the blood of a Dragon. By the same Logick we may infer, the Crystalline humour of the eye, or rather the Crystalline heaven above, to be of the substance of Crystal here below; Or that God sendeth down Crystal, because it is delivered in the vulgar translation, Psal. 147, *Mittit Crystallum suum sicut Buccellas.* Which translation although it literally express the Septuagint; yet is there no more meant thereby, then what our translation in plain English expresseth; that is, he casteth forth his Ice like morsels, or what *Tremellius* and *Junius* as clearly deliver, *Dejicit gelu suum sicut frusta, coram frigore ejus quis consistet?* which proper and latine expressions, had they been observed in ancient translations, elder Expositors had not been misguided by the Synonymy: nor had they afforded occasion unto *Austin*, the Gloss, *Lyranus*, and many others, to have taken up the common conceit, and spoke of this Text conformably unto the opinion rejected.

CHAPTER II

Concerning the Loadstone

Of things particularly spoken thereof evidently or probably true. Of things generally believed, or particularly delivered, manifestly or probably false. In the first of the Magnetical vertue of the Earth, of the four motions of the stone, that is, its Verticity or Direction, its Attraction or Coition, its Declination, its Variation, and also of its Antiquity. In the second a rejection of sundry opinions and relations thereof, Natural, Medical, Historical, Magical.

And first we conceive the earth to be a Magnetical body. A Magnetical body, we term not onely that which hath a power attractive, but that which seated in a convenient medium, naturally disposeth it self to one invariable and fixed situation. And such a Magnetical vertue we conceive to be in the Globe of the Earth, whereby as unto its natural points and proper terms, it disposeth it self unto the poles; being so framed, constituted, and ordered unto these points, that those parts which are now at the poles, would not naturally abide under the Æquator, nor *Greenland* remain in the place of *Magellanica*. And if the whole earth were violently removed, yet would it not foregoe its primitive points, nor pitch in the East or West, but return unto its polary position again. For though by compactness or gravity it may acquire the lowest place, and become the center of the universe, yet that it makes good that point, not varying at all by the accession of bodies upon, or secession thereof from its surface, perturbing the equilibration of either Hemisphere (whereby the altitude of the stars might vary) or that it strictly maintains the North and Southern points; that neither upon the motions of the heavens, air, and winds without, large eruptions and division of parts within, its polary parts should never incline or veer unto the Equator (whereby the latitude of places should also vary) it cannot so well be salved from gravity as a Magnetical verticity. This is probably, that foundation the wisdom of the Creator hath laid unto the earth; in this sense we may more nearly apprehend, and sensibly make out the expressions of holy Scripture, as *Firmavit orbem terræ qui non commovebitur,* he hath made the round world so sure that it cannot be moved: as when it is said by Job, *Extendit Aquilonem super vacuo,* &c. He stretcheth forth the North upon the empty place, and hangeth the earth upon nothing. And this is the most probable answer unto that great question. Whereupon are the foundations of the Earth fastened, or who laid the corner stone thereof? Had they been acquainted with this principle, *Anaxagoras, Socrates,* and *Democritus,* had better made out the ground of this stability; *Xenophanes* had not been fain to say the Earth had no bottom, and *Thales Milesius* to make it swim in water.

Nor is the vigour of this great body included only in its self, or circumferenced by its surface, but diffused at indeterminate distances through the air, water, and all bodies circumjacent. Exciting and impregnating Magnetical bodies within its surface or without it, and performing in a secret and invisible way what we evidently behold effected by the Loadstone. For these effluxions penetrate all bodies, and like the species of visible objects are ever ready in the medium, and lay hold on all bodies proportionate or capable of their action, those bodies likewise being of a congenerous nature, do readily receive the impressions of their motor; and if not fettered by their gravity, conform themselves to situations, wherein they best unite unto their Animator. And this will sufficiently appear from the observations that are to follow, which can no better way be made out then by this we speak of, the Magnetical vigour of the Earth. Now whether these effluviums do flye by striated Atoms and winding particles as *Renatus des Cartes* conceiveth; or glide by streams attracted from either Pole and Hemisphere of the Earth unto the Equator, as Sir *Kenelm Digby* excellently declareth, it takes not away this vertue of the Earth, but more distinctly sets down the gests and progress thereof, and are conceits of eminent use to salve Magnetical Phenomena's. And as in Astronomy those hypotheses though never so strange are best esteemed which best do salve apparencies; so surely in Philosophy those principles (though seeming monstrous) may with advantage be embraced, which best confirm experiment, and afford the readiest reason of observation. And truly the doctrine of effluxions, their penetrating natures, their invisible paths, and insuspected effects, are very considerable; for besides this Magnetical one of the Earth, several effusions there may be from divers other bodies, which invisibly act their parts at any time, and perhaps through any medium; a part of Philosophy but yet in discovery, and will, I fear, prove the last leaf to be turned over in the Book of Nature.

First, Therefore it is true, and confirmable by every experiment, that Steel and good Iron never excited by the Loadstone, discover in themselves a verticity; that is, a directive or polary faculty, whereby, conveniently placed, they do septentrionate at one extream, and Australize at another. This is manifestable in long and thin plates of Steel perforated in the middle and equiliberated; or by an easier way in long wires equiponderate with untwisted Silk and soft Wax; for in this manner pendulous, they will conform themselves Meridionally, directing one extream unto the North, another to the South. The same is also manifest in Steel wires thrust through little sphears or globes of Cork and floated on the water, or in naked Needles gently let fall thereon; for so disposed they will not rest, until they have found out the Meridian, and as near as they can lye parallel unto the Axis of the Earth: Sometimes the eye, sometimes the point Northward in divers Needles, but the same point always in most: Conforming themselves unto the whole Earth, in the same manner as they do unto every Loadstone. For if a Needle untouch be hanged above a Loadstone, it will convert into a parallel position thereto; for in this situation it can best receive its verticity and be excited proportionably at both extreams. Now this direction proceeds not primitively from themselves, but is derivative and contracted from the Magnetical effluctions of the Earth; which they have winded in their hammering and formation; or else by long continuance in one position, as we shall declare hereafter.

It is likewise true what is delivered of Irons heated in the fire, that they contract a verticity in their refrigeration; for heated red hot and cooled in the Meridian from North to South, they presently contract a polary power, and being poised in air or water, convert that part unto the North which respected that point in its refrigeration, so that if they had no sensible verticity before, it may be acquired by this way; or if they had any, it might be exchanged by contrary position in the cooling. For by the fire they omit not onely many drossie and scorious parts, but whatsoever they had received from the Earth or Loadstone;

and so being naked and despoiled of all verticity, the Magnetical Atomes invade their bodies with more effect and agility.

Neither is it only true what *Gilbertus* first observed, that Irons refrigerated North and South acquire a Directive faculty; but if they be cooled upright and perpendicularly, they will also obtain the same. That part which is cooled toward the North on this side the Equator, converting it self unto the North, and attracting the South point of the Needle: the other and highest extream respecting the South, and attracting the Northern, according unto Laws Magnetical: For (what must be observed) contrary Poles or faces attract each other, as the North the South; and the like decline each other, as the North the North. Now on this side of the Equator, that extream which is next the Earth is animated unto the North, and the contrary unto the South; so that in coition it applies it self quite oppositely, the coition or attraction being contrary to the Verticity or Direction. Contrary, If we speak according unto common use, yet alike, if we conceive the vertue of the North Pole to diffuse it self and open at the South, and the South at the North again.

This polarity from refrigeration upon extremity and in defect of a Loadstone might serve to invigorate and touch a Needle any where; and this, allowing variation, is also the readiest way at any season to discover the North or South; and surely far more certain then what is affirmed of the grains and circles in trees, or the figure in the root of Fern. For if we erect a red hot wire until it cool, then hang it up with wax and untwisted Silk, where the lower end and that which cooled next the earth doth rest, that is the Northern point; and this we affirm will still be true, whether it be cooled in the air or extinguished in water, oyl of Vitriol, *Aqua fortis*, or Quicksilver. And this is also evidenced in culinary utensils and Irons that often feel the force of fire, as Tongs, Fire-shovels, Prongs, and Andirons; all which acquire a Magnetical and polary condition, and being suspended, convert their lower extreams unto the North; with the same attracting the Southern point of the Needle. For easier experiment, if we place a Needle touched at the foot of Tongs or Andirons, it will obvert or turn aside its lillie or North point, and conform its cuspis or South extream unto the Andiron. The like verticity though more obscurely is also contracted by Bricks and Tiles, as we have made trial in some taken out of the backs of Chimneys. Now to contract this Direction, there needs not a total ignition, nor is it necessary the Irons should be red hot all over.

82

For if a wire be heated only at one end, according as that end is cooled upward or downward, it respectively acquires a verticity, as we have declared in wires totally candent. Nor is it absolutely requisite they should be cooled perpendicularly, or strictly lie in the Meridian; for whether they be refrigerated inclinatorily or somewhat Æquinoxially, that is toward the Eastern or Western points; though in a lesser degree, they discover some verticity.

Nor is this onely true in Irons, but in the Loadstone it self. For if a Loadstone be made red hot, it loseth the magnetical vigour it had before in it self, and acquires another from the Earth in its refrigeration; for that part which cooleth toward the Earth will acquire the respect of the North, and attract the Southern point or cuspis of the Needle. The experiment hereof we made in a Loadstone of a parallelogram or long square figure; wherein onely inverting the extreams, as it came out of the fire, we altered the poles or faces thereof at pleasure.

It is also true what is delivered of the Direction and coition of Irons, that they contract a verticity by long and continued position; that is, not onely being placed from North to South, and lying in the Meridian, but respecting the Zenith and perpendicular unto the Center of the Earth; as is manifest in bars of windows, casements, hinges and the like. For if we present the Needle unto their lower extreams, it wheels about and turns its Southern point unto them. The same condition in long time do Bricks contract which are placed in walls, and therefore it may be a fallible way to find out the Meridian by placing the Needle on a wall; for some Bricks therein by a long and continued position, are often magnetically enabled to distract the polarity of the Needle. And therefore those Irons which are said to have been converted into Loadstones; whether they were real conversions, or onely attractive augmentations, might be much promoted by this position: as the Iron cross of a hundred weight upon the Church of St. *John* in *Ariminum*, or that Loadston'd Iron of *Cæsar Moderatus*, set down by *Aldrovandus*.

Lastly, Irons do manifest a verticity not only upon refrigeration and constant situation, but (what is wonderful and advanceth the magnetical Hypothesis) they evidence the same by meer position according as they are inverted, and their extreams disposed respectively unto the Earth. For if an Iron or Steel not formerly excited, be held perpendicularly or inclinatorily unto the Needle, the lower end thereof will attract the *cuspis* or Southern point; but if the same extream be inverted and held under the Needle, it will then attract the lilly or Northern point; for by inversion it changeth its direction acquired before, and receiveth a new and Southern polarity from the Earth, as being the upper extream. Now if an Iron be touched before, it varieth not in this manner; for then it admits not this magnetical impression, as being already informed by the Loadstone, and polarily determined by its preaction.

And from these grounds may we best determine why the Northern Pole of the Loadstone attracteth a greater weight then the Southern on this side of the Æquator; why the stone is best preserved in a natural and polary situation; and why as *Gilbertus* observeth, it respecteth that Pole out of the Earth, which it regarded in its Mineral bed and subterraneous position.

It is likewise true and wonderful what is delivered of the Inclination or Declination of the Loadstone; that is, the descent of the Needle below the plain of the Horizon. For long Needles which stood before upon their *axis, parallel* unto the Horizon, being vigorously excited, incline and bend downward, depressing the North extream below the Horizon. That is the North on this, the South on the other side of the Equator; and at the very Line or middle circle stand without deflexion. And this is evidenced not onely from observations of the Needle in several parts of the earth, but sundry experiments in any part thereof, as in a long Steel wire, equilibrated or evenly ballanced in the air; for excited by a vigorous Loadstone it will somewhat depress its animated extream, and intersect the horizontal circumference. It is also manifest in a Needle pierced through a Globe of Cork so cut away and pared by degrees, that it will swim under water, yet sink not unto the bottom, which may be well effected; for if the Cork be a thought too light to sink under the surface, the body of the water may be attenuated with spirits of wine; if too heavy, it may be incrassated with salt; and if by chance too much be added, it may again be thinned by a proportionable addition of fresh water. If then the Needle be taken out, actively touched and put in again, it will depress and bow down its Northern head toward the bottom, and advance its Southern extremity toward the brim. This way invented by *Gilbertus* may seem of difficulty; the same with less labour may be observed in a needled sphere of Cork equally contiguous unto the surface of the water; for if the Needle be not exactly equiponderant, that end which is a thought too light, if touched becometh even; that Needle also which will but just swim under the water, if forcibly touched will sink deeper, and sometime unto the bottom. If likewise that inclinatory vertue be destroyed by a touch from the contrary Pole, that end which before was elevated will then decline, and this perhaps might be observed in some scales exactly ballanced, and in such Needles which for their bulk can hardly be supported by the water. For if they be powerfully excited and equally let fall, they commonly sink down and break the water at that extream whereat they were septentrionally excited: and by this way it is conceived there may be some fraud in the weighing of precious commodities, and such as carry a value in quarter-grains; by placing a powerful Loadstone above or below, according as we intend to depress or elevate one extream.

Now if these Magnetical emissions be onely qualities, and the gravity of bodies incline them onely unto the earth; surely that which alone moveth other bodies to descent, carrieth not the stroak in this, but rather the Magnetical alliciency of the Earth; unto which with alacrity it applieth it self, and in the very same way unto the whole Earth, as it doth unto a single Loadstone. For if an untouched Needle be at a distance suspended over a Loadstone, it will not hang parallel, but decline at the North extream, and at that part will first salute its Director. Again, what is also wonderful, this inclination is not invariable; for just under the line the Needle lieth parallel with the Horizon, but sailing North or South it beginneth to incline, and encreaseth according as it approacheth unto either Pole; and would at least endeavour to erect it self. And this is no more then what it doth upon the Loadstone, and that more plainly upon the Terella or spherical magnet Cosmographically set out with circles of the Globe. For at the Equator thereof, the Needle will stand rectangularly; but approaching Northward toward the Tropick it will regard the stone obliquely, and when it attaineth the Pole, directly; and if its bulk be no impediment, erect it self and stand perpendicularly thereon. And therefore upon strict observation of this inclination in several latitudes and due records preserved, instruments are made whereby without the help of Sun or Star, the latitude of the place may be discovered; and yet it appears the observations of men have not as yet been so just and equal as is desireable; for of those Tables of declination which I have perused, there are not any two that punctually agree; though some have been thought exactly calculated, especially that which *Ridley* received from Mr. *Brigs*, in our time Geometry Professor in *Oxford*.

It is also probable what is delivered concerning the variation of the Compass that is the cause and ground thereof, for the manner as being confirmed by observation we shall not at all dispute. The variation of the Compass is an Arch of the Horizon intercepted between the true and Magnetical Meridian; or more plainly, a deflexion and siding East and West from the true Meridian. The true Meridian is a major Circle passing through the Poles of the World, and the Zenith or Vertex of any place, exactly dividing the East from the West. Now on this line the Needle exactly lieth not, but diverts and varieth its point, that is, the North point on this side the Equator, the South on the other; sometimes on the East, sometime toward the West, and in some few places varieth not at all. First, therefore it is observed that betwixt the Shore of *Ireland, France, Spain, Guiny,* and the *Azores,* the North point varieth toward the East, and that in some variety; at *London* it varieth eleven degrees, at *Antwerp* nine, at *Rome* but five: at some parts of the *Azores* it deflecteth not, but lieth in the true Meridian; on the other side of the *Azores,* and this side of the Equator, the North point of the Needle wheeleth to the West; so that in the latitude of 36 near the shore, the variation is about eleven degrees; but on the other side the Equator, it is quite otherwise: for about *Capo Frio* in *Brasilia,* the South point varieth twelve degrees unto the West, and about the mouth of the Straits of *Magellan* five or six; but elongating from the coast of *Brasilia* toward the shore of *Africa* it varieth Eastward, and arriving at *Capo de las Aguillas,* it resteth in the Meridian, and looketh neither way.

Now the cause of this variation was thought by *Gilbertus* to be the inequality of the Earth, variously disposed, and indifferently intermixed with the Sea: withal the different disposure of its Magnetical vigor in the eminencies and stronger parts thereof. For the Needle naturally endeavours to conform unto the Meridian, but being distracted, driveth that way where the greater and powerfuller part of the Earth is placed. Which may be illustrated from what hath been delivered and may be conceived by any, that understands the generalities of Geography. For whereas on this side of the Meridian, or the Isles of *Azores,* where the first Meridian is placed, the Needle varieth Eastward; it may be occasioned by that vast Tract of Earth, that is, of *Europe, Asia,* and *Africa,* seated toward the East, and disposing the Needle that way. For arriving at some part of the *Azores,* or Islands of Saint *Michael,* which have a middle situation between these Continents, and that a vast and almost answerable Tract of America, it seemeth equally distracted by both; and diverting unto neither, doth parallel and place it self upon the true Meridian. But sailing farther, it veers its Lilly to the West, and regardeth that quarter wherein the Land is nearer or greater; and in the same latitude as it approacheth the shore augmenteth its variation. And therefore as some observe, if *Columbus* or whosoever first discovered *America*, had apprehended the cause of this variation, having passed more then half the way, he might have been confirmed in the discovery, and assuredly foretold there lay a vast and mighty continent toward the West. The reason I confess and inference is good, but the instance perhaps not so. For *Columbus* knew not the variation of the compass, whereof *Sebastian Cabot* first took notice, who after made discovery in the Northern part of that continent. And it happened indeed that part of *America* was first discovered, which was on this side farthest distant, that is, *Jamaica*, *Cuba*, and the Isles in the Bay of *Mexico*. And from this variation do some new discoverers deduce a probability in the attempts of the Northern passage toward the *Indies*.

Now because where the greater continents are joyned, the action and effluence is also greater; therefore those Needles do suffer the greatest variation which are in Countries which most do feel that action. And therefore hath *Rome* far less variation then *London*; for on the West side of *Rome* are seated the great continents of *France*, *Spain*, *Germany*, which take off the exuperance, and in some way ballance the vigor of the Eastern parts. But unto *England* there is almost no Earth West, but the whole extent of *Europe* and *Asia* lieth Eastward; and therefore at *London* it varieth eleven degrees, that is almost one *Rhomb*. Thus also by reason of the great continent of *Brasilia*, *Peru*, and *Chili*, the Needle deflecteth toward the Land twelve degrees; but at the straits of *Magellan* where the Land is narrowed, and the Sea on the other side, it varieth but five or six. And so likewise, because the Cape *de las Agullas* hath Sea on both sides near it, and other Land remote, and as it were æquidistant from it, therefore at that point the Needle conforms unto the true Meridian, and is not distracted by the vicinity of Adjacencies. This is the general and great cause of variation. But if in certain Creeks and Vallies the Needle prove irregular, and vary beyond expectation, it may be imputed unto some vigorous part of the Earth, or Magnetical eminence not far distant. And this was the invention of *D[r]. Gilbert*, not many years past, a Physitian in *London*. And therefore although some assume the invention of its direction, and other have had the glory of the Card; yet in the experiments, grounds, and causes thereof, *England* produced the Father Philosopher, and discovered more in it then *Columbus* or *Americus* did ever by it.

Unto this in great part true the reason of *Kircherus* may be added: That this variation proceedeth not only from terrestrious eminencies, and magnetical veins of the Earth, laterally respecting the Needle, but the different coagmentation of the Earth disposed unto the Poles, lying under the Sea and Waters, which affect the Needle with great or lesser variation, according to the vigour or imbecility of these subterraneous lines, or the entire or broken compagination of the magnetical fabrick under it. As is observable from several Loadstones placed at the bottom of any water, for a Loadstone or Needle upon the surface, will variously conform it self, according to the vigour or faintness of the Loadstones under it.

Thus also a reason may be alledged for the variation of the variation, and why, according to observation, the variation of the Needle hath after some years been found to vary in some places. For this may proceed from mutations of the earth, by subterraneous fires, fumes, mineral spirits, or otherwise: which altering the constitution of the magnetical parts, in process of time, doth vary the variation over the place.

It is also probable what is conceived of its Antiquity, that the knowledge of its polary power and direction unto the North was unknown unto the Ancients; and though *Levinus Lemnius*, and *Cælius Colcagninus*, are of another belief, is justly placed with new inventions by *Pancirollus*. For their *Achilles* and strongest argument is an expression in *Plautus*, a very ancient Author, and contemporary unto *Ennius. Hic ventus jam secundus est, cape modo versoriam.* Now this *versoriam* they construe to be the compass, which notwithstanding according unto *Pineda*, who hath discussed the point, *Turnebus, Cabeus,* and divers others, is better interpreted the rope that helps to turn the Ship, or as we say, doth make it tack about; the Compass declaring rather the Ship is turned, then conferring unto its conversion. As for the long expeditions and sundry voyages of elder times, which might confirm the Antiquity of this invention, it is not improbable they were performed by the help of Stars; and so might the Phœnicean navigators, and also *Ulisses* sail about the Mediterranean. By the flight of Birds, or keeping near the shore; and so might *Hanno* coast about *Af-*

rica; or by the help of Oars, as is expressed in the voyage of *Jonah*. And whereas it is contended that this verticity was not unknown unto *Solomon*, in whom is presumed an universality of knowledge; it will as forcibly follow, he knew the Art of Typography, Powder and Guns, or had the Philosopher's Stone, yet sent unto *Ophir* for Gold. It is not to be denied, that beside his Political wisdom, his knowledge in Philosophy was very large; and perhaps from his Works therein, the ancient Philosophers, especially *Aristotle*, who had the assistance of *Alexanders* acquirements, collected great observables. Yet if he knew the use of the Compass, his Ships were surely very slow, that made a three years voyage from *Eziongeber* in the red Sea unto *Ophir*; which is supposed to be *Taprobana* or *Malaca* in the *Indies*, not many moneths sail; and since in the same or lesser time, *Drake* and *Candish* performed their voyage about the Earth.

And as the knowledge of its verticity is not so old as some conceive, so is it more ancient then most believe; nor had its discovery with Guns, Printing, or as many think, some years before the discovery of *America*. For it was not unknown unto *Petrus Peregrinus*, a Frenchman, who two hundred years since left a Tract of the Magnet, and a perpetual motion to be made thereby, preserved by *Gasserus*. *Paulus Venetus*, and about five hundred years past *Albertus Magnus* make mention hereof, and quote for it a Book of *Aristotle*, *De Lapide*, which Book although we find in the Catalogue of *Laertius*, yet with *Cabeus* we may rather judge it to be the work of some Arabick Writer, not many years before the dayes of *Albertus*.

Lastly, It is likewise true what some have delivered of *Crocus Martis*, that is Steel corroded with Vinegar, Sulphur, or otherwise, and after reverberated by fire. For the Loadstone will not at all attract it, nor will it adhere, but lye therein like Sand. This to be understood of *Crocus Martis* well reverberated and into a violet colour; for common chalybs *præparatus,* or corroded and powdered Steel, the Loadstone attracts like ordinary filings of Iron; and many times most of that which passeth for *Crocus Martis*. So that this way may serve as a test of its preparation; after which it becometh a very good medicine in fluxes. The like may be affirmed of flakes of Iron that are rusty and begin to tend unto Earth; for their cognation then expireth, and the Loadstone will not regard them.

And therefore this may serve as a trial of good Steel. The

Loadstone taking up a greater mass of that which is most pure, it may also decide the conversion of Wood into Iron, as is pretended from some Waters: and the common conversion of Iron into Copper by the mediation of blew Coperose, for the Loadstone will not attract it. Although it may be questioned, whether in this operation, the Iron or Coperose be transmuted, as may be doubted from the cognation of Coperose with Copper; and the quantity of Iron remaining after the conversion. And the same may be useful to some discovery concerning Vitriol or Coperose of Mars, by some called Salt of Steel, made by the spirits of Vitriol or Sulphur. For the corroded powder of Steel will after ablution be actively attracted by the Loadstone, and also remaineth in little diminished quantity. And therefore whether those shooting Salts partake but little of Steel, and be not rather the vitriolous spirits fixed into Salt by the effluvium or odor of Steel, is not without good question.

CHAPTER III

Concerning the Loadstone; therein of sundry common Opinions, and received several relations: Natural, Historical, Medical, Magical.

And first not only a simple Heterodox, but a very hard Paradox, it will seem, and of great absurdity unto obstinate ears, if we say, attraction is unjustly appropriated unto the Loadstone, and that perhaps we speak not properly, when we say vulgarly and appropriately the Loadstone draweth Iron; and yet herein we should not want experiment and great Authority. The words of *Renatus des Cartes* in his Principles of Philosophy are very plain: *Præterea magnes trahet ferrum, sive potius magnes & ferrum ad invicem accedunt, neque enim ulla ibi tractio est.* The same is solemnly determined by *Cabeus. Nec magnes trahit proprie ferrum, nec ferrum ad se magnetum provocat, sed ambo pari conatu ad invicem confluunt.* Concordant hereto is the assertion of Doctor *Ridley*, Physitian unto the Emperour of *Russia*, in his Tract of Magnetical Bodies, defining Magnetical attraction to be a natural incitation and disposition conforming unto contiguity, an union of one Magnetical Body with another, and no violent haling of the weak unto the stronger. And this is also the Doctrine of *Gilbertus*, by whom this motion is termed Coition, and that not made by any faculty attractive of one, but a Syndrome and concourse of each; a Coition alway of their vigours, and also of their bodies, if bulk or impediment prevent not. And therefore those contrary actions which flow from opposite Poles or Faces, are not so properly expulsion and attraction, as *Sequela* and *Fuga*, a mutual flight and following. Consonant whereto are also the determinations of *Helmontius, Kircherus*, and *Licetus.*

The same is also confirmed by experiment; for if a piece of Iron be fastened in the side of a bowl or bason of water, a Loadstone swimming freely in a Boat of Cork, will presently make unto it. So if a Steel or Knife untouched, be offered toward the Needle that is touched, the Needle nimbly moveth toward it, and conformeth unto union with the Steel that moveth not. Again, If a Loadstone be finely filed, the Atoms or dust thereof will adhere unto Iron that was never touched, even as the powder of Iron doth also unto the Loadstone. And lastly, if in two Skiffs of Cork, a Loadstone and Steel be placed within the Orb of their activities, the one doth not move, the other standing still, but both hoise sail and steer unto each other. So that if the Loadstone attract, the Steel hath also its attraction ; for in this action the Alliciency is reciprocal, which joyntly felt, they mutually approach and run into each others arms.

And therefore surely more moderate expressions become this action, then what the Ancients have used; which some have delivered in the most violent terms of their language; so *Austin* calls it *Mirabilem ferri raptorem: Hippocrates*, λίθος hοτι τον οἰδηρον αρπάζει, *Lapis qui ferrum rapit. Galen* disputing against *Epicurus* useth the term ελκειν, but this also is too violent: among the Ancients *Aristotle* spake most warily, λίθος hοστις τον οἰδηρον κινεῖ, *Lapis qui ferrum movet*: and in some tolerable acception do run the expressions of *Aquinas, Scaliger*, and *Cusanus*.

Many relations are made, and great expectations are raised from the *Magnes Carneus*, or a Loadstone, that hath a faculty to attract not only iron but flesh; but this upon enquiry, and as *Cabeus* also observed, is nothing else but a weak and inanimate kind of Loadstone, veined here and there with a few magnetical and ferreous lines, but consisting of a bolary and clammy substance, whereby it adheres like *Hæmatites*, or *Terra Lemnia*, unto the Lips. And this is that stone which is to be understood, when Physitians joyn it with *Ætites*, or the Eagle stone, and promise therein a vertue against abortion.

There is sometime a mistake concerning the variation of the Compass, and therein one point is taken for another. For beyond the Equator some men account its variation by the diversion of the Northern point, whereas beyond that Circle the Southern point is Soveraign, and the North submits his preheminency. For in the Southern coast either of *America* or *Africa*; the Southern point deflects and varieth toward the Land, as being disposed and spirited that way by the Meridional and proper Hemisphere. And therefore on that side of the Earth the varying point is best accounted by the South. And therefore also the writings of some, and Maps of others, are to be enquired, that make the Needle decline unto the East twelve degrees at *Capo Frio*, and six at the straits of *Magellan*; accounting hereby one point for another, and preferring the North in the Liberties and Province of the South.

But certainly false it is what is commonly affirmed and believed, that Garlick doth hinder the attraction of the Loadstone, which is notwithstanding delivered by grave and worthy Writers, by *Pliny*, *Solinus*, *Ptolomy*, *Plutarch*, *Albertus*, *Mathiolus*, *Rueus*, *Langius*, and many more. An effect as strange as that of *Homers Moly*, and the Garlick that *Mercury* bestowed upon *Ulysses*. But that it is evidently false, many experiments declare. For an Iron wire heated red hot and quenched in the juice of Garlick, doth notwithstanding contract a verticity from the Earth, and attracteth the Southern point of the Needle. If also the tooth of a Loadstone be covered or stuck in Garlick, it will notwithstanding attract; and Needles excited and fixed in Garlick until they begin to rust, do yet retain their attractive and polary respects.

Of the same stamp is that which is obtruded upon us by Authors ancient and modern, that an Adamant or Diamond prevents or suspends the attraction of the Loadstone: as is in open terms delivered by *Pliny*. *Adamas dissidet cum Magnete lapide, ut juxta positus ferrum non patiatur abstrahi, aut si admotus magnes apprehenderit, rapiat atque auferat*. For if a Diamond be placed between a Needle and a Loadstone, there will nevertheless ensue a Coition even over the body of the Diamond. And an easie matter it is to touch or excite a Needle through a Diamond, by placing it at the tooth of a Loadstone; and therefore the relation is false, or our estimation of these gemms untrue; nor are they Diamonds which carry that name amongst us.

It is not suddenly to be received what *Paracelsus* affirmeth, that if a Loadstone be anointed with Mercurial oyl, or onely put into Quicksilver, it omitteth its attraction for ever. For we have found that Loadstones and touched Needles which have laid long time in Quicksilver have not amitted their attraction. And we also find that red hot Needles or wires extinguished in Quicksilver, do yet acquire a verticity according to the Laws of position in extinction. Of greater repugnancy unto reason is that which he delivers concerning its graduation, that heated in fire and often extinguished in oyl of Mars or Iron, it acquires an ability to extract or draw forth a nail fastened in a wall; for, as we have declared before, the vigor of the Loadstone is destroyed by fire, nor will it be re-impregnated by any other Magnete then the Earth.

Nor it is to be made out what seemeth very plausible, and formerly hath deceived us, that a Loadstone will not attract an Iron or Steel red hot. The falsity hereof discovered first by *Kircherus*, we can confirm by iterated experiment; very sensibly in armed Loadstones, and obscurely in any other.

True it is, that besides fire some other wayes there are of its destruction, as Age, Rust; and what is least dreamt on, an unnatural or contrary situation. For being impolarily adjoyned unto a more vigorous Loadstone, it will in a short time exchange its Poles; or being kept in undue position, that is, not lying on the Meridian, or else with its poles inverted, it receives in longer time impair in activity, exchange of Faces; and is more powerfully preserved by position then by the dust of Steel. But the sudden and surest way is fire; that is, fire not onely actual but potential; the one surely and suddenly, the other slowly and imperfectly; the one changing, the other destroying the figure. For if distilled Vinegar or *Aqua fortis* be poured upon the powder of Loadstone, the subsiding powder dryed, retains some Magnetical vertue, and will be attracted by the Loadstone; but if the menstruum or dissolvent be evaporated to a consistence, and afterward doth shoot into Icycles or Crystals, the Loadstone hath no power upon them; and if in a full dissolution of Steel a separation of parts be made by precipitation or exhalation, the exsiccated powder hath lost its wings and ascends not unto the Loadstone. And though a Loadstone fired doth presently omit its proper vertue, and according to the position in cooling contracts a new verticity from the Earth; yet if the same be laid awhile in *aqua fortis* or other corrosive water, and taken out before a considerable corrosion, it still reserves its attraction, and will convert the Needle according to former polarity. And that duly preserved from violent corrosion, or the natural disease of rust, it may long conserve its vertue, beside the Magnetical vertue of the Earth, which hath lasted since the Creation, a great example we have from the observation of our learned friend Mr. *Graves*, in an Ægyptian Idol cut out of Loadstone, and found among the *Mummies*; which still retains its attraction, though probably taken out of the Mine about two thousand years ago.

It is improbable what *Pliny* affirmeth concerning the object of its attraction, that it attracts not only ferreous bodies, but also *liquorem vitri*; for in the body of Glass there is no ferreous or magnetical nature which might occasion attraction. For of the Glass we use, the purest is made of the finest sand and the ashes of Chali or Glaswort, and the courser or green sort of the ashes of Brake or other plants. True it is that in the making of Glass, it hath been an ancient practice to cast in pieces of magnet, or perhaps manganes: conceiving it carried away all ferreous and earthy parts, from the pure and running portion of Glass, which the Loadstone would not respect; and therefore if that attraction were not rather Electrical then Magnetical, it was a wondrous effect what *Helmont* delivereth concerning a Glass wherein the Magistery of Loadstone was prepared, which after retained an attractive quality.

But whether the Magnet attracteth more then common Iron, may be tried in other bodies. It seems to attract the Smyris or Emery in powder; It draweth the shining or glassie powder brought from the *Indies*, and usually implied in writing-dust. There is also in Smiths Cinders by some adhesion of Iron whereby they appear as it were glazed, sometime to be found a magnetical operation; for some thereof applied have power to move the Needle. But whether the ashes of vegetables which grow over Iron Mines contract a magnetical quality, as containing some mineral particles, which by sublimation ascend unto their Roots, and are attracted together with their nourishment; according as some affirm from the like observations upon the Mines of Silver, Quick silver, and Gold; we must refer unto further experiment.

It is also improbable and something singular what some conceive, and *Eusebius Nierembergius*, a learned Jesuit of *Spain* delivers, that the body of man is magnetical, and being placed in a Boat, the Vessel will never rest until the head respecteth the North. If this be true, the bodies of Christians do lye unnaturally in their Graves. King *Cheops* in his Tomb, and the *Jews* in their beds have fallen upon the natural position: who reverentially declining the situation of their Temple, nor willing to lye as that stood, do place their Beds from North to South, and delight to sleep Meridionally. This Opinion confirmed would much advance the Microcosmical conceit, and commend the Geography of *Paracelsus*, who according to the Cardinal points of the World, divideth the body of man; and therefore working upon humane ordure, and by long preparation rendring it odiferous, he terms it *Zibeta Occidentalis*, Western *Civet*; making the face the East, but the posteriours the *America* or Western part of his Microcosm. The verity hereof might easily be tried in *Wales*, where there are portable Boats, and made of Leather, which would convert upon the impulsion of any verticity; and seem to be the same whereof in his description of *Britain Cæsar* hath left some mention.

Another kind of verticity, is that which *Angelus doce mihi jus, alias, Michael Sundevogis*, in a Tract *De Sulphure*, discovereth in Vegetables, from sticks let fall or depressed under water; which equally framed and permitted unto themselves, will ascend at the upper end, or that which was vertical in their vegetation; wherein notwithstanding, as yet, we have not found satisfaction. Although perhaps too greedy of Magnalities, we are apt to make but favourable experiments concerning welcom Truths, and such desired verities.

It is also wondrous strange what *Lælius Bisciola* reporteth, that if unto ten ounces of Loadstone one of Iron be added, it encreaseth not unto eleven, but weighs ten ounces still. A relation inexcusable in a work of leisurable hours: the examination being as ready as the relation, and the falsity tried as easily as delivered. Nor is it to be omitted what is taken up by the *Cæsius Bernardus* a late Mineralogist, and originally confirmed by *Porta*, that Needles touched with a *Diamond* contract a verticity, even as they do with a Loadstone, which will not consist with experiment. And therefore, as *Gilbertus* observeth, he might be deceived, in touching such Needles with *Diamonds*, which had a verticity before, as we have declared most Needles to have; and so had he touched them with Gold or Silver, he might have concluded a magnetical vertue therein.

In the same form may we place *Frascatorius* his attraction of silver, *Philostratus* his *Pantarbes*; *Apollodorus* and *Beda* his relation of the Loadstone that attracted onely in the night. But most inexcusable is *Franciscus Rueus*, a man of our own profession; who in his discourse of *Gemms* mentioned in the *Apocalyps*, undertakes a Chapter of the Loadstone. Wherein substantially and upon experiment he scarce delivereth any thing: making long enumeration of its traditional qualities, whereof he seemeth to believe many, and some above convicted by experience, he is fain to salve as impostures of the Devil. But

Boetius de Boot Physitian unto *Rodulphus* the second, hath recompenced this defect; and in his Tract, *De Lapidibus & Gemmis*, speaks very materially hereof; and his Discourse is consonant unto Experience and Reason.

As for Relations Historical, though many there be of less account, yet two alone deserve consideration: The first concerneth magnetical Rocks, and attractive Mountains in several parts of the Earth. The other the Tomb of *Mahomet* and bodies suspended in the air. Of Rocks magnetical there are likewise two relations; for some are delivered to be in the *Indies*, and some in the extremity of the North, and about the very Pole. The Northern account is commonly ascribed unto *Olaus Magnus* Archbishop of *Upsale*, who out of his Predecessor *Joannes, Saxo*, and others, compiled a History of some Northern Nations; but this assertion we have not discovered in that Work of his which commonly passeth amongst us, and should believe his Geography herein no more then that in the first line of his Book; when he affirmeth that *Biarmia* (which is not seventy degrees in latitude) hath the Pole for its Zenith, and Equinoctial for the Horizon.

Now upon this foundation, how uncertain soever men have erected mighty illations, ascribing thereto the cause of the Needles direction, and conceiving the effluctions from these Mountains and Rocks invite the Lilly toward the North. Which conceit though countenanced by learned men, is not made out either by experience or reason, for no man hath yet attained or given a sensible account of the Pole by some degrees. It is also observed the Needle doth very much vary as it approacheth the Pole; whereas were there such direction from the Rocks, upon a nearer approachment it would more directly respect them. Beside, were there such magnetical Rocks under the Pole, yet being so far removed they would produce no such effect. For they that sail by the Isle of *Ilua* now called *Elba* in the Thuscan Sea which abounds in veins of Loadstone, observe no variation or inclination of the Needle, much less may they expect a direction from Rocks at the end of the Earth. And lastly, men that ascribe thus much unto Rocks of the North, must presume or discover the like magneticals at the South: For in the Southern Seas and far beyond the Equator, variations are large, and declinations as constant as in the Northern Ocean.

The other relation of Loadstone Mines and Rocks, in the shore of *India* is delivered of old by *Pliny*; wherein, saith he, they are so placed both in abundance and vigour, that it proves an adventure of hazard to pass those Coasts in a Ship with Iron nails. *Serapion* the Moor, an Author of good esteem and reasonable Antiquity, confirmeth the same, whose expression in the word *magnes* is this. The Mine of this Stone is in the Sea-coast of *India*, whereto when Ships approach, there is no Iron in them which flies not like a Bird unto those Mountains; and therefore their Ships are fastened not with Iron but Wood, for otherwise they would be torn to pieces. But this assertion, how positive soever, is contradicted by all Navigators that pass that way; which are now many, and of our own Nation, and might surely have been controled by *Nearchus* the Admiral of *Alexander*; who not knowing the Compass, was fain to coast that shore.

For the relation concerning *Mahomet*, it is generally believed his Tomb at *Medina Talnabi*, in *Arabia*, without any visible supporters hangeth in the air between two Loadstones artificially contrived both above and below; which conceit is fabulous and evidently false from the testimony of Ocular Testators, who affirm his Tomb is made of Stone, and lyeth upon the ground; as besides others the learned *Vossius* observeth from *Gabriel Sionita*, and *Joannes Hesronita*, two *Maronites* in their relations hereof. Of such intentions and attempt by *Mahometans* we read in some Relators, and that might be the occasion of the Fable, which by tradition of time and distance of place enlarged into the Story of being accomplished. And this hath been promoted by attempts of the like nature; for we read in *Pliny* that one *Dinocrates* began to Arch the Temple of *Arsinoe* in *Alexandria* with Loadstone, that so her Statue might be suspended in the air to the amazement of the beholders. And to lead on our credulity herein, confirmation may be drawn from History and Writers of good authority. So is it reported by *Ruffinus*, that in the Temple of *Serapis* there was an Iron Chariot suspended by Loadstones in the air; which stones removed, the Chariot fell and dashed into pieces. The like doth *Beda* report of *Bellerophons* Horse, which framed of Iron, was placed between two Loadstones, with wings expansed, pendulous in the air.

The verity of these Stories we shall not further dispute, their possibility we may in some way determine; if we conceive what no man will deny, that bodies suspended in the air have this suspension from one or many Loadstones placed both above and below it; or else by one or many placed only above it. Likewise the body to be suspended in respect of the Loadstone above, is either placed first at a pendulous distance in the medium, or else attracted unto that site by the vigor of the Loadstone. And so we first affirm that possible it is a body may be suspended between two Loadstones; that is, it being so equally attracted unto both, that it determineth it self unto neither. But surely this position will be of no duration; for if the air be agitated or the body waved either way, it omits the equilibration, and disposeth it self unto the nearest attractor. Again, It is not impossible (though hardly feasible) by a single Loadstone to suspend an Iron in the air, the Iron being artificially placed and at a distance guided toward the stone, until it find the neutral point, wherein its gravity just equals the magnetical quality, the one exactly extolling as much as the other depresseth. And lastly, Impossible it is that if an Iron rest upon the ground, and a Loadstone be placed over it, it should ever so arise as to hang in the way or medium; for that vigor which at a distance is able to overcome the resistance of its gravity and to lift up it from the Earth, will as it approacheth nearer be still more able to attract it; never remaining in the middle that could not abide in the extreams. Now the way of *Baptista Porta* that by a thred fastneth a Needle to a Table, and then so guides and orders the same, that by the attraction of the Loadstone it abideth in the air, infringeth not this reason; for this is a violent retention, and if the thred be loosened, the Needle ascends and adheres unto the Attractor.

The third consideration concerneth Medical relations; wherein what ever effects are delivered, they are either derived from its mineral and ferreous condition, or else magnetical operation. Unto the ferreous and mineral quality pertaineth what *Dioscorides* an ancient Writer and Souldier under *Anthony* and *Cleopatra* affirmeth, that half a dram of Loadstone given with Honey and Water, proves a purgative medicine, and evacuateth gross humours. But this is a quality of great incertainty; for omitting the vehicle of Water and Honey, which is of a laxative power it self, the powder of some Loadstones in this dose doth rather constipate and binde, then purge and loosen the belly. And if sometimes it cause any laxity, it is probably in the same way with Iron and Steel unprepared, which will disturb some bodies, and work by Purge and Vomit. And therefore, whereas it is delivered in a Book ascribed unto *Galen*, that it is a good medicine in dropsies, and evacuates the waters of persons so affected: It may I confess by siccity and astriction afford a confirmation unto parts relaxed, and such as be hydropically disposed; and by these qualities it may be useful in *Hernias* or *Ruptures*, and for these it is commended by *Ætius, Ægineta,* and *Oribasius*; who only affirm that it contains the vertue of *Hæma-tites*, and being burnt was sometimes vended for it. Wherein notwithstanding there is an higher vertue; and in the same prepared, or in rich veins thereof, though crude, we have observed the effects of Chalybeat Medicines; and the benefits of Iron and Steel in strong obstructions. And therefore that was probably a different vein of Loadstone; or infected with other mineral mixture, which the Ancients commended for a purgative medicine, and ranked the same with the violentest kinds thereof: with *Hippophae, Cneoron,* and *Thymelæa,* as we find it in *Hippocrates*; and might be somewhat doubtful, whether by the magnesian stone, he understood the Loadstone, did not *Achilles Statius* define the same, the Stone that loveth Iron.

To this mineral condition belongeth what is delivered by some, that wounds which are made with weapons excited by the Loadstone, contract a malignity, and become of more difficult cure; which nevertheless is not to be found in the incision of Chyrurgions with knives and lancets touched; which leave no such effect behind them. Hither we also refer that affirmative, which sayes the Loadstone is poison; and therefore in the lists of poisons we find it in many Authors. But this our experience cannot confirm, and the practice of the King of *Zeilan* clearly contradicteth; who as *Garcias ab Horto*, Physitian unto the *Spanish* Viceroy delivereth, hath all his meat served up in Loadstone, and conceives thereby he preserveth the vigour of youth.

But surely from a magnetical activity must be made out what is let fall by *Ætius*, that a Loadstone held in the hand of one that is podagrical, doth either cure or give great ease in the Gout. Or what *Marcellus Empericus* affirmeth, that as an amulet, it also cureth the headach; which are but additions unto its proper nature, and hopeful enlargements of its allowed attraction. For perceiving its secret power to draw magnetical bodies, men have invented a new attraction, to draw out the dolour and pain of any part. And from such grounds it surely became a philter, and was conceived a medicine of some venereal attraction; and therefore upon this stone they graved the Image of *Venus*, according unto that of *Claudian, Venerem magnetica gemma figura.* Hither must we also refer what is delivered concerning its power to draw out of the body bullets and heads of arrows, and for the like intention is mixed up in plaisters. Which course, although as vain and ineffectual it be rejected by many good Authors, yet is it not methinks so readily to be denied, nor the Practice of many Physicians which have thus compounded plaisters, thus suddenly to be condemned, as may be observed in the *Emplastrum divinum Nicolai*, the *Emplastrum nigrum* of *Augspurg*, the *Opodeldoch* and *Attractium* of *Parcelsus*, with several more in the Dispensatory of *Wecker*, and practice of *Sennertus*. The cure also of *Hernias*, or *Ruptures* in *Pareus*: and the method also of curation lately delivered by Daniel Beckherus, and approved by the Professors of *Leyden*, that is, of a young man of *Spruceland* that casually swallowed a knife about ten inches long, which was cut out of his stomach, and the wound healed up. In which cure to attract the knife to a convenient situation, there was applied a plaister made up with the powder of Loadstone. Now this kind of practice *Libavius*, *Gilbertus*, and lately *Swickardus* condemn, as vain, and altogether unuseful; because a Loadstone in powder hath no attractive power; for in that form it omits his polary respects, and loseth those parts which are the rule of attraction.

Wherein to speak compendiously, if experiment hath not deceived us, we first affirm that a Loadstone in powder omits not all attraction. For if the powder of a rich vein be in a reasonable quantity presented toward the Needle freely placed, it will not appear to be void of all activity, but will be able to stir it. Nor hath it only a power to move the Needle in powder and by it self, but this will it also do, if incorporated and mixed with plaisters; as we have made trial in the *Emplastrum de Minio*; with half an ounce of the mass, mixing a dram of Loadstone. For applying the magdaleon or roal unto the Needle, it would both stir and attract it; not equally in all parts, but more vigorously in some, according unto the Mine of the Stone, more plentifully dispersed in the mass. And lastly, In the Loadstone powdered, the polary respects are not wholly destroyed. For those diminutive particles are not atomical or meerly indivisible, but consist of dimensions sufficient for their operations, though in obscurer effects. Thus if unto the powder of Loadstone or Iron we admove the North Pole of the Loadstone, the Powders or small divisions will erect and conform themselves thereto; but if the South pole approach, they will subside, and inverting their bodies, respect the Loadstone with the other extream. And this will happen not only in a body of powder together, but in any particle or dust divided from it.

Now though we disavow not these plaisters, yet shall we not omit two cautions in their use, that therein the Stone be not too subtilly powdered, for it will better manifest its attraction in a more sensible dimension. That where is desired a speedy effect, it may be considered whether it were not better to relinquish the powdered plaisters, and to apply an entire Loadstone unto the part: And though the other be not wholly ineffectual, whether this way be not more powerful, and so might have been in the cure of the young man delivered by *Beckerus*.

The last consideration concerneth Magical relations; in which account we comprehend effects derived and fathered upon hidden qualities, specifical forms, Antipathies, and Sympathies, whereof from received grounds of Art, no reasons are derived. Herein relations are strange and numerous; men being apt in all Ages to multiply wonders, and Philosophers dealing with admirable bodies, as Historians have done with excellent men, upon the strength of their great atcheivements, ascribing acts unto them not only false but impossible; and exceeding truth as much in their relations, as they have others in their actions. Hereof we shall briefly mention some delivered by Authors of good esteem: whereby we may discover the fabulous inventions of some, the credulous supinity of others, and the great disservice unto truth by both: multiplying obscurities in Nature, and authorising hidden qualities that are false: whereas wide men are ashamed there are so many true.

And first, *Dioscorides* puts a shrewd quality upon it, and such as men are apt enough to experiment, who therewith discovers the incontinency of a wife, by placing the Loadstone under her pillow, whereupon she will not be able to remain in bed with her husband. The same he also makes a help unto thievery. For Thieves saith he, having a design upon a house, do make a fire at the four corners thereof, and cast therein the fragments of Loadstone: whence ariseth a fume that so disturbeth the inhabitants, that they forsake the house and leave it to the spoil of the Robbers. This relation, how ridiculous soever, hath *Albertus* taken up above a thousand years after, and *Marbodeus* the Frenchman hath continued the same in Latine Verse, which with the Notes of *Pictorius* is currant unto our dayes. As strange must be the Lithomancy or divination from this Stone, whereby as *Tzetzes* delivers, *Helenus* the Prophet foretold the destruction of *Troy*: and the Magick thereof not safely to be believed, which was delivered by *Orpheus*, that sprinkled with water it will upon a question emit a voice not much unlike an Infant. But surely the Loadstone of *Laurentius Guascus* the Physitian, is never to be matched; wherewith, as *Cardan* delivereth, whatsoever Needles or Bodies were touched, the wounds and punctures made thereby, were never felt at all. And yet as strange is that which is delivered by some, that a Loadstone preserved in the salt of a *Remora*, acquires a power to attract gold out of the deepest Wells. Certainly a studied absurdity, not casually cast out, but plotted for perpetuity: for the strangeness of the effect ever to be admired, and the difficulty of the trial never to be convicted.

These conceits are of that monstrosity that they refute themselves in their recitements. There is another of better notice, and whispered thorow the World with some attention; credulous and vulgar auditors readily believing it, and more judicious and distinctive heads, not altogether rejecting it. The conceit is excellent, and if the effect would follow, somewhat divine; whereby we might communicate like spirits, and confer on earth with *Menippus* in the Moon. And this is pretended with the sympathy of two Needles touched with the same Loadstone, and placed in the center of two Abecedary circles or rings, with letters described round about them, one friend keeping one, and another the other, and agreeing upon an hour wherein they will communicate. For then, saith Tradition, at what distance of place soever, when one Needle shall be removed unto any letter; the other by a wonderful sympathy will move unto the same. But herein I confess my experience can find no truth; for having expressly framed two circles of Wood, and according to the number of the Latine letters divided each into twenty three parts, placing therein two stiles or Needles composed of the same steel, touched with the same Loadstone, and at the same point: of these two, whensoever I removed the one, although but at the distance of half a span, the other would stand like *Hercules* pillars, and if the Earth stand still, have surely no motion at all. Now as it is not possible that any body should have no boundaries, or Sphear of its activity, so it is improbable it should effect that at distance, which nearer hand it cannot at all perform.

Again, The conceit is ill contrived, and one effect inferred, whereas the contrary will ensue. For if the removing of one of the Needles from *A* to *B*, should have any action or influence on the other, it would not intice it from *A* to *B*, but repell it from *A* to *Z*: for Needles excited by the same point of the stone, do not attract, but avoid each other, even as those also do, when their invigorated extreams approach unto one another.

Lastly, Were this conceit assuredly true, yet were it not a conclusion at every distance to be tried by every head: it being no ordinary or Almanack business, but a Problem Mathematical, to finde out the difference of hours in different places; nor do the wisest exactly satisfie themselves in all. For the hours of several places anticipate each other, according unto their Longitudes, which are not exactly discovered of every place; and therefore the trial hereof at a considerable interval, is best performed at the distance of the *Antoeci*; that is, such habitations as have the same Meridian and equal parallel, on different sides of the Æquator; or more plainly, the same Longitude and the same Latitude unto the South, which we have in the North. For unto such situations it is noon and midnight at the very same time.

And therefore the Sympathy of these Needles is much of the same mould with that intelligence which is pretended from the flesh of one body transmuted by incision into another. For if by the Art of *Taliacotius*, a permutation of flesh, or transmutation be made from one man's body into another, as if a piece of flesh be exchanged from the bicipital muscle of either parties arm, and about them both, an Alphabet circumscribed; upon a time appointed as some conceptions affirm, they may communicate at what distance soever. For if the one shall prick himself in *A*, the other at the same time will have a sense thereof in the same part: and upon inspection of his arm perceive what letters the other points out in his. Which is a way of intelligence very strange: and would require the lost art of *Pythagoras*, who could read a reverse in the Moon.

Now this magnetical conceit how strange soever, might have some original in Reason; for men observing no solid body whatsoever did interrupt its action, might be induced to believe no distance would terminate the same; and most conceiving it pointed unto the Pole of Heaven, might also opinion that nothing between could restrain it. Whosoever was the Author, the *Æolus* that blew it about, was *Famianus Strada*, that Elegant Jesuit, in his Rhetorical prolusions, who chose out this subject to express the stile of *Lucretius*. But neither *Baptista Porta, De Furtivis Literarum notis*; *Trithemius* in his Steganography, *Selenus* in his Cryptography, or *Nuncius inanimatus* make any consideration hereof, although they deliver many ways to communicate thoughts at distance. And this we will not deny may in some manner be effected by the Loadstone; that is, from one room into another; by placing a table in the wall common unto both, and writing thereon the same letters one against another: for upon the approach of a vigorous Loadstone unto a letter on this side, the Needle will move unto the same on the other. But this is a very different way from ours at present; and hereof there are many ways delivered, and more may be discovered which contradict not the rule of its operations.

As for *Unguentum Armarium*, called also *Magneticum*, it belongs not to this discourse, it neither having the Loadstone for its ingredient, nor any one of its actions: but supposeth other principles, as common and universal spirits, which convey the action of the remedy unto the part, and conjoins the vertue of bodies far disjoyned. But perhaps the cures it doth, are not worth so mighty principles; it commonly healing but simple wounds, and such as mundified and kept clean, do need no other hand then that of Nature, and the Balsam of the proper part. Unto which effect there being fields of Medicines, it may be a hazardous curiosity to rely on this; and because men say the effect doth generally follow, it might be worth the experiment to try, whether the same will not ensue, upon the same Method of cure, by ordinary Balsams, or common vulnerary plaisters.

Many other Magnetisms may be pretended, and the like attractions through all the creatures of Nature. Whether the same be verified in the action of the Sun upon inferiour bodies, whether there be *Æolian* Magnets, whether the flux and reflux of the Sea be caused by any Magnetism from the Moon; whether the like be really made out, or rather Metaphorically verified in the sympathies of Plants and Animals, might afford a large dispute; and *Kircherus* in his *Catena Magnetica* hath excellently discussed the same; which work came late unto our hand, but might have much advantaged this Discourse.

Other Discourses there might be made of the Loadstone: as Moral, Mystical, Theological; and some have handsomely done them; as *Ambrose*, *Austine*, *Gulielmus Parisiensis*, and many more, but these fall under no Rule, and are as boundless as mens inventions. And though honest minds do glorifie God hereby; yet do they most powerfully magnifie him, and are to be looked on with another eye, who demonstratively set forth its Magnalities; who not from postulated or precarious inferences, entreat a courteous assent; but from experiments and undeniable effects, enforce the wonder of its Maker.

CHAPTER IV

Of Bodies Electrical

Having thus spoken of the Loadstone and Bodies Magnetical, I shall in the next place deliver somewhat of Electrical, and such as may seem to have attraction like the other. Hereof we shall also deliver what particularly spoken or not generally known is manifestly or probably true, what generally believed is also false or dubious. Now by Electrical bodies, I understand not such as are Metallical, mentioned by *Pliny*, and the Ancients; for their Electrum was a mixture made of Gold, with the Addition of a fifth part of Silver; a substance now as unknown as true *Aurichaleum*, or *Corinthian* Brass, and set down among things lost by *Pancirollus*. Nor by Electrick Bodies do I conceive such only as take up shavings, straws, and light bodies, in which number the Ancients only placed *Jet* and *Amber*; but such as conveniently placed unto their objects attract all bodies palpable whatsoever. I say conveniently placed, that is, in regard of the object, that it be not too ponderous, or any way affixed; in regard of the Agent, that it be not foul or sullied, but wiped, rubbed, and excited; in regard of both, that they be conveniently distant, and no impediment interposed. I say, all bodies palpable, thereby excluding fire, which indeed it will not attract, nor yet draw through it; for fire consumes its effluxions by which it should attract.

Now although in this rank but two were commonly mentioned by the Ancients, *Gilbertus* discovereth many more; as *Diamonds*, *Saphyrs*, *Carbuncles*, *Iris*, *Opalls*, *Amethysts*, *Beril*, *Crystal*, *Bristol stones*, *Sulphur*, *Mastick*, hard *wax*, hard *Rosin*, *Arsenic*, *Sal-gemm*, *Roch-Allum*, common Glass, *Stibium*, or Glass of *Antimony*. Unto these *Cabeus* addeth white *wax*, *Gum Elemi*, *Gum Guaici*, *Pix Hispanica*, and *Gipsum*. And unto these we add *Gum Anime*, *Benjamin*,

Talcum, China-dishes, Sandaraca, Turpentine, Styrax Liquida, and *Caranna* dried into a hard consistence. And the same attraction we find, not onely in simple bodies, but such as are much compounded; as in the *Oxycroceum* plaister, and obscurely that *ad Herniam,* and *Gratia Dei*; all which smooth and rightly prepared, will discover a sufficient power to stir the Needle, setled freely upon a well-pointed pin; and so as the Electrick may be applied unto it without all disadvantage.

But the attraction of these Electricks we observe to be very different. Resinous or unctuous bodies, and such as will flame, attract most vigorously, and most thereof without frication; as *Anime, Benjamin,* and most powerfully good hard *Wax,* which will convert the Needle almost as actively as the Loadstone. And we believe that all or most of this substance if reduced to hardness tralucency or clearness, would have some attractive quality. But juices concrete, or Gums easily dissolving in water, draw not at all: As *Aloe, Opium, Sanguis Draconis, Lacca, Galbanum, Sagapenum.* Many stones also both precious and vulgar, although terse and smooth, have not this power attractive: As *Emeralds, Pearl, Jaspis, Corneleans, Agathe, Heliotropes, Marble, Alablaster, Touchstone, Flint,* and *Bezoar.* Glass attracts but weakly, though clear; some slick stones and thick Glasses indifferently: *Arsenic* but weakly, so likewise Glass of *Antimony,* but *Crocus Metallorum* not at all. Salts generally but weakly, as *Sal Gemma, Allum,* and also *Talke*; nor very discoverably by any frication, but if gently warmed at the fire, and wiped with a dry cloth, they will better discover their Electricities.

No Metal attracts, nor Animal concretion we know, although polite and smooth; as we have made trial in *Elks* Hoofs, Hawks-Talons, the Sword of a *Sword-fish, Tortois-shells, Sea-horse,* and *Elephants* Teeth, in Bones, in *Harts-horn,* and what is usually conceived *Unicorns-horn.* No Wood though never so hard and polished, although out of some thereof Electrick bodies proceed; as *Ebony, Box, Lignum vitæ, Cedar,* &c. And although *Jet* and *Amber* be reckoned among *Bitumens,* yet neither do we find *Asphaltus,* that is *Bitumens* of *Judea,* nor *Sea-cole,* nor *Camphire,* nor *Mummia* to attract, although we have tried in large and polished pieces. Now this attraction have we tried in straws and paleous bodies, in Needles of Iron, equilibrated, Powders of Wood and Iron, in Gold and Silver foliate. And not only in solid but fluent and liquid bodies, as oyls made both by expression and distillation; in Water, in spirits of Wine, *Vitriol* and *Aqua fortis*.

But how this attraction is made, is not so easily determined; that 'tis performed by effluviums is plain, and granted by most; for Electricks will not commonly attract, except they grow hot or become perspirable. For if they be foul and obnubilated, it hinders their effluxion; nor if they be covered, though but with Linen or Sarsenet, or if a body be interposed, for that intercepts the effluvium. If also a powerful and broad Electrick of Wax or *Anime* be held over fine powder, the Atoms or small particles will ascend most numerously unto it; and if the Electrick be held unto the light, it may be observed that many thereof will fly, and be as it were discharged from the Electrick to the distance sometime of two or three inches. Which motion is performed by the breath of the effluvium issuing with agility; for as the Electrick cooleth, the projection of the Atoms ceaseth.

The manner hereof *Cabeus* wittily attempteth, affirming that this effluvium attenuateth and impelleth the neighbor air, which returning home in a gyration, carrieth with it the obvious bodies unto the Electrick. And this he labours to confirm by experiments; for if the straws be raised by a vigorous Electrick, they do appear to wave and turn in their ascents. If likewise the Electrick be broad, and the straws light and chaffy, and held at a reasonable distance, they will not arise unto the middle, but rather adhere toward the Verge or Borders thereof. And lastly, if many straws be laid together, and a nimble Electrick approach, they will not all arise unto it, but some will commonly start aside, and be whirled a reasonable distance from it. Now that the air impelled returns unto its place in a gyration or whirling, is evident from the Atoms or Motes in the Sun. For when the Sun so enters a hole or window, that by its illumination the Atoms or Motes become perceptible, if then by our breath the air be gently impelled, it may be perceived, that they will circularly return and in a gyration unto their places again.

Another way of their attraction is also delivered; that is, by a tenuous emanation or continued effluvium, which after some distance retracteth into it self; as is observable in drops of Syrups, Oyl, and seminal Viscosities, which spun at length, retire into their former dimensions. Now these effluviums advancing from the body of the Electrick, in their return do carry back the bodies whereon they have

108

laid hold within the Sphere or Circle of their continuities; and these they do not onely attract, but with their viscous arms hold fast a good while after. And if any shall wonder why these effluviums issuing forth impel and protrude not the straw before they can bring it back; it is because the effluvium passing out in a smaller thred and more enlengthened filament, it stirreth not the bodies interposed, but returning unto its original, falls into a closer substance, and carrieth them back unto it self. And this way of attraction is best received, embraced by Sir *Kenelm Digby* in his excellent Treaty of bodies, allowed by *Des Cartes* in his principles of Philosophy, as far as concerneth fat and resinous bodies, and with exception of Glass, whose attraction he also deriveth from the recess of its effluction. And this in some manner the words of *Gilbertus* will bear: *Effluvia illa tenuiora concipiunt & amplectuntur corpora, quibus uniuntur, & electris tanquam extensis brachiis, & ad fontem propinquitate invalescentibus effluviis, deducuntur.* And if the ground were true, that the Earth were an Electrick body, and the air but the effluvium thereof, we might have more reason to believe that from this attraction, and by this effluction, bodies tended to the Earth, and could not remain above it.

Our other discourse of Electricks concerneth a general opinion touching *Jet* and *Amber*, that they attract all light bodies, except *Ocymum* or *Basil*, and such as be dipped in oyl or oyled; and this is urged as high as *Theophrastus*: but *Scaliger* acquitteth him; And had this been his assertion, *Pliny* would probably have taken it up, who herein stands out, and delivereth no more but what is vulgarly known. But *Plutarch* speaks positively in his *Symposiacks*, that *Amber* attracteth all bodies, excepting Basil and oyled substances. With *Plutarch* consent many Authors both Ancient and Modern; but the most inexcusable are *Lemnius* and *Rueus*, whereof the one delivering the nature of Minerals mentioned in Scripture, the infallible fountain of Truth, confirmeth their vertues with erroneous traditions; the other undertaking the occult and hidden Miracles of Nature, accepteth this for one; and endeavoureth to alledge a reason of that which is more then occult, that is, not existent.

Now herein, omitting the authority of others, as the Doctrine of experiment hath informed us, we first affirm, That *Amber* attracts not Basil, is wholly repugnant unto truth. For if the leaves thereof or dried stalks be stripped into small straws, they arise unto *Amber*, *wax*, and other Electrics, no otherwise then those of Wheat and Rye: nor is

109

there any peculiar fatness or singular viscosity in that plant that might cause adhesion, and so prevent its ascension. But that *Jet* and *Amber* attract not straws oyled, is in part true and false. For if the straws be much wet or drenched in oyl, true it is that *Amber* draweth them not; for then the oyl makes the straws to adhere unto the part whereon they are placed, so that they cannot rise unto the Attractor; and this is true, not onely if they be soaked in Oyl, but spirits of Wine or Water. But if we speak of Straws or festucous divisions lightly drawn over oyl, and so that it causeth no adhesion; or if we conceive an Antipathy between Oyl and *Amber*, the Doctrine is not true. For *Amber* will attract straws thus oyled, it will convert the Needles of Dials made either of Brass or Iron, although they be much oyled; for in these Needles consisting free upon their Center, there can be no adhesion. It will likewise attract Oyl it self, and if it approacheth unto a drop thereof, it becometh conical, and ariseth up unto it, for Oyl taketh not away his attraction, although it be rubbed over it. For if you touch a piece of Wax already excitated with common oyl, it will notwithstanding attract, though not so vigorously as before. But if you moisten the same with any Chymical Oyl, Water, or spirits of Wine, or only breath upon it, it quite omits its attraction, for either its influencies cannot get through, or will not mingle with those substances.

It is likewise probable the Ancients were mistaken concerning its substance and generation; they conceiving it a vegetable concretion made of the gums of Trees, especially *Pine* and *Poplar* falling into the water, and after indurated or hardened, whereunto accordeth the Fable of *Phaetons* sisters: but surely the concretion is Mineral, according as is delivered by *Boetius*. For either it is found in Mountains and mediterraneous parts; and so it is a fat and unctuous sublimation in the Earth, concreted and fixed by salt and nitrous spirits wherewith it meeteth. Or else, which is most usual, it is collected upon the Sea-shore; and so it is a fat and bituminous juice coagulated by the saltness of the Sea. Now that salt spirits have a power to congeal and coagulate unctuous bodies, is evident in Chymical operations; in the distillations of *Arsenick*, sublimate and *Antimony*; in the mixture of oyl of *Juniper*, with the salt and acide spirit of *Sulphur*, for thereupon ensueth a concretion unto the consistence of *Birdlime*; as also in spirits of salt, or *Aqua fortis* poured upon oyl of Olive, or more plainly in the Manufacture of Soap. And many bodies will coagulate upon commixture, whose separated natures promise no concretion. Thus upon a solution of *Tin* by *Aqua fortis*, there will ensue a coagulation, like that of whites of Eggs. Thus the volatile salt of Urine will coagulate *Aqua vitæ*, or spirits of Wine; and thus perhaps (as *Helmont* excellently declareth) the stones or calculous concretions in Kidney or Bladder may be produced: the spirits or volatile salt or Urine conjoyning with the *Aqua vitæ* potentially lying therein; as he illustrateth from the distillation of fermented Urine. From whence ariseth an *Aqua vitæ* or spirit, which the volatile salt of the same Urine will congeal; and finding an earthy concurrence, strike into a lapideous substance.

Lastly, We will not omit what *Bellabonus* upon his own experiment writ from *Dantzich* unto *Mellichius*, as he hath left recorded in his Chapter, *De succino*, that the bodies of *Flies*, *Pismires*, and the like, which are said oft-times to be included in *Amber*, are not real but representative, as he discovered in several pieces broke for that purpose. If so, the two famous Epigrams hereof in *Martial* are but Poetical, the *Pismire* of *Brassavolus* Imaginary, and *Cardans Mousoleum* for a Flie, a meer phansie. But hereunto we know not how to assent, as having met with some whose reals made good their representments.

CHAPTER V

Compendiously of sundry other common Tenents, concerning Mineral and Terreous Bodies, which examined, prove either false or dubious.

1. And first we hear it in every mouth, and in many good Authors read it, That a *Diamond*, which is the hardest of stones, not yielding unto *Steel*, *Emery*, or any thing but its own powder, is yet made soft, or broke by the blood of a Goat. Thus much is affirmed by *Pliny, Solinus, Albertus, Cyprian, Austin, Isidore*, and many Christian Writers; alluding herein unto the heart of man and the precious bloud of our Saviour, who was typified by the Goat that was slain, and the scape-Goat in the Wilderness; and at the effusion of whose bloud, not only the hard hearts of his enemies relented, but the stony rocks and vail of the Temple were shattered. But this I perceive is easier affirmed then proved. For *Lapidaries*, and such as profess the art of cutting this stone, do generally deny it; and they that seem to countenance it, have in their deliveries so qualified it, that little from thence of moment can be inferred for it. For first, the holy Fathers, without a further enquiry did take it for granted, and rested upon the authority of the first deliverers. As for *Albertus*, he promiseth this effect, but conditionally, not except the Goat drink wine, and be fed with *Siler montanum, petroselinum*, and such herbs as are conceived of power to break the stone in the bladder. But the words of *Pliny*, from whom most likely the rest at first derived it, if strictly considered, do rather overthrow, then any way advantage this effect. His words are these: *Hircino rumpitur sanguine, nec aliter quam recenti, calidoque macerata, & sic quoque multis ictibus, tunc etiam præterquam eximias incudes malleosque ferreos frangens.* That is, it is broken with Goat's blood, but not except

it be fresh and warm, and that not without many blows, and then also it will break the best Anvils and Hammers of Iron. And answerable hereto, is the assertion of *Isidore* and *Solinus*. By which account, a Diamond steeped in Goats bloud, rather increaseth in hardness, then acquireth any softness by the infusion; for the best we have are comminuible without it; and are so far from breaking hammers, that they submit unto pistillation, and resist not an ordinary pestle.

Upon this conceit arose perhaps the discovery of another; that the bloud of a Goat was soveraign for the Stone, as it stands commended by many good Writers, and brings up the composition in the powder of *Nicolaus*, and the Electuary of the Queen of *Colein*. Or rather because it was found an excellent medicine for the Stone, and its ability commended by some to dissolve the hardest thereof; it might be conceived by amplifying apprehensions, to be able to break a *Diamond*; and so it came to be ordered that the Goat should be fed with saxifragous herbs, and such as are conceived of power to break the stone. However it were, as the effect is false in the one, so is it surely very doubtful in the other. For although inwardly received it may be very diuretick, and expulse the stone in the Kidneys; yet how it should dissolve or break that in the bladder, will require a further dispute; and perhaps would be more reasonably tried by a warm injection thereof, then as it is commonly used. Wherein notwithstanding, we should rather rely upon the urine in a castling's bladder, a resolution of Crabs eyes, or the second distillation of Urine, as *Helmont* hath commended; or rather (if any such might be found) a Chilifactory menstruum or digestive preparation drawn from species or individuals, whose stomacks peculiarly dissolve lapideous bodies.

2. *That Glass is poison*, according unto common conceit, I know not how to grant. Not onely from the innocency of its ingredients, that is, fine Sand, and the ashes of Glass-wort or Fearn, which in themselves are harmless and useful; or because I find it by many commended for the Stone, but also from experience, as having given unto Dogs above a dram thereof, subtilly powdered in Butter and Paste, without any visible disturbance.

The conceit is surely grounded upon the visible mischief of Glass grosly or coursly powdered, for that indeed is mortally noxious, and effectually used by some to destroy Mice and Rats; for by reason of its acuteness and angularity, it commonly excoriates the parts through which it passeth, and solicits them unto a continual expulsion. Whereupon there ensues fearful symptomes, not much unlike those which attend the action of poison. From whence notwithstanding, we cannot with propriety impose upon it that name, either by occult or elementary quality, which he that concedeth will much enlarge the Catalogue or Lists of Poisons. For many things, neither deleterious by substance or quality, are yet destructive by figure, or some occasional activity. So are Leeches destructive, and by some accounted poison; not properly, that is by temperamental contrariety, occult form, or so much as elemental repugnancy; but because being inwardly taken they fasten upon the veins, and occasion an effusion of bloud, which cannot be easily stanched. So a Sponge is mischievous, not in it self, for in its powder it is harmless; but because being received unto the stomach it swelleth, and occasioning a continual distension, induceth a strangulation. So Pins, Needles, ears of Rye or Barley may be poison. So *Daniel* destroyed the Dragon by a composition of three things, whereof neither was poison alone, nor properly all together, that is, Pitch, Fat, and Hair, according as is expressed in the History. Then *Daniel* took Pitch, and Fat, and Hair, and did seeth them together, and made lumps thereof, these he put in the Dragons mouth, and so he burst asunder. That is, the Fat and Pitch being cleaving bodies, and the Hair continually extimulating the parts: by the action of the one, Nature was provoked to expell, but by the tenacity of the other forced to retain: so that there being left no passage in or out, the Dragon brake in pieces. It must therefore be taken of grosly-powdered Glass, what is delivered by *Grevinus*: and from the same must that mortal dysentery which is related by *Sanctorius*. And in the same sense shall we only allow a *Diamond* to be poison; and whereby as some relate *Paracelsus* himself was poisoned. So even the precious fragments and cordial gems which are of frequent use in Physick, and in themselves confessed of useful faculties; received in gross and angular Powders, may so offend the bowels, as to procure desperate languors, or cause most dangerous fluxes.

That Glass may be rendred malleable and pliable unto the hammer, many conceive, and some make little doubt, when they read in *Dio*, *Pliny*, and *Petronius*, that one unhappily effected it for *Tiberius*. Which notwithstanding must needs seem strange unto such as consider, that bodies are ductile from a tenacious humidity, which so holdeth the parts together; that though they dilate or extend, they part not from each other. That bodies run into Glass, when the volatile parts are exhaled, and the continuating humour separated: the Salt and Earth, that is, the fixed parts remaining. And therefore vitrification maketh bodies brittle, as destroying the viscous humours which hinder the disruption of parts. Which may be verified even in the bodies of Metals. For Glass of Lead or Tin is fragile, when that glutinous Sulphur hath been fired out, which made their bodies ductile.

He that would most probably attempt it, must experiment upon Gold. Whose fixed and flying parts are so conjoined, whose Sulphur and continuating principle is so united unto the Salt, that some may be hoped to remain to hinder fragility after vitrification. But how to proceed, though after frequent corrosion, as that upon the agency of fire, it should not revive into its proper body before it comes to vitrifie, will prove no easie discovery.

3. That Gold inwardly taken, either in substance, infusion, decoction or extinction, is a cordial of great efficacy, in sundry Medical uses, although a practice much used, is also much questioned, and by no man determined beyond dispute. There are hereof I perceive two extream opinions; some excessively magnifying it, and probably beyond its deserts; others extreamly vilifying it, and perhaps below its demerits. Some affirming it a powerful Medicine in many diseases, others averring that so used, it is effectual in none: and in this number are very eminent Physicians, *Erastus, Duretus, Rondeletius, Brassavolus*, and many other; who beside the strigments and sudorous adhesions from mens hands, acknowledge that nothing proceedeth from Gold in the usual decoction thereof. Now the capital reason that led men unto this opinion, was their observation of the inseparable nature of Gold: it being excluded in the same quantity as it was received, without alteration of parts, or diminution of its gravity.

Now herein to deliver somewhat which in a middle way may be entertained; we first affirm, that the substance of Gold is invincible by the powerfullest action of natural heat; and that not only alimentally in a substantial mutation, but also medicamentally in any corporeal conversion. As is very evident, not only in the swallowing of golden bullets, but in the lesser and foliate divisions thereof: passing the stomach and guts even as it doth the throat, that is, without abatement of weight or consistence. So that it entereth not the veins with those electuaries, wherein it is mixed: but taketh leave of the permeant parts, at the mouths of the *Meseraicks*, or Lacteal Vessels, and accompanieth the inconvertible portion unto the siege. Nor is its substantial conversion expectible in any composition or aliment wherein it is taken. And therefore that was truly a starving absurdity, which befel the wishes of *Midas*. And little credit there is to be given to the golden Hen, related by *Wendlerus*. So in the extinction of Gold, we must not conceive it parteth with any of its salt or dissoluble principle thereby, as we may affirm of Iron; for the parts thereof are fixed beyond division, nor will they separate upon the strongest test of fire. This we affirm of pure Gold: for that which is currant and passeth in stamps amongst us, by reason of its allay, which is a proportion of Silver or Copper mixed therewith, is actually dequantitated by fire, and possibly by frequent extinction.

Secondly, Although the substance of Gold be not immuted or its gravity sensibly decreased, yet that from thence some vertue may proceed either in substantial reception or infusion we cannot safely deny. For possible it is that bodies may emit vertue and operation without abatement of weight; as is evident in the Loadstone, whose effluencies are continual, and communicable without a minoration of gravity. And the like is observable in Bodies electrical, whose emissions are less subtile. So will a Diamond or Saphire emit an effluvium sufficient to move the Needle or a Straw, without diminution of weight. Nor will polished Amber although it send forth a gross and corporal exhalement, be found a long time defective upon the exactest scales. Which is more easily conceivable in a continued and tenacious effluvium, whereof a great part retreats into its body.

Thirdly, If amulets do work by emanations from their bodies, upon those parts whereunto they are appended, and are not yet observed to abate their weight; if they produce visible and real effects by imponderous and invisible emissions, it maybe unjust to deny the possible efficacy of Gold, in the non-omission of weight, or deperdition of any ponderous particles.

Lastly, Since *Stibium* or Glass of Antimony, since also its *Regulus* will manifestly communicate unto Water or Wine, a purging and vomitory operation; and yet the body it self, though after iterated infusions, cannot be found to abate either vertue or weight: we shall not deny but Gold may do the like, that is, impart some effluences unto the infusion, which carry with them the separable subtilties thereof.

116

That therefore this Metal thus received, hath any undeniable effect, we shall not imperiously determine, although beside the former experiments, many more may induce us to believe it. But since the point is dubious and not yet authentically decided, it will be no discretion to depend on disputable remedies; but rather in cases of known danger, to have recourse unto medicines of known and approved activity. For, beside the benefit accruing unto the sick, hereby may be avoided a gross and frequent errour, commonly committed in the use of doubtful remedies, conjointly with those which are of approved vertues; that is to impute the cure unto the conceited remedy, or place it on that whereon they place their opinion. Whose operation although it be nothing, or its concurrence not considerable, yet doth it obtain the name of the whole cure: and carrieth often the honour of the capital energie, which had no finger in it.

Herein exact and critical trial should be made by publick enjoinment, whereby determination might be setled beyond debate: for since thereby, not only the bodies of men, but great Treasures might be preserved, it is not only an errour of Physick, but folly of State, to doubt thereof any longer.

4. That a pot full of ashes, will still contain as much water as it would without them, although by *Aristotle* in his Problems taken for granted, and so received by most, is not effectable upon the strictest experiment I could ever make. For when the airy intersticies are filled, and as much of the salt of the ashes as the water will imbibe is dissolved, there remains a gross and terreous portion at the bottom, which will possess a space by it self, according whereto there will remain a quantity of Water not receivable; so will it come to pass in a pot of salt, although decrepitated; and so also in a pot of Snow. For so much it will want in reception, as its solution taketh up, according unto the bulk whereof, there will remain a portion of Water not to be admitted. So a Glass stuffed with pieces of Sponge will want about a sixth part of what it would receive without it. So Sugar will not dissolve beyond the capacity of the Water, nor a Metal in *aqua fortis* be corroded beyond its reception. And so a pint of salt of Tartar exposed unto a moist air until it dissolve, will make far more liquor, or as some term it oyl, then the former measure will contain.

Nor is it only the exclusion of air by water, or repletion of cavities possessed thereby, which causeth a pot of ashes to admit so

117

great a quantity of Water, but also the solution of the salt of the ashes into the body of the dissolvent. So a pot of ashes will receive somewhat more of hot Water then of cold, for the warm water imbibeth more of the Salt; and a vessel of ashes more then one of pin-dust or filings of Iron; and a Glass full of Water will yet drink in a proportion of Salt or Sugar without overflowing.

Nevertheless to make the experiment with most advantage, and in which sense it approacheth nearest the truth, it must be made in ashes throughly burnt and well reverberated by fire, after the salt thereof hath been drawn out by iterated decoctions. For then the body being reduced nearer unto Earth, and emptied of all other principles, which had former ingression unto it, becometh more porous, and greedily drinketh in water. He that hath beheld what quantity of Lead the test of saltless ashes will imbibe, upon the refining of Silver, hath encouragement to think it will do very much more in water.

5. Of white powder and such as is discharged without report, there is no small noise in the World: but how far agreeable unto truth, few I perceive are able to determine. Herein therefore to satisfie the doubts of some, and amuse the credulity of others, We first declare, that Gunpowder consisteth of three ingredients, Salt-petre, Small-coal, and Brimstone. Salt-petre although it be also natural and found in several places, yet is that of common use as an artificial Salt, drawn from the infusion of salt Earth, as that of Stales, Stables, Dove-houses, Cellers, and other covered places, where the rain can neither dissolve, nor the Sun approach to resolve it. Brimstone is a Mineral body of fat and inflamable parts, and this is either used crude, and called Sulphur Vive, and is of a sadder colour; or after depuration, such as we have in magdeleons or rolls, of a lighter yellow. Small-coal is known unto all, and for this use is made of *Sallow*, *Willow*, *Alder*, *Hazel*, and the like; which three proportionably mixed, tempered, and formed into granulary bodies, do make up that Powder which is in use for Guns.

Now all these, although they bear a share in the discharge, yet have they distinct intentions, and different offices in the composition. From Brimstone proceedeth the piercing and powerful firing; for Small-coal and Petre together will onely spit, nor vigorously continue the ignition. From Small-coal ensueth the black colour and quick accension; for neither Brimstone nor Petre, although in Powder, will take fire like Small-coal, nor will they easily kindle upon the sparks of a

Flint; as neither will *Camphire*, a body very inflamable: but Small-coal is equivalent to Tinder, and serveth to light the Sulphur. It may also serve to diffuse the ignition through every part of the mixture; and being of more gross and fixed parts, may seem to moderate the activity of Salt-petre, and prevent too hasty rarefaction. From Salt-petre proceedeth the force and the report; for Sulphur and Small-coal mixed will not take fire with noise, or exilition, and Powder which is made of impure and greasie Petre hath but a weak emission, and giveth a faint report. And therefore in the three sorts of Powder the strongest containeth most Salt-petre, and the proportion thereof is about ten parts of Petre, unto one of Coal and Sulphur.

But the immediate cause of the Report, is the vehement commotion of the air upon the sudden and violent eruption of the Powder; for that being suddenly fired, and almost together, upon this high rarefacation, requireth by many degrees a greater space then before its body occupied; but finding resistance, it actively forceth his way, and by concussion of the air occasioneth the Report. Now with what violence it forceth upon the air, may easily be conceived, if we admit what *Cardan* affirmeth, that the Powder fired doth occupy an hundred times a greater space then its own bulk; or rather what *Snellius* more exactly accounteth; that it exceedeth its former space no less then 12000 and 500 times. And this is the reason not only of this fulminating report of Guns, but may resolve the cause of those terrible cracks, and affrighting noises of Heaven; that is, the nitrous and sulphureous exhalations, set on fire in the Clouds; whereupon requiring a larger place, they force out their way, not only with the breaking of the cloud, but the laceration of the air about it. When if the matter be spirituous, and the cloud compact, the noise is great and terrible: If the cloud be thin, and the Materials weak, the eruption is languid, ending in coruscations and flashes without noise, although but at the distance of two miles; which is esteemed the remotest distance of clouds. And therefore such lightnings do seldom any harm. And therefore also it is prodigious to have thunder in a clear sky, as is observably recorded in some Histories.

From the like cause may also proceed subterraneous Thunders and Earthquakes, when sulphureous and nitreous veins being fired, upon rarefaction do force their way through bodies that resist them. Where if the kindled matter be plentiful, and the Mine close and firm about it, subversion of Hills and Towns doth sometimes follow: If scanty, weak, and the Earth hollow or porous, there only ensueth some faint concussion or tremulous and quaking Motion. Surely, a main reason why the Ancients were so imperfect in the doctrine of Meteors, was their ignorance of Gun-powder and Fire-works, which best discover the causes of many thereof.

Now therefore he that would destroy the report of Powder, must work upon the Petre; he that would exchange the colour, must think how to alter the Small-coal. For the one, that is, to make white Powder, it is surely many ways feasible: The best I know is by the powder of rotten Willows, Spunk, or Touch-wood prepared, might perhaps make it Russet: and some, as *Beringuccio* affirmeth, have promised to make it Red. All which notwithstanding doth little concern the Report, for that, as we have shewed, depends on another Ingredient. And therefore also under the colour of black, this principle is very variable; for it is made not onely by *Willow*, *Alder*, *Hazel*, &c. But some above all commend the coals of *Flax* and *Rushes*, and some also contend the same may be effected with Tinder.

As for the other, that is, to destroy the Report, it is reasonably attempted but two ways; either by quite leaving out, or else by silencing the Salt-petre. How to abate the vigour thereof, or silence its bombulation, a way is promised by *Porta*, not only in general terms by some fat bodies, but in particular by *Borax* and butter mixed in a due proportion; which saith he, will so go off as scarce to be heard by the discharger; and indeed plentifully mixed, it will almost take off the Report, and also the force of the charge. That it may be thus made without Salt-petre, I have met with but one example, that is, of *Alphonsus* Duke of *Ferrara*, who in the relation of *Brassavolus* and *Cardan*, invented such a Powder as would discharge a bullet without Report.

That therefore white Powder there may be, there is no absurdity; that also such a one as may give no report, we will not deny a possibility. But this however, contrived either with or without Salt-petre, will surely be of little force, and the effects thereof no way to be feared: For as it omits of Report so will it of effectual exclusion, and so the charge be of little force which is excluded. For thus much is reported of that famous Powder of *Alphonsus*, which was not of force enough to kill a Chicken, according to the delivery of *Brassavolus*.

Jamque pulvis inventus est qui glandem sine bombo projicit, nec tamen vehementer ut vel pullum interficere possit.

It is not to be denied, there are ways to discharge a bullet, not only with Powder that makes no noise, but without any Powder at all; as is done by Water and Wind guns, but these afford no fulminating Report, and depend on single principles. And even in ordinary Powder there are pretended other ways to alter the noise and strength of the discharge; and the best, if not only way, consists in the quality of the Nitre: for as for other ways which make either additions or alterations in the Powder, or charge, I find therein no effect: That unto every pound of Sulphur, an adjection of one ounce of Quick-silver, or unto every pound of Petre, one ounce of *Sal Armoniac* will much intend the force, and consequently the Report, as *Beringuccio* hath delivered, I find no success therein. That a piece of *Opium* will dead the force and blow, as some have promised, I find herein no such peculiarity, no more then in any Gun or viscose body: and as much effect there is to be found from *Scammony*. That a bullet dipped in oyl by preventing the transpiration of air, will carry farther, and pierce deeper, as *Porta* affirmeth, my experience cannot discern. That Quick-silver is more destructive then shot, is surely not to be made out; for it will scarce make any penetration, and discharged from a Pistol, will hardly pierce through a Parchment. That Vinegar, spirits of Wine, or the distilled water of Orange-pills, wherewith the Powder is tempered, are more effectual unto the Report then common Water, as some do promise, I shall not affirm; but may assuredly more conduce unto the preservation and durance of the Powder, as *Cataneo* hath well observed.

That the heads of arrows and bullets have been discharged with that force, as to melt or grow red hot in their flight, though commonly received, and taken up by *Aristotle* in his Meteors, is not so easily allowable by any, who shall consider, that a Bullet of Wax will mischief without melting; that an Arrow or Bullet discharged against Linen or Paper do not set them on fire; and hardly apprehend how an Iron should grow red hot, since the swiftest motion at hand will not keep one red that hath been made red by fire; as may be observed in swinging a red hot Iron about, or fastning it into a Wheel; which under that motion will sooner grow cold then without it. That a Bullet also mounts upward upon the horizontall or point-blank discharge, many Artists do not allow: who contend that it describeth a parabolical and bowing line, by reason of its natural gravity inclining it always downward.

But, Beside the prevalence from Salt-petre, as Master-ingredient in the mixture; Sulphur may hold a greater use in the composition and further activity in the exclusion, then is by most conceived. For Sulphur vive makes better Powder then common Sulphur, which nevertheless is of a quick accension. For Small-coal, Salt-petre, and *Camphire* made into Powder will be of little force, wherein notwithstanding there wants not the accending ingredient. And *Camphire* though it flame well, yet will not flush so lively, or defecate Salt-petre, if you inject it thereon, like Sulphur; as in the preparation of *Sal prunellæ*. And lastly, though many ways may be found to light this Powder, yet is there none I know to make a strong and vigorous Powder of Salt-petre, without the admixtion of Sulphur. *Arsenic* red and yellow, that is *Orpement* and *Sandarach* may perhaps do something, as being inflamable and containing Sulphur in them; but containing also a salt, and mercurial mixtion, they will be of little effect; and white or crystalline *Arsenic* of less, for that being artificial, and sublimed with salt, will not endure flammation.

This Antipathy or contention between Salt-petre and Sulphur upon an actual fire, in their compleat and distinct bodies, is also manifested in their preparations, and bodies which invisibly contain them. Thus in the preparation of *Crocus Metallorum*; the matter kindleth and flusheth like Gunpowder, wherein notwithstanding, there is nothing but *Antimony* and Salt-petre. But this may proceed from the Sulphur of *Antimony*, not enduring the society of Salt-petre; for after three or four accensions, through a fresh addition of Petre, the Powder will flush no more, for the sulphur of the *Antimony* is quite exhaled. Thus Iron in *Aqua fortis* will fall into ebullition, with noise and emication, as also a crass and fumid exhalation, which are caused from this combat of the sulphur of Iron, with the acid and nitrous spirits of *Aqua fortis*. So is it also in *Aurum fulminans*, or Powder of Gold dissolved in *Aqua Regis*, and precipitated with oyl of *Tartar*, which will kindle without an actual fire, and afford a report like Gun-powder; that is not as *Crollius* affirmeth from any Antipathy between *Sal Armoniac* and *Tartar*, but rather between the nitrous spirits of *Aqua Regis*, commixed *per minima* with the sulphur of Gold, as *Sennertus* hath observed.

6. That *Coral* (which is a *Lithophyton* or stone-plant, and groweth at the bottom of the Sea) is soft under Water, but waxeth hard in the air, although the assertion of *Dioscorides, Pliny,* and consequently *Solinus, Isidore, Rueus,* and many others, and stands believed by most, we have some reason to doubt, especially if we conceive with common Believers, a total softness at the bottom, and this induration to be singly made by the air, not only from so sudden a petrifaction and strange induration, not easily made out from the qualities of air, but because we find it rejected by experimental enquiries. *Johannes Beguinus* in his Chapter of the tincture of *Coral,* undertakes to clear the World of this Error, from the express experiment of *John Baptista de Nicole,* who was Over-seer of the gathering of *Coral* upon the Kingdom of *Thunis.* This Gentleman, saith he, desirous to find the nature of *Coral,* and to be resolved how it groweth at the bottom of the Sea, caused a man to go down no less then a hundred fathom, with express to take notice whether it were hard or soft in the place where it groweth. Who returning, brought in each hand a branch of *Coral,* affirming it was as hard at the bottom, as in the air where he delivered it. The same was also confirmed by a trial of his own, handling it a fathom under water before it felt the air. *Bœtius* in his acurate Tract *De Gemmis,* is of the same opinion, not ascribing its concretion unto the air, but the coagulating spirits of Salt, and lapidifical juice of the Sea, which entring the parts of that Plant, overcomes its vegetability, and converts it into a lapideous substance. And this, saith he, doth happen when the Plant is ready to decay; for all *Coral* is not hard, and in many concreted Plants some parts remain unpetrified, that is the quick and livelier parts remain as Wood, and were never yet converted. Now that Plants and ligneous bodies may indurate under Water without approachment of air, we have experiments in *Coralline,* with many Coralloidal concretions; and that little stony Plant which Mr. *Johnson* nameth, *Hippuris coralloides,* and *Gesner, foliis mansu Arenosis,* we have found in fresh water, which is the less concretive portion of that Element. We have also with us the visible petrification of Wood in many waters, whereof so much as is covered with water converteth into stone; as much as is above it and in the air, retaineth the form of Wood, and continueth as before.

Now though in a middle way we may concede, that some are soft and others hard; yet whether all *Coral* were first a woody substance, and afterward converted; or rather some thereof were never such, but from the sprouting spirit of Salt, were able even in their stony natures to ramifie and send forth branches; as is observable in some stones, in silver and metallick bodies, is not without some question. And such at least might some of those be, which *Fioravanti* observed to grow upon Bricks at the bottom of the Sea, upon the coast of Barbarie.

7. We are not thoroughly resolved concerning *Porcellane* or *China* dishes, that according to common belief they are made of Earth, which lieth in preparation about an hundred years under ground; for the relations thereof are not onely divers, but contrary, and Authors agree not herein. *Guido Pancirollus* will have them made of Egg-shells, Lobster-shells, and *Gypsum* laid up in the Earth the space of 80 years: of the same affirmation is *Scaliger*, and the common opinion of most. *Ramuzuius* in his Navigations is of a contrary assertion, that they are made out of Earth, not laid under ground, but hardned in the Sun and Wind, the space of forty years. But *Gonzales de Mendoza*, a man imployed into *China* from *Philip* the second King of *Spain*, upon enquiry and ocular experience, delivered a way different from all these. For inquiring into the artifice thereof, he found they were made of a Chalky Earth; which beaten and steeped in water, affordeth a cream or fatness on the top, and a gross subsidence at the bottom; out of the cream of superfluitance, the finest dishes, saith he, are made, out of the residence thereof the courser; which being formed, they gild or paint, and not after an hundred years, but presently commit unto the furnace. This, saith he, is known by experience, and more probable then what *Odoardus Barbosa* hath delivered, that they are made of shells, and buried under earth an hundred years. And answerable in all points hereto, is the relation of *Linschotten*, a diligent enquirer, in his Oriental Navigations. Later confirmation may be had from *Alvarez* the Jesuit, who lived long in those parts, in his relations of *China*. That *Porcellane* Vessels were made but in one Town of the Province of *Chiamsi*: That the earth was brought out of other Provinces, but for the advantage of water, which makes them more polite and perspicuous, they were only made in this. That they were wrought and fashioned like those of other Countries, whereof some were tincted blew, some red, others yellow, of which colour only they presented unto the King.

The latest account hereof may be found in the voyage of the Dutch Embassadors sent from *Batavia* unto the Emperour of *China*, printed in *French* 1665. which plainly informeth, that the Earth whereof *Porcellane* dishes are made, is brought from the Mountains of

Hoang, and being formed into square loaves, is brought by water, and marked with the Emperour's Seal: that the Earth it self is very lean, fine, and shining like Sand: and that it is prepared and fashioned after the same manner which the *Italians* observe in the fine Earthen Vessels of *Faventia* or *Fuenca*: that they are so reserved concerning that Artifice, that 'tis only revealed from Father unto Son: that they are painted with *Indico* baked in a fire for fifteen days together, and with very dry and not smoaking Wood: which when the Author had seen he could hardly contain from laughter at the common opinion above rejected by us.

Now if any enquire, why being so commonly made, and in so short a time, they are become so scarce, or not at all to be had? The Answer is given by these last Relators, that under great penalties it is forbidden to carry the first sort out of the Country. And of those surely the properties must be verified, which by *Scaliger* and others are ascribed unto China-dishes: That they admit no poison, that they strike fire, that they will grow hot no higher then the liquor in them ariseth. For such as pass amongst us, and under the name of the finest, will only strike fire, but not discover *Aconite*, *Mercury*, or *Arsenic*; but may be useful in dysenteries and fluxes beyond the other.

8. Whether a Carbuncle (which is esteemed the best and biggest of Rubies) doth flame in the dark, or shine like a coal in the night, though generally agreed on by common Believers, is very much questioned by many. By *Milius*, who accounts it a Vulgar Error: By the learned *Bœtius*, who could not find it verified in that famous one of *Rodulphus*, which was a big as an Egg, and esteemed the best in *Europe*. Wherefore although we dispute not the possibility, and the like is said to have been observed in some Diamonds, yet whether herein there be not too high an apprehension, and above its natural radiancy, is not without just doubt: however it be granted a very splendid *Gem*, and whose sparks may somewhat resemble the glances of fire, and Metaphorically deserve that name. And therefore when it is conceived by some, that this Stone in the Brest-plate of *Aaron* respected the Tribe of *Dan*, who burnt the City of *Laish*; and *Sampson* of the same Tribe, who fired the Corn of the *Philistines*; in some sense it may be admitted, and is no intollerable conception.

As for that *Indian* Stone that shined so brightly in the Night, and pretended to have been shewn to many in the Court of *France*, as

Andreus Chioccus hath declared out of *Thuanus*, it proved but an imposture, as that eminent Philosopher *Licetus* hath discovered, and therefore in the revised Editions of *Thuanus*, it is not to be found. As for the *Phosphorus* or *Bononian* Stone, which exposed unto the Sun, and then closely shut up, will afterward afford a light in the dark; it is of unlike consideration, for that requireth the calcination or reduction into a dry powder by fire, whereby it imbibeth the light in the vaporous humidity of the air about it, and therefore maintaineth its light not long, but goes out when the vaporous vehicle is consumed.

9. Whether the *Ætites* or *Eagle*-stone hath that eminent property to promote delivery or restrain abortion, respectively applied to lower or upward parts of the body, we shall not discourage common practice by our question: but whether they answer the account thereof, as to be taken out of *Eagles* nests, co-operating in Women unto such effects, as they are conceived toward the young *Eagles*: or whether the single signature of one stone included in the matrix and belly of another, were not sufficient at first, to derive this vertue of the pregnant Stone, upon others in impregnation, may yet be farther considered. Many sorts there are of this ratling Stone, beside the *Geodes*, containing a softer substance in it. Divers are found in *England*, and one we met with on the Sea-shore, but because many of eminent use are pretended to be brought from *Iseland*, wherein are divers airies of *Eagles*; we cannot omit to deliver what we received from a learned person in that Country, *Ætites an in nidis Aquilarum aliquando fuerit repertus, nescio. Nostra certè memoria, etiam inquirentibus non contiget invenisse, quare in fabulis habendum.*

10. Terrible apprehensions and answerable unto their names, are raised of *Fayrie* stones, and *Elves* spurs, found commonly with us in Stone, Chalk, and Marl-pits, which notwithstanding are no more then *Echinometrites* and *Belemnites*, the Sea-Hedg-Hog, and the *Dart*-stone, arising from some siliceous Roots, and softer then that of Flint, the Master-stone, lying more regularly in courses, and arising from the primary and strongest spirit of the Mine. Of the *Echinites*, such as are found in Chalk-pits are white, glassie, and built upon a Chalky inside; some of an hard and flinty substance, are found in Stone-pits and elsewhere. Common opinion commendeth them for the Stone, but are most practically used against Films in Horses eyes.

11. Lastly, He must have more heads then *Rome* had Hills, that makes out half of those vertues ascribed unto stones, and their not only Medical, but Magical proprieties, which are to be found in Authors of great Name. In *Psellus, Serapian, Evax, Albertus, Aleazar, Marbodetus*; in *Maiolus, Rueus, Mylius*, and many more.

That *Lapis Lazuli* hath in it a purgative faculty we know; that *Bezoar* is Antidotal, *Lapis Judaicus* diuretical, *Coral* Antepileptical, we will not deny. That *Cornelians, Jaspis, Heliotropes*, and Bloodstones, may be of vertue to those intentions they are implied, experience and visible effects will make us grant. But that an *Amethyst* prevents inebriation, that an *Emerald* will break if worn in copulation. That a *Diamond* laid under the pillow, will betray the incontinency of a wife. That a *Saphire* is preservative against inchantments; that the fume of an *Agath* will avert a tempest, or the wearing of a *Crysoprase* make one out of love with Gold; as some have delivered, we are yet, I confess, to believe, and in that infidelity are likely to end our dayes. And therefore, they which in the explication of the two Beryls upon the *Ephod*, or the twelve stones in the Rational or Brest-plate of *Aaron*, or those twelve which garnished the wall of the holy City in the Apocalyps, have drawn their significations from such as these; or declared their symbolical verities from such traditional falsities, have surely corrupted the sincerity of their Analogies, or misunderstood the mystery of their intentions.

Most men conceive that the twelve stones in *Aarons* brestplate made a Jewel surpassing any, and not to be parallel'd; which notwithstanding will hardly be made out from the description of the Text, for the names of the Tribes were engraven thereon, which must notably abate their lustre. Beside, it is not clear made out that the best of Gemms, a Diamond, was amongst them; nor is to be found in the list thereof, set down by the *Jerusalem Thargum*, wherein we find the darker stones of *Sardius, Sardonix*, and *Jasper*; and if we receive them under those names wherein they are usually described, it is not hard to contrive a more illustrious and splendent Jewel. But being not ordained for meer lustre by diaphanous and pure tralucencies, their mysterious significations became more considerable then their Gemmary substances; and those no doubt did nobly answer the intention of the Institutor. Beside some may doubt whether there be twelve distinct species of noble tralucent Gemms in nature, at least yet known unto us, and such as may not be referred unto some of those in high esteem among us, which come short of the number of twelve; which to make up we must find out some others to match and join with the Diamond, *Beryl, Saphyr, Emerald, Amethyst, Topaz, Crysolit, Jacynth, Ruby,* and if we may admit it in this number, the Oriental Granat.

CHAPTER VI

Of sundry Tenets concerning Vegetables or Plants, which examined, prove either false or dubious.

1. Many Mola's and false conceptions there are of *Mandrakes*, the first from great Antiquity, conceiveth the Root thereof resembleth the shape of Man; which is a conceit not to be made out by ordinary inspection, or any other eyes, then such as regarding the Clouds, behold them in shapes conformable to pre-apprehensions.

Now whatever encouraged the first invention, there have not been wanting many ways of its promotion. The first a Catachrestical and far derived similitude it holds with Man; that is, in a bifurcation or division of the Root into two parts, which some are content to call Thighs; whereas notwithstanding they are oft-times three, and when but two, commonly so complicated and crossed, that men for this deceit are fain to effect their design in other plants; And as fair a resemblance is often found in *Carrots*, *Parsnips*, *Briony*, and many others. There are, I confess, divers Plants which carry about them not only the shape of parts, but also of whole Animals, but surely not all thereof, unto whom this conformity is imputed. Whoever shall peruse the signatures of *Crollius*, or rather the Phytognomy of *Porta*, and strictly observe how vegetable Realities are commonly forced into Animal Representations, may easily perceive in very many, the semblance is but postulatory, and must have a more assimilating phansie then mine to make good many thereof.

Illiterate heads have been led on by the name, which in the first syllable expresseth its Representation; but others have better observed the Laws of *Etymology*, and deduced it from a word of the same language, because it delighteth to grow in obscure and shady places; which derivation, although we shall not stand to maintain, yet the other seemeth answerable unto the Etymologies of many Authors, who often confound such nominal Notations. Not to enquire beyond our own profession, the Latine Physitians which most adhered unto the *Arabick* way, have often failed herein; particularly *Valescus de Tarranta*, a received Physitian, in whose *Philonium* or Medical practice these may be observed: *Diarhea*, saith he, *Quia pluries venit in die. Herisepela, quasi hærens pilis, Emorrohis, ab emach sanguis & morrhois quod est cadere. Lithargia à Litos quod est oblivio, & Targus morbus, Scotomia à Scotus quod est videre, & mias musca. Opthalmia ab opus Grœce quod est succus, & Talmon, quod est occulus. Paralisis, quasi lœsio partis. Fistula à fos sonus & stolon quod est emissio, quasi emissio soni vel vocis.* Which are derivations as strange indeed as the other, and hardly to be parallel'd elsewhere; confirming not only the words of one language with another, but creating such as were never yet in any.

The received distinction and common Notation by Sexes, hath also promoted the conceit; for true it is, that *Herbalists* from ancient times, have thus distinguished them; naming that the Male, whose leaves are lighter, and Fruit and Apples rounder; but this is properly no generative division, but rather some note of distinction in colour, figure or operation. For though *Empedocles* affirm, there is a mixt, and undivided Sex in Vegetables; and *Scaliger* upon *Aristotle*, doth favourably explain that opinion; yet will it not consist with the common and ordinary acception, nor yet with *Aristotles* definition. For if that be Male which generates in another, that Female which procreates in it self; if it be understood of Sexes conjoined, all Plants are Female; and if of disjoined and congressive generation, there is no Male or Female in them at all.

But the Atlas or main Axis which supported this opinion, was dayly experience, and the visible testimony of sense. For many there are in several parts of *Europe*, who carry about Roots and sell them unto ignorant people, which handsomely make out the shape of Man or Woman. But these are not productions of Nature, but contrivances of Art, as divers have noted, and *Mathiolus* plainly detected, who

130

learned this way of Trumpery from a vagabond cheater lying under his cure for the French disease. His words are these, and may determine the point, *Sed profectò vanum & fabulosum, &c.* But this is vain and fabulous, which ignorant people, and simple women believe; for the roots which are carried about by impostors to deceive unfruitful women, are made of the roots of Canes, Briony and other plants: for in these yet fresh and virent, they carve out the figures of men and women, first sticking therein the grains of Barley or Millet, where they intend the hair should grow; then bury them in sand until the grains shoot forth their roots, which at the longest will happen in twenty days; they afterward clip and trim those tender strings in the fashion of beards and other hairy tegument. All which like other impostures once discovered is easily effected, and in the root of white *Briony* may be practised every spring.

What is therefore delivered in favour thereof, by Authors ancient or modern, must have its root in tradition, imposture, far derived similitude, or casual and rare contingency. So may we admit of the Epithet of *Pythagoras*, who calls it *Anthropomorphus*, and that of *Columella*, who terms it *Semihomo*; more appliable unto the Man-Orchis, whose flower represents a Man. Thus is *Albertus* to be received when he affirmeth, that *Mandrakes* represent man-kind with the distinction of either Sex. Under these restrictions may those Authors be admitted, which for this opinion are introduced by *Drusius*; nor shall we need to question the monstrous root of *Briony* described in *Aldrovandus*.

Thesecond assertion concerneth its production, That it naturally groweth under Gallowses and places of execution, arising from fat or urine that drops from the body of the dead; a story somewhat agreeable unto the fable of the Serpents teeth sowed in the earth by *Cadmus*; or rather the birth of *Orion* from the Urine of *Jupiter*, *Mercury*, and *Neptune*. Now this opinion seems grounded on the former, that is, a conceived similitude it hath with man; and therefore from him in some way they would make out its production: Which conceit is not only erroneous in the foundation, but injurious unto Philosophy in the superstructure. Making putrifactive generations, correspondent unto seminal productions, and conceiving in equivocal effects an univocal conformity unto the efficient. Which is so far from being verified of animals in their corruptive mutations into Plants, that they maintain not this similitude in their nearer translation into animals. So

131

when the Oxe corrupteth into Bees, or the Horse into Hornets, they come not forth in the image of their originals. So the corrupt and excrementous humours in man are animated into Lice; and we may observe, that Hogs, Sheep, Goats, Hawks, Hens and others, have one peculiar and proper kind of vermine; not resembling themselves according to seminal conditions, yet carrying a setled and confined habitude unto their corruptive originals. And therefore come not forth in generations erratical, or different from each other; but seem specifically and in regular shapes to attend the corruption of their bodies, as do more perfect conceptions, the rule of seminal productions.

The third affirmeth the roots of *Mandrakes* do make a noise, or give a shriek upon eradication; which is indeed ridiculous, and false below confute; arising perhaps from a small and stridulous noise, which being firmly rooted, it maketh upon divulsion of parts. A slender foundation for such a vast conception: for such a noise we sometimes observe in other Plants, in Parsenips, Liquorish, Eringium, Flags, and others.

The last concerneth the danger ensuing, That there follows an hazard of life to them that pull it up, that some evil fate pursues them, and they live not very long after. Therefore the attempt hereof among the Ancients, was not in ordinary way, but as *Pliny* informeth, when they intended to take up the root of this Plant, they took the wind thereof, and with a sword describing three circles about it, they digged it up, looking toward the *west*. A conceit not only injurious unto truth, and confutable by daily experience, but somewhat derogatory unto the providence of God; that is, not only to impose so destructive a quality on any Plant, but to conceive a Vegetable, whose parts are useful unto many, should in the only taking up prove mortal unto any. To think he suffereth the poison of *Nubia* to be gathered, *Napellus*, *Aconite*, and *Thora*, to be eradicated, yet this not to be moved. That he permitteth Arsenick and mineral poisons to be forced from the bowels of the Earth, yet not this from the surface thereof. This were to introduce a second forbidden fruit, and inhance the first malediction, making it not only mortal for *Adam* to taste the one, but capital unto his posterity to eradicate or dig up the other.

Now what begot, at least promoted so strange conceptions, might be the magical opinion hereof; this being conceived the Plant so much in use with *Circe*, and therefore named *Circea*, as *Dioscorides* and *Theophrastus* have delivered, which being the eminent Sorcerers of elder story, and by the magick of simples believed to have wrought many wonders: some men were apt to invent, others to believe any tradition or magical promise thereof.

Analogus relations concerning other plants, and such as are of near affinity unto this, have made its currant smooth, and pass more easily among us. For the same effect is also delivered by *Josephus*, concerning the root *Baaras*; by *Ælian* of *Cynospastus*; and we read in *Homer* the very same concerning Moly,

The Gods it Moly call, whose Root to dig away, Is dangerous unto Man; but Gods, they all things may.

Now parallels or like relations alternately relieve each other, when neither will pass asunder, yet are they plausible together; their mutual concurrences supporting their solitary instabilities.

Signaturists have somewhat advanced it; who seldom omitting what Ancients delivered; drawing into inference received distinction of sex, not willing to examine its humane resemblance; and placing it in the form of strange and magical simples, have made men suspect there was more therein, then ordinary practice allowed; and so became apt to embrace whatever they heard or read conformable unto such conceptions.

Lastly, The conceit promoteth it self: for concerning an effect whose trial must cost so dear, it fortifies it self in that invention; and few there are whose experiment it need to fear. For (what is most contemptible) although not only the reason of any head, but experience of every hand may well convict it, yet will it not by divers be rejected; for prepossessed heads will ever doubt it, and timorous beliefs will never dare to trie it. So these Traditions how low and ridiculous soever, will find suspition in some, doubt in others, and serve as tests or trials of Melancholy and superstitious tempers for ever.

2. That Cinamon, Ginger, Clove, Mace, and Nutmeg, are but the several parts and fruits of the same tree, is the common belief of those which daily use them. Whereof to speak distinctly, Ginger is the root of neither Tree nor Shrub, but of an herbaceous Plant, resembling

the Water Flower-De-luce, as *Garcias* first described; or rather the common Reed, as *Lobelius* since affirmed. Very common in many parts of *India*, growing either from Root or Seed, which in *December* and *January* they take up, and gently dried, roll it up in earth, whereby occluding the pores, they conserve the natural humidity, and so prevent corruption.

Cinamon is the inward bark of a Cinamon Tree, whereof the best is brought from *Zeilan*; this freed from the outward bark, and exposed unto the Sun, contracts into those folds wherein we commonly receive it. If it have not a sufficient insolation it looketh pale, and attains not its laudable colour; if it be sunned too long, it suffereth a torrefaction, and descendeth somewhat below it.

Clove seems to be either the rudiment of a fruit, or the fruit it self growing upon the Clove tree, to be found but in a few Countries. The most commendable is that of the Isles of *Molucca*; it is first white, afterward green, which beaten down, and dried in the Sun, becometh black, and in the complexion we receive it.

Nutmeg is the fruit of a Tree differing from all these, and as *Garcias* describeth it, somewhat like a Peach; growing in divers places, but fructifying in the Isle of *Banda*. The fruit hereof consisteth of four parts; the first or outward part is a thick and carnous covering like that of a Wal-nut. The second a dry and flosculous coat, commonly called Mace. The third a harder tegument or shell, which lieth under the Mace. The fourth a Kernel included in the shell, which is the same we call Nutmeg. All which both in their parts and order of disposure, are easily discerned in those fruits, which are brought in preserves unto us.

Now if because Mace and Nutmeg proceed from one Tree, the rest must bear them company; or because they are all from the *East Indies*, they are all from one Plant: the Inference is precipitous, nor will there such a Plant be found in the Herbal of Nature.

3. That Viscous Arboreus or Misseltoe is bred upon Trees, from seeds which Birds, especially Thrushes and Ring-doves let fall thereon, was the Creed of the Ancients, and is still believed among us, is the account of its production, set down by *Pliny*, delivered by *Virgil*,

and subscribed by many more. If so, some reason must be assigned, why it groweth onely upon certain Trees, and not upon many whereon these Birds do light. For as Exotick observers deliver, it groweth upon Almond-trees, Chesnut, Apples, Oaks, and Pine-trees. As we observe in *England* very commonly upon Apple, Crabs, and White-thorn; sometimes upon Sallow, Hazel, and Oak: rarely upon Ash, Limetree, and Maple; never, that I could observe, upon Holly, Elm, and many more. Why it groweth not in all Countries and places where these Birds are found; for so *Brassavolus* affirmeth, it is not to be found in the Territory of *Ferrara*, and was fain to supply himself from other parts of *Italy*. Why if it ariseth from a seed, if sown it will not grow again, as *Pliny* affirmeth, and as by setting the Berries thereof, we have in vain attempted its production; why if it cometh from seed that falleth upon the tree, it groweth often downwards, and puts forth under the bough, where seed can neither fall nor yet remain. Hereof beside some others, the Lord *Verulam* hath taken notice. And they surely speak probably who make it an arboreous excrescence, or rather super plant, bred of a viscous and superfluous sap which the tree it self cannot assimilate. And therefore sprouteth not forth in boughs and surcles of the same shape, and similary unto the Tree that beareth it; but in a different form, and secondary unto its specifical intention, wherein once failing, another form succeedeth: and in the first place that of Misseltoe, in Plants and Trees disposed to its production. And therefore also where ever it groweth, it is of constant shape, and maintains a regular figure; like other supercrescences, and such as living upon the stock of others, are termed parasitical Plants, as Polypody, Moss, the smaller Capillaries, and many more: So that several regions produce several Misseltoes; *India* one, *America* another, according to the law and rule of their degenerations.

Now what begot this conceit, might be the enlargement of some part of truth contained in its story. For certain it is, that some Birds do feed upon the berries of this Vegetable, and we meet in *Aristotle* with one kind of Trush called the Missel Trush, or feeder upon Misseltoe. But that which hath most promoted it, is a received proverb, *Turdus sibi malum cacat*; appliable unto such men as are authors of their own misfortune. For according unto ancient tradition and *Plinies* relation, the Bird not able to digest the fruit whereon she feedeth; from her inconverted muting ariseth this Plant, of the Berries whereof Bird-lime is made, wherewith she is after entangled. But although Proverbs be popular principles, yet is not all true that is proverbial; and in many

135

thereof, there being one thing delivered, and another intended; though the verbal expression be false, the Proverb is true enough in the verity of its intention.

As for the Magical vertues in this Plant, and conceived efficacy unto veneficial intentions, it seemeth a *Pagan* relique derived from the ancient *Druides*, the great admirers of the Oak, especially the Misseltoe that grew thereon; which according unto the particular of *Pliny*, they gathered with great solemnity. For after sacrifice the Priest in a white garment ascended the tree, cut down the Misseltoe with a golden hook, and received it in a white coat; the vertue whereof was to resist all poisons, and make fruitful any that used it. Vertues not expected from Classical practice; and did they fully answer their promise which are so commended, in Epileptical intentions, we would abate these qualities. Country practice hath added another, to provoke the after-birth, and in that case the decoction is given unto Cows. That the Berries are poison as some conceive, we are so far from averring, that we have safely given them inwardly; and can confirm the experiment of *Brassavolus*, that they have some purgative quality.

4. The Rose of *Jericho*, that flourishes every year just about Christmas Eve, is famous in Christian reports; which notwithstanding we have some reason to doubt, and are plainly informed by *Bellonius*, it is but a Monastical imposture, as he hath delivered in his observations, concerning the Plants in *Jericho*. That which promoted the conceit, or perhaps begot its continuance, was a propriety in this Plant. For though it be dry, yet will it upon imbibition of moisture dilate its leaves, and explicate its flowers contracted, and seemingly dried up. And this is to be effected not only in the Plant yet growing, but in some manner also in that which is brought exuccous and dry unto us. Which quality being observed, the subtilty of contrivers did commonly play this shew upon the Eve of our Saviours Nativity, when by drying the Plant again, it closed the next day, and so pretended a double mystery: referring unto the opening and closing of the womb of *Mary*.

There wanted not a specious confirmation from a text in *Ecclesiasticus, Quasi palma exaltata sum in Cades, & quasi plantatio Rosæ in Jericho*; I was exalted like a Palm-tree in *Engaddi*, and as a Rose in *Jericho*. The sound whereof in common ears, begat an extraordinary opinion of the Rose of that denomination. But herein there seemeth a mistake: for by the Rose in the Text, is implied the true and

136

proper Rose, as first the Greek, and ours accordingly rendreth it. But that which passeth under this name, and by us is commonly called the Rose of *Jericho*, is properly no Rose, but a small thorny shrub or kind of Heath, bearing little white flowers, far differing from the Rose; whereof *Bellonius* a very inquisitive *Herbalist*, could not find any in his travels thorow *Jericho*. A Plant so unlike a Rose, it hath been mistaken by some good *Simplist* for *Amomum*; which truly understood is so unlike a Rose, that as *Dioscorides* delivers, the flowers thereof are like the white Violet, and its leaves resemble *Briony*.

Suitable unto this relation almost in all points is that of the Thorn at *Glassenbury*, and perhaps the daughter hereof; herein our endeavours as yet have not attained satisfaction, and cannot therefore enlarge. Thus much in general we may observe, that strange effects, are naturally taken for miracles by weaker heads, and artificially improved to that apprehension by wiser. Certainly many precocious Trees, and such as spring in the Winter, may be found in most parts of *Europe*, and divers also in *England*. For most Trees do begin to sprout in the Fall of the leaf or Autumn, and if not kept back by cold and outward causes, would leaf about the Solstice. Now if it happen that any be so strongly constituted, as to make this good against the power of Winter, they may produce their leaves or blossoms in that season. And perform that in some singles, which is observable in whole kinds; as in *Ivy*, which blossoms and bears at least twice a year, and once in the Winter; as also in *Furze*, which flowereth in that season.

5. That *ferrum Equinum*, or *Sferra Cavallo* hath a vertue attractive of Iron, a power to break locks, and draw off the shoes of a Horse that passeth over it: whether you take it for one kind of *Securdiaca*, or will also take in *Lunaria*, we know it to be false; and cannot but wonder at *Mathiolus*, who upon a parallel in *Pliny* was staggered into suspension. Who notwithstanding in the imputed vertue to open things, close and shut up, could laugh himself at that promise from the herb *Æthiopis* or *Æthiopian* mullen; and condemn the judgment of *Scipio*, who having such a picklock, would spend so many years in battering the Gates of *Carthage*. Which strange and Magical conceit, seems to have no deeper root in reason, then the figure of its seed; for therein indeed it somewhat resembles a Horse-shoe; which notwithstanding *Baptista Porta* hath thought too low a signification, and raised the same unto a Lunary representation.

6. That *Bayes* will protect from the mischief or Lightning and Thunder, is a quality ascribed thereto, common with the Fig-tree, Eagle, and skin of a Seal. Against so famous a quality, *Vicomercatus* produceth experiment of a Bay-tree blasted in *Italy*. And therefore although *Tiberius* for this intent, did wear a Lawrel upon his Temples; yet did *Augustus* take a more probable course, who fled under arches and hollow vaults for protection. And though *Porta* conceive, because in a streperous eruption, it riseth against fire, it doth therefore resist lightning, yet is that no emboldning Illation. And if we consider the threefold effect of *Jupiters* Trisulk, to burn, discuss, and terebrate; and if that be true which is commonly delivered, that it will melt the blade, yet pass the scabbard; kill the child, yet spare the mother; dry up the wine, yet leave the hogshead entire: though it favour the amulet, it may not spare us; it will be unsure to rely on any preservative, 'tis no security to be dipped in Styx, or clad in the armour of *Ceneus*. Now that Beer, Wine, and other Liquors, are spoiled with lightning and thunder, we conceive it proceeds not onely from noise and concussion of the air, but also noxious spirits, which mingle therewith, and draw them to corruption; whereby they become not only dead themselves, but sometime deadly unto others, as that which *Seneca* mentioneth; whereof whosoever drank, either lost his life, or else his wits upon it.

7. It hath much deceived the hope of good fellows, what is commonly expected of bitter Almonds, and though in *Plutarch* confirmed from the practice of *Claudius* his Physitian, that Antidote against ebriety hath commonly failed. Surely men much versed in the practice do err in the theory of inebriation; conceiving in that disturbance the brain doth only suffer from exhalations and vaporous ascensions from the stomack, which fat and oyly substances may suppress. Whereas the prevalent intoxication is from the spirits of drink dispersed into the veins and arteries; from whence by common conveyances they creep into the brain, insinuate into its ventricles, and beget those vertigoes, accompanying that perversion. And therefore the same effect may be produced by a Glister, the Head may be intoxicated by a medicine at the Heel. So the poisonous bites of Serpents, although on parts at distance from the head, yet having entered the veins, disturb the animal faculties, and produce the effects of drink, or poison swallowed. And so as the Head may be disturbed by the skin, it may the same way be relieved; as is observable in balneations, washings, and fomentations, either of the whole body, or of that part alone.

138

CHAPTER VII

Of some Insects, and the properties of several Plants

1. Few ears have escaped the noise of the Dead-watch, that is, the little clickling sound heard often in many rooms, somewhat resembling that of a Watch; and this is conceived to be of an evil omen or prediction of some persons death: wherein notwithstanding there is nothing of rational presage or just cause of terrour unto melancholy and meticulous heads. For this noise is made by a little sheath-winged gray Insect found often in Wainscot, Benches, and Wood-work, in the Summer. We have taken many thereof, and kept them in thin boxes, wherein I have heard and seen them work and knack with a little *proboscis* or trunk against the side of the box, like *Apicus Martius*, or Woodpecker against a tree. It worketh best in warm weather, and for the most part, giveth not over under nine or eleven stroaks at a time. He that could extinguish the terrifying apprehensions hereof, might prevent the passions of the heart, and many cold sweats in Grandmothers and Nurses, who in the sickness of children, are so startled with these noises.

2. The presage of the year succeeding, which is commonly made from Insects or little Animals in Oak apples, according to the kinds thereof, either Maggot, Fly, or Spider; that is, of Famine, War, or Pestilence; whether we mean that woody excrescence, which shooteth from the branch about *May*, or that round and Apple-like accretion which groweth under the leaf about the latter end of Summer, is I doubt too distinct, nor verifiable from event.

For Flies and Maggots are found every year, very seldom Spiders: And *Helmont* affirmeth he could never find the Spider and the Fly upon the same Trees, that is the signs of War and Pestilence, which often go together: Beside, That the Flies found were at first Maggots, experience hath informed us; for keeping these excrescencies, we have observed their conversions, beholding in Magnifying Glasses the daily progression thereof. As may be also observed in other Vegetable excretions, whose Maggots do terminate in Flies of constant shapes; as in the Nutgalls of the Out-landish Oak, and the Mossie tuft of the wild Briar; which having gathered in *November* we have found the little Maggots which lodged in wooden Cells all *Winter*, to turn into Flies in *June*.

We confess the opinion may hold some verity in the Analogy, or Emblematical phansie. For Pestilence is properly signified by the Spider, whereof some kinds are of a very venemous Nature. Famine by Maggots, which destroy the fruits of the Earth. And War not improperly by the Fly; if we rest in the phansie of *Homer*, who compares the valiant *Grecian* unto a Fly.

Some verity it may also have in it self, as truly declaring the corruptive constitution in the present sap and nutrimental juice of the Tree; and may consequently discover the disposition of that year, according to the plenty or kinds of these productions. For if the putrifying juices of bodies bring forth plenty of Flies and Maggots, they give forth testimony of common corruption, and declare that the Elements are full of the seeds of putrifaction, as the great number of Caterpillars, Gnats, and ordinary Insects do also declare. If they run into Spiders, they give signs of higher putrifaction, as plenty of Vipers and Scorpions are confessed to do; the putrifying Materials producing Animals of higher mischiefs, according to the advance and higher strain of corruption.

3. Whether all Plants have seed, were more easily determinable, if we could conclude concerning Harts-tongue, Fern, the Capillaries, Lunaria, and some others. But whether those little dusty particles, upon the lower side of the leaves, be seeds and seminal parts; or rather, as it is commonly conceived, excremental separations; we have not as yet been able to determine by any germination or univocal production from them when they have been sowed on purpose: but having set the roots of Harts tongue in a garden, a year or two after

there came up three or four of the same Plants, about two yards distance from the first. Thus much we observe, that they seem to renew yearly, and come not fully out till the Plant be in his vigour: and by the help of Magnifying Glasses we find these dusty Atoms to be round at first, and fully representing seeds, out of which at last proceed little Mites almost invisible; so that such as are old stand open, as being emptied of some bodies formerly included; which though discernable in Harts-tongue, is more notoriously discoverable in some differencies of Brake or Fern.

But exquisite Microscopes and Magnifying Glasses have at last cleared this doubt, whereby also long ago the noble *Federicus Cæsius* beheld the dusts of Polypody as bigg as Pepper corns; and as *Johannes Faber* testifieth, made draughts on Paper of such kind of seeds, as bigg as his Glasses represented them: and set down such Plants under the Classis of *Herbæ Tergifætæ*, as may be observed in his notable Botanical Tables.

4. Whether the sap of Trees runs down to the roots in Winter, whereby they become naked and grow not: or whether they do not cease to draw any more, and reserve so much as sufficeth for conservation, is not a point indubitable. For we observe, that most Trees, as though they would be perpetually green, do bud at the Fall of the leaf, although they sprout not much forward untill the Spring, and warmer weather approacheth; and many Trees maintain their leaves all Winter, although they seem to receive very small advantage in their growth. But that the sap doth powerfully rise in the Spring, to repair that moisture whereby they barely subsisted in the Winter, and also to put the Plant in a capacity of fructification: he that hath beheld how many gallons of water may in a small time be drawn from a Birch-tree in the Spring, hath slender reason to doubt.

5. That *Camphire* Eunuchates, or begets in Men an impotency unto Venery, observation will hardly confirm; and we have found it to fail in Cocks and Hens, though given for many days; which was a more favourable trial then that of *Scaliger*, when he gave it unto a Bitch that was proud. For the instant turgescence is not to be taken off, but by Medicines of higher Natures; and with any certainty but one way that we know, which notwithstanding, by suppresing that natural evacuation, may encline unto Madness, if taken in the Summer.

141

6. In the History of Prodigies we meet with many showrs of Wheat; how true or probable, we have not room to debate. Only this much we shall not omit to inform, That what was this year found in many places, and almost preached for Wheat rained from the clouds, was but the seed of Ivy-berries, which somewhat represent it; and though it were found in Steeples and high places, might be conveyed thither, or muted out by Birds: for many feed thereon, and in the crops of some we have found no less then three ounces.

7. That every Plant might receive a Name according unto the disease it cureth, was the wish of *Paracelsus*. A way more likely to multiply Empericks then Herbalists: yet what is practised by many is advantagious unto neither; that is, relinquishing their proper appellations to re-baptize them by the name of Saints, Apostles, Patriarchs, and Martyrs, to call this the herb of *John*, that of *Peter*, this of *James*, or *Joseph*, that of *Mary* or *Barbara*. For hereby apprehensions are made additional unto their proper Natures; whereon superstitious practises ensue; and stories are framed accordingly to make good their foundations.

8. We cannot omit to declare the gross mistake of many in the Nominal apprehension of Plants; to instance but in few. An herb there is commonly called *Betonica Pauli*, or *Pauls Betony*; hereof the People have some conceit in reference to St. *Paul*; whereas indeed that name is derived from *Paulus Ægineta*, an ancient Physitian of *Ægina*, and is no more then Speed-well, or *Fluellen*. The like expectations are raised from *Herba Trinitatis*; which notwithstanding obtaineth that name from the figure of its leaves, and is one kind of Liverwort, or *Hepatica*. In *Milium Solis*, the Epithete of the Sun hath enlarged its opinion; which hath indeed no reference thereunto, it being no more then *Lithospermon*, or *Grummel*, or rather *Milium Soler*; which as *Serapion* from *Aben Juliel* hath taught us, because it grew plentifully in the Mountains of *Soler*, received that appellation. In Jews-ears something is conceived extraordinary from the Name, which is in propriety but *Fungus sambucinus*, or an excrescence about the Roots of Elder, and concerneth not the Nation of the *Jews*, but *Judas Iscariot*, upon a conceit, he hanged on this Tree; and is become a famous Medicine in Quinsies, sore Throats, and strangulations ever since. And so are they deceived in the name of the Horse-Raddish, Horse-Mint, Bull-rush, and many more: conceiving therein some prenominal consideration, whereas indeed that expression is but a Grecism, by the prefix of *Hip-*

pos and *Bous*, that is, Horse and Bull, intending no more then Great. According whereto the great Dock is called *Hippollapathum*; and he that calls the Horse of *Alexander*, *Great-head*, expresseth the same which the *Greeks* do in *Bucephalus*.

9. Lastly, Many things are delivered and believed of other Plants, wherein at least we cannot but suspend. That there is a property in *Basil* to propagate Scorpions, and that by the smell thereof they are bred in the brains of men, is much advanced by *Hollerius*, who found this Insect in the brains of a man that delighted much in this smell. Wherein beside we find no way to conjoin the effect unto the cause assigned; herein the Moderns speak but timorously, and some of the Ancients quite contrarily. For, according unto *Oribasius*, Physitian unto *Julian*, The *Affricans*, Men best experienced in poisons, affirm, whosoever hath eaten *Basil*, although he be stung with a Scorpion, shall feel no pain thereby: which is a very different effect, and rather antidotally destroying, then seminally promoting its production.

That the leaves of *Cataputia* or Spurge, being plucked upward or downward, respectively perform their operations by Purge or Vomit, as some have written, and old wives still do preach, is a strange conceit, ascribing unto Plants positional operations, and after the manner of the Loadstone; upon the Pole whereof if a Knife be drawn from the handle unto the point, it will take up a Needle; but if drawn again from the point to the handle, it will attract it no more.

That Cucumbers are no commendable fruits, that being very waterish, they fill the veins with crude and windy serosities; that containing little Salt or spirit, they may also debilitate the vital acidity, and fermental faculty of the Stomach, we readily concede. But that they should be so cold, as be almost poison by that quality, it will be hard to allow, without the contradiction of *Galen*: who accounteth them cold but in the second degree, and in that Classis have most Physitians placed them.

That Elder Berries are poison, as we are taught be tradition, experience will unteach us. And beside the promises of *Blochwitius*, the healthful effects thereof daily observed will convict us.

That an Ivy Cup will separate Wine from Water, if filled with both, the Wine soaking through, but the Water still remaining, as after *Pliny* many have averred, we know not how to affirm; who making trial thereof, found both the liquors to soak indistinctly through the bowl.

That Sheep do often get the Rot, by feeding in boggy grounds where *Ros-solis* groweth, seems beyond dispute. That this herb is the cause thereof, Shepherds affirm and deny; whether it hath a cordial vertue by sudden refection, sensible experiment doth hardly confirm, but that it may have a Balsamical and resumptive Vertue, whereby it becomes a good Medicine in Catarrhes and Consumptive dispositions, Practice and Reason conclude. That the lentous drops upon it are not extraneous, and rather an exudation from it self, then a rorid concretion from without: beside other grounds, we have reason to conceive; for having kept the Roots moist and earthed in close chambers, they have, though in lesser plenty, sent out these drops as before.

That *Flos Affricanus* is poison, and destroyeth Dogs, in two experiments we have not found.

That Yew and the Berries thereof are harmless, we know.

That a Snake will not endure the shade of an Ash, we can deny. Nor is it inconsiderable what is affirmed by *Bellonius*; for if his Assertion be true, our apprehension is oftentimes wide in ordinary simples, and in common use we mistake one for another. We know not the true Thyme; the Savourie in our Gardens, is not that commended of old; and that kind of Hysop the Ancients used, is unknown unto us, who make great use of another.

We omit to recite the many Vertues, and endless faculties ascribed unto Plants, which sometime occur in grave and serious Authors; and we shall make a bad transaction for truth to concede a verity in half. To reckon up all, it were imployment for *Archimedes*, who undertook to write the number of the Sands. Swarms of others there are, some whereof our future endeavours may discover; common reason I hope will save us a labour in many: Whose absurdities stand naked unto every eye; Errours not able to deceive the Embleme of Justice, and need no *Argus* to decry them. Herein there surely wants

144

expurgatory animadversions, whereby we might strike out great numbers of hidden qualities; and having once a serious and conceded list, we might with more encouragement and safety, attempt their Reasons.

End of Book II

THE THIRD
BOOK

Of divers popular and received Tenets concerning Animals, which examined, prove either false
or dubious.

CHAPTER I

Of the Elephant

The first shall be of the Elephant, whereof there generally passeth an opinion it hath no joints; and this absurdity is seconded with
another, that being unable to lie down, it sleepeth against a Tree;
which, the Hunters observing, do saw it almost asunder; whereon the
Beast relying, by the fall of the Tree, falls also down it self, and is able
to rise no more. Which conceit is not the daughter of later times, but
an old and gray-headed error, even in the days of *Aristotle*, as he delivereth in his Booke, *De incessu Animalium,* and stands successively
related by several other Authors: by *Diodorus Siculus*, *Strabo*,
Ambrose, *Cassiodore*, *Solinus*, and many more. Now herein methinks
men much forget themselves, not well considering the absurdity of
such assertions.

For first, they affirm it hath no joints, and yet concede it walks
and moves about; whereby they conceive there may be a progression
or advancement made in Motion without inflexion of parts. Now all
progression or Animals locomotion being (as *Aristotle* teacheth) performed *tractu & pulsu*; that is, by drawing on, or impelling forward
some part which was before in station, or at quiet; where there are no
joints or flexures, neither can there be these actions. And this is true,
not onely in Quadrupedes, Volatils, and Fishes, which have distinct
and prominent Organs of Motion, Legs, Wings, and Fins; but in such
also as perform their progression by the Trunk, as Serpents, Worms,
and Leeches. Whereof though some want bones, and all extended articulations, yet have they arthritical Analogies, and by the motion of
fibrous and musculous parts, are able to make progression. Which to
conceive in bodies inflexible, and without all protrusion of parts, were
to expect a Race from *Hercules* his pillars; or hope to behold the ef-

fects of *Orpheus* his Harp, when trees found joints, and danced after his Musick.

Again, While men conceive they never lie down, and enjoy not the position of rest, ordained unto all pedestrious Animals, hereby they imagine (what Reason cannot conceive) that an Animal of the vastest dimension and longest duration, should live in a continual motion, without that alternity and vicissitude of rest whereby all others continue; and yet must thus much come to pass, if we opinion they lye not down and enjoy no decumbence at all. For station is properly no rest, but one kind of motion, relating unto that which Physitians (from *Galen*) do name extensive or tonical; that is, an extension of the muscles and organs of motion maintaining the body at length or in its proper figure.

Wherein although it seem to be unmoved, it is not without all Motion; for in this position the muscles are sensibly extended, and labour to support the body; which permitted unto its proper gravity, would suddenly subside and fall unto the earth; as it happeneth in sleep, diseases, and death. From which occult action and invisible motion of the muscles in station (as *Galen* declareth) proceed more offensive lassitudes then from ambulation. And therefore the Tyranny of some have tormented men with long and enforced station, and though *Ixion* and *Sisiphus* which always moved, do seem to have the hardest measure; yet was not *Titius* favoured, that lay extended upon *Caucasus*; and *Tantalus* suffered somewhat more then thirst, that stood perpetually in Hell. Thus *Mercurialis* in his Gymnasticks justly makes standing one kind of exercise; and *Galen* when we lie down, commends unto us middle figures, that is, not to lye directly, or at length, but somewhat inflected, that the muscles may be at rest; for such as he termeth *Hypobolemaioi* or figures, of excess, either shrinking up or stretching out, are wearisome positions, and such as perturb the quiet of those parts. Now various parts do variously discover these indolent and quiet positions, some in right lines, as the wrists: some at right angles, as the cubit: others at oblique angles, as the fingers and the knees: all resting satisfied in postures of moderation, and none enduring the extremity of flexure and extension.

Moreover men herein do strangely forget the obvious relations of history, affirming they have no joints, whereas they dayly read of several actions which are not performable without them. They forget what is delivered by *Xiphilinus*, and also by *Suetonius* in the lives of *Nero* and *Galba*, that Elephants have been instructed to walk on ropes, in publick shews before the people. Which is not easily performed by man, and requireth not only a broad foot, but a pliable flexure of joints, and commandible disposure of all parts of progression. They pass by that memorable place in *Curtius*, concerning the Elephant of King *Porus*, *Indus qui Elephantem regebat, descendere eum ratus, more solito procumbere jussit in genua, cæteri quoque (ita enim instituti erant) demisere corpora in terram*. They remember not the expression of *Osorius*, when he speaks of the Elephant presented to *Leo* the tenth, *Pontificem ter genibus flexis, & demisso corporis habitu venerabundus salutavit*. But above all, they call not to mind that memorable shew of *Germanicus*, wherein twelve Elephants danced unto the sound of Musick, and after laid them down in the *Tricliniums*, or places of festival Recumbency.

They forget the Etymologie of the Knee, approved by some Grammarians. They disturb the position of the young ones in the womb: which upon extension of legs is not easily conceivable; and contrary unto the general contrivance of Nature. Nor do they consider the impossible exclusion thereof, upon extension and rigour of the legs.

Lastly, they forget or consult not experience, whereof not many years past, we have had the advantage in *England*, by an Elephant shewn in many parts thereof, not only in the posture of standing, but kneeling and lying down. Whereby although the opinion at present be well suppressed, yet from some strings of tradition, and fruitful recurrence of errour, it is not improbable, it may revive in the next generation again. This being not the first that hath been seen in *England*; for (besides some others) as *Polydore Virgil* relateth, *Lewis* the French King sent one to Henry the third, and *Emanuel* of *Portugal* another to *Leo* the tenth into *Italy*, where notwithstanding the errour is still alive and epidemical, as with us.

The hint and ground of this opinion might be the gross and somewhat Cylindrical composure of the legs, the equality and less perceptible disposure of the joints, especially in the former legs of this Animal; they appearing when he standeth, like Pillars of flesh, without any evidence of articulation. The different flexure and order of the joints might also countenance the same, being not disposed in the Elephant, as they are in other quadrupedes, but carry a nearer conformity unto those of Man; that is, the bought of the fore-legs, not directly backward, but laterally and somewhat inward; but the hough or suffraginous flexure behind rather outward. Somewhat different unto many other quadrupedes, as Horses, Camels, Deer, Sheep, and Dogs; for their fore-legs bend like our legs, and their hinder legs like our arms, when we move them to our shoulders. But quadrupedes oviparous, as Frogs, Lizards, Crocadiles, have their joints and motive flexures more analogously framed unto ours: and some among viviparous, that is, such thereof as can bring their fore-feet and meat therein unto their mouths, as most can do that have the clavicles or collerbones: whereby their brests are broader, and their shoulders more asunder, as the Ape, the Monkey, the Squirrel and some others. If therefore any shall affirm the joints of Elephants are differently framed from most of other quadrupedes, and more obscurely and grosly almost then any, he doth herein no injury unto truth. But if *à dicto secundam quid ad dictum simpliciter*, he affirmeth also they have no articulations at all, he incurs the countroulment of reason, and cannot avoid the contradiction also of sense.

As for the manner of their venation, if we consult historical experience, we shall find it to be otherwise then as is commonly presumed, by sawing away of Trees. The accounts whereof are to be seen at large in *Johannes, Hugo, Edwardus Lopez, Garcias ab horto, Cadamustus*, and many more.

Other concernments there are of the Elephant, which might admit of discourse; and if we should question the teeth of Elephants, that is, whether they be properly so termed, or might not rather be called horns: it were no new enquiry of mine, but a Paradox as old as *Oppianus*. Whether as *Pliny* and divers since affirm it, that Elephants are terrified, and make away upon the grunting of Swine, *Garcias ab horto* may decide, who affirmeth upon experience, they enter their stalls, and live promiscuously in the Woods of *Malavar*. That the situation of the genitals is averse, and their copulation like that which some believe of Camels, as *Pliny* hath also delivered, is not to be received; for we have beheld that part in a different position; and their coition is made by supersaliency, like that of horses, as we are informed by some who have beheld them in that act. That some Elephants have not only written whole sentences, as *Ælian* ocularly testifieth, but have also spoken, as *Oppianus* delivereth, and *Christo-*

phorus à Costa particularly relateth; although it sound like that of *Achilles* Horse in *Homer*, we do not conceive impossible. Nor beside the affinity of reason in this Animal any such intollerable incapacity in the organs of divers quadrupedes, whereby they might not be taught to speak, or become imitators of speech like Birds. Strange it is how the curiosity of men that have been active in the instruction of Beasts, have never fallen upon this artifice; and among those, many paradoxical and unheard of imitations, should not attempt to make one speak. The Serpent that spake unto *Eve*, the Dogs and Cats that usually speak unto Witches, might afford some encouragement. And since broad and thick chops are required in Birds that speak, since lips and teeth are also organs of speech; from these there is also an advantage in quadrupedes, and a proximity of reason in Elephants and Apes above them all. Since also an Echo will speak without any mouth at all, articulately returning the voice of man, by only ordering the vocal spirit in concave and hollow places; whether the musculous and motive parts about the hollow mouths of Beasts, may not dispose the passing spirit into some articulate notes, seems a query of no great doubt.

CHAPTER II

Of the Horse

The second Assertion, that an Horse hath no gall, is very general, nor only swallowed by the people, and common Farriers, but also received by good *Veterinarians*, and some who have laudably discoursed upon Horses. It seemeth also very ancient; for it is plainly set down by *Aristotle*, an Horse and all solid ungulous or whole hoofed animals have no gall; and the same is also delivered by *Pliny*, which notwithstanding we find repugnant unto experience and reason. For first, it calls in question the providence or wise provision of Nature; who not abounding in superfluities, is neither deficient in necessities. Wherein nevertheless there would be a main defect, and her improvision justly accusable; if such a feeding Animal, and so subject unto diseases from bilious causes, should want a proper conveyance for choler; or have no other receptacle for that humour then the Veins, and general mass of bloud.

It is again controllable by experience, for we have made some search and enquiry herein; encouraged by *Absyrtus* a Greek Author, in the time of *Constantine*, who in his Hippiatricks, obscurely assigneth the gall a place in the liver; but more especially by *Carlo Ruini* the *Bononian*, who in his *Anatomia del Cavallo*, hath more plainly described it, and in a manner as I found it. For in the particular enquiry into that part, in the concave or simous part of the Liver, whereabout the Gall is usually seated in quadrupedes, I discover an hollow, long and membranous substance, of a pale colour without, and lined with Choler and Gall within; which part is by branches diffused into the lobes and several parcels of the Liver; from whence receiving the fiery superfluity , or cholerick remainder, by a manifest and open passage, it conveyeth it into the *duodenum* or upper gut, thence into the lower bowels; which is the manner of its derivation in Man and other Animals. And therefore although there be no eminent and circular follicle, no round bag or vesicle which long containeth this humour: yet is there a manifest receptacle and passage of choler from the Liver into the Guts: which being not so shut up, or at least not so long detained;, as it is in other Animals: procures that frequent excretion, and occasions the Horse to dung more often then many other, which considering the plentiful feeding, the largeness of the guts, and their various circumvolution, was prudently contrived by providence in this Animal. For choler is the natural Glister, or one excretion whereby Nature excludeth another; which descending daily into the bowels, extimulates those parts, and excites them unto expulsion. And therefore when this humour aboundeth or corrupteth, there succeeds ofttimes a *cholerica passio*, that is, a sudden and vehement Purgation upward and downward: and when the passage of gall becomes obstructed, the body grows costive, and the excrements of the belly white; as it happeneth in the Jaundice.

If any therefore affirm an Horse hath no gall, that is, no receptacle, or part ordained for the separation of Choler, or not that humour at all; he hath both sense and reason to oppose him. But if he saith it hath no bladder of Gall, and such as is observed in many other Animals, we shall oppose our sense, if we gain-say him. Thus must *Aristotle* be made out when he denieth this part; by this distinction we may relieve *Pliny* of a contradiction, who in one place affirming an Horse hath no gall, delivereth yet in another, that the gall of an Horse was accounted poison; and therefore at the sacrifices of Horses in *Rome*, it was unlawful for the *Flamen* to touch it. But with more difficulty, or hardly at all is that reconcileable which is delivered by our Countryman, and received *Veterinarian*; whose words in his Masterpiece, and Chapter of diseases from the Gall, are somewhat too strict, and scarce admit a Reconciliation. The fallacie therefore of this conceit is not unlike the former; *A dicto secundum quid ad dictum simpliciter.* Because they have not a bladder of gall, like those we usually observe in others, they have no gall at all. Which is a Paralogism not admittible; a fallacy that dwels not in a cloud, and needs not the Sun to scatter it.

CHAPTER III

Of the Dove

The Third assertion is somewhat like the second, that a Dove or Pigeon hath no gall; which is affirmed from very great antiquity; for as *Pierius* observeth from this consideration the Egyptians did make it the Hieroglyphick of Meekness. It hath been averred by many holy Writers, commonly delivered by *Postillers* and *Commentators*; who from the frequent mention of the Dove in the *Canticles*, the precept of our Saviour, to be wise as Serpents, and innocent as Doves: and especially the appearance of the Holy Ghost in the similitude of this Animal, have taken occasion to set down many affections of the Dove, and what doth most commend it, is, that it hath no gall. And hereof have made use not only Minor Divines, but *Cyprian, Austin, Isidore, Beda, Rupertus, Jansenius*, and many more.

Whereto notwithstanding we know not how to assent, it being repugnant unto the Authority and positive determination of ancient Philosophy. The affirmative of *Aristotle* in his *History of Animals* is very plain, *Fel aliis ventri, aliis intestino jungitur*: Some have the gall adjoined to the guts, as the Crow, the Swallow, Sparrow, and the Dove; the same is attested by *Pliny*, and not without some passion by *Galen*, who in his Book *De Atra bile*, accounts him ridiculous that denies it.

It is not agreeable to the constitution of this Animal, nor can we so reasonably conceive there wants a Gall: that is, the hot and fiery humour in a body so hot of temper, which Flegm or Melancholy could not effect. Now of what complexion it is, *Julius Alexandrinus* declareth, when he affirmeth that some upon the use thereof, have fallen into Feavers and Quinsies. The temper of their Dung and intestinal

Excretions do also confirm the same; which Topically applied become a *Phænigmus* or Rubifying Medicine, and are of such fiery parts, that as we read in *Galen*, they have of themselves conceived fire, and burnt a house about them. And therefore when in the famine of *Samaria* (wherein the fourth part of a Cab of Pigeons dung was sold for five pieces of silver,) it is delivered by *Josephus*, that men made use hereof in stead of common Salt: although the exposition seem strange, it is more probable then many other. For that it containeth very much Salt, as beside the effects before expressed, is discernable by taste, and the earth of Columbaries or Dove-houses, so much desired in the artifice of Salt-petre. And to speak generally, the excrement of Birds hath more of Salt and acrimony, then that of other pissing animals. Now if because the Dove is of a mild and gentle nature, we cannot conceive it should be of an hot temper; our apprehensions are not distinct in the measure of constitutions, and the several parts which evidence such conditions. For the Irascible passions do follow the temper of the heart, but the concupiscible distractions the crasis of the liver. Now many have hot livers, which have but cool and temperate hearts; and this was probably the temper of *Paris*, a contrary constitution to that of *Ajax*, and both but short of *Medea*, who seemed to exceed in either.

Lastly, it is repugnant to experience, for Anatomical enquiry discovereth in them a gall: and that according to the determination of *Aristotle*, not annexed unto the liver, but adhering unto the guts: nor is the humour contained in smaller veins, or, obscurer capillations, but in a vescicle, or little bladder, though some affirm it hath no bag at all. And therefore the Hieroglyphick of the Ægyptians, though allowable in the sense, is weak in the foundation: who expressing meekness and lenity by the portract of a Dove with a tail erected, affirmed it had no gall in the inward parts, but only in the rump, and as it were out of the body. And therefore also if they conceived their gods were pleased with the sacrifice of this Animal, as being without gall, the ancient Heathens were surely mistaken in the reason, and in the very oblation. Whereas in the holocaust or burnt-offering of *Moses*, the gall was cast away: for as *Ben Maimon* instructeth, the inwards whereto the gall ad-hereth were taken out with the crop, according unto the Law: which the Priest did not burn, but cast unto the East, that is, behind his back, and readiest place to be carried out of the Sanctuary. And if they also conceived that for this reason, they were the Birds of *Venus*, and want-ing the furious and discording part, were more acceptable unto the Deity of Love, they surely added unto the conceit, which was at first venereal: and in this Animal may be sufficiently made out from that conception.

The ground of this conceit is partly like the former, the obscure situation of the gall, and out of the liver, wherein it is commonly enquired. But this is a very injust illation, not well considering with what variety this part is seated in Birds. In some both at the stomach and the liver, as in the Capriceps; in some at the liver only, as in Cocks, Turkeys, and Pheasants; in others at the guts and liver, as in Hawks and Kites, in some at the guts alone, as Crows, Doves, and many more. And these perhaps may take up all the ways of situation, not only in Birds, but also in other Animals; for what is said of the Anchovie, that answerable unto its name, it carrieth the gall in the head, is farther to be enquired. And though the discoloured particles in the skin of an Heron, be commonly termed Galls, yet is not this Animal deficient in that part, but containeth it in the Liver. And thus when it is conceived that the eyes of *Tobias* were cured by the gall of the fish *Callyonimus*, or *Scorpius marinus*, commended to that effect by *Dioscorides*, although that part were not in the liver, yet there were no reason to doubt that probability. And whatsoever Animal it was, it may be received without exception, when its delivered, the married couple as a testimony of future concord, did cast the gall of the sacrifice behind the Altar.

A strict and literal acception of a loose and tropical expression was a second ground hereof. For while some affirmed it had no gall, intending only thereby no evidence of anger or fury; others have construed it anatomically, and denied that part at all. By which illation we may infer, and that from sacred Text, a Pigeon hath no heart, according to that expression, *Factus est Ephraim sicut Columba seducta non habens Cor.* And so from the letter of the Scripture we may conclude it is no mild, but a fiery and furious animal, according to that of *Jeremy, Facta est terra in desolationum à facie iræ Columbæ*: and again, *Revertamur ad terram nativitatis nostræ à facie gladii Columbæ.* Where notwithstanding the Dove is not literally intended; but thereby may be implied the *Babylonians*, whose Queen *Semiramis* was called by that name, and whose successors did bear the Dove in their Standard. So is it proverbially said, *Formicæ sua bilis inest, habet & musca splenem*; whereas we know Philosophy doubteth these parts, nor hath *Anatomy* so clearly discovered them in those insects.

If therefore any affirm a Pigeon hath no gall, implying no more thereby then the lenity of this Animall, we shall not controvert his affirmation. Thus may we make out the assertions of ancient Writers, and safely receive the expressions of Divines and worthy Fathers. But if by a transition from Rhetorick to Logick, he shall contend, it hath no such part or humour, he committeth an open fallacy, and such as was probably first committed concerning *Spanish* Mares, whose swiftness tropically expressed from their generation by the wind; might after be grosly taken, and a real truth conceived in that conception.

CHAPTER IV

Of the Bever

That a Bever to escape the Hunter, bites off his testicles or stones, is a Tenet very ancient; and hath had thereby advantage of propagation. For the same we find in the Hieroglyphicks of the Egyptians, in the Apologue of *Æsop*, an Author of great Antiquity, who lived in the beginning of the *Persian* Monarchy, and in the time of *Cyrus*: the same is touched by *Aristotle* in his Ethicks, but seriously delivered by *Ælian*, *Pliny*, and *Solinus*: the same we meet with in *Juvenal*, who by an handsome and Metrical expression more welcomly engrafts it in our junior Memories:

> —— imitatus Castora, qui se
> Eunuchum ipse facit, cupiens evadere damno
> Testiculorum, adeo medicatum intellegit inguen.

it hath been propagated by Emblems: and some have been so bad Grammarians as to be deceived by the Name, deriving *Castor à castrando*, whereas the proper Latine word is *Fiber*, and *Castor* but borrowed from the Greek, so called *quasi γάστωρ*, that is, *Animal ventricosum*, from his swaggy and prominent belly.

Herein therefore to speak compendiously, we first presume to affirm that from strict enquiry, we cannot maintain the evulsion or biting off any parts, and this is declarable from the best and most professed Writers: for though some have made use hereof in a Moral or Tropical way, yet have the professed Discoursers by silence deserted, or by experience rejected this assertion. Thus was it in ancient times discovered, and experimentally refuted by one *Sestius* a Physitian, as it stands related by *Pliny*; by *Dioscorides*, who plainly affirms that this tradition is false; by the discoveries of Modern Authors, who have expressly discoursed hereon, as *Aldrovandus, Mathiolus, Gesnerus, Bellonius*; by *Olaus Magnus, Peter Martyr*, and others, who have described the manner of their Venations in *America*; they generally omitting this way of their escape, and have delivered several other, by which they are daily taken.

The original of this conceit was probably Hieroglyphical, which after became Mythological unto the Greeks, and so set down by *Æsop*; and by process of tradition, stole into a total verity, which was but partially true, that is in its covert sense and Morality. Now why they placed this invention upon the Bever (beside the Medicable and Merchantable commodity of *Castoreum*, or parts conceived to be bitten away) might be the sagacity and wisdom of that Animal, which from the works it performs, and especially its Artifice in building, is very strange, and surely not to be matched by any other. Omitted by *Plutarch, De solertia Animalium*, but might have much advantaged the drift of that Discourse.

If therefore any affirm a wise man should demean himself like the Bever, who to escape with his life, contemneth the loss of his genitals, that is in case of extremity, not strictly to endeavour the preservation of all, but to sit down in the enjoyment of the greater good, though with the detriment and hazard of the lesser: we may hereby apprehend a real and useful Truth. In this latitude of belief, we are content to receive the Fable of *Hippomanes*, who redeemed his life with the loss of a Golden Ball; and whether true or false, we reject not the Tragœdy of *Absyrtus*, and the dispersion of his Members by *Medea*, to perplex the pursuit of her Father. But if any shall positively affirm this act, and cannot believe the Moral, unless he also credit the Fable; he is surely greedy of delusion, and will hardly avoid deception in theories of this Nature. The Error therefore and Alogy in this opinion, is worse then in the last; that is, not to receive Figures for Realities, but to expect a verity in Apologues; and believe, as serious affirmations, confessed and studied Fables.

Again, If this were true, and that the Bever in chase makes some divulsion of parts, as that which we call *Castoreum*; yet are not the same to be termed Testicles or Stones; for these Cods or Follicles are found in both Sexes, though somewhat more protuberant in the

Male. There is hereto no derivation of the seminal parts, nor any passage from hence, unto the Vessels of Ejaculation: some perforations onely in the part it self, through which the humour included doth exudate: as may be observed in such as are fresh, and not much dried with age. And lastly, The Testicles properly so called, are of a lesser magnitude, and seated inwardly upon the loins: and therefore it were not only a fruitless attempt, but impossible act, to Eunuchate or castrate themselves: and might be an hazardous practice of Art, if at all attempted by others.

Now all this is confirmed from the experimental Testimony of five very memorable Authors: *Bellonius, Gesnerus, Amatus, Rondeletius*, and *Mathiolus*: who receiving the hint hereof from *Rondeletius* in the Anatomy of two Bevers, did find all true that had been delivered by him, whose words are these in his learned Book *De Piscibus: Fibri in inguinibus geminos tumores habent, utrinque unicum, ovi Anserini magnitudine, inter hos est mentula in maribus, in foeminis pudendum, hi tumores testes non sunt, sed folliculi membrana contecti, in quorum medio singuli sunt meatus è quibus exudat liquor pinguis & cerosus, quem ipse Castor sæpe admoto ore lambit & exugit, postea veluti oleo, corporis partes oblinit; Hos tumores testes non esse hinc maxime colligitur, quod ab illis nulla est ad mentulam via neque ductus quo humor in mentulæ miatum derivetur, & foras emittatur; præterea quod testes intus reperiuntur, eosdem tumores Moscho animali inesse puto, è quibus odoratum illud plus emanat.* Then which words there can be no plainer, nor more evidently discovering the impropriety of this appellation. That which is included in the cod or visible bag about the groin, being not the Testicle, or any spermatical part; but rather a collection of some superfluous matter deflowing from the body, especially the parts of nutrition as unto their proper emunctories: and as it doth in Musk and Civet Cats, though in a different and offensive odour; proceeding partly from its food, that being especially Fish; whereof this humour may be a garous excretion and olidous separation.

Most thereof of the Moderns before *Rondeletius*, and all the Ancients excepting *Sestius*, have misunderstood this part, conceiving *Castoreum* the Testicles of the *Bever*: as *Dioscorides, Galen, Ægineta, Ætius*, and others have pleased to name it. The Egyptians also failed in the ground of their Hieroglyphick, when they expressed the punishment of Adultery by the Bever depriving himself of his testicles, which was amongst them the penalty of such incontinency. Nor is *Ætius* perhaps too strictly to be observed, when he prescribeth the stones of the Otter, or River-dog, as succedaneous unto *Castoreum*. But most inexcusable of all is *Pliny*; who having before him in one place the experiment of *Sestius* against it, sets down in another, that the *Bevers* of *Pontus* bite off their testicles: and in the same place affirmeth the like of the *Hyena*. Which was indeed well joined with the Bever, as having also a bag in those parts; if thereby we understand the *Hyena odorata*, or Civet Cat, as is delivered and graphically described by *Castellus*.

Now the ground of this mistake might be the resemblance and situation of these tumours about those parts, wherein we observe the testicles in other animals. Which notwithstanding is no well founded illation, for the testicles are defined by their office, and not determined by place or situation; they having one office in all, but different seats in many. For beside that, no Serpent, or Fishes oviparous, that neither biped nor quadruped oviparous have testicles exteriourly, or prominent in the groin; some also that are viviparous contain these parts within, as beside this Animal, the Elephant and Hedg-hog.

If any therefore shall term these testicles, intending metaphorically, and in no strict acception; his language is tolerable, and offends our ears no more then the Tropical names of Plants: when we read in Herbals, of Dogs, Fox, and Goat-stones. But if he insisteth thereon, and maintaineth a propriety in this language: our discourse hath overthrown his assertion, nor will Logick permit his illation; that is, from things alike, to conclude a thing the same; and from an accidental convenience, that is a similitude in place or figure, to infer a specifical congruity or substantial concurrence in Nature.

CHAPTER V

Of the Badger

That a Brock or Badger hath the legs on one side shorter then of the other, though an opinion perhaps not very ancient, is yet very general; received not only by Theorists and unexperienced believers, but assented unto by most who have the opportunity to behold and hunt them daily. Which notwithstanding upon enquiry I find repugnant unto the three Determinators of Truth, Authority, Sense, and Reason. For first, *Albertus Magnus* speaks dubiously, confessing he could not confirm the verity hereof; but *Aldrovandus* plainly affirmeth, there can be no such inequality observed. And for my own part, upon indifferent enquiry, I cannot discover this difference, although the regardable side be defined, and the brevity by most imputed unto the left.

Again, It seems no easie affront unto Reason, and generally repugnant unto the course of Nature; for if we survey the total set of Animals, we may in their legs, or Organs of progression, observe an equality of length, and parity of Numeration; that is, not any to have an odd legg, or the supporters and movers of one side not exactly answered by the other. Although the hinder may be unequal unto the fore and middle legs, as in Frogs, Locusts, and Grasshoppers; or both unto the middle, as in some Beetles and Spiders, as is determined by *Aristotle, De incessu Animalium*. Perfect and viviparous quadrupeds, so standing in their position of proneness, that the opposite joints of Neighbour-legs consist in the same plane; and a line descending from their Navel intersects at right angles the axis of the Earth. It happeneth often I confess that a Lobster hath the Chely or great claw of one side longer than the other; but this is not properly their leg, but a part of apprehension, and whereby they hold or seize upon their prey; for the legs and proper parts of progression are inverted backward, and stand in a position opposite unto these.

Lastly, The Monstrosity is ill contrived, and with some disadvantage; the shortness being affixed unto the legs of one side, which might have been more tolerably placed upon the thwart or Diagoniall Movers. For the progression of quadrupeds being performed *per Diametrum*, that is the cross legs moving or resting together, so that two are always in motion, and two in station at the same time; the brevity had been more tolerable in the cross legs. For then the Motion and station had been performed by equal legs; whereas herein they are both performed by unequal Organs, and the imperfection becomes discoverable at every hand.

CHAPTER VI

Of the Bear

That a Bear brings forth her young informous and unshapen, which she fashioneth after by licking them over, is an opinion not only vulgar, and common with us at present: but hath been of old delivered by ancient Writers. Upon this Foundation it was an Hieroglyphick with the Egyptians: *Aristotle* seems to countenance it; *Solinus, Pliny,* and *Ælian* directly affirm it, and *Ovid* smoothly delivereth it:

> *Nec catulus partu quem reddidit ursa recenti*
> *Sed male viva caro est, lambendo mater in artus*
> *Ducit, & in formam qualem cupit ipsa reducit.*

Which notwithstanding is not only repugnant unto the sense of every one that shall enquire into it, but the exact and deliberate experiment of three Authentick Philosophers. The first of *Mathiolus* in his Comment on *Dioscorides*, whose words are to this effect. In the Valley of *Anania* about *Trent*, in a Bear which the Hunters eventerated or opened, I beheld the young ones with all their parts distinct: and not without shape, as many conceive; giving more credit unto *Aristotle* and *Pliny*, then experience and their proper senses. Of the same assurance was *Julius Scaliger* in his Exercitations, *Ursam foetus informes potius ejicere, quam parere, si vera dicunt, quos postea linctu effingat: Quid hujusce fabulæ authoribus fidei habendum ex hac historia cognosces; In nostris Alpibus venatores fœtam Ursam cepere, dissecta ea fœtus plane formatus intus inventus est.* And lastly, *Aldrovandus* who from the testimony of his own eyes affirmeth, that in the Cabinet of the Senate of *Bononia*, there was preserved in a Glass a Cub taken out of a Bear perfectly formed, and compleat in every part.

It is moreover injurious unto Reason, and much impugneth the course and providence of Nature, to conceive a birth should be ordained before there is a formation. For the conformation of parts is necessarily required, not onely unto the pre-requisites and previous conditions of birth, as Motion and Animation: but also unto the parturition or very birth it self: Wherein not only the Dam, but the younglings play their parts; and the cause and act of exclusion proceedeth from them both. For the exclusion of Animals is not meerly passive like that of Eggs, nor the total action of delivery to be imputed unto the Mother: But the first attempt beginneth from the Infant: Which at the accomplished period attempteth to change his Mansion: and strugling to come forth, dilacerates and breaks those parts which restrained him before.

Beside (what few take notice of) Men hereby do in an high measure vilifie the works of God, imputing that unto the tongue of a Beast, which is the strangest Artifice in all the Acts of Nature; that is the formation of the Infant in the Womb, not only in Mankind, but all viviparous Animals. Wherein the plastick or formative faculty, from matter appearing Homogeneous, and of a similary substance, erecteth Bones, Membranes, Veins, and Arteries: and out of these contriveth every part in number, place, and figure, according to the law of its species. Which is so far from being fashioned by any outward agent, that once omitted or perverted by a slip of the inward *Phidias*, it is not reducible by any other whatsoever. And therefore *Mire me plasmaverunt manu tuae*, though it originally respected the generation of Man, yet is it applicable unto that of other Animals; who entring the Womb in bare and simple Materials, return with distinction of parts, and the perfect breath of life. He that shall consider these alterations without, must needs conceive there have been strange operations within; which to behold, it were a spectacle almost worth ones beeing, a sight beyond all; except that Man had been created first, and might have seen the shew of five days after.

Now as the opinion is repugnant both unto sense and Reason, so hath it probably been occasioned from some slight ground in either. Thus in regard the Cub comes forth involved in the Chorion, a thick and tough Membrane obscuring the formation, and which the Dam doth after bite and tear asunder; the beholder at first sight conceives it a rude and informous lump of flesh, and imputes the ensuing shape unto the Mouthing of the Dam; which addeth nothing thereunto, but

167

only draws the curtain, and takes away the vail which concealed the Piece before. And thus have some endeavoured to enforce the same from Reason; that is, the small and slender time of the Bears gestation, or going with her young; which lasting but few days (a Month some say) the exclusion becomes precipitous, and the young ones consequently informous; according to that of *Solinus, Trigesimus dies uterum liberat ursæ; unde evenit ut præcipitata fœcunditas informes creet partus.* But this will overthrow the general Method of Nature in the works of generation. For therein the conformation is not only antecedent, but proportional unto the exclusion; and if the period of the birth be short, the term of conformation will be as sudden also. There may I confess from this narrow time of gestation ensue a Minority or smalness in the exclusion; but this however inferreth no informity, and it still receiveth the Name of a natural and legitimate birth; whereas if we affirm a total informity, it cannot admit so forward a term as an Abortment, for that supposeth conformation. So we must call this constant and intended act of Nature, a slip or effluxion, that is an exclusion before conformation: before the birth can bear the name of the Parent, or be so much as properly called an *Embryon.*

CHAPTER VII

Of the Basilisk

Many opinions are passant concerning the Basilisk or little King of Serpents, commonly called the Cockatrice: some affirming, others denying, most doubting the relations made hereof. What therefore in these uncertainties we may more safely determine: that such an Animal there is, if we evade not the testimony of Scripture and humane Writers, we cannot safely deny. So is it said, *Psalm* 91. *Super Aspidem & Basiliscum ambulabis*, wherein the Vulgar Translation retaineth the Word of the Septuagint, using in other places the Latine expression *Regulus*, as *Proverbs* 23. *Mordebit ut coluber, & sicut Regulus venena diffundet*: and *Jeremy* 8. *Ecce ego mittam vobis serpentes Regulos, &c.* That is, as ours translate it, *Behold I wil send Serpents, Cockatrices among you which will not be charmed, and they shall bite you.* And as for humane Authors, or such as have discoursed of Animals, or Poisons, it is to be found almost in all: in *Dioscorides, Galen, Pliny, Solinus, Ælian, Ætius, Avicen, Ardoynus, Grevinus,* and many more. In *Aristotle* I confess we find no mention thereof, but *Scaliger* in his Comment and enumeration of Serpents, hath made supply; and in his Exercitations delivereth that a Basilisk was found in *Rome,* in the days of *Leo* the fourth. The like is reported by *Sigonius*; and some are so far from denying one, that they have made several kinds thereof: for such is the *Catoblepas* of *Pliny* conceived to be by some, and the *Dryinus* of *Ætius* by others.

But although we deny not the existence of the Basilisk, yet whether we do not commonly mistake in the conception hereof, and call that a Basilisk which is none at all, is surely to be questioned. For certainly that which from the conceit of its generation we vulgarly call a Cockatrice, and wherein (but under a different name) we intend a formal Identity and adequate conception with the Basilisk; is not the Basilisk of the Ancients, whereof such wonders are delivered. For this of ours is generally described with legs, wings, a Serpentine and winding tail, and a crist or comb somewhat like a Cock. But the Basilisk of elder times was a proper kind of Serpent, not above three palms long, as some account; and differenced from other Serpents by advancing his head, and some white marks or coronary spots upon the crown, as all authentick Writers have delivered.

Nor is this Cockatrice only unlike the Basilisk, but of no real shape in Nature; and rather an Hieroglyphical fansie, to express different intentions, set forth in different fashions. Sometimes with the head of a Man, sometime with the head of an Hawk, as *Pierius* hath delivered; and as with addition of legs the Heralds and Painters still describe it. Nor was it only of old a symbolical and allowable invention, but is now become a manual contrivance of Art, and artificial imposture; whereof besides others, *Scaliger* hath taken notice: *Basilisci formam mentiti sunt vulgo Gallinaceo similem, & pedibus binis; neque enim absimiles sunt cæteris serpentibus, nisi macula quasi in vertice candida, unde illi nomen Regium*; that is, men commonly counterfeit the form of a Basilisk with another like a Cock, and with two feet; whereas they differ not from other Serpents, but in a white speck upon their Crown. Now although in some manner it might be counterfeited in *Indian* Cocks, and flying Serpents, yet is it commonly contrived out of the skins of Thornbacks, Scaits, or Maids, as *Aldrovand* hath observed, and also graphically described in his excellent Book of Fishes; and for satisfaction of my own curiosity I have caused some to be thus contrived out of the same Fishes.

Nor is onely the existency of this animal considerable, but many things delivered thereof, particularly its poison and its generation. Concerning the first, according to the doctrine of the Ancients, men still affirm, that it killeth at a distance, that it poisoneth by the eye, and by priority of vision. Now that deleterious it may be at some distance, and destructive without corporal contaction, what uncertainty soever there be in the effect, there is no high improbability in the relation. For if Plagues or pestilential Atoms have been conveyed in the Air from distant Regions, if men at a distance have infected each other, if the shadows of some trees be noxious, if *Torpedoes* deliver their opium at a distance, and stupifie beyond themselves; we cannot reasonably deny, that (beside our gross and restrained poisons requiring contiguity unto their action) there may proceed from subtiller seeds, more agile emanations, which contemn those Laws, and invade at distance unexpected.

That this venenation shooteth from the eye, and that this way a Basilisk may empoison, although thus much be not agreed upon by Authors, some imputing it unto the breath, others unto the bite, it is not a thing impossible. For eyes receive offensive impressions from their objects, and may have influences destructive to each other. For the visible species of things strike not our senses immaterially, but streaming in corporal raies, do carry with them the qualities of the object from whence they flow, and the medium through which they pass. Thus through a green or red Glass all things we behold appear of the same colours; thus sore eyes affect those which are sound, and themselves also by reflection, as will happen to an inflamed eye that beholds it self long in a Glass; thus is fascination made out, and thus also it is not impossible, what is affirmed of this animal, the visible rayes of their eyes carrying forth the subtilest portion of their poison, which received by the eye of man or beast, infecteth first the braine, and is from thence communicated unto the heart.

But lastly, That this destruction should be the effect of the first beholder, or depend upon priority of aspection, is a point not easily to be granted, and very hardly to be made out upon the principles of *Aristotle, Alhazen, Vitello*, and others, who hold that sight is made by Reception, and not by extramission; by receiving the raies of the object into the eye, and not by sending any out. For hereby although he behold a man first, the Basilisk should rather be destroyed, in regard he first receiveth the rayes of his Antipathy, and venomous emissions which objectively move his sense; but how powerful soever his own poison be, it invadeth not the sense of man, in regard he beholdeth him not. And therefore this conceit was probably begot by such as held the opinion of sight by extramission; as did *Pythagoras, Plato, Empedocles, Hipparchus, Galen, Macrobius, Proclus, Simplicius*, with most of the Ancients, and is the postulate of *Euclide* in his Opticks, but now sufficiently convicted from observations of the Dark Chamber.

As for the generation of the Basilisk, that it proceedeth from a Cocks egg hatched under a Toad or Serpent, it is a conceit as monstrous as the brood it self. For if we should grant that Cocks growing

171

old, and unable for emission, amass within themselves some seminal matter, which may after conglobate into the form of an egg, yet will this substance be unfruitful. As wanting one principle of generation, and a commixture of both sexes, which is required unto production, as may be observed in the eggs of Hens not trodden; and as we have made trial in some which are termed Cocks' eggs. It is not indeed impossible that from the sperm of a Cock, Hen, or other Animal, being once in putrescence, either from incubation or otherwise, some generation may ensue; not univocal and of the same species, but some imperfect or monstrous production, even as in the body of man from putrid humours, and peculiar ways of corruption; there have succeeded strange and unseconded shapes of worms; whereof we have beheld some our selves, and read of others in medical observations. And so may strange and venomous Serpents be several ways engendered; but that this generation should be regular, and alway produce a Basilisk, is beyond our affirmation, and we have good reason to doubt.

Again, It is unreasonable to ascribe the equivocacy of this form unto the hatching of a Toad, or imagine that diversifies the production. For Incubation alters not the species, nor if we observe it, so much as concurs either to the sex or colour: as appears in the eggs of Ducks or Partridges hatched under a Hen, there being required unto their exclusion only a gentle and continued heat: and that not particular or confined unto the species or parent. So have I known the seed of Silk-worms hatched on the bodies of women: and *Pliny* reports that *Livia* the wife of *Augustus* hatched an egg in her bosome. Nor is only an animal heat required hereto, but an elemental and artificial warmth will suffice: For as *Diodorus* delivereth, the Ægyptians were wont to hatch their eggs in Ovens, and many eye-witnesses confirm that practice unto this day. And therefore this generation of the Basilisk, seemes like that of *Castor* and *Helena*; he that can credit the one, may easily believe the other: that is, that these two were hatched out of the egg, which *Jupiter* in the form of a Swan, begat on his Mistress *Leda*.

The occasion of this conceit might be an Ægyptian tradition concerning the Bird *Ibis*: which after became transferred unto Cocks. For an opinion it was of that Nation, that the *Ibis* feeding upon Serpents, that venomous food so inquinated their oval conceptions, or eggs within their bodies, that they sometimes came forth in Serpentine shapes, and therefore they always brake their eggs, nor would they endure the Bird to sit upon them. But how causeless their fear was herein, the daily incubation of Ducks, Pea-hens, and many other testi-fie, and the Stork might have informed them; which Bird they honoured and cherished, to destroy their Serpents.

That which much promoteth it, was a misapprehension in holy Scripture upon the Latine translation in *Esa.* 51. *Ova aspidum rupe-runt, & telas Aranearum texuerunt, qui comedent de ovis eorum morietur, & quod confotum est, erumpet in Regulum.* From whence notwithstanding, beside the generation of Serpents from eggs, there can be nothing concluded; and what kind of Serpents are meant, not easie to be determined, for Translations are very different: *Tremellius* rendering the Asp Hæmorrhous, and the Regulus or Basilisk a Viper, and our translation for the Asp sets down a Cockatrice in the Text, and an Adder in the margin.

Another place of *Esay* doth also seem to countenance it, Chap. 14. *Ne Læteris Phillistœa quoniam diminuta est virga percussoris tui, de radice enim colubri egredietur Regulus, & semen ejus absorbens volucrem*; which ours somewhat favorably rendereth: *Out of the Ser-pents Root shall come forth a Cockatrice, and his fruit shall be a fiery flying Serpent.* But *Tremellius, è radice Serpentis prodit Hœmorrhous, & fructus illius præster volans*; wherein the words are different, but the sense is still the same; for therein are figuratively intended *Uzziah* and *Ezechias*; for though the Philistines had escaped the minor Serpent *Uzziah*, yet from his stock a fiercer Snake should arise, that would more terribly sting them, and that was *Ezechias*.

But the greatest promotion it hath received from a misunder-standing of the Hieroglyphical intention. For being conceived to be the Lord and King of Serpents, to aw all others, nor to be destroyed by any; the Ægyptians hereby implied Eternity, and the awful power of the supreme Deitie: and therefore described a crowned Asp or Basilisk upon the heads of their gods. As may be observed in the Bembine ta-ble, and other Ægyptian monuments.

CHAPTER VIII

Of the Wolf

Such a Story as the Basilisk is that of the Wolf concerning priority of vision, that a man becomes hoarse or dumb, if a Wolf have the advantage first to eye him. And this is a plain language affirmed by *Pliny*: *In Italia ut creditur, Luporum visus est noxius, vocemque homini, quem prius contemplatur adimere*; so is it made out what is delivered by *Theocritus*, and after him by *Virgil*:

————*Vox quoque Moerim*
Jam fugit ipsa, Lupi Moerim videre priores.

Thus is the Proverb to be understood, when during the discourse, if the party or subject interveneth, and there ensueth a sudden silence, it is usually said, *Lupus est in fabula*. Which conceit being already convicted, not only by *Scaliger, Riolanus* and others; but daily confutable almost every where out of *England*, we shall not further refute.

The ground or occasional original hereof, was probably the amazement and sudden silence the unexpected appearance of Wolves do often put upon Travellers; not by a supposed vapour, or venomous emanation, but a vehement fear which naturally produceth obmutescence; and sometimes irrecoverable silence. Thus Birds are silent in presence of an Hawk, and *Pliny* saith that Dogs are mute in the shadow of an Hyæna. But thus could not the mouths of worthy Martyrs be silenced, who being exposed not onely unto the eyes, but the merciless teeth of Wolves, gave loud expressions of their faith, and their holy clamours were heard as high as Heaven.

That which much promoteth it beside the common Proverb,

was an expression in *Theocritus*, a very ancient Poet, *Edere non poteris vocem, Lycus est tibi visus*; which *Lycus* was Rival unto another, and suddenly appearing stopped the mouth of his Corrivall; now *Lycus* signifying also a Wolf, occasioned this apprehension; men taking that appellatively, which was to be understood properly, and translating the genuine acception. Which is a fallacy of Æquiviocation, and in some opinions begat the like conceit concerning *Romulus* and *Remus*, that they were fostered by a Wolf; the name of the nurse being *Lupa*, and founded the Fable of *Europa*, and her carriage over Sea by a Bull, because the Ship or Pilots name was *Taurus*. And thus have some been startled at the Proverb, *Bos in lingua*, confusedly apprehending how a man should be said to have an Oxe in his tongue, that would not speak his mind; which was no more then that a piece of money had silenced him: for by the Oxe was onely implied a piece of coin stamped with that figure, first currant with the *Athenians*, and after among the *Romans*.

CHAPTER IX

Of the Deer

The common Opinion concerning the long life of Animals, is very ancient, especially of Crows, Choughs and Deer; in moderate accounts exceeding the age of man, in some the days of *Nestor*, and in others surmounting the years of *Artephius* or *Methuselah*. From whence Antiquity hath raised proverbial expressions, and the real conception of their duration, hath been the Hyperbolical expression of many others. From all the rest we shall single out the Deer, upon concession a long-lived Animal, and in longævity by many conceived to attain unto hundreds; wherein permitting every man his own belief, we shall our selves crave liberty to doubt, and our reasons are those ensuing.

The first is that of *Aristotle*, drawn from the increment and gestation of this Animal, that is, its sudden arrivance unto growth and maturity, and the small time of its remainder in the Womb. His words in the translation of *Scaliger* are these; *De ejus vitæ longitudine fabulantur; neque enim aut gestatio aut incrementum hinnulorum ejusmodi sunt, ut præstent argumentum longævi animalis*; that is, Fables are raised concerning the vivacity of Deer; for neither are their gestation or increment, such as may afford an argument of long life. And these, saith *Scaliger*, are good Mediums conjunctively taken, that is, not one without the other. For of Animals viviparous such as live long, go long with young, and attain but slowly to their maturity and stature. So the Horse that liveth above thirty, arriveth unto his stature about six years, and remaineth above ten moneths in the womb; so the Camel that liveth unto fifty, goeth with young no less then ten moneths, and ceaseth not to grow before seven; and so the Elephant that liveth an hundred, beareth its young above a year, and arriveth unto perfection at twenty. On the contrary, the Sheep and Goat, which live but eight or ten years, go but five moneths, and attain to their perfection at two years: and the like proportion is observable in Cats, Hares, and Conies. And so the Deere that endureth the womb but eight moneths, and is compleat at six years, from the course of Nature, we cannot expect to live an hundred; nor in any proportional allowance much more then thirty. As having already passed two general motions observable in all animations, that is, its beginning and encrease; and having but two more to run thorow, that is, its state and declination; which are proportionally set out by Nature in every kind: and naturally proceeding admit of inference from each other.

The other ground that brings its long life into question, is the immoderate salacity, and almost unparallel'd excess of venery, which every *September* may be observed in this Animal: and is supposed to shorten the lives of Cocks, Partridges, and Sparrows. Certainly a confessed and undeniable enemy unto longævity, and that not only as a sign in the complexional desire and impetuosity, but also as a cause in the frequent act, or iterated performance thereof. For though we consent not with that Philosopher, who thinks a spermatical emission unto the weight of one drachm, is æquivalent unto the effusion of sixty ounces of bloud; yet considering the exolution and languor ensuing that act in some, the extenuation and marcour in others, and the visible acceleration it maketh of age in most: we cannot but think it much abridgeth our days. Although we also concede that this exclusion is natural, that Nature it self will finde a way hereto without either act or object: And although it be placed among the six Non-naturals, that is, such as neither naturally constitutive, nor meerly destructive, do preserve or destroy according unto circumstance; yet do we sensibly observe an impotency or total privation thereof, prolongeth life: and they live longest in every kind that exercise it not at all. And this is true not only in Eunuchs by Nature, but Spadoes by Art: for castrated Animals in every species are longer lived then they which retain their virilities. For the generation of bodies is not meerly effected as some conceive, of souls, that is, by Irradiation, or answerably unto the propagation of light, without its proper diminution: but therein a transmission is made materially from some parts, with the Idea of every one: and the propagation of one, is in a strict acception, some minoration of another. And therefore also that axiom in Philosophy, that the generation of one thing, is the corruption of another: although it be substantially true concerning the form and matter, is also dispositively verified in the efficient or producer.

As for more sensible arguments, and such as relate unto experiment: from these we have also reason to doubt its age, and presumed vivacity: for where long life is natural, the marks of age are late: and when they appear, the journey unto death cannot be long. Now the age of Deer (as *Aristotle* not long ago observed) is best conjectured, by view of the horns and teeth. From the horns there is a particular and annual account unto six years: they arising first plain, and so successively branching: after which the judgment of their years by particular marks becomes uncertain. But when they grow old, they grow less branched, and first do lose their *propugnacula*; that is, their brow-antlers, or lowest furcations next the head, which *Aristotle* saith the young ones use in fight: and the old as needless, have them not at all. The same may be also collected from the loss of their Teeth, whereof in old age they have few or none before in either jaw. Now these are infallible marks of age, and when they appear, we must confess a declination: which notwithstanding (as men inform us in *England*, where observations may well be made,) will happen between twenty and thirty. As for the bone, or rather induration of the Roots of the arterial vein and great artery, which is thought to be found only in the heart of an old Deer, and therefore becomes more precious in its Rarity; it is often found in Deer much under thirty, and we have known some affirm they have found it in one of half that age. And therefore in that account of *Pliny*, of a Deer with a Collar about his neck, put on by *Alexander* the Great, and taken alive an hundred years after, with other relations of this nature, we much suspect imposture or mistake. And if we grant their verity, they are but single relations, and very rare contingencies in individuals, not affording a regular deduction upon the species. For though *Ulysses* his Dog lived unto twenty, and the *Athenian* Mule unto fourscore, yet do we not measure their days by those years, or usually say, they live thus long. Nor can the three hundred years of *John* of times, or *Nestor*, overthrow the assertion of *Moses*, or afford a reasonable encouragement beyond his septuagenary determination.

The ground and authority of this conceit was first Hierogliphical, the *Ægyptians* expressing longævity by this Animal; but upon what uncertainties, and also convincible falsities they often erected such Emblems, we have elsewhere delivered. And if that were true

178

which *Aristotle* delivers of his time, and *Pliny* was not afraid to take up long after, the *Ægyptians* could make but weak observations herein; for though it be said that *Æneas* feasted his followers with Venison, yet *Aristotle* affirms that neither Deere nor Boar were to be found in *Africa*. And how far they miscounted the lives and duration of Animals, is evident from their conceit of the Crow, which they presume to live five hundred years; and from the lives of Hawks, which (as *Ælian* delivereth) the *Ægyptians* do reckon no less then at seven hundred.

The second which led the conceit unto the *Grecians*, and probably descended from the Egyptians was Poetical; and that was a passage of *Hesiod*, thus rendered by *Ausonius*.

> *Ter binos deciesque novem super exit in annos,*
> *Justa senescentum quos implet vita vivorum.*
> *Hos novies superat vivendo garrula cornix,*
> *Et quater egreditur cornicis sæcula cervus,*
> *Alipidem cervum ter vincit corvus.* —

> To ninety six the life of man ascendeth,
> Nine times as long that of the Chough extendeth,
> Four times beyond the life of Deer doth go,
> And thrice is that surpassed by the Crow.

So that according to this account, allowing ninety six for the age of Man, the life of a Deer amounts unto three thousand four hundred fifty six. A conceit so hard to be made out, that many have deserted the common and literal construction. So *Theon* in *Aratus* would have the number of nine not taken strictly, but for many years. In other opinions the compute so far exceedeth the truth, that they have thought it more probable to take the word *Genea*, that is, a generation consisting of many years, but for one year, or a single revolution of the Sun; which is the remarkable measure of time, and within the compass whereof we receive our perfection in the womb. So that by this construction, the years of a Deer should be but thirty six, as is discoursed at large in that Tract of *Plutarch*, concerning the cessation of Oracles; and whereto in his discourse of the Crow, *Aldrovandus* also inclineth. Others not able to make it out, have rejected the whole account, as may be observed from the words of *Pliny, Hesiodus qui primus aliquid de longævitate vitæ prodidit, fabulose (reor) multa de hominum ævo referens, cornici novem nostras attribuit ætates, quadruplum ejus cervis, id triplicatum corvis, & reliqua fabulosius de Phoenice & nymphis.* And this how slender soever, was probably the strongest ground Antiquity had for this longævity of Animals; that made *Theophrastus* expostulate with Nature concerning the long life of Crows; that begat that Epithete of Deer in *Oppianus*, and that expression of *Juvenal*,

——— Longa & cervina senectus.

The third ground was Philosophical, and founded upon a probable Reason in Nature, that is, the defect of a Gall, which part (in the opinion of *Aristotle* and *Pliny*) this Animal wanted, and was conceived a cause and reason of their long life: according (say they) as it happeneth unto some few men, who have not this part at all. But this assertion is first defective in the verity concerning the Animal alledged: for though it be true, a Deer hath no Gall in the Liver like many other Animals, yet hath it that part in the Guts, as is discoverable by taste and colour: and therefore *Pliny* doth well correct himself, when having affirmed before it had no Gall, he after saith, some hold it to be in the guts; and that for their bitterness, dogs will refuse to eat them. The assertion is also deficient in the verity of the Induction or connumeration of other Animals conjoined herewith, as having also no Gall; that is, as *Pliny* accounteth, *Equi, Muli,* &c. Horses, Mules, Asses, Deer, Goats, Boars, Camels, Dolphins, have no Gall. In Dolphins and Porpoces I confess I could find no Gall. But concerning Horses, what truth there is herein we have declared before; as for Goats we find not them without it; what Gall the Camel hath, *Aristotle* declareth: that Hogs also have it, we can affirm; and that not in any obscure place, but in the Liver, even as it is seated in man.

That therefore the Deer is no short-lived Animal, we will acknowledge: that comparatively, and in some sense long-lived we will concede; and thus much we shall grant if we commonly account its days by thirty six or forty: for thereby it will exceed all other cornigerous Animals. But that it attaineth unto hundreds, or the years delivered by Authors, since we have no authentick experience for it, since we have reason and common experience against it, since the grounds are false and fabulous which do establish it: we know no ground to assent.

Concerning Deer there also passeth another opinion, that the Males thereof do yearly lose their pizzel. For men observing the decidence of their horns, do fall upon the like conceit of this part, that it annually rotteth away, and successively reneweth again. Now the ground hereof was surely the observation of this part in Deer after immoderate venery, and about the end of their Rut, which sometimes becomes so relaxed and pendulous, it cannot be quite retracted: and being often beset with flies, it is conceived to rot, and at last to fall from the body. But herein experience will contradict us: for Deer which either die or are killed at that time, or any other, are always found to have that part entire. And reason will also correct us: for spermatical parts, or such as are framed from the seminal principles of parents, although homogeneous or similary, will not admit a Regeneration, much less will they receive an integral restauration, which being organical and instrumental members, consist of many of those. Now this part, or Animal of *Plato*, containeth not only sanguineous and reparable particles: but is made up of veins, nerves, arteries, and in some Animals, of bones: whose reparation is beyond its own fertility, and a fruit not be expected from the fructifying part it self. Which faculty were it communicated unto Animals, whose originals are double, as well as unto Plants, whose seed is within themselves: we might abate the Art of *Taliacotius*, and the new in-arching of Noses. And therefore the fansies of Poets have been so modest, as not to set down such renovations, even from the powers of their deities: for the mutilated shoulder of *Pelops* was pieced out with Ivory, and that the limbs of *Hippolitus* were set together, not regenerated by *Æsculapius*, is the utmost assertion of Poetry.

CHAPTER X

Of the King-fisher

That a King-fisher hanged by the bill, sheweth in what quarter the wind is by an occult and secret propriety, converting the breast to that point of the Horizon from whence the wind doth blow, is a received opinion, and very strange; introducing natural Weather-cocks, and extending Magnetical positions as far as Animal Natures. A conceit supported chiefly by present practice, yet not made out by Reason or Experience.

Unto Reason it seemeth very repugnant, that a carcass or body disanimated, should be so affected with every wind, as to carry a conformable respect and constant habitude thereto. For although in sundry Animals we deny not a kind of natural Meteorology or innate presention both of wind and weather, yet that proceeding from sense receiving impressions from the first mutation of the air, they cannot in reason retain that apprehension after death, as being affections which depend on life, and depart upon disanimation. And therefore with more favourable Reason may we draw the same effect or sympathie upon the Hedg-hog, whose presention of winds is so exact, that it stoppeth the North or Southern hole of its nest, according to the prenotion of these winds ensuing; which some men observing, have been able to make predictions which way the wind would turn, and been esteemed hereby wise men in point of weather. Now this proceeding from sense in the creature alive, it were not reasonable to hang up an Hedg-hogs head, and to expect a conformable motion unto its living conversion. And though in sundry Plants their vertues do live after death, and we know that Scammony, Rhubarb, and Scena will purge without any vital assistance; yet in Animals and sensible creatures, many actions are mixt, and depend upon their living form, as well as that of mistion; and though they wholly seem to retain unto the body, depart upon disunion. Thus Glow-worms alive, project a lustre in the dark, which fulgour notwithstanding ceaseth after death; and thus the Torpedo which being alive stupifies at a distance, applied after death, produceth no such effect; which had they retained in places where they abound, they might have supplied Opium, and served as frontals in Phrensies.

As for experiment, we cannot make it out by any we have attempted; for if a single King-fisher be hanged up with untwisted silk in an open room, and where the air is free, it observes not a constant respect unto the mouth of the wind, but variously converting, doth seldom breast it right. If two be suspended in the same room, they will not regularly conform their breasts, but oft-times respect the opposite points of Heaven. And if we conceive that for exact exploration, they should be suspended where the air is quiet and unmoved, that clear of impediments, they may more freely convert upon their natural verticity; we have also made this way of inquisition, suspending them in large and capacious glasses closely stopped; wherein nevertheless we observed a casual station, and that they rested irregularly upon conversion. Wheresoever they rested, remaining inconverted, and possessing one point of the Compass, whilst the wind perhaps had passed the two and thirty.

The ground of this popular practice might be the common opinion concerning the vertue prognostick of these Birds; as also the natural regard they have unto the winds, and they unto them again; more especially remarkable in the time of their nidulation, and bringing forth their young. For at that time, which happeneth about the brumal Solstice, it hath been observed even unto a proverb, that the Sea is calm, and the winds do cease, till the young ones are excluded; and forsake their nest which floateth upon the Sea, and by the roughness of winds might otherwise be overwhelmed. But how far hereby to magnifie their prediction we have no certain rule; for whether out of any particular prenotion they chuse to sit at this time, or whether it be thus contrived by concurrence of causes, and providence of Nature, securing every species in their production, is not yet determined. Surely many things fall out by the design of the general motor, and undreamt of contrivance of Nature, which are not imputable unto the intention or knowledge of the particular Actor. So though the seminality of Ivy be almost in every earth, yet that it ariseth and groweth not, but where it may be supported; we cannot ascribe the same unto the distinction of the seed, or conceive any science therein which suspends and conditionates its eruption. So if, as *Pliny* and *Plutarch* report, the Crocodils of *Ægypt* so aptly lay their Eggs, that the Natives thereby are able to know how high the floud will attain; it will be hard to make out, how they should divine the extent of the inundation depending on causes so many miles remote; that is, the measure of shores in *Æthiopia*; and whereof, as *Athanasius* in the life of *Anthony* delivers, the Devil himself upon demand could make no clear prediction. So are there likewise many things in nature, which are the fore runners or signs of future effects, whereto they neither concur in causality or prenotion, but are secretly ordered by the providence of causes, and concurrence of actions collateral to their signations.

It was also a custom of old to keep these Birds in chests, upon opinion that they prevented Moths; whether it were not first hanged up in Rooms to such effects, is not beyond all doubt. Or whether we mistake not the posture of suspension, hanging it by the bill, whereas we should do it by the back; that by the bill it might point out the quarters of the wind: for so hath *Kircherus* described the Orbis and the Sea Swallow. But the eldest custom of hanging up these birds was founded upon a tradition that they would renew their feathers every year as though they were alive: In expectation whereof four hundred years ago *Albertus Magnus* was deceived.

CHAPTER XI

Of Griffins

That there are Griffins in Nature, that is a mixt and dubious Animal, in the fore-part resembling an Eagle, and behind the shape of a Lion, with erected ears, four feet and a long tail, many affirm, and most, I perceive, deny not. The same is averred by *Ælian, Solinus, Mela,* and *Herodotus,* countenanced by the Name sometimes found in Scripture, and was an Hieroglyphick of the Egyptians.

Notwithstanding we find most diligent enquirers to be of a contrary assertion. For beside that *Albertus* and *Pliny* have disallowed it, the learned *Aldrovandus* hath in a large discourse rejected it; *Mathias Michovius* who writ of those Northern parts wherein men place these Griffins, hath positively concluded against it; and if examined by the Doctrine of Animals, the invention is Monstrous, nor much inferiour unto the figment of Sphynx, Chimæra, and Harpies, for though there be some flying Animals of mixed and participating Natures, that is, between Bird and quadruped, yet are their wings and legs so set together, that they seem to make each other. For though some species there be of middle and participating Natures, that is, of Bird and Beast, as Bats and some few others, yet are there parts so conformed and set together, that we cannot define the beginning or end of either; there being a commixtion of both in the whole, rather then an adaptation or cement of the one unto the other.

Now for the word γρύψ or *Gryps,* sometimes mentioned in Scripture, and frequently in humane Authors, properly understood, it signifies some kind of Eagle or Vulture, from whence the Epithete *Grypus* for an hooked or Aquiline Nose. Thus when the Septuagint makes use of this word, *Tremellius* and our Translation hath rendered it the Ossifrage, which is one kind of Eagle. And although the Vulgar Translation, and that annexed unto the Septuagint, retain the word *Gryps*, which in ordinary and school construction is commonly rendred a Griffin, yet cannot the Latine assume any other sense then the Greek, from whence it is borrowed. And though the Latine *Gryphes* be altered somewhat by the addition of an *h*, or aspiration of the letter π, yet is not this unusual; so what the Greeks call τρόπαιον, the Latine will call *Trophæum*; and that person which in the Gospel is named Κλέοπας, the Latines will render *Cleophas*. And therefore the quarrel of *Origen* was unjust, and his conception erroneous, when he conceived the food of Griffins forbidden by the Law of *Moses*: that is, Poetical Animals, and things of no existence. And therefore when in the Hecatombs and mighty Oblations of the Gentiles, it is delivered they sacrificed Gryphes or Griffins; hereby we may understand some stronger sort of Eagles. And therefore also when 'tis said in *Virgil* of an improper Match, or *Mopsus* marrying *Nysa, Jungentur jam gryphes equis*; we need not hunt after other sense, then that strange unions shall be made, and different Natures be conjoined together.

As for the testimonies of ancient Writers, they are but derivative, and terminate all in one *Aristeus* a Poet of *Proconesus*; who affirmed that near the *Arimaspi*, or one-eyed Nation, Griffins defended the Mines of Gold. But this, as *Herodotus* delivereth, he wrote by hear-say; and *Michovius* who hath expresly written of those parts, plainly affirmeth, there is neither Gold nor Griffins in that Country, nor any such Animal extant; for so doth he conclude, *Ego vero contra veteres authores, Gryphes nec in illa septentrionis, nec in aliis orbis partibus inveniri affirmarim.*

Lastly, Concerning the Hieroglyphical authority, although it nearest approach the truth, it doth not infer its existency. The conceit of the *Griffin* properly taken being but a symbolical phansie, in so intollerable a shape including allowable morality. So doth it well make out the properties of a *Guardian*, or any person entrusted; the ears implying attention, the wings celerity of execution, the Lion-like shape, courage and audacity, the hooked bill, reservance and tenacity. It is also an Emblem of valour and magnanimity, as being compounded of the Eagle and Lion, the noblest Animals in their kinds; and so it is appliable unto Princes, Presidents, Generals, and all heroick

Commanders; and so is it also born in the Coat-arms of many noble Families of *Europe*.

But the original invention seems to be Hieroglyphical, derived from the Egyptians, and of an higher signification. By the mystical conjunction of Hawk and Lion, implying either the Genial or the sydereous Sun, the great celerity thereof, and the strength and vigour in its operations. And therefore under such Hieroglyphicks *Osyris* was described; and in ancient Coins we meet with Gryphins conjointly with *Apollo's*, *Tripodes* and Chariot wheels; and the marble Gryphins at Saint *Peters* in *Rome*, as learned men conjecture, were first translated from the Temple of *Apollo*. Whether hereby were not also mystically implied the activity of the Sun in Leo, the power of God in the Sun, or the influence of the Cœlestial *Osyris*, by *Moptha* the Genius of *Nilus*, might also be considered. And then the learned *Kircherus*, no man were likely to be a better *Oedipus*.

CHAPTER XII

Of the Phœnix

That there is but one Phœnix in the World, which after many hundred years burneth it self, and from the ashes thereof ariseth up another, is a conceit not new or altogether popular, but of great Antiquity; not only delivered by humane Authors, but frequently expressed also by holy Writers: by *Cyril*, *Epiphanius*, and others, by *Ambrose* in his Hexameron, and *Tertullian* in his Poem *De Judicio Domini*; but more agreeably unto the present sense, in his excellent Tract, *De Resurrectione carnis. Illum dico alitem orientis peculiarem, de singularitate famosum, de posteritate monstruosum; qui semetipsum libenter funerans renovat, natali fine decedens, atque succedens iterum Phœnix. Ubi jam nemo, iterum ipse; quia non jam, alius idem.* The Scripture also seems to favour it, particularly that of Job 21. In the interpretation of *Beda, Dicebam in nidulo meo moriar, & sicut Phœnix multiplicabo dies*: and *Psal.* 31, *vir justus ut Phœnix florebit*, as *Tertullian* renders it, and so expounds it in his Book before alledged.

All which notwithstanding, we cannot presume the existence of this Animal; nor dare we affirm there is any Phœnix in Nature. For, first there wants herein the definitive confirmator and test of things uncertain, that is, the sense of man. For though many Writers have much enlarged hereon, yet is there not any ocular describer, or such as presumeth to confirm it upon aspection. And therefore *Herodotus* that led the story unto the *Greeks*, plainly saith, he never attained the sight of any, but only in the picture.

Again, Primitive Authors, and from whom the stream of relations is derivative, deliver themselves very dubiously; and either by a doubtful parenthesis, or a timerous conclusion overthrow the whole relation. Thus *Herodotus* in his *Euterpe*, delivering the story hereof, presently interposeth, *emoi men ou pista legontes*, that is, which account seems to me improbable. *Tacitus* in his annals affordeth a larger story, how the Phœnix was first seen at *Heliopolis* in the reign of *Sesostris*, then in the reign of *Amasis*, after in the dayes of *Ptolomy*, the third of the *Macedonian* race; but at last thus determineth, *Sed Antiquitas obscura, & nonnulli falsum esse hunc Phœnicem, neque Arabum è terris credidere*. *Pliny* makes yet a fairer story, that the Phœnix flew into *Egypt* in the Consulship of *Quintus Plancius*, that it was brought to *Rome* in the Censorship of *Claudius*, in the eight hundred year of the City, and testified also in their records; but after all concludeth, *Sed quœ falsa nemo dubitabit*, As we read it in the fair and ancient impression of *Brixia*; as *Aldrovandus* hath quoted it, and as it is found in the manuscript Copy, as *Dalechampius* hath also noted.

Moreover, Such as have naturally discoursed hereon, have so diversly, contrarily, or contradictorily delivered themselves, that no affirmative from thence can reasonably be deduced. For most have positively denied it, and they which affirm and believe it, assign this name unto many, and mistake two or three in one. So hath that bird been taken for the Phœnix which liveth in *Arabia*, and buildeth its nest with Cinnamon; by *Herodotus* called *Cinnamulgus*, and by *Aristotle*, *Cinnamomus;* and as a fabulous conceit is censured by *Scaliger*. Some have conceived that bird to be the Phœnix, which by a *Persian* name with the *Greeks* is called *Rhyntace*; but how they made this good we find occasion of doubt; whilest we read in the life of *Artaxerxes*, that this is a little bird brought often to their Tables, and herewith *Parysatis* cunningly poisoned the Queen. The *Manucodiata* or Bird of Paradise, hath had the honour of this name, and their feathers brought from the *Molucca's* do pass for those of the Phœnix. Which though promoted by rarity with us, the *Eastern* Travellers will hardly admit; who know they are common in those parts, and the ordinary plume of *Janizaries* among the *Turks*. And lastly, the Bird *Semenda* hath found the same appellation, for so hath *Scaliger* observed and refuted; nor will the solitude of the Phœnix allow this denomination; for many there are of that species, and whose trifistulary bill and crany we have beheld our selves. Nor are men only at variance in regard of the Phœnix it self, but very disagreeing in the accidents ascribed thereto: for some affirm it liveth three hundred, some five, others six, some a thousand, others no less then fifteen hundred years; some say it liveth in *Æthiopia*, others in *Arabia*, some in *Egypt*, others in *India*, and some in *Utopia*; for such a one must that be which is described by *Lactantius*; that is, which neither was singed in the combustion of *Phœton*, or overwhelmed by the innundation of *Deucalion*.

Lastly, Many Authors who have discoursed hereof, have so delivered themselves, and with such intentions, that we cannot from thence deduce a confirmation. For some have written Poetically, as *Ovid, Mantuan, Lactantius, Claudian* and others: Some have written mystically, as *Paracelsus* in his Book *De Azoth*, or *De ligno & linea vitœ*; and as several Hermetical Philosophers, involving therein the secret of their Elixir, and enigmatically expressing the nature of their great work. Some have written Rhetorically, and concessively, not controverting, but assuming the question, which taken as granted, advantaged the illation. So have holy men made use hereof so far as thereby to confirm the Resurrection; for discoursing with Heathens who granted the story of the Phœnix, they induced the Resurrection from principles of their own, and positions received among themselves. Others have spoken Emblematically and Hieroglyphically; and so did the *Egyptians*, unto whom the Phœnix was the Hieroglyphick of the Sun. And this was probably the ground of the whole relation; succeeding Ages adding fabulous accounts, which laid together built up this singularity, which every Pen proclaimeth.

As for the Texts of Scripture, which seem to confirm the conceit, duly perpended, they add not thereunto. For whereas in that of *Job*, according to the Septuagint or Greek Translation we find the work Phœnix, yet can it have no animal signification; for therein it is not expressed φοινιξ, but στέλεχος φοίνικος, the trunk of the Palmtree, which is also called Phœnix; and therefore the construction will be very hard, if not applied unto some vegetable nature. Nor can we safely insist upon the Greek expression at all; for though the Vulgar translates it *Palma*, and some retain the word Phœnix, others do render it by a word of a different sense; for so hath *Tremellius* delivered it: *Dicebam quod apud nidum meum expirabo, & sicut arena multiplicabo dies*; so hath the *Geneva* and ours translated it, *I said I shall die in my Nest, and shall multiply my days as the sand*. As for that in the Book of Psalms, *Vir justus ut Phœnix florebit*, as *Epiphanius* and *Tertullian* render it, it was only a mistake upon the Homonymy of the Greek word Phœnix, which signifies also a Palm-tree. Which is a fallacy of equivocation, from a community in name inferring a common nature; and whereby we may as firmly conclude, that Diaphœnicon a purging Electuary hath some part of the Phœnix for its ingredient; which receiveth that name from Dates, or the fruit of the Palm-tree, from whence, as *Pliny* delivers, the Phœnix had its name.

Nor do we only arraign the existence of this Animal, but many things are questionable which are ascribed thereto, especially its unity, long life, and generation. As for its unity or conceit there should be but one in nature, it seemeth not only repugnant unto Philosophy, but also holy Scripture; which plainly affirms, there went of every sort two at least into the Ark of *Noah,* according to the Text, *Every Fowl after his kind, every bird of every sort, they went into the Ark, two and two of all flesh, wherein there is the breath of life, and they that went in, went in both male and female of all flesh.* It infringeth the benediction of God concerning multiplication. God blessed them, saying, *Be fruitful and multiply, and fill the waters in the seas, and let fowl multiply in the earth*: And again, *Bring forth with thee every living thing, that they may breed abundantly in the earth, and be fruitful and multiply upon the earth*: which terms are not appliable unto the Phœnix, whereof there is but one in the world, and no more now living then at the first benediction. For the production of one, being the destruction of another, although they produce and generate, they encrease not; and must not be said to multiply, who do not transcend an unity.

As for longævity, that it liveth a thousand years or more; beside that from imperfect observations and rarity of appearance, no confirmation can be made; there may be probable a mistake in the compute. For the tradition being very ancient and probably Egyptian, the *Greeks* who dispersed the Fable, might summ up the account by their own numeration of years; whereas the conceit might have its original in times of shorter compute. For if we suppose our present calculation, the Phœnix now in nature will be the sixth from the Creation, but in the middle of its years; and if the *Rabbins* Prophecie succeed, shall conclude its days not in his own but the last and general flames, without all hope of Reviviction.

Concerning its generation, that without all conjunction it begets and reseminates it self, hereby we introduce a vegetable production in Animals, and unto sensible natures, transfer the propriety of Plants; that is, to multiply within themselves, according to the Law of the Creation, *Let the earth bring forth grass, the herb yielding seed, and the tree yielding fruit, whose seed is in it self.* Which is indeed the natural way of Plants, who having no distinction of sex, and the power of the species contained in every *individuum*, beget and propagate themselves without commixtion; and therefore their fruits proceeding from simpler roots, are not so unlike, or distinguishable from each other, as are the off-springs of sensible creatures and prolifications descending from double originals. But Animal generation is accomplished by more, and the concurrence of two sexes is required to the constitution of one. And therefore such as have no distinction of sex, engender not at all, as *Aristotle* conceives of Eels, and testaceous animals. And though Plant-animals do multiply, they do it not by copulation, but in a way analogous unto Plants. So *Hermaphrodites* although they include the parts of both sexes, and may be sufficiently potent in either; yet unto a conception require a separated sex, and cannot impregnate themselves. And so also though *Adam* included all humane nature, or was (as some opinion) an *Hermaphrodite*, yet had he no power to propagate himself; and therefore God said, *It is not good that man should be alone, let us make him an help meet for him*; that is, an help unto generation; for as for any other help, it had been fitter to have made another man.

Now whereas some affirm that from one Phœnix there doth not immediately proceed another, but the first corrupteth into a worm, which after becometh a Phœnix, it will not make probable this production. For hereby they confound the generation of perfect animals with imperfect, sanguineous with exanguineous, vermiparous with oviparous, and erect Anomalies, disturbing the laws of Nature. Nor will this corruptive production be easily made out in most imperfect generations: for although we deny not that many animals are vermiparous, begetting themselves at a distance, and as it were at the second hand (as generally Insects, and more remarkably Butter-flies and Silk-worms) yet proceeds not this generation from a corruption of themselves, but rather a specifical and seminal diffusion, retaining still the Idea of themselves, though it act that part a while in other shapes. And this will also hold in generations equivocal, and such as are not begotten from Parents like themselves; so from Frogs corrupting, proceed not Frogs again; so if there be anatiferous Trees, whose corruption breaks forth into Bernacles, yet if they corrupt, they generate into Maggots, which produce not them again. For this were a confusion of corruptive and seminal production, and a frustration of that seminal power committed to animals at the Creation. The problem might have been spared, *Why we love not our lice as well as our children?* Noahs

Ark had been needless, the graves of Animals would be the fruitful'st wombs; for death would not destroy, but empeople the world again.

Since therefore we have so slender grounds to confirm the existence of the Phœnix, since there is no ocular witness of it, since as we have declared, by Authors from whom the story is derived, it rather stands rejected; since they who have seriously discoursed hereof, have delivered themselves negatively, diversly, or contrarily; since many others cannot be drawn into Argument, as writing Poetically, Rhetorically, Enigmatically, Hieroglyphically; since holy Scripture alledged for it duly perpended, doth not advantage it; and lastly, since so strange a generation, unity and long life, hath neither experience nor reason to confirm it, how far to rely on this tradition, we refer unto consideration.

But surely they were not well-wishers unto parable Physick, or remedies easily acquired, who derived medicines from the Phœnix; as some have done, and are justly condemned by *Pliny*: *Irridere est, vitæ remedia post millesimum annum redditura monstrare*; It is a folly to find out remedies that are not recoverable under a thousand years; or propose the prolonging of life by that which the twentieth generation may never behold. More veniable is a dependance upon the Philosophers stone, potable gold, or any of those Arcana's whereby *Paracelsus* that died himself at forty seven, gloried that he could make other men immortal. Which, although extreamly difficult, and *tantum non* infesible, yet are they not impossible, nor do they (rightly understood) impose any violence on Nature. And therefore if strictly taken for the Phœnix, very strange is that which is delivered by *Plutarch*, That the brain is a pleasant bit, but that it causeth head-ach. Which notwithstanding the luxurious Emperour could never taste, though he had at his Table many a Phœnicopterus, yet had he not one Phœnix; for though he expected and attempted it, we read not in *Lampridius* that he performed it; and considering the unity thereof, it was a vain design, that is, to destroy any species, or mutilate the great accomplishment of six days. And although some conceive, and it may seem true, that there is in man a natural possibility to destroy the world in one generation, that is, by a general conspire to know no woman themselves, and disable all others also: yet will this never be effected. And therefore *Cain* after he had killed *Abel*, were there no other woman living, could not have also destroyed *Eve*: which although he had a natural power to effect, yet the execution thereof, the providence of

God would have resisted; for that would have imposed another creation upon him, and to have animated a second Rib of *Adam*.

CHAPTER XIII

Of Frogs, Toads, and Toad-stone

Concerning the venomous Urine of Toads, of the stone in the Toads head, and of the generation of Frogs, conceptions are entertained which require consideration. And first, that a Toad pisseth, and this way diffuseth its venome, is generally received, not only with us, but also in other parts; for so hath *Scaliger* observed in his Comment, *Aversum urinam reddere ob oculos persecutoris perniciosam ruricolis persuasum est*; and *Mathiolus* hath also a passage, that a Toad communicates its venome, not only by Urine, but by the humidity and slaver of its mouth; which notwithstanding strictly understood, may admit of examination: for some doubt may be made whether a Toad properly pisseth, that is distinctly and separately voideth the serous excretion: for though not only birds, but oviparous quadrupeds and Serpents have kidneys and ureters, and some Fishes also bladders: yet for the moist and dry excretion they seem at last to have but one vent and common place of exclusion: and with the same propriety of language, we may ascribe that action unto Crows and Kites. And this not onely in Frogs and Toads, but may be enquired in Tortoyses: that is, whether that be strictly true, or to be taken for a distinct and separate miction, when *Aristotle* affirmeth, that no oviparous animal, that is, which either spawneth or layeth Eggs, doth Urine except the Tortois.

The ground or occasion of this expression might from hence arise, that Toads are sometimes observed to exclude or spit out a dark and liquid matter behind: which we have observed to be true, and a venomous condition there may be perhaps therein, but some doubt there may be, whether this is to be called their urine: not because it is emitted aversly or backward, by both sexes, but because it is confounded with the intestinal excretions and egestions of the belly: and this way is ordinarily observed, although possible it is that the liquid excretion may sometimes be excluded without the other.

As for the stone commonly called a Toad-stone, which is presumed to be found in the head of that animal, we first conceive it not a thing impossible: nor is there any substantial reason why in a Toad there may not be found such hard and lapideous concretions. For the like we daily observe in the heads of Fishes, as Cods, Carps, and Pearches: the like also in Snails, a soft and exosseous animal, whereof in the naked and greater sort, as though she would requite the defect of a shell on their back, Nature near the head hath placed a flat white stone, or rather testaceous concretion. Which though *Aldrovandus* affirms, that after dissection of many, he found but in some few: yet of the great gray Snails, I have not met with any that wanted it: and the same indeed so palpable, that without dissection it is discoverable by the hand.

Again, though it be not impossible, yet it is surely very rare: as we are induced to believe from some enquiry of our own, from the trial of many who have been deceived, and the frustrated search of *Porta*, who upon the explorement of many, could scarce find one. Nor is it only of rarity, but may be doubted whether it be of existencie, or really any such stone in the head of a Toad at all. For although *Lapidaries* and questuary enquirers affirm it, yet the Writers of Minerals and natural speculators, are of another belief: conceiving the stones which bear this name, to be a Mineral concretion; not to be found in animals, but in fields. And therefore *Bœtius* refers to *Asteria* or some kind of *Lapis stellaris*, and plainly concludeth, *reperiuntur in agris, quos tamen alii in annosis, ac qui diu in Arundinetis, inter rubos sentesque delituerunt, bufonis capitibus generari pertinaciter affirmant.*

Lastly, If any such thing there be, yet must it not, for ought I see, be taken as we receive it, for a loose and moveable stone, but rather a concretion or induration of the crany it self; for being of an earthy temper, living in the earth, and as some say feeding thereon, such indurations may sometimes happen. Thus when *Brassavolus* after a long search had discovered one, he affirms it was rather the forehead bone petrified, then a stone within the crany; and of this belief was *Gesner*. Which is also much confirmed from what is delivered in *Al-*

drovandus, upon experiment of very many Toads, whose cranies or sculs in time grew hard, and almost of a stony substance. All which considered, we must with circumspection receive those stones which commonly bear this name, much less believe the traditions, that in envy to mankind they are cast out, or swallowed down by the Toad; which cannot consist with *Anatomy*, and with the rest, enforced this censure from *Bœtius*, *Ab eo tempore pro nugis habui quod de Bufonio lapide, ejusque orgine traditur.*

What therefore best reconcileth these divided determinations, may be a middle opinion; that of these stones some may be mineral, and to be found in the earth; some animal, to be met with in Toads, at least by the induration of their cranies. The first are many and manifold, to be found in *Germany* and other parts; the last are fewer in number, and in substance not unlike the stones in Carps heads. This is agreeable unto the determination of *Aldrovandus*, and is also the judgment of learned *Spigelius* in his Epistle unto *Pignorius*.

But these Toadstones, at least very many thereof, which are esteemed among us, are at last found to be taken not out of Toads heads, but out of a Fishes mouth, being handsomely contrived out of the teeth of the *Lupus Marinus*, a Fish often taken in our Northern Seas, as was publickly declared by an eminent and Learned Physitian. But because men are unwilling to conceive so low of of their Toadstones which they so highly value, they may make some trial thereof by a candent or red hot Iron applied unto the hollow and unpolished part thereof, whereupon if they be true stones they will not be apt to burn or afford a burnt odour, which they may be apt to do, if contrived out of animal parts or the teeth of fishes.

Concerning the generation of Frogs, we shall briefly deliver that account which observation hath taught us. By Frogs I understand not such as arising from putrefaction, are bred without copulation, and because they subsist not long, are called *Temporariæ*; nor do I mean the little Frog of an excellent Parrat green, that usually sits on Trees and Bushes, and is therefore called *Ranunculus viridis*, or *arboreus*; but hereby I understand the aquatile or Water-Frog, whereof in ditches and standing plashes we may behold many millions every Spring in *England*. Now these do not as *Pliny* conceiveth, exclude black pieces of Flesh, which after become Frogs; but they let fall their spawn in the water, of excellent use in Physick, and scarce unknown unto any. In this spawn of a lentous and transparent body, are to be discerned many specks, or little conglobulations, which in a small time become of deep black, a substance more compacted and terrestrious then the other; for it riseth not in distillation, and affords a powder when the white and aqueous part is exhaled. Now of this black or duskie substance is the Frog at last formed; as we have beheld, including the spawn with water in a glass, and exposing it unto the Sun. For that black and round substance, in a few days began to dilate and grow longer, after a while the head, the eyes, the tail to be discernable, and at last to become that which the Ancients called *Gyrinus*, we a *Porwigle* or Tadpole. This in some weeks after becomes a perfect Frog, the legs growing out before, and the tail wearing away, to supply the other behind; as may be observed in some which have newly forsaken the water; for in such, some part of the tail will be seen, but curtailed and short, not long and finny as before. A part provided them a while to swim and move in the water, that is, untill such time as Nature excluded legs, whereby they might be provided not only to swim in the water, but move upon the land, according to the amphibious and mixt intention of Nature, that is, to live in both. So that whoever observeth the first progression of the seed before motion, or shall take notice of the strange indistinction of parts in the Tadpole, even when it moveth about, and how successively the inward parts do seem to discover themselves, until their last perfection; may easily discern the high curiosity of Nature in these inferiour animals, and what a long line is run to make a Frog.

And because many affirm, and some deliver, that in regard it hath lungs and breatheth, a Frog may be easily drowned; though the reason be probable, I find not the experiment answerable; for fastning one about a span under water, it lived almost six days. Nor is it only hard to destroy one in water, but difficult also at land: for it will live long after the lungs and heart be out; how long it will live in the seed, or whether the spawn of this year being preserved, will not arise into Frogs in the next, might also be enquired: and we are prepared to trie.

CHAPTER XIV

Of the Salamander

That a Salamander is able to live in flames, to endure and put out fire, is an assertion, not only of great antiquity, but confirmed by frequent, and not contemptible testimony. The *Egyptians* have drawn it into their Hieroglyphicks, *Aristotle* seemeth to embrace it; more plainly *Nicander, Sarenus Sammonicus, Ælian* and *Pliny*, who assigns the cause of this effect: An Animal (saith he) so cold that it extinguisheth the fire like Ice. All which notwithstanding, there is on the negative, Authority and Experience: *Sextius* a Physitian, as *Pliny* delivereth, denied this effect; *Dioscorides* affirmed it a point of folly to believe it; *Galen* that it endureth the fire a while, but in continuance is consumed therein. For experimental conviction, *Mathiolus* affirmeth, he saw a Salamander burnt in a very short time: and of the like assertion is *Amatus Lusitanus*; and most plainly *Pierius*, whose words in his Hieroglyphicks are these; *Whereas it is commonly said that a Salamander extinguisheth the fire, we have found by experience, that it is so far from quenching hot coals, that it dieth immediately therein.* As for the contrary assertion of *Aristotle*, it is but by hear-say, as common opinion believeth, *Hæc enim (ut aiunt) ignem ingrediens, eum extinguit*; and therefore there was no absurdity in *Galen*, when as a Septical medicine he commended the ashes of a Salamander; and *Magicians* in vain from the power of this Tradition, at the burning of Towns or Houses expect a relief from Salamanders.

The ground of this opinion, might be some sensible resistance of fire observed in the Salamander: which being, as *Galen* determineth, cold in the fourth, and moist in the third degree, and having also a mucous humidity above and under the skin, by vertue thereof it may a while endure the flame; which being consumed, it can resist no more. Such an humidity there is observed in Newtes, or Water-Lizards, especially if their skins be perforated or pricked. Thus will Frogs and Snails endure the flame: thus will whites of Eggs, vitreous or glassie flegm extinguish a coal: thus are unguents made which protect a while from the fire: and thus beside the Hirpini there are later stories of men that have passed untoucht through the fire. And therefore some truth we allow in the tradition: truth according unto *Galen*, that it may for a time resist a flame, or as *Scaliger* avers, extinguish or put out a coal: for thus much will many humid bodies perform: but that it perseveres and lives in that destructive element, is a fallacious enlargement. Nor do we reasonably conclude, because for a time it endureth fire, it subdueth and extinguisheth the same, because by a cold and aluminous moisture, it is able a while to resist it: from a peculiarity of Nature it subsisteth and liveth in it.

It hath been much promoted by Stories of incombustible napkins and textures which endure the fire, whose materials are called by the name of Salamanders wool. Which many too literally apprehending, conceive some investing part, or tegument of the Salamander: wherein beside that they mistake the condition of this Animal (which is a kind of Lizard, a quadruped corticated and depilous, that is, without wool, fur or hair) they observe not the method and general rule of nature: whereby all Quadrupeds oviparous, as Lizards, Frogs, Tortois, Chamelions, Crocodiles, are without hair, and have no covering part or hairy investment at all. And if they conceive that from the skin of the Salamander, these incremable pieces are composed; beside the experiments made upon the living, that of *Brassavolus* will step in, who in the search of this truth, did burn the skin of one dead.

Nor is this Salamanders wooll desumed from any Animal, but a Mineral substance Metaphorically so called from this received opinion. For beside *Germanicus* his heart, and *Pyrrhus* his great Toe, which would not burn with the rest of their bodies, there are in the number of Minerals some bodies incombustible; more remarkably that which the Ancients named *Asbeston*, and *Pancirollus* treats of in the Chapter of *Linum vivum*. Whereof by Art were weaved Napkins, Shirts, and Coats, inconsumable by fire; and wherein in ancient times to preserve their ashes pure, and without commixture, they burnt the bodies of Kings. A Napkin hereof *Pliny* reports that *Nero* had, and the like saith *Paulus Venetus* the Emperour of *Tartary* sent unto Pope *Alexander*; and also affirms that in some part of *Tartary* there were

Mines of Iron whose filaments were weaved into incombustible cloth. Which rare Manufacture, although delivered for lost by *Pancirollus*, yet *Salmuth* his Commentator affirmeth, that one *Podocaterus* a Cyprian, had shewed the same at *Venice*; and his materials were from *Cyprus*, where indeed *Dioscorides* placeth them; the same is also ocularly confirmed by *Vives* upon *Austin*, and *Maiolus* in his Colloquies. And thus in our days do men practise to make long-lasting Snasts for Lamps out of Alumen plumosum; and by the same we read in *Pausanius*, that there always burnt a Lamp before the Image of *Minerva*.

CHAPTER XV

Of the Amphisbæna

That the Amphisbæna, that is, a smaller kind of Serpent, which moveth forward and backward, hath two heads, or one at either extream, was affirmed first by *Nicander*, and after by many others, by the Author of the Book *De Theriaca ad Pisonem*, ascribed unto *Galen*; more plainly *Pliny, Geminum habet caput, tanquam parum esset uno ore effundi venenum*: But *Ælian* most confidently, who referring the conceit of *Chimera* and *Hydra* unto Fables, hath set down this as an undeniable truth.

Whereunto while men assent, and can believe a bicipitous conformation in any continued species, they admit a gemination of principle parts, not naturally discovered in any Animal. True it is that other parts in Animals are not equal: for some make their progression with many legs, even to the number of an hundred, as *Juli, Scolopendræ*, or such as are termed *Centipedes*: some fly with two wings, as Birds and many Insects, some with four, as all farinaceous or mealy-winged Animals, as Butter-flies, and Moths: all vaginipennous or sheath-winged Insects, as Beetles and Dorrs. Some have three Testicles, as *Aristotle* speaks of the Buzzard; and some have four stomachs, as horned and ruminating Animals: but for the principle parts, the Liver, Heart, and especially the brains regularly they are but one in any kind or species whatsoever.

And were there any such species or natural kind of animal, it would be hard to make good those six positions of body, which according to the three dimensions are ascribed unto every animal, that is, *infra, supra, ante, retro, dextrosum, sinistrosum*: for if (as it is determined) that be the anterior and upper part, wherein the senses are placed, and that the posterior and lower part which is opposite there-unto, there is no inferiour or former part in this Animal; for the senses being placed at both extreams, doth make both ends anterior, which is impossible; the terms being Relative, which mutually subsist, and are not without each other. And therefore this duplicity was ill contrived to place one head at both extreams, and had been more tolerable to have setled three or four at one. And therefore also Poets have been more reasonable then Philosophers, and *Geryon* or *Cerberus* less monstrous than *Amphisbæna*.

Again, If any such thing there were, it were not to be obtruded by the name of *Amphisbæna*, or as an Animal of one denomination; for properly that Animal is not one, but multiplicious or many, which hath a duplicity or gemination of principal parts. And this doth *Aristotle* define, when he affirmeth a monster is to be esteemed one or many, according to its principle, which he conceived the heart, whence he derived the original of Nerves, and thereto ascribed many acts which Physitians assign unto the brain: and therefore if it cannot be called one, which hath a duplicity of hearts in his sense, it cannot receive that appellation with a plurality of heads in ours. And this the practice of Christians hath acknowledged, who have baptized these geminous births, and double connascencies with several names, as conceiving in them a distinction of souls, upon the divided execution of their functions; that is, while one wept, the other laughing; while one was silent, the other speaking; while one awaked, the other sleeping; as is declared by three remarkable examples in *Petrarch*, *Vincentius*, and the *Scottish* History of *Buchanan*.

It is not denied there have been bicipitous Serpents with the head at each extream, for an example hereof we find in *Aristotle*, and of the like form in *Aldrovandus* we meet with the Icon of a Lizzard; and of this kind perhaps might that *Amphisbæna* be, the picture whereof *Cassianus Puteus* shewed unto the learned *Faber*. Which double formations do often happen unto multiparous generations, more especially that of Serpents; whose productions being numerous, and their Eggs in chains or links together (which sometime conjoyn and inoculate into each other) they may unite into various shapes and come out in mixed formations. But these are monstrous productions, beside the intention of Nature, and the statutes of generation, neither begotten of like parents, nor begetting the like again, but irregularly produced, do stand as Anomalies in the general Book of Nature. Which being shifts and forced pieces, rather then genuine and proper effects, they afford us no illation; nor is it reasonable to conclude, from a monstrosity unto a species, or from accidental effects, unto the regular works of Nature.

Lastly, The ground of the conceit was the figure of this Animal, and motion oft-times both ways; for described it is to be like a worm, and so equally framed at both extreams, that at an ordinary distance it is no easie matter to determine which is the head; and therefore some observing them to move both ways, have given the appellation of heads unto both extreams, which is no proper and warrantable denomination; for many Animals with one head, do ordinarily perform both different and contrary Motions; Crabs move sideling, Lobsters will swim swiftly backward, Worms and Leeches will move both ways; and so will most of those Animals, whose bodies consist of round and annulary fibers, and move by undulation; that is, like the waves of the Sea, the one protruding the other, by inversion whereof they make a backward Motion.

Upon the same ground hath arisen the same mistake concerning the Scolopendra or hundred-footed Insect, as is delivered by *Rhodoginus* from the Scholiast of *Nicander*: *Dicitur à Nicandro*, ἀμφικαρες, *id est, dicephalus aut biceps fictum vero, quoniam retrorsum (ut scribit Aristoteles) arrepit*, observed by *Aldrovandus*, but most plainly by *Muffetus*, who thus concludeth upon the Text of *Nicander*: *Tamen pace tanti authoris dixerim, unicum illi duntaxat caput licet pari facilitate, prorsum capite, retrorsum ducente cauda, incedat, quod Nicandro aliisque imposuisse dubito*: that is, under favour of so great an Author, the Scolopendra hath but one head, although with equal facility it moveth forward and backward, which I suspect deceived *Nicander*, and others.

And therefore we must crave leave to doubt of this double-headed Serpent until we have the advantage to behold or have an iterated ocular testimony concerning such as are sometimes mentioned by *American* relators; and also such as *Cassianus Puteus*, shewed in a picture to *Johannes Faber*; and that which is set down under the name of *Amphisbœna Europœa* in his learned discourse upon *Hernandez* his History of *America*.

CHAPTER XVI

Of the Viper

That the young Vipers force their way through the bowels of their Dam, or that the female Viper in the act of generation bites off the head of the male, in revenge whereof the young ones eat through the womb and belly of the female, is a very ancient tradition. In this sense entertained in the Hieroglyphicks of the *Egyptians*; affirmed by *Herodotus, Nicander, Pliny, Plutarch, Ælian, Jerome, Basil, Isidore*, seems countenanced by *Aristotle*, and his Scholar *Theophrastus*: from hence is commonly assigned the reason why the Romans punished *Parricides* by drowning them in a Sack with a Viper. And so perhaps upon the same opinion the men of *Mileta* when they saw a Viper upon the hand of *Paul*, said presently without conceit of other sin, *No doubt this man is a murderer, who though he have escaped the Sea, yet vengeance suffereth him not to live*: that is, he is now paid in his own way, the parricidous Animal and punishment of murderers is upon him. And though the tradition were currant among the Greeks, to confirm the same the Latine name is introduced, *Vipera quasi vi pariat*; That passage also in the Gospel, *O ye generation of Vipers!* hath found expositions which countenance this conceit. Notwithstanding which authorities, transcribed relations and conjectures, upon enquiry we find the same repugnant unto experience and reason.

And first, it seems not only injurious unto the providence of Nature, to ordain a way of production which should destroy the producer, or contrive the continuation of the species by the destruction of the Continuator; but it overthrows and frustrates the great Benediction of God, *God blessed them, saying, Be fruitful and multiply*. Now if it be so ordained that some must regularly perish by multiplication, and these be the fruits of fructifying in the Viper: it cannot be said that God did bless, but curse this Animal: *Upon thy belly shalt thou go, and dust shalt thou eat all thy life*, was not so great a punishment unto the Serpent after the fall, as *encrease, be fruitful and multiply*, was before. This were to confound the Maledictions of God, and translate the curse of the Woman upon the Serpent: that is, *in dolore paries, in sorrow shalt thou bring forth*; which being proper unto the Woman, is verified best in the Viper, whose delivery is not only accompanied with pain, but also with death it self. And lastly, it overthrows the careful course, and parental provision of Nature, whereby the young ones newly excluded are sustained by the Dam, and protected until they grow up to a sufficiency for themselves. All which is perverted in this eruptive generation; for the Dam being destroyed, the younglings are left to their own protection: which is not conceivable they can at all perform, and whereof they afford us a remarkable confirmation many days after birth. For the young one supposed to break through the belly of the Dam, will upon any fright for protection run into it; for then the old one receives them in at her mouth, which way the fright being past, they will return again, which is a peculiar way of refuge; and although it seem strange, is avowed by frequent experience and undeniable testimony.

As for the experiment, although we have thrice attempted it, it hath not well succeeded; for though we fed them with Milk, Bran, Cheese, &c. the females always died before the young ones were mature for this eruption; but rest sufficiently confirmed in the experiments of worthy enquirers. Wherein to omit the ancient conviction of *Apollonius*, we shall set down some few of Modern Writers. The first, of *Amatus Lusitanus* in his Comment upon *Dioscorides*, *Vidimus nos viperas prægnantes inclusas pixidibus parere, quæ inde ex partu nec mortuæ, nec visceribus perforatæ mansuerunt.* The second is that of *Scaliger*, *Viperas ab impatientibus moræ foetibus numerosissimis rumpi atque interire falsum esse scimus, qui in Vincentii Camerini circulatoris lignea theca vidimus, enatas viperellas, parente salva.* The last and most plain of *Franciscus Bustamantinus*, a Spanish Physitian of *Alcala de Henares*, whose words in his third *de Animantibus Scripturæ*, are these: *Cum vero per me & per alios hæc ipsa disquisissem servata Viperina progenie*, &c. that is, when by my self and others I had enquired the truth hereof, including Vipers in a glass, and feeding them with Cheese and Bran, I undoubtedly found that the Viper was not delivered by tearing of her bowels; but I beheld the young ones excluded by the passage of generation, near the orifice of the seidge. Whereto we might also add the ocular confirmation of *Lacuna* upon *Dioscorides, Ferdinandus Imperatus,* and that learned Physician of *Naples, Aurelius Severinus.*

Now although the Tradition be untrue, there wanted not many grounds which made it plausibly received. The first was a favourable indulgence and special contrivance of Nature; which was the conceit of *Herodotus,* who thus delivereth himself. Fearful Animals, and such as serve for food, Nature hath made more fruitful: but upon the offensive and noxious kind, she hath not conferred fertility. So the Hare that becometh a prey unto Man, unto Beasts, and Fowls of the air, is fruitful even to superfætation; but the Lion, a fierce and ferocious Animal hath young ones but seldom, and also but one at a time; Vipers indeed although destructive, are fruitful; but lest their number should increase, Providence hath contrived another way to abate it: for in copulation the female bites off the head of the male, and the young ones destroy the mother. But this will not consist with reason, as we have declared before. And if we more nearly consider the condition of Vipers and noxious Animals, we shall discover an higher provision of Nature: how although in their paucity she hath not abridged their malignity, yet hath she notoriously effected it by their secession or latitancy. For not only offensive insects, as Hornets, Wasps, and the like; but sanguineous corticated Animals, as Serpents, Toads, and Lizzards, do lie hid and betake themselves to coverts in the Winter. Whereby most Countries enjoying the immunity of Ireland and Candie, there ariseth a temporal security from their venoms; and an intermission of their mischiefs, mercifully requiting the time of their activities.

A second ground of this effect, was conceived the justice of Nature, whereby she compensates the death of the father by the matricide or murder of the mother: and this was the expression of *Nicander.* But the cause hereof is as improbable as the effect; and were indeed an improvident revenge in the young ones, whereby in consequence, and upon defect of provision they must destroy themselves. And whereas he expresseth this decollation of the male by so full a term as ἀποκόπτειν, that is, to cut or lop off, the act is hardly conceiveable; for the Viper hath but two considerable teeth, and those so disposed, so slender and needle-pointed, that they are apter for puncture then any act of incision. And if any like action there be, it may be only some fast retention or sudden compression in the *Orgasmus* or fury of their

207

lust; according as that expression of *Horace* is construed concerning *Lydia* and *Telephus*.

————Sive puer furens,
Impressit memorem dente labris notam.

Others ascribe this effect unto the numerous conception of the Viper; and this was the opinion of *Theophrastus*. Who though he denieth the exesion or forcing through the belly, conceiveth nevertheless that upon a full and plentiful impletion there may perhaps succeed a disruption of the matrix, as it happeneth sometimes in the long and slender fish *Acus*. Now although in hot Countries, and very numerous conceptions, in the Viper or other Animals, there may sometimes ensue a dilaceration of the genital parts; yet is this a rare and contingent effect, and not a natural and constant way of exclusion. For the wise Creator hath formed the organs of Animals unto their operations, and in whom he ordaineth a numerous conception, in them he hath prepared convenient receptacles, and a sutable way of exclusion.

Others do ground this disruption upon their continued or protracted time of delivery, presumed to last twenty days; whereat excluding but one a day, the latter brood impatient, by a forcible proruption anticipate their period of exclusion; and this was the assertion of *Pliny, Cæteri tarditatis impatientes prorumpunt latera, occisâ parente*; which was occasioned upon a mistake of the Greek Text in *Aristotle*, which is literally thus translated, *Parit autem una die secundum unum, parit autem plures quam viginti*, and may be thus Englished, *She bringeth forth in one day, one by one, and sometimes more then twenty*: and so hath *Scaliger* rendred it, *Sigillatim parit, absolvit una die, interdum plures quam viginti*; But *Pliny*, whom *Gaza* followeth, hath differently translated it, *Singulos diebus singulis parit, numero ferè viginti*; whereby he extends the exclusion unto twenty days, which in the textuary sense is fully accomplished in one.

But what hath most advanced it, is a mistake in another text of *Aristotle*, which seemeth directly to determine this disruption, which Gaza hath thus translated, *Parit catulos obvolutos membranis, quæ tertio die rumpuntur, evenit interdum ut qui in utero adhuc sunt abrosis membranis prorumpant*. Now herein probably *Pliny*, and many since have been mistaken; for the disruption of the membranes or skins, which include the young ones, conceiving a dilaceration of the matrix and belly of the Viper: and concluding from a casual dilaceration, a regular and constant disruption.

As for the Latine word *Vipera*, which in the Etymologie of *Isidore* promoteth this conceit; more properly it may imply *vivipera*. For whereas other Serpents lay Eggs, the Viper excludeth living Animals; and though the *Cerastes* be also viviparous, and we have found formed Snakes in the belly of the *Cicilia* or Slow-worm; yet may the Viper emphatically bear the name. For the notation or Etymology is not of necessity adequate unto the name; and therefore though animal be deduced from *anima*, yet are there many animations beside, and Plants will challenge a right therein as well as sensible Creatures.

As touching the Text of Scripture, and compellation of the *Pharisees*, by Generation of Vipers, although constructions be made hereof conformable to this Tradition; and it may be plausibly expounded, that out of a viperous condition, they conspired against their Prophets, and destroyed their spiritual parents; yet (as *Jansenius* observeth) *Gregory* and *Jerome*, do make another construction; apprehending thereby what is usually implied by that Proverb, *Mali corvi, malum ovum*; that is, of evil parents, an evil generation, a posterity not unlike their majority; of mischievous progenitors, a venomous and destructive progeny.

And lastly, Concerning the Hieroglyphical account, according to the Vulgar conception set down by *Orus Apollo*, the Authority thereof is only Emblematical; for were the conception true or false, to their apprehensions, it expressed filial impiety. Which strictly taken, and totally received for truth, might perhaps begin, but surely promote this conception.

More doubtful assertions have been raised of no Animal then the Viper, as we have dispersedly noted: and *Francisco Redi* hath amply discovered in his noble observations of Vipers; from good reasons and iterated experiments affirming, that a Viper containeth no humour, excrement, or part which either dranke or eat, is able to kill any: that the *remorses* or dog-teeth, are not more then two in either sex: that these teeth are hollow, and though they bite and prick therewith, yet are they not venomous, but only open a way and entrance unto the

209

poyson, which notwithstanding is not poysonous except it touch or attain unto the bloud. And that there is no other poyson in this Animal, but only that almost insipid liquor like oyl of Almonds, which stagnates in the sheaths and cases that cover the teeth; and that this proceeds not from the bladder of gall, but is rather generated in the head, and perhaps demitted and sent from thence into these cases by salival conducts and passages, which the head communicateth unto them.

CHAPTER XVII

Of Hares

The double sex of single Hares, or that every Hare is both male and female, beside the vulgar opinion, was the affirmative of Archelaus, of Plutarch, Philostratus, and many more. Of the same belief have been the Jewish Rabbins: The same is likewise confirmed from the Hebrew word; which, as though there were no single males of that kind, hath only obtained a name of the feminine gender. As also from the symbolical foundation of its prohibition in the law, and what vices therein are figured; that is, not only pusillanimity and timidity from its temper, feneration or usury from its foecundity and superfetation; but from this mixture of sexes, unnatural venery and degenerous effemination. Nor are there hardly any who either treat of mutation or mixtion of sexes, who have not left some mention of this point; some speaking positively, others dubiously, and most resigning it unto the enquiry of the Reader. Now hereof to speak distinctly, they must be male and female by mutation and succession of sexes; or else by composition, mixture or union thereof.

As for the mutation of sexes, or transition into one another, we cannot deny it in Hares, it being observable in Man. For hereof beside Empedocles or Tiresias there are not a few examples: and though very few, or rather none which have emasculated or turned women, yet very many who from an esteem or reality of being Women have infallibly proved Men. Some at the first point of their menstruous eruptions, some in the day of their marriage, others many years after: which occasioned disputes at Law, and contestations concerning a restore of the dowry. And that not only mankind, but many other Animals may suffer this transexion, we will not deny, or hold it at all impossible: although I confess by reason of the postick and backward position of the feminine part in quardrupedes, they can hardly admit the substitution of a protrusion, effectual unto masculine generation; except it be in Retromingents, and such as couple backward.

Nor shall we only concede the succession of sexes in some, but shall not dispute the transition of reputed species in others; that is, a transmutation, or (as Paracelsians term it) Transplantation of one into another. Hereof in perfect Animals of a congenerous seed, or near affinity of natures, examples are not unfrequent, as in Horses, Asses, Dogs, Foxes, Pheasants, Cocks, &c. but in imperfect kinds, and such where the discrimination of sexes is obscure, these transformations are more common: and in some within themselves without commixtion, as particularly, in Caterpillars or Silkworms, wherein there is a visible and triple transfiguration. But in Plants, wherein there is no distinction of sex, these transplantations are conceived more obvious then any: as that of Barley into Oats, of Wheat into Darnel; and those grains which generally arise among Corn, as Cockle, Aracus, Ægilops, and other degenerations; which come up in unexpected shapes, when they want the support and maintenance of the primary and master-forms. And the same do some affirm concerning other Plants in less analogy of figures: as the mutation of Mint into Cresses, Basil into Serpoile, and Turneps into Radishes. In all which, as Severinus conceiveth, there may be equivocal seeds and Hermaphroditical principles, which contain the radicality and power of different forms; thus in the seed of Wheat there lieth obscurely the seminality of Darnel, although in a secondary or inferiour way, and at some distance of production; which nevertheless if it meet with convenient promotion, or a conflux and conspiration of causes more powerful then the other; it then beginneth to edifie in chief, and contemning the superintendent form, produceth the signatures of it self.

Now therefore although we deny not these several mutations, and do allow that Hares may exchange their sex, yet this we conceive doth come to pass but sometimes, and not in that vicissitude or annual alteration as is presumed. That is, from imperfection to perfection, from perfection to imperfection; from female unto male, from male to female again, and so in a circle to both without a permansion in either. For beside the inconceivable mutation of temper, which should yearly alternate the sex; this is injurious unto the order of nature, whose operations do rest in the perfection of their intents; which having once attained, they maintain their accomplished ends, and relapse not again into their progressional imperfections. So if in the minority of natural vigor, the parts of seminality take place; when upon encrease or growth thereof the masculine appear, the first design of nature is atchieved, and those parts are after maintained.

But surely it much impeacheth this iterated transection of Hares, if that be true which Cardan and other Physicians affirm, that Transmutation of sex is only so in opinion; and that these transfeminated persons were really men at first; although succeeding years produced the manifesto or evidence of their virilities. Which although intended and formed, was not at first excluded: and that the examples hereof have undergone no real or new transection, but were Androgynally born, and under some kind of *Hermaphrodites.* For though Galen do favour the opinion, that the distinctive parts of sexes are only different in Position, that is, inversion or protrusion; yet will this hardly be made out from the Anatomy of those parts. The testicles being so seated in the female, that they admit not of protrusion; and the neck of the matrix wanting those parts which are discoverable in the organs of virility.

The second and most received acception, is, that Hares are male and female by conjunction of both sexes; and such as are found in mankind, Poetically called Hermaphrodites; supposed to be formed from the equality, or *non victorie* of either seed; carrying about them the parts of Man and Woman; although with great variety in perfection, site, and ability; not only as Aristotle conceived, with a constant impotency in one; but as later observers affirm, sometimes with the ability of either venery. And therefore the providence of some Laws have thought good, that at the years of maturity they should elect one sex, and the errors in the other should suffer a severer punishment. Whereby endeavouring to prevent incontinency, they unawares enjoyned perpetual chastity; for being executive in both parts, and confined unto one, they restrained a natural power, and ordained a partial virginity. Plato and some of the Rabbins proceeded higher; who conceived the first Man an Hermaphrodite; and Marcus Leo the learned Jew, in some sense hath allowed it; affirming that Adam in one suppositum without division, contained both Male and Female. And therefore whereas it is said in the text, That God *created man in his own Image, in the Image of God created he him, male and female created he them;* applying the singular and plural unto Adam, it might denote, that in one substance, and in himself he included both sexes, which was after divided, and the female called Woman. The opinion of Aristotle extendeth farther, from whose assertion all men should be Hermaphrodites; for affirming that Women do not spermatize, and confer a place or receptacle rather then essential principles of generation, he deductively includes both sexes in mankind; for from the father proceed not only males and females, but from him also must Hermaphroditical and masculo-feminine generations be derived, and a commixtion of both sexes arise from the seed of one. But the School-men have dealt with that sex more hardly then any other; who though they have not much disputed their generation, yet have they controverted their Resurrection, and raisen a querie, whether any at the last day should arise in the sex of Women; as may be observed in the supplement of Aquinas.

Now as we must acknowledge this Androgynal condition in Man, so can we not deny the like doth happen in beasts. Thus do we read in Pliny, that Neroes Chariot was drawn by four Hermaphroditical Mares, and Cardan affirms he also beheld one at Antwerp. And thus may we also concede, that Hares have been of both sexes, and some have ocularly confirmed it; but that the whole species or kind should be bisexuous or double-sexed, we cannot affirm, who have found the parts of male and female respectively distinct and single in any wherein we have enquired: and the like success had Bacchinus in such as he dissected. And whereas it is conceived that being an harmless Animal and delectable food unto man, nature hath made them with double sexes, that actively and passively performing they might more numerously increase; we forget an higher providence of nature whereby she especially promotes the multiplication of Hares, which is by superfetation; that is, a conception upon a conception, or an improvement of a second fruit before the first be excluded; preventing hereby the usual intermission and vacant time of generation; which is very common and frequently observable in Hares, mentioned long ago by Aristotle, Herodotus, and Pliny; and we have often observed, that after the first cast, there remain successive conceptions, and other younglings very immature, and far from their term of exclusion.

Nor need any man to question this in Hares, for the same we observe doth sometime happen in Women; for although it be true, that upon conception the inward orifice of the matrix exactly closeth, so that it commonly admitteth nothing after; yet falleth it out sometime, that in the act of coition, the avidity of that part dilateth it selfe, and

214

receiveth a second burden; which if it happen to be near in time unto the first, they do commonly both proceed unto perfection, and have legitimate exclusions, periodically succeeding each other. But if the superfetation be made with considerable intermission, the latter most commonly proves abortive; for the first being confirmed, engrosseth the aliment from the other. How ever therefore the project of Julia, seem very plausible, and that way infallible, when she received not her passengers, before she had taken in her lading, yet was there a fallibility therein: nor indeed any absolute security in the policy of adultery after conception. For the Matrix (which some have called another Animal within us, and which is not subjected unto the law of our will) after reception of its proper Tenant, may yet receive a strange and spurious inmate. As is confirmable by many examples in Pliny; by Larissæa in Hippocrates and that merry one in Plautus urged also by Aristotle: that is, of Iphicles and Hercules, the one begat by Jupiter, the other by Amphitryon upon Alcmæna as also in those super-conceptions, where one child was like the father, the other like the adulterer, the one favoured the servant, the other resembled the master.

Now the grounds that begat, or much promoted the opinion of a double sex in Hares, might be some little bags or tumours, at first glance representing stones or Testicles, to be found in both sexes about the parts of generation; which men observing in either sex, were induced to believe a masculine sex in both. But to speak properly, these are no Testicles or parts official unto generation, but glandulous substances that seem to hold the nature of Emunctories. For herein may be perceived slender perforations, at which may be expressed a black and foeculent matter. If therefore from these we shall conceive a mixtion of sexes in Hares, with fairer reason we may conclude it in Bevers; whereof both sexes contain a double bag or Tumour in the groin, commonly called the Cod or Castor, as we have delivered before.

Another ground were certain holes or cavities observable about the siedge; which being perceived in Males, made some conceive thee might be also a foeminine nature in them. And upon this very ground, the same opinion hath passed upon they Hyæna, and is declared by Aristotle, and thus translated by Scaliger; *Quod autem aiunt utriusque sexus habere genitalia, falsum est, quod videtur esse foemineum sub cauda est simile figura foeminino, verum pervium non est;* and thus is it also in Hares, in whom these holes, although they seem to make a deep cavity, yet do they not perforate the skin, nor

215

hold a community with any part of generation: but were (as Pliny delivereth), esteemed the marks of their age, the number of those deciding their number of years. In which opinion what truth there is we shall not contend; for if in other Animals there be authentick notations, if the characters of years be found in the horns of Cows, or in the Antlers of Deer; if we conjecture the age of Horses from joints in their docks, and undeniably presume it from their teeth; we cannot affirm, there is in this conceit, any affront unto nature; although who ever enquireth shall find no assurance therein.

The last foundation was Retromingency or pissing backward; for men observing both sexes to urine backward, or aversly between their legs, they might conceive there was a foeminine part in both; wherein they are deceived by the ignorance of the just and proper site of the Pizzel, or part designed unto the Excretion of urine; which in the Hare holds not the common position, but is aversly seated, and in its distension enclines unto the Coccix or Scut. Now from the nature of this position, there ensueth a necessity of Retrocopulation, which also promoteth the conceit: for some observing them to couple without ascension, have not been able to judge of male or female, or to determine the proper sex in either. And to speak generally, this way of copulation is not appropriate unto Hares, nor is there one, but many ways of coition: according to divers shapes and different conformations. For some couple laterally or sidewise, as Worms: some circularly or by complication, as Serpents; some pronely, that is, by contaction of the ventral parts in both, as Apes, Porcupines, Hedgehogs, and such as are termed Mollia, as the Cuttle-fish and the Purple; some mixtly, that is, the male ascending the female, or by application of the ventral parts of the one, unto the postick parts of the other, as most Quadrupeds: Some aversly, as all Crustaceous Animals, Lobsters, Shrimps, and Crevises, and also Retromingents, as Panthers, Tygers, and Hares. This is the constant Law of their Coition, this they observe and transgress not: onely the vitiosity of man hath acted the varieties hereof; nor content with a digression from sex or species, hath in his own kind run thorow the Anomalies of venery; and been so bold, not only to act, but represent to view, the irregular wayes of Lust.

CHAPTER XVIII

Of Moles, or Molls

That Moles are blind and have no eyes, though a common opinion, is received with much variety; some affirming only they have no sight, as *Oppianus*, the Proverb *Talpa Cæcior*, and the word σπαλαχία, or *Talpitas*, which in *Hesychius* is made the same with *Cæcitas*: some that they have eyes, but no sight, as the text of *Aristotle* seems to imply; some neither eyes nor sight, as *Albertus*, *Pliny*, and the vulgar opinion; some both eyes and sight, as *Scaliger*, *Aldrovandus*, and some others. Of which opinions the last with some restriction, is most consonant unto truth: for that they have eyes in their head is manifest unto any, that wants them not in his own; and are discoverable, not only in old ones, but as we have observed in young and naked conceptions, taken out of the belly of the Dam. And he that exactly enquires into the cavity of their cranies, may perhaps discover some propagation of nerves communicated unto these parts. But that the humours together with their coats are also distinct (though *Galen* seem to affirm it) transcendeth our discovery; for separating these little Orbs, and including them in magnifying Glasses, we discerned no more then *Aristotle* mentions, *ton ophthalmon melaina*, that is, a black humour, nor any more if they be broken. That therefore they have eyes we must of necessity affirm; but that they be comparatively incomplete we need not to deny: So *Galen* affirms the parts of generation in women are imperfect, in respect of those of men, as the eyes of Moles in regard of other Animals; So *Aristotle* terms them πηρουμενους, which *Gaza* translates *Oblæsos*, and *Scaliger* by a word of imperfection *inchoatos*.

Now as that they have eyes is manifest unto sense, so that they have sight not incongruous unto reason; if we call not in question the providence of this provision, that is, to assign the Organs, and yet deny the Office, to grant them eyes and withhold all manner of vision. For as the inference is fair, affirmatively deduced from the action to the Organ, that they have eyes because they see; so is it also from the organ to the action, that they have eyes, therefore some sight designed, if we take the intention of Nature in every species, and except the casual impediments, or morbosities in individuals. But as their eyes are more imperfect then others, so do we conceive of their sight or act of vision, for they will run against things, and hudling forwards fall from high places. So that they are not blind, nor yet distinctly see; there is in them no Cecity, yet more then a Cecutiency; they have sight enough to discern the light, though not perhaps to distinguish of objects or colours; so are they not exactly blind, for light is one object of vision. And this (as *Scaliger* observeth) might be as full a sight as Nature first intended, for living in darkness under the earth, they had no further need of eyes then to avoid the light; and to be sensible when ever they lost that darkness of earth, which was their natural confinement. And therefore however Translators do render the word of *Aristotle* or *Galen*, that is, *imperfectos oblæsos*, or *inchoatos*, it is not much considerable; for their eyes are sufficiently begun to finish this action, and competently perfect for this imperfect Vision.

And lastly, although they had neither eyes nor sight, yet could they not be termed blind. For blindness being a privative term unto sight, this appellation is not admittible in propriety of speech, and will overthrow the doctrine of privations: which presuppose positive forms or habits, and are not indefinite negations, denying in all subjects, but such alone wherein the positive habits are in their proper Nature, and placed without repugnancy. So do we improperly say a Mole is blind, if we deny it the Organs or a capacity of vision from its created Nature; so when the text of *John* had said, that person was blind from his nativity, whose cecity our Saviour cured, it was not warrantable in *Nonnus* to say he had no eyes at all, as in the judgment of *Heinsius*, he describeth in his paraphrase; and as some ancient Fathers affirm, that by this Miracle they were created in him. And so though the sense may be accepted, that Proverb must be candidly interpreted, which maketh fishes Mute; and calls them silent when they have no voice in Nature.

Now this conceit is erected upon a misapprehension or mistake in the symtomes of vision; men confounding abolishment, diminution and depravement, and naming that an abolition of sight, which indeed is but an abatement. For if vision be abolished, it is called *cæcitas*, or blindness; if depraved and receive its objects erroneously, Hallucination; if diminished, *hebetudo visus, caligatio*, or dimness. Now instead of a diminution or imperfect vision in the Mole, we affirm an abolition or total privation; instead of a caligation or dimness, we conclude a cecity or blindness. Which hath been frequently inferred concerning other Animals, so some affirm the Water-Rat is blind, so *Sammonicus* and *Nicander* do call the Mus-Araneus, the shrew or Ranny, blind: And because darkness was before light, the *Ægyptians* worshipped the same. So are *Cæciliæ* or Slow-Worms accounted blind, and the like we affirm proverbially of the Beetle; although their eyes be evident, and they will flye against lights, like many other Insects, and though also *Aristotle* determines, that the eyes are apparent in all flying Insects, though other senses be obscure, and not perceptible at all. And if from a diminution we may infer a total privation, or affirm that other Animals are blind which do not acutely see, or comparatively unto others, we shall condemn unto blindness many not so esteemed; for such as have corneous or horney eyes, as Lobsters and crustaceous Animals, are generally dim-sighted; all Insects that have *antennæ*, or long horns to feel out their way, as Butter-flyes and Locusts; or their fore-legs so disposed, that they much advance before their heads, as may be observed in Spiders; and if the Eagle were judg, we might be blind our selves. The expression therefore of scripture in the story of *Jacob* is surely with circumspection: *And it came to pass when Jacob was old, and his eyes were dim, quando caligarunt oculi*, saith *Jerome* and *Tremellius*, which are expressions of diminution, and not of absolute privation.

Other concerns there are of Molls, which though not commonly opinioned are not commonly enough considered: As the peculiar formation of their feet, the slender ossa Fugalia, and Dog-teeth, and how hard it is to keep them alive out of the Earth: As also the ferity and voracity of these animals; for though they be contented with Roots, and stringy parts of Plants, or Wormes under ground, yet when they are above it will sometimes tear and eat one another, and in a large glass wherein a Moll, a Toad, and a Viper were inclosed, we have known the Moll to dispatch them and to devour a good part of them both.

219

CHAPTER XIX

Of Lampries

Whether Lampries have nine eyes, as is received, we durst re-fer it unto *Polyphemus*, who had but one, to judg it. An error concerning eyes, occasioned by the error of eyes; deduced from the appearance of divers cavities or holes on either side, which some call eyes that carelessly behold them; and is not only refutable by experi-ence, but also repugnant unto Reason. For beside the monstrosity they fasten unto Nature, in contriving many eyes, who hath made but two unto any Animal, that is, one of each side, according to the division of the brain; it were a superfluous inartificial act to place and settle so many in one plane; for the two extreams would sufficiently perform the office of sight without the help of the intermediate eyes, and be-hold as much as all seven joyned together. For the visible base of the object would be defined by these two; and the middle eyes, although they behold the same thing, yet could they not behold so much thereof as these; so were it no advantage unto man to have a third eye between those two he hath already; and the fiction of *Argus* seems more rea-sonable then this; for though he had many eyes, yet were they placed in circumference and positions of advantage, and so are they placed in several lines in Spiders.

Again, These cavities which men calls eyes are seated out of the head, and where the Gils of other fish are placed; containing no Organs of sight, nor having any Communication with the brain. Now all sense proceeding from the brain, and that being placed (as *Galen* observeth) in the upper part of the body, for the fitter situation of the eyes, and conveniency required unto sight; it is not reasonable to imagine that they are any where else, or deserve that name which are seated in other parts. And therefore we relinquish as fabulous what is delivered of *Sternophthalmi*, or men with eyes in their breast, and when it is said by *Solomon*, A wise mans eyes are in his head, it is to be taken in a second sense, and affordeth no objection. True it is that the eyes of Animals are seated with some difference, but in sanguineous animals in the head, and that more forward then the ear or hole of hearing. In quadrupedes, in regard of the figure of their heads, they are placed at some distance; in latirostrous and flat-bild birds they are more laterally seated; and therefore when they look intently they turn one eye upon the object, and can convert their heads to see before and behind, and to behold two opposite points at once. But at a more easie distance are they situated in man, and in the same circumference with the ear; for if one foot of the compass be placed upon the Crown, a circle described thereby will intersect, or pass over both the ears.

The error in this conceit consists in the ignorance of these cavities, and their proper use in nature; for this is a particular disposure of parts, and a peculiar conformation whereby these holes and sluces supply the defect of Gils, and are assisted by the conduit in the head; for like cetaceous Animals and Whales, the Lamprie hath a fistula, spout or pipe at the back part of the head, whereat it spurts out water. Nor is it only singular in this formation, but also in many other; as in defect of bones, whereof it hath not one; and for the spine or back-bone, a cartilaginous substance without any spondyles, processes or protuberance whatsoever. As also in the provision which Nature hath made for the heart; which in this Animal is very strangely secured, and lies immured in a cartilage or gristly substance. And lastly, in the colour of the liver: which is in the Male of an excellent grass green: but of a deeper colour in the Female, and will communicate a fresh and durable verdure.

CHAPTER XX

Of Snayls

Whether *Snayls* have eyes some Learned men have doubted. For *Scaliger* terms them but imitations of eyes; and *Aristotle* upon consequence denyeth them, when he affirms that *Testaceous* Animals have no eyes. But this now seems sufficiently asserted by the help of exquisite Glasses, which discover those black and atramentous spots or globales to be their eyes.

That they have two eyes is the common opinion, but if they have two eyes, we may grant them to have no less then four, that is, two in the larger extensions above, and two in the shorter and lesser horns below, and this number may be allowed in these inferiour and exanguious animals; since we may observe the articulate and latticed eyes in Flies, and nine in some Spiders: and in the great *Phalangium* Spider of America, we plainly number eight.

But in sanguineous animals, quadrupeds, bipeds, or man, no such number can be regularly verified, or multiplicity of eyes confirmed. And therefore what hath been under this kind delivered, concerning the plurality, paucity or anomalous situation of eyes, is either monstrous, fabulous, or under things never seen includes good sense or meaning. And so may we receive the figment of *Argus*, who was an Hieroglyphick of heaven, in those centuries of eyes expressing the stars; and their alternate wakings, the vicissitude of day and night. Which strictly taken cannot be admitted; for the subject of sleep is not the eye, but the common sense, which once asleep, all eyes must be at rest. And therefore what is delivered as an Embleme of vigilancy, that the Hare and Lion do sleep with one eye open, doth not evince they are any more awake then if they were both closed. For the open eye be-holds in sleep no more then that which is closed; and no more one eye in them then two in other Animals that sleep with both open; as some by disease, and others naturally which have no eye-lids at all.

As for Polyphemus, although the story be fabulous, the mon-strosity is not impossible. For the act of Vision may be performed with one eye; and in the deception and fallacy of sight, hath this advantage of two, that it beholds not objects double, or sees two things for one. For this doth happen when the axis of the visive cones, diffused from the object, fall not upon the same plane; but that which is conveyed into one eye, is more depressed or elevated then that which enters the other. So if beholding a Candle, we protrude either upward or down-ward the pupill of one eye, the object will appear double; but if we shut the other eye, and behold it with one, it will then appear but sin-gle; and if we abduce the eye unto either corner, the object will not duplicate: for in that position the axis of the cones remain in the same plane, as is demonstrated in the opticks, and delivered by *Galen*, in his tenth *De usu partium*.

Relations also there are of men that could make themselves invisible, which belongs not to this discourse; but may serve as notable expressions of wise and prudent men, who so contrive their affairs, that although their actions be manifest, their designs are not discover-able. In this acception there is nothing left of doubt, and *Giges* Ring remaineth still amongst us: for vulgar eyes behold no more of wise men then doth the Sun: they may discover their exteriour and outward ways, but their interiour and inward pieces he only sees, that sees into their beings.

CHAPTER XXI

Of the Chameleon

Concerning the *Chameleon* there generally passeth an opinion that it liveth only upon air, and is sustained by no other aliment: Thus much is in plain terms affirmed by *Solinus*, *Pliny*, and others, and by this periphrasis is the same described by *Ovid*. All which notwithstanding, upon enquiry I find the assertion mainly controvertible, and very much to fail in the three inducements of belief.

And first for its verity, although asserted by some, and traditionally delivered by others, yet is it very questionable. For beside *Ælian*, who is seldom defective in these accounts: *Aristotle* distinctly treating hereof, hath made no mention of this remarkable propriety: which either suspecting its verity, or presuming its falsity, he surely omitted: for that he remained ignorant of this account it is not easily conceiveable: it being the common opinion, and generally received by all men. Some have positively denied it, as *Augustinus*, *Niphus*, *Stobæus*, *Dalechampius*, *Fortunius*, *Licetus*, with many more; others have experimentally refuted it, as namely *Johannes Landius*, who in the relation of *Scaliger*, observed a *Chameleon* to lick up a fly from his breast: But *Bellonius* hath been more satisfactorily experimental, not only affirming they feed on Flies, Caterpillars, Beetles and other Insects, but upon exenteration he found these Animals in their bellies: whereto we might also add the experimental decisions of the worthy *Peireschius* and learned *Emanuel Vizzanius*, in that *Chameleon* which had been often observed to drink water, and delight to feed on Mealworms. And although we have not had the advantage of our own observation, yet have we received the like confirmation from many ocular spectators.

As touching the verisimility or probable truth of this relation, several reasons there are which seem to overthrow it. For first, there are found in this Animal, the guts, the stomack, and other parts official unto nutrition; which were its aliment the empty reception of air, their provisions had been superfluous. Now the wisdom of nature abhorring superfluities, and effecting nothing in vain, unto the intention of these operations, respectively contriveth the Organs; and therefore where we find such Instruments, we may with strictness expect their actions; and where we discover them not, we may with safety conclude the non-intention of their operations. So when we perceive that Bats have teats, it is not unreasonable to infer they suckle their younglings with milk; but whereas no other flying Animal hath these parts, we cannot from them expect a viviparous exclusion; but either a generation of eggs, or some vermiparous separation, whose navel is within it self at first, and its nutrition after not connexedly depending of its original.

Again, Nature is so far from leaving any one part without its proper action, that she oft-times imposeth two or three labours upon one, so the Pizel in Animals is both official unto Urine and to generation, but the first and primary use is generation; for some creatures enjoy that part which urine not. So the nostrils are useful both for respiration and smelling, but the principal use is smelling; for many have nostrils which have no lungs, as fishes, but none have lungs or respiration, which have not some shew, or some analogy of nostrils. Thus we perceive the providence of Nature, that is, the wisdom of God, which disposeth of no part in vain, and some parts unto two or three uses, will not provide any without the execution of its proper office, nor where there is no digestion to be made, make any parts inservient to that intention.

Beside the remarkable teeth, the tongue of this animal is a second argument to overthrow this airy nutrication: and that not only in its proper nature, but also its peculiar figure. For of this part properly taken there are two ends; that is, the formation of the voice, and the execution of tast: for the voice, it can have no office in *Chameleons*, for they are mute Animals; as beside fishes, are most other sorts of Lizards. As for their tast, if their nutriment be air, neither can it be an Instrument thereof, for the body of that element is ingustible, void of all sapidity, and without any action of the tongue, is by the rough artery or wezon conducted into the lungs. And therefore *Pliny* much forgets the strictness of his assertion, when he alloweth excrements unto that Animal, that feedeth only upon Air; which notwithstanding the urine of an Ass, he commends as a magicall Medicine upon our enemies.

The figure of the tongue seems also to overthrow the presumption of this aliment, which according to exact delineation, is in this Animal peculiar, and seemeth contrived for prey, For in so little a creature it is at the least a palm long, and being it self very slow in motion, hath in this part a very great agility; withall its food being flies and such as suddenly escape, it hath in the tongue a mucous and slimy extremity, whereby upon a sudden emission it inviscates and tangleth those Insects. And therefore some have thought its name not unsuitable unto its nature; the nomination in Greek is a little Lion; not so much for the resemblance of shape, as affinity of condition; that is for vigilancy in its prey, and sudden rapacity thereof, which it performeth not like the Lion with its teeth, but a sudden and unexpected ejaculation of the tongue. This exposition is favoured by some, especially the old gloss upon *Leviticus*, whereby in the Translation of *Jerome* and the Septuagint, this Animal is forbidden: what ever it be, it seems as reasonable as that of *Isidore*, who derives this name *à Camelo & Leone*, as presuming herein resemblance with a Camell.

As for the possibility hereof, it is not also unquestionable; and wise men are of opinion, the bodies of Animals cannot receive a proper aliment from air; for beside that tast being (as *Aristotle* terms it) a kind of touch, it is required the aliment should be tangible, and fall under the palpable affections of touch; beside also that there is some sapor in all aliments, as being to be distinguished and judged by the gust; which cannot be admitted in air: Beside these, I say, if we consider the nature of aliment, and the proper use of air in respiration, it will very hardly fall under the name hereof, or properly attain the act of nutrication.

And first concerning its nature, to make a perfect nutrition into the body nourished, there is required a transmutation of the nutriment; now where this conversion or aggeneration is made, there is also required in the aliment a familiarity of matter, and such a community or vicinity unto a living nature, as by one act of the soul may be converted into the body of the living, and enjoy one common soul. Which cannot be effected by air, it concurring only with our flesh in common principles, which are at the largest distance from life, and common also unto inanimated constitutions. And therefore when it is said by *Fernelius*, and asserted by divers others, that we are only nourished by living bodies, and such as are some way proceeding from them, that is, the fruits, effects, parts, or seeds thereof; they have laid out an object very agreeable unto assimilation; for these indeed are fit to receive a quick and immediate conversion, as holding some community with our selves, and containing approximate dispositions unto animation.

Secondly, (as is argued by *Aristotle* against the *Pythagorians*) whatsoever properly nourisheth before its assimilation, by the action of natural heat it receiveth a corpulency or incrassation progressional unto its conversion; which notwithstanding cannot be effected upon air; for the action of heat doth not condense but rarifie that body, and by attenuation, rather then for nutrition, disposeth it for expulsion.

Thirdly, (which is the argument of *Hippocrites*) all aliment received into the body, must be therein a considerable space retained, and not immediately expelled. Now air but momentally remaining in our bodies, it hath no proportionable space for its conversion; only of length enough to refrigerate the heart; which having once performed, lest being it self heated again, it should suffocate that part, it maketh no stay, but hasteth back the same way it passed in.

Fourthly, The use of air attracted by the lungs, and without which there is no durable continuation in life, is not the nutrition of parts, but the contemperation and ventilation of that fire always maintained in the forge of life; whereby although in some manner it concurreth unto nutrition, yet can it not receive the proper name of nutriment. And therefore by *Hippocrates* it is termed *Alimentum non Alimentum*, a nourishment and no nourishment. That is, in a large acception, but not in propriety of language; conserving the body, not nourishing the same; not repairing it by assimilation, but preserving it by ventilation; for thereby the natural flame is preserved from extinction, and so the individuum supported in some way like nutrition.

And though the air so entreth the Lungs, that by its nitrous Spirit, doth affect the heart, and several ways qualifie the blood; and though it be also admitted into other parts, even by the meat we chew, yet that it affordeth a proper nutriment alone, is not easily made out.

Again, Some are so far from affirming the air to afford any nutriment, that they plainly deny it to be any Element, or that it entreth into mixt bodies as any principle in their compositions, but performeth other offices in the Universe; as to fill all vacuities about the earth or beneath it, to convey the heat of the sun, to maintain fires and flames, to serve for the flight of volatils, respiration of breathing Animals, and refrigeration of others. And although we receive it as an Element, yet since the transmutation of Elements and simple bodies, is not beyond great question, since also it is no easie matter to demonstrate that air is so much as convertible into water; how transmutable it is into flesh, may be of deeper doubt.

And although the air attracted may be conceived to nourish the invisible flame of life, in as much as common and culinary flames are nourished by the air about them; we make some doubt whether air is the pabulous supply of fire, much less that flame is properly air kindled. And the same before us, hath been denied by the Lord of *Verulam*, in his Tract of life and death, and also by Dr. *Jorden* in his book of Mineral waters. For that which substantially maintaineth the fire, is the combustible matter in the kindred body, and not the ambient air, which affordeth exhalation to its fuliginous atomes; nor that which causeth the flame properly to be termed air, but rather as he expresseth it, the accension of fuliginous exhalations, which contain an unctuosity in them, and arise from the matter of fuel, which opinion will salve may doubts, whereof the common conceit affordeth no solution.

As first, How fire is stricken out of flints? that is, not by kindling the air from the collision of two hard bodies; for then Diamonds should do the like better then Flints: but rather from sulphureous inflamed and even vitrified effluviums and particles, as hath been observed of late. The like saith *Jorden* we observe we observe in canes and woods, that are unctuous and full of oyl, which will yield fire by frication, or collision, not by kindling the air about them, but the inflamable oyl within them. Why the fire goes out without air? that is, because the fuliginous exhalations wanting evaporation recoil upon the flame and choak it, as is evident in cupping glasses; and the artifice of charcoals, where if the air be altogether excluded, the fire goes out. Why some lamps included in those bodies have burned many hundred years, as that discovered in the Sepulchre of *Tullia*, the sister of *Cicero*, and that of *Olibius* many years after, near *Padua*, because whatever was their matter, either a preparation of gold, or *Naptha*, the duration proceeded from the purity of their oyl which yielded no fuliginous exhalations to suffocate the fire; For if air had nourished the flame, it had not continued many minutes, for it would have been spent and wasted by the fire. Why a piece of flax will kindle, although it touch not the flame? because the fire extendeth further, then indeed it is visible, being at some distance from the week, a pellucide and transparent body, and thinner then the air it self. Why Mettals in their liquation, although they intensly heat the air above their surface, arise not yet into a flame, nor kindle the air about them; because their sulphur is more fixed, and they emit not inflamable exhalations. And lastly, why a lamp or candle burneth only in the air about it, and inflameth not the air at a distance from it? because the flame extendeth not beyond the inflamable effluence, but closely adheres unto the original of its inflamation; and therefore it only warmeth, not kindleth the air about it. Which notwithstanding it will do, if the ambient air be impregnate with subtile inflamabilities, and such as are of quick accension; as experiment is made in a close room; upon an evaporation of spirits of wine and Camphire; as subterraneous fires do sometimes happen; and as *Creusa* and *Alexanders* boy in the bath were set on fire by *Naptha*.

Lastly, The Element of air is so far from nourishing the body, that some have questioned the power of water; many conceiving it enters not the body in the power of aliment, or that from thence there proceeds a substantial supply. For beside that some creatures drink not at all; Even unto our selves, and more perfect Animals, though many ways assistent thereto, it performs no substantial nutrition, serving for refrigeration, dilution of solid aliment, and its elixation in the stomack; which from thence as a vehicle it conveys through less accessible cavities, and so in a rorid substance through the capillary cavities, into every part; which having performed, it is afterward excluded by Urine, sweat and serous separations. And this opinion surely possessed the Ancients; for when they so highly commended that water which is suddenly hot and cold, which is without all savour, the lightest, the thinnest, and which will soonest boil Beans or Pease, they had no consideration of nutrition; whereunto had they had respect, they would have surely commended gross and turbid streams, in whose confusion at least, there might be contained some nutriment; and not jejune or limped water, nearer the simplicity of its Element. Although, I confess, our clearest waters and such as seem simple unto sense, are much compounded unto reason, as may be observed in the evaporation of large quantities of water; wherein beside a terreous residence some salt is also found, as is also observable in rain water; which appearing pure and empty, is full of seminal principles, and carrieth vital atomes of plants and Animals in it, which have not perished in the great circulation of nature; as may be discovered from several Insects generated in rain water, from the prevalent fructification of plants thereby; and (beside the real plant of *Cornerius*) from vegetable figurations, upon the sides of glasses, so rarely delineated in frosts.

All which considered, severer heads will be apt enough to conceive the opinion of this Animal, not much unlike that of the Astomi, or men without mouths, in *Pliny*; sutable unto the relation of the Mares in *Spain*, and their subventaneous conceptions, from the Western wind; and in some way more unreasonable then the figment of *Rabican* the famous horse in *Ariosto*, which being conceived by flame and wind, never tasted grass, or fed on any grosser provender then air: for this way of nutrition was answerable unto the principles of his generation. Which being of no airy, but gross and seminal in the *Chameleon*; unto its conservation there is required a solid pasture, and a food congenerous unto the principles of its nature.

The grounds of this opinion are many; the first observed by *Theophrastus*, was the inflation or swelling of the body, made in this Animal upon inspiration or drawing in its breath; which people observing, have thought it to feed upon air. But this effect is rather occasioned upon the greatness of its lungs, which in this Animal are very large, and by their backward situation, afford a more observable dilatation; and though their lungs be less, the like inflation is also observable in Toads, but especially in Seatortoises.

A second is the continual hiation or holding open its mouth, which men observing, conceive the intention thereof to receive the aliment of air; but this is also occasioned by the greatness of its lungs; for repletion whereof not having a sufficient or ready supply by its nostrils; it is enforced to dilate and hold open the jaws.

The third is the paucity of blood observed in this Animal, scarce at all to be found but in the eye, and about the heart; which defect being observed, inclined some into thoughts, that the air was a sufficient maintenance for these exanguious parts. But this defect or rather paucity of blood, is also agreeable unto many other Animals, whose solid nutriment we do not controvert; as may be observed in other sorts of Lizards, in Frogs and divers Fishes; and therefore an Horse-leech will not readily fasten upon every fish; and we do not read of much blood that was drawn from Frogs by Mice, in that famous battel of *Homer*.

The last and most common ground which begat or promoted this opinion, is the long continuation hereof without any visible food, which some observing, precipitously conclude they eat not any at all. It cannot be denied it is (if not the most of any) a very abstemious Animal, and such as by reason of its frigidity, paucity of blood, and latitancy in the winter (about which time the observations are often made) will long subsist without a visible sustentation. But a like condition may be also observed in many other Animals; for Lizards and Leeches, as we have made trial, will live some months without sustenance; and we have included Snails in glasses all winter, which have returned to feed again the in spring. Now these notwithstanding, are not conceived to pass all their lives without food; for so to argue is fallacious, and is moreover sufficiently convicted by experience. And therefore probably other relations are of the same verity, which are of the like affinity; as is the conceit of the *Rhintace* in *Persia*, the *Canis Levis* of *America*, and the *Manucodiata* or bird of Paradise in *India*.

To assign a reason of this abstinence in Animals, or declare how without a supply there ensueth no destructive exhaustion, exceedeth the limits and intention of my discourse. *Fortunius Licetus*, in his excellent Tract, *de his qui diu vivunt sine alimento*, hath very ingeniously attempted it; deducing the cause hereof from an equal conformity of natural heat and moisture, at least no considerable exuperancy in either; which concurring in an unactive proportion, the natural heat consumeth not the moisture (whereby ensueth no exhaustion) and the condition of natural moisture is able to resist the slender action of heat (whereby it needeth no reparation) and this is evident in Snakes, Lizards, Snails, and divers Insects latitant many months in the year; which being cold creatures, containing a weak heat in a crass or copious humidity, do long subsist without nutrition. For the activity of the agent, being not able to over-master the resistance of the patient, there will ensue no deperdition. And upon the like grounds it is, that cold and phlegmatick bodies, and (as *Hippocrates* determineth) that old men will best endure fasting. Now the same harmony and stationary constitution, as it happeneth in many species, so doth it fall out sometime in Individuals. For we read of many who have lived long time without aliment; and beside deceits and impostures, there may be veritable Relations of some, who without a miracle, and by peculiarity of temper, have far out-fasted *Elias*. Which notwithstanding doth not take off the miracle; for that may be miraculously effected in one, which is naturally causable in another. Some naturally living unto an hundred; unto which age, others notwithstanding could not attain without a miracle.

CHAPTER XXII

Of the Ostrich

The common opinion of the *Ostrich, Struthiocamelus* or *Sparrow-Camel*, conceives that it digesteth Iron; and this is confirmed by the affirmations of many; beside swarms of others, *Rhodiginus* in his prelections taketh it for granted, *Johannes Langius* in his Epistles pleadeth experiment for it; the common picture also confirmeth it, which usually describeth this Animal with an Horshoe in its mouth. Notwithstanding upon enquiry we find it very questionable, and the negative seems most reasonably entertained; whose verity indeed we do the rather desire, because hereby we shall relieve our ignorance of one occult quality; for in the list thereof it is accounted, and in that notion imperiously obtruded upon us. For my part, although I have had the sight of this Animal, I have not had the opportunity of its experiment, but have received great occasion of doubt, from learned discourses thereon.

For *Aristotle* and *Oppianus* who have particularly treated hereof are silent in this singularity; either omitting it as dubious, or as the Comment saith, rejecting it as fabulous. *Pliny* speaketh generally, affirming only, the digestion is wonderful in this Animal; *Ælian* delivereth, that it digesteth stones without any mention of Iron; *Leo Africanus*, who lived in those Countries wherein they most abound, speaketh diminutively, and but half way into this assertion; *Surdum ac simplex animal est, quicquid invenit, absque delectu, usque ad ferum devorat*: *Fernelius* in his second *De abditis rerum causis*, extenuates it, and *Riolanus* in his Comment thereof positively denies it. Some have experimentally refuted it, as *Albertus Magnus*; and most plainly *Ulysses Aldrovandus*, whose words are these; *Ego ferri frustra devorare, dum Tridenti essem, observavi, sed quæ incocta rursus ex-*

cerneret, that is, at my being at Trent, I observed the *Ostrich* to swallow Iron, but yet to exclude it undigested again.

Now beside experiment, it is in vain to attempt against it by Philosophical argument, it being an occult quality, which contemns the law of Reason, and defends it self by admitting no reason at all. As for its possibility we shall not at present dispute; nor will we affirm that Iron indigested, receiveth in the stomack of the *Ostrich* no alteration at all; but if any such there be, we suspect this effect rather from some way of corrosion, then any of digestion; nor any liquid reduction or tendance to chilification by the power of natural heat, but rather some attrition from an acide and vitriolous humidity in the stomack, which may absterse and shave the scorious parts thereof. So rusty Iron crammed down the throat of a Cock, will become terse and clear again in its gizzard: So the Counter which according to the relation of *Amatus* remained a whole year in the body of a youth, and came out much consumed at last; might suffer this diminution, rather from sharp and acide humours, then the strength of natural heat, as he supposeth. So silver swallowed and retained some time in the body, will turn black, as if it had been dipped in *Aqua fortis*, or some corrosive water, but Lead will remain unaltered; for that mettal containeth in it a sweet salt or sugar, whereby it resisteth ordinary corrosion, and will not easily dissolve even in *Aqua fortis*. So when for medical uses, we take down the filings of Iron or Steel, we must not conceive it passeth unaltered from us; for though the grosser parts be excluded again, yet are the dissoluble parts extracted, whereby it becomes effectual in deopilations; and therefore for speedier operation we make extinctions, infusions, and the like, whereby we extract the salt and active parts of the Medicine; which being in solution, more easily enter the veins. And this is that the Chymists mainly drive at in the attempt of their *Aurum Potabile*, that is, to reduce that indigestible substance into such a form as may not be ejected by seidge, but enter the cavities, and less accessible parts of the body, without corrosion.

The ground of this conceit is its swallowing down fragments of Iron, which men observing, by a froward illation, have therefore conceived it digesteth them; which is an inference not to be admitted, as being a fallacy of the consequent, that is, concluding a position of the consequent, from the position of the antecedent. For many things are swallowed by animals, rather for condiment, gust or medicament, then any substantial nutriment. So Poultrey, and especially the Turkey, do of themselves take down stones; and we have found at one time in the gizzard of a Turkey no less then seven hundred. Now these rather concur unto digestion, then are themselves digested, for we have found them also in the guts and excrements, but their descent is very slow, for we have given them stones and small pieces of Iron, which eighteen days after we have found remaining in the giazard. And therefore the experiment of *Langius* and others might be fallible, whilst after the taking they expected it should come down within a day or two after. Thus also we swallow Cherry-stones, but void them unconcocted, and we usually say they preserve us from surfet; for being hard bodies they conceive a strong and durable heat in the stomack, and so prevent the crudities of their fruit: And upon the like reason do culinary operators observe, that flesh boiles best, when the bones are boiled with it. Thus dogs will eat grass, which they digest not: Thus Camels to make water sapid, do raise the mud with their feet: Thus horses will knable at walls, Pigeons delight in salt stones. Rats will gnaw Iron, and *Aristotle* saith the Elephant swalloweth stones. And thus may also the *Ostrich* swallow Iron; not as his proper aliment, but for the ends above expressed, and even as we observe the like in other Animals.

And whether these fragments of Iron and hard substances swallowed by the *Ostrich*, have not also that use in their stomacks, which they have in other birds; that is, in some way to supply the use of teeth, by commolition, grinding and compression of their proper aliment, upon the action of the strongly conformed muscles of the stomack; as the honor'd Dr. *Harvey* discourseth, may also be considered.

What effect may therefore be expected from the stomack of an *Ostrich* by application alone to further digestion in ours, beside the experimental refute of *Galen*, we refer it unto considerations above alledged; Or whether there be any more credit to be given unto the Medicine of *Ælian*, who affirms the stones they swallow have a peculiar vertue for the eyes, then that of *Hermolaus* and *Pliny* drawn from the urine of this Animal; let them determine who can swallow so strange a transmission of qualities, or believe that any Bird or flying Animal doth separately and distinctly urine beside the Bat.

That therefore an *Ostrich* will swallow and take down Iron, is easily to be granted: that oftentimes it pass entire away, if we admit of ocular testimony not to be denied. And though some experiment may also plead, that sometimes they are so altered, as not to be found or excluded in any discernable parcels: yet whether this be not effected by some way of corrosion, from sharp and dissolving humidities, rather then any proper digestion, chilifactive mutation, or alimental conversion,

CHAPTER XXIII

Of Unicorns horn

Great account and much profit is made of *Unicorns horn*, at least of that which beareth the name thereof; wherein notwithstanding, many I perceive suspect an Imposture, and some conceive there is no such Animal extant. Herein therefore to draw up our determinations; beside the several places of Scripture mentioning this Animal (which some may well contend to be only meant of the Rhinoceros we are so far from denying there is any *Unicorn* at all, that we affirm there are many kinds thereof. In the number of Quadrupedes, we will concede no less then five; that is, the *Indian* Ox, the *Indian* Ass, the Rhinoceros, the Oryx, and that which is more eminently termed *Monoceros*, or *Unicornis*. Some in the list of fishes; as that described by *Olaus*, *Albertus* and others: and some Unicorns we will allow even among Insects; as those four kinds of nasicornous Beetles described by *Muffetus*.

Secondly, Although we concede there be many *Unicorns*, yet are we still to seek; for whereunto to affix this Horn in question, or to determine from which thereof we receive this magnified Medicine, we have no assurance, or any satisfactory decision. For although we single out one, and eminently thereto assign the name of the *Unicorn*; yet can we not be secure what creature is meant thereby; what constant shape it holdeth, or in what number to be received. For as far as our endeavours discover, this animal is not uniformly described, but differently set forth by those that undertake it. *Pliny* affirmeth it is a fierce and terrible creature; *Vartomannus* a tame and mansuete Animal: those which *Garcias ab Horto* described about the cape of good hope, were beheld with heads like horses; those which *Vartomannus* beheld, he described with the head of a Deer; *Pliny, Ælian, Solinus*, and after these from ocular assurance, *Paulus Venetus* affirmeth the feet of the *Unicorn* are undivided, and like the Elephants: But those two which *Vartomannus* beheld at *Mecha*, were as he describeth, footed like a Goat. As *Ælian* describeth, it is in the bigness of an Horse, as *Vartomannus*, of a Colt; that which *Thevet* speaketh of was not so big as an Heifer; but *Paulus Venetus* affirmeth, they are but little less then Elephants. Which are discriminations very material, and plainly declare, that under the same name Authors describe not the same Animal: so that the *Unicorns* Horn of one, is not that of another, although we proclaim an equal vertue in all.

Thirdly, Although we were agreed what Animal this was, or differed not in its description, yet would this also afford but little satisfaction; for the Horn we commonly extol, is not the same with that of the Ancients. For that in the description of *Ælian* and *Pliny* was black: this which is shewed amongst us is commonly white, none black; and of those five which *Scaliger* beheld, though one spadiceous, or of a light red, and two enclining to red, yet was there not any of this complexion among them.

Fourthly, What Horns soever they be which pass amongst us, they are not surely the Horns of any one kind of Animal, but must proceed from several sorts of *Unicorns*. For some are wreathed, some not: That famous one which is preserved at St. *Dennis* near *Paris*, hath wreathy spires, and chocleary turnings about it, which agreeth with the description of the *Unicorns* Horn in *Ælian*. Those two in the treasure of St. *Mark* are plain, and best accord with those of the *Indian* Ass, or the descriptions of other *Unicorns*: That in the Repository of the electour of Saxonie is plain and not hollow, and is believed to be a true Land *Unicorns* Horn. *Albertus Magnus* describeth one ten foot long, and at the base about thirteen inches compass: and that of *Antwerp* which *Goropius Becanus* describeth, is not much inferiour unto it; which best agree unto the descriptions of the *Sea-Unicorns*; for these, as *Olaus* affirmeth, are of that strength and bigness, as able to penetrate the ribs of ships. The same is more probable, because it was brought from Island, from whence, as *Becanus* affirmeth, three other were brought in his days: And we have heard of some which have been found by the Sea-side, and brought unto us from *America*. So that while we commend the *Unicorns* Horn, and conceive it peculiar but unto one animal; under apprehension of the same vertue, we use very many; and commend that effect from all, which every one confineth unto some one he hath either seen or described.

Fifthly, Although there be many *Unicorns*, and consequently many Horns, yet many there are which bear that name, and currantly pass among us, which are no Horns at all. Such are those fragments and pieces of *Lapis Ceratites*, commonly termed *Cornu fossile*, whereof *Bœtius* had no less then twenty several sorts presented him for *Unicorns* Horn. Hereof in subterraneous cavities, and under the earth there are many to be found in several parts of *Germany*; which are but the lapidescencies and petrifactive mutations of hard bodies; sometimes of Horn, of teeth, of bones, and branches of trees, whereof there are some so imperfectly converted, as to retaine the odor and qualities of their originals: as he relateth of pieces of Ash and Walnut. Again, in most if not all which pass amongst us, and are extolled for precious Horns, we discover not an affection common unto other Horns; that is, they mollifie not with fire, they soften not upon decoction or infusion, nor will they afford a jelly, or mucilaginous concretion in either; which notwithstanding we may effect in Goats horns, Sheeps, Cows and Harts-horn, in the Horn of the *Rhinoceros*, the horn of the Pristis or Sword-fish. Nor do they become friable or easily powderable by Philosophical calcination, that is, from the vapor or steam of water, but split and rift contrary to other horns. Briefly, many of those commonly received, and whereof there be so many fragments preserved in *England*, are not only no Horn, but a substance harder then a bone, that is, parts of the tooth of a Morse or Sea-horse; in the midst of the solider part containing a curdled grain, which is not to be found in Ivory. This in Northern Regions is of frequent use for hafts of knives or hilts of swords, and being burnt becomes a good remedy for fluxes: but Antidotally used, and exposed for *Unicorns* Horn, it is an insufferable delusion; and with more veniable deceit, it might have beene practised in Harts-horn.

The like deceit may be practised in the teeth of other Sea-animals; in the teeth also of the *Hippopotamus*, or great Animal which frequenteth the River *Nilus*: For we read that the same was anciently used instead of Ivory or Elephants tooth. Nor is it to be omitted, what hath been formerly suspected, but now confirmed by *Olaus Wormius*, and *Thomas Bartholinus* and others, that those long Horns preserved as pretious rarities in many places, are but the teeth of Narhwales; to be found about Island, Greenland, and other Northern regions; of many feet long, commonly wreathed, very deeply fastned in the upper jaw, and standing directly forward, graphically described in *Bartholinus*, according unto one sent from a Bishop of Island, not separated from the crany. Hereof *Mercator* hath taken notice in his description of Island: some relations hereof there seem to be in *Purchas*, who also delivereth that the horn at *Windsor*, was in his second voyage brought hither by *Frobisher*. These before the Northern discoveries, as unknown rarities, were carried by Merchants into all parts of *Europe*; and though found on the Sea-shore, were sold at very high rates; but are now become more common, and probably in time will prove of little esteem; and the bargain of *Julius* the third, be accounted a very hard one, who stuck not to give many thousand crowns for one.

Nor is it great wonder we may be so deceived in this, being daily gulled in the brother Antidote Bezoar; whereof though many be false, yet one there passeth amongst us of more intollerable delusion; somewhat paler then the true stone, and given by women in the extremity of great diseases, which notwithstanding is no stone, but seems to be the stony seed of some Lithospermum or greater Grumwell; or the Lobus Echinatus of *Clusius*, called also the Bezoar Nut; for being broken, it discovereth a kernel of a leguminous smell and tast, bitter like a Lupine, and will swell and sprout if set in the ground, and therefore more serviceable for issues, then dangerous and virulent diseases.

Sixthly, Although we were satisfied we had the *Unicorns* Horn, yet were it no injury unto reason to question the efficacy thereof, or whether those virtues pretended do properly belong unto it. For what we observe (and it escaped not the observation of *Paulus Jovius* many years past) none of the Ancients ascribed any medicinal or antidotal vertue unto the *Unicorns* Horn; and that which *Ælian* extolleth, who was the first and only man of the Ancients who spake of the medical virtue of any *Unicorn*, was the Horn of the *Indian* Ass; whereof, saith he, the Princes of those parts make bowls and drink therein, as preservatives against Poyson, Convulsions, and the Falling-sickness. Now the description of that Horn is not agreeable unto that we commend; for that (saith he) is red above, white below, and black in the middle; which is very different from ours, or any to be seen amongst us. And thus, though the description of the *Unicorn* be very ancient, yet was there of old no vertue ascribed unto it; and although this amongst us receive the opinion of the same vertue, yet is it not the same Horn whereunto the Antients ascribed it.

Lastly, although we allow it an Antidotal efficacy, and such as the Ancients commended, yet are there some vertues ascribed thereto by Moderns not easily to be received; and it hath surely faln out in this, as other magnified medicines, whose operations effectual in some diseases, are presently extended unto all. That some Antidotal quality it may have, we have no reason to deny; for since Elks Hoofs and Horns are magnified for Epilepsies, since not only the bone in the heart, but the Horn of a Deer is Alexipharmacal, and ingredient into the confection of Hyacinth, and the Electuary of Maximilian; we cannot without prejudice except against the efficacy of this. But when we affirm it is not only Antidotal to proper venoms, and substances destructive by qualities we cannot express; but that it resisteth also Sublimate, Arsenick, and poysons which kill by second qualities, that is, by corrosion of parts; I doubt we exceed the properties of its nature, and the promises of experiment will not secure the adventure. And therefore in such extremities, whether there be not more probable relief from fat oyly substances, which are the open tyrants over salt and corrosive bodies, then precious and cordial medicines which operate by secret and disputable proprieties; or whether he that swallowed Lime, and dranke down Mercury water, did not more reasonably place his cure in milk, butter or oyl, then if he had recurred unto Pearl and Bezoar, common reason at all times, and necessity in the like case would easily determine.

Since therefore there be many *Unicorns*; since that whereto we appropriate a Horn is so variously described, that it seemeth either never to have been seen by two persons, or not to have been one animal; Since though they agreed in the description of the animal, yet is not the Horn we extol the same with that of the Ancients; Since what Horns soever they be that pass among us, they are not the Horns of one, but several animals; Since many in common use and high esteem are no Horns at all; Since if they were true Horns, yet might their vertues be questioned; Since though we allowed some vertues, yet were not others to be received; with what security a man may rely on this remedy, the mistress of fools hath already instructed some, and to wisdom (which is never too wise to learn) it is not too late to consider.

CHAPTER XXIV

That all Animals of the Land, are in their kind in the Sea.

That all Animals of the Land, are in their kind in the Sea, although received as a principle, is a tenent very questionable, and will admit of restraint. For some in the Sea are not to be matcht by any enquiry at Land, and hold those shapes which terrestrious forms approach not; as may be observed in the Moon fish, or Orthragoriscus, the several sorts of Raia's, Torpedo's, Oysters, and many more, and some there are in the Land which were never maintained to be in the Sea, as Panthers, Hyæna's, Camels, Sheep, Molls, and others, which carry no name in Ichthyology, nor are to be found in the exact descriptions of *Rondeletius*, *Gesner*, or *Aldrovandus*.

Again, Though many there be which make out their nominations, as the Hedg-Hog, Sea-serpents and others; yet are there also very many that bear the name of animals at Land, which hold no resemblance in corporal configuration; in which account we compute *Vulpecula, Canis, Rana, Passer, Cuculus, Asellus, Turdus, Lepus*, &c. Wherein while some are called the Fox, the Dog, the Sparrow or Frog-fish, and are known by common names with those at Land; yet as their describers attest, they receive not these appellations from a total similitude in figure, but any concurrence in common accidents, in colour, condition or single conformation. As for Sea-horses which much confirm this assertion; in their common descriptions, they are but Grotesco deliniations which fill up empty spaces in Maps, and meer pictorial inventions, not any Physical shapes: sutable unto those which (as *Pliny* delivereth) *Praxiteles* long ago set out in the Temple of *Domitius*. For that which is commonly called a Sea-horse, is properly called a Morse, and makes not out that shape. That which the Ancients named *Hippocampus* is a little animal about six inches long, and not preferred beyond the classis of Insects. That which they termed *Hippopotamus* an amphibious animal, about the River *Nile*, so little resembleth an horse, that as *Mathiolus* observeth, in all except the feet, it better makes out a swine. That which they termed a Lion, was but a kind of Lobster: that which they called the Bear, was but one kind of Crab: and that which they named *Bos marinus*, was not as we conceive a fish resembling an Ox, but a Skait or Thornback, so named from its bigness, expressed by the Greek word *Bous*, which is a prefix of augmentation to many words in that language.

And therefore although it be not denied that some in the water do carry a justifiable resemblance to some at Land, yet are the major part which bear their names unlike; nor do they otherwise resemble the creatures on earth, then they on earth the constellations which pass under animal names in heaven: nor the Dog-fish at Sea much more make out the Dog of the Land, then that his cognominal or name-sake in the heavens. Now if from a similitude in some, it be reasonable to infer a correspondence in all, we may draw this analogy of animals upon plants; for vegetables there are which carry a near and allowable similitude unto animals. We might also conclude that animal shapes were generally made out in minerals: For several stones there are that bare their names in relation to animals or their parts, as *Lapis anguinus*, *Conchites*, *Echinites*, *Encephalites*, *Ægopthalmus*, and many more; as will appear in the Writers of Minerals, and especially in *Bœtius* and *Aldrovandus*.

Moreover if we concede, that the animals of one Element, might bear the names of those in the other, yet in strict reason the watery productions should have the prenomination: and they of the land rather derive their names, then nominate those of the Sea. For the watery plantations were first existent, and as they enjoyed a priority in form, had also in nature precedent denominations: but falling not under than Nomenclature of *Adam*, which unto terrestrious animals assigned a name appropriate unto their natures: from succeeding spectators they received arbitrary appellations; and were respectively denominated unto creatures known at Land; who in themselves had independent names and not to be called after them, which were created before them.

Lastly, By this assertion we restrain the hand of God, and abridge the variety of the creation; making the creatures of one Element, but an acting over those of another, and conjoyning as it were the species of things which stood at distance in the intellect of God; and though united in the Chaos, had several seeds of their creation. For although in that distinguisht mass, all things seemed one; yet separated by the voice of God, according to their species, they came out in incommunicate varieties, and irrelative seminalities, as well as divided places; and so although we say the world was made in six days, yet was there as it were a world in every one; that is, a distinct creation of distinguisht creatures; a distinction in time of creatures divided in nature, and a several approbation and survey in every one.

CHAPTER XXV

Concerning the common course of Diet, in making choice of some Animals, and abstaining from eating others.

Why we confine our food unto certain Animals, and totally reject some others; how these distinctions crept into several Nations; and whether this practice be built upon solid reason, or chiefly supported by custom or opinion; may admit consideration.

For first there is no absolute necessity to feed on any; and if we resist not the stream of Authority, and several diductions from holy Scripture: there was no *Sarcophagie* before the flood; and without the eating of flesh, our fathers from vegetable aliments, preserved themselves unto longer lives, then their posterity by any other. For whereas it is plainly said, I have given you every herb which is upon the face of all the earth, and every tree, to you it shall be for meat; presently after the deluge, when the same had destroyed or infirmed the nature of vegetables, by an expression of enlargement, it is again delivered: Every moving thing that liveth, shall be meat for you, even as the green herb, have I given you all things.

And therefore although it be said that Abel was a Shepherd, and it be not readily conceived, the first men would keep sheep, except they made food thereof: great Expositors will tell us, that it was partly for their skins, wherewith they were cloathed, partly for their milk, whereby they were sustained; and partly for Sacrifices, which they also offered.

And though it may seem improbable, that they offered flesh, yet eat not thereof; and *Abel* can hardly be said to offer the firstlings of his flock, and the fat or acceptable part, if men used not to tast the same, whereby to raise such distinctions: some will confine the eating of flesh unto the line of *Cain*, who extended their luxury, and confined not unto the rule of God. That if at any time the line of *Seth* eat flesh, it was extraordinary, and only at their sacrifices; or else (as *Grotius* hinteth) if any such practice there were, it was not from the beginning; but from that time when the waies of men were corrupted, and whereof it is said, that the wickedness of mans heart was great; the more righteous part of mankind probably conforming unto the diet prescribed in Paradise, and the state of innocency. And yet however the practice of men conformed, this was the injunction of God, and might be therefore sufficient, without the food of flesh.

That they fed not on flesh, at least the faithful party before the flood, may become more probable, because they refrained the same for some time after. For so was it generally delivered of the golden age and raign of *Saturn*; which is conceived the time of *Noah*, before the building of *Babel*. And he that considereth how agreeable this is unto the traditions of the *Gentiles*; that that age was of one tongue: that *Saturn* devoured all his sons but three, that he was the son of *Oceanus* and *Thetis*; that a Ship was his Symbole, that he taught the culture of vineyards, and that art of husbandry, and was therefore described with a sickle, may well conceive, these traditions had their original in *Noah*. Nor did this practice terminate in him, but was continued at least in many after: as (beside the *Pythagorians* of old, *Bannyans* now in *India*, who upon single opinions refrain the food of flesh) ancient records do hint or plainly deliver. Although we descend not so low, as that of *Æsclepiades* delivered by *Porphyrius*, that men began to feed on flesh in the raign of *Pygmaleon* brother of *Dido*, who invented several torments, to punish the eaters of flesh.

Nor did men only refrain from the flesh of beasts at first, but as some will have it, beasts from one another. And if we should believe very grave conjecturers, carnivorous animals now, were not flesh devourers then, according to the expression of the divine provision for them. To every beast of the earth, and to every fowl of the air, I have given every green herb for meat, and it was so. As is also collected from the store laid up in the Ark; wherein there seems to have been no fleshly provision for carnivorous Animals. For of every kind of un-

246

clean beast there went but two into the Ark: and therefore no stock of flesh to sustain them many days, much less almost a year.

But when ever it be acknowledged that men began to feed on flesh, yet how they betook themselves after to particular kinds thereof, with rejection of many others, is a point not clearly determined. As for the distinction of clean and unclean beasts, the original is obscure, and salveth not our practice, For no Animal is naturally unclean, or hath this character in nature; and therefore whether in this distinction there were not some mystical intention: whether *Moses* after the distinction made of unclean beasts, did not name these so before the flood by anticipation: whether this distinction before the flood, were not only in regard of sacrifices, as that delivered after was in regard of food: (for many were clean for food, which were unclean for sacrifice) or whether the denomination were but comparative, and of beasts less commodious for food, although not simply bad, is not yet resolved.

And as for the same distinction in the time of *Moses*, long after the flood, from thence we hold no restriction, as being no rule unto Nations beside the *Jews* in dietetical consideration, or natural choice of diet, they being enjoyned or prohibited certain foods upon remote and secret intentions. Especially thereby to avoid community with the Gentiles upon promiscuous commensality: or to divert them from the Idolatry of *Egypt* whence they came, they were enjoyned to eat the Gods of *Egypt* in the food of Sheep and Oxen. Withall in this distinction of Animals the consideration was hieroglyphical; in the bosom and inward sense implying an abstinence from certain vices symbolically intimated from the nature of those animals; as may be well made out in the prohibited meat of Swine, Cony, Owl, and many more.

At least the intention was not medical, or such as might oblige unto conformity or imitation; For some we refrain which that Law alloweth, as Locusts and many others; and some it prohibiteth, which are accounted good meat in strict and Medical censure: as (beside many fishes which have not finns and scales,) the Swine, Cony and Hare, a dainty dish with the Ancients; as is delivered by *Galen*, testified by *Martial*, as the popular opinion implied, that men grew fair by the flesh thereof: by the diet of *Cato*, that is Hare and Cabbage; and the *Jus nigrum*, or Black broth of the *Spartans*, which was made with the blood and bowels of an Hare.

And if we take a view of other Nations, we shall discover that they refrained many meats upon the like considerations. For in some the abstinence was symbolical; so *Pythagoras* enjoyned abstinence from fish: that is, luxurious and dainty dishes; So according to *Herodotus*, some *Egyptians* refrained swines flesh, as an impure and sordid animal: which whoever but touched, was fain to wash himself.

Some abstained superstitiously or upon religious consideration: So the *Syrians* refrained Fish and Pigeons; the *Egyptians* of old, Dogs, Eeles, and Crocodiles; though *Leo Africanus* delivers, that many of late, do eat them with good gust: and *Herodotus* also affirmeth, that the *Egyptians* of *Elephantina* (unto whom they were not sacred,) did eat thereof in elder times: and Writers testify, that they are eaten at this day in *India* and *America*. And so, as *Cæsar* reports, unto the ancient *Britains* it was piaculous to tast a Goose, which dish at present no table is without.Unto some Nations the abstinence was political and for some civil advantage: So the *Thessalians* refrained Storks, because they destroyed their Serpents; and the like in sundry animals is observable in other Nations.

And under all these considerations were some animals refrained: so the *Jews* abstained from swine at first symbolically, as an Emblem of impurity; and not for fear of the Leprosie, as *Tacitus* would put upon them. The *Cretians* superstitiously, upon tradition that *Jupiter* was suckled in that countrey by a Sow. Some *Egyptians* politically, because they supplyed the labour of plowing by rooting up the ground. And upon like considerations perhaps the Phœnicians and *Syrians* fed not on this Animal: and as *Solinus* reports, the *Arabians* also and *Indians*. A great part of mankind refraining one of the best foods, and such as Pythagoras himself would eat; who, as Aristoxenus records refused not to feed on Pigs.

Moreover while we single out several dishes and reject others, the selection seems but arbitrary, or upon opinion; for many are commended and cryed up in one age, which are decryed and nauseated in another. Thus in the dayes of *Mecenas*, no flesh was preferred before young Asses; which notwithstanding became abominable unto succeeding appetites. At the table of *Heliogabalus* the combs of Cocks were an esteemed service; which country stomacks will not admit at ours. The Sumen or belly and dugs of swine with Pig, and sometimes beaten and bruised unto death: the womb of the same Animal, especially that was barren, or else had cast her young ones, though a tough and membranous part, was magnified by Roman Pallats; whereunto nevertheless we cannot perswade our stomacks. How *Alec, Muria*, and *Garum*, would humour our gust I know not; but surely few there are that could delight in the *Cyceon*; that is, the common draught of Honey, Cheese, parcht Barley-flower, Oyl and Wine; which notwithstanding was a commended mixture, and in high esteem among them. We mortifie our selves with the diet of fish, and think we fare coursly if we refrain from the flesh of other animals. But antiquity held another opinion hereof: When *Pythagoras* in prevention of luxury advised, not so much as to tast on fish. Since the *Rhodians* were wont to call them clowns that eat flesh: and since *Plato* to evidence the temperance of the noble *Greeks* before *Troy*, observed, that it was not found they fed on fish, though they lay so long near the *Helespont*; and was only observed in the companions of *Menelaus*, that being almost starved, betook themselves to fishing about *Pharos*.

Nor will (I fear) the attest or prescript of Philosophers and Physitians, be a sufficient ground to confirm or warrant common practice, as is deducible from ancient Writers, from *Hippocrates, Galen, Simeon, Sethi*: and the later tracts of *Nonnus* and *Castellanus*. So *Aristotle* and *Albertus* commend the flesh of young Hawks: *Galen* the flesh of Foxes about Autumn when they feed on Grapes: but condemneth Quails, and ranketh Geese but with Ostriches: which notwithstanding, present practice and every table extolleth. Men think they have fared hardly, if in times of extremity they have descended so low as Dogs: but *Galen* delivereth, that young, fat and gelded, they were the food of Many Nations: and *Hippocrates* ranketh the flesh of Whelps with that of Birds: who also commends them against the Spleen, and to promote conception. The opinion in *Galens* time, which *Pliny* also followeth, deeply condemned Horse-flesh, and conceived the very blood thereof destructive; but no diet is more common among the *Tartars*, who also drink their blood. And though this may only seem an adventure of *Northern* stomacks, yet as *Herodotus* tells us, in the hotter clime of *Persia*, the same was a convivial dish, and solemnly eaten at the feasts of their nativities: whereat they dressed whole Horses, Camels and Asses; contemning the Poverty of *Grecian* feasts, as unfurnish'd of dishes sufficient to fill the bellies of their guests.

Again, while we confine our diet in several places, all things almost are eaten, if we take in the whole earth: for that which is refused in one country, is accepted in another, and in the collective judgment of the world, particular distinctions are overthrown. Thus were it not hard to shew, that Tigers, Elephants, Camels, Mice, Bats and others, are the food of several countries; and *Lerius* with others delivers, that some *Americans* eat of all kinds, not refraining Toads and Serpents: and some have run so high, as not to spare the flesh of man: a practice inexcusable, not to be drawn into example, a diet beyond the rule and largest indulgence of God.

As for the objection against beasts and birds of prey, it acquitteth not our practice, who observe not this distinction in fishes: nor regard the same in our diet of Pikes, Perches and Eels; Nor are we excused herein, if we examine the stomacks of Mackerels, Cods, and Whitings. Nor is the foulness of food sufficient to justifie our choice; for (beside their natural heat is able to convert the same into laudable aliment) we refuse not many whose diet is more impure then some which we reject; as may be considered in hogs, ducks, puets, and many more.

Thus we perceive the practise of diet doth hold no certain course, nor solid rule of selection or confinement; Some in an indistinct voracity eating almost any, other out of a timerous pre-opinion, refraining very many. Wherein indeed necessity, reason and Physick, are the best determinators. Surely many animals may be fed on, like many plants; though not in alimental, yet medical considerations: Whereas having raised Antipathies by prejudgement or education, we often nauseate proper meats, and abhor that diet which disease or temper requireth.

Now whether it were not best to conform unto the simple diet of our fore-fathers, whether pure and simple waters were not more healthfull then fermented liquors; whether there be not an ample sufficiency without all flesh, in the food of honey, oyl, and the several parts of milk: in the variety of grains, pulses, and all sorts of fruits; since either bread or beverage may be made almost of all? whether nations have rightly confined unto several meats? or whether the common food of one countrey be not more agreeable unto another? how indistinctly all tempers apply unto the same, and how the diet of youth and old age is confounded: were considerations much concerning health, and might prolong our days, but must not this discourse.

CHAPTER XXVI

Of Sperma-Ceti, and the Sperma-Ceti Whale

What Sperma-Ceti is, men might justly doubt, since the learned *Hofmanus* in his work of Thirty years, saith plainly, *Nescio quid sit*. And therefore need not wonder at the variety of opinions; while some conceived it to be *flos maris*, and many, a bituminous substance floating upon the sea.

That it was not the spawn of the Whale, according to vulgar conceit, or nominal appellation Phylosophers have always doubted: not easily conceiving the Seminal humour of Animals, should be inflamable; or of a floating nature.

That it proceedeth from a Whale, beside the relation of *Clusius* and other learned observers, was indubitably determined, not many years since by a Sperma-Ceti Whale, cast on our coast of *Norfolk*. Which, to lead on further inquiry, we cannot omit to inform. It contained no less then sixty foot in length, the head somewhat peculiar, with a large prominency over the mouth; teeth only in the lower Jaw, received into fleshly sockets in the upper. The Weight of the largest about two pound: No gristly substances in the mouth, commonly called Whale-bones; Only two short finns seated forwardly on the back; the eyes but small, the pizell large, and prominent. A lesser Whale of this kind above twenty years ago, was cast upon the same shore.

The description of this Whale seems omitted by *Gesner, Rondeletius*, and the first Editions of *Aldrovandus*; but described in the Latin impression of *Pareus*, in the *Exoticks* of *Clusius*, and the natural history of *Nirembergius*; but more amply in Icons and figures of *Johnstonus*.

Mariners (who are not the best Nomenclators) called it a *Jubartus*, or rather *Gibbartas*. Of the same appellation we meet with one in *Rondeletius*, called by the *French* Gibbar, from its round and Gibbous back. The name *Gibbarta* we find also given unto one kind of *Greenland* Whales: But this of ours seemed not to answer the Whale of that denomination; but was more agreeable unto the *Trumpa* or Sperma-Ceti Whale: according to the account of our *Greenland* describers in *Purchas*. And maketh the third among the eight remarkable Whales of that Coast.

Out of the head of this Whale, having been dead divers days, and under putrifaction, flowed streams of oyl and Sperma-Ceti; which was carefully taken up and preserved by the Coasters. But upon breaking up, the Magazin of Sperma-Ceti, was found in the head lying in folds and courses, in the bigness of goose eggs, encompassed with large flaxie substances, as large as a mans head, in form of honycombs, very white and full of oyl.

Some resemblance or trace hereof there seems to be in the *Physiter* or *Capidolio* of *Rondeletius*; while he delivers, that a fatness more liquid then oyl, runs from the brain of that animal; which being out, the Reliques are like the scales of *Sardinos* pressed into a mass; which melting with heat, are again concreted by cold. And this many conceive to have been the fish which swallowed *Jonas*. Although for the largeness of the mouth, and frequency in those seas, it may possibly be the *Lamia*.

Some part of the Sperma-Ceti found on the shore was pure, and needed little depuration; a great part mixed with fetid oyl, needing good preparation, and frequent expression, to bring it to a flakie constituency. And not only the head, but other parts contained it. For the carnous parts being roasted, the oyl dropped out, an axungious and thicker part subsiding; the oyl it self contained also much in it, and still after many years some is obtained from it.

Greenland Enquirers seldom meet with a Whale of this kind: and therefore it is but a contingent Commodity, not reparable from any other. It flameth white and candent like Camphire, but dissolveth not in *aqua fortis*, like it. Some lumps containing about two ounces, kept ever since in water, afford a fresh, and flosculous smell. Well prepared and separated from the oyl, it is of a substance unlikely to decay, and may out last the oyl required in the Composition of *Mathiolus*.

Of the large quantity of oyl, what first came forth by expression from the Sperma-Ceti, grew very white and clear, like that of Almonds or Ben. What came by decoction was red. It was found to spend much in the vessels which contained it: It freezeth or coagulateth quickly with cold, and the newer soonest. It seems different from the oyl of any other animal, and very much frustrated the expectation of our soap-boylers, as not incorporating or mingling with their lyes. But it mixeth well with painting Colours, though hardly drieth at all. Combers of wooll made use hereof, and Country people for cuts, aches and hard tumours. It may prove of good Medical use; and serve for a ground in compounded oyls and Balsams. Distilled, it affords a strong oyl, with a quick and piercing water. Upon Evaporation it gives a balsame, which is better performed with Turpentine distilled with Sperma-Ceti.

Had the abominable scent permitted, enquiry had been made into that strange composure of the head, and hillock of flesh about it. Since the Work-men affirmed, they met with *Sperma-Ceti* before they came to the bone, and the head yet preserved, seems to confirm the same. The Sphincters inserving unto the Fistula or spout, might have been examined, since they are so notably contrived in other cetaceous Animals; as also the Larynx or Throtle, whether answerable unto that of Dolphins and Porposes in the strange composure and figure which it maketh. What figure the stomack maintained in this Animal of one jaw of teeth, since in Porposes, which abound in both, the ventricle is trebly divided, and since in that formerly taken nothing was found but Weeds and a Loligo. The heart, lungs, and kidneys, had not escaped; wherein are remarkable differences from Animals of the land, likewise what humor the bladder contained, but especially the seminal parts, which might have determined the difference of that humor, from this which beareth its name.

In vain it was to rake for Ambergreece in the panch of this *Leviathan*, as *Greenland* discovers, and attests of experience dictate, that they sometimes swallow great lumps thereof in the Sea; insufferable fetour denying that enquiry. And yet if, as *Paracelsus* encourageth, Ordure makes the best Musk, and from the most fetid substances may be drawn the most odoriferous Essences; all that had not *Vespasians* Nose, might boldly swear, here was a subject fit for such extractions

CHAPTER XXVII

Compendiously of sundry Tenents concerning other Animals, which examined, prove either false or dubious.

1. And first from great Antiquity, and before the Melody of *Syrens*, the Musical note of Swans hath been commended, and that they sing most sweetly before their death. For thus we read in *Plato*, that from the opinion of *Metempsuchosis*, or transmigration of the souls of men into the bodies of beasts most sutable unto their humane condition, after his death, *Orpheus* the Musician became a Swan. Thus was it the bird of *Apollo* the god of Musick by the *Greeks*; and an Hieroglyphick of music among the *Egyptians*, from whom the *Greeks* derived the conception; hath been the affirmation of many Latines, and hath not wanted assertors almost from every Nation.

All which notwithstanding, we find this relation doubtfully received by *Ælian*, as an hear-say account by *Bellonius*, as a false one by *Pliny*, expresly refuted by *Myndius* in *Athenæus*; and severely rejected by *Scaliger*; whose words unto *Cardan* are these. *De Cygni vero cantu suavissimo quem cum parente mendaciorum Græcia jactare ausus est, ad Luciani tribunal, apud quem novi aliquid dicas, statuo.* Authors also that countenance it, speak not satisfactorily of it. Some affirming they sing not till they die; some that they sing, yet die not. Some speak generally, as though this note were in all; some but particularly, as though it were only in some; some in places remote, and where we can have no trial of it; others in places where every experience can refute it; as *Aldrovandus* upon relation delivered, concerning the Musick of the Swans on the river of *Thames* near *London*.

Now that which countenanceth, and probably confirmeth this opinion, is the strange and unusual conformation of the wind pipe, or vocal organ in this animal: observed first by *Aldrovandus*, and conceived by some contrived for this intention. For in its length it far exceedeth the gullet; and hath in the chest a sinuous revolution, that is, when it ariseth from the lungs, it ascendeth not directly unto the throat, but descending first into a capsulary reception of the breast bone; by a Serpentine and Trumpet recurvation it ascendeth again into the neck; and so by the length thereof a great quantity of air is received, and by the figure thereof a Musical modulation effected. But to speak indifferently, this formation of the Weazon, is not peculiar unto the Swan, but common also unto the Platea or Shovelard, a bird of no Musical throat; And as *Aldrovandus* confesseth, may thus be contrived in the Swan to contain a larger stock of air, whereby being to feed on weeds at the bottom, they might the longer space detain their heads under water. But were this formation peculiar, or had they unto this effect an advantage from this part: yet have they a known and open disadvantage from another; that is, a flat bill. For no Latirostrous animal (whereof nevertheless there are no slender numbers) were ever commended for their note, or accounted among those animals which have been instructed to speak.

When therefore we consider the dissention of Authors, the falsity of relations, the indisposition of the Organs, and the immusical note of all we ever beheld or heard of; if generally taken and comprehending all Swans, or of all places, we cannot assent thereto. Surely he that is bit with a Tarantula, shall never be cured by this Musick; and with the same hopes we expect to hear the harmony of the Spheres.

2. That there is a special propriety in the flesh of Peacocks, roast or boiled, to preserve a long time incorrupted, hath been the assertion of many; stands yet confirmed by *Austin, De Civitate Dei*; by *Gygas Sempronius* in *Aldrovandus*; and the same experiment we can confirm our selves, in the brawn or fleshly parts of Peacocks so hanged up with thred, that they touch no place whereby to contract a moisture; and hereof we have made trial both in summer and winter. The reason, some, I perceive, attempt to make out from the siccity and driness of its flesh, and some are content to rest in a secret propriety thereof. As for the siccity of the flesh, it is more remarkable in other animals, as Eagles, Hawks, and birds of prey; That it is a propriety or agreeable unto none other, we cannot, with reason admit; for the same

preservation, or rather incorruption we have observed in the flesh of Turkeys, Capons, Hares, Partridge, Venison, suspended freely in the air, and after a year and a half, dogs have not refused to eat them.

As for the other conceit, that a Peacock is ashamed when he looks on his legs, as is commonly held, and also delivered by *Cardan*; beside what hath been said against it by *Scaliger*; let them believe that hold specificial deformities; or that any part can seem unhandsome to their eyes, which hath appeared good and beautiful unto their makers. The occasion of this conceit, might first arise from a common observation, that when they are in their pride, that is, advance their train, if they decline their neck to the ground, they presently demit, and let fall the same: which indeed they cannot otherwise do; for contracting their body, and being forced to draw in their foreparts to establish the hinder in the elevation of the train; if the foreparts depart and incline to the ground, the hinder grow too weak, and suffer the train to fall. And the same in some degree is also observable in the Turkeys.

3. That Storks are to be found, and will only live in Republikes or free States, is a petty conceit to advance the opinion of popular policies, and from Antipathies in nature, to disparage Monarchical government. But how far agreeable unto truth, let them consider who read in *Pliny*, that among the *Thessalians* who were governed by Kings, and much abounded with Serpents, it was no less then capital to kill a Stork. That the Ancient *Egyptians* honoured them, whose government was from all times Monarchical. That *Bellonius* affirmeth, men make them nests in *France*. That relations make them common in *Persia*, and the dominions of the great *Turk*. And lastly, how *Jeremy* the Prophet delivered himself unto his countreymen, whose government was at that time Monarchical. The Stork in the heaven knowing her appointed time, the Turtile, Crane, and Swallow observe the time of their coming, but my people know not the judgment of the Lord. Wherein to exprobrate their stupidity, he induceth the providence of Storks. Now if the bird had been unknown, the illustration had been obscure, and the exprobration not so proper.

4. That a Bittor maketh that mugient noise, or as we term it Bumping, by putting its bill into a reed as most believe, or as *Bellonius* and *Aldrovandus* conceive, by putting the same in water or mud, and after a while retaining the air by suddenly excluding it again, is not so easily made out. For my own part, though after diligent enquiry, I

could never behold them in this motion; Notwithstanding by others whose observations we have expressly requested, we are informed, that some have beheld them making this noise on the shore, their bils being far enough removed from reed or water; that is, first strongly attracting the air, and unto a manifest distention of the neck, and presently after with great contention and violence excluding the same again. As for what Authors affirm of putting their bill in water or mud, it is also hard to make out. For what may be observed from any that walketh the Fens, there is little intermission, nor any observable pawse, between the drawing in and sending forth of their breath. And the expiration or breathing forth doth not only produce a noise, but the inspiration or hailing in of the air, affordeth a sound that may be heard almost a flight-shot.

Now the reason of this strange and peculiar noise, is deduced from the conformation of the wind-pipe, which in this bird is different from other volatiles. For at the upper extream it hath no fit Larinx, or throttle to qualify the sound, and at the other end, by two branches deriveth it self into the lungs. Which division consisteth only of Semicircular fibers, and such as attain but half way round the part; By which formation they are dilatable into larger capacities, and are able to contain a fuller proportion of air; which being with violence sent up the weazon, and finding no resistance by the Larinx, it issueth forth in a sound like that from caverns, and such as sometimes subterraneous eruptions, from hollow rocks afford. As *Aristotle* observeth in a Problem, and is observable in pitchers, bottles, and that instrument which *Aponensis* upon that Problem describeth, wherewith in *Aristotles* time Gardiners affrighted birds.

Whether the large perforations of the extremities of the weazon, in the *abdomen*, admitting large quantity of ayr within the cavity of its membrans, as it doth in Frogs; may not much assist this mugiency or boation, may also be considered. For such as have beheld them making this noise out of the water, observe a large distention in their bodies; and their ordinary note is but like that of a Raven.

5. That whelps are blind nine days and then begin to see, is the common opinion of all, and some will be apt enough to descend unto oaths upon it. But this I find not answerable unto experience, for upon a strict observation of many, I have scarce found any that see the ninth day, few before the twelfth, and the eyes of some not open before the

fourteenth day. And this is agreeable unto the determination of *Aristotle*: who computeth the time of their anopsie or non-vision by that of their gestation. For some, saith he, do go with their young the sixt part of a year, two days over or under, that is, about sixty days or nine weeks; and the whelps of these see not till twelve days. Some go the fifth part of a year, that is, seventy one days, and these saith he, see not before the fourteenth day. Others do go the fourth part of the year, that is, three whole months, and these, saith he, are without sight no less then seventeen days. Wherein although the accounts be different, yet doth the least thereof exceed the term of nine days, which is so generally received. And this compute of *Aristotle* doth generally overthrow the common cause alleadged for this effect, that is , a precipitation or over-hasty exclusion before the birth be perfect, according unto the vulgar Adage, *Festinans canis cæcos parit catulos*: for herein the whelps of longest gestation, are also the latest in vision. The manner hereof is this. At the first littering, their eyes are fastly closed, that is, by coalition or joining together of the eyelids, and so continue untill about the twelfth day; at which time they begin to separate, and may be easily divelled or parted asunder; they open at the inward Canthis or greater Angle of the eye, and so by degrees dilate themselves quite open. An effect very strange, and the cause of much obscurity, wherein as yet mens enquiries are blind, and satisfaction not easily acquirable. What ever it be, thus much we may observe, those animals are only excluded without sight, which are multiparous and multifidous, that is, which have many at a litter, and have also their feet divided into many portions. For the Swine, although multiparous, yet being bisulcous, and only cloven hoofed, is not excluded in this manner, but farrowed with open eyes, as other bisulcous animals.

6. The Antipathy between a Toad and a Spider, and that they poisonously destroy each other, is very famous, and solemn stories have been written of their combats; wherein most commonly the victory is given unto the Spider. Of what Toads and Spiders it is to be understood would be considered. For the Phalangium and deadly Spiders, are different from those we generally behold in *England*. However the verity hereof, as also of many others, we cannot, but desire; for hereby we might be surely provided of proper Antidotes in cases which require them; But what we have observed herein, we cannot in reason conceal; who having in a Glass included a Toad with several Spiders, we beheld the Spiders without resistance to sit upon his head and pass over all his body; what at last upon advantage he

swallowed down, and that in few hours, unto the number of seven. And in the like manner will Toads also serve Bees, and are accounted enemies unto their Hives.

7. Whether a Lion be also afraid of a Cock, as is related by many, and believed by most, were very easie in some places to make trial. Although how far they stand in fear of that animal, we may sufficiently understand, from what is delivered by *Camerarius*, whose words in his *Symbola* are these: *Nostris temporibus in Aula serenissimi Principis Bavariæ, unus ex Leonibus miris saltibus in vicinam cujusdam domus aream sese dimisit, ubi Gallinaciorum cantum aut clamores nihil reformidans, ipsos una cum plurimis gallinis devoravit.* That is, In our time in the Court of the Prince of *Bavaria*, one of the Lions leaped down into a Neighbours yard, where nothing regarding the crowing or noise of the Cocks, he eat them up with many other Hens. And therefore a very unsafe defensative it is against the fury of this animal (and surely no better then Virginity or bloud Royal) which *Pliny* doth place in Cock broth: For herewith, saith he whoever is anointed (especially if Garlick be boiled therein) no Lion or Panther will touch him. But of an higher nature it were, and more exalted Antipathy, if that were certain which *Proclus* delivers, that solary *Dæmons*, and such as appear in the shape of Lions, will disappear and vanish, if a Cock be presented upon them.

8. It is generally conceived, an Ear-wig hath no Wings, and is reckoned amongst impennous insects by many; but he that shall narrowly observe them, or shall with a needle put a side the short and sheathy cases on their back, may extend and draw forth two wings of a proportionable length for flight, and larger then in many flies. The experiment of *Pennius* is yet more perfect, who with a Rush or Bristle so pricked them as to make them flie.

9. That Worms are exanguious Animals, and such as have no bloud at all, is the determination of Phylosophy, the general opinion of Scholars, and I know not well to dissent from thence my self. If so, surely we want a proper term whereby to express that humour in them which so strictly resembleth bloud: and we refer it unto the discernment of others what to determine of that red and sanguineous humor, found more plentifully about the Torquis or carneous Circle of great Worms in the Spring, affording in Linnen or Paper an indiscernable tincture from bloud. Or wherein that differeth from a vein, which in an

260

apparent blew runneth along the body, and if dexterously pricked with a lancet, emitteth a red drop, which pricked on either side it will not readily afford.

In the upper parts of Worms, there are likewise found certain white and oval Glandulosities, which Authors term Eggs, and in magnifying Glasses, they also represent them; how properly, may also be enquired; since if in them there be distinction of Sexes, these Eggs are to be found in both. For in that which is presumed to be their coition, their usual complication, or lateral adhesion above the ground, dividing suddenly with two Knives the adhering parts of both, I have found these Eggs, in either.

10. That Flies, Bees, &c. Do make that noise or humming sound by their mouth, or as many believe with their wings only, would be more warily asserted, if we consulted the determination of *Aristotle*, who as in sundry other places, so more expresly in his book of respiration, affirmeth this sound to be made by the illision of an inward spirit upon a pellicle or little membrane about the precinct or pectoral division of their body. If we also consider that a Bee or Flie, so it be able to move the body, will buz, though its head be off; that it will do the like if deprived of wings, reserving the head, whereby the body may be the better moved. And that some also which are big and lively will hum without either head or wing.

Nor is it only the beating upon this little membrane, by the inward and con-natural spirit as *Aristotle* determines, or the outward air as *Scaliger* conceiveth, which affordeth this humming noise, but most of the other parts may also concur hereto; as will be manifest, if while they hum we lay our finger on the back or other parts; for thereupon will be felt a serrous or jarring motion like that which happeneth while we blow on the teeth of a comb through paper; and so if the head or other parts of the trunk be touched with oyl, the sound will be much impaired, if not destroyed: for those being also dry and membranous parts, by attrition of the spirit do help to advance the noise: And therefore also the sound is strongest in dry weather, and very weak in rainy season, and toward winter; for then the air is moist, and the inward spirit growing weak, makes a languid and dumb allision upon the parts.

11. There is found in the Summer a kind of Spider called a Tainct, of a red colour, and so little of body that ten of the largest will hardly outway a grain; this by Country people is accounted a deadly poison unto Cows and Horses; who, if they suddenly die, and swell thereon, ascribe their death hereto, and will commonly say, they have licked a Tainct. Now to satisfie the doubts of men we have called this tradition unto experiment; we have given hereof unto Dogs, Chickens, Calves and Horses, and not in the singular in number; yet never could find the least disturbance ensue. There must be therefore other causes enquired of the sudden death and swelling of cattle; and perhaps this insect is mistaken, and unjustly accused for some other. For some there are which from elder times have been observed pernicious unto cattle, as the Buprestis or Burstcow, the Pityocampe or Eruca Pinnum, by *Dioscorides, Galen* and *Ætius*, the Staphilinus described by *Aristotle* and others, or those red Phalangious Spiders like Cantharides mentioned by *Muffetus*. Now although the animal may be mistaken and the opinion also false, yet in the ground and reason which makes men most to doubt the verity hereof, there may be truth enough, that is, the inconsiderable quantity of this insect. For that a poison cannot destroy in so small a bulk; we have no reason to affirm. For if as *Leo Africanus* reporteth, the tenth part of a grain of the poison of *Nubia*, will dispatch a man in two hours; if the bite of a Viper and sting of a Scorpion, is not conceived to impart so much; if the bite of an Asp will kill within an hour, yet the impression scarce visible, and the poison communicated not ponderable; we cannot as impossible reject this way of destruction; or deny the power of death in so narrow a circumscription.

12. Wondrous things are promised from the Glow-worm; from thence perpetual lights are pretended, and waters said to be distilled which afford a lustre in the night; and this is asserted by *Cardan, Albertus, Gaudentinus, Mizaldus* and many more. But hereto we cannot with reason assent: for the light made by this animal depends much upon its life. For when they are dead they shine not, nor alwaies while they live; but are obscure or light, according to the protrusion of their luminous parts, as observation will instruct us. For this flammeous light is not over all the body, but only visible on the inward side; in a small white part near the tail. When this is full and seemeth protruded, there ariseth a flame of a circular figure and Emerald green colour; which is discernable in any dark place in the day; but when it falleth and seemeth contracted, the light disappeareth, and the colour of the

part only remaineth. Now this light, as it appeareth and disappeareth in their life, so doth it go quite out at their death. As we have observed in some, which preserved in fresh grass have lived and shined eighteen days; but as they declined, and the luminous humor dryed, their light grew languid, and at last went out with their lives. Thus also the *Torpedo*, which alive hath a power to stupifie at a distance, hath none upon contaction being dead, as *Galen* and *Rondeletius* particularly experimented. And this hath also disappointed the mischief of those intentions, which study the advancement of poisons; and fancy destructive compositions from Asps or Vipers teeth, from Scorpions or Hornet stings. For these omit their efficacy in the death of the individual, and act but dependantly on their forms. And thus far also those Philosophers concur with us, which held the Sun and Stars were living creatures, for they conceived their lustre depended on their lives; but if they ever died, their light must also perish.

It were a Notable piece of Art to translate the light from the *Bononian* Stone into another Body; he that would attempt to make a shining Water from *Glow-worms*, must make trial when the Splendent part is fresh and turgid. For even from the great *American Glow-Worms*, and Flaming *Flies*, the light declineth as the luminous humour dryeth.

Now whether the light of animals, which do not occasionally shine from contingent causes, be of Kin unto the light of Heaven; whether the invisible flame of life received in a convenient matter, may not become visible, and the diffused ætherial light make little Stars by conglobation in idoneous parts of the compositum: whether also it may not have some original in the seed and spirit analogous unto the Element of Stars, whereof some glympse is observable in the little refulgent humor, at the first attempts of formation: Philosophy may yet enquire.

True it is, that a Glow-worm will afford a faint light, almost a day's space when many will conceive it dead; but this is a mistake in the compute of death, and term of disanimation; for indeed, it is not then dead, but if it be distended will slowly contract it self again, which when it cannot do, it ceaseth to shine any more. And to speak strictly, it is no easie matter to determine the point of death in Insects and Creatures who have not their vitalities radically confined unto one part; for they are not dead when they cease to move or afford the visible evidences of life; as may be observed in Flies, who, when they appear even desperate and quite forsaken of their forms, by vertue of the Sun or warm ashes will be revoked into life, and perform its functions again.

Now whether this lustre, a while remaining after death, dependeth not still upon the first impression, and light communicated or raised from an inward spirit, subsisting a while in a moist and apt recipient, nor long continuing in this, or the more remarkable *Indian* Glow-worm; or whether it be of another Nature, and proceedeth from different causes of illumination; yet since it confessedly subsisteth so little a while after their lives, how to make perpetual lights, and sublunary moons thereof as is pretended, we rationally doubt, thought not so sharply deny, with *Scaliger* and *Muffetus*.

13. The wisdom of the Pismire is magnified by all, and in the Panegyricks of their providence we alwaies meet with this, that to prevent the growth of Corn which they store up, they bite off the end thereof: And some have conceived that from hence they have their name in Hebrew: From whence ariseth a conceit that Corn will not grow if the extreams be cut or broken. But herein we find no security to prevent its germination; as having made trial in grains, whose ends cut off have notwithstanding suddenly sprouted, and accordingly to the Law of their kinds; that is, the roots of barley and oats at contrary ends, of wheat and rye at the same. And therefore some have delivered that after rainy weather they dry these grains in the Sun; which if effectual, we must conceive to be made in a high degree and above the progression of Malt; for that Malt will grow, this year hath informed us, and that unto a perfect ear.

And if that be true which is delivered by many, and we shall further experiment, that a decoction of Toad-stools if poured upon earth, will produce the same again: If Sow-thistles will abound in places manured with dung of Hogs, which feeds much upon that plant: If Horse-dung reproduceth oats; If winds and rains will transport the seminals of plants; it will not be easie to determine where the power of generation ceaseth. The forms of things may lie deeper then we conceive them; seminal principles may not be dead in the divided atoms of plants; but wandering in the ocean of nature, when they hit upon proportionable materials, may unite, and return to their visible selves again.

But the prudence of this animal is by knawing, piercing, or otherwise to destroy the little nebbe or principle of germination. Which notwithstanding is not easily discoverable; it being no ready business to meet with such grains in Ant-hils; and he must dig deep, that will seek them in Winter.

Chap XXVIII

Of some Others

That a Chicken is formed out of the yelk of the Egg, was the opinion of some Ancient Philosophers. Whether it be not the nutriment of the Pullet, may also be considered: Since umbilical vessels are carried unto it: Since much of the yelk remaineth after the Chicken is formed: Since in a Chicken newly hatched, the stomack is tinted yellow, and the belly full of yelk, which is drawn in at the navel or vessels towards the vent, as may be discerned in Chickens within a day or two before exclusion.

Whether the Chicken be made out of the white, or that be not also its aliment, is likewise very questionable: Since an umbilical vessal is derived unto it: Since after the formation and perfect shape of the Chicken, much of the white remaineth.

Whether it be not made out of the *grando*, gallature, germ or tred of the Egg, As *Aquapendente* informeth us, seemed to many of doubt: for at the blunter end it is not discovered after the Chicken is formed; by this also the yelk and white are continued, whereby it may conveniently receive its nutriment from them both.

Now that from such slender materials, nature should effect this production it is no more then is observed in other animals; and even in grains and kernels, the greatest part is but the nutriment of that generative particle, so disproportionable unto it.

A greater difficulty in the doctrine of Eggs, is, how the sperm of the Cock prolificates and makes the oval conception fruitful, or how it attaineth unto every Egg, since the vitellary or place of the yelk is very high: Since the ovary or part where the white involveth it, is in the second region of the matrix, which is somewhat long and inverted: Since also a Cock will in one day fertilitate the whole racemation or cluster of Eggs, which are not excluded in many weeks after.

But these at last, and how in the Cicatricula or little pale circle formation first beginneth, how the Grando or tredle, are but the poles and establishing particles of the tender membrans, firmly conserving the floating parts in their proper places, with many other observables, that ocular Philosopher, and singular discloser of truth, Dr. *Harvey* hath discovered, in that excellent discourse of Generation; So strongly erected upon the two great pillars of truth, experience and solid reason.

That the sex is discernable from the figure of Eggs, or that Cocks or Hens proceed from long or round ones, as many contend, experiment will easily frustrate.

The *Ægyptians* observed a better way to hatch their Eggs in Ovens, then the *Babylonians* to roast them at the bottom of a sling, by swinging them round about, till heat from motion had concocted them; for that confuseth all parts without any such effect.

Though slight distinction be made between boiled and roasted Eggs, yet is there no slender difference, for the one is much drier then the other: the Egg expiring less in the elixation or boiling; whereas in the assation or roasting, it will sometimes abate a dragm; that is, three-score grains in weight. So a new laid Egg will not so easily be boiled hard, because it contains a greater stock of humid parts; which must be evaporated, before the heat can bring the inexhalable parts into consistence.

Why the Hen hatcheth not the Egg in her belly, or maketh not at least some rudiment thereof within her self, by the natural heat of inward parts, since the same is performed by incubation from an outward warmth after; Why the Egg is thinner at one extream? Why there is some cavity or emptiness at the blunter end? Why we open them at that part? Why the greater end is first excluded? Why some Eggs are all red, as the Kestrils; some only red at one end, as those of Kites and Buzzards? why some Eggs are not Oval but Round, as those of fishes?

&c. Are problems, whose decisions would too much enlarge this discourse.

That Snakes and Vipers do sting or transmit their mischief by the tail, is a common expression not easily to be justified; and a determination of their venoms unto a part, wherein we could never find it; the poison lying about the teeth, and communicated by bite, in such as are destructive. And therefore when biting Serpents are mentioned in the Scripture, they are not differentially set down from such as mischief by stings; nor can conclusions be made conformable to this opinion, because when the Rod of Moses was turned into a Serpent, God determinately commanded him to take up the same by the tail.

Nor are all Snakes of such empoisoning qualities, as common opinion presumeth; as is confirmable from the ordinary green Snake with us, from several histories of domestick Snakes, from Ophiophagous nations, and such as feed upon Serpents.

Surely the destructive delusion of Satan in this shape, hath much enlarged the opinion of their mischief. Which notwithstanding was not so high with the heathens, in whom the Devil had wrought a better opinion of this animal, it being sacred unto the *Egyptians*, *Greeks* and *Romans*, and the common symbole of sanity. In the shape whereof *Æsculapius* the God of health appeared unto the *Romans*, accompanied their Embassadors to *Rome* from *Epidaurus*; and the same did stand in the *Tiberine* Isle upon the Temple of *Æsculapius*.

Some doubt many have of the Tarantula, or poisonous Spider of *Calabria*, and that magical cure of the bite thereof by Musick. But since we observe that many attest it from experience: Since the learned *Kircherus* hath positively averred it, and set down the songs and tunes solemnly used for it; Since some also affirm the Tarantula it self will dance upon certain stroaks, whereby they set their instruments against its poison; we shall not at all question it.

Much wonder is made of the Boramez, that strange plant-animal or vegetable Lamb of *Tartary*, which Wolves delight to feed on, which hath the shape of a Lamb, affordeth a bloody juyce upon breaking, and liveth while the plants be consumed about it. And yet if all this be no more, then the shape of a Lamb in the flower or seed, upon the top of the stalk, as we meet with the forms of Bees, Flies and Dogs in some others; he hath seen nothing that shall much wonder at it.

It may seem too hard to question the swiftness of Tigers, which hath therefore given names unto horses, Ships and Rivers, nor can we deny what all have thus affirmed; yet cannot but observe, that *Jacobus Bontius* late Physitian at *Java* in the East *Indies*, as an ocular and frequent witness is not afraid to deny it; to condemn *Pliny* who affirmeth it, and that indeed it is but a slow and tardigradous animal, and preying upon advantage, and otherwise may be escaped.

Many more there are whose serious enquiries we must request of others, and shall only awake considerations. Whether that common opinion that Snakes do breed out of the back or spinal marrow of man, doth build upon any constant root or seed in nature; or did not arise from contingent generation, in some single bodies remembered by *Pliny* or others, and might be paralleld since in living corruptions of the guts and other parts; which regularly proceed not to putrifactions of that nature.

Whether the story of the Remora be not unreasonably amplified; whether that of Bernacles and Goose-trees be not too much enlarged; whether the common history of Bees will hold, as large accounts have delivered; whether the brains of Cats be attended with such destructive malignities, as *Dioscorides* and others put upon them.

As also whether there be not some additional help of Art, unto the Numismatical and Musical shells, which we sometimes meet with in conchylious collections among us.

Whether the fasting spittle of man be poison unto Snakes and Vipers, as experience hath made us doubt? Whether the Nightingals setting with her breast against a thorn, be any more then that she placeth some prickels on the outside of her nest, or roosteth in thorny and prickly places, where Serpents may least approach her? Whether Mice may be bred by putrifaction as well as univocall production, as may easily be believed, if that receit to make Mice out of wheat will hold, which *Helmont* hath delivered. Whether Quails from any idiosyncracy or peculiarity of constitution, do innocuously feed upon

Hellebore, or rather sometime but medically use the same; because we perceive that Stares, which are commonly said harmlessly to feed on Hemlock, do not make good the tradition; and he that observes what vertigoes, cramps, and convulsions follow thereon in these animals, will be of our belief.

End of Book III

THE FOURTH

BOOK

Of many popular Tenents concerning Man,
which examined, prove either false or dubious.

Chapter I

Of the erectness of Man

That onely *Man* hath an Erect figure, and for to behold and look up toward heaven, according to that of the Poet,

Pronaque cum spectant animalia cætera terram,
Os homini sublime dedit, cælumque tueri
Jussit, & erectos ad sydera tollere vultus,

is a double assertion, whose first part may be true, if we take Erectness strictly, and so as *Galen* hath defined it; for they onely, saith he, have an Erect figure, whose spine and thigh-bone are carried in right lines; and so indeed of any we yet know *Man* only is Erect. For the thighs of other animals do stand at Angles with their spine, and have rectangular positions in Birds, and perfect Quadrupeds. Nor doth the Frog, though stretched out, or swimming, attaine the rectitude of *Man*, or carry its thigh without all angularity. And thus is it also true, that Man onely sitteth, if we define sitting to be a firmation of the body upon the *Ischias*: wherein if the position be just and natural, the Thigh-bone lyeth at right angles to the Spine, and the Leg-bone or Tibia to the Thigh. For others when they seem to sit, as *Dogs*, *Cats*, or *Lions*, doe make unto their Spine acute angles with their Thigh, and acute to the Thigh with their Shank. Thus is it likewise true, what *Aristotle* alledgeth in that Problem: why *Man* alone suffereth pollutions in the night? because *Man* only lyeth upon his Back; if we define not the same by every supine position, but when the Spine is in rectitude with the Thigh, and both with the arms lie parallel to the *Horizon*: so that a line through their Navel will pass through the Zenith and Centre of the Earth. And so cannot other Animals lie upon their Backs; for though the Spine lie parallel with the *Horizon*, yet will their Legs incline, and lie at angles unto it. And upon these three divers positions in *Man* wherein the Spine can only be at right lines with the Thigh, arise those remarkable postures, prone, supine, and Erect; which are but differenced in situation, or unangular postures upon the Back, the Belly and the Feet.

But if Erectness be popularly taken, and as it is largely opposed unto proneness, or the posture of animals looking downwards, carrying their venters or opposite part to the Spine directly towards the Earth, it may admit of question. For though in *Serpents* and *Lizards* we may truly allow a proneness, yet *Galen* acknowledgeth that perfect Quadrupeds, as *Horses*, *Oxen*, and *Camels*, are but partly prone, and have some part of Erectness. And *Birds* or flying Animals, are so far from this kind of proneness, that they are almost Erect; advancing the Head and Breast in their progression, and only prone in the Act of volitation or flying. And if that be true which is delivered of the *Penguin* or *Anser Magellanicus* often described in Maps about those *Straits*, that they goe Erect like *Men*, and with their Breast and Belly do make one line perpendicular unto the axis of the Earth; it will almost make up the exact Erectness of *Man*. Nor will that insect come very short which we have often beheld, that is, one kind of Locust which stands not prone, or a little inclining upward, but in a large Erectness, elevating alwaies the two fore Legs, and sustaining it self in the middle of the other four; by *Zoographers* called *Mantis*, and by the Common people of *Province*, *Prega Dio*, the Prophet and praying Locust; as being generally found in the posture of supplication, or such as resembleth ours, when we lift up our hands to Heaven.

As for the end of this Erection, to looke up toward Heaven; though confirmed by several testimonies, and the *Greek* Etymology of *Man*, it is not so readily to be admitted; and as a popular and vain conceit was Anciently rejected by *Galen*; who in his third, *De usu partium*, determines, that *Man* is Erect, because he was made with hands, and was therewith to exercise all Arts, which in any other figure he could not have performed; as he excellently declareth in that place where he also proves that *Man* could have beene made neither Quadruped nor Centaur.

And for the accomplishment of this intention, that is, to look up and behold the Heavens, *Man* hath a notable disadvantage in the Eye lid; whereof the upper is far greater then the lower, which abridgeth the sight upwards; contrary to those of *Birds*, who herein have the advantage of *Man*: Insomuch that the learned *Plempius* is bold to affirm, that if he had had the formation of the Eye-lids, he would have contrived them quite otherwise.

The ground and occasion of this conceit was a literall apprehension of a figurative expression in *Plato*, as *Galen* thus delivers; To opinion that *Man* is Erect to look up and behold the Heavens, is a conceit only fit for those that never saw the *Fish* Uranoscopus, that is, the Beholder of Heaven; which hath its Eyes so placed, that it looks up directly to Heaven, which *Man* doth not, except he recline, or bend his head backward: and thus to look up to Heaven, agreeth not onely unto *Men*, but *Asses*; to omit *Birds* with long necks, which look not only upwards, but round about at pleasure. And therefore *Men* of this opinion understood not *Plato* when he said that *Man* doth *Sursum aspicere*; for thereby was not meant to gape, or look upward with the Eye, but to have his thoughts sublime, and not only to behold, but speculate their Nature, with the Eye of the understanding.

Now although *Galen* in this place makes instance but in one, yet are there other fishes, whose eyes regard the heavens, as *Plane*, and Cartilagineous *Fishes*; as *Pectinals*, or such as have their bones made laterally like a Combe; for when they apply themselves to sleep or rest upon the white side, their Eyes on the other side look upward toward Heaven. For *Birds*, they generally carry their heads Erectly like *Man*, and have advantage in their upper Eye-lid; and many that have long necks, and bear their heads somewhat backward, behold far more of the Heavens, and seem to look above the æquinoxial Circle. And so also in many Quadrupeds, although their progression be partly prone, yet is the sight of their Eye direct, not respecting the Earth but Heaven, and makes an higher Arch of altitude then our own. The position of a *Frog* with his head above water exceedeth these; for therein he seems to behold a large part of the Heavens, and the acies of his Eye to ascend as high as the Tropick; but he that hath behold the posture of a *Bittor*, will not deny that it beholds almost the very *Zenith*.

Chapter II

Of the Heart.

That the *Heart* of Man is seated in the left side, is an asseveration, which strictly taken, is refutable by inspection, whereby it
appeares the base and centre thereof is in the midst of the chest; true it
is, that the Mucro or Point thereof inclineth unto the left; for by this
position it giveth way unto the ascension of the midriff, and by reason
of the hollow vein could not commodiously deflect unto the right.
From which diversion, neverthelesse we cannot so properly say tis
placed in the left, as that it consisteth in the middle, that is, where its
centre resteth; for so doe we usually say a Gnomon or Needle is in the
middle of a Dial, although the extreams may respect the North or
South, and approach the circumference thereof.

The ground of this mistake is a general observation from the
pulse or motion of the *Heart*, which is more sensible on this side; but
the reason hereof is not to be drawne from the situation of the *Heart*,
but the site of the left ventricle wherein the vital Spirits are laboured;
and also the great Artery that conveieth them out; both which are situated on the left. Upon this reason Epithems or cordial Applications are
justly applied unto the left Breast; and the wounds under the fifth Rib
may be more suddenly destructive if made on the sinister side, and the
Spear of the Souldier that peirced our Saviour, is not improperly described, when Painters direct it a little towards the left.

The other ground is more particular and upon inspection; for
in dead Bodies especially lying upon the Spine, the *Heart* doth seem to
incline unto the left. Which happeneth not from its proper site; but besides its sinistrous gravity, is drawn that way by the great Artery,

which then subsideth and haileth the *Heart* unto it. And therefore strictly taken, the *Heart* is seated in the middle of the Chest; but after a careless and inconsiderate aspection, or according to the readiest sense of pulsation, we shall not Quarrel, if any affirm it is seated toward the left. And in these considerations must *Aristotle* be salved, when he affirmeth the *Heart* of Man is placed in the left side, and thus in a popular acception may we receive the periphrasis of *Persius* when he taketh the part under the left Pap for the *Heart*; and if rightly apprehended, it concerneth not this controversie, when it is said in *Ecclesiastes*; The *Heart* of a wise Man is in the right side, but that of a Fool in the left, for thereby may be implied, that the *Heart* of a wise Man delighteth in the right way, or in the path of Vertue; that of a Fool in the left, or road of Vice; according to the mystery of the Letter of *Pythagoras*, or that expression in *Jonah*, concerning sixscore thousand, that could not discern between their right hand and their left, or knew not good from evil.

That assertion also that Man proportionally hath the largest brain, I did I confess somewhat doubt; and conceived it might have failed in Birds, especially such as having little Bodies, have yet large Cranies, and seeme to contain much Brain, as *Snipes*, *Woodcocks*, &c. But upon trial I find it very true. The Brains of a Man, *Archangelus* and *Bauhinus* observe to weigh four pound, and sometime five and a half. If therefore a Man weigh one hundred and forty pounds, and his Brain but five, his Weight is 27. times as much as his brain, deducting the weight of that five pound which is allowed for it. Now in a Snipe, which weighed four ounces two dragms, I find the Brains to weigh but half a dragm, so that the weight of body (allowing for the Brain) exceeded the weight of the Brain, sixty seven times and an half.

More controvertible it seemeth in the Brains of Sparrows, whose Cranies are rounder, and so of larger capacity: and most of all in the Heads of Birds, upon the first formation in the Egg, wherein the Head seems larger then all the Body, and the very Eyes almost as big as either. A Sparrow in the total we found to weigh seven dragms and four and twenty grains; whereof the Head a dragm, but the Brain not fifteen grains; which answereth not fully the proportion of the brain of Man. And therefore it is to be taken of the whole Head with the Brains, when *Scaliger* objecteth that the Head of a Man is the fifteenth part of his Body; that of a Sparrow, scarce the fifth.

CHAPTER III

Of Pleurisies

That *Pleurisies* are only on the left side, is a popular Tenent not only absurd but dangerous. From the misapprehension hereof, men omitting the opportunity of remedies, which otherwise they would not neglect. Chiefly occasioned by the ignorance of *Anatomie* and the extent of the part affected; which in an exquisite *Pleurisie* is determined to be the skin or membrane which investeth the Ribs, for so it is defined, *Inflammatio membranæ costas succingentis;* An Inflammation, either simple, consisting only of an hot and sanguineous affluxion; or else denominable from other humours, according to the predominancy of melancholy, flegm, or choler. The membrane thus inflamed, is properly called *Pleura*; from whence the disease hath its name; and this investeth not only one side, but overspreadeth the cavity of the chest, and affordeth a common coat unto the parts contained therein.

Now therefore the *Pleura* being common unto both sides, it is not reasonable to confine the inflammation unto one, nor strictly to determine it is alwaies in the side; but sometimes before and behind, that is, inclining to the Spine or Breast-bone; for thither this Coat extendeth; and therefore with equal propriety we may affirm, that ulcers of the lungs, or Apostems of the brain do happen oney in the left side; or that Ruptures are confinable unto one side, whereas the Peritoneum or Rim of the Belly may be broke, or its perforations relaxed in either.

CHAPTER IV

Of the Ring-finger

AN opinion there is, which magnifies the fourth *Finger* of the left Hand; presuming therein a cordial relation, that a particular vessel, nerve, vein or artery is conferred thereto from the heart, and therefore that especially hath the honour to bear our Rings. Which was not only the Christian practice in Nuptial contracts, but observed by Heathens, as *Alexander ab Alexandro, Gellius, Macrobius*, and *Pierius* have delivered, as *Levinus Lemnius* hath confirmed, who affirms this peculiar vessel to be an artery, and not a Nerve, as Antiquity conceived it; adding moreover that *Rings* hereon peculiarly affect the Heart; that in Lipothymies or swoundings he used the frication of this *Finger* with saffron and gold: that the ancient Physitians mixed up their Medicines herewith; that this is seldom or last of all affected with the Gout, and when that becometh nodous, Men continue not long after. Notwithstanding all which we remain unsatisfied, nor can we think the reasons alleadged sufficiently establish the preheminency of this *Finger*.

For first, Concerning the practice of Antiquity, the custom was not general to weare their *Rings* either on this Hand or *Finger*; for it is said, and that emphatically in *Jeremiah, Si fuerit Jeconias filius Joachim regis Judæ annulus in manu dextrâ meâ, inde evallam eum*; Though *Coniah* the son of *Joachim* King of *Judah*, were the signet on my right Hand, yet would I pluck thee thence. So is it observed by *Pliny*, that in the portraits of their Gods, the *Rings* were worn on the *Finger* next the *Thumb*; that the *Romans* wore them on the middle *Finger*, as the ancient *Gaules* and *Britans*; and some upon the *forefinger*, as is deduceable from *Julius Pollux*: who names that Ring *Corionos*.

Again, That the practice of the ancients, had any such respect of cordiality or reference unto the Heart, will much be doubted, if we consider their Rings were made of Iron; such was that of *Prometheus*, who is conceived the first that brought them in use. So, as *Pliny* affirmeth, for many yeares the *Senators* of *Rome* did not wear any Rings of Gold: but the slaves wore generally Iron Rings until their manumission or preferment to some dignity. That the *Lacedemonians* continued their Iron Rings unto his daies, *Pliny* also delivereth, and surely they used few of Gold; for beside that *Lycurgus* prohibited that mettal, we read in *Athenæus*, that having a desire to guild the face of *Apollo*, they enquired of the Oracle where they might purchase so much Gold, and were directed into *Cræsus* King of *Lydia*.

Moreover whether the Ancients had any such intention, the grounds which they conceived in vein, Nerve or Artery, are not to be justified, nor will inspection confirm a peculiar vessel in this Finger. For as *Anatomy* informeth the Basilica vein dividing into two branches below the cubit, the outward sendeth two surcles unto the thumb, two unto the fore-finger, and one unto the middle finger in the inward side; the other branch of the Basilica sendeth one surcle unto the outside of the middle finger, two unto the Ring, and as many unto the little fingers; so that they all proceed from the Basilica, and are in equal numbers derived unto every one: In the same manner are the branches of the axillary artery distributed into the Hand; for below the cubit it divideth into two parts, the one running along the *Radius*, and passing by the wrest or place of the pulse, is at the *Fingers* subdivided into three Branches; whereof the first conveyeth two surcles unto the *Thumb*, the second as many to the fore-*Finger*, and the third one unto the middle *Finger*; the other or lower division of the artery descendeth by the ulna, and furnisheth the other *Fingers*; that is the middle with one Surcle, and the *Ring* and little *Fingers* with two. As for the Nerves, they are disposed much after the same manner, and have their original from the Brain, and not the Heart, as many of the Ancients conceived; which is so far from affording Nerves unto other parts, that it receiveth very few it self from the sixth conjugation, or paire of Nerves in the Brain.

Lastly, These propagations being communicated unto both Hands, we have no greater reason to weare our *Rings* on the left, then on the right; nor are there cordial considerations in the one, more then the other. And therefore when *Forestus* for the stanching of blood makes use of Medical applications unto the fourth *Finger*, he confines not that practice unto the left, but varieth the side according to the nostril bleeding. So in Feavers, where the Heart primarily suffereth, we apply Medicines unto the wrests of either arm; so we touch the pulse of both, and judge of the affections of the Heart by the one as well as the other. And although in indispositions of Liver or Spleen, considerations are made in *Phlebotomy* respectively to their situation; yet when the Heart is affected, Men have thought it as effectual to bleed on the right as the left; and although also it may be thought, a nearer respect is to be had of the left, because the great artery proceeds from the left ventricle, and so is nearer that arm; it admits not that consideration. For under the channel bones the artery divideth into two great branches, from which trunk or point of division, the distance unto either Hand is equal, and the consideration also answerable.

All which with many respective Niceties, in order unto parts, sides, and veines, are now become of less consideration, by the new and noble doctrine of the circulation of the blood.

And therefore *Macrobius* discussing the point, hath alleadged another reason; affirming that the gestation of *Rings* upon this Hand and *Finger*, might rather be used for their conveniency and preservation, then any cordial relation. For at first (saith he) it was both free and usual to weare *Rings* on either Hand; but after that luxury encreased, when pretious gems and rich insculptures were added, the custom of wearing them on the right Hand was translated unto the left; for that Hand being lesse imployed, thereby they were best preserved. And for the same reason they placed them on this *Finger*; for the *Thumb* was too active a *Finger*, and is commonly imployed with either of the rest: the Index or fore-*Finger* was too naked whereto to commit their pretiosities, and hath the tuition of the *Thumb* scarce unto the second joint: the middle and little *Finger* they rejected as extreams, and too big or too little for their *Rings*, and of all chose out the fourth, as being least used of any, as being guarded on either side, and having in most this peculiar condition that it cannot be extended alone and by it self, but will be accompanied by some *Finger* on either side. And to this opinion assenteth *Alexander ab Alexandro, Annulum nuptialem prior ætas in sinistrâ ferebat, crediderim ne attereretur.*

Now that which begat or promoted the common opinion, was the common conceit that the Heart was seated on the left side; but how far this is verified, we have before declared. The *Egyptian* practice hath much advanced the same, who unto this *Finger* derived a Nerve from the Heart; and therefore the Priest anointed the same with precious oyls before the Altar. But how weak *Anatomists* they were, which were so good Embalmers, we have already shewed. And though this reason took most place, yet had they another which more commended that practice: and that was the number whereof this *Finger* was an Hieroglyphick. For by holding down the fourth *Finger* of the left Hand, while the rest were extended, they signified the perfect and magnified number of six. For as *Pierius* hath graphically declared, Antiquity expressed numbers by the *Fingers* of either Hand: on the left they accounted their digits and articulate numbers unto an hundred; on the right Hand hundreds and thousands; the depressing this *Finger*, which in the left Hand implied but six, in the right indigitated six hundred. In this way of numeration, may we construe that of *Juvenal* concerning *Nestor*,

> Qui per tot sæcula mortem
> Distulit, atque suos jam dextrâ computat annos.

And however it were intended, in this sense it will be more elegant what is delivered of Wisdom, *Prov.* 3. Length of daies is in her right Hand, and in her left Hand riches and honour.

As for the observation of *Lemnius* an eminent Physitian, concerning the Gout; however it happened in his Country, we may observe it otherwise in ours; that is, that chiragricall persons do suffer in this *Finger* as well as in the rest, and sometimes first of all, and sometimes no where else. And for the mixing up medicines herewith; it is rather an argument of opinion, then any considerable effect; and we as highly conceive of the practice in *Diapalma*, that is in the making of that plaster, to stir it with the stick of a Palm.

CHAPTER V

Of the right and left Hand

It is also suspicious, and not with that certainty to be received, what is generally believed concerning the right and left hand; that Men naturally make use of the right, and that the use of the other is a digression or aberration from that way which nature generally intendeth. We do not deny that almost all Nations have used this hand, and ascribed a preheminence thereto: hereof a remarkable passage there is in the 48. of *Genesis*, And *Joseph* took them both, *Ephraim* in his right hand towards *Israels* left hand, and *Manasses* in his left hand towards *Israels* right hand, and *Israel* stretched out his right hand and laid it upon *Ephraims* head, who was the younger, and his left hand upon *Manasses* head, guiding his hands wittingly, for *Manasses* was the first-born; and when *Joseph* saw that his father laid his right hand upon the head of *Ephraim*, it displeased him, and he held up his fathers hand to remove it from *Ephraims* head unto *Manasses* head, and *Joseph* said, Not so my father, for this is the first-born, put thy right hand upon his head: The like appeareth from the ordinance of *Moses* in the consecration of their Priests, Then shalt thou kill the Ram, and take of his blood, and put it upon the tip of the right ear of *Aaron*, and upon the tip of the right ear of his sons, and upon the thumb of the right hand, and upon the great toe of the right foot, and sprinkle the blod on the Altar round about. That the *Persians* were wont herewith to plight their faith, is testified by *Diodorus*: That the *Greeks* and *Romans* made use hereof, beside the testimony of divers Authors, is evident from their custom of discumbency at their meals, which was upon their left side, for so their right hand was free, and ready for all service. As also from the conjunction of the right hands and not the left observable in the *Roman* medals of concord. Nor was this only in use with divers Nations of Men, but was the custom of whole Nations of Women; as is deduceable from the Amazons in the amputation of their right breast, whereby they had the freer use of their bow. All which do seem to declare a natural preferment of the one unto motion before the other; wherein notwithstanding in submission to future information, we are unsatisfied unto great dubitation.

For first, if there were a determinate prepotency in the right, and such as ariseth from a constant root in nature, we might expect the same in other animals, whose parts are also differenced by dextrality; wherein notwithstanding we cannot discover a distinct and complying account; for we find not that *Horses, Buls,* or *Mules,* are generally stronger on this side. As for Animals whose forelegs more sensibly supply the use of arms, they hold, if not an equality in both, a prevalency oft-times in the other, as *Squirrels, Apes,* and *Monkies*; the same is also discernable in *Parrets,* who feed themselves more commonly by the left-leg, and Men observe that the Eye of a Tumbler is biggest, not constantly in one, but in the bearing side.

That there is also in men a natural prepotency in the right, we cannot with constancy affirm, if we make observation in children; who permitted the free-dom of both, do oft-times confine unto the left, and are not without great difficulty restrained from it. And therefore this prevalency is either uncertainly placed in the laterality, or custom determines its difference. Which is the resolution of *Aristotle* in that Problem, which enquires why the right side being better then the left, is equal in the senses? because, saith he, the right and left do differ by use and custom, which have no place in the senses. For right and left as parts inservient unto the motive faculty, are differenced by degrees from use and assuefaction, according whereto the one grows stronger, and oft-times bigger then the other. But in the senses it is otherwise; for they acquire not their perfection by use or custom, but at the first we equally hear and see with one Eye, as well as with another. And therefore, were this indifferency permitted, or did not institution, but Nature determine dextrality, there would be many more Scevolaes then are delivered in story; nor needed we to draw examples of the left, from the sons of the right hand; as we read of seven thousand in the Army of the *Benjamites*. True it is, that although there be an indifferency in either, or a prevalency indifferent in one, yet is it most reasonable for uniformity, and sundry respective uses, that Men should apply themselves to the constant use of one; for there will otherwise arise anomalous disturbances in manual actions, not only in civil and artificial, but also in Military affairs, and the severall actions of war.

Secondly, the grounds and reasons alleadged for the right, are not satisfactory, and afford no rest in their decision. *Scaliger* finding a defect in the reason of *Aristotle*, introduceth one of no less deficiency himself; *Ratio materialis* (saith he) *sanguinis crassitudo simul & multitudo*; that is, the reason of the vigour of this side, is the crassitude and plenty of blood; but this is not sufficient; for the crassitude or thickness of blood affordeth no reason why one arm should be enabled before the other, and the plenty thereof, why both not enabled equally. *Fallopius* is of another conceit, deducing the reason from the Azygos or *vena sine pari*, a large and considerable vein arising out of the *cava* or hollow vein, before it enters the right ventricle of the Heart, and placed only in the right side. But neither is this perswasory; for the Azygos communicates no branches unto the arms or legs on either side, but disperseth into the Ribs on both, and in its descent doth furnish the left Emulgent with one vein, and the first vein of the loins on the right side with another; which manner of derivation doth not confer a peculiar addition unto either. *Cælius Rodiginus* undertaking to give a reason of Ambidexters and *Left handed* Men, delivereth a third opinion: Men, saith he, are Ambidexters, and use both *Hands* alike, when the heat of the Heart doth plentifully disperse into the left side, and that of the Liver into the right, and the spleen be also much dilated; but Men are *Left-handed* when ever it happeneth that the Heart and Liver are seated on the left-side; or when the Liver is on the right side, yet so obducted and covered with thick skins, that it cannot diffuse its vertue into the right. Which reasons are no way satisfactory; for herein the spleen is injustly introduced to invigorate the sinister side, which being dilated it would rather infirm and debilitate. As for any tunicles or skins which should hinder the Liver from enabling the dextral parts; we must not conceive it diffuseth its vertue by meer irradiation, but by its veins and proper vessels, which common skins and teguments cannot impede. And for the seat of the Heart and Liver in one side, whereby Men become *Left-handed*, it happeneth too rarely to countenance an effect so common; for the seat of the Liver on the left side is monstrous, and rarely to be met with in the observations of Physitians. Others not considering ambidextrous and *Left-handed* Men, do totally submit unto the efficacy of the Liver, which though seated on the right side, yet by the subclavian division doth equidistantly communicate its activity unto either Arm; nor will it salve the doubts of observation:

for many are *Right-handed* whose Livers are weakely constituted, and many use the left, in whom that part is strongest; and we observe in Apes, and other animals, whose Liver is in the right, no regular prevalence therein.

And therefore the Braine, especially the spinal marrow, which is but the brain prolonged, hath a fairer plea hereto; for these are the principles of motion, wherein dextrality consists; and are divided within and without the Crany. By which division transmitting Nerves respectively unto either side; according to the indifferency, or original and native prepotency, there ariseth an equality in both, or prevalency in either side. And so may it be made out, what many may wonder at, why some most actively use the contrary Arm and Leg; for the vigour of the one dependeth upon the upper part of the spine, but the other upon the lower.

And therefore many things are Philosophically delivered concerning right and left, which admit of some suspension. That a Woman upon a masculine conception advanceth her right Leg, will not be found to answer strick observation. That males are conceived in the right side of the womb, females in the left, though generally delivered, and supported by ancient testimony, will make no infallible account; it happening oft times that males and females do lie upon both sides, and Hermaphrodites for ought we know on either. It is also suspitious what is delivered concerning the right and left testicle, that males are begotten from the one, and females from the other. For though the left seminal vein proceedeth from the emulgent, and is therefore conceived to carry down a serous and feminine matter; yet the seminal Arteries which send forth the active materials, are both derived from the great Artery. Besides this original of the left vein was thus contrived, to avoid the pulsation of the great Artery, over which it must have passed to attain unto the testicle. Nor can we easily infer such different effects from the divers situation of parts which have one end and office; for in the kidneys which have one office, the right is seated lower then the left, whereby it lieth free, and giveth way unto the Liver. And therefore also that way which is delivered for masculine generation, to make a strait ligature about the left testicle, thereby to intercept the evacuation of that part, deserveth consideration. For one sufficeth unto generation, as hath beene observed in semicastration, and oft times in carnous ruptures. Beside, the seminal ejaculation proceeds not immediately from the testicle, but from the spermatick glandules; and therefore *Aristotle* affirms (and reason cannot deny) that although there be nothing diffused from the testicles, an *Horse* or *Bull* may generate after castration; that is, from the stock and remainder of seminal matter, already prepared and stored up in the Prostates or glandules of generation.

Thirdly, Although we should concede a right and left in Nature, yet in this common and received account we may err from the proper acception; mistaking one side for another, calling that in Man and other animals the right which is the left, and that the left which is the right, and that in some things right and left, which is not properly either.

For first the right and left, are not defined by Phylosophers according to common acception, that is, respectively from one Man unto another, or any constant site in each; as though that should be the right in one, which upon confront or facing, stands athwart or diagonially unto the other; but were distinguished according to the activity and predominant locomotion upon either side. Thus *Aristotle* in his excellent Tract *de incessu animalium*, ascribeth six positions unto Animals, answering the three dimensions; which he determineth not by site or position unto the Heavens, but by their faculties and functions; and these are *Imum summum, Ante Retro, Dextra & Sinistra*: that is, the superiour part, where the aliment is received, that the lower extream where it is last expelled; so he termeth a Man a plant inverted; for he supposeth the root of a Tree the head or upper part thereof, whereby it receiveth its aliment, although therewith it respects the Center of the Earth, but with the other the Zenith; and this position is answerable unto longitude. Those parts are anteriour and measure profundity, where the senses, especially the Eyes are placed, and those posterior which are opposite hereunto. The dextrous and sinistrous parts of the body, make up the latitude; and are not certain and inalterable like the other; for that, saith he, is the right side, from whence the motion of the body beginneth, that is, the active or moving side; but that the sinister which is the weaker or more quiescent part. Of the same determination were the *Platonicks* and *Pythagorians* before him; who conceiving the heavens an animated body, named the *East*, the right or dextrous part, from whence began their motion: and thus the *Greeks*, from whence the *Latins* have borrowed their appellation, have named this hand δέξια, denominating it not from the site, but office, from

287

δέχομαι, *capio,* that is, the hand which receiveth, or is usually implied in that action.

Now upon these grounds we are most commonly mistaken, defining that by situation which they determined by motion; and giving the term of right hand to that which doth not properly admit it. For first, Many in their infancy are sinistriously disposed, and divers continue all their life Αριστεροί, that is, left handed, and have but weak and imperfect use of the right; now unto these, that hand is properly the right, and not the other esteemed so by situation. Thus may *Aristotle* be made out, when he affirmeth the right claw of *Crabs* and *Lobsters* is biggest, if we take the right for the most vigorous side, and not regard the relative situation: for the one is generally bigger then the other, yet not alwayes upon the same side. So may it be verified what is delivered by *Scaliger* in his Comment, that Palsies do oftnest happen upon the left side, if understood in this sense; the most vigorous part protecting it self, and protruding the matter upon the weaker and less resistive side. And thus the Law of Common-Weales, that cut off the right hand of Malefactors, if Philosophically executed, is impartial; otherwise the amputation not equally punisheth all.

Some are αμφιδέξιοι, that is, ambidexterous or right handed on both sides; which happeneth only unto strong and Athletical bodies, whose heat and spirits are able to afford an ability unto both. And therefore *Hippocrates* saith, that Women are not ambidexterous, that is, not so often as Men; for some are found, which indifferently make use of both. And so may *Aristotle* say, that only Men are ambidexterous; of this constitution was *Asteropæus* in *Homer,* and *Parthenopeus* the *Theban* Captain in *Statius*: and of the same, do some conceive our Father *Adam* to have been, as being perfectly framed, and in a constitution admitting least defect. Now in these Men the right hand is on both sides, and that is not the left which is opposite unto the right, according to common accepcion.

Againe, some are αμφαριστεροί, as *Galen* hath expressed it; that is, ambilevous or left-handed on both sides; such as with agility and vigour have not the use of either: who are not gymnastically composed: nor actively use those parts. Now in these there is no right hand: of this constitution are many Women, and some Men, who though they accustom themselves unto either hand, do dexterously make use of neither. And therefore although the Political advice of *Aristotle* be very good, that Men should accustom themselves to the command of either hand: yet cannot the execution or performance thereof be general: for though there be many found that can use both, yet will there divers remain that can strenuously make use of neither.

Lastly, These lateralities in Man are not only fallible, if relatively determined unto each other, but made in reference unto the heavens and quarters of the Globe: for those parts are not capable of these conditions in themselves, nor with any certainty respectively derived from us, nor from them to us again. And first in regard of their proper nature, the heavens admit not these sinister and dexter respects; there being in them no diversity or difference, but a simplicity of parts, and equiformity in motion continually succeeding each other; so that from what point soever we compute, the account will be common unto the whole circularity. And therefore though it be plausible, it is not of consequence hereto what is delivered by *Solinus*, That Man was therefore a Microcosme or little World, because the dimensions of his positions were answerable unto the greater. For as in the Heavens the distance of the North and Southern pole, which are esteemed the superiour and inferiour points, is equal unto the space between the East and West, accounted the dextrous and sinistrous parts thereof; so is it also in Man, for the extent of his fathome or distance betwixt the extremity of the fingers of either hand upon expansion, is equal unto the space between the sole of the foot and the crown. But this doth but petitionarily infer a dextrality in the Heavens, and we may as reasonably conclude a right and left laterallity in the Ark or naval edifice of *Noah*. For the length thereof was three hundred cubits, the bredth fifty, and the heighth or profundity thirty; which well agreeth unto the proportion of Man, whose length, that is a perpendicular from the vertex unto the sole of the foot is sextuple unto his breadth, or a right line drawn from the ribs of one side to another; and decuple unto his profundity; that is a direct line between the breast bone and the spine.

Againe, They receive not these conditions with any assurance or stability from our selves. For the relative foundations and points of denomination, are not fixed and certain, but variously designed according to imagination. The Philosopher accounts that East from whence the Heavens begin their motion. The Astronomer regarding the South and Meridian Sun, calls that the dextrous part of Heaven which respecteth his right hand; and that is the West. Poets respecting the West, assign the name of right unto the North which regardeth their right hand; and so must that of *Ovid* be explained, *utque duæ dextrâ Zonæ totidemque sinistrâ*. But Augurs or Southsayers turning their face to the East, did make the right in the South; which was also observed by the *Hebrews* and *Chaldæans*. Now if we name the quarters of Heaven respectively unto our sides, it will be no certain or invariable denomination. For if we call that the right side of Heaven which is seated Easterly unto us, when we regard the Meridian Sun; the inhabitants beyond the Æquator and Southern Tropick when they face us, regarding the Meridian, will contrarily define it; for unto them, the opposite part of Heaven will respect the left, and the Sun arise to their right.

And thus have we at large declared that although the right be most commonly used, yet hath it no regular or certaine root in nature. Since it is not confirmable from other Animals: Since in Children it seems either indifferent or more favourable in the other; but more reasonable for uniformity in action, that Men accustom unto one: Since the grounds and reasons urged for it, do not sufficiently support it: Since if there be a right and stronger side in nature, yet may we mistake in its denomination; calling that the right which is the left, and the left which is the right. Since some have one right, some both, some neither. And lastly, Since these affections in Man are not only fallible in relation unto one another, but made also in reference unto the Heavens, they being not capable of these conditions in themselves, nor with any certainty from us, nor we from them again.

And therefore what admission we ow unto many conceptions concerning right and left, requireth circumspection. That is, how far we ought to rely upon the remedy in *Kiranides*, that is, the left eye of an *Hedg-hog* fried in oyle to procure sleep, and the right foot of a *Frog* in a *Dears* skin for the *Gout*; or that to dream of the loss of right or left tooth, presageth the death of male or female kindred, according to the doctrine of *Artemidorus*. What verity there is in that numeral conceit in the lateral division of Man by even and odd, ascribing the odd unto the right side, and even unto the left; and so by parity or imparity of letters in Mens names to determine misfortunes on either side of their bodies; by which account in Greek numeration, *Hephæstus* or *Vulcan* was lame in the right foot, and *Anibal* lost his right eye. And lastly, what substance there is in that Auspicial principle, and fundamental doctrine of Ariolation, that the left hand is ominous, and that good things do pass sinistrously upon us, because the left hand of man re-spected the right hand of the Gods, which handed their favours unto us.

CHAPTER VI

Of Swimming, and Floating

That Men swim naturally, if not disturbed by fear; that Men being drowned and sunk, do float the ninth day when their gall breaketh; that Women drowned, swim prone, but Men supine, or upon their backs: are popular affirmations, whereto we cannot assent. And first, that Man should swim naturally, because we observe it is no lesson unto other Animals, we are not forward to conclude; for other Animals swim in the same Manner as they go, and need no other way of motion for natation in the water, then for progression upon the land. And this is true whether they move *per latera*, that is two legs of one side together, which is Tollutation or ambling; or *per diametrum*, lifting one foot before, and the cross foot behind, which is succussation or trotting; or whether *per frontem* or *quadratum* as *Scaliger* terms it, upon a square base, the legs of both sides moving together, as *Frogs* and salient Animals, which is properly called leaping. For by these motions they are able to support and impell themselves in the water, without alteration in the stroak of their legs, or position of their bodies.

But with Man it is performed otherwise: for in regard of site he alters his natural posture and swimmeth prone, whereas he walketh erect. Again, in progression the arms move parallel to the legs, and the arms and legs unto each other; but in natation they intersect and make all sorts of angles, And lastly, in progressive motion, the arms and legs do move successively, but in natation both together; all which aptly to perform, and so as to support and advance the body, is a point of Art, and such as some in their young and docile years could never attain. But although swimming be acquired by art, yet is there somewhat more of nature in it then we observe in other habits, nor will it strictly fall under that definition; for once obtained, it is not to be removed; nor is there any who from disuse did ever yet forget it.

Secondly, That persons drowned arise and float the ninth day when their gall breaketh, is a questionable determination both in the time and cause. For the time of floating, it is uncertain according to the time of putrefaction, which shall retard or accelerate according to the subject and season of the year; for as we observed, *Cats* and *Mice* will arise unequally, and at different times, though drowned at the same. Such as are fat do commonly float soonest, for their bodies soonest ferment, and that substance approacheth nearest unto air: and this is one of *Aristotles* reasons why dead *Eels* will not float, because saith he, they have but slender bellies, and little fat.

As for the cause, it is not so reasonably imputed unto the breaking of the gall as the putrefaction or corruptive fermentation of the body, whereby the unnatural heat prevailing, the putrifying parts do suffer a turgescence and inflation, and becoming aery and spumous affect to approach the air, and ascend unto the surface of the water. And this is also evidenced in Eggs, whereof the sound ones sink, and such as are addled swim, as do also those which are termed hypenemia or wind-eggs; and this is also a way to separate seeds, whereof such as are corrupted and steril, swim; and this agreeth not only unto the seed of plants lockt up and capsulated in their husks, but also unto the sperm and seminal humor of Man; for such a passage hath *Aristotle* upon the Inquisition and test of its fertility.

That the breaking of the gall is not the cause hereof, experience hath informed us. For opening the *abdomen*, and taking out the gall in *Cats* and *Mice*, they did notwithstanding arise. And because we had read in *Rhodiginus* of a Tyrant, who to prevent the emergency of murdered bodies, did use to cut off their lungs, and found Mens minds possessed with this reason; we committed some unto the water without lungs, which notwithstanding floated with the others. And to compleat the experiment, although we took out the guts and bladder, and also perforated the Cranium, yet would they arise, though in a longer time. From these observations in other Animals, it may not be unreasonable to conclude the same in Man, who is too noble a subject on whom to make them expressely, and the casual opportunity too rare almost to make any. Now if any should ground this effect from gall or choler, because it is the lightest humor and will be above the rest; or being the fiery humor will readiest surmount the water, we must confess in the common putrescence it may promote elevation, which the breaking of the bladder of gall, so small a part in Man, cannot considerably advantage.

Lastly, That Women drowned float prone, that is, with their bellies downward, but Men supine or upward, is an assertion wherein the *hoti* or point it self is dubious; and were it true, the reason alledged for it, is of no validity. The reason yet currant was first expressed by *Pliny, veluti pudori defunctorum parcente naturâ,* nature modestly ordaining this position to conceale the shame of the dead, which hath been taken up by *Solinus, Rhodiginus,* and many more. This indeed (as *Scaliger* termeth it) is *ratio civilis non philosophica,* strong enough for morality or Rhetoricks, not for Philosophy or Physicks. For first, in nature the concealment of secret parts is the same in both sexes, and the shame of their reveal equal: so *Adam* upon the tast of the fruit was ashamed of his nakedness as well as *Eve.* And so likewise in *America* and Countries unacquainted with habits, where modesty conceals these parts in one sex, it doth it also in the other; and therefore had this been the intention of nature, not only Women, but Men also had swimmed downwards; the posture in reason being common unto both, where the intent is also common.

Again, While herein we commend the modesty, we condemn the wisdom of nature: for that prone position we make her contrive unto the Woman, were best agreeable unto the Man, in whom the secret parts are very anteriour and more discoverable in a supine and upward posture. And therefore *Scaliger* declining this reason, hath recurred unto another from the difference of parts in both sexes; *Quod ventre vastro sunt mulieres plenoque intestinis, itaque minus impletur & subsidet, inanior maribus quibus nates præponderant*: If so, then Men with great bellies will float downward, and only *Callipygae,* and Women largely composed behind, upward. But *Anatomists* observe, that to make the larger cavity for the Infant, the hanch bones in Women, and consequently the parts appendant are more protuberant then they are in Men. They who ascribe the cause unto the breasts of Women, take not away the doubt; for they resolve not why children float downward, who are included in that sex, though not in the reason alleadged. But hereof we cease to discourse lest we undertake to afford a reason of the golden tooth, that is to invent or assign a cause, when we remain unsatisfied or unassured of the effect.

That a *Mare* will sooner drown then a *Horse,* though commonly opinion'd, is not I fear experienced: nor is the same observed, in the drowning of *Whelps* and *Kitlins*. But that a Man cannot shut or open his eyes under water, easie experiment may convict. Whether Cripples or mutilated Persons, who have lost the greatest part of their thighs, will not sink but float, their lungs being abler to waft up their bodies, which are in others overpoised by the hinder legs; we have not made experiment. Thus much we observe, that Animals drown downwards, and the same is observable in *Frogs*, when the hinder legges are cut off. But in the air most seem to perish headlong from high places; however *Vulcan* thrown from heaven, be made to fall on his feet.

CHAPTER VII

Concerning Weight

That Men weigh heavier dead then alive, if experiment hath not failed us, we cannot reasonably grant. For though the trial hereof cannot so well be made on the body of Man, nor will the difference be sensible in the abate of scruples or dragms, yet can we not confirm the same in lesser Animals, from whence the inference is good; and the affirmative of *Pliny* saith, that it is true in all. For exactly weighing and strangling a *Chicken* in the Scales; upon an immediate ponderation, we could discover no sensible difference in weight; but suffering it to lie eight or ten hours, until it grew perfectly cold, it weighed most sensibly lighter; the like we attempted, and verified in *Mice*, and performed their trials in Scales, that would turn upon the eighth or tenth part of a graine.

Now whereas some alledge that spirits are lighter substances, and naturally ascending, do elevate and waft the body upward, whereof dead bodies being destitute, contract a greater gravity; although we concede that spirits are light, comparatively unto the body, yet that they are absolutely so, or have no weight at all, we cannot readily allow. For since Phylosophy affirmeth, that spirits are middle substances between the soul and body, they must admit of some corporiety, which supposeth weight or gravity. Beside, in carcasses warm, and bodies newly disanimated, while transpiration remaineth, there do exhale and breath out vaporous and fluid parts, which carry away some power of gravitation. Which though we allow, we do not make answerable unto living expiration; and therefore the *Chicken* or *Mice* were not so light being dead, as they would have been after ten hours kept alive; for in that space a man abateth many ounces. Nor if it had slept, for in that space of sleep, a Man will sometimes abate forty ounces; nor if it had been in the middle of summer, for then a Man weigheth some pounds less, then in the height of winter; according to experience, and the statick Aphorisms of *Sanctorius*.

Againe, Whereas Men affirm they perceive an addition of ponderosity in dead bodies, comparing them usually unto blocks and stones, whensoever they lift or carry them; this accesional preponderancy is rather in appearance then reality. For being destitute of any motion, they confer no relief unto the Agents; or Elevators; which makes us meet with the same complaints of gravity in animated and living bodies, where the Nerves subside, and the faculty locomotive seems abolished; as may be observed in the lifting or supporting of persons inebriated, Apoplectical, or in Lipothymies and swoundings.

Many are also of opinion, and some learned Men maintain, that Men are lighter after meals then before, and that by a supply and addition of spirits obscuring the gross ponderosity of the aliment ingested; but the contrary hereof we have found in the trial of sundry persons in different sex and ages. And we conceive Men may mistake if they distinguish not the sense of levity uno themselves, and in regard of the scale or decision of trutination. For after a draught of wine, a Man may seem lighter in himself from sudden refection, although he be heavier in the balance, from a corporal and ponderous addition; but a Man in the morning is lighter in the scale, because in sleep some pounds have perspired; and is also lighter unto himself, because he is refected.

And to speak strictly, a Man that holds his breath is weightier while his lungs are full, then upon expiration. For a bladder blown is weightier then one empty, and if it containe a quart, expressed and emptied it will abate about a quarter of a grain. And therefore we somewhat mistrust the experiment of a pumice stone taken up by *Montanus*, in his Comment upon *Avicenna*, where declaring how the rarity of parts, and numerosity of pores, occasioneth a lightness in bodies, he affirms that a pumice-stone powdered, is lighter then one entire; which is an experiment beyond our satisfaction; for beside that abatement can hardly be avoided in the Trituration; if a bladder of good capacity will scarce include a graine of ayre, a pumice of three or foure dragms, cannot be presumed to containe the hundredth part thereof; which will not be sensible upon the exactest beams we use. Nor is it to be taken strictly which is delivered by the learned Lord *Verulam*, and referred unto further experiment; That a dissolution of Iron in *aqua fortis*, will bear as good weight as their bodies did before, notwithstanding a great deal of wast by a thick vapour that issueth during the working; for we cannot find it to hold neither in Iron nor Copper, which is dissolved with less ebullition; and hereof we made trial in Scales of good exactness: wherein if there be a defect, or such as will not turn upon quarter grains, there may be frequent mistakes in experiments of this nature. That also may be considered which is delivered by *Hamerus Poppius*, that *Antimony* calcin'd or reduced to ashes by a burning glass, although it emit a gross and ponderous exhalation, doth rather exceed then abate its former gravity. Nevertheless, strange it is, how very little and almost insensible abatement there will be sometimes in such operations, or rather some encrease, as in the refining of metals, in the test of bone ashes, according to experience: and in a burnt brick, as *Monsieur de Clave* affirmeth. Mistake may be made in this way of trial, when the *Antimony* is not weighed immediately upon the calcination; but permitted the air, it imbibeth the humidity thereof, and so repaireth its gravity.

CHAPTER VIII

Of the passage of Meat and Drink

That there are different passages for Meat and Drink, the Meat or dry aliment descending by the one, the Drink or moistning vehicle by the other, is a popular Tenent in our daies, but was the assertion of learned men of old. For the same was affirmed by *Plato*, maintained by *Eustathius* in *Macrobius*, and is deducible from *Eratosthenes*, *Eupolis* and *Euripides*. Now herein Men contradict experience, not well understanding *Anatomy*, and the use of parts. For at the Throat there are two cavities or conducting parts: the one the Oesophagus or Gullet, seated next the spine, a part official unto nutrition, and whereby the aliment both wet and dry is conveied unto the stomack; the other (by which tis conceived the Drink doth pass) is the weazon, rough artery, or wind-pipe, a part inservient to voice and respiration; for thereby the air descendeth into the lungs, and is communicated unto the heart. And therefore all Animals that breath or have lungs, have also the weazon, but many have the gullet or feeding channel, which have no lungs or wind-pipe; as fishes which have gils, whereby the heart is refrigerated; for such thereof as have lungs and respiration, are not without the weazon, as Whales and cetaceous Animals.

Again, Beside these parts destin'd to divers offices, there is a peculiar provision for the wind-pipe, that is, a cartilagineous flap upon the opening of the Larinx or Throttle, which hath an open cavity for the admission of the air; but lest thereby either meat or drink should descend, Providence hath placed the *Epiglottis, Ligula*, or flap like an Ivy leaf, which alwaies closeth when we swallow, or when the meat and drink passeth over it into the gullet. Which part although all have not that breath, as all cetaceous and oviparous Animals, yet is the weazon secured some other way; and therefore in Whales that breath, least the water should get into the lungs, an ejection thereof is contrived by a Fistula or spout at the head. And therefore also though birds have no Epiglottis, yet can they so contract the rim or chink of their Larinx, as to prevent the admission of wet or dry ingested; either whereof getting in, occasioneth a cough, until it be ejected. And this is the reason why a Man cannot drink and breath at the same time; why, if we laugh while we drink, the drink flies out at the nostrils; why, when the water enters the weazon, Men are suddenly drowned; and thus must it be understood, when we read of one that dyed by the seed of a Grape, and another by an hair in milke.

Now if any shall still affirm, that some truth there is in the assertion, upon the experiment of *Hippocrates*, who killing an Hog after a red potion, found the tincture thereof in the Larinx; if any will urge the same from medical practice, because in affections both of Lungs and weazon, Physitians make use of syrupes, and lambitive medicines; we are not averse to acknowledge, that some may distil and insinuate into the wind-pipe, and medicines may creep down, as well as the rheum before them; yet to conclude from hence, that air and water have both one common passage, were to state the question upon the weaker side of the distinction, and from a partial or guttulous irrigation, to conclude a totall descension.

CHAPTER IX

Of Sneezing

Concerning Sternutation or Sneezing, and the custom of saluting or blessing upon that motion, it is pretended, and generally believed to derive its original from a disease, wherein Sternutation proved mortal, and such as Sneezed, died. And this may seeme to be proved from *Carolus Sigonius*, who in his History of *Italy*, makes mention of a Pestilence in the time of *Gregory* the Great, that proved pernitious and deadly to those that Sneezed. Which notwithstanding will not sufficiently determine the grounds hereof: that custom having an elder *Æra*, then this Chronology affordeth.

For although the age of *Gregory* extend above a thousand, yet is this custom mentioned by *Apuleius*, in the Fable of the Fullers wife, who lived three hundred years before; by *Pliny* in that Probleme of his, *Cur Sternutantes salutantur*; and there are also reports that *Tiberius* the Emperour, otherwise a very sower Man, would perform this rite most punctually unto others, and expect the same from others, unto himself. *Petronius Arbiter*, who lived before them both, and was Proconsul of *Bythinia* in the raign of *Nero*, hath mentioned it in these words, *Gyton collectione spiritus plenus, ter continuo ita sternutavit ut grabatum concuteret, ad quem motum Eumolpus conversus, Salvere Gytona jubet*, *Cælius Rhodiginus* hath an example hereof among the *Greeks*, far antienter then these, that is, in the time of *Cyrus* the younger; when consulting about their retreat, it chanced that one among them Sneezed; at the noise whereof, the rest of the Souldiers called upon *Jupiter Soter*. There is also in the Greeke Anthology a remarkeable mention hereof in an Epigram, upon one *Proclus*; the Latin whereof we shall deliver, as we find it often translated.

Non potis est Proclus digitis emungere nasum,
Namque est pro nasi mole pusilla manus,
Non vocat ille Jovem sternutans, quippe nec audit
Sternutamentum, tam procul aure sonat.
Proclus with his hand his nose can never wipe,
His hand too little is his nose to gripe;
He Sneezing calls not Jove, for why? he hears
Himself not Sneeze, the sound's so far from's ears.

Nor was this onely an ancient custom among the *Greeks* and *Romans*, and is still in force with us, but is received at this day in remotest parts of *Africa*. For so we read in *Codignus*; that upon a Sneeze of the Emperour of *Monomotapa*, there passed acclamations successively through the City. And as remarkable an example there is of the same custom, in the remotest parts of the East, recorded in the travels of *Pinto*.

But the history will run much higher, if we should take in the *Rabbinical* account hereof; that Sneezing was a mortal sign even from the first Man; until it was taken off by the special supplication of *Jacob*. From whence, as a thankful acknowledgment, this salutation first began; and was after continued by the expression of *Tobim Chaiim*, or *vita bona*, by standers by, upon all occasion of Sneezing.

Now the ground of this ancient custom was probably the opinion the ancients held of Sternutation: which they generally conceived to be a good signe or a bad, and so upon this motion according used, a Salve or Ζευ σοσον, as a gratulation for the one, and a deprecation for the other. Now of the waies whereby they enquired and determined its signality; the first was natural, arising from Physical causes, and consequencies oftentimes naturally succeeding this motion; and so it might be justly esteemed a good sign. For Sneezing being properly a motion of the brain, suddenly expelling through the nostrils what is offensive unto it, it cannot but afford some evidence of its vigour; and therefore saith *Aristotle*, they that heare it προσκυνουσιν Ος hιερον, honour it as somewhat Sacred, and a sign of Sanity in the diviner part; and this he illustrates from the practise of Physitians, who in persons near death, do use Sternutatories, or such medicines as provoke unto Sneezing; when if the facultie awaketh, and Sternutation ensueth, they conceive hopes of life, and with gratulation receive the signs of safety.

302

And so is it also of good signality, according to that of *Hippocrates*, that Sneezing cureth the hicket, and is profitable unto Women in hard labour; and so is it good in Lethargies, Apoplexies, Catalepsies, and Coma's. And in this natural way it is sometime likewise of bad effects or signs, and may give hints of deprecation; as in diseases of the chest; for therein *Hippocrates* condemneth it as too much exagitating: in the beginning of *Catarrhs* according unto *Avicenna*, as hindering concoction, in new and tender conceptions (as *Pliny* observeth) for then it endangers abortion.

The second way was superstitious and Augurial, as *Cælius Rhodiginus* hath illustrated in testimonies, as ancient as *Theocritus* and *Homer*: as appears from the *Athenian* Master, who would have retired, because a Boatman Sneezed; and the testimony of *Austin*, that the Ancients were wont to go to bed again if they Sneezed while they put on their shoe. And in this way it was also of good and bad signification; so *Aristotle* hath a Problem, why Sneezing from noon unto midnight was good, but from night to noon unlucky? So *Eustathius* upon *Homer* observes, that Sneezing to the left hand was unlucky, but prosperous unto the right; so, as *Plutarch* relateth, when *Themistocles* sacrificed in his galley before the battle of *Xerxes*, and one of the assistants upon the right hand Sneezed, *Euphrantides* the Southsayer, presaged the victory of the *Greeks*, and the overthrow of the *Persians*.

Thus we may perceive the custom is more ancient then commonly conceived; and these opinions hereof in all ages, nor any one disease to have been the occasion of this salute and deprecation. Arising at first from this vehement and affrighting motion of the brain, inevitably observable unto the standers by; from whence some finding dependent effects to ensue; others ascribing hereto as a cause what perhaps but casually or inconnexedly succeeded; they might proceed unto forms of speeches, felicitating the good, or deprecating the evil to follow.

CHAPTER X

Of the Jews

That the *Jews* stink naturally, that is, that in their race and nation there is an evil savour, is a received opinion we know not how to admit; although concede many questionable points, and dispute not the verity of sundry opinions which are of affinity hereto. We will acknowledg that certain odours attend on animals, no less then certain colours; that pleasant smels are not confined unto vegitables, but found in divers animals, and some more richly then in plants. And though the Problem of *Aristotle* enquire why no animal smells sweet beside that Parde? yet later discoveries adde divers sorts of *Monkeys*, the *Civet Cat* and *Gazela*, from which our Musk proceedeth. We confess that beside the smell of the species, there may be individual odours, and every Man may have a proper and peculiar savour; which although not perceptible unto Man, who hath this sense, but weak, yet sensible unto *Dogs*, who hereby can single out their masters in the dark. We will not deny that particular Men have sent forth a pleasant savour, as *Theophrastus* and *Plutarch* report of *Alexander* the great, and *Tzetzes* and *Cardan* do testifie of themselves. That some may also emit an unsavoury odour, we have no reason to deny; for this may happen from the quality of what they have taken; the Fætor whereof may discover it self by sweat and urine, as being unmasterable by the natural heat of Man, not to be dulcified by concoction beyond an unsavoury condition: the like may come to pass from putrid humours, as is often discoverable in putrid and malignant feavers. And sometime also in gross and humid bodies even in the latitude of sanity; the natural heat of the parts being insufficient for a perfect and through digestion, and the errors of one concoction not rectifiable by another. But that an unsavoury odour is gentilitious or national unto the *Jews*, if rightly understood, we cannot well concede; nor will the information of reason or sence induce it.

For first, Upon consult of reason, there will bee found no easie assurance to fasten a material or temperamental propriety upon any nation; there being scarce any condition (but what depends upon clime) which is not exhausted or obscured from the commixture of introvenient nations either by commerce or conquest; much more will it be difficult to make out this affection in the *Jews*; whose race however pretended to be pure, must needs have suffered inseparated commixtures with nations of all sorts, not only in regard of their proselytes, but their universal dispersion; some being posted from several parts of the earth, others quite lost, and swallowed up in those nations where they planted. For the tribes of *Ruben*, *Gad*, part of *Manasses* and *Naphthali*, which were taken by *Assur*, and the rest at the sacking of *Samaria* which were led away by *Salmanasser* into *Assyria*, and after a year and half arrived at *Arseereth*, as is delivered in *Esdras*; these I say never returned, and are by the *Jews* as vainly expected as their *Messias*. Of those of the tribe of *Judah* and *Benjamin*, which were led captive into *Babylon* by *Nebuchadnezzar*, many returned under *Zorobabel*; the rest remained, and from thence long after upon invasion of the *Saracens*, fled as far as *India*; where yet they are said to remain, but with little difference from the *Gentiles*.

The Tribes that returned to *Judea*, were afterward widely dispersed; for beside sixteen thousand which *Titus* sent to *Rome* unto the triumph of his father *Vespasian*, he sold no less then an hundred thousand for slaves. Not many years after *Adrian* the Emperour, who ruined the whole Countrey, transplanted many thousands into *Spain*, from whence they dispersed into divers Countreys, as into *France* and *England*, but were banished after from both. From Spain they dispersed into *Africa*, *Italy*, *Constantinople*, and the Dominions of the *Turk*, where they remain as yet in very great numbers. And if (according to good relations) where they must freely speak it, they forbear not to boast that there are at present many thousand Jews in *Spane*, *France*, and *England*, and some dispensed withall even to the degree of Priesthood; it is a matter very considerable, and could they be smelled out, would much advantage, not only the Church of Christ, but also the coffers of Princes.

Now having thus lived in several Countries, and alwaies in subjection, they must needs have suffered many commixtures; and we are sure they are not exempted from the common contagion of Venery contracted first from Christians. Nor are fornications unfrequent between them both; there commonly passing opinions of invitement, that their Women desire copulation with them rather then their own Nation, and affect Christian carnality above circumcised venery. It being therefore acknowledged, that some are lost, evident that others are mixed, and not assured that any are distinct, it will be hard to establish this quality upon the *Jews*, unless we also transfer the same unto those whose generations are mixed, whose genealogies are *Jewish*, and naturally derived from them.

Again, if we concede a National unsavourinesse in any people, yet shall we find the *Jews* less subject hereto then any, and that in those regards which most powerfully concur to such effects, that is, their diet and generation. As for their diet, whether in obedience unto the precepts of reason, or the Injunctions of parsimony, therein they are very temperate; seldom offending in ebrietie or excess of drink, nor erring in gulosity or superfluity of meats; whereby they prevent indigestion and crudities, and consequently putrescence of humors. They have in abomination all flesh maimed, or the inwards any way vitiated; and therefore eat no meat but of their own killing. They observe not only fasts at certain times, but are restrained unto very few dishes at all times; so few, that whereas St. *Peters* sheet will hardly cover our Tables, their Law doth scarce permit them to set forth a Lordly feast; nor any way to answer the luxury of our times, or those of our fore-father. For of flesh their Law restrains them many sorts, and such as compleat our feasts: That Animal, *Propter convivia natum*, they touch not, nor any of its preparations, or parts so much in respect at *Roman* Tables, nor admit they unto their board, *Hares, Conies, Herons, Plovers* or *Swans*. Of *Fishes* they only tast of such as have both fins and scales; which are comparatively but few in number, such only, saith *Aristotle*, whose Egg or spawn is arenaceous; whereby are excluded all cetaceous and cartilagineous *Fishes*, many pectinal, whose ribs are rectilineal; many costal, which have their ribs embowed; all spinal, or such as have no ribs, but only a back bone, or somewhat analogous thereto, as *Eels, Congers, Lampries*; all that are testaceous, as *Oysters, Cocles, Wilks, Scollops, Muscles*; and likewise all crustaceous, as *Crabs, Shrimps*, and *Lobsters*. So that observing a spare and simple diet, whereby they prevent generation of crudities;

306

and fasting often whereby they might also digest them; they must be less inclinable unto this infirmity then any other Nation, whose proceedings are not so reasonable to avoid it.

As for their generations and conceptions (which are the purer from good diet,) they become more pure and perfect by the strict observation of their Law; upon the injunctions whereof, they severely observe the times of Purification, and avoid all copulation, either in the uncleanness of themselves, or impurity of their Women. A Rule, I fear, not so well observed by Christians; whereby not only conceptions are prevented, but if they proceed, so vitiated and defiled, that durable inquinations, remain upon the birth. Which, when the conception meets with these impurities, must needs be very potent; since in the purest and most fair conceptions, learned Men derive the cause of *Pox* and *Meazels*, from principles of that nature; that is, the menstruous impurities in the Mothers blood, and virulent tinctures contracted by the Infant, in the nutriment of the womb.

Lastly, Experience will convict it; for this offensive odor is no way discoverable in their Synagogues where many are, and by reason of their number could not be concealed: nor is the same discernible in commerce or conversation with such as are cleanly in Apparel, and decent in their Houses. Surely the Viziars and *Turkish* Basha's are not of this opinion, who as Sr. *Henry Blunt* informeth, do generally keep a *Jew* of their private Counsel. And were this true, the *Jews* themselves do not strictly make out the intention of their Law, for in vain do they scruple to approach the dead, who livingly are cadaverous, or fear any outward pollution, whose temper pollutes themselves. And lastly, were this true, yet our opinion is not impartial; for unto converted *Jews* who are of the same seed, no Man imputeth this unsavoury odor; as though Aromatized by their conversion, they lost their scent with their Religion, and smelt no longer then they savoured of the *Jew*.

Now the ground that begat or propagated this assertion, might be the distasteful averseness of the Christian from the *Jew*, upon the villany of that fact, which made them abominable and stink in the nostrils of all Men. Which real practise, and metaphorical expression, did after proceed into a literal construction; but was a fraudulent illation; for such an evil savour their father *Jacob* acknowledged in himself, when he said, his sons had made him stink in the land, that is, to be abominable unto the inhabitants thereof. Now how dangerous it is in sensible things to use metaphorical expressions unto the people, and what absurd conceits they will swallow in their literals; an impatient example we have in our profession; who having called an eating *Ulcer* by the name of a *Woolf*, common apprehension conceives a reality therein; and against our selves, ocular affirmations are pretended to confirm it.

The nastiness of that Nation, and sluttish course of life hath much promoted the opinion, occasioned by their servile condition at first, and inferiour wayes of parsimony ever since; as is delivered by Mr. *Sandys*, They are generally fat, saith he, and rank of the savours which attend upon sluttish corpulency: The *Epithetes* assigned them by ancient times, have also advanced the same; for *Ammianus Marcellinus* describeth them in such language; and *Martial* more ancient, in such a relative expression sets forth unsavoury *Bassa*.

> Quod jejunia Sabbatariorum
> Mallem, quàm quod oles, olere Bassa.

From whence notwithstanding we cannot infer an inward imperfection in the temper of that Nation; it being but an effect in the breath from outward observation, in their strict and tedious fasting; and was a common effect in the breaths of other Nations, became a Proverb among the *Greeks*, and the reason thereof begot a Problem in *Aristotle*.

Lastly, If all were true, and were this savour conceded, yet are the reasons alleadged for it no way satisfactory. *Hucherius*, and after him *Alsarius Crucius*, imputes this effect unto their abstinence from salt or salt meats; which how to make good in the present diet of the *Jews* we know not; nor shall we conceive it was observed of old, if we consider they seasoned every Sacrifice, and all oblations whatsoever; whereof we cannot deny a great part was eaten by the Priests. And if the offering were of flesh, it was salted no lesse then thrice, that is, once in the common chamber of salt, at the foot-step of the Altar, and upon the top thereof, as is at large delivered by *Maimonides*. Nor if they refrained all salt, is the illation very urgent; for many there are not noted for ill odours, which eat no salt at all; as all carnivorous Animals, most Children, many whole Nations, and probably our Fathers after the Creation; there being indeed in every thing we eat, a natural and concealed salt, which is separated by digestions, as doth appear in our tears, sweat, and urines, although we refrain all salt, or what doth seem to contain it.

Another cause is urged by *Campegius*, and much received by Christians; that this ill savour is a curse derived upon them by Christ, and stands, as a badge or brand of a generation that crucified their *Salvator*. But this is a conceit without all warrant; and an easie way to take off dispute in what point of obscurity soever. A method of many Writers, which much depreciates the esteem and value of miracles: that is, therewith to salve not only real verities, but also nonexistencies. Thus have elder times, not only ascribed the immunity of *Ireland* from any venemous beast, unto the staff or rod of *Patrick*; but the long tails of *Kent*, unto the malediction of *Austin*.

Thus therefore, although we concede that many opinions are true which hold some conformity unto this, yet in assenting hereto, many difficulties must arise: it being a dangerous point to annex a constant property unto any Nation, and much more this unto the *Jew*; since this quality is not verifiable by observation; since the grounds are feeble that should establish it; and lastly: since if all were true, yet are the reasons alleadged for it, of no sufficiency to maintain it.

CHAPTER XI

Of Pigmies

By *Pigmies* we understand a dwarfish race of people, or lower diminution of mankind, comprehended in one cubit, or as some will have it, in two foot, or three spans; not taking them single, but nationally considering them, and as they make up an aggregated habitation. Whereof although affirmations be many, and testimonies more frequent then in any other point which wise men have cast into the list of fables, yet that there is, or ever was such a race or Nation, upon exact and confirmed testimonies, our strictest enquiry receaves no satisfaction.

I say, exact testimonies, first, In regard of the Authors, from whom we derive the account, for though we meet herewith in *Herodotus*, *Philostratus*, *Mela*, *Pliny*, *Solinus*, and many more; yet were they derivative Relators, and the primitive Author was *Homer*; who, using often similies, as well to delight the ear, as to illustrate his matter, in the third of his Iliads, compareth the *Trojans* unto *Cranes*, when they descend against the *Pigmies*; which was most largely set out by *Oppian*, *Juvenal*, *Mantuan*, and many Poets since; and being only a pleasant figment in the fountain, became a solemn story in the stream, and current still among us.

Again, Many professed enquirers have rejected it; *Strabo* an exact and judicious Geographer, hath largely condemned it as a fabulous story, *Julius Scaliger* a diligent enquirer, accounts thereof, but as a Poetical fiction; *Ulysses Aldrovandus* a most exact Zoographer in an express discourse hereon, concludes the story fabulous, and a Poetical account of *Homer*; and the same was formerly conceived by *Eustathius* his excellent Commentator. *Albertus Magnus* a man oft-times too credulous, herein was more then dubious; for he affirmeth, if any such dwarfs were ever extant, they were surely some kind of *Apes*; which is a conceit allowed, by *Cardan*, and not esteemed improbable by many others.

There are I confesse two testimonies, which from their authority admit of consideration. The first of *Aristotle*, whose words are these, *esti de ho topos*, etc. That is, *Hic locus est quem incolunt Pygmæi, non enim id fabula est, sed pusillum genus ut aiunt.* Wherein indeed *Aristotle* plaies the *Aristotle*, that is, the wary and evading assertor; For though with *non est fabula*, he seems at first to confirm it, yet at the last he claps in, *Sicut aiunt*, and shakes the beliefe he put before upon it. And therefore I observe *Scaliger* hath not translated the first; perhaps supposing it surreptitious or unworthy so great an assertor. And truly for those books of animals, or work of eight hundred talents, as *Athenæus* terms it, although ever to be admired, as containing most excellent truths; yet are many things therein delivered upon relation, and some repugnant unto the history of our senses; as we are able to make out in some, and *Scaliger* hath observed in many more, as he hath freely declared in his Comment upon that piece.

The second testimony is deduced from holy Scripture; *Sed & Pygmæi qui erant in turribus tuis, pharetras suas suspenderunt in muris tuis per gyrum*: from whence notwithstanding we cannot infer this assertion, for first the Translators accord not, and the Hebrew word *Gammadim* is very variously rendered. Though *Aquila, Vatablus* and *Lyra* will have it *Pygmæi*, yet in the Septuagint, it is no more then Watchmen; and so in the *Arabick* and high *Dutch*. In the *Chaldie, Cappadocians*, in *Symmachus, Medes*, and in the *French*, those of *Gamad. Theodotian* of old, and *Tremellius* of late, have retained the Textuary word; and so have the *Italian*, Low *Dutch* and *English* Translators, that is, the Men of *Arvad* were upon thy walls round about, and the *Gammadims* were in thy Towers.

Nor do men only dissent in the Translation of the word, but in the Exposition of the sense and meaning thereof; for some by *Gammadims* understand a people of *Syria*, so called from the City *Gamala*; some hereby understand the *Cappadocians*, many the *Medes*: and hereof *Forerius* hath a singular Exposition, conceiving the Watchmen of *Tyre*, might well be called *Pigmies*, the Towers of that City being so high, that unto Men below, they appeared in a cubital stature. Others

311

expounded it quite contrary to common acception, that is not Men of the least, but of the largest size; so doth *Cornelius* construe *Pygmœi*, or *viri cubitales*, that is, not Men of a cubit high, but of the largest stature, whose height like that of Giants is rather to be taken by the cubit then the foot; in which phrase we read the measure of *Goliath*, whose height is said to be six cubits and a span. Of affinity hereto is also the Exposition of *Jerom*; not taking *Pigmies* for dwarfs, but stout and valiant Champions; not taking the sense of πυγμὶ, which signifies the cubit measure, but that which expresseth Pugils; that is, Men fit for combat and the exercise of the fist. Thus can there be no satisfying illation from this Text, the diversity or rather contrariety of Expositions and interpretations, distracting more then confirming the truth of the story.

Again, I say, exact testimonies; in reference unto circumstantial relations so diversly or contrarily delivered. Thus the Relation of *Aristotle* placeth them above *Egypt* towards the head of *Nyle* in *Africa*; *Philostratus* affirms they are about *Ganges* in *Asia*, and *Pliny* in a third place, that is *Gerania* in *Scythia*: some write they fight with Cranes, but *Menecles* in *Athenæus* affirms they fight with *Partridges*, some say they ride on *Partridges*, and some on the backs of *Rams*.

Lastly, I say, confirmed testimonies; for though *Paulus Jovinus* delivers there are *Pigmies* beyond *Japan*; *Pigafeta*, about the *Molucca's*; and *Olaus Magnus* placeth them in *Greenland*; yet wanting frequent confirmation in a a matter so confirmable, their affirmation carrieth but slow perswasion; and wise men may think there is as much reality in the *Pigmies* of *Paracelsus*; that is, his non-Adamical men, or middle natures betwixt men and spirits.

There being thus no sufficient confirmation of their verity, some doubt may arise concerning their possibility, wherein, since it is not defined in what dimensions the soul may exercise her faculties, we shall not conclude impossibility; or that there might not be a race of *Pigmies*, as there is sometimes of Giants. So may we take in the opinion of *Austin*, and his Comment *Ludovicus*, but to believe they should be in the stature of a foot or span, requires the preaspection of such a one as *Philetas* the Poet in *Athenæus*; who was faine to fasten lead unto his feet lest the wind should blow him away. Or that other in the same Author, who was so little *ut ad obolum accederet*, a story so strange, that we might herein accuse the printer, did not the account of *Ælian* accord unto it, as *Casaubon* hath observed in his learned Animadversions.

Lastly, If any such Nation there were, yet is it ridiculous what Men have delivered of them; that they fight with *Cranes* upon the backs of *Rams* or *Partridges*: or what is delivered by *Ctesias*, that they are *Negroes* in the middest of *India*; whereof the King of that Country, entertaineth three thousand Archers for his guard. Which is a relation below the tale of *Oberon*; nor could they better defend him, then the Emblem saith, they offended *Hercules* whilest he slept; that is to wound him no deeper, then to awake him.

CHAPTER XII

Of the great Climacterical year, that is, Sixty three

Certainly the Eyes of the understanding, and those of the sense are differently deceived in their greatest objects; the sense apprehending them in lesser magnitudes then their dimensions require; so it beholdeth the Sun, the Stars, and the Earth it selfe. But the understanding quite otherwise: for that ascribeth unto many things far larger horizons then their due circumscriptions require: and receiveth them with amplifications which their reality will not admit. Thus hath it fared with many Heroes and most worthy persons, who being sufficiently commendable from true and unquestionable merits, have received advancement from falshood and the fruitful stock of Fables. Thus hath it happened unto the Stars, and Luminaries of heaven: who being sufficiently admirable in themselves, have been set out by effects, no way dependent on their efficiencies, and advanced by amplifications to the questioning of their true endowments. Thus is it not improbable it hath also fared with number, which though wonderful in it self, and sufficiently magnifiable from its demonstrable affections, hath yet received adjections from the multiplying conceits of men, and stands laden with additions, which its equity will not admit.

And so perhaps hath it happened unto the numbers, 7 and 9, which multiplied into themselves do make up Sixty three, commonly esteemed the great Climacterical of our lives. For the daies of men are usually cast up by Septenaries, and every seventh yeare conceived to carry some altering character with it, either in the temper of body, mind, or both. But among all other, three are most remarkable, that is 7 times 7 or forty nine, 9 times 9 or eighty one, and 7 times 9 or the year of Sixty three; which is conceived to carry with it the most considerable fatality, and consisting of both the other numbers was apprehended to comprise the vertue of either: is therefore expected and entertained with fear, and esteemed a favour of fate to pass it over. Which notwithstanding many suspect to be but a Panick terrour, and men to fear they justly know not what: and to speak indifferently, I find no satisfaction: nor any sufficiency in the received grounds to establish a rationall fear.

Now herein to omit Astrological considerations (which are but rarely introduced) the popular foundation whereby it hath continued, is first, the extraordinary power and secret vertue conceived to attend these numbers: whereof we must confess there have not wanted not only especial commendations, but very singular conceptions. Among Philosophers, *Pythagoras* seems to have played the leading part; which was long after continued by his disciples, and the *Italick* School. The Philosophy of *Plato*, and most of the *Platonists* abounds in numeral considerations; above all, *Philo* the learned *Jew*, hath acted this part even to superstition: bestowing divers pages in summing up every thing, which might advantage this number. Which notwithstanding, when a serious Reader shall perpend, he will hardly find any thing that may convince his judgment, or any further perswade, then the lenity of his belief, or prejudgment of reason inclineth.

For first, not only the number of 7 and 9 from considerations abstruse, have been extolled by most, but all or most of the other digits have been as mystically applauded. For the number of One and Three have not been only admitted by the Heathens, but from adorable grounds, the unity of God, and mystery of the Trinity admired by many Christians. The number of four stands much admired, not only in the quaternity of the Elements, which are the principles of bodies, but in the letters of the Name of God, which in the *Greek*, *Arabian*, *Persian*, *Hebrew*, and *Egyptian*, consisteth of that number; and was so venerable among the *Pythagorians*, that they swore by the number four. That of six hath found many leaves in its favour; not only for the daies of the Creation, but its natural consideration, as being a perfect number, and the first that is compleated by its parts; that is, the sixth, the half, and the third, 1. 2. 3. Which drawn into a sum, make six. The number of Ten hath been as highly extolled, as containing even, odd, long, plain, quadrate and cubical numbers; and *Aristotle* observed with admiration, that *Barbarians* as well as *Greeks*, did use numeration unto Ten, which being so general, was not to be judged casual, but to have a foundation in nature. So that not only 7 and 9, but all the rest have had their Elogies, as may be observed at large in *Rhodiginus*, and in several Writers since: every one extolling number, according to his subject, and as it advantaged the present discourse in hand.

Again, they have been commended not only from pretended grounds in nature, but from artificial, casual, or fabulous foundations: so have some endeavoured to advance their admiration, from the 9 Muses, from the 7 Wonders of the World, from the 7 Gates of *Thebes*: in that 7 Cities contended for *Homer*, in that there are 7 stars in *Ursa minor*, and 7 in Charles wayn, or Plaustrum of *Ursa major*. Wherein indeed although the ground be natural, yet either from constellations or their remarkable parts, there is the like occasion to commend any other number, the number 5 from the stars in *Sagitta*, 3 from the girdle of *Orion*, and 4 from *Equiculus*, *Crusero*, or the feet of the Centaur: yet are such as these clapt in by very few good Authors, and some not omitted by *Philo*.

Nor are they only extolled from Arbitrary and Poetical grounds, but from foundations and principles, false, or dubious. That Women are menstruant, and Men pubescent at the year of twice seven is accounted a punctual truth: which period nevertheless we dare not precisely determine, as having observed a variation and latitude in most, agreeable unto the heat of clime or temper, Men arising variously into virility, according to the activity of causes that promote it. *Sanguis mentruosus ad diem, ut plurimum, septimum durat*, saith *Philo*. Which notwithstanding is repugnant unto experience, and the doctrine of *Hippocrates*, who in his book, *de diæta*, plainly affirmeth, it is thus but with few women, and only such as abound with pituitous and watery humours.

It is further conceived to receive addition, in that there are 7 heads of *Nyle*, but we have made manifest elsewhere by the description of Geographers, they have beene sometime more, and are at present fewer.

In that there were 7 Wise men of *Greece*, which though generally received, yet having enquired into the verity thereof we cannot so readily determine it; for in the life of *Thales*, who was accounted in that number, *Diogenes Laertius* plainly saith *Magna de eorum numero discordia est*; some holding but four, some ten, others twelve, and none agreeth in their names, though according in their number.

In that there are just 7 Planets or errant Stars in the lower orbs of Heaven, but it is now demonstrable unto sense, that there are many more; as *Galileo* hath declared, that is, two more in the orb of Saturn, and no less then four more in the sphere of Jupiter. And the like may be said of the *Pleiades* or 7 Stars, which are also introduced to magnifie this number, for whereas scarce discerning six, we account them 7, by his relation, there are no less then fourty.

That the Heavens are encompassed with 7 Circles, is also the allegation of *Philo*; which are in his account, The Artick, Antartick, the Summer and Winter Tropicks, the Æquator, Zodiack, and the Milky circle; whereas by Astronomers they are received in greater number. For though we leave out the Lacteous circle (which *Aratus*, *Geminus*, and *Proclus*, out of him hath numbered among the rest) yet are there more by four then *Philo* mentions; that is, the Horizon, Meridian and both the Colures; circles very considerable, and generally delivered, not only by *Ptolomie*, and the Astronomers since his time, but such as a flourished long before, as *Hipparchus* and *Eudoxus*. So that for ought I know, if it make for our purpose, or advance the theme in hand, with equal liberty, we may affirm there were 7 Sybils, or but 7 signs in the Zodiack circle of Heaven.

That verse in *Virgil* translated out of *Homer*, *O terque quaterque beati*; that is, as men will have it, 7 times happy, hath much advanced this number in critical apprehensions; yet is not this construction so indubitably to be received, as not at all to be questioned; for though *Rhodiginus*, *Beroaldus* and others from the authority of *Macrobius* so interpret it, yet *Servius* his ancient commentator conceives no more thereby then a finite number for indefinite, and that no more is implied then often happy. *Strabo* the ancientist of them all, conceives no more by this in *Homer*, then a full and excessive expression; whereas in common phrase and received language, he should have termed them thrice happy; herein exceeding that number, he called them four times happy; that is, more then thrice. And this he illustrates by the like expression of *Homer* in the speech of *Circe*; who to express the dread and terrour of the Ocean, sticks not unto the common form of speech in the strict account of its reciprocations, but largely speaking, saith, it ebbs and flows no less then thrice a day, *terque die revomit fluctus, iterumque resorbet.* And so when 'tis said by *Horace, fælices ter & amplius,* the exposition is sufficient, if we conceive no more then the letter fairly beareth, that is, four times, or indefinitly more then thrice.

But the main considerations which most set off this number, are observations drawn from the motions of the Moon, supposed to be measured by sevens; and the critical or decretory daies dependent on that number. As for the motion of the Moon, though we grant it to be measured by sevens, yet will not this advance the same before its fellow numbers; for hereby the motions of other Stars are not measured, the fixed Stars by many thousand years, the Sun by 365 daies, the superiour Planets by more, the inferiour by somewhat less. And if we consider the revolution of the first Movable, and the daily motion from East to West, common unto all the Orbs, we shall find it measured by another number, for being performed in four and twenty hours, it is made up of 4 times 6: and this is the measure and standard of other parts of time, of months, of years, Olympiades, Lustres, Indictions, Cycles, Jubilies, &c.

Again, Months are not only Lunary, and measured by the Moon, but also Solary, and determined by the motion of the Sun; that is, the space wherein the Sun doth pass 30 degrees of the Ecliptick. By this month *Hippocrates* computed the time of the Infants gestation in the womb; for 9 times 30, that is, 270 daies, or compleat 9 months, make up forty weeks, the common compute of women. And this is to be understood, when he saith, 2 daies makes the fifteenth, and 3 the tenth part of a month. This was the month of the ancient *Hebrews* before their departure out of *Egypt:* and hereby the compute will fall out right, and the account concur, when in one place it is said, the waters of the flood prevailed an hundred and fifty daies, and in another it is delivered, that they prevailed from the seventeenth day of the second month, unto the seventeenth day of the seventh. As for the hebdomadal periods or weeks, although in regard of their Sabbaths, they were observed by the *Hebrews,* yet it is not apparent, the ancient *Greeks* or *Romans* used any: but had another division of their months into Ides, Nones and Calends.

Moreover, Moneths howsoever taken, are not exactly divisible into septenaries or weeks, which fully containe seven daies: whereof four times do make compleatly twenty eight. For, beside the usual or Calendary month, there are but four considerable: the month of Peragration, of Apparition, of Consecution, and the medical or Decretorial month; whereof some come short, others exceed this account. A month of Peragration, is the time of the Moons revolution from any part of the Zodiack, unto the same again: and this containeth but 27 daies, and about 8 hours: which cometh short to compleat the septenary account. The month of Consecution, or as some will terme it, of progression, is the space between one conjunction of the Moon with the Sun, unto another: and this containeth 29 daies and an half: for the Moon returning unto the same point wherein it was kindled by the Sun, and not finding it there again, (for in the mean time, by its proper motion it hath passed through 2 signes) it followeth after, and attaines the Sun in the space of 2 daies and 4 hours more, which added unto the account of Peragration, makes 29 daies and an half: so that this month exceedeth the latitude of Septenaries, and the fourth part comprehendeth more then 7 daies. A month of Apparition, is the space wherein the Moon appeareth (deducting three daies wherein it commonly disappeareth; and being in combustion with the Sun, is presumed of less activity,) and this containeth but 26 daies and 12 hours. The medical month, not much exceedeth this, consisting of 26 daies and 22 hours, and is made up out of all the other months. For if out of 29 and an half, the month of Consecution, we deduct 3 daies of disappearance, there will remain the month of Apparition 26 daies, and 12. hours: whereto if we add 27 daies and 8 hours, the month of Peragration, there will arise 53 daies and 10. hours, which divided by 2, makes 26 daies and 22 hours: called by Physitians the medical month; introduced by *Galen* against *Archigenes*, for the better compute of Decretory or Critical daies.

As for the Critical daies (such I mean wherein upon a decertation betweene the disease and nature, there ensueth a sensible alteration, either to life or death,) the reasons thereof are rather deduced from Astrology, then Arithmetick: for accounting from the beginning of the disease, and reckoning on unto the seventh day, the Moon will be in a Tetragonal or Quadrate aspect, that is, 4 signs removed from that wherein the disease began: in the fourteenth day it will be in an opposite aspect: and at the end of the third septenary,

Tetragonal again: as will most graphically appeare in the figures of Astrologers, especially *Lucas Gauricus, De Diebus decretoriis.*

Again, (Beside that computing by the Medical month the first hebdomade or septenary consists of 6 daies, seventeen hours and an half, the second happeneth in 13 daies and eleven hours, and the third but in the twentieth natural day) what *Galen* first, and *Aben-Ezra* since observed in his Tract of Critical daies, in regard of Eccentricity and the Epicycle or lesser orb wherein it moveth, the motion of the Moon is various and unequal; whereby the Critical account must also vary. For though its middle motion be equal, and of 13 degrees, yet in the other it moveth sometimes fifteen, sometimes less then twelve. For moving in the upper part of its orb, it performeth its motion more slowly then in the lower; insomuch that being at the lwest, it arriveth at the Tetragonal and opposite signs sooner, and the Critical day will be in 6 and 13; and being at the height, the critical account will be out of the latitude of 7, nor happen before the eigth or ninth day. Which are considerations not to be neglected in the compute of decretory daies, and manifestly declare that other numbers must have a respect herein as well as 7 and fourteen.

Lastly, Some things to this intent are deduced from holy Scripture; thus is the yeare of *Jubile* introduced to magnifie this number, as being a yeare made out of 7 times 7; wherein notwithstanding there may be a misapprehension; for this ariseth not from 7 times 7, that is 49; but was observed the fiftieth yeare, as is expressed, And you shall hallow the fiftieth year, a *Jubile* shall that fiftieth year be unto you. Answerable whereto is the Exposition of the *Jews* themselves; as is delivered by *Ben-Maimon*; that is, the year of Jubile, cometh not into the account of the years of 7, but the forty ninth is the Release, and the fiftieth the yeare of *Jubile.* Thus is it also esteemed no small advancement unto this number, that the Genealogy of our Saviour is summed up by 14, that is, this number doubled; according as is expressed. So all the generations from *Abraham* to *David* are fourteen generations, and from *David* unto the carrying away into *Babylon,* are fourteen generations; and from the carrying away into *Babylon* unto *Christ,* are fourteen generations. Which nevertheless must not be strictly understood as numeral relations require; for from *David* unto *Jeconiah* are accounted by *Matthew* but 14 generations; whereas according to the exact account in the History of Kings, there were at least 17; and 3 in this account, that is, *Ahazias, Joas* and *Amazias* are left out. For so it is delivered by the Evangelist: And *Joram* begat *Ozias*: whereas in the Regal Genealogy there are 3 successions between: for *Ozias* or *Uzziah* was the son of *Amazias*, *Amazias* of *Joas*, *Joas* of *Azariah*, and *Azariah* of *Joram*: so that in strict account, *Joram* was the *Abavus* or Grand-father twice removed, and not the Father of *Ozias*. And these second omitted descents made a very considerable measure of time, in the Royal chronology of *Judah*: for although *Azariah* reigned but one year, yet *Joas* reigned fourty, and *Amazias* no less then nine and twenty. However therefore these were delivered by the Evangelist, and carry (no doubt) an incontroulable conformity unto the intention of his delivery: yet are they not appliable unto precise numerality, nor strictly to be drawn unto the rigid test of numbers.

Lastly, Though many things have been delivered by Authors concerning number, and they transferred unto the advantage of their nature, yet are they oft-times otherwise to be understood, then as they are vulgarly received in active and causal considerations; they being many times delivred Hieroglyphically, Metaphorically, Illustratively, and not with reference unto action or causality. True it is, that God made all things in number, weight and measure, yet nothing by them or through the efficacy of either. Indeed our daies, actions and motions being measured by time (which is but motion measured) what ever is observable in any, fals under the account of some number; which notwithstanding cannot be denominated the cause of those events. So do we injustly assign the power of Action even unto Time it self; nor do they speak properly who say that Time consumeth all things; for Time is not effective, nor are bodies destroyed by it, but from the action and passion of their Elements in it; whose account it only affordeth, and measuring out their motion, informs us in the periods and terms of their duration, rather then effecteth, or physically produceth the same.

A second consideration which promoteth this opinion, are confirmations drawn from Writers, who have made observations, or set down favourable reasons for this Climacterical yeare; so have *Henricus Ranzovius*, *Baptista Codronchus*, and *Levinus Lemnius* much confirmed the same; but above all, that memorable Letter of *Augustus* sent unto his Nephew *Caius*, wherein he encourageth him to celebrate his nativity, for he had now escaped Sixty three, the great Climacterical and dangerous year unto man: which notwithstanding rightly perpended, it can be no singularity to question it, nor any new Paradox to deny it.

For first, It is implicitely, and upon consequence denied by *Aristotle* in his Politicks, in that discourse against *Plato*, who measured the vicissitude and mutation of States, by a periodical fatality of number. *Ptolomie* that famous Mathematician plainly saith, he will not deliver his doctrines by parts and numbers which are ineffectual, and have not the nature of causes; now by these numbers saith *Rhodiginus* and *Mirandula*, he implyeth Climacterical years, that is, septenaries, and novenaries set down by the bare observation of numbers. *Censorinus* an Author of great authority, and sufficient antiquity, speaks yet more amply in his book *De die Natali*, wherein expresly treating of Climacterical daies, he thus delivereth himself. Some maintain that 7 times 7, that is, fourty nine, is most dangerous of any other, and this is the most general opinion; others unto 7 times 7, add 9 times 9, that is, the year of eighty one, both which consisting of square and quadrate numbers, were thought by *Plato* and others to be of great consideration; as for this year of Sixty three or 7 times 9, though some esteem it of most danger, yet do I conceive it less dangerous then the other; for though it containeth both numbers above named, that is 7 and 9, yet neither of them square or quadrate; and as it is different from them both, so is it not potent in either. Nor is this year remarkable in the death of many famous men. I find indeed that *Aristotle* died this year, but he by the vigour of his mind, a long time sustained a natural infirmity of stomack; so that it was a greater wonder he attained unto Sixty three, then that he lived no longer. The Psalm of *Moses* hath mentioned a year of danger differing from all these: and that is ten times 7 or seventy; for so it is said, The daies of Man are threescore and ten. And the very same is affirmed by *Solon*, as *Herodotus* relates in a speech of his unto *Crœsus*, *Ego annis septuaginta humanœ vitœ modum definio*; and surely that year must be of greatest danger, which is the Period of all the rest, and fewest safely passe thorow that, which is set as a bound for few or none to pass. And therefore the consent of elder times, setling their conceits upon Climacters, not only differing from this of ours, but one another; though several Nations and Ages do fancy unto themselves different years of danger, yet every one expects the same event, and constant verity in each.

Again, Though *Varro* divided the daies of man into five proportions, *Hippocrates* into 7, and *Solon* into 10; yet probably their divisions were to be received with latitude, and their considerations not strictly to be confined unto their last unities. So when *Varro* extendeth *Pueritia* unto 15. *Adolescentia* unto 30. *Juventus* unto 35. There is a latitude between the terms or Periods of compute, and the verity holds good in the accidents of any years between them. So when *Hippocrates* divideth our life into 7 degrees or stages, and maketh the end of the first 7. Of the second 14. Of the third 28. Of the fourth 35. Of the fift 47. Of the sixt 56. And of the seventh, the last year when ever it happeneth; herein we observe, he maketh not his divisions precisely by 7 and 9, and omits the great Climacterical; beside there is between every one at least the latitude of 7 years, in which space or interval, that is either in the third of fourth year, what ever falleth out is equally verified of the whole degree, as though it had happened in the seventh. *Solon* divided it into ten Septenaries, because in every one thereof, a man received some sensible mutation; in the first is Dedentition or falling of teeth; in the second Pubescence; in the third the beard groweth; in the fourth strength prevails; in the fift maturity for issue; in the sixth moderation of apetite; in the seventh prudence, &c. Now herein there is a tolerable latitude, and though the division proceed by 7, yet is not the total verity to be restrained unto the last year; nor constantly to be expected the beard should be compleat at 21. or wisedom acquired just in 49. and thus also though 7 times 9, contain one of those septenaries, and doth also happen in our declining years; yet might the events thereof be imputed unto the whole septenary; and be more reasonably entertained with some latitude, then strictly reduced unto the last number, or all the accidents from 56. imputed unto Sixty three.

Thirdly, Although this opinion may seem confirmed by observation, and men may say it hath been so observed, yet we speak also upon experience, and do believe that men from observation will collect no satisfaction. That other years may be taken against it; especially if they have the advantage to precede it; as sixty against sixty three, and sixty three against sixty six. For fewer attain to the latter then the former; and so surely in the first septenary do most die, and probably also in the very first year; for all that ever lived were in the account of that year; beside the infirmities that attend it are so many, and the body that receives them so tender and inconfirmed, we scarce count any alive that is not past it.

Fabritius Paduanius, discoursing of the great Climacterical, attempts a numeration of eminent men, who died in that year; but in so small a number, as not sufficient to make a considerable Induction. He mentioneth but four, *Diogenes Cynicus*, *Dionysius Heracleoticus*,

Xenocrates Platonicus, and *Plato*: as for *Dionysius,* as *Censorinus* witnesseth, he famished himself in the 82 year of his life; *Xenocrates* by the testimony of *Laertius* fell into a cauldron, and died the same year; and *Diogenes* the *Synick* by the same testimony lived almost unto ninety. The date of *Plato's* death is not exactly agreed on, but all dissent from this which he determineth: *Neanthes* in *Laertius* extendeth his daies unto 84. *Suidas* unto 82. But *Hermippus* defineth his death in 81. And this account seemeth most exact; for if, as he delivereth, *Plato* was borne in the 88 Olympiade, and died in the first year of the 108, the account will not surpass the year of 81, and so in his death he verified the opinion of his life, and of the life of man, whose Period, as *Censorinus* recordeth, he placed in the Quadrate of 9 or 9 times 9, that is, eighty one: and therefore as *Seneca* delivereth, the *Magicians* at *Athens* did sacrifice unto him, as declaring in his death somewhat above humanity; because he died in the day of his nativity, and without deduction justly accomplished the year of eighty one. *Bodine* I confess, delivers a larger list of men that died in this year, *Moriuntur innumerabiles anno sexagesimo tertio, Aristoteles, Chrysippus, Bocatius, Bernardus, Erasmus, Lutherus, Melancthon, Sylvius, Alexander, Jacobus Sturmius, Nicolaus Cusanus, Thomas Linacer, eodem anno Cicero cæsus est.* Wherein, beside that it were not difficult to make a larger Catalogue of memorable persons that died in other years, we cannot but doubt the verity of his Induction. As for *Silvius* and *Alexander*, which of that name he meaneth I know not; but for *Chrysippus*, by the testimony of *Laertius*, he dyed in the 73 year, *Bocatius* in the 62, *Linacer* the 64, and *Erasmus* exceeded 70, as *Paulus Jovius* hath delivered in his Elogy of learned men. And as for *Cicero*, as *Plutarch* in his life affirmeth, he was slain the year of 46; and therefore sure the question is hard set, and we have no easy reason to doubt, when great and entire Authors shall introduce injustifiable examples, and authorize their assertions by what is not authentical.

Fourthly, They which proceed upon strict numerations, and will by such regular and determined waies measure out the lives of men, and periodically define the alterations of their tempers; conceive a regularity in mutations, with an equalitie in constitutions, and forget that variety, which Physitians therein discover. For seeing we affirm that women do naturally grow old before men, that the cholerick fall short in longævity of the sanguine, that there is *senium ante senectutem*, and many grow old before they arrive at age; we cannot affix unto them all one common point of danger, but should rather assign a respective fatality unto each. Which is concordant unto the doctrin of the numerists, and such as maintain this opinion: for they affirm that one number respecteth Men, another Women, as *Bodin* explaining that of *Seneca, Septimus quisque annus ætati signum imprimit,* subjoins *Hoc de maribus dictum, oportuit, hoc primum intueri licet, perfectum numerum, id est, sextum fœminas septenarium mares immutare.*

Fiftly, Since we esteem this opinion to have some ground in nature, and that nine times seven revolutions of the Sun, imprints a dangerous Character on such as arrive unto it; it will leave some doubt behind, in what subjection hereunto were the lives of our forefathers presently after the flood, and more especially before it; who attaining unto 8 or 900 years, had not their Climacters Computable by digits, or as we do account them; for the great Climacterical was past unto them before they begat Children, or gave any Testimony of their virility; for we read not that any begat children before the age of sixty five. And this may also afford a hint to enquire, what are the Climacters of other animated creatures; whereof the lives of some attain not so far as this of ours, and that of others extends a considerable space beyond it.

Lastly, The imperfect accounts that Men have kept of time, and the difference thereof both in the same and divers common Wealths, will much distract the certainty of this assertion. For though there were a fatality in this year, yet divers were, and others might be out in their account, aberring several waies from the true and just compute, and calling that one year, which perhaps might be another.

For first, They might be out in the commencement or beginning of their account; for every man is many months elder then he computeth. For although we begin the same from our nativity, and conceive that no arbitrary, but natural term of compute, yet for the duration of life or existence, we are liable in the Womb unto the usual distinctions of time; and are not to be exempted from the account of age and life, where we are subject to diseases, and often suffer death. And therefore *Pythagoras, Hippocrates, Diocles, Avicenna* and others, have set upon us, numeral relations and temporal considerations in the womb; not only affirming the birth of the seventh month to be vital, that of the eighth mortal, but the progression thereto to be measured by rule, and to hold a proportion unto motion and formation. As what receiveth motion in the seventh, to be perfected in the Triplicities; that is, the time of conformation unto motion is double, and that from motion unto the birth, treble; So what is formed the 35 day, is moved the seventy, and born the 210 day. And therefore if any invisible causality there be, that after so many years doth evidence it selfe at Sixty three, it will be questionable whether its activity only set out at our nativity, and begin not rather in the womb, wherein we place the like considerations. Which doth not only entangle this assertion, but hath already embroiled the endeavours of Astrology in the erection of Schemes, and the judgement of death or diseases; for being not incontroulably determined, at what time to begin, whether at conception, animation or exclusion (it being indifferent unto the influence of Heaven to begin at either) they have invented another way, that is, to begin *ab Hora quæstionis*, as *Haly*, *Messahallach*, *Ganivetus*, and *Guido Bonatus* have delivered.

Again, In regard of the measure of time by months and years, there will be no small difficulty; and if we shall strictly consider it, many have been and still may be mistaken. For neither the motion of the Moon, whereby months are computed; nor of the Sun, whereby years are accounted, consisteth of whole numbers, but admits of fractions, and broken parts, as we have already declared concerning the Moon. That of the Sun consisteth of 365 daies, and almost 6 hours, that is, wanting eleven minutes; which 6 hours omitted, or not taken notice of, will in process of time largely deprave the compute; and this is the occasion of the Bisextile or leap-year, which was not observed in all times, nor punctually in all Common-Wealths; so that in Sixty three years there may be lost almost 18 daies, omitting the intercalation one day every fourth year, allowed for this quadrant, or 6 hours supernumerary. And though the same were observed, yet to speak strictly a man may be somewhat out in the account of his age at Sixty three, for although every fourth year we insert one day, and so fetch up the quadrant, yet those eleven minutes whereby the year comes short of perfect 6 hours, will in the circuit of those years arise unto certain hours; and in a larger progression of time unto certaine daies. Whereof at present we find experience in the Calender we observe. For the *Julian* year of 365 daies being eleven minutes larger then the annual revolution of the Sun, there will arise an anticipation in the Æquinoxes; and as *Junctinus* computeth, in every 136 year they will anticipate almost one day. And therefore those ancient men and Nestors of old times, which yearly observed their nativities, might be mistaken in the day; nor that to be construed without a grain of Salt, which is delivered by *Moses*; At the end of four hundred years, even the self same day, all the hoast of *Israel* went out of the land of *Egypt*. For in that space of time the Æquinoxes had anticipated, and the eleven minutes had amounted far above a day. And this compute rightly considered will fall fouler on them who cast up the lives of Kingdoms, and sum up their duration by particular numbers; as *Plato* first began, and some have endeavoured since by perfect and spherical numbers, by the square and cube of 7 and 9 and 12, the great number of *Plato*. Wherein indeed Bodine hath attempted a particular enumeration; but (beside the mistakes committible in the solary compute of years) the difference of Chronology disturbs the satisfaction and quiet of his computes; some adding, others detracting, and few punctually according in any one year; whereby indeed such accounts should be made up; for the variations in an unite destroyes the total illation.

Thirdly, The compute may be unjust not only in a strict acception, of few daies or houres, but in the latitude also of some years; and this may happen from the different compute of years in divers Nations, and even such as did maintain the most probable way of account: their year being not only different from one another, but the civil and common account disagreeing much from the natural year, whereon the consideration is founded. Thus from the testimony of *Herodotus*, *Censorinus* and others, the *Greeks* observed the Lunary yeare, that is, twelve revolutions of the Moon, 354 daies; but the *Egyptians*, and many others adhered unto the Solary account, that is, 365 daies, that is eleven daies longer. Now hereby the account of the one would very much exceed the other: A man in the one would account himself 63, when one in the other would think himself but 61; and so although their nativities were under the same hour, yet did they at different years believe the verity of that which both esteemed affixed and certain unto one. The like mistake there is in a tradition of our daies; men conceiving a peculiar danger in the beginning daies of *May*, set out as a fatal period unto consumptions and Chronical diseases; wherein notwithstanding we compute by Calenders, not only different from our ancestors, but one another; the compute of the one anticipating that of the other; so that while we are in *April*, others begin *May*, and the danger is past unto one, while it beginneth with another.

Fourthly, Men were not only out in the number of some daies, the latitude of a few years, but might be wide by whole Olympiades and divers Decades of years. For as *Censorinus* relateth, the ancient *Arcadians* observed a year of three months, the *Carians* of six, the

Iberians of four; and as *Diodorus* and *Xenophon de Æquivocis*, al-leadgeth, the ancient *Egyptians* have used a year of three, two, and one moneth, so that the Climacterical was not only different unto those Nations, but unreasonably distant from ours; for Sixty three will pass in their account, before they arrive so high as ten in ours.

Nor if we survey the account of *Rome* it self, may we doubt they were mistaken; and if they feared Climacterical years, might err in their numeration. For the civil year whereof the people took notice, did sometimes come short, and sometimes exceed the natural. For ac-cording to *Varro, Suetonius,* and *Censorinus,* their year consisted first of ten months; which comprehended but 304 daies, that is 61 less then ours containeth; after by *Numa* or *Tarquine* from a superstitious con-ceit of imparity were added 51 daies, which made 355, one day more then twelve revolutions of the Moon. And thus a long time it contin-ued, the civil compute exceeding the natural; the correction whereof, and the due ordering of the Leap-year was referred unto the Pontifices; who either upon favour or malice, that some might continue their of-fices a longer or shorter time; or from the magnitude of the year that men might be advantaged, or endamaged in their contracts, by arbi-trary intercalations depraved the whole account. Of this abuse *Cicero* accused *Verres,* which at last proceeded so far, that when *Julius Cæsar* came unto that office, before the redress hereof he was fain to insert two intercalary months unto *November* and *December,* when he had already inserted 23 daies unto *February;* so that the year consisted of 445 daies; a quarter of a year longer then that we observe, and though at the last the year was reformed, yet in the mean time they might be out, wherein they summed up Climacterical observations.

Lastly, One way more there may be of mistake, and that not unusual among us, grounded upon a double compute of the year; the one beginning from the 25 of *March,* the other from the day of our birth, unto the same again which is the natural account. Now hereupon many men frequently miscast their daies; for in their age they deduce the account not from the day of their birth, but the year of our Lord, wherein they were born. So a man that was born in *January* 1582, if he live to fall sick in the latter end of *March* 1645, will sum up his age, and say I am now Sixty three, and in my Climacterical and dangerous year; for I was born in the yeare 1582, and now it is 1645, whereas indeed he wanteth many months of that year, considering the true and natural account unto his birth; and accounteth two months for a year:

and though the length of time and accumulation of years do render the mistake insensible; yet is it all one, as if one born in *January* 1644, should be accounted a year old the 25 of *March* 1645.

All which perpended, it may be easily perceived with what insecurity of truth we adhere unto this opinion; ascribing not only effects depending on the natural period of time unto arbitrary calculations, and such as vary at pleasure; but confirming our tenets by the uncertain account of others and our selves. There being no positive or indisputable ground where to begin our compute; that if there were, men have been several waies mistaken; the best in some latitude, others in greater, according to the different compute of divers states, the short and irreconcilable years of some, the exceeding error in the natural frame of others, and the lapses and false deductions of ordinary accountants in most.

Which duly considered, together with a strict account and critical examen of reason, will also distract the witty determinations of Astrology. That Saturn the enemy of life, comes almost every seventh year, unto the quadrate or malevolent place; that as the Moon about every seventh day arriveth unto a contrary sign, so Saturn, which remaineth about as many years, as the Moon doth daies in one sign, and holdeth the same consideration in years as the Moon in daies; doth cause these periculous periods. Which together with other Planets, and profection of the Horoscope, unto the seventh house, or opposite signs every seventh year; oppresseth living natures, and causeth observable mutations, in the state of sublunary things.

Further satisfaction may yet be had from the learned discourse of *Salmasius* lately published, if any desire to be informed how different the present observations are from those of the ancients; how every one hath different Climactericals; with many other observables, impugning the present opinion.

CHAPTER XIII

Of the Canicular or Dog-daies

Whereof to speak distinctly: among the Southern Constellations two there are which bear the name of the Dog: the one in 16 degrees of latitude, containing on the left thigh a Star of the first magnitude, usually called Procyon or Anticanis, because say some it riseth before the other; which if truly understood, must be restrained unto those habitations, who have elevation of pole above thirty two degrees. Mention thereof is in *Horace*, who seems to mistake or confound the one with the other; and after him in *Galen*, who is willing, the remarkablest Star of the other should be called by this name: because it is the first that ariseth in the constellation; which notwithstanding, to speak strictly, it is not, unless we except one of the third magnitude in the right paw in his own and our elevation, and two more on his head in and beyond the degree of Sixty. A second and more considerable one there is, and neighbour unto the other, in 40 degrees of latitude, containing 18 Stars, whereof that in his mouth of the first magnitude, the *Greeks* call Σέιριος, the *Latines canis major*, and we emphatically the Dog-Star.

Now from the rising of this Star, not cosmically, that is, with the Sun, but Heliacally, that is, its emersion from the raies of the Sun, the Ancients computed their canicular daies; concerning which there generally passeth an opinion, that during those daies, all medication or use of Physick is to be declined, and the cure committed unto Nature. And therefore as though there were any feriation in nature or justitiums imaginable in professions, whose subject is natural, and under no intermissive, but constant way of mutation; this season is commonly termed the Physitians vacation, and stands so received by most men. Which conceit however general, is not only erroneous, but unnatural, and subsisting upon foundations either false, uncertain, mistaken or misapplied, deserves not of mankind that indubitable assent it findeth.

For first, which seems to be the ground of this assertion, and not to be drawn into question, that is, the magnified quality of this Star conceived to cause, or intend the heat of this season, whereby these daies become more observable then the rest: We finde that wiser Antiquity was not of this opinion. For, seventeen hundred years ago it was as a vulgar error rejected by *Geminus*, a learned Mathematician in his Elements of Astronomy; wherein he plainly affirmeth, that common opinion made that a cause, which was at first observed but as a sign. The rising and setting both of this Star and others being observed by the Ancients, to denote and testifie certain points of mutation, rather then conceived to induce or effect the same. For our forefathers, saith he, observing the course of the Sun, and marking certaine mutations to happen in his progress through particular parts of the Zodiack, they registred and set them down in their Parapegmes, or Astronomical Canons; and being not able to design these times by daies, months or years (the compute thereof, and the beginning of the year being different, according unto different Nations) they thought best to settle a general account unto all; and to determine these alterations by some known and invariable signs; and such did they conceive the rising and setting of the fixed Stars; not ascribing thereto any part of causality, but notice and signification. And thus much seems implied in that expression of *Homer*, when speaking of the Dog-Star, he concludeth — κακόν δε τε σίμα τέτυκται, *Malum autem signum est*; the same as *Petavius* observeth, is implied in the words of *Ptolomy*, and the Ancients, περί επισημασιον, that is, of the signification of Stars. The terme of Scripture also favours it, as that of *Isaiah*. *Nolite timere a signis cœli*, and that in *Genesis*, *Ut sint in signa et tempora*: Let there be lights in the firmament, and let them be for signes and for seasons.

The Primitive and leading magnifiers of this Star, were the *Egyptians*, the great admirers of Dogs in Earth and Heaven. Wherein they worshipped *Anubis* or *Mercurius*, the Scribe of *Saturn*, and Counseller of *Osyris*, the great inventor of their religious rites, and Promoter of good unto *Egypt*. Who was therefore translated into this Star; by the *Egyptians* called *Sothis*, and *Siris* by the *Ethiopians*; from whence that *Sirias* or the Dog-Star had its name, is by some conjectur'd.

And this they looked upon, not with reference unto heat, but cœlestial influence upon the faculties of man, in order to religion and all sagacious invention; and from hence derived the abundance and great fertility of *Egypt*, the overflow of *Nylus* happening about the ascent hereof. And therefore in hieroglyphical monuments, *Anubis* is described with a Dogs-head, with a Crocodile between his legs, with a sphere in his hand, with two Stars, and a water Pot standing by him; implying thereby, the rising and setting of the Dog-star, and the inundation of the River *Nylus*.

But if all were silent, *Galen* hath explained this point unto the life; who expounding the reason why *Hippocrates* declared the affections of the year by the rising and setting of Stars; it was saith he, because he would proceed on signs and principles best known unto all Nations. And upon his words in the first of the Epidemicks, *In Thaso Autumno circa Equinoxium & sub virgilias pluviæ erant multæ*, he thus enlargeth: If (saith he) the same compute of times and months were observed by all Nations, *Hippocrates* had never made any mention either of Arcturus, Pleiades or the Dog-star; but would have plainly said, in *Macedonia*, in the month Dion, thus or thus was the air disposed. But for as much as the month Dion is only known unto the *Macedonians*, but obscure unto the *Athenians* and other Nations, he found more general distinctions of time, and instead of naming months, would usually say, at the Æquinox, the rising of the Pleiades, or the Dog-star. And by this way did the Ancients divide the seasons of the year, the Autumn, Winter, Spring, and Summer. By the rising of the Pleiades, denoting the beginning of Summer, and by that of the Dog-star, the declination thereof. By this way *Aristotle* through all his books of Animals, distinguisheth their times of generation, latitancy, migration, sanity and venation. And this were an allowable way of compute, and still to be retained, were the site of the Stars as inalterable, and their ascents as invariable as primitive Astronomy conceaved them. And therefore though *Aristotle* frequently mentioneth this Star, and particularly affirmeth that Fishes in the Bosphorus are best catched from the arise of the Dog-star, we must not conceive the same a meer effect thereof. Nor though *Scaliger* from hence be willing to infer the efficacy of this Star, are we induced hereto; except because the same Philosopher affirmeth, that Tunny is fat about the rising of the Pleiades, and depart upon Arcturus, or that most insects are latent, from the setting of the 7 Stars; except, I say, he give us also leave to infer that these particular effects and alterations proceed from those

Stars; which were indeed but designations of such quarters and portions of the year, wherein the same were observed. Now what *Pliny* affirmeth of the Orix, that it seemeth to adore this Star, and taketh notice thereof by voyce and sternutation; until we be better assured of its verity, we shall not salve the sympathy.

Secondly, What slender opinion the Ancients held of the efficacy of this Star; is declarable from their compute. For as *Geminus* affirmeth, and *Petavius* his learned Commentator proveth, they began their account from its Heliacal emersion, and not its cosmical ascent. The cosmical ascension of a Star we term that, when it ariseth together with the Sun, or the same degree of the Ecliptick wherein the Sun abideth: and that the Heliacal, when a Star which before for the vicinity of the Sun was not visible, being further removed, beginneth to appear. For the annual motion of the Sun from West to East being far swifter then that of the fixed Stars, he must of necessity leave them on the East while he hastneth forward, and obscureth others to the West: and so the Moon who performs its motion swifter then the Sun (as may be observed in their Conjunctions and Eclipses) gets Eastward out of his raies; and appears when the Sun is set. If therefore the Dog-star had this effectual heat which is ascribed unto it, it would afford best evidence thereof, and the season would be most fervent, when it ariseth in the probablest place of its activity, that is, the cosmical ascent; for therein it ariseth with the Sun, and is included in the same irradiation. But the time observed by the Ancients was long after this ascent, and in the Heliacal emersion, when it becomes at greater distance from the Sun, neither rising with it nor near it. And therefore had they conceived any more then a bare signality in this Star, or ascribed the heat of the season thereunto; they would not have computed from its Heliacal ascent, which was of inferiour efficacy; nor imputed the vehemency of heat unto those points wherein it was more remiss, and where with less probability they might make out its action.

Thirdly, Although we derive the authority of these daies from observations of the Ancients, yet are our computes very different, and such as confirm not each other. For whereas they observed it Heliacally, we seem to observe it Cosmically; for before it ariseth Heliacally unto our latitude, the Summer is even at an end. Again, we compute not only from different ascents, but also from divers Stars; they from the greater Dog-star, we from the lesser; they from *Orions*, we from *Cephalus* his dog; they from *Seirius*, we from *Procyon*; for the beginning of the Dog-daies with us is set down the 19 of *July*, about which time the lesser Dog-star ariseth with the Sun; whereas the Star of the greater Dog ascendeth not until after that month. And this mistake will yet be larger, if the compute be made stricter, and as Dr. *Bainbrigge* late professor of Astronomy in *Oxford*, hath set it down. Who in the year 1629 computed, that in the Horizon of *Oxford*, the Dog-Star arose not before the fifteenth day of *August*; when in our Almanack accounts, those daies are almost ended. So that the common and received time not answering the true compute, it frustrates the observations of our selves. And being also different from the calculations of the Ancients, their observations confirm not ours, nor ours theirs, but rather confute each other.

Nor will the computes of the Ancients be so Authentick unto those, who shall take notice, how commonly they applied the celestial descriptions of other climes unto their own; wherein the learned *Bainbrigius* justly reprehendeth *Manilius*, who transferred the *Ægyptian* descriptions unto the *Roman* account; confounding the observation of the *Greek* and *Barbarick* Spheres.

Fourthly, (which is the Argument of *Geminus*) were there any such effectual heat in this Star, yet could it but weakly evidence the same in Summer; it being about 40 degrees distant from the Sun; and should rather manifest its warming power in the Winter, when it remains conjoyned with the Sun in its Hybernal conversion. For about the 29 of *October*, and in the 16 of *Scorpius*, and so again in *January*, the Sun performes his revolution in the same parallel with the Dog-star. Again, If we should impute the heat of this season, unto the co-operation of any Stars with the Sun, it seems more favourable for our times, to ascribe the same unto the constellation of *Leo*. Where besides that the Sun is in his proper house, it is conjoyned with many Stars: whereof two of the first magnitude; and in the 8th of *August* is corporally conjoyned with *Basiliscus*; a Star of eminent name in Astrology, and seated almost in the Ecliptick.

Fifthly, If all were granted, that observation and reason were also for it, and were it an undeniable truth, that an effectual fervour proceeded from this Star; yet would not the same determine the opinion now in question; it necessarily suffering such restrictions as take off general illations. For first in regard of different latitudes, unto some the canicular daies are in the Winter; as unto such as have no latitude, but live in a right Sphere, that is, under the Equinoctial line; for unto them it ariseth when the Sun is about the Tropick of Cancer; which season unto them is Winter, and the Sun remotest from them. Nor hath the same position in the Summer, that is, in the Equinoctial points, any advantage from it; for in the one point the Sun is at the Meridian, before the Dog-star ariseth; in the other the Star is at the Meridian, before the Sun ascendeth.

Some latitudes have no canicular daies at all; as namely all those which have more then 73 degrees of Northern Elevation; as the territory of *Nova Zembla*, part of *Greenland* and *Tartary*; for unto that habitation the Dog star is invisible, and appeareth not above the Horizon.

Unto such Latitudes wherein it ariseth, it carrieth a various and very different respect; unto some it ascendeth when Summer is over, whether we compute Heliacally or Cosmically; for though unto *Alexandria* it ariseth in Cancer, yet it ariseth not unto *Biarmia* Cosmically before it be in Virgo, and Heliacally about the Autumnal Equinox. Even unto the Latitude of 52, the efficacy thereof is not much considerable, whether we consider its ascent, Meridian altitude or abode above the Horizon. For it ariseth very late in the year, about the eighteenth of *Leo*, that is, the 31 of *July*. Of Meridian Altitude it hath but 23 degrees, so that it plaies but oblickly upon us, and as the Sun doth about the 23 of *January*. And lastly, his abode above the Horizon is not great; for in the eighteenth of *Leo*, the 31 of *July*, although they arise together; yet doth it set above 5 houres before the Sun, that is, before two of the clock, after which time we are more sensible of heat, then all the day before.

Secondly, In regard of the variation of the longitude of the Stars, we are to consider (what the Ancients observed not) that the site of the fixed Stars is alterable, and that since elder times they have suffered a large and considerable variation of their longitudes. The longitude of a Star, to speak plainly, is its distance from the first point of numeration toward the East; which first point unto the Ancients was the vernall æquinox. Now by reason of their motion from West to East, they have very much varied from this point: The first Star of Aries in the time of *Meton* the *Athenian* was placed in the very intersection, which is now elongated and removed Eastward 28 degrees; insomuch that now the sign of Aries possesseth the place of

335

Taurus, and Taurus that of Gemini. Which variation of longitude must very much distract the opinion of the Dog-star; not only in our daies, but in times before and after; for since the World began it hath arisen in Taurus, and if the World last, may have its ascent in Virgo; so that we must place the canicular daies, that is the hottest time of the year in the Spring in the first Age, and in the Autumn in Ages to come.

Thirdly, The Stars have not only varied their longitudes, whereby their ascents have altered; but they have also changed their declinations, whereby their rising at all, that is, their appearing hath varied. The declination of a Star we call its distance from the Equator. Now though the Poles of the world and the Equator be immovable, yet because the Stars in their proper motions from West to East, do move upon the poles of the Ecliptick, distant 23 degrees and an half from the Poles of the Equator, and describe circles parallel not unto the Equator, but the Ecliptick; they must be therefore sometimes nearer, sometimes removed further from the Equator. All Stars that have their distance from the Ecliptick Northward not more then 23 degrees and an half (which is the greatest distance of the Ecliptick from the Equator) may in progression of time have declination Southward, and move beyond the Equator: but if any Star hath just this distance of 23 and an half (as hath Capella on the backe of Erichthonius) it may hereafter move under the Equinoctial; and the same will happen respectively unto Stars which have declination Southward. And therefore many Stars may be visible in our Hemisphere, which are not so at present; and many which are at present, shall take leave of our Horizon, and appear unto Southern habitations. And therefore the time may come that the Dog star may not be visible in our Horizon, and the time hath been, when it hath not shewed it self unto our neighbour latitudes. So that canicular daies there have beene none, nor shall be; yet certainly in all times some season the yeare more notably hot then other.

Lastly, We multiply causes in vain; and for the reason hereof, we need not have recourse unto any Star but the Sun, and continuity of its action. For the Sun ascending into the Northern signs, begetteth first a temperate heat in the air; which by his approach unto the solstice he intendeth; and by continuation increaseth the same even upon declination. For running over the same degrees again, that is, in Leo, which he hath done in Taurus, in *July* which he did in *May*; he augmenteth the heat in the latter which he began in the first; and easily intendeth the same by continuation which was well promoted before.

So it is observed that they which dwell between the Tropicks and the Equator, have their second summer hotter and more maturative of fruits then the former. So we observe in the day (which is a short year) the greatest heat about two in the afternoon, when the Sun is past the Meridian (which is his diurnal solstice) and the same is evident from the Thermometer or observations of the weather-glass. So are the colds of the night sharper in the Summer about two or three after midnight, and the frosts in Winter stronger about those houres. So likewise in the year we observe the cold to augment, when the daies begin to increase, though the Sun be then ascensive, and returning from the Winter Tropick. And therefore if we rest not in this reason for the heat in the declining part of Summer, we must discover freezing Stars that may resolve the latter colds of Winter; which who ever desires to invent, let him study the Stars of *Andromeda*, or the nearer constellation of *Pegasus*, which are about that time ascendent.

It cannot therefore seeme strange, or savour of singularity that we have examined this point. Since the same hath beene already denied by some, since the authority and observations of the Ancients rightly understood, do not confirm it, since our present computes are different from those of the Ancients, whereon notwithstanding they depend; since there is reason against it, and if all were granted, yet must it be maintained with manifold restraints, far otherwise then is received. And lastly, since from plain and natural principles, the doubt may be fairly salved, and not clapt up from petitionary foundations and principles unestablished.

But that which chiefly promoted the consideration of these daies, and medically advanced the same, was the doctrine of *Hippocrates*; a Physitian of such repute, that he received a testimony from a Christian, that might have beene given unto Christ. The first in his book *de Aere, Aquis, & locis. Syderum ortus*, &. That is, we are to observe the rising of Stars, especially the Dog-star, Arcturus, and the setting of the Pleiades or seven Stars. From whence notwithstanding we cannot infer the general efficacy of these Stars, or co-efficacy particular in medications. Probably expressing no more hereby then if he should have plainly said, especial notice we are to take of the hottest time in Summer, of the beginning of Autumn and Winter; for by the rising and setting of those Stars were these times and seasons defined. And therefore subjoyns this reason, *Quoniam bis temporibus morbi finiuntur*, because at these times diseases have their ends; as Physitions

337

well know, and he else where affirmeth, that seasons determine diseases, beginning in their contraries; as the spring the diseases of Autumn, and the Summer those of Winter. Now (what is very remarkable) whereas in the same place he adviseth to observe the times of notable mutations, as the Equinoxes, and the Solstices, and to decline Medication ten daies before and after; how precisely soever canicular cautions be considered, this is not observed by Physitians, nor taken notice of by the people. And indeed should we blindly obey the restraints both of Physitions and Astrologers, we should contract the liberty of our prescriptions, and confine the utility of Physick unto a very few daies. For observing the Dog-daies, and as is expressed, some daies before, likewise ten daies before and after the Equinoctial and Solsticial points; by this observation alone are exempted an hundred daies. Whereunto if we adde the two *Egyptian* daies in every moneth, the interlunary and plenilunary exemptions, the Eclipses of Sun and Moon, conjunctions and oppositions Planetical, the houses of Planets, and the site of the Luminaries under the signs (wherein some would induce a restraint of Purgation or Phlebotomy) there would arise above an hundred more; so that of the whole year the use of Physick would not be secure much above a quarter. Now as we do not strictly observe these days, so need we not the other; and although consideration be made hereof, yet must we prefer the nearer Indications, before those which are drawn from the time of the year, or other cælestial relations.

The second Testimony is taken out of the last piece of his Age, and after the experience (as some think) of no less then an hundred years, that is, his book of Aphorisms, or short and definitive determinations in Physick. The Aphorism alleadged is this *Sub Cane & ante Canem difficiles sunt purgationes. Sub Cane & Anticane,* say some including both the Dog stars; but that cannot consist with the Greek: *hupo kuna kai pro kunos,* nor had that Criticism been ever omitted by *Galen.* Now how true this sentence was in the mouth of *Hippocrates,* and with what restraint it must be understood by us, will readily appear from the difference between us both, in circumstantial relations.

And first, Concerning his time and Chronology: he lived in the reign of *Artaxerxes Longimanus,* about the 82 Olympiade, 450 years before Christ; and from our times above two thousand. Now since that time (as we have already declared) the Stars have varied their longitudes; and having made large progressions from West to East, the time of the Dog stars ascent must also very much alter. For it ariseth later now in the year, then it formerly did in the same latitude; and far later unto us who have a greater elevation; for in the daies of *Hippocrates* this Star ascended in Cancer, which now ariseth in Leo; and will in progression of time arise in Virgo. And therefore in regard of the time wherein he lived, the Aphorism was more considerable in his daies then in ours, and in times far past then present, and in his Countrey then ours.

The place of his nativity was *Coos*, an Island in the *Myrtoan* Sea, not far from *Rhodes*, described in Maps by the name of *Lango*, and called by the *Turks* who are Masters thereof, *Stancora*; according unto *Ptolomy* of Northern latitude 36 degrees. That he lived and writ in these parts, is not improbably collected from the Epistles that passed betwixt him and *Artaxerxes*; as also between the Citizens of *Abdera*, and *Coos*, in the behalf of *Democritus*. Which place being seated from our latitude of 52, 16 degrees Southward, there will arise a different consideration; and we may much deceive our selves if we conform the ascent of Stars in one place unto another, or conceive they arise the same day of the month in *Coos* and in *England*. For as *Petavius* computes in the first *Julian* yeare, at *Alexandria* of latitude 31, the Star arose cosmically in the twelfth degree of Cancer, Heliacally the 26, by the compute of *Geminus* about this time at *Rhodes* of latitude 37, it ascended cosmically the 16 of Cancer, Heliacally the first of Leo; and about that time at *Rome* of latitude 42, cosmically the 22 of Cancer, and Heliacally the first of Leo. For unto places of great latitude it ariseth ever later; so that in some latitudes the cosmical ascent happeneth not before the twentieth degree of Virgo, ten daies before the Autumnal Equinox, and if they compute Heliacally, after it, in Libra.

Again, Should we allow all, and only compute unto the latitude of *Coos*; yet would it not impose a total omission of Physick. For if in the hottest season of that clime, all Physick were to be declined, then surely in many other none were to be used at any time whatsoever; for unto many parts, not only in the Spring and Autumn, but also in the Winter, the Sun is nearer, then unto the Clime of *Coos* in the Summer.

The third consideration concerneth purging medicines, which are at present far different from those implied in this Aphorism, and such as were commonly used by *Hippocrates*. For three degrees we make of purgative medicines: The first thereof is very benign, nor far removed from the nature of Aliment, into which, upon defect of working, it is oft-times converted; and in this form do we account *Manna, Cassia, Tamarindes,* and many more; whereof we find no mention in *Hippocrates.* The second is also gentle having a familiarity with some humor, into which it is but converted if it fail of its operation: of this sort are *Aloe, Rhabarb, Senna,* &c. Whereof also few or none were known unto Hippocrates: The third is of a violent and venemous quality, which frustrate of its action, assumes as it were the nature of poison; such as are Scammoneum, Colocynthis, Elaterium, Euphorbium, Tithymallus, Laureola, Peplum, &c. Of this sort *Hippocrates* made use, even in Fevers, Pleurisies and Quinsies; and that composition is very remarkable which is ascribed unto *Diogenes* in *Ætius,* that is of Pepper, Sal Armoniac, Euphorbium, of each an ounce, the Dosis whereof four scruples and an half; which whosoever should take, would find in his bowells more then a canicular heat, though in the depth of Winter; many of the like nature may be observed in *Ætius,* or in the book *De Dinamidiis,* ascribed unto *Galen,* which is the same *verbatim* with the other.

Now in regard of the second, and especially the first degree of Purgatives, the Aphorism is not of force; but we may safely use them, they being benign and of innoxious qualities. And therefore *Lucas Gauricus,* who hath endeavoured with many testimonies to advance this consideration, at length concedeth that lenitive Physick may be used, especially when the Moon is well affected in Cancer or in the watery signes. But in regard of the third degree the Aphorism is considerable: purgations may be dangerous; and a memorable example there is in the medical Epistles of *Crucius,* of a *Roman* Prince that died upon an ounce of Diaphænicon, taken in this season. From the use whereof we refrain not only in hot seasons, but warily exhibit it at all times in hot diseases. Which when necessity requires, we can perform more safely then the Ancients, as having better ways of preparation and correction; that is, not only by addition of other bodies, but separation of noxious parts from their own.

But beside these differences between *Hippocrates* and us, the Physitians of these times and those of Antiquity; the condition of the disease, and the intention of the Physitian, hold a main consideration in what time and place soever. For Physick is either curative or preventive; Preventive we call that which by purging noxious humors, and the causes of diseases, preventeth sickness in the healthy, or the recourse thereof in the valetudinary; this is of common use at the spring and fall, and we commend not the same at this season. Therapeutick or curative Physicke, we term that, which restoreth the Patient unto Sanity, and taketh away diseases actually affecting. Now of diseases some are cronical and of long duration, as quartane Agues, Scurvy, &c. Wherein because they admit of delay, we defer the cure to more advantagious seasons; Others we term acute, that is, of short duration and danger, as Fevers, Pleurisies, &c. In which, because delay is dangerous, and they arise unto their state before the Dog-daies determine; we apply present remedies according unto Indications; respecting rather the acuteness of the disease, and precipitancy of occasion, then the rising or setting of Stars; the effects of the one being disputable, of the other assured and inevitable.

And although Astrology may here put in, and plead the secret influence of this Star; yet *Galen* in his Comment, makes no such consideration; confirming the truth of the Aphorism from the heat of the year; and the operation of Medicines exhibited. In regard that bodies being heated by the Summer, cannot so well endure the acrimony of purging Medicines; and because upon purgations contrary motions ensue, the heat of the air attracting the humours outward, and the action of the Medicine retracting the same inward. But these are readily salved in the distinctions before alleadged; and particularly in the constitution of our climate and divers others, wherein the air makes no such exhaustion of spirits. And in the benignity of our Medicines; whereof some in their own natures, others well prepared, agitate not the humors, or make a sensible perturbation.

Nor do we hereby reject or condemn a sober and regulated Astrology; we hold there is more truth therein then in Astrologers; in some more then many allow, yet in none so much as some pretend. We deny not the influence of the Stars, but often suspect the due application thereof; for though we should affirm that all things were in all things; that heaven were but earth celestified, and earth but heaven terrestrified, or that each part above had an influence upon its divided affinity below; yet how to single out these relations, and duly to apply their actions is a worke oft times to be effected by some revelation, and *Cabala* from above, rather then any Philosophy, or speculation here below. What power soever they have upon our bodies, it is not requisite they should destroy our reasons, that is, to make us rely on the strength of Nature, when she is least able to relieve us; and when we conceive the heaven against us, to refuse the assistance of the earth created for us. This were to suffer from the mouth of the Dog above, what others do from the teeth of Dogs below; that is, to be afraid of their proper remedy, and refuse to approach any water, though that hath often proved a cure unto their disease. There is in wise men a power beyond the Stars; and *Ptolomy* encourageth us, that by fore-knowledge, we may evade their actions; for, being but universal causes, they are determined by particular agents; which being inclined, not constrained, contain within themselves the casting act, and a power to command the conclusion.

Lastly, If all be conceded, and were there in this Aphorism an unrestrained truth, yet were it not reasonable from a caution to infer a non usance or abolition, from a thing to be used with discretion, not to be used at all. Because the Apostle bids us beware of Philosophy, heads of extremity will have none at all; an usual fallacie in vulgar and less distinctive brains, who having once overshot the mean, run violently on, and find no rest but in the extreams.

Now hereon we have the longer insisted, because the error is material, and concerns oft-times the life of man; an error to be taken notice of by State, and provided against by Princes, who are of the opinion of *Solomon*, that their riches consists in the multitude of their subjects. An error worse then some reputed *Heresies*; and of greater danger to the body, then they unto the soul; which whosoever is able to reclaim, he shall save more in one summer then *Themison* destroyed in any Autumn; he shall introduce a new way of cure, preserving by Theory, as well as practice, and men not only from death, but from destroying themselves.

End of Book IV

THE FIFTH

BOOK

Of many things questionable as they are commonly described in Pictures.

CHAPTER I

Of the Picture of the Pelecan

And first in every place we meet with the picture of the Pelecan, opening her breast with her bill, and feeding her young ones with the blood distilling from her. Thus is it set forth not onely in common Signs, but in the Crest and Scutcheon of many Noble families; hath been asserted by many holy Writers, and was an Hieroglyphick of piety and pitty among the *Ægyptians*; on which consideration, they spared them at their tables.

Notwithstanding upon enquiry we find no mention hereof in Ancient Zodiographers, and such as have particularly discoursed upon Animals, as *Aristotle, Elian, Pliny, Solinus* and many more; who seldom forget proprieties of such a nature, and have been very punctual in less considerable Records. Some ground hereof I confess we may allow, nor need we deny a remarkable affection in Pelecans toward their young; for *Elian* discoursing of Storks, and their affection toward their brood, whom they instruct to fly, and unto whom they re-deliver up the provision of their Bellies, concludeth at last, that Herons and Pelecans do the like.

As for the testimonies of Ancient Fathers, and Ecclesiasticall Writers, we may more safely conceive therein some Emblematical than any reall Story: so doth *Eucherius* confess it to bee the Emblem of Christ. And we are unwilling literally to receive that account of *Jerome*, that perceiving her young ones destroyed by Serpents, she openeth her side with her bill, by the blood whereof they revive and return unto life again. By which relation they might indeed illustrate the destruction of man by the old Serpent, and his restorement by the blood of Christ: and in this sense we shall not dispute the like relations of *Austine, Isidore, Albertus,* and many more, and under an Emblematical intention, we accept it in coat-armour.

As for the Hieroglyphick of the *Egyptians,* they erected the same upon other consideration, which was parentall affection; manifested in the protection of her young ones, when her nest was set on fire. For as for letting out her blood, it was not the assertion of the *Egyptians,* but seems translated unto the Pelecan from the Vulture, as *Pierius* hath plainly delivered. *Sed quod Pelicanum (ut etiam aliis plerisque persuasum est) rostro pectus dissecantem pingunt, ita ut suo sanguine filios alat, ab Ægyptiorum historia valde alienum est, illi enim vulturem tantum id facere tradiderunt.*

And lastly, as concerning the picture, if naturally examined, and not Hieroglyphically conceived, it containeth many improprieties, disagreeing almost in all things from the true and proper description. For whereas it is commonly set forth green or yellow, in its proper colour, it is inclining to white; excepting the extremities or tops of the wing feathers, which are brown. It is described in the bigness of a Hen, whereas it approacheth and sometimes exceedeth the magnitude of a Swan. It is commonly painted with a short bill; whereas that of the Pelecan attaineth sometimes the length of two spans. The bill is made acute or pointed at the end; whereas it is flat and broad, though somewhat inverted at the extream. It is described like fissipedes, or birds which have their feet or claws divided; whereas it is palmipedous, or fin-footed like Swans and Geese; according to the method of nature, in latirostrous or flat-bild birds; which being generally swimmers, the organ is wisely contrived unto the action, and they are framed with fins or oars upon their feet; and therefore they neither light, nor build on trees, if we except Cormorants, who make their nests like Herons. Lastly, there is one part omitted more remarkable then any other, that is, the chowle or crop adhering unto the lower side of the bill, and so descending by the throat; a bag or sachel very observable, and of a capacity almost beyond credit; which notwithstanding, this animal could not want; for therein it receiveth Oysters, Cochels, Scollops, and other testaceous animals; which being not able to break, it retains them until they open, and vomitting them up, takes out the meat contained. This is that part preserved for a rarity, and wherein (as *Sanctius* delivers) in one dissected, a *Negro* child was found.

A possibility there may be of opening and bleeding their

breast; for this may be done by the uncous and pointed extremity of their bill; and some probability also that they sometimes do it, for their own relief, though not for their young ones; that is by nibbling and biting themselves on the itching part of their breast, upon fullness or acrimony of blood. And the same may be better made out; if (as some relate) their feathers on that part are sometimes observed to be red and tincted with blood.

Chapter II

Of the Picture of Dolphins

That Dolphins are crooked, is not only affirmed by the hand of the Painter, but commonly conceived their natural and proper figure; which is not only the opinion of our times, but seems the belief of elder times before us. For beside the expressions of *Ovid* and *Pliny*, their Pourtraicts in some ancient Coyns are framed in this figure, as will appear in some thereof in *Gesner*, others in *Goltsius*, and *Lævinus Hulsius* in his description of Coyns, from *Julius Cæsar* unto *Rhodulphus* the Second.

Notwithstanding, to speak strictly in their natural figure they are streight, nor have their spine convexed, or more considerably embowed, then Sharks, Porposes, Whales, and other Cetaceous animalls, as *Scaliger* plainly affirmeth; *Corpus habet non magis curvum quam reliqui pisces.* As ocular enquiry informeth; and as unto such as have not had the opportunity to behold them, their proper pourtraicts will discover in *Rondeletius, Gesner,* and *Aldrovandus.* And as indeed is deducible from pictures themselves; for though they be drawn repandous, or convexedly crooked in one piece, yet the Dolphin that carrieth Arion is concavously inverted, and hath its spine depressed in another. And answerably hereto may we behold them differently bowed in medalls, and the Dolphins of *Tarus* and *Fulius* do make another flexure from that of *Commodus* and *Agrippa.*

And therefore what is delivered of their incurvity, must either be taken Emphatically, that is, not really but in appearance; which happeneth, when they leap above water, and suddenly shoot down again; which is a fallacy in vision, whereby straight bodies in a sudden motion protruded obliquely downward, appear unto the eye crooked;

and this is the construction of *Bellonius*. Or if it be taken really, it must not universally and perpetually; that is, not when they swim and remain in their proper figures, but only when they leap, or impetuously whirl their bodies any way; and this is the opinion of *Gesnerus*. Or lastly, It may be taken neither really nor emphatically, but only Emblematically: for being the Hieroglyphick of celerity, and swifter than other animals, men best expressed their velocity by incurvity, and under some figure of a bow: and in this sense probably do Heralds also receive it, when from a Dolphin extended, they distinguish a Dolphin embowed.

And thus also must that picture be taken of a Dolphin clasping an Anchor: that is, not really, as is by most conceived out of affection unto man, conveighing the Anchor unto the ground: but emblematically, according as *Pierius* hath expressed it, The swiftest animal conjoyned with that heavy body, implying that common moral, *Festina lentè*: and that celerity should always be contempered with cunctation.

Chapter III.

Of the Picture of a Grashopper

There is also among us a common description and picture of a Grashopper, as may be observed in the pictures of Emblematists, in the coats of severals families, and as the word *Cicada* is usually translated in Dictionaries. Wherein to speak strictly, if by this word Grashopper, we understand that animal which is implied by τέτιξ with the *Greeks*, and by *Cicada* with the *Latines*; we may with safety affirm the picture is widely mistaken, and that for ought enquiry can inform, there is no such insect in *England*. Which how paradoxical soever, upon a strict enquiry, will prove undeniable truth.

For first, That animal which the French term *Sauterelle*, we a Grashopper, and which under this name is commonly described by us, is named ακρις by the *Greeks*, by the *Latines Locusta*, and by our selves in proper speech a Locust; as in the diet of John *Baptist*, and in our Translation, The *Locusts* have no King, yet go they forth all of them by bands. Again, Between the *Cicada* and that we call a Grashopper, the differences are very many, as may be observed in themselves, or their descriptions in *Mathiolus, Aldrovandus* and *Muffetus*. For first, They are differently cucullated or capuched upon the head and back, and in the *Cicada* the eyes are more prominent: the Locusts have *Antennæ* or long horns before, with a long falcation or forcipated tail behind; and being ordained for saltation, their hinder legs do far exceed the other. The Locust or our Grashopper hath teeth, the *Cicada* none at all; nor any mouth according unto *Aristotle*: the Cicada is most upon trees; and lastly, the fritinnitus or proper note thereof is far more shrill then that of the Locust; and its life so short in

Summer, that for provision it needs not have recourse unto the providence of the Pismire in Winter.

And therefore where the *Cicada* must be understood, the pictures of Heralds and Emblematists are not exact, nor is it safe to adhere unto the interpretation of Dictionaries; and we must with candour make our owne Translations: for in the plague of *Ægypt*, *Exodus* 10. the word ακρις is translated a Locust, but in the same sense and subject, *Wisdom* 16. It is translated a Grashopper; For them the bitings of Grashoppers and flIes killed: whereas we have declared before, the *Cicada* hath no teeth, but is conceived to live upon dew; and the possibility of its subsistence is disputed by *Licetus*. Hereof I perceive *Muffetus* hath taken notice, dissenting from *Langius* and *Lycostenes*, while they deliver, the *Cicada's* destroyed the fruits in *Germany*, where that insect is not found; and therefore concludeth, *Tam ipsos quam aliios deceptos fuisse autumo, dum locustas cicadas esse vulgari errore crederent.*

And hereby there may be some mistake in the due dispensation of medicines desumed from this animal; particularly of Diatettigon commended by *Ætius* in the affections of the kidnies. It must be likewise understood with some restriction what hath been affirmed by *Isidore*, and yet delivered by many, that Cicadas are bred out of Cuccow spittle or Woodsear; that is, that spumous, frothy dew or exudation or both, found upon Plants, especially about the joynts of Lavender and Rosemary, observable with us about the latter end of May. For here the true *Cicada* is not bred, but certain it is, that out of this, some kind of Locust doth proceed; for herein may be discovered a little insect of a festucine or pale green, resembling in all parts a Locust, or what we call a Grashopper.

Lastly, The word it self is improper, and the term of Grashopper not appliable unto the *Cicada*; for therein the organs of motion are not contrived for saltation, nor are the hinder legs of such extension, as is observable in salient animals, and such as move by leaping. Whereto the Locust is very well conformed; for therein the legs behind are longer than all the body, and make at the second joynt acute angles, at a considerable advancement above their backs.

The mistake therefore with us might have its original from a defect in our language; for having not the insect with us, we have not fallen upon its proper name, and so make use of a term common unto it and the Locust; whereas other countries have proper expressions for it. So the *Italian* calls it *Cicada*, the *Spaniard Cigarra*, and the *French Cigale*; all which appellations conform unto the original, and properly express this animal. Whereas our word is borrowed from the Saxon Gærsthopp, which our forefathers, who never beheld the *Cicada*, used for that insect which we yet call a Grashopper.

Chapter IV

Of the Picture of the Serpent tempting Eve

In the Picture of Paradise, and delusion of our first Parents, the Serpent is often described with humane visage, not unlike unto *Cadmus* or his wife, in the act of their Metamorphosis. Which is not a meer pictorial contrivance or invention of the Picturer, but an ancient tradition and conceived reality, as it stands delivered by *Beda* and Authors of some antiquity; that is, that Sathan appeared not unto *Eve* in the naked form of a Serpent, but with a Virgins head, that thereby he might become more acceptable, and his temptation find the easier entertainment. Which nevertheless is a conceit not to be admitted, and the plain and received figure, is with better reason embraced.

For first, as *Pierius* observeth from *Barcephas*, the assumption of humane shape had proved a disadvantage unto Sathan; affording not only a suspicious amazement in *Eve*, before the fact, in beholding a third humanity beside her self and *Adam*; but leaving some excuse unto the woman, which afterward the man took up with lesser reason; that is, to have been deceived by another like her self.

Again, There was no inconvenience in the shape assumed, or any considerable impediment that might disturb that performance in the common form of a Serpent. For whereas it is conceived the woman must needs be afraid thereof, and rather flie than approach it; it was not agreeable unto the condition of Paradise and state of innocency therein; if in that place as most determine, no creature was hurtful or terrible unto man, and those destructive effects they now discover succeeded the curse, and came in with thorns and briars. And therefore *Eugubinus* (who affirmeth this serpent was a Basilisk) incurreth no absurdity, nor need we infer that *Eve* should be destroyed immediatly upon that Vision. For noxious animals could offend them no more in the Garden, than *Noah* in the Ark: as they peaceably received their names, so they friendly possessed their natures: and were their conditions destructive unto each other, they were not so unto man, whose constitutions then were antidotes, and needed not fear poisons. And if (as most conceive) there were but two created of every kind, they could not at that time destroy either man or themselves; for this had frustrated the command of multiplication, destroyed a species, and imperfected the Creation. And therefore also if *Cain* were the first man born, with him entred not only the act, but the first power of murther; for before that time neither could the Serpent nor *Adam* destroy *Eve*, nor *Adam* and *Eve* each other; for that had overthrown the intention of the world, and put its Creator to act the sixt day over again.

Moreover, Whereas in regard of speech, and vocal conference with *Eve*, it may be thought he would rather assume an humane shape and organs, then the improper form of a Serpent, it implies no material impediment. Nor need we to wonder how he contrived a voice out of the mouth of a Serpent, who hath done the like out of the belly of a Pythonissa, and the trunk of an Oak; as he did for many yeares at *Dodona*.

Lastly, Whereas it might be conceived that an humane shape was fitter for this enterprise, it being more than probable she would be amazed to hear a Serpent speak; some conceive she might not yet be certain that only man was priviledged with speech; and being in the novity of the Creation, and in experience of all things, might not be affrighted to hear a Serpent speak. Beside she might be ignorant of their natures, who was not versed in their names, as being not present at the general survey of Animals, when *Adam* assigned unto every one a name concordant unto its nature. Nor is this my opinion, but the determination of *Lombard* and *Tostatus*; and also the reply of *Cyrill* unto the objection of *Julian*, who compared this story unto the fables of the *Greeks*.

Chapter V

Of the picture of Adam and Eve with Navels

Another mistake there may be in the Picture of our first Parents, who after the manner of their posterity are both delineated with a Navel. And this is observable not only in ordinary and stained pieces, but in the Authentick draughts of *Urbin*, *Angelo* and others. Which notwithstanding cannot be allowed, except we impute that unto the first cause, which we impose not on the second; or what we deny unto nature, we impute unto Naturity it self; that is, that in the first and most accomplished piece, the Creator affected superfluities, or ordained parts without use or office.

For the use of the Navel is to continue the Infant unto the Mother, and by the vessels thereof to convey its aliment and sustentation. The vessels whereof it consisteth, are the umbilical vein, which is a branch of the Porta, and implanted in the Liver of the Infant; two Arteries likewise arising from the Iliacal branches, by which the Infant receiveth the purer portion of blood and spirits from the mother; and lastly, the Urachos or ligamental passage derived from the bottom of the bladder, whereby it dischargeth the waterish and urinary part of its aliment. Now upon the birth, when the Infant forsaketh the womb, although it dilacerate, and break the involving membranes, yet do these vessels hold, and by the mediation thereof the Infant is connected unto the womb, not only before, but a while also after the birth. These therefore the midwife cutteth off, contriving them into a knot close unto the body of the Infant; from whence ensueth that tortuosity or complicated nodosity we usually call the Navel; occasioned by the colligation of vessels before mentioned. Now the Navel being a part, not precedent, but subsequent unto generation, nativity or parturition, it cannot be well imagined at the creation or extraordinary formation of *Adam*, who immediately issued from the Artifice of God; nor also that of *Eve*, who was not solemnly begotten, but suddenly framed, and anomalously proceeded from *Adam*.

And if we be led into conclusions that *Adam* had also this part, because we behold the same in our selves, the inference is not reasonable; for if we conceive the way of his formation, or of the first animals, did carry in all points a strict conformity unto succeeding productions, we might fall into imaginations that *Adam* was made without Teeth; or that he ran through those notable alterations in the vessels of the heart, which the Infant suffereth after birth: we need not dispute whether the egg or bird were first; and might conceive that Dogs were created blind, because we observe they are littered so with us. Which to affirm, is to confound, at least to regulate creation unto generation, the first Acts of God, unto the second of Nature; which were determined in that general indulgence, Encrease and Multiply, produce or propagate each other; that is, not answerably in all points, but in a prolonged method according to seminal progression. For the formation of things at first was different from their generation after; and although it had nothing to precede it, was aptly contrived for that which should succeed it. And therefore though *Adam* were framed without this part, as having no other womb then that of his proper principles, yet was not his posterity without the same: for the seminality of his fabrick contained the power thereof; and was endued with the science of those parts whose predestinations upon succession it did accomplish.

All the Navel therefore and conjunctive part we can suppose in *Adam*, was his dependency on his Maker, and the connexion he must needs have unto heaven, who was the Son of God. For holding no dependence on any preceding efficient but God; in the act of his production there may be conceived some connexion, and *Adam* to have been in a momental Navel with his Maker. And although from his carnality and corporal existence, the conjunction seemeth no nearer than of causality and effect; yet in his immortal and diviner part he seemed to hold a nearer coherence, and an umbilicality even with God himself. And so indeed although the propriety of this part be found but in some animals, and many species there are which have no Navel at all; yet is there one link and common connexion, one general ligament, and necessary obligation of all whatever unto God. Whereby although they act themselves at distance, and seem to be at loose; yet do they hold a continuity with their Maker. Which catenation or conserving union when ever his pleasure shall divide, let go, or separate, they shall fall from their existence, essence, and operations: in brief, they must retire unto their primative nothing, and shrink into their Chaos again.

They who hold the egg was before the Bird, prevent this doubt in many other animals, which also extendeth unto them: For birds are nourished by umbilical vessels, and the Navel is manifest sometimes a day or two after exclusion. The same is probable in all oviparous exclusions, if the lesser part of eggs must serve for the formation, the greater part for nutriment. The same is made out in the eggs of Snakes; and is not improbable in the generation of Porwiggles or Tadpoles, and may be also true in some vermiparous exclusions; although (as we have observed in the daily progresse in some) the whole Maggot is little enough to make a Fly, without any part remaining.

CHAPTER VI

Of the Pictures of Eastern Nations, and the Jews at their Feasts, especially our Saviour at the Passover.

Concerning the pictures of the *Jews*, and Eastern Nations at their Feasts, concerning the gesture of our Saviour at the Passover, who is usually described sitting upon a stoole or bench at a square table, in the middest of the twelve, many make great doubt; and (though they concede a table-gesture) will hardly allow this usuall way of Session.

Wherein restraining no mans enquiry, it will appear that accubation, or lying down at meals was a gesture used by very many Nations. That the *Persians* used it, beside the testimony of humane Writers, is deducible from that passage in *Esther*. That when the Kindg returned unto the place of the banquet of wine, *Haman* was fallen upon the bed whereon *Esther* was. That the *Parthians* used it, is evident from *Athenæus*, who delivereth out of *Possidonius*, that their King lay down at meals, on an higher bed then others. That *Cleopatra* thus entertained *Anthony*, the same Author manifesteth when he saith, she prepared twelve Tricliniums. That it was in use among the *Greeks*, the word Triclinium implieth, and the same is also declarable from many places in the Symposiacks of *Plutarch*. That it was not out of fashion in the days of *Aristotle*, he declareth in his politicks; when among the Institutionary rules of youth, he adviseth they might not be permitted to heare Iambicks and Tragedies before they were admitted unto discumbency or lying along with others at their meals. That the *Romans* used this gesture at repast, beside many more, is evident from *Lipsius*,

Mercurialis, *Salmasius*, and *Ciaconius*, who have expresly and distinctly treated hereof.

Now of their accumbing places, the one was called Stibadion and Sigma, carrying the figure of an half Moon, and of an uncertain capacity, whereupon it received the name of Hexaclinon, Octoclinon, according unto that of *Martial*,

> Accipe Lunata scriptum testudine Sigma:
> Octo capit, veniat quisquis amicus erit.

Hereat in several ages the left and right horn were the principal places, and the most honorable person, if he were not master of the feast, possessed one of those rooms. The other was termed Triclinium, that is, Three beds about a table, as may be seen in the figures thereof, and particularly in the *Rhamnusian* Triclinium, set down by Mercurialis. The customary use hereof was probably deduced from the frequent use of bathing, after which they commonly retired to bed, and refected themselves with repast; and so that custom by degrees changed their cubiculary beds into discubitory, and introduced a fashion to go from the bathes unto these.

As for their gesture or position, the men lay down leaning on their left elbow, their back being advanced by some pillow or soft substance: the second lay so with his back towards the first, that his head attained about his bosom; and the rest in the same order: For women, they sat sometimes distinctly with their sex, sometime promiscuously with men, according to affection or favour, as is delivered by Juvenal

> Gremio jacuit nova nupta mariti.

And by *Suetonius* of *Caligula*, that at his feasts he placed his sisters, with whom he had been incontinent, successively in order below him.

Again, As their beds were three, so the guests did not usually exceed that number in every one; according to the ancient Laws, and proverbial observations to begin with the Graces, and make up their feasts with the Muses. And therefore it was remarkable in the Emperour *Lucius Verus*, that he lay down with twelve: which was, saith

Julius Capitolinus, præter exempla majorum, not according to the custom of his Predecessors, except it were at publick and nuptial suppers. The regular number was also exceeded in this last supper, whereat there were no lesse than thirteen, and in no place fewer then ten, for, as *Josephus* delivereth, it was not lawful to celebrate the Passover with fewer than that number.

Lastly, For the disposing and ordering of the persons: The first and middle beds were for the guests, the third and lowest for the Master of the house and his family; he always lying in the first place of the last bed, that is, next the middle bed; but if the wife and children were absent, their rooms were supplied by the Umbræ, or hangers on, according to that of *Juvenal — Locus est & pluribus Umbris*. For the guests, the honourablest place in every bed was the first, excepting the middle or second bed; wherein the most honourable Guest of the feast was placed in the last place, because by that position he might be next the Master of the feast. For the Master lying in the first of the last bed, and the principal Guest in the last place of the second, they must needs be next each other; as this figure doth plainly declare, and whereby we may apprehend the feast of *Perpenna* made unto *Sertorius*, described by *Salustius*, whose words we shall thus read with *Salmasius: Igitur discubuere, Sertorius inferior in medio lecto, supra Fabius; Antonius*

360

in summo; Infra Scriba Sertorii Versius, alter scriba Mæcenas in Imo, medius inter Tarquitium & Dominum Perpennam.

At this feast there were but seven; the middle places of the highest and middle bed being vacant; and hereat was *Sertorius* the General and principal guest slain. And so may we make out what is delivered by *Plutarch* in his life, that lying on his back, and raising himself up, *Perpenna* cast himself upon his stomack; which he might very well do, being Master of the feast, and lying next unto him. And thus also from this Tricliniary disposure, we may illustrate that obscure expression of *Seneca*; That the Northwind was in the middle, the North-East on the higher side, and the North-West on the lower. For as appeareth in the circle of the winds, the North-East will answer the bed of Antonius, and the North-West that of Perpenna.

That the custom of feasting upon beds was in use among the *Hebrews*, many deduce from Ezekiel. Thou sattest upon a stately bed, and a table prepared before it. The custom of Discalceation or putting off their shoes at meals, is conceived to confirm the same; as by that means keeping their beds clean; and therefore they had a peculiar charge to eat the Passover with their shoes on; which Injunction were needless, if they used not to put them off. However it were in times of high antiquity, probable it is that in after ages they conformed unto the fashions of the *Assyrians* and Eastern Nations, and lastly of the *Romans*, being reduced by *Pompey* unto a Provincial subjection.

That this discumbency at meals was in use in the days of our Saviour, is conceived probable from several speeches of his expressed in that phrase, even unto common Auditors, as *Luke* 14. *Cum invitatus fueris ad nuptias, non discumbas in primo loco*, and besides many more, *Matthew* 23. When reprehending the *Scribes* and *Pharises*, he saith, *Amant protoclisias, id est, primos recubitus in cœnis, & protocathedrias, sive, primas cathedras, in Synagogis*: wherein the terms are very distinct, and by an Antithesis do plainly distinguish the posture of sitting, from this of lying on beds. The consent of the *Jews* with the *Romans* in other ceremonies and rites of feasting, makes probable their conformity in this. The *Romans* washed, were anointed, and wore a cenatory garment: and that the same was practised by the *Jews*, is deduceable from that expostulation of our Saviour with *Simon*, that he washed not his feet, nor anointed his head with oyl: the common civilities at festival entertainments: and that expression of his concerning the cenatory or wedding garment; and as some conceive of the linnen garment of the young man or St. *John*; which might be the same he wore the night before at the last Supper.

That they used this gesture at the Passover, is more than probable from the testimony of *Jewish* Writers, and particularly of *Benmaimon* recorded by *Scaliger De emendatione temporum*. After the second cup according to the Institution. The Son asketh, what meaneth this service? Then he that maketh the declaration saith, How different is this night from all other nights! for all other nights we wash but once, but this night twice; all other we eat leavened or unleavened bread, but this only leavened; all other we eat flesh roasted, boyled, or baked, but this only roasted; all other nights we eat together lying or sitting, but this only lying along. And this posture they used as a token of rest and security which they enjoyed. far different from that, at the eating of the Passover in *Ægypt*.

That this gesture was used when our Saviour ate the Passover, is not conceived improbable from the words where by the Evangelists expresse the same, that is, αναπίπειν, ανακεῖθαι, κατακεῖσθαι, ανακλιθεναι, which terms do properly signifie, this Gesture in *Aristotle*, *Athenœus*, *Euripides*, *Sophocles*, and all humane Authors; and the like we meete with in the paraphrastical expression of *Nonnus*.

Lastly, If it be not fully conceded, that this gesture was used at the Passover, yet that it was observed at the last supper, seems almost incontrovertible: for at this feast or cenatory convention, learned men make more than one supper, or at least many parts thereof. The first was that Legal one of the Passover, or eating of the Paschal Lamb with bitter herbs, and ceremonies described by *Moses*. Of this it is said, that when the even was come he sat down with the twelve. This is supposed when it is said, that the Supper being ended, our Saviour arose, took a towel and washed the disciples feet. The second was common and Domestical, consisting of ordinary and undefined provisions; of this it may be said, that our Saviour took his garment, and sat down again, after he had washed the Disciples feet, and performed the preparative civilities of suppers; at this 'tis conceived the sop was given unto *Judas*, the Original word implying some broath or decoction, not used at the Passover. The third or latter part was Eucharistical, which began at the breaking and blessing of the bread, according to that of *Matthew*, And as they were eating, Jesus took bread and blessed it.

Now although at the Passover or first supper, many have doubted this Reclining posture, and some have affirmed that our Saviour stood; yet that he lay down at the other, the same men have acknowledged, as *Chrysostom, Theophylact, Austin*, and many more. And if the tradition will hold, the position is unquestionable; for the very Triclinium is to be seen at *Rome*, brought thither by *Vespasian*, and graphically set forth by *Casalius*.

Thus may it properly be made out; what is delivered, *John* 13. *Erat recumbens unus ex Discipulis ejus in sinu Jesu quem diligebat*; Now there was leaning on Jesus bosom one of his Disciples whom Jesus loved; which gesture will not so well agree unto the position of sitting, but is natural, and cannot be avoided in the Laws of accubation. And the very same expression is to be found in *Pliny*, concerning the Emperour *Nerva* and *Veiento* whom he favoured; *Coenabat Nerva cum paucis, Veiento recumbebat propius atque etiam in sinu*; and from this custom arose the word ἐπιστήθιος, that is, a near and bosom friend. And therefore *Casaubon* justly rejecteth *Theophylact*; who not considering the ancient manner of decumbency, imputed this gesture of the beloved Disciple unto Rusticity, or an act of incivility. And thus also have some conceived, it may be more plainly made out what is delivered of *Mary Magdalen*, That she stood at Christs feet behind him weeping, and began to wash his feet with tears, and did wipe them with the hairs of her head. Which actions, if our Saviour sat, she could not perform standing, and had rather stood behind his back, than at his feet. And therefore it is not allowable, what is observable in many pieces, and even of *Raphael Urbin*, wherein *Mary Magdalen* is pictured before our Saviour, washing his feet on her knees; which will not consist with the strict description and letter of the Text.

Now whereas this position may seem to be discountenanced by our Translation, which usually renders it sitting, it cannot have that illation, for the *French* and *Italian* Translations expressing neither position of session or recubation, do only say that he placed himself at the table; and when ours expresseth the same by sitting, it is in relation unto our custom, time, and apprehension. The like upon occasion is not unusual: so when it is said, *Luke* 4. πτύξας τὸ βιβλίον, and the

Vulgar renders it, *Cum plicasset librum*, ours translateth it, he shut or closed the book; which is an expression proper unto the paginal books of our times, but not so agreeable unto volumes or rolling books in use among the *Jews*, not only in elder times, but even unto this day. So when it is said, the *Samaritan* delivered unto the host two pence for the provision of the *Levite*; and when our Saviour agreed with the Labourers for a penny a day, in strict translation it should be seven pence half penny; and is not to be conceived our common penny, the sixtieth part of an ounce. For the word in the Originall is δηνάριον, in Latine, *Denarius*, and with the Romans did value the eight part of an ounce, which after five shillings the ounce amounteth unto seven pence half penny of our money.

Lastly, Whereas it might be conceived that they eat the Passover standing rather then sitting, or lying down, according to the Institution, *Exod.* 12. Thus shall you eat, with your loins girded, your shooes on your feet, and your staff in your hand; the *Jews* themselves reply, this was not required of succeeding generations, and was not observed, but in the Passover of *Ægypt*. And so also many other injunctions were afterward omitted, as the taking up of the Paschal Lamb, from the tenth day, the eating of it in their houses dispersed; the striking of the blood on the door posts, and the eating thereof in hast. Solemnities and Ceremonies primatively enjoyned, afterward omitted; as was also this of station, for the occasion ceasing, and being in security, they applied themselves unto gestures in use among them.

Now in what order of recumbency Christ and the Disciples were disposed, is not so easily determined. *Casalius* from the Lateran Triclinium will tell us, that there being thirteen, five lay down in the first bed, five in the last, and three in the middle bed; and that our Saviour possessed the upper place thereof. That *John* lay in the same bed seems plain, because he leaned on our Saviours bosom. That *Peter* made the third in that bed, conjecture is made, because he beckened unto *John*, as being next him, to ask of Christ, who it was that should betray him. That *Judas* was not far off seems probable, not only because he dipped in the same dish, but because he was so near, that our Saviour could hand the sop unto him.

CHAPTER VII

Of the picture of our Saviour with long haire

Another picture there is of our Saviour described with long haire, according to the custome of the Jews, and his description sent by Lentulus unto the Senate; wherein indeed the hand of the Painter is not accusable, but the judgement of the common Spectator, conceaving he observed this fashion of his hayre, because he was a Nazarite, and confounding a Nazarite by vow, with those by birth or education.

The Nazarite by vow is declared Numb. 6 and was to refraine three things, drinking of Wine, cutting the hayre, and approaching unto the dead, and such a one was Sampson: Now that our Saviour was a Nazarite after this kinde, we have no reason to determine, for he dranke wine, and was therefore called by the Pharisees a Wine bibber; he approached also the dead, as when he raised from death Lazarus, and the daughter of Jairus.

The other Nazarite was a Topicall appellation, and applyable unto such as were borne in Nazareth, a City of Galiliee, and in the Tribe of Napthali; neither if strictly taken, was our Saviour in this sense a Nazarite; for he was borne in Bethlehem in the Tribe of Judah; but might receave that name, because he abode in that City, and was not onely conceaved therein, but there also passed the silent part of his life, after his returne from Ægypt, as is delivred by Matthew, And he came and dwelt in a City called Nazareth, that it might be fulfilled which was spoken by the Prophet, he shall be called a Nazarene; both which kinds of Nazarites, as they are distinguishable by Zaid, and Tsade in the Hebrew, so in the Greeke, by Alpha and Omega; for, as Jansenius observeth, where the votary Nazarite is mentioned, it is written Ναζαραιος, as Levit. 6. and Lament. 4. Where it is spoken of our Saviour, we reade it Ναζωραιος, as in Matthew, Luke, and John; onely Marke who writ his Gospell at Rome did Latinize and write it

CHAPTER VIII

Of the Picture of Abraham sacrificing Isaac

In the Picture of the Immolation of *Isaac*, or *Abraham* sacrificing his son, *Isaac* is described as a little boy; which notwithstanding is not consentaneous unto the authority of Expositors, or the circumstance of the Text. For therein it is delivered that *Isaac* carried on his back the wood for the sacrifice; which being an holocaust or burnt offering to be consumed unto ashes, we cannot well conceive a burthen for a boy; but such a one unto *Isaac*, as that which it typified was unto Christ, that is, the wood or cross whereon he suffered; which was too heavy a load for his shoulders, and was fain to be relieved therein by *Simon* of *Cyrene*.

Again, He was so far from a boy, that he was a man grown, and at his full stature, if we believe *Josephus* who placed him in the last of *Adolescency*, and makes him twenty five years old. And whereas in the Vulgar Translation he is termed *puer*, it must not be strictly apprehended, (for that age properly endeth in puberty, and extendeth but unto fourteen) but respectively unto *Abraham*, who was at that time above sixscore. And therefore also herein he was not unlike unto him, who was after led dumb unto the slaughter, and commanded by others, who had legions at command; that is in meekness and humble submission. For had he resisted, it had not been in the power of his aged parent to have enforced; and many at his years have performed such acts, as few besides at any. *David* was too strong for a Lion and a Bear; *Pompey* had deserved the name of Great; *Alexander* of the same cognomination was *Generalissimo* of *Greece*; and *Anibal* but one year after, succeeded *Asdruball* in that memorable War against the *Romans*.

CHAPTER IX

Of the Picture of Moses with Horns

In many pieces, and some of ancient Bibles, *Moses* is described with horns. The same description we finde in a silver Medal; that is, upon one side *Moses* horned, and on the reverse the commandment against sculptile Images. Which is conceived to be a coynage of some *Jews*, in derision of Christians, who first began that Pourtract.

The ground of this absurdity, was surely a mistake of the Hebrew Text, in the history of *Moses* when he descended from the Mount; upon the affinity of *Kæren* and *Karan,* that is, an horn, and to shine, which is one quality of horn: The Vulgar Translation conforming unto the former. *Ignorabat quod cornuta esset facies ejus. Qui videbant faciem Moses esse cornutam.* But the *Chaldee* paraphrase, translated by Paulus Fagius, hath otherwise expressed it. *Moses nesciebat quod multus esset splendor gloriæ vultus ejus. Et viderunt filii Israel quod multa esset claritas gloriæ faciei Moses.* The expression of the Septuagint is as large, δεδόξασται he οψις του χρώματος του προσώπου, *Glorificatus est aspectus cutis, seu coloris faciei.*

And this passage of the Old Testament, is well explained by another of the New; wherein it is delivered, that they could not stedfastly behold the face of *Moses,* Δια τεν δόξαν του προσώπου; that is, for the glory of his countenance. And surely the exposition of one Text is best performed by another; men vainly interposing their constructions, where the Scripture decideth the controversie. And therefore some have seemed too active in their expositions, who in the story of *Rahab* the harlot, have given notice that the word also signifieth an

Hostess; for in the Epistle to the *Hebrews*, she is plainly termed πόρνη, which signifies not an Hostess, but a pecuniary and prostituting Harlot; a term applyed unto *Lais* by the *Greeks*, and distinguished from εταιρα, or *amica,* as may appear in the thirteenth of *Athenæus.*

And therefore more allowable is the Translation of *Tremellius*, *Quod splendida facta esset cutis faciei ejus*; or as *Estius* hath interpreted it, *facies ejus erat radiosa*, his face was radiant, and dispersing beams like many horns and cones about his head; which is also consonant unto the original signification, and yet observed in the pieces of our Saviour, and the Virgin *Mary*, who are commonly drawn with scintillations, or radiant Halo's about their head; which after the *French* expression are usually termed, the Glory.

Now if besides this occasional mistake, any man shall contend a propriety in this picture, and that no injury is done unto Truth by this description, because an horn is the Hieroglyphick of authority, power and dignity, and in this Metaphor is often used in Scripture; the piece I confess in this acception is harmeless and agreeable unto *Moses*: and under emblematical constructions, we finde that *Alexander* the Great, and *Attila* King of *Hunnes*, in ancient Medals are described with horns. But if from the common mistake, or any solary consideration we persist in this description; we vilify the mystery of the irradiation, and authorize a dangerous piece conformable unto that of *Jupiter Hammon*; which was the Sun, and therefore described with horns; as is delivered by *Macrobius*; *Hammonem quem Deum solem occidentem Lybies existimant, arietinis cornibus fingunt, quibus id animal valet, sicut radiis sol.* We herein also imitate the Picture of *Pan*, and *Pagan* emblem of Nature. And if (as *Macrobius* and very good Authors concede) *Bacchus*, (who is also described with horns) be the same Deity with the Sun, and if (as *Voßius* well contendeth) *Moses* and *Bacchus* were the same person; their descriptions must be relative, or the Tauricornous picture of the one, perhaps the same with the other.

CHAPTER X

Of the Scutcheons of the Tribes of Israel

We will not pass over the Scutcheons of the Tribes of *Israel*, as they are usually described in the Maps of *Canaan* and several other pieces, generally conceived to be the proper coats, and distinctive badges of their several Tribes. So *Reuben* is conceived to bear three Bars wave, *Judah* a Lyon Rampant, *Dan* a Serpent nowed, *Simeon* a sword impale the point erected, &c. The ground whereof is the last Benediction of *Jacob*, wherein he respectively draweth comparisons from things here represented.

Now herein although we allow a considerable measure of truth, yet whether as they are usually described, these were the proper cognizances, and coat-arms of the Tribes; whether in this manner applyed, and upon the grounds presumed material doubts remain.

For first, They are not strictly made out, from the Prophetical blessing of *Jacob*; for *Simeon* and *Levi* have distinct coats, that is, a Sword, and the two Tables, yet are they by *Jacob* included in one Prophesie, *Simeon* and *Levi* are brethren, Instruments of cruelties are in their habitations. So *Joseph* beareth an Ox, whereof notwithstanding there is no mention in this Prophesie; for therein it is said *Joseph* is a fruitful bough, even a fruitful bough by a well; by which repetition are intimated the two Tribes descending from him, *Ephraim* and *Manasses*; whereof notwithstanding *Ephraim* only beareth an Ox: True it is, that many years after in the benediction of *Moses*, it is said, of *Joseph*, *His glory is like the firstlings of his Bullock*; and so we may concede, what *Voßius* learnedly declareth, that the *Ægyptians* represented *Joseph*, in the Symbole of an Ox; for thereby was best implied the dream of *Pharoah*, which he interpreted, the benefit by Agriculture, and provident provision of corn which he performed; and therefore did *Serapis* bear a bushel upon his head.

Again, If we take these two benedictions together, the resemblances are not appropriate, and *Moses* therein conforms not unto *Jacob*; for that which in the Prophesie of *Jacob* is appropriated unto one, is in the blessing of *Moses* made common unto others. So whereas *Judah* is compared unto a Lion by *Jacob*, *Judah* is Lions whelp, the same is applied unto *Dan* by *Moses*, *Dan* is a Lions whelp, he shall leap from *Bashan*, and also unto *Gad*; he dwelleth as a Lion.

Thirdly, If a Lion were the proper coat of *Judah*, yet were it not probably a Lion Rampant, as it is commonly described, but rather couchant or dormant, as some *Heralds* and *Rabbins* do determine; according to the letter of the Text, *Recumbens dormisti ut Leo*, He couched as a Lion, and as a young Lion, who shall rouse him?

Lastly, when it is said, Every man of the Children of *Israel* shall pitch by his own standard with the Ensign of their fathers house; upon enquiry what these standards and Ensigns were there is no small incertainty; and men conform not unto the Prophesie of *Jacob*. Christian Expositors are fain herein to rely upon the *Rabbins*, who notwithstanding are various in their traditions, and confirm not these common descriptions. For as for inferiour ensigns, either of particular bands or houses, they determine nothing at all; and of the four principal or Legionary standards, that is, of *Judah, Reuben, Ephraim*, and *Dan* (under every one whereof marched three Tribes) they explain them very variously. *Jonathan* who compiled the Thargum conceives the colours of these banners to answer the precious stones in the breast-plate, and upon which the names of the Tribes were engraven. So the standard for the Camp of *Judah*, was of three colours, according unto the stones, Chalcedony, Saphir and Sardonix; and therein were expressed the names of the three Tribes, *Judah, Isachar*, and *Zabulon*, and in the middest thereof was written, Rise up Lord, and let they enemies be scattered, and let them that hate thee flee before thee; in it was also the pourtrait of a Lion. The standard of *Reuben* was also of three colours, Sardine, Topaz, and Amethyst; therein were expressed the names of *Reuben, Simeon*, and *Gad*, in the middest was written, Hear, O *Israel*, The Lord our God, the Lord is one: Therein was also the pourtraiture of a Hart. But Abenezra and others, beside the colours of the field, do set down other charges, in *Reubens* the form of a man or mandrake, in that of *Judah* a Lion, in *Ephraims* an Ox, in *Dans* the figure of an Eagle.

And thus indeed the four figures in the banners of the principal squadrons of *Israel* are answerable unto the Cherubins in the vision of *Ezekiel*; every one carrying the form of all these. As for the likeness of their faces, they four had the likeness of the face of a Man, and the face of a Lion on the right side, and they four had the face of an Ox on the left side, they four had also the face of an Eagle. And conformable hereunto the pictures of the Evangelists (whose Gospels are the Christian banners) are set forth with the addition of a man or Angel, an Ox, a Lion, and an Eagle. And these symbolically represent the office of Angels, and Ministers of Gods Will; in whom is required understanding as in a man, courage and vivacity as in the Lion, service and ministerial officiousness, as in the Ox, expedition or celerity of execution, as in the Eagle.

From hence therefore we may observe that these descriptions, the most authentick of any, are neither agreeable unto one another, nor unto the Scutcheons in question. For though they agree in *Ephraim* and *Judah*, that is, the Ox and the Lion, yet do they differ in those of *Dan*, and *Reuben*, as far as an Eagle is different from a Serpent, and the figure of a Man, Hart, or Mandrake, from three Bars wave. Wherein notwithstanding we rather declare the incertainty of Arms in this particular, than any way question their antiquity; for hereof more ancient examples there are, than the Scutcheons of the Tribes, if *Osyris*, *Mizraim* or *Jupiter* the Just, were the Son of *Cham*; for of his two Sons, as *Diodorus* delivereth, the one for his Device gave a Dog, the other a Wolf. And, beside the shield of *Achilles*, and many ancient *Greeks*: if we receive the conjecture of *Voßius*, that the Crow upon *Corvinus* his head, was but the figure of that Animal upon his helmet, it is an example of Antiquity among the *Romans*.

But more widely must we walk, if we follow the doctrine of the *Cabalists*, who in each of the four banners inscribe a letter of the Tetragrammaton or quadriliteral name of God: and mysterizing their ensigns, do make the particular ones of the twelve Tribes, accommodable unto the twelve signes in the Zodiack, and twelve moneths in the year: But the Tetrachical or general banners, of *Judah*, *Reuben*, *Ephraim*, and *Dan*, unto the signs of Aries, Cancer, Libra and Capricornus: that is, the four cardinal parts of the Zodiack, and seasons of the year. .

CHAPTER XI

Of the Pictures of the Sibyls

The Pictures of the *Sibyls* are very common, and for their Prophesies of Christ in high esteem with Christians; described commonly with youthful faces, and in a defined number. Common pieces making twelve, and many precisely ten; observing therein the account of *Varro*, that is, *Sibylla Delphica, Erythræa, Samia, Cumana, Cumæa,* or *Cimmeria, Hellespontiaca, Lybica, Phrygia, Tiburtina, Persica.* In which enumeration I perceive learned men are not satisfied, and many conclude an irreconcilable incertainty; some making more, others fewer, and not this certain number. For *Suidas,* though he affirm that in divers ages there were ten, yet the same denomination he affordeth unto more; *Boysardus* in his Tract of Divination hath set forth the Icons of these Ten, yet addeth two others, *Epirotica,* and *Ægyptia;* and some affirm that Prophesying women were generally named *Sibyls.*

Others make them fewer: *Martianus Capella* two, *Pliny* and *Solinus* three, *Ælian* four; and *Salmasius* in effect but seven. For discoursing hereof in his *Plinian* Exercitations, he thus determineth; *Ridere licet hodiernos Pictores, qui tabulas proponunt Cumanæ, Cumeæ, & Erythræœ, quasi trium diversarum Sibyllarum; cum una eademque fuerit Cumana, Cumæa, & Erythræa, ex plurium et doctissimorum Authorum sententia;* *Boysardus* gives us leave to opinion there was no more then one; for so doth he conclude, *In tanta Scriptorum varietate liberum relinquimus Lectori credere, an una & eadem in diversis regionibus peregrinata, cognomen sortita sit ab iis locis ubi oracula redidisse comperitur, an plures extiterint:* And therefore not discovering a resolution of their number from pens of the best Writers, we have not reason to determine the same from the hand and pencil of Painters.

As touching their age, that they are generally described as young women, History will not allow; for the Sibyl whereof *Virgil* speaketh is termed by him *longæva sacerdos*, and *Servius* in his Comment amplifieth the same. The other that sold the books unto *Tarquin*, and whose History is plainer than any, by *Livie* and *Gellius* is tearmed *Anus*; that is, properly no woman of ordinary age, but full of years, and in the dayes of dotage, according to the Etymology of *Festus*; and consonant unto the History; wherein it is said, that *Tarquin* thought she doted with old age. Which duly perpended, the *Licentia pictoria* is very large; with the same reason they may delineate old *Nestor* like *Adonis*, *Hecuba* with *Helens* face, and Time with *Absalons* head. But this absurdity that eminent Artist *Michael Angelo* hath avoided, in the Pictures of the *Cumean* and *Persian* Sibyls, as they stand described from the printed sculptures of *Adam Mantuanus*.

CHAPTER XII

Of the Picture describing the death of Cleopatra

The Picture concerning the death of *Cleopatra* with two Asps or venemous Serpents unto her arms, or breasts, or both, requires consideration: for therein (beside that this variety is not excusable) the thing it self is questionable; nor is it indisputably certain what manner of death she died. *Plutarch* in the life of *Antony* plainly delivereth, that no man knew the manner of her death; for some affirmed she perished by poison, which she always carried in a little hollow comb, and wore it in her hair. Beside, there were never any Asps discovered in the place of her death, although two of her Maids perished also with her; only it was said, two small and almost insensible pricks were found upon her arm; which was all the ground that *Cæsar* had to presume the manner of her death. *Galen* who was contemporary unto *Plutarch*, delivereth two wayes of her death: that she killed her self by the bite of an Asp, or bit an hole in her arm, and poured poison therein. *Strabo* that lived before them both hath also two opinions; that she died by the bite of an Asp, or else a poisonous ointment.

We might question the length of the Asps, which are sometimes described exceeding short; whereas the Chersæa or land-Asp which most conceive she used, is above four cubits long. Their number is not unquestionable; for whereas there are generally two described, *Augustus* (as *Plutarch* relateth) did carry in his triumph the Image of *Cleopatra* but with one Asp unto her arm. As for the two pricks, or little spots in her arm, they infer not their plurality: for like the Viper, the Asp hath two teeth; whereby it left this impression, or double puncture behind it.

And lastly, We might question the place; for some apply them unto her breast, which notwithstanding will not consist with the History; and *Petrus Victorius* hath well observed the same. But herein the mistake was easie; it being the custom in capital malefactors to apply them unto the breast, as the Author of *De Theriaca ad Pisonum*, an eye witness hereof in *Alexandria*, where *Cleopatra* died, determineth: I beheld, saith he, in *Alexandria*, how suddenly these Serpents bereave a man of life; for when any one is condemned to this kind of death, if they intend to use him favourably, that is, to dispatch him suddenly, they fasten an Asp unto his breast; and bidding him walk about, he presently perisheth thereby.

CHAPTER XIII

Of the Pictures of the Nine Worthies

The pictures of the nine Worthies are not unquestionable, and to critical spectators may seem to contain sundry improprieties. Some will enquire why *Alexander* the Great is described upon an Elephant: for, we do not find he used that animal in his Armies, much less in his own person; but his Horse is famous in History, and its name is alive to this day. Beside, he fought but one remarkable battel, wherein there were any Elephants, and that was with *Porus* King of *India*; In which notwithstanding, as *Curtius*, *Arrianus*, and *Plutarch* report, he was on Horseback himself. And if because he fought against Elephants, he is with propriety set upon their backs; with no less or greater reason is the same description agreeable unto *Judas Maccabeus*, as may be observed in the history of the *Macabees*; and also unto *Julius Cæsar*, whose triumph was honoured with captive Elephants, as may be observed in the order thereof, set forth by *Jacobus Laurus*. And if also we should admit this description upon an Elephant, yet were not the manner thereof unquestionable, that is, in his ruling the beast alone; for beside the Champion upon their back, there was also a guide or ruler, which sat more forward to command or guide the beast. Thus did King *Porus* ride when he was overthrown by *Alexander*; and thus are also the towred Elephants described, *Maccab*. 1.6. Upon the beasts there were strong towers of wood, which covered every one of them, and were girt fast unto them by devices: there were also upon every one of them thirty two strong men, beside the *Indian* that ruled them.

Others will demand, not only why *Alexander* upon an Elephant, but *Hector* upon an Horse: whereas his manner of fighting, or presenting himselfe in battel, was in a Chariot, as did the other noble

Trojans, who as *Pliny* affirmeth were the first inventers thereof. The same way of fight is testified by *Diodorus*, and thus delivered by Sir Walter *Raleigh*. Of the vulgar little reckoning was made, for they fought all on foot, slightly armed, and commonly followed the success of their Captains; who rode not upon Horses, but in Chariots drawn by two or three Horses. And this was also the ancient way of fight among the *Britains*, as is delivered by *Diodorus*, *Cæsar*, and *Tacitus*; and there want not some who have taken advantage hereof, and made it one argument of their original from *Troy*.

Lastly, By any man versed in Antiquity, the question can hardly be avoided, why the Horses of these Worthies, especially of *Cæsar*, are described with the furniture of great saddles, and stirrops; for saddles largely taken, though some defence there may be, yet that they had not the use of stirrops, seemeth of lesser doubt; as *Pancirollus* hath observed, as *Polydore Virgil* and *Petrus Victorius* have confirmed, expresly discoursing hereon; as is observable from *Pliny*, and cannot escape our eyes in the ancient monuments, medals, and Triumphant arches of the *Romans*. Nor is there any ancient classical word in Latine to express them; for *Staphia, Stapes* or *Stapeda* is not to be found in Authors of this Antiquity. And divers words which may be urged of this signification, are either later, or signified not thus much in the time of *Cæsar*. And therefore as *Lipsius* observeth, lest a thing of common use should want a common word, *Franciscus Philelphus* named them *Stapedas*, and *Bodinus Subicus Pedaneos*. And whereas the name might promise some Antiquity, because among the three small bones in the Auditory Organ, by Physitians termed *Incus, Malleus*, and *stapes*, one thereof from some resemblance doth bear this name; these bones were not observed, much less named by *Hippocrates*, *Galen* or any ancient Physitian. But as *Laurentius* observeth concerning the invention of the stapes or stirrop bone, there is some contention between *Columbus* and *Ingrassias*; the one of *Scicilia*, the other of *Cremona*, and both within the compass of this Century.

The same is also deduceable from very approved Authors: *Polybius* speaking of the way which *Anibal* marched into *Italy*, useth the word βεβημάτισται, that is saith *Petrus Victorius*, it was stored with devices for men to get upon their horses, which ascents were termed *Bemata*; and in the life of *Caius Gracchus*, *Plutarch* expresseth as much. For endeavouring to ingratiate himself with the people, besides the placing of stones at every miles end; he made at nearer distances certain elevated places, and Scalary ascents, that by the help thereof they might with better ease ascend or mount their horses. Now if we demand how Cavaliers then destitute of stirrops did usually mount their horses; as *Lipsius* informeth, the unable and softer sort of men had their Stratores, which helped them up on horse back, as in the practise of *Crassus* in *Plutarch*, and *Caracalla* in *Spartianus*, and the later example of *Valentinianus*, who because his horse rised before that he could not be setled on his back, cut off the right hand of his Strator. But how the active and hardy persons mounted, *Vegetius* resolves us, that they used to vault or leap up, and therefore they had wooden horses in their houses and abroad: that thereby young men might enable themselves in this action: wherein by instruction and practice they grew so perfect, that they could vault up on the right or left, and that with their sword in hand, according to that of *Virgil*

> *Poscit equos, atque arma simul, saltuque superbus*
> *Emicat.*

And againe:

> *Infrænant alii currus & corpora saltu*
> *Injiciunt in equos. —*

So *Julius Pollux* adviseth to teach horses to incline, dimit, and bow down their bodies, that their riders may with better ease ascend them. And thus may it more causally be made out, what *Hippocrates* affirmeth of the *Scythians*, that using continual riding, they were generally molested with the Sciatica or hip-gout. Or what *Suetonius* delivereth of *Germanicus*, that he had slender legs, but encreased them by riding after meals; that is, the humours descending upon their pendulosity, they having no support or suppedaneous stability.

Now if any shall say that these are petty errors and minor lapses not considerably injurious unto truth, yet is it neither reasonable nor safe to contemn inferiour falsities; but rather as between falshood and truth, there is no medium, so should they be maintained in their distances: nor the contagion of the one, approach the sincerity of the other.

CHAPTER XIV

Of the Picture of Jephthah sacrificing his daughter

The hand of the Painter confidently setteth forth the picture of *Jephthah* in the posture of *Abraham*, sacrificing his only daughter: Thus is it commonly received, and hath had the attest of many worthy Writers. Notwithstanding upon enquiry we find the matter doubtful, and many upon probable grounds to have beene of another opinion: conceiving in this oblation not a natural but a civil kind of death, and a separation only unto the Lord. For that he pursued not his vow unto a literal oblation, there want not arguments both from the Text and reason.

For first, It is evident that she deplored her Virginity, and not her death; Let me go up and down the mountains, and bewail my Virginity, I and my fellows.

Secondly, When it is said, that *Jephthah* did unto her according unto his vow, it is immediately subjoyned, *Et non cognovit virum*, and she knew no man; which as immediate in words, was probably most near in sense unto the vow.

Thirdly, It is said in the Text, that the daughters of *Israel* went yearly to talk with the daughter of *Jephthah* four dayes in the year; which had she been sacrificed, they could not have done: For whereas the word is sometime translated to lament, yet doth it also signifie to talk or have conference with one, and by *Tremellius*, who was well able to Judge of the Original, it is in this sense translated: *Ibant filiæ*

Israelitarum, ad confabulandum cum filia Jephthaci, quatuor diebus quotannis: And so it is also set down in the marginal notes of our Translation. And from this annual concourse of the daughters of *Israel*, it is not improbable in future Ages, the daughter of *Jephthah* came to be worshipped as a Deity; and had by the *Samaritans* an annual festivity observed unto her honour, as *Epiphanius* hath left recorded in the Heresie of the *Melchisedicians*.

It is also repugnant unto reason; for the offering of mankind was against the Law of God, who so abhorred humane sacrifice, that he admitted not the oblation of unclean beasts, and confined his Altars but unto few kinds of Animals, the Ox, the Goat, the Sheep, the Pigeon and its kinds: In the cleansing of the Leper, there is I confess, mention made of the Sparrow; but great dispute may be made whether it be properly rendred. And therefore the Scripture with indignation oft-times makes mention of humane sacrifice among the *Gentiles*; whose oblations scarce made scruple of any Animal, sacrificing not only Man, but Horses, Lions, Ӕagles; and though they come not into holocausts, yet do we read the *Syrians* did make oblations of fishes unto the goddes *Derceto*. It being therefore a sacrifice so abominable unto God, although he had pursued it, it is not probable the Priests and Wisdom of *Israel* would have permitted it; and that not only in regard of the subject or sacrifice it self, but also the sacrificator, which the Picture makes to be *Jephthah*; who was neither Priest, nor capable of that Office: for he was a *Gileadite*, and as the Text affirmeth, the son also of an harlot. And how hardly the Priest-hood woud endure encroachment upon their function, a notable example there is in the Story of *Ozias*.

Secondly, The offering up of his daughter was not only unlawful, and entrenched upon his Religion, but had been a course that had much condemned his discretion; that is, to have punished himself in the strictest observance of his vow, when as the Law of God had allowed an evasion; that is, by way of commutation or redemption, according as is determined, *Levit.* 27. Whereby if she were between the age of five and twenty, she was to be estimated but at ten shekels, and if between twenty and sixty, not above thirty. A sum that could never discourage an indulgent Parent; it being but the value of a servant slain; the inconsiderable Salary of *Judas*; and will make no greater noise than three pound fifteen shillings with us. And therefore their conceit is not to be exploded, who say that from the Story of

Jephthah sacrificing his owne daughter, might spring the fable of *Agamemnon*, delivering unto sacrifice his daughter *Iphigenia*, who was also contemporary unto *Jephthah*:: wherein to answere the ground that hinted it, *Iphigenia* was not sacrificed her self, but redeemed with an Hart, which *Diana* accepted for her.

Lastly, Although his vow run generally for the words, Whatsoever shall come forth, &c., Yet might it be restrained in the sense, for whatsoever was sacrificable, and justly subject to lawful immolation: and so would not have sacrificed either Horse or Dog, if they had come out upon him. Nor was he obliged by oath unto a strict observation of that which promissorily was unlawful; or could he be qualified by vow to commit a fact which naturally was abominable. Which doctrine had *Herod* understood, it might have saved *Iohn Baptists* head; when he promised by oath to give unto *Herodias* whatsoever she would ask; that is, if it were in the compass of things, which he could lawfully grant. For his oath made not that lawful which was illegal before: and if it were unjust to murder *John*, the supervenient Oath did not extenuate the fact, or oblige the Juror unto it.

Now the ground at least which much promoted the opinion, might be the dubious words of the text, which contain the sense of his vow; most men adhering unto their common and obvious acception. Whatsoever shall come forth of the doors of my house shall surely be the Lords, and I will offer it up for a burnt offering. Now whereas it is said, *Erit Jehovæ, & offeram illud holocaustum*, The word signifying both *&* and *aut*, it may be taken disjunctively, *aut offeram*, that is, it shall either be the Lords by separation, or else, an holocaust by common oblation, even as our marginal translation advertiseth; and as *Tremellius* rendreth it, *Erit inquam Jehovæ, aut offeram illud holocaustum*; and for the vulgar translation, it useth often *&* where *aut* must be presumed, as *Exod.* 21. *Si quis percusserit patrem & matrem,* that is not both, but either. There being therefore two waies to dispose of her, either to separate her unto the Lord, or offer her as a sacrifice, it is of no necessity the latter should be necessary; and surely less derogatory unto the sacred text and history of the people of God, must be the former.

CHAPTER XV

Of the Picture of John the Baptist

The picture of *John* the Baptist, in a Camels skin is very questionable, and many I perceive have condemned it. The ground or occasion of this description are the words of the holy Scripture, especially of *Matthew* and *Mark*, for *Luke* and *John* are silent herein; by them it is delivered, his garment was of Camels hair, and had a leather girdle about his loins. Now here it seemes the Camels hair is taken by Painters for the skin or pelt with the hair upon it. But this Exposition will not so well consist with the strict acceptation of the words; for *Mark* 1. It is said, he was ενδεδυμενός τρίχας καμήλου, and Matthew 3, εἶχε το ενδυμα αυτο τριχον καμήλου, that is, as the vulgar translation, that of *Beza*, that of *Sixtus Quintus*, and *Clement* the eight hath rendred it, *vestimentum habebat è pilis camelinis*; which is as ours translateth it, a garment of Camels hair; that is, made of some texture of that hair, a course garment; a cilicious or sackcloth habit; sutable to the austerity of his life; the severity of his Doctrin, Repentance; and the place thereof, the wilderness, his food and diet, locusts and wild hony. Agreeable unto the example of *Elias*, who is said to be *vir pilosus*, that is, as *Tremellius* interprets, *Veste villoso cinctus*; answerable unto the habit of the ancient Prophets, according to that of *Zachary*. In that day the Prophets shall be ashamed, neither shall they wear a rough garment to deceive; and sutable to the Cilicious and hairy Vests of the strictest Orders of Fryers, who derive the institution of their Monastick life from the example of *John* and *Elias*.

As for the wearing of skins, where that is properly intended, the expression of the Scripture is plain; so it is said, *Heb.* 11. They wandred about in Goats skins; and so it is said of our first Parents, *Gen.* 3 that God made them coats of skins; which though a natural habit unto all, before the invention of Texture, was something more unto *Adam*, who had newly learned to die; for unto him a garment from the dead, was but a dictate of death, and an habit of mortality.

Now if any man will say this habit of *John*, was neither of Camels skin, nor any course Texture of its hair, but rather some finer Weave of Camelot, Grograin or the like, in as much as these stuffs are supposed to be made of the hair of that Animal, or because that *Ælian* affirmeth, that Camels hair of *Persia*, is as fine as *Milesian* wool, wherewith the great ones of that place were clothed; they have discovered an habit, not onely unsutable unto his leathern cincture, and the coursness of his life; but not consistent with the words of our Saviour, when reasoning with the people concerning *John*, he saith, What went you out into the wilderness to see? a man clothed in soft raiment? Behold, they that wear soft raiment, are in Kings houses.

CHAPTER XVI

Of the Picture of St. Christopher

The Picture of St. *Christopher*, that is a man of a Giantlike stature, bearing upon his shoulders our Saviour Christ, and with a staff in his hand, wading thorow the water, is known unto Children, common over all *Europe*, and stands *Colossus* like in the entrance of *Nostre Dame* in *Paris*.

Now from hence, common eyes conceive an history sutable unto this description, that he carried our Saviour in his Minority over some river or water; which notwithstanding we cannot at all make out. For we read not thus much in any good Author, nor of any remarkable *Christopher*, before the reigne of *Decius*: who lived 250 years after Christ. This man indeed according unto History suffered as a Martyr in the second year of that Emperour, and in the *Roman Calendar* takes up the 21 of *July*.

The ground that begat or promoted this opinion, was, first the fabulous adjections of succeeding ages, unto the veritable acts of this Martyr, who in the most probable accounts was remarkable for his staff, and a man of goodly stature.

The second might be a mistake or misapprehension of the Picture, most men conceiving that an History which was contrived at first but as an Emblem or Symbolical fancy: as from the Annotations of *Baronius* upon the *Roman* Martyrologie, *Lipellous* in the life of St. *Christopher* hath observed in these words; *Acta S. Christophori à multis depravata inveniuntur: quod quidem non aliunde originem sumpsisse certum est: quam quod symbolicas figuras imperiti ad veritatem successu temporis transtulerint: itaque cuncta illa de Sancto Christophoro pingi consueta, symbola potius, quam historiæ alicujus existimandum est esse expressam imaginem*; that is, The Acts of St Christopher are depraved by many: which surely began from no other ground, then, that in process of time, unskilful men translated symbolical figures unto real verities: and therefore what is usually described in the Picture of St. *Christopher*, is rather to be received as an Emblem, or Symbolical description, then any real History. Now what Emblem this was, or what its signification, conjectures are many: *Pierius* hath set down one, that is, of the Disciple of Christ; for he that will carry Christ upon his shoulders, must rely upon the staff of his direction, whereon if he firmeth himself, he may be able to overcome the billows of resistance, and in the vertue of this staff, like that of *Jacob*, pass over the waters of *Jordan*. Or otherwise thus: He that will submit his shoulders unto Christ, shall by the concurrence of his power encrease into the strength of a Giant; and being supported by the staff of his holy Spirit, shall not be overwhelmed by the waves of the world, but wade through all resistance.

Add also the mystical reasons of this pourtract alleadged by *Vida* and *Xerisanus*: and the recorded story of *Christopher*, that before his Martyrdom he requested of God, that where ever his body were, the places should be freed from pestilence and mischiefs, from infection. And therefore his picture or pourtract, was usually placed in publick wayes, and at the entrance of Towns and Churches, according to the received Distick.

Christophorum videas, postea tutus eris.

CHAPTER XVII

Of the Picture of S. George

The picture of St. *George* killing the Dragon, and, as most ancient draughts do run, with the daughter of a King standing by, is famous amongst Christians. And upon this description dependeth a solemn story, how by this atchievement he redeemed a Kings daughter: which is more especially believed by the *English*, whose Protector he is, and in which form and history, according to his description in the *English* Colledge at *Rome*, he is set forth in the Icons or Cuts of Martyrs by *Cevalerius*; and all this according to the *Historia Lombardica*, or golden legend of *Iacobus de Voragine*. Now of what authority soever this piece be amongst us, it is I perceive received with different beliefs: for some believe the person and the story; some the person, but not the story; and others deny both.

That such a person there was, we shall not contend: for besides others, Dr. *Heilin* hath clearly asserted it in his History of St. *George*. The indistinction of many in the community of name, or the misapplication of the acts of one unto another, have made some doubt thereof. For of this name we meet with more then one in History, and no less then two conceived of *Cappadocia*. The one an *Arrian*, who was slain by the *Alexandrians* in the time of *Iulian*; the other a valiant Souldier and Christian Martyr, beheaded in the reign of *Dioclesian*. This is the *George* conceived in this Picture, who hath his day in the *Roman* Calender, on whom so many fables are delivered, whose story is set forth by *Metaphrastes*, and his myracles by *Turonensis*.

As for the story depending hereon, some conceive as lightly thereof, as of that of *Perseus* and *Andromeda*; conjecturing the one to be the father of the other; and some too highly assert it. Others with better moderation, doe either entertain the same as a fabulous addition unto the true and authentick story of St. *George*; or else conceive the literal acception to be a misconstruction of the symbolical expression; apprehending a veritable history, in an Emblem or piece of Christian Poesie. And this Emblematical construction hath been received by men not forward to extenuate the acts of Saints, as from *Baronius, Lipellous* the *Carthusian* hath delivered in the life of St. *George, Picturam illam St.* Georgii *quâ effingitur eques armatus, qui hastæ cuspide hostem interficit, juxta quam etiam virgo posita manus supplices tendens ejus explorat auxilium, Symboli potius quam historiæ alicujus censenda expressa Imago. Consuevit quidem ut equestris militiæ miles equestri imagine referri*: that is, The Picture of St. *George*, wherein he is described like a Curassier or horseman compleatly armed, &c. is rather a symbolical image, then any proper figure.

Now in the picture of this Saint and Souldier, might be implied the Christian Souldier and true Champion of Christ. A horseman armed *Cap a pe*, intimating the *Panoplia* or compleat armour of a Christian; combating with the Dragon, that is, with the Devil; in defence of the Kings daughter, that is the Church of God. And therefore although the history be not made out, it doth not disparage the Knights and Noble order of St. *George*, whose cognisance is honourable in the Emblem of the Souldier of Christ, and is a worthy memorial to conform unto its mystery. Nor, were there no such person at all, had they more reason to be ashamed, then the Noble order of *Burgundy*, and Knights of the Golden Fleece, whose badge is a confessed fable.

CHAPTER XVIII

Of the Picture of Jerom

The Picture of *Jerom* usually described at his study, with a Clock hanging by, is not to be omitted; for though the meaning be allowable, and probable it is that industrious Father did not let slip his time without account; yet must not perhaps that Clock be set down to have been his measure thereof. For Clocks or Automatous organs, whereby we now distinguish of time, have found no mention in any ancient Writers, but are of late invention, as *Pancirollus* observeth. And *Polydore Virgil* discoursing of new inventions whereof the authors are not known, makes instance in Clocks and Guns. Now *Jerom* is no late Writer, but one of the ancient Fathers, and lived in the fourth Century, in the reign of *Theodosius* the first.

It is not to be denied that before the dayes of *Jerom* there were Horologies, and several accounts of time; for they measured the hours not only by drops of water in glasses called Clepsydræ, but also by sand in glasses called Clepsammia. There were also from great antiquity, Scioterical or Sun Dials, by the shadow of a stile or gnomon denoting the hours of the day: an invention ascribed unto *Anaximenes* by *Pliny*. Hereof a memorable one there was in *Campus Martius*, from an obelisk erected, and golden figures placed horizontally about it, which was brought out of *Egypt* by *Augustus*, and described by *Jacobus Laurus*. And another of great antiquity we meet with in the story of *Ezechias*; for so it is delivered in *King.* 2.20. That the Lord brought the shadow backward ten degrees by which it had gone down in the Diall of Ahaz; that is, say some, ten degrees, not lines, for the hours were denoted by certain divisions or steps in the Dial, which others distinguished by lines according to that of *Persius*.

> Stertimus indomitum quod despumare Falernum
> Sufficiat, quintâ dum linea tangitur umbra.

That is, the line next the Meridian, or within an houre of noon.

Of later years there succeeded new inventions, and horologies composed by Trochilick or the artifice of wheels, whereof some are kept in motion by weight, others perform without it. Now as one age instructs another, and time that brings all things to ruin, perfects also every thing; so are these indeed of more general and ready use then any that went before them. By the Water-glasses the account was not regular: for from attenuation and condensation, whereby that Element is altered, the hours were shorter in hot weather then in cold, and in Summer then in Winter. As for Scioterical Dials, whether of the Sun or Moon, they are only of use in the actual radiation of those Luminaries, and are of little advantage unto those inhabitants, which for many months enjoy not the Lustre of the Sun.

It is I confess no easie wonder how the horometry of Antiquity discovered not this Artifice, how *Architas* that contrived the moving Dove, or rather the *Helicosophie* of *Archimedes*, fell not upon this way. Surely as in many things, so in this particular, the present age hath far surpassed Antiquity; whose ingenuity hath been so bold not only to proceed below the account of minutes; but to attempt perpetual motions, and engines whose revolutions (could their substance answer their design) might out-last the exemplary mobility, and out measure time it self. For such a one is that mentioned by *John Dee*, whose words are these in his learned Preface unto *Euclide*: By Wheels strange works and incredible are done: A wondrous example was seen in my time in a certain Instrument, which by the Inventer and Artificer was sold for twenty talents of gold; and then by chance had received some injury, and one *Janellus* of *Cremona* did mend the same, and presented it unto the Emperour *Charls* the fift. *Jeronimus Cardanus*, can be my witness, that therein was one Wheel that moved at such a rate, that in seven thousand years his own period should be finished; a thing almost incredible, but how far I keep within my bounds, many men yet alive can tell.

CHAPTER XIX

Of the Pictures of Mermaids, Unicorns, and some others

Few eyes have escaped the Picture of *Mermaids*; that is, according to *Horace* his Monster, with womans head above, and fishy extremity below: and these are conceived to answer the shape of the ancient *Syrens* that attempted upon *Ulysses*. Which notwithstanding were of another description, containing no fishy composure, but made up of Man and Bird; the humane mediety variously placed not only above, but below: according unto *Ælian, Suidas, Servius, Boccatius,* and *Aldrovandus*: who hath referred their description unto the story of fabulous Birds; according to the description of *Ovid*, and the account thereof in *Hyginus*, that they were the daughters of *Melpomene*, and metamorphosed into the shape of man and bird by *Ceres*.

And therefore these pieces so common among us, do rather derive their original, or are indeed the very descriptions of *Dagon*; which was made with human figure above, and fishy shape below; whose stump, or as *Tremellius* and our margin renders it, whose fishy part only remained, when the hands and upper part fell before the Ark. Of the shape of *Atergates*, or *Derceto* with the *Phœniceans*; in whose fishy and feminine mixture, as some conceive, were implyed the Moon and the Sea, or the Deity of the waters; and therefore, in their sacrifices, they made oblations of fishes. From whence were probably occasioned the pictures of *Nereides* and *Tritons* among the *Grecians*, and such as we read in *Macrobius*, to have been placed on the top of the Temple of *Saturn*.

We are unwilling to question the Royal Supporters of *England*, that is, the approved descriptions of the Lion and the Unicorn.

Although, if in the Lion the position of the pizell be proper, and that the natural situation; it will be hard to make out their retrocopulation, or their coupling and pissing backward, according to the determination of *Aristotle*; All that urine backward do copulate πυγηδον, *clunatim*, or aversly, as Lions, Hares, Linxes.

As for the Unicorn, if it have the head of a Deer, and the tail of a Boar, as *Vartomannus* describeth it, how agreeable it is to this picture every eye may discerne. If it be made bisulcous or cloven footed, it agreeth unto the description of *Vartomannus*, but scarce of any other; and *Aristotle* supposeth that such as divide the hoof, do also double the horn; they being both of the same nature, and admitting division together. And lastly if the horn have this situation and be so forwardly affixed, as is described, it will not be easily conceived, how it can feed from the ground; and therefore we observe, that Nature in other cornigerous animals, hath placed the horns higher and reclining, as in Bucks; in some inverted upwards, as in the Rhinoceros, the *Indian* Ass, and Unicornous Beetles; and thus have some affirmed it is seated in this animal.

We cannot but observe that in the Picture of *Jonah* and others, Whales are described with two prominent spouts on their heads; whereas indeed they have but one in the forehead, and terminating over the windepipe. Nor can we overlook the Picture of Elephants with Castles on their backs, made in the form of land Castles, or stationary fortifications, and answerable unto the Arms of *Castile*, or Sr. *John* Old Castle; whereas the towers they bore, were made of wood, and girt unto their bodies; as is delivered in the books of *Maccabees*, and as they were appointed in the Army of *Antiochus*.

We will not dispute the Pictures of Retiary Spiders, and their position in the web, which is commonly made laterall, and regarding the Horizon; although, if observed, we shall commonly find it downward, and their heads respecting the Center. We will not controvert the Picture of the seven Stars; although if thereby be meant the Pleiades, or subconstellation upon the back of Taurus, with what congruity they are described, either in site or magnitude, in a clear night an ordinary eye may discover, from July unto April. We will not question the tongues of Adders and Vipers, described like an Anchor; nor the picture of the Flower *de Luce*: though how farre they agree unto their naturall draughts, let every Spectator determine.

Whether the Cherubims about the Ark be rightly described in the common Picture, that is, only in humane heads, with two wings; or rather in the shape of Angels or young men, or somewhat at least with feet, as the Scripture seems to imply. Whether the Cross seen in the air by *Constantine*, were of that figure wherein we represent it; or rather made out of *X* and *P*, the two first letters of χριστος. Whether the Cross of Christ did answer the common figure; whether so far advanced above his head; whether the feet were so disposed, that is, one upon another, or separately nailed, as some with reason describe it: we shall not all contend. Much less whether the house of *Diogenes* were a Tub framed of wood, and after the manner of ours; or rather made of earth, as learned men conceive, and so more clearly make out that expression of *Juvenal*. We should be too critical to question the letter Y, or bicornous element of Pythagoras, that is, the making of the hornes equal: or the left less then the right, and so destroying the Symbolical intent of the figure; confounding the narrow line of Vertue, with the larger roade of vice; answerable unto the narrow door of Heaven, and the ample gates of Hell, expressed by our Saviour, and not forgotten by *Homer*, in that Epithete of *Pluto's* house.

Many more there are whereof our pen shall take no notice, nor shall we urge their enquiry; we shall not enlarge with what incongruity, and how dissenting from the pieces of Antiquity, the Pictures of their gods and goddesses are described, and how hereby their symbolical sense is lost; although herein it were not hard to be informed from *Phornutus*, *Fulgentius*, and *Albricus*. Whether *Hercules* be more properly described strangling than tearing the Lion, as *Victorius* hath disputed; nor how the characters and figures of the Signs and Planets be now perverted, as *Salmasius* hath learnedly declared. We will dispense with Bears with long tails, such as are described in the figures of heaven; We shall tolerate flying Horses, black Swans, Hydra's, Centaur's, Harpies, and Satyrs; for these are monstrosities, rarities, or else Poetical fancies, whose shadowed moralities requite their substantial falsities. Wherein indeed we must not deny a liberty; nor is the hand of the Painter more restrainable than the pen of the Poet. But where the real works of Nature, or veritable acts of stories are to be described, digressions are aberrations; and Art being but the imitator or secondary representor, it must not vary from the verity of the example; or describe things otherwise than they truly are or have been. For hereby introducing false Idea's of things it perverts and deforms the face and symmetry of truth.

CHAPTER XX

Of the Hieroglyphical pictures of the Egyptians

Certainly of all men that suffered from the confusion of *Babel*, the *Ægyptians* found the best evasion; for, though words were confounded, they invented a language of things, and spake unto each other by common notions in Nature. Whereby they discoursed in silence, and were intuitively understood from the theory of their Expresses. For, they assumed the shapes of animals common unto all eyes; and by their conjunctions and compositions were able to communicate their conceptions, unto any that coapprehended the Syntaxis of their Natures. This many conceive to have been the primitive way of writing, and of greater antiquity than letters; and this indeed might *Adam* well have spoken, who understanding the nature of things, had the advantage of natural expressions. Which the *Egyptians* but taking upon trust, upon their own or common opinion; from conceded mistakes they authentically promoted errors; describing in their Hieroglyphicks creatures of their own invention; or from known and conceded animals, erecting significations not inferrible from their natures.

And first, Although there were more things in Nature than words which did express them; yet even in these mute and silent discourses, to expresss complexed significations, they took a liberty to compound and piece together creatures of allowable forms into mixtures inexistent. Thus began the descriptions of Griphins, Basilisks, Phœnix, and many more; which Emblematists and Heralds have entertained with significations answering their institutions; Hieroglyphically adding Martegres, Wivernes, Lion fishes, with divers others. Pieces of good and allowable invention unto the prudent Spectator, but are lookt on by vulgar eyes as literal truths, or absurd impossibilities; whereas indeed, they are commendable inventions, and of laudable significations.

Again, Beside these pieces fictitiously set down, and having no Copy in Nature; they had many unquestionably drawn, of inconsequent signification, nor naturally verifying their intention. We shall instance but in few, as they stand recorded by *Orus*: The male sex they expressed by a Vulture, because of Vultures all are females, and impregnated by the wind: which authentically transmitted hath passed many pens, and became the assertion of *Ælian, Ambrose, Basil, Isidore, Tzetzes, Philes*, and others. Wherein notwithstanding what injury is offered unto the Creation in this confinement of sex, and what disturbance unto Philosophy in the concession of windy conceptions, we shall not here declare. By two dragms they thought it sufficient to signifie an heart, because the heart at one year weigheth two dragms, that is, a quarter of an ounce, and unto fifty years annually encreaseth the weight of one dragm, after which in the same proportion it yearly decreaseth; so that the life of a man doth not naturally extend above an hundred. And this was not only a popular conceit, but consentaneous unto their Physical principles, as *Heurnius* hath accounted it.

A Woman that hath but one Child, they express by a Lioness; for that conceiveth but once. Fecundity they set forth by a Goat, because but seven daies old, it beginneth to use coition. The abortion of a Woman they describe by an Horse kicking a Wolf; because a Mare will cast her foal if she tread in the track of that animal. Deformity they signifie by a Bear; and an unstable Man by an Hyæna, because that animal yearly exchangeth its sex. A Woman delivered of a female Child, they imply by a Bull looking over his left shoulder; because if in coition a Bull part from a Cow on that side, the Calf will prove a female.

All which, with many more, how far they consent with the truth, we shall not disparage our Reader to dispute; and though some way allowable unto wiser conceits, who could distinctly receive their significations: yet carrying the majesty of Hieroglyphicks, and so transmitted by Authors: they crept into a belief with many, and favourable doubt with most. And thus, I fear, it hath fared with the Hieroglyphical Symboles of Scripture: which excellently intended in the species of things sacrificed, in the prohibited meats, in the dreams of *Pharaoh, Joseph*, and many other passages: are oft-times wrackt beyond their symbolizations, and inlarg'd into constructions disparaging their true intentions.

CHAPTER XXI

Of the Picture of Haman hanged

In common draughts, *Haman* is hanged by the Neck upon an high Gibbet, after the usual and now practised way of suspension, but whether this description truly answereth the Original, Learned pens consent not, and good grounds there are to doubt. For it is not easily made out that this was an ancient way of Execution, in the publick punishment of Malefactors among the *Persians*; but we often read of Crucifixion in their Stories. So we find that *Orostes* a *Persian* Governour crucified *Polycrates* the *Samian* Tyrant. And hereof we have an example in the life of *Artaxerxes* King of *Persia*; (whom some will have to be *Ahasuerus* in this Story) that his Mother *Parysatis* flead and crucified her *Eunuch*. The same also seems implied in the letters patent of King *Cyrus*. *Omnis qui hanc mutaverit jussionem, tollatur lignum de domo ejus, & erigatur & configatur in eo.*

The same kind of punishment was in use among the *Romans*, *Syrians*, *Egyptians*, *Carthaginians* and *Grecians*. For though we find in *Homer*, that *Ulysses* in a fury hanged the strumpets of those who courted *Penelope*, yet is it not so easie to discover, that this was the publick practice or open course of justice among the *Greeks*.

And even that the *Hebrews* used this present way of hanging, by illaqueation or pendulous suffocation in publick justice and executions; the expressions and examples in scripture conclude not beyond good doubt.

That the King of *Hai* was hanged, or destroyed by the common way of suspension, is not conceded by the learned *Masius* in his comment upon that text; who conceiveth thereby rather some kind of crucifixion; at least some patibulary affixion after he was slain; and so represented unto the people until toward the evening.

Though we read in our translation, that *Pharoah* hanged the chief Baker, yet learned expositors understand hereby some kind of crucifixion, according to the mode of *Egypt*, whereby he exemplarily hanged out till the fowls of the air fed on his head or face, the first part of their prey being the eyes. And perhaps according to the signal draught hereof in a very old manuscript of *Genesis*, now kept in the Emperors Library at *Vienna*; and accordingly set down by the learned *Petrus Lambecius*, in the second Tome of the description of that Library.

When the *Gibeonites* hanged the bodies of those of the house of *Saul*, thereby was intended some kind of crucifying, according unto good expositors, and the vulgar translation; *crucifixerunt eos in monte coram domino*; many both in Scripture and humane writers might be said to be crucified, though they did not perish immediately by crucifixion: But however otherwise destroyed, their bodies might be afterward appended or fastned unto some elevated engine; as exemplary objects unto the eyes of the people: So sometimes we read of the crucifixion of only some part, as of the Heads of *Julianus* and *Albinus*, though their bodies were cast away.

That legal Text which seems to countenance the common way of hanging, if a man hath committed a sin worthy of Death, and they hang him on a Tree; is not so received by Christian and Jewish expositors. And as a good Annotator of ours delivereth, out of *Maimonides*: The *Hebrews* understand not this of putting him to death by hanging, but of hanging a Man after he was stoned to death; and the manner is thus described. After he is stoned to death, they fasten a piece of timber in the Earth, and out of it there cometh a piece of wood, and then they tye both his hands one to another, and hang him unto the setting of the Sun.

Beside, the original word *Hakany* determineth not the doubt. For that by *Lexicographers* or *Dictionarie* interpreters, is rendred suspension and crucifixion; there being no *Hebrew* word peculiarly and fully expressing the proper word of crucifixion, as it was used by the *Romans*; nor easie to prove it the custom of the *Jewish* Nation to nail them by distinct parts unto a Cross, after the manner of our Saviour crucified: wherein it was a special favour indulged unto *Joseph* to take down the Body.

Lipsius lets fall a good caution to take off doubts about suspension delivered by ancient Authors, and also the ambiguous sence of κρεμάσαι among the Greeks. *Tale apud Latinos ipsum suspendere, quod in crucem referendum moneo juventutem,* as that also may be understood of *Seneca. Latrocinium fecit aliquis, quid ergo meruit? ut suspendatur.* And this way of crucifying he conceiveth to have been in general use among the *Romans,* until the latter daies of *Constantine,* who in reverence unto our Saviour abrogated that opprobrious and infamous way of crucifixion. Whereupon succeeded the common and now practised way of suspension.

But how long before this abrogation of the Cross, the *Jewish* Nation had known the true sense of crucifixion: whereof no Nation had a sharper apprehension, while *Adrian* crucified five hundred of them every day, until Wood was wanting for that service. So they which had nothing but *crucifie* in their mouths, were therewith paid home in their own bodies: Early suffering the reward of their imprecations, and properly in the same kind.

CHAPTER XXII

Compendiously of many questionable Customs, Opinions, Pictures, Practices, and Popular Observations.

If an Hare crosse the high way, there are few above threescore years that are not perplexed thereat: which notwithstanding is but an Augurial terror, according to that received expression, *Inauspicatum dat iter oblatus Lepus*. And the ground of the conceit was probably no greater then this, that a fearful animal passing by us, portended unto us some thing to be feared: as upon the like consideration the meeting of a Fox presaged some future imposture; which was a superstitious observation prohibited unto the *Jews*, as is expressed in the Idolatry of *Maimonides*, and is referred unto the sin of an observer of Fortunes, or one that abuseth events unto good or bad signs, forbidden by the Law of *Moses*; which notwithstanding sometimes succeeding, according to fears or desires, have left impressions and timerous expectations in credulous minds for ever.

2. That Owls and Ravens are ominous appearers, and presignifying unlucky events, as Christians yet conceit, was also an Augurial conception. Because many Ravens were seen when *Alexander* entered *Babylon*, they were thought to pre-ominate his death; and because an Owl appeared before the battle, it presaged the ruin of *Crassus*. Which though decrepite superstitions, and such as had their nativity in times beyond all history, are fresh in the observation of many heads, and by the credulous and feminine party still in some Majesty among us. And therefore the Emblem of Superstition was well

set out by Ripa, in the picture of an Owl, an Hare, and an Old Woman. And it no way confirmeth the Augurial consideration, that an Owl is a forbidden food in the Law of *Moses*; or that *Jerusalem* was threatned by the Raven and the Owl, in that expression of *Esay* 34. That it should be a court for Owls, that the Cormorant and the Bittern should possess it, and the Owl and the Raven dwell in it. For thereby was only implied their ensuing desolation, as is expounded in the words succeeding: He shall draw upon it the line of confusion, and the stones of emptiness.

3. The falling of Salt is an authentick presagement of ill luck, nor can every temper contemn it; from whence notwithstanding nothing can be naturally feared: nor was the same a generall prognostick of future evil among the Ancients, but a particular omination concerning the breach of friendship. For Salt as incorruptible, was the Symbole of friendship, and before the other service was offered unto their guests; which if it casually fell, was accounted ominous, and their amity of no duration. But whether Salt were not only a Symbole of friendship with man, but also a figure of amity and reconciliation with God, and was therefore observed in sacrifices; is an higher speculation.

4. To break the egg shell after the meat is out, we are taught in our childhood, and practise it all our lives; which neverthelesse is but a superstitious relict, according to the judgement of *Pliny*: *Huc pertinet ovorum, ut exorbuerit quisque, calices protinus frangi, aut eosdem cochlearibus perforari*, and the intent hereof was to prevent witchcraft; for lest witches should draw or prick their names therein, and veneficiously mischiefe their persons, they broke the shell, as *Dalecampius* hath observed.

5. The true Lovers knot is very much magnified, and still retained in presents of Love among us; which though in all points it doth not make it out, had perhaps its original from the *Nodus Herculanus*, or that which was called *Hercules* his knot, resembling the snaky complication in the caduceus or rod of *Hermes*; and in which form the Zone or woolen girdle of the Bride was fastened, as *Turnebus* observeth in his *Adversaria*.

6. When our cheek burneth or ear tingleth, we usually say that some body is talking of us, which is an ancient conceit, and ranked

among superstitious opinions by *Pliny*. *Absentes tinnitu aurium præsentire sermones de se receptum est*, according to that disticke noted by *Dalecampius*.

> Garrula quid totis resonas mihi noctibus auris?
> Nescio quem dicis nunc meminisse mei.

Which is a conceit hardly to be made out without the concession of a signifying *Genius*, or universal *Mercury*; conducting sounds unto their distant subjects, and teaching us to hear by touch.

7. When we desire to confine our words we commonly say they are spoken under the Rose; which expression is commendable, if the Rose from any natural property may be the Symbole of silence, as *Nazianzene* seems to imply in these translated verses:

> Utque latet Rosa Verna suo putamine clausa,
> Sic os vincla ferat, validisque arctetur habenis,
> Indicatque suis prolixa silentia labris:

And is also tolerable, if by desiring a secrecy to words spoke under the Rose, we only mean in society and compotation, from the ancient custom in Symposiack meetings, to wear chaplets of Roses about their heads: and so we condemn not the *German* custom, which over the Table describeth a Rose in the cieling. But more considerable it is, if the original were such as *Lemnius*, and others have recorded; that the Rose was the flower of *Venus*, which *Cupid* consecrated unto *Harpocrates* the God of silence, and was therefore an Emblem thereof, to conceal the pranks of Venery; as is declared in this Tetrastick:

> Est Rosa flos veneris, cujus quo facta laterent
> Harpocrati matris, dona dicavit Amor;
> Inde Rosam mensis hospes suspendit Amicis,
> Convivæ ut sub ea dicta tacenda sciant.

8. That smoak doth follow the fairest is an usual saying with us, and in many parts of *Europe*; whereof although there seem no natural ground, yet is it the continuation of a very ancient opinion, as *Petrus Victorius* and *Casaubon* have observed from a passage in *Athenæus*: wherein a *Parasite* thus describeth himselfe.

To every Table first I come,
Whence Porridge I am call'd by some:
A Capaneus at Stares I am,
To enter any Room a Ram;
Like whips and thongs to all I ply,
Like smoake unto the Fair I fly.

9. To set cross leg'd, or with our fingers pectinated or shut together is accounted bad, and friends will perswade us from it. The same conceit religiously possessed the Ancients, as is observable from Pliny. *Poplites alternis genibus imponere nefas olim*; and also from *Athenæus*, that it was an old veneficious practice, and *Juno* is made in this posture to hinder the delivery of *Alcmæna*. And therefore, as *Pierius* observeth, in the Medal of *Julia Pia*, the right hand of *Venus* was made extended with the inscription of *Venus, Genetrix*; for the complication or pectination of the fingers was an Hieroglyphick of impediment, as in that place he declareth.

10. The set and statary times of pairing of nails, and cutting of hair, is thought by many a point of consideration; which is perhaps but the continuation of an ancient superstition. For piaculous it was unto the *Romans* to pare their nails upon the Nundinæ, observed every ninth day; and was also feared by others in certain daies of the week; according to that of *Ausonius, Ungues Mercurio, Barbam Jove, Cypride Crines*; and was one part of the wickedness that filled up the measure of *Manasses*, when 'tis delivered, that he observed times.

11. A common fashion it is to nourish hair upon the mouls of the face; which is the perpetuation of a very ancient custom; and though innocently practised among us, may have a superstitious original, according to that of *Pliny. Nævos in facie tondere religiosum habent nunc multi.* From the like might proceed the fears of poling Elvelocks or complicated hairs of the head, and also of locks longer than the other hair; they being votary at first, and dedicated upon occasion; preserved with great care, and accordingly esteemed by others, as appears by that of *Apuleius, Adjuro per dulcem capilli tui nodulum.*

12. A custom there is in most parts of *Europe* to adorn Aqueducts, spouts and Cisterns with Lions head: which though no illaudable ornament, is of an *Egyptian* geneology, who practised the

same under a symbolical illation. For because the Sun being in Leo, the flood of *Nilus* was at the full, and water became conveyed into every part, they made the spouts of their Aqueducts through the head of a Lion. And upon some cœlestial respects it is not improbable the great Mogul or *Indian* King doth bear for his Arms a Lion and the Sun.

13. Many conceive there is somewhat amiss, and that as we usually say, they are unblest until they put on their girdle. Wherein (although most know not what they say) there are involved unknown considerations. For by a girdle or cincture are symbolically implied Truth, Resolution, and Readiness unto action, which are parts and vertues required in the service of God. According whereto we find that the *Israelites* did eat the Paschal Lamb with their loins girded; and the Almighty challenging *Job*, bids him gird up his loins like a man. So runneth the expression of *Peter*, Gird up the loins of your minds, be sober and hope to the end: so the high Priest was girt with the girdle of fine linnen: so is it part of the holy habit to have our loins girt about with truth; and so is it also said concerning our Saviour, Righteousness shall be the girdle of his loins, and faithfulness the girdle of his reines.

Moreover by the girdle, the heart and parts which God requires are divided from the inferiour and concupiscential organs; implying thereby a memento unto purification and cleanness of heart, which is commonly defiled from the concupiscence and affection of those parts; and therefore unto this day the *Jews* do bless themselves when they put on their zone or cincture. And thus may we make out the doctrin of *Pythagoras*, to offer sacrifice with our feet naked, that is, that our inferiour parts and farthest removed from Reason might be free, and of no impediment unto us. Thus *Achilles*, though dipped in Styx, yet having his heel untouched by that water; although he were fortified elsewhere, he was slain in that part, as only vulnerable in the inferiour and brutal part of Man. This is that part of *Eve* and her posterity the devil still doth bruise, that is, that part of the soul which adhereth unto earth, and walks in the paths thereof. And in this secondary and symbolical sense it may be also understood, when the Priests in the Law washed their feet before the sacrifice; when our Saviour washed the feet of his Disciples, and said unto *Peter*, If I wash not thy feet thou hast no part in me. And thus is it symbollically explainable and implyeth purification and cleanness, when in the burnt offerings the Priest is commanded to wash the inwards and legs thereof in water; and in the peace and sin-offerings, to burn the two kidneys, the fat which is about the flanks, and as we translate it, the Caul above the Liver. But whether the *Jews* when they blessed themselves, had any eye unto the words of *Jeremy*, wherein God makes them his Girdle; or had therein any reference unto the Girdle, which the Prophet was commanded to hide in the hole of the rock of *Euphrates*, and which was the type of their captivity, we leave unto higher conjecture.

14. The Picture of the Creator, or God the Father in the shape of an old Man, is a dangerous piece, and in this Fecundity of sects may revive the Anthropomorphites. Which although maintained from the expression of *Daniel*, I beheld where the Ancient of dayes did sit, whose hair of his head was like the pure wool; yet may it be also derivative from the Hieroglyphical description of the *Ægyptians*; who to express their Eneph, or Creator of the world, described an old man in a blew mantle, with an egge in his mouth; which was the Emblem of the world. Surely those heathens, that notwithstanding the exemplary advantage in heaven, would endure no pictures of Sun or Moon, as being visible unto all the world, and needing no representation; do evidently accuse the practise of those pencils, that will describe invisibles. And he that challenged the boldest hand unto the picture of an Echo, must laugh at this attempt, not only in the description of invisibility, but circumscription of Ubiquity, and fetching under lines incomprehensible circularity.

The Pictures of the *Ægyptians* were more tolerable, and in their sacred letters more veniably expressed the apprehension of Divinity. For though they implied the same by an eye upon a Scepter, by an Ægles head, a Crocodile, and the like: yet did these manual descriptions pretend no corporal representations; nor could the people misconceive the same unto real correspondencies. So though the Cherub carried some apprehension of Divinity, yet was it not conceived to be the shape thereof: and so perhaps because it is metaphorically predicated of God, that he is a consuming fire, he may be harmlessly described by a flaming representation; Yet if, as some will have it, all mediocrity of folly is foolish, and because an unrequitable evil may ensue, an indifferent convenience must be omitted; we shall not urge such representments; we could spare the holy Lamb for the picture of our Saviour, and the Dove or fiery Tongues to represent the holy Ghost.

15. The Sun and Moon are usually described with humane faces; whether herein there be not a *Pagan* imitation, and those visages at first implied *Apollo* and *Diana*, we may make some doubt; and we find the statua of the Sun was framed with raies about the head, which were the indeciduous and unshaven locks of *Apollo*. We should be too Iconomical to question the pictures of the winds, as commonly drawne in humane heads, and with their cheeks distended; which notwithstanding we find condemned by *Minutius*, as answering poetical fancies, and the gentile discription of *Æolus*, *Boreas*, and the feigned Deities of winds.

16. We shall not, I hope, disparage the Resurrection of our Redeemer, if we say the Sun doth not dance on Easter day. And though we would willingly assent unto any sympathetical exultation, yet cannot conceive therein any more then a Tropical expression. Whether any such motion there were in that day wherein Christ arised, Scripture hath not revealed, which hath been punctual in other records concerning solary miracles: and the Areopagite that was amazed at the Eclipse, took no notice of this. And if metaphorical expressions go so far, we may be bold to affirm, not only that one Sun danced, but two arose that day: That light appeared at his nativity, and darkenesse at his death, and yet a light at both; for even that darkness was a light unto the *Gentiles*, illuminated by that obscurity. That 'twas the first time the Sun set above the Horizon; that although there were darkness above the earth, there was light beneath it, nor dare we say that hell was dark if he were in it.

17. Great conceits are raised of the involution or membranous covering, commonly called the Silly-how, that sometimes is found about the heads of children upon their birth; and is therefore preserved with great care, not onely as medical in diseases, but effectual in success, concerning the Infant and others; which is surely no more than a continued superstition. For hereof we read in the life of *Antoninus* delivered by *Spartianus*, that children are born sometimes with this natural cap; which Midwives were wont to sell unto credulous Lawyers, who had an opinion it advantaged their promotion.

But to speake strictly the effect is natural, and thus may be conceived; Animal conceptions have largely taken three teguments, or membranous films which cover them in the womb, that is, the Corion, Amnios, and Allantois; the Corion is the outward membrane wherein

407

are implanted the Veins, Arteries, and umbilical vessels, whereby its nourishment is conveyed: the Allantois a thin coat seated under the Corion, wherein are received the watery separations conveyed by the Urachus, that the acrimony thereof should not offend the skin. The Amnios is a general investment, containing the sudorus or thin serosity perspirable through the skin. Now about the time when the Infant breaketh these coverings, it sometime carrieth with it about the head a part of the Amnios or nearest coat; which saith *Spiegelius*, either proceedeth from the toughness of the membrane or weakness of the Infant that cannot get clear thereof. And therefore herein significations are natural and concluding upon the Infant, but not to be extended unto magical signalities, or any other person.

18. That 'tis good to be drunk once a month, is a common flattery of sensuality, supporting it self upon Physick, and the healthful effects of inebriation. This indeed seems plainly affirmed by *Avicenna*, a Physitian of great authority, and whose religion prohibiting Wine, could less extenuate ebriety. But *Averroes* a man of his own faith was of another belief; restraining his ebriety unto hilarity, and in effect making no more thereof than *Seneca* commendeth, and was allowable in *Cato*; that is, a sober incalescence and regulated æstuation from wine; or what may be conceived between *Joseph* and his brethren, when the text expresseth they were merry, or drank largely, and whereby indeed the commodities set down by *Avicenna*, that is, alleviation of spirits, resolution of superfluities, provocation of sweat and urine may also ensue. But as for dementation, sopition of reason, and the diviner particle from drink; though *American* religion approve, and *Pagan* piety of old hath practised it, even at their sacrifices; Christian morality and the doctrine of Christ will not allow. And surely that religion which excuseth the fact of *Noah*, in the aged surprisal of six hundred years, and unexpected inebriation from the unknown effects of wine, will neither acquit ebriosity nor ebriety, in their known and intended perversions.

And indeed, although sometimes effects succeed which may relieve the body, yet if they carry mischief or peril unto the soul, we are therein restrainable by Divinity, which circumscribeth Physick, and circumstantially determines the use thereof. From natural considerations, Physick commendeth the use of venery; and happily, incest, adultery, or stupration may prove as Physically advantagious, as conjugal copulation; which notwithstanding must not be drawn into practise. And truly effects, consequents, or events which we commend, arise oft-times from wayes which we all condemn. Thus from the fact of *Lot*, we derive the generation of *Ruth*, and blessed Nativity of our Saviour; which notwithstanding did not extenuate the incestuous ebriety of the generator. And if, as is commonly urged, we think to extenuate ebriety from the benefit of vomit oft succeeding, *Egyptian* sobriety will condemn us, who purged both wayes twice a month, without this perturbation: and we foolishly contemn the liberal hand of God, and ample field of medicines which soberly produce that action.

19. A conceit there is, that the Devil commonly appeareth with a cloven hoof; wherein although it seem excessively ridiculous, there may be somewhat of truth; and the ground thereof at first might be his frequent appearing in the shape of a Goat, which answers that description. This was the opinion of ancient Christians concerning the apparition of Panites, Fauns and Satyres; and in this form we read of one that appeared unto *Antony* in the wildernesse. The same is also confirmed from expositions of holy Scripture; for whereas is it said, Thou shalt not offer unto Devils, the Original word is *Seghnirim*, that is, rough and hairy Goats, because in that shape the Devil most often appeared; as is expounded by the *Rabbins*, as *Tremellius* hath also explained; and as the word *Ascimah*, the god of *Emath* is by some conceived. Nor did he only assume this shape in elder times, but commonly in later dayes, especially in the place of his worship: If there be any truth in the confession of Witches, and as in many stories it stands confirmed by *Bodinus*. And therefore a Goat is not improperly made the Hieroglyphick of the devil, as *Pierius* hath expressed it. So might it be the Emblem of sin, as it was in the sin-offering; and so likewise of wicked and sinful men, according to the expression of Scripture in the method of the last distribution; when our Saviour shall separate the Sheep from the Goats, that is, the Sons of the Lamb from the children of the devil.

CHAPTER XXIII

Of some others

1.That temperamental dignotions, and conjecture of prevalent humours, may be collected from spots in our nails, we are not averse to concede. But yet not ready to admit sundry divinations, vulgarly raised upon them. Nor do we observe it verified in others, what *Cardan* discovered as a property in himself: to have found therein some signs of most events that ever happened unto him. Or that there is much considerable in that doctrine of Cheiromancy, that spots in the top of the nails do signifie things past; in the middle, things present; and at the bottom, events to come. That white specks presage our felicity, blew ones our misfortunes. That those in the nail of the thumb have significations of honour, those in the forefinger, of riches, and so respectively in other fingers, (according to Planetical relations, from whence they receive their names) as *Tricassus* hath taken up, and *Picciolus* well rejecteth.

We shall not proceed to querie, what truth there is in Palmistry, or divination from those lines in our hands, of high denomination. Although if any thing be therein, it seems not confinable unto man; but other creatures are also considerable: as is the forefoot of the Moll, and especially of the Monkey; wherein we have observed the table line, that of life, and of the liver.

2. That Children committed unto the school of Nature, without institution would naturally speak the primitive language of the world, was the opinion of ancient heathens, and continued since by Christians: who will have it our *Hebrew* tongue, as being the language of *Adam*. That this were true, were much to be desired, not only for the easy attainment of that useful tongue, but to determine the true and

primitive Hebrew. For whether the present Hebrew, be the unconfounded language of *Babel*, and that which remaining in *Heber* was continued by *Abraham* and his posterity, or rather the language of *Phœnicia* and *Canaan*, wherein he lived, some learned men I perceive do yet remain unsatisfied. Although I confess probability stands fairest for the former: nor are they without all reason, who think that at the confusion of tongues, there was no constitution of a new speech in every family: but a variation and permutation of the old; out of one common language raising several Dialects: the primitive tongue remaining still intire. Which they who retained, might make a shift to understand most of the rest. By vertue whereof in those primitive times and greener confusions, *Abraham* of the family of *Heber* was able to converse with the *Chaldeans*, to understand *Mesopotamians*, *Canaanites*, *Philistins*, and *Egyptians*: whose several Dialects he could reduce unto the Original and primitive tongue, and so be able to understand them.

3. Though useless unto us, and rather of molestation, we commonly refrain from killing Swallows, and esteem it unlucky to destroy them: whether herein there be not a *Pagan* relique, we have some reason to doubt. For we read in *Elian*, that these birds were sacred unto the *Penates* or houshold gods of the ancients, and therefore were preserved. The same they also honoured as the nuncio's of the spring; and we finde in *Athenæus* that the *Rhodians* had a solemn song to welcome in the Swallow.

4. That Candles and Lights burn dim and blew at the apparition of spirits, may be true, if the ambient ayr be full of sulphurious spirits, as it happeneth oft-times in mines; where damps and acide exhalations are able to extinguish them. And may be also verified, when spirits do make themselves visible by bodies of such effluviums. But of lower consideration is the common foretelling of strangers, from the fungous parcels about the weeks of Candles: which only signifieth a moist and pluvious ayr about them, hindering the avolation of the light and favillous particles; whereupon they are forced to settle upon the Snast.

5. Though Coral doth properly preserve and fasten the Teeth in men, yet is it used in Children to make an easier passage for them; and for that intent is worn about their necks. But whether this custom were not superstitiously founded, as presumed an amulet or defensa-

tive against fascination, is not beyond all doubt. For the same is delivered by *Pliny. Aruspices religiosum Coralli gestamen amoliendis
periculis arbitrantur; & surculi infantiæ alligati, tutelam habere cre-
duntur.*

6. A strange kind of exploration and peculiar way of Rhabdomancy is that which is used in mineral discoveries; that is, with a
forked hazel, commonly called *Moses* his Rod, which freely held forth,
will stir and play if any mine be under it. And though many there are
who have attempted to make it good, yet until better information, we
are of opinion with *Agricola*, that in it self it is a fruitless exploration,
strongly scenting of *Pagan* derivation, and the *virgula Divina*, proverbially magnified of old. The ground whereof were the Magical rods in
Poets: that of *Pallas* in *Homer*, that of *Mercury* that charmed *Argus*,
and that of *Circe* which transformed the followers of *Ulysses*. Too
boldly usurping the name of *Moses* rod, from which notwithstanding,
and that of *Aaron*, were probably occasioned the fables of all the rest.
For that of *Moses* must needs be famous unto the *Ægyptians*; and that
of *Aaron* unto many other Nations, as being preserved in the Ark, until
the destruction of the Temple built by *Solomon*.

7. A practice there is among us to determine doubtful matters,
by the opening of a book, and letting fall a staff; which notwithstanding are ancient fragments of *Pagan* divinations. The first an imitation
of *sortes Homericæ*, or *Virgilinæ*, drawing determinations from verses
casually occurring. The same was practised by *Severus*, who entertained ominous hopes of the Empire, from that verse in *Virgil, Tu
regere imperio populos Romane memento*; and *Gordianus* who
reigned but few dayes was discouraged by another, that is, *Ostendunt
terris hunc tantum fata, nec ultra esse sinunt*. Nor was this only performed in heathen Authors, but upon the sacred text of Scripture, as
Gregorius Turonensis hath left some account, and as the practise of
the Emperour *Heraclius*, before his Expedition into *Asia* minor, is delivered by *Cedrenus*.

As for the Divination or decision from the staff, it is an Augurial relique, and the practise thereof is accused by God himselfe; My
people ask counsel of their stocks, and their staff declareth unto them.
Of this kind of Rhabdomancy was that practised by *Nabuchadonozor*
in that *Caldean* miscellany, delivered by *Ezekiel*; the King of *Babylon*
stood at the parting of the way, at the head of the two wayes to use

412

divination, he made his arrows bright, he consulted with Images, he looked in the Liver; at the right hand were the divinations of *Jerusalem*. That is, as *Estius* expoundeth it, the left way leading into *Rabbah*, the chief City of the *Ammonites*, and the right unto *Jerusalem*, he consulted *Idols* and entrails, he threw up a bundle of arrows to see which way they would light; and falling on the right hand he marched towards *Jerusalem*. A like way of Belomancy or Divination by Arrows hath been in request with *Scythians*, *Alanes*, *Germans*, with the *Africans* and *Turks* of *Algier*. But of another nature was that which was practised by *Elisha*, when by an arrow shot from an Eastern window, he pre-signified the destruction of *Syria*; or when according unto the three stroaks of *Joash*, with an arrow upon the ground, he foretold the number of his victories. For thereby the spirit of God particular'd the same; and determined the stroaks of the King, unto three, which the hopes of the Prophet expected in twice that number.

8. We cannot omit to observe, the tenacity of ancient customs, in the nominal observation of the several dayes of the week, according to *Gentile* and *Pagan* appellations: for the Original is very high, and as old as the ancient *Ægyptians*, who named the same according to the seven Planets, the admired stars of heaven, and reputed Deities among them. Unto every one assigning a several day; not according to their celestial order, or as they are disposed in heaven; but after a diatesseron or musical fourth. For beginning Saturday with Saturn, the supremest Planet, they accounted by Jupiter and Mars unto Sol, making Sunday. From Sol in like manner by Venus and Mercurie unto Luna, making Munday; and so through all the rest. And the same order they confirmed by numbring the hours of the day unto twenty four, according to the natural order of the Planets. For beginning to account from Saturn, Jupiter, Mars, and so about unto twenty four, the next day will fall unto Sol; whence accounting twenty four, the next will happen unto Luna, making Munday. And so with the rest, according to the account and order still observed among us.

The *Jews* themselves in their Astrological considerations, concerning Nativities, and Planetary hours, observe the same order, upon as witty foundations. Because by an equal interval, they make seven triangles, the bases whereof are the seven sides of a septilateral figure, described within a circle. That is, If a figure of seven sides be described in a circle, and at the angles thereof the names of the Planets be placed, in their natural order on it: if we begin with Saturn, and successively draw lines from angle to angle, until seven equicrural triangles be described, whose bases are the seven sides of the septilateral figure, the triangles will be made by this order. The first being made by Saturn, Sol and Luna, that is, Saturday, Sunday and Munday; and so the rest in the order still retained.

But thus much is observable, that however in cœlestial considerations they embraced the received order of the Planets, yet did they not retain either characters, or names in common use amongst us; but declining humane denominations, they assigned them names from some remarkable qualities; as is very observable in their red and splendent Planets, that is, of Mars and Venus. But the change of their names disparaged not the consideration of their natures; nor did they thereby reject all memory of these remarkable Stars; which God himself admitted in his Tabernacle, if conjecture will hold concerning the Golden Candlestick; whose shaft resembled the Sun, and six branches the Planets about it.

9. We are unwilling to enlarge concerning many other; only referring unto sober examination, what natural effects can reasonably be expected, when to prevent the Ephialtes or night-Mare we hang up an hollow stone in our stables; when for amulets against Agues we use the chips of Gallows and places of execution. When for Warts we rub our hands before the Moon, or commit any maculated part unto touch of the dead. What truth there is in those common female doctrines, that the first Rib of Roast Beef powderd is a peculiar remedy against Fluxes. That to urine upon earth newly cast up by a Moll, bringeth down the menses in Women. That if a Child dieth, and the neck becometh not stiff, but for many howers remaineth Lythe and Flaccid, some other in the same house will dye not long after. That if a woman with child looketh upon a dead body, her child will be of a pale complexion. Swarms hereof our learned Philosophers and critical Philosophers might illustrate, whose exacter performances our adventures doe but solicite; mean while, I hope, they will plausibly receive our attempts, or candidly correct our misconjectures.

Disce, sed ira cadat naso, rugosaque sanna,
Dum veteres avias tibi de pulmone revello.

End of Book V

414

THE SIXTH
BOOK

Of sundry common opinions
Cosmographical and Historical.

The first Discourse comprehended in several
Chapters.

CHAPTER I

Concerning the beginning of the World, that the
time thereof is not precisely to be known, as
men generally suppose: Of mens enquiries in
what season or point of the Zodiack it began.
That as they are generally made they are in vain,
and as particularly applied uncertain. Of the division of the seasons and four quarters of the
year, according to Astronomers and Physitians.
That the common compute of the Ancients, and
which is yet retained by most, is unreasonable
and erroneous. Of some Divinations and ridiculous diductions from one part of the year to
another. And of the Providence and Wisdom of
God in the site and motion of the Sun.

Concerning the World and its temporal circumscriptions, who
ever shall strictly examine both extreams, will easily perceive there is
not only obscurity in its end, but its beginning; that as its period is inscrutable, so is its nativity indeterminable: That as it is presumption to
enquire after the one, so is there no rest or satisfactory decision in the
other. And hereunto we shall more readily assent, if we examine the
informations, and take a view of the several difficulties in this point;
which we shall more easily doe, if we consider the different conceits
of men, and duly perpend the imperfections of their discoveries.

And first, The histories of the *Gentiles* afford us slender satis-faction, nor can they relate any story, or affix a probable point to its beginning. For some thereof (and those of the wisest amongst them) are so far from determining its beginning, that they opinion and main-tain it never had any at all; as the doctrin of *Epicurus* implieth, and more postively *Aristotle* in his books *De Cœo* declareth. Endeavouring to confirm it with arguments of reason, and those appearingly demon-strative; wherein his labours are rational, and uncontroulable upon the grounds assumed, that is, of Physical generation, and a Primary or first matter, beyond which no other hand was apprehended. But herein we remain sufficiently satisfied from *Moses*, and the Doctrin delivered of the Creation; that is, a production of all things out of nothing, a forma-tion not only of matter, but of form, and materiation even of matter it self.

Others are so far from defining the Original of the World or of mankind, that they have held opinions not only repugnant unto Chro-nology, but Philosophy; that is, that they had their beginning in the soil where they inhabited; assuming or receiving appellations conformable unto such conceits. So did the *Athenians* tearm themselves αὐτόχθονες or *Aborigines*, and in testimony thereof did wear a golden insect on their heads; the same is also given unto the Inlanders, or *Midland* in-habitants of this Island by *Cæsar*. But this is a conceit answerable unto the generation of the Giants; not admittable in Philosophy, much less in Divinity, which distinctly informeth we are all the seed of *Adam*, that the whole world perished unto eight persons before the flood, and was after peopled by *Colonies* of the sons of *Noah*. There was there-fore never any *Autochthon*, or man arising from the earth but *Adam*; for the Woman being formed out of the rib, was once removed from earth, and framed from that Element under incarnation. And so al-though her production were not by copulation, yet was it in a manner seminal: For if in every part from whence the seed doth flow, there be contained the Idea of the whole; there was a seminality and contracted *Adam* in the rib, which by the information of a soul, was individuated into *Eve*. And therefore this conceit applyed unto the Original of man, and the beginning of the world, is more justly appropriable unto its end. For then indeed men shall rise out of the earth: the grave shall shoot up their concealed seeds, and in that great Autumn, men shall spring up, and awake from their Chaos again.

Others have been so blind in deducing the Original of things, or delivering their own beginnings, that when it hath fallen unto controversie, they have not recurred unto Chronologie or the Records of time: but betaken themselves unto probabilities, and the conjecturalities of Philosophy. Thus when the two ancient Nations, *Egyptians*, and *Scythians* contended for antiquity, the *Egyptians* pleaded their antiquity from the fertility of their soil, inferring that men there first inhabited, where they were most facility sustained; and such a land did they conceive was *Egypt*.

The *Scythians*, although a cold and heavier Nation urged more acutely, deducing their arguments from the two active Elements and Principles of all things, Fire and Water. For if of all things there was first an union, and that Fire over-ruled the rest: surely that part of earth which was coldest, would first get free, and afford a place of habitation. But if all the earth were first involved in Water, those parts would surely first appear, which were most high, and of most elevated situation, and such was theirs, These reasons carried indeed the antiquity from the *Egyptians*, but confirmed it not in the *Scythians*: for as *Herodotus* relateth from *Pargitaus*, their first King unto *Darius*, they accounted but two thousand years.

As for the *Egyptians* they invented another way of trial; for as the same Author relateth, *Psammitichus* their King attempted this decision by a new and unknown experiment, bringing up two Infants with Goats, and where they never heard the voice of man; concluding that to be the ancientest Nation, whose language they should first deliver. But herein he forgot that speech was by instruction not instinct, by imitation, not by nature; that men do speak in some kind but like Parrets, and as they are instructed, that is, in simple terms and words, expressing the open notions of things; which the second act of Reason compoundeth into propositions, and the last into Syllogisms and Forms of ratiocination. And howsoever the account of *Manethon* the *Egyptian* Priest run very high, and it be evident that *Mizraim* peopled that Country (whose name with the *Hebrews* it beareth unto this day) and there be many things of great antiquity related in Holy Scripture, yet was their exact account not very ancient; for *Ptolomy* their Country-man beginneth his Astronomical compute no higher then *Nabonasser*, who is conceived by some the same with *Salmanasser*. As for the argument deduced from the Fertility of the soil, duly enquired, it rather overthroweth then promoteth their antiquity; if that

Country whose Fertility they so advance, was in ancient times no firm or open land, but some vast lake or part of the Sea, and became a gained ground by the mud and limous matter brought downe by the River *Nilus*, which setled by degrees into a firm land. According as is expressed by *Strabo*, and more at large by *Herodotus*, both from the *Egyptian* tradition and probable inducements from reason, called therefore *fluvii donum*, an accession of earth, or tract of land acquired by the River.

Lastly, Some indeed there are, who have kept Records of time, and of a considerable duration, yet do the exactest thereof afford no satisfaction concerning the beginning of the world, or any way point out the time of its creation. The most authentick Records and best approved antiquity are those of the *Chaldeans*; yet in the time of *Alexander* the Great, they attained not so high as the flood. For as *Simplicius* relateth, *Aristotle* required of *Calisthenes*, who accompanied that Worthy in his Expedition, that at his arrival in *Babylon*, he would enquire of the antiquity of their Records; and those upon compute he found to amount unto 1903 years: which account notwithstanding ariseth no higher then 95 years after the flood. The *Arcadians* I confess, were esteemed of great antiquity, and it was usually said they were before the Moon, according unto that of *Seneca*, *Sydus post veteres Arcades editum*; and that of *Ovid*, *Luna gens prior illa fuit*. But this as *Censorinus* observeth, must not be taken grossly, as though they were existent before that Luminary; but were so esteemed, because they observed a set course of year, before the *Greeks* conformed their year unto the course and motion of the Moon.

Thus the Heathens affording no satisfaction herein, they are most likely to manifest this truth, who have been acquainted with Holy Scripture, and the sacred Chronology delivered by *Moses*, who distinctly sets down this account, computing by certain intervals, by memorable *Æras*, *Epoches*, or terms of time. As from the Creation unto the flood, from thence unto *Abraham*, from *Abraham* unto the departure from *Egypt*, &c.. Now in this number have only been *Samaritans*, *Jews*, and *Christians*. For the *Jews* they agree not in their accounts, as *Bodine* in his method of History hath observed out of *Baal Seder*, *Rabbi Nassom*, *Gersom*, and others; in whose compute the age of the World is not yet 5400 years. The same is more evidently observable from two most learned *Jews*, *Philo* and *Josephus*; who very much differ in the accounts of time, and variously sum up these Intervalls assented unto by all. Thus *Philo* from the departure out of *Egypt* unto the building of the Temple, accounts but 920 years, but *Josephus* sets down 1062. *Philo* from the building of the Temple to its destruction 440, *Josephus* 470: *Philo* from the Creation to the Destruction of the Temple 3373, but *Josephus* 3513. *Philo* from the Deluge to the Destruction of the Temple 1718, but *Josephus* 1913. In which Computes there are manifest disparities, and such as much divide the concordance and harmony of times.

For the *Samaritans*; their account is different from these or any others; for they account from the Creation to the Deluge, but 1302 years; which cometh to pass upon the different account of the ages of the Patriarks set down when they begat children. For whereas the *Hebrew*, *Greek* and *Latin* texts account *Jared* 162 when he begat *Enoch*, they account but 62, and so in others. Now the *Samaritans* were no incompetent Judges of times and the Chronology thereof; for they embraced the five books of *Moses*, and as it seemeth, preserved the Text with far more integrity then the *Jews*; who as *Tertullian, Chrysostom,* and others observe, did several wayes corrupt the same, especially in passages concerning the prophesies of Christ; So that as *Jerom* professeth, in his translation he was fain sometime to relieve himselfe by the *Samaritan* Pentateuch; as amongst others in that Text, *Deuteronomy* 27, *Maledictus omnis qui non permanserit in omnibus quæ scripta sunt in libro Legis.* From hence Saint *Paul* inferreth there is no justification by the Law, and urgeth the Text according to the Septuagint. Now the Jews to afford a latitude unto themselves, in their copies expunged the word לב or Syncategorematical term *omnis*: wherein lieth the strength of the Law, and of the Apostles argument; but the *Samaritan* Bible retained it right, and answerable unto what the Apostle had urged.

As for Christians from whom we should expect the exactest and most concurring account, there is also in them a manifest disagreement, and such as is not easily reconciled. For first, the Latins accord not in their account: to omit the calculation of the Ancients, of *Austin, Bede,* and others, the Chronology of the Moderns doth manifestly dissent. *Josephus Scaliger,* whom *Helvicus* seems to follow, accounts the Creation in 765 of the *Julian* period; and from thence unto the Nativity of our Saviour alloweth 3947 years; But *Dionysius Petavius* a learned Chronologer dissenteth from this compute almost 40 years; placing the Creation in the 730 of the *Julian* period, and from thence unto the Incarnation accounteth 3983 years.

For the Greeks; their accounts are more anomalous: for if we recur unto ancient computes; we shall find that *Clemens Alexandrinus*, an ancient Father and *Præceptor* unto *Origen*, accounted from the Creation unto our Saviour, 5664 years; for in the first of his Stromaticks, he collecteth the time from *Adam* unto the death of *Commodus* to be 5858 years; now the death of *Commodus* he placeth in the year after Christ 194, which number deducted from the former, there remaineth 5664. *Theophilus* Bishop of *Antioch* accounteth unto the Nativity of Christ 5515, deduceable from the like way of compute, for in his first book *ad Autolychum*, he accounteth from *Adam* unto *Aurelius Verus* 5695 years; now that Emperour died in the year of our Lord 180, which deducted from the former sum there remaineth 5515. *Julius Africanus* an ancient Chronologer, accounteth somewhat less, that is, 5500. *Eusebius*, *Orosius*, and others dissent not much from this, but all exceed five thousand.

The latter compute of the Greeks, as *Petavius* observeth, hath been reduced unto two or three accounts. The first accounts unto our Saviour 5501, and this hath been observed by *Nicephorus*, *Theophanes*, and *Maximus*. The other accounts 5509; and this of all at present is generally received by the Church of *Constantinople*, observed also by the Moscovite, as I have seen in the date of the Emperours letters; wherein this year of ours 1645 is from the year of the world 7154, which doth exactly agree unto this last account 5509, for if unto that sum be added 1645, the product will be 7154, by this Chronology are many Greek Authors to be understood: and thus is *Martinus Crusius* to be made out, when in his Turcogrecian history he delivers, the City of *Constantinople* was taken by the Turks in the year ϛ͵υξα, that is, 6961. Now according unto these Chronologists, the Prophecy of *Elias* the Rabbin, so much in request with the Jews, and in some credit also with Christians, that the world should last but six thousand years; unto these I say, it hath beene long and out of memory disproved, for the Sabbatical and 7000 year wherein the world should end (as did the Creation on the seventh day) unto them is long ago expired; they are proceeding in the eight thousand year, and numbers exceeding those days which men have made the types and shadows of these. But certainly what *Marcus Leo* the Jew conceiveth of the end of the heavens, exceedeth the account of all that ever shall be; for though he conceiveth the Elemental frame shall end in the Seventh or Sabbatical Millenary, yet cannot he opinion the heavens and more durable part of the Creation shall perish before seven times seven, or 49, that is, the Quadrant of the other seven, and perfect Jubilee of thousands.

Thus may we observe the difference and wide dissent of mens opinions, and therefore the great incertainty in this establishment. The Hebrews not only dissenting from the Samaritans, the Latins from the Greeks, but every one from another. Insomuch that all can be in the right it is impossible; that any one is so, not with assurance determinable. And therefore as *Petavius* confesseth, to effect the same exactly without inspiration it is impossible, and beyond the Arithmetick of any but God himselfe. And therefore also what satisfaction may be obtained from those violent disputes, and eager enquirers in what day of the month the world began either of March or October; likewise in what face or position of the Moon, whether at the prime or full, or soon after, let our second and serious considerations determine.

Now the reason and ground of this dissent, is the unhappy difference betweene the Greek and Hebrew Editions of the Bible, for unto these two Languages have all Translations conformed; the holy Scripture being first delivered in Hebrew, and first translated into Greek. For the Hebrew; it seems the primitive and surest text to rely on, and to preserve the same entire and uncorrupt there hath been used the highest caution humanity could invent. For as *R. Ben Maimon* hath declared, if in the copying thereof one letter were written twice, or if one letter but touched another, that copy was not admitted into their Synagogues, but only allowable to be read in Schools and private families. Neither were they careful only in the exact number of their Sections of the Law, but had also the curiosity to number every word, and affixed the account unto their several books. Notwithstanding all which, divers corruptions ensued, and several depravations slipt in, arising from many and manifest grounds, as hath been exactly noted by *Morinus* in his preface unto the Septuagint.

As for the Septuagint, it is the first and most ancient Translation; and of greater antiquity than the Chaldee version; occasioned by the request of *Ptolomeus Philadelphus* King of *Egypt*, for the ornament of his memorable Library; unto whom the high Priest addressed six Jews out of every Tribe, which amounteth unto 72; and by these was effected that Translation we usually term the Septuagint, or Translation of seventy. Which name however it obtain from the number of their persons, yet in respect of one common Spirit, it was the Translation but as it were of one man; if as the story relateth, although they were set apart and severed from each other, yet were their Translations found to agree in every point, according as is related by *Philo* and *Josephus*; although we finde not the same in *Aristæus*, who hath expresly treated thereof. But of the Greek compute there have passed some learned dissertations not many years ago, wherein the learned *Isacius Vossius* makes the nativity of the world to anticipate the common account one thousand four hundred and forty years.

This Translation in ancient times was of great authority, by this many of the Heathens received some notions of the Creation and the mighty works of God; This in express terms is often followed by the Evangelists, by the Apostles, and by our Saviour himself in the quotations of the Old Testament. This for many years was used by the Jews themselves, that is, such as did Hellenize and dispersedly dwelt out of Palestine with the Greeks; and this also the succeeding Christians and ancient Fathers observed; although there succeeded other Greek versions, that is, of *Aquila*, *Theodosius* and *Symmachus*; for the Latin translation of *Jerom* called now the Vulgar, was about 800 years after the Septuagint; although there was also a Latin translation before, called the Italick version. Which was after lost upon the general reception of the translation of St *Jerom*. Which notwithstanding (as he himself acknowledgeth) had been needless, if the Septuagint copys had remained pure, and as they were first translated. But, (beside that different copys were used, that *Alexandria* and *Egypt* followed the copy of *Hesychius*, *Antioch* and *Constantinople* that of *Lucian* the Martyr, and others that of *Origen*) the Septuagint was much depraved, not only from the errors of the Scribes, and the emergent corruptions of time, but malicious contrivance of the Jews; as *Justin Martyr* hath declared, in his learned dialogue with *Tryphon*, and *Morinus* hath learnedly shewn from many confirmations.

Whatsoever Interpretations there have been since, have been especially effected with reference unto these, that is, the Greek and Hebrew text, the Translators sometimes following the one, sometimes adhering unto the other, according as they found them consonant unto truth, or most correspondent unto the rules of faith. Now however it commeth to pass, these two are very different in the enumeration of Genealogies, and particular accounts of time; for in the second intervail, that is, betweene the Flood and *Abraham*, there is by the Septuagint introduced one *Cainan* to be the son of *Arphaxad* and father of *Salah*; whereas in the Hebrew there is no mention of such a person, but *Arphaxad* is set down to be the father of *Salah*. But in the first intervail, that is, from the Creation unto the Flood, their disagreement is more considerable; for therein the Greek exceedeth the Hebrew, and common account almost 600 years. And 'tis indeed a thing not very strange, to be at the difference of a third part, in so large and collective an account, if we consider how differently they are set forth in minor and less mistakable numbers. So in the Prophesie of *Jonah*, both in the Hebrew and Latin text, it is said, Yet forty dayes and *Ninevy* shall be overthrown: But the Septuagint saith plainly, and that in letters at length, τρεῖς ἡμέρας, that is, yet three dayes and *Ninevy* shall be destroyed. Which is a difference not newly crept in, but an observation very ancient, discussed by *Austin* and *Theodoret*, and was conceived an error committed by the Scribe. Men therefore have raised different computes of time, according as they have followed their different texts; and so have left the history of times far more perplexed then Chronology hath reduced.

Again, However the texts were plain, and might in their numerations agree, yet were there no small difficulty to set down a determinable Chronology, or establish from hence any fixed point of time. For the doubts concerning the time of the Judges are inexplicable; that of the Reigns and succession of Kings is as perplexed; it being uncertain whether the years both of their lives and reigns ought to be taken as compleat, or in their beginning and but currant accounts. Nor is it unreasonable to make some doubt whether in the first ages and long lives of our fathers, *Moses* doth not sometime account by full and round numbers, whereas strictly taken they might be some few years above or under; as in the age of *Noah*, it is delivered to be just five hundred when he begat *Sem*; whereas perhaps he might be somewhat above or below that round and compleat number. For the same way of speech is usual in divers other expressions: Thus do we say the Septuagint, and using the full and articulate number, do write the Translation of Seventy; whereas we have shewen before, the precise number was Seventy two. So is it said that Christ was three days in the grave; according to that of *Mathew*, as *Jonas* was three days and three nights in the Whales belly, so shall the Son of man be three days and three nights in the heart of the earth: which notwithstanding must be taken Synechdochically; or by understanding a part for an whole day; for he remained but two nights in the grave, for he was buried in the afternoon of the first day; and arose very early in the morning on the third; that is, he was interred in the eve of the Sabbath, and arose the morning after it.

Moreover, although the number of years be determined and rightly understood, and there be without doubt a certain truth herein; yet the text speaking obscurely or dubiously, there is oft-times no slender difficulty at what point to begin or terminate the account. So when it is said, *Exod.* 12. the sojourning of the children of *Israel* who dwelt in *Egypt* was 430 years, it cannot be taken strictly, and from their first arrival into *Egypt*, for their habitation in that land was far less; but the account must begin from the Covenant of God with *Abraham*, and must also comprehend their sojourn in the land of *Canaan*, according as is expressed, *Gal.* 3. The Covenant that was confirmed before of God in Christ, the Law which was 430 yeares after cannot disanul. Thus hath it also happened in the account of the 70 years of their captivity, according to that of *Jeremy*, This whole land shall be a desolation, and these nations shall serve the King of *Babylon* 70 years. Now where to begin or end this compute, ariseth no small difficulties; for there were three remarkable captivities, and deportations of the Jews. The first was in the third or fourth year of *Joachim*, and the first of *Nabuchodonozer*, when *Daniel* was carried away; the second in the reign of *Ieconiah*, and the eighth year of the same King; the third and most deplorable in the reign of *Zedechias*, and in the nineteenth year of *Nabuchodonozer*, whereat both the Temple and City were burned. Now such is the different conceit of these times, that men have computed from all; but the probablest account and most concordant unto the intention of *Ieremy*, is from the first of *Nabuchodonozer* unto the first of King *Cyrus* over *Babylon*; although the Prophet *Zachary* accounteth from the last. O Lord of hosts, How Long! Wilt thou not have mercy on *Ierusalem*, against which thou hast had indignation these three score and ten years? for he maketh this expostulation in the second year of *Darius Histaspes*, wherein he prophesied, which is about eighteen years in account after the other.

Thus also there be a certain truth therein, yet is there no easie doubt concerning the seventy weeks, or seventy times seven years of *Daniel*; whether they have reference unto the nativity or passion of our Saviour, and especially from whence, or what point of time they are to be computed. For thus is it delivered by the Angel *Gabriel*: Seventy weeks are determined upon thy people; and again in the following verse: Know therefore and understand, that from the going forth of the

Commandment to restore and to build *Ierusalem* unto the Messias the Prince, shall be seven weeks, and threescore and two weeks, the street shall be built again, and the wall even in troublesome times; and after threescore and two weeks shall Messiah be cut off. Now the going out of the Commandment to build the City, being the point from whence to compute, there is no slender controversie when to begin. For there are no less then four several Edicts to this effect, the one in the first year of *Cyrus*, the other in the second of *Darius*, the third and fourth in the seventh, and in the twentieth of *Artaxerxes Longimanus*; although as *Petavius* accounteth, it best accordeth unto the twenty year of *Artaxerxes*, from whence *Nehemiah* deriveth his Commission. Now that computes are made uncertainly with reference unto Christ, it is no wonder, since I perceive the time of his Nativity is in controversie, and no less his age at his Passion, For *Clemens* and *Tertullian* conceive he suffered at thirty; but *Irenæus* a Father neerer his time, is further off in his account, that is, between forty and fifty.

Longomontanus a late Astronomer, endeavours to discover this secret from Astronomical grounds, that is, the Apogeum of the Sun; conceiving the Excentricity invariable, and the Apogeum yearly to move one scruple, two seconds, fifty thirds, &c. Wherefore if in the time of *Hipparchus*, that is, in the year of the *Iulian* period 4557 it was in the fifth degree of *Gemini*, and in the daies of *Tycho Brahe*, that is, in the year of our Lord 1588, or of the world 5554. the same was removed unto the fift degree of *Cancer*; by the proportion of its motion, it was at the Creation first in the beginning of *Aries*, and the Perigeum or nearest point in *Libra*. But this conceit how ingenious or subtile soever, is not of satisfaction; it being not determinable, or yet agreed in what time precisely the Apogeum absolveth one degree, as *Petavius* hath also delivered.

Lastly, However these or other difficulties intervene, and that we cannot satisfie our selves in the exact compute of time, yet may we sit down with the common and usual account; nor are these differences derogatory unto the Advent or Passion of Christ, unto which indeed they all do seem to point, for the Prophecies concerning our Saviour were indefinitely delivered before that of *Daniel*; so was that pronounced unto *Eve* in paradise, that after of *Balaam*, those of *Isaiah* and the Prophets, and that memorable one of *Iacob*, the Scepter shall not depart from *Israel* until *Shilo* come; which time notwithstanding it did not define at all. In what year therefore soever, either from the destruction of the Temple, from the re-edifying thereof, from the flood, or from the Creation he appeared, certain it is, that in the fulness of time he came. When he therefore came is not so considerable, as that he is come: in the one there is consolation, in the other no satisfaction. The greater Quere is, when he will come again; and yet indeed is no Quere at all; for that is never to be known, and therefore vainly enquired; 'tis a professed and authentick obscurity, unknown to all but to the omniscience of the Almighty. Certainly the ends of things are wrapt up in the hands of God, he that undertakes the knowledge thereof, forgets his own beginning, and disclaims his principles of earth. No man knows the end of the world, nor assuredly of any thing in it: God sees it, because unto his Eternity it is present; he knoweth the ends of us, but not of himself: and because he knowes not this, he knoweth all things, and his knowledge is endless, even in the object of himself.

CHAPTER II

Of mens Enquiries in what season or Point of the Zodiack it began, that as they are generally made, they are in vain, and as particularly, uncertain.

Concerning the Seasons, that is, the quarters of the year, some are ready to enquire, others to determine, in what season, whether in the Autumn, Spring, Winter or Summer the World had its beginning. Wherein we affirm, that as the question is generally, and in respect of the whole earth proposed, it is with manifest injury unto reason in any particular determined; because when ever the world had its beginning it was created in all these four. For, as we have elsewhere delivered, whatsoever sign the Sun possesseth (whose recess or vicinity defineth the quarters of the year) those four seasons were actually existent; it being the nature of that Luminary to distinguish the several seasons of the year; all which it maketh at one time in the whole earth, and successively in any part thereof. Thus if we suppose the Sun created in Libra, in which sign unto some it maketh Autumn; at the same time it had been winter unto the Northern-pole, for unto them at that time the Sun beginneth to be invisible, and to shew it self again unto the Pole of the South. Unto the position of a right Sphere or directly under the Æquator, it had been Summer; for unto that situation the Sun is at that time vertical. Unto the latitude of Capricorn, or the Winter Solstice it had been Spring; for unto that position it had been in a middle point, and that of ascent, or approximation, but unto the latitude of Cancer or the Summer Solstice it had been Autumn; for then had it been placed in a middle point, and that of descent, or elongation.

And if we shall take it literally what *Moses* described popularly, this was also the constitution of the first day. For when it was evening unto one longitude, it was morning unto another; when night unto one, day unto another. And therefore that question, whether our Saviour shall come again in the twilight (as is conceived he arose) or whether he shall come upon us in the night, according to the comparison of a thief, or the *Jewish* tradition, that he will come about the time of their departure out of *Ægypt*, when they eat the Passover, and the Angel passed by the doors of their houses; this Quere I say needeth not further dispute. For if the earth be almost every where inhabited, and his coming (as Divinity affirmeth) must needs be unto all; then must the time of his appearance be both in the day and night. For if unto *Jerusalem*, or what part of the world soever he shall appear in the night, at the same time unto the *Antipodes*, it must be day; if twilight unto them, broad day unto the *Indians*; if noon unto them, yet night unto the *Americans*; and so with variety according unto various habitations, or different positions of the Sphere, as will be easily conceived by those who understand the affections of different habitations, and the conditions of *Antœci*, *Periœci*, and *Antipodes*. And so although he appear in the night, yet may the day of Judgement or Dooms-day well retain that name; for that implieth one revolution of the Sun, which maketh the day and night, and that one natural day. And yet to speak strictly, if (as the Apostle affirmeth) we shall be changed in the twinckling of an eye (and as the Schools determine) the destruction of the world shall not be successive but in an instant; we cannot properly apply thereto the usual distinctions of time; calling that twelve houres, which admits not the parts thereof, or use at all the name of the time, when the nature thereof shall perish.

But if the enquiry be made unto a particular place, and the question determined unto some certain Meridian; as namely, unto *Mesopotamia*, wherein the seat of paradise is presumed, the Query becomes more reasonable, and is indeed in nature also determinable. Yet positively to define that season, there is no slender difficulty; for some contend that it began in the Spring; as (beside *Eusebius*, *Ambrose*, *Bede*, and *Theodoret*) some few years past *Henrico Philippi* in his Chronology of the Scripture. Others are altogether for Autumn; and from hence doe our Chronologers commence their compute; as may be observed in *Helvicus*, *Jo. Scaliger*, *Calvisius*, and *Petavius*.

CHAPTER III

Of the Divisions of the seasons and four Quarters of the year, according unto Astronomers and Physitians: that the common compute of the Ancients, and which is still retained by some is very questionable.

As for the divisions of the year, and the quartering out this remarkable standard of time, there have passed especially two distinctions; the first in frequent use with Astronomers, according to the cardinal intersections of the Zodiack, that is, the two Æquinoctials and both the Solsticial points; defining that time to be the Spring of the year, wherein the Sun doth pass from the Æquinox of Aries unto the Solstice of Cancer; the time between the Solstice and the Æquinox of Libra, Summer; from thence unto the Solstice of Capricornus, Autumn; and from thence unto the Æquinox of Aries again, Winter. Now this division although it be regular and equal, is not universal; for it includeth not those latitudes which have the seasons of the year double; as have the inhabitants under the Æquator, or else between the Tropicks. For unto them the Sun is vertical twice a year, making two distinct Summers in the different points of verticality. So unto those which live under the Æquator, when the Sun is in the Æquinox it is Summer, in which points it maketh Spring or Autumn unto us; and unto them it is also Winter when the Sun is in either Tropick; whereas unto us it maketh alwayes Summer in the one: And the like will happen unto those habitations, which are between the Tropicks and the Æquator.

A second and more sensible division there is observed by *Hippocrates*, and most of the ancient *Greeks*, according to the rising and setting of divers stars; dividing the year, and establishing the account of the seasons from usual alterations, and sensible mutations in the air, discovered upon the rising and setting of those stars; accounting the Spring from the Æquinoxial point of Aries; from the rising of the Pleiades, or the several stars on the back of Taurus, Summer; from the rising of Arcturus, a star between the thighes of Boots, Autumn; and from the setting of the Pleiades, Winter. Of these divisions because they were unequal, they were fain to subdivide the two larger portions, that is of the Summer and Winter quarters; the first part of the Summer they named θέρος, the second unto the rising of the Dogstar, from thence unto the setting of Arcturus. The Winter they divided also into three parts; the first part, or that of seed time they named σπόρητον, the middle or proper Winter, χειμον, the last, which was their planting or grafting time φυταλίαν. This way of division was in former ages received, is very often mentioned in Poets, translated from one Nation to another; from the *Greeks* unto the *Latines* as is received by good Authors; and delivered by Physitians, even into our times.

Now of these two, although the first in some latitude may be retained, yet is not the other in any to be admitted. For in regard of time (as we elsewhere declare) the stars do vary their longitudes, and consequently the times of their ascension and discention. That star which is the term of numeration, or point from whence we commence the account, altering his site and longitude in process of time, and removing from West to East, almost one degree in the space of 72 years, so that the same star, since the age of *Hippocrates* who used this account, is removed in *consequentia* about 27 degrees. Which difference of their longitudes, doth much diversifie the times of their ascents, and rendereth the account unstable which shall proceed thereby.

Again, In regard of different latitudes, this cannot be a setled rule, or reasonably applied unto many Nations. For whereas the setting of the Pleiades or seven stars, is designed the term of Autumn, and the beginning of Winter; unto some latitudes these stars do never set, as unto all beyond 67 degrees. And if in several and far distant latitudes we observe the same star as a common term of account unto both, we shall fall upon an unexpected, but an unsufferable absurdity; and by the same account it will be Summer unto us in the North, before it be so unto those, which unto us are Southward, and many degrees approaching nearer the Sun. For if we consult the Doctrine of the sphere, and observe the ascention of the Pleiades, which maketh the beginning of Summer, we shall discover that in the latitude of 40, these stars arise in the 16 degree of Taurus; but in the latitude of 50, they ascend in the eleventh degree of the same sign, that is, 5 dayes sooner; so shall it be Summer unto *London* before it be unto *Toledo*, and begin to scorch in *England*, before it grow hot in *Spaine*.

This is therefore no general way of compute, nor reasonable to be derived from one Nation unto another; the defect of which consideration hath caused divers errors in Latine Poets, translating these expressions from the *Greeks*; and many difficulties even in the *Greeks* themselves; which living in divers latitudes, yet observed the same compute. So that to make them out, we are fain to use distinctions; sometime computing cosmically what they intended heliacally, and sometime in the same expression accounting the rising heliacally, the setting cosmically. Otherwise it will be hardly made out, what is delivered by approved Authors; and is an observation very considerable unto those which meet with such expressions, as they are very frequent in the poets of elder times, especially *Hesiod*, *Aratus*, *Virgil*, *Ovid*, *Manilius*; and Authors Geoponical, or which have treated *de re rustica*, as *Constantine*, *Marcus Cato*, *Columella*, *Palladius* and *Varro*.

Lastly, The absurdity in making common unto many Nations those considerations whose verity is but particular unto some, will more evidently appear, if we examine the Rules and Precepts of some one climate, and fall upon consideration with what incongruity they are transferrible unto others. Thus is it advised by *Hesiod*,

Pleiadibus Atlante natis orientibus
Incipe messem, Arationem vero occidentibus.

Implying hereby the Heliacal ascent and Cosmical descent of those stars. Now herein he setteth down a rule to begin harvest at the arise of the Pleiades; which in his time was in the beginning of *May*. This indeed was consonant unto the clime wherein he lived, and their harvest began about that season; but is not appliable unto our own, for therein we are so far from expecting an harvest, that our Barley-seed is not ended. Again, correspondent unto the rule of *Hesiod*, *Virgil* affordeth another,

Ante tibi Eoæ Atlantides abscondantur,
Debita quam sulcis committas semina.

Understanding hereby their Cosmical descent, or their setting
when the Sun ariseth, and not their Heliacal obscuration, or their inclu-
sion in the lustre of the Sun, as *Servius* upon this place would have it;
for at that time these stars are many signs removed from that luminary.
Now herein he strictly adviseth, not to begin to sow before the setting
of these stars; which notwithstanding without injury to agriculture,
cannot be observed in *England*; for they set unto us about the 12 of
November, when our Seed-time is almost ended.

And this diversity of clime and cœlestial observations, precisely observed unto certaine stars and moneths, hath not only
overthrown the deductions of one Nation to another, but hath perturbed the observation of festivities and statary Solemnities, even with
the *Jews* themselves. For unto them it was commanded that at their
entrance into the land of *Canaan*, in the fourteenth of the first moneth
(that is *Abib* or *Nisan* which is Spring with us) they should observe the
celebration of the Passover; and on the morrow after, which is the fifteenth day, the feast of unleavened bread; and in the sixteenth of the
same moneth, that they should offer the first sheaf of the harvest. Now
all this was feasible and of an easie possibility in the land of *Canaan*,
or latitude of *Jerusalem*; for so is it observed by several Authors in
later times; and is also testified by holy Scripture in times very far before. For when the children of *Israel* passed the river *Jordan*, it is
delivered by way of parenthesis, that the river overfloweth its banks in
the time of harvest; which is conceived the time wherein they passed;
and it is after delivered, that in the fourteenth day they celebrated the
Passover: which according to the Law of *Moses* was to be observed in
the first moneth, or moneth of *Abib*.

And therefore it is no wonder, what is related by *Luke*, that the
Disciples upon the *Deuteroproton*, as they passed by, plucked the ears
of corn. For the *Deuteroproton* or second first Sabbath, was the first
Sabbath after the Deutera or second of the Passover, which was the
sixteenth of *Nisan* or *Abib*. And this is also evidenced from the received construction of the first and latter rain. I will give you the rain
of your land in his due season, the first rain and the latter rain. For the
first rain fell upon the seed-time about October, and was to make the
seed to root, the latter was to fill the ear, and fell in Abib or March, the

first moneth: according as is expressed. And he will cause to come down for you the rain, the former rain, and the latter rain in the first moneth; that is the moneth of *Abib* wherein the Passover was observed. This was the Law of *Moses*, and this in the land of *Canaan* was well observed, according to the first institution: but since their dispersion and habitation in Countries, whose constitutions admit not such tempestivity of harvests; and many not before the latter end of Summer; notwithstanding the advantage of their Lunary account, and intercalary moneth Veader, affixed unto the beginning of the year, there will be found a great disparity in their observations; nor can they strictly and at the same season with their forefathers observe the commands of God.

To add yet further, those Geoponical rules and precepts of Agriculture which are delivered by divers Authors, are not to be generally received; but respectively understood unto climes whereto they are determined. For whereas one adivseth to sow this or that at one season, a second to set this or that at another, it must be conceived relatively, and every Nation must have its Country Farm; for herein we may observe a manifest and visible difference, not only in the seasons of harvest, but in the grains themselves. For with us Barley-harvest is made after wheat-harvest but with the *Israelites* and *Ægyptians* it was otherwise; so is it expressed by way of priority, *Ruth* the 2. So *Ruth* kept fast by the maidens of *Boaz* to glean unto the end of Barley-harvest and of Wheat-harvest, which in the plague of hayl in *Ægypt* is more plainly delivered *Exod.* 9. And the Flax and the Barley were smitten, for the Barley was in the eare and the Flax was bolled, but the Wheat and the Rye were not smitten, for they were not grown up.

And thus we see the account established upon the arise or descent of the stars can be no reasonable rule unto distant Nations at all, and by reason of their retrogression but temporary unto any one. Nor must these respective expressions be entertained in absolute considerations; for so distinct is the relation, and so artificial the habitude of this inferiour globe unto the superiour, and even of one thing in each unto the other: that general rules are dangerous; and applications most safe that run with security of circumstance. Which rightly to effect, is beyond the subtlety of sense, and requires the artifice of reason.

CHAPTER IV

Of some computations of days and deductions of one part of the year unto another.

Fourthly, there are certain vulgar opinions concerning days of the year, and conclusions popularly deduced from certain days of the moneth: men commonly believing the days increase and decrease equally in the whole year: which notwithstanding is very repugnant unto truth. For they increase in the moneth of March, almost as much as in the two moneths of January and February: and decrease as much in September, as they do in July and August. For the days increase or decrease according to the declination of the Sun, that is, its deviation Northward or Southward from the Æquator. Now this digression is not equal but near the Æquinoxial intersections, it is right and greater, near the Solstices more oblique and lesser. So from the eleventh of March the vernal Æquinox, unto the eleventh of April the Sun declineth to the North twelve degrees; from the eleventh of April unto the eleventh of May but eight, from thence unto the fifteenth of June, or the Summer Solstice but three and a half; all which make twenty three degrees and an half, the greatest declination of the Sun.

And this inequality in the declination of the Sun in the Zodiack or line of life, is correspondent unto the growth or declination of man. For setting out from infancy we increase not equally, or regularly attain to our state or perfection: nor when we descend from our state, is our declination equal, or carrieth us with even paces unto the grave. For as *Hippocrates* affirmeth, a man is hottest in the first day of his life, and coldest in the last: his natural heat setteth forth most vigorously at first, and declineth most sensibly at last. And so though the growth of man end not perhaps until twenty one, yet is his stature more advanced in the first septenary than in the second, and in the second, more than in the third, and more in the first seven years, than in the fourteen succeeding; for what stature we attain unto at seven years, we do sometimes but double, most times come short of at one and twenty. And so do we decline again: For in the latter age upon the Tropick and first descension from our solstice, we are scarce sensible of declination: but declining further, our decrement accelerates, we set apace, and in our last days precipitate into our graves. And thus are also our progressions in the womb, that is, our formation, motion, our birth or exclusion. For our formation is quickly effected, our motion appeareth later, and our exclusion very long after: if that be true which *Hippocrates* and *Avicenna* have declared, that the time of our motion is double unto that of formation, and that of exclusion treble unto that of motion. As if the Infant be formed at thirty five days, it moveth at seventy, and is born the two hundred and tenth day, that is, the seventh month; or if it receives not formation before forty five days, it moveth the ninetieth day, and is excluded in two hundred and seventy, that is, the ninth month.

There are also certain popular prognosticks drawn from festivals in the Calendar, and conceived opinions of certain days in months; so is there a general tradition in most parts of *Europe*, that inferreth the coldness of succeeding winter from the shining of the Sun upon *Candlemas* day, or the Purification of the Virgin Mary, according to the proverbial distich,

> Si Sol splendescat Maria purificante,
> Major erit glacies post festum quam fuit ante.

So is it usual among us to qualifie and conditionate the twelve months of the year, answerably unto the temper of the twelve days in *Christmas*; and to ascribe unto March certain borrowed days from April; all which men seem to believe upon annual experience of their own, and the received traditions of their fore-fathers.

Now it is manifest, and most men likewise know, that the Calenders of these computers, and the accounts of these days are very different; the Greeks dissenting from the Latins, and the Latins from each other; the one observing the *Julian* or ancient account, as great *Britain* and part of *Germany*; the other adhering to the *Gregorian* or new account, as *Italy*, *France*, *Spain*, and the united Provinces of the

Netherlands. Now this later account by ten days at least anticipateth the other; so that before the one beginneth the account, the other is past it; yet in the several calculations, the same events seem true, and men with equal opinion of verity, expect and confess a confirmation from them all. Whereby it is evident that Oraculous authority of tradition, and the easie seduction of men, neither enquiring into the verity of the substance, nor reforming upon repugnance of circumstance.

And thus may divers easily be mistaken who superstitiously observe certain times, or set down unto themselves an observation of unfortunate months, or dayes, or hours; As did the *Egyptians*, two in every month, and the *Romans*, the days after the Nones, Ides and Calends. And thus the Rules of Navigators must often fail, setting down, as *Rhodiginus* observeth, suspected and ominous days in every month, as the first and seventh of March, the fift and sixt of April, the sixt, the twelfth and fifteenth of February. For the accounts hereof in these months are very different in our days, and were different with several nations in Ages past; and how strictly soever the account be made, and even by the self-same Calendar, yet is it possible that Navigators may be out. For so were the Hollanders, who passing Westward through *fretum le Mayre*, and compassing the Globe, upon their return into their own Country, found that they had lost a day. For if two men at the same time travel from the same place, the one Eastward, the other Westward round about the earth, and meet in the same place from whence they first set forth; it will so fall out, that he which hath moved Eastward against the diurnal motion of the Sun, by anticipating dayly something of its circle with his own motion, will gain one day; but he that travelleth Westward, with the motion of the Sun, by seconding its revolution, shall lose or come short a day. And therefore also upon these grounds that *Delos* was seated in the middle of the earth, it was no exact decision, because two Eagles let fly East and West by *Jupiter*, their meeting fell out just in the Island Delos

CHAPTER V

A Digression of the Wisdom of God in the site and motion of the Sun

Having thus beheld the ignorance of man in some things, his error and blindness in others, that is, in the measure of duration both of years and seasons, let us a while admire the Wisdom of God in this distinguisher of times, and visible Deity (as some have termed it) the Sun. Which though some from its glory adore, and all for its benefits admire, we shall advance from other considerations, and such as illustrate the artifice of its Maker. Nor do we think we can excuse the duty of our knowledg, if we only bestow the flourish of Poetry hereon, or those commendatory conceits which popularly set forth the eminency of this creature; except we ascend unto subtiler considerations, and such as rightly understood, convincingly declare the wisdom of the Creator. Which since a Spanish Physitian hath begun, we will enlarge with our deductions; and this we shall endeavour from two considerations; its proper situation, and wisely ordered motion.

And first, we cannot pass over his providence, in that it moveth at all; for had it stood still, and were it fixed like the earth, there had been then no distinction of times, either of day or year, of Spring, of Autumn, of Summer, or of Winter; for these seasons are defined by the motions of the Sun; when that approacheth nearest our Zenith, or vertical Point, we call it Summer, when furthest off, Winter, when in the middle spaces, Spring or Autumn, whereas remaining in one place these distinctions had ceased, and consequently the generation of all things depending on their vicissitudes; making in one hemisphere a perpetuall Summer, in the other a deplorable and comfortless Winter. And thus had it also been continual day unto some, and perpetual night unto others; for the day is defined by the abode of the Sun above the Horizon, and the night by its continuance below; so should we have needed another Sun, one to illustrate our Hemisphere, a second to enlighten the other; which inconvenience will ensue in what site soever we place it, whether in the Poles, or the Æquator, or between them both; no spherical body of what bigness soever illuminating the whole sphere of another, although it illuminate something more then half of a lesser, according unto the doctrin of Opticks.

His wisdom is againe discernable, not only in that it moveth at all, and in its bare motion, but wonderful in contriving the line of its revolution; which is so prudently effected, that by a vicissitude in one body and light it sufficeth the whole earth, affording thereby a possible or pleasurable habitation in every part thereof; and this is the line Ecliptick; all which to effect by any other circle it had been impossible. For first, if we imagine the Sun to make his course out of the Ecliptick, and upon a line without any obliquity, let it be conceaved within that Circle, that is either on the Æquator, or else on either side: (Fo, if we should place it either in the Meridian or Colures, beside the subversion of its course from East to West, there would ensue the like incommodities.) Now if we conceave the Sun to move between the obliquity of this Ecliptick in a line upon one side of the Æquator, then would the Sunne be visible but unto one pole, that is the same which was nearest unto it. So that unto the one it would be perpetual day, unto the other perpetual night; the one would be oppressed with constant heat, the other with insufferable cold; and so the defect of alternation would utterly impugn the generation of all things; which naturally require a vicissitude of heat to their production, and no less to their increase and conservation.

But if we conceive it to move in the Æquator; first, unto a parallel sphere, or such as have the pole for their Zenith, it would have made neither perfect day nor night. For being in the Æquator it would intersect their Horizon, and be half above and half beneath it: or rather it would have made perpetual night to both; for though in regard of the rational Horizon, which bisecteth the Globe into equal parts, the Sun in the Æquator would intersect the Horizon: yet in respect of the sensible Horizon (which is defined by the eye) the Sun would be visible unto neither. For if as ocular witnesses report, and some also write, by reason of the convexity of the Earth the eye of man under the Æquator cannot discover both the poles; neither would the eye under the poles discover the Sun in the Æquator. Thus would there nothing fructifie either near or under them: The Sun being Horizontal to the poles, and of no considerable altitude unto parts a reasonable distance from them. Again, unto a right sphere, or such as dwell under the Æquator, although it made a difference in day and night, yet would it not make any distinction of seasons: for unto them it would be constant Summer, it being alwaies vertical, and never deflecting from them: So had there been no fructification at all, and the Countries subjected would be as unhabitable, as indeed antiquity conceived them.

Lastly, It moving thus upon the Æquator, unto what position soever, although it had made a day, yet could it have made no year: for it could not have had those two motions now ascribed unto it, that is, from East to West, whereby it makes the day, and likewise from West to East, whereby the year is computed. For according to received Astronomy, the poles of the Æquator are the same with those of the *Primum Mobile*. Now it is impossible that on the same circle, having the same poles, both these motions from opposite terms, should be at the same time performed, all which is salved, if we allow an obliquity in his annual motion, and conceive him to move upon the Poles of the Zodiack, distant from these of the world 23 degrees and an half. Thus may we discern the necessity of its obliquity, and how inconvenient its motion had been upon a circle parallel to the Æquator, or upon the Æquator it self.

Now with what Providence this obliquity is determined, we shall perceive upon the ensuing inconveniences from any deviation. For first, if its obliquity had been less (as instead of twenty three degrees, twelve or the half thereof) the vicissitude of seasons appointed for the generation of all things, would surely have been too short; for different seasons would have hudled upon each other; and unto some it had not been much better then if it had moved on the Æquator. But had the obliquity been greater then now it is, as double, or of 40 degrees; several parts of the earth had not been able to endure the disproportionable differences of seasons, occasioned by the great recess, and distance of the Sun. For unto some habitations the Summer would have been extream hot, and the Winter extream cold; likewise the Summer temperate unto some, but excessive and in extremity unto others, as unto those who should dwell under the Tropick of Cancer, as then would do some part of *Spain*, or ten degrees beyond, as *Germany*, and some part of *England*; who would have Summers as now the

Moors of *Africa*. For the Sun would sometime be vertical unto them: but they would have Winters like those beyond the Artick Circle; for in that season the Sun would be removed above 80 degrees from them. Again, it would be temperate to some habitations in the Summer, but very extream in the Winter: temperate to those in two or three degrees beyond the Artick Circle, as now it is unto us; for they would be equidistant from that Tropick, even as we are from this at present. But the Winter would be extream, the Sun being removed above an hundred degrees, and so consequently would not be visible in their Horizon; no position of sphere discovering any star distant above 90 degrees, which is the distance of every Zenith from the Horizon. And thus if the obliquity of this Circle had been less, the vicissitude of seasons had been so small as not to be distinguished; if greater, so large and disproportionable as not to be endured.

Now for its situation, although it held this Ecliptick line, yet had it been seated in any other Orb, inconveniences would ensue of condition like the former; for had it been placed in the lowest sphere of the Moon, the year would have consisted but of one moneth; for in that space of time it would have passed through every part of the Ecliptick; so would there have been no reasonable distinction of seasons required for the generation and fructifying of all things; contrary seasons which destroy the effects of one another, so suddenly succeeding. Besides by this vicinity unto the earth, its heat had been intollerable: for if (as many affirm) there is a different sense of heat from the different points of its proper Orb, and that in the Apogeum or highest point (which happeneth in Cancer) it is not so hot under that Tropick, on this side of the Æquator, as unto the other side in the Perigeum or lowest part of the Eccentrick (which happeneth in Capricornus) surely being placed in an Orb far lower, its heat would be unsufferable, nor needed we a fable to set the world on fire.

Now whether we adhere unto the hypothesis of *Copernicus*, affirming the Earth to move, and the Sun to stand still; or whether we hold, as some of late have concluded from the spots in the Sun, which appear and disappear again; that besides the revolution it makes with its Orbs, it hath also a dinetical motion, and rowls upon its own Poles, whether I say we affirm these or no, the illations before mentioned are not thereby infringed. We therefore conclude this contemplation, and are not afraid to believe, it may be literally said of the wisdom of God, what men will have but figuratively spoken of the words of Christ; that if the wonders thereof were duly described, the whole world, that is, all within the last circumference, would not contain them. For as his Wisdom is infinite, so cannot the due expressions thereof be finite, and if the world comprise him not, neither can it comprehend the story of him.

CHAPTER VI

Concerning the vulgar opinion, that the Earth, was slenderly peopled before the Flood

Beside the slender consideration men of latter times do hold of the first ages, it is commonly opinioned, and at first thought generally imagined, that the Earth was thinly inhabited, at least not remotely planted before the flood; whereof there being two opinions, which seem to be of some extremity, the one too largely extending, the other too narrowly contracting the populosity of those times; we shall not pass over this point without some enquiry into it.

Now for the true enquiry thereof, the means are as obscure as the matter, which being naturally to be explored by History, Humane or Divine, receiveth thereby no small addition of obscurity. For as for humane relations, they are so fabulous in *Deucalions* flood, that they are of little credit about *Ogyges* and *Noahs*. For the Heathens (as *Varro* accounteth) make three distinctions of time: the first from the beginning of the World unto the general Deluge of *Ogyges*, they term, *Adelon*, that is, a time not much unlike that which was before time, immanifest and unknown; because thereof there is almost nothing or very obscurely delivered: for though divers Authors have made some mention of the Deluge, as *Manethon* the *Egyptian* Priest, *Xenophon* de æquivocis, *Fabius Pictor* de Aureo seculo, *Mar. Cato* de orginibus, and *Archiolochus* the Greek, who introduceth also the Testimony of *Moses* in his fragment *de temporibus*; yet have they delivered no account of what preceded or went before. *Josephus* I confess in his Discourse against *Appion* induceth the antiquity of the *Jews* unto the flood, and before from the testimony of humane Writers; insisting especially upon *Maseas* of *Damascus*, *Jeronmus Ægyptius*, and *Berosus*;

and confirming the long duration of their lives, not only from these, but the authority of *Hesiod, Erathius, Hellanicus* and *Agesilaus*. *Berosus* the *Chaldean* Priest, writes most plainly, mentioning the City of *Enos*, the name of *Noah* and his sons, the building of the Ark, and also the place of its landing. And *Diodorus Siculus* hath in his third book a passage, which examined, advanced as high as *Adam*: for the *Chaldeans*, saith he, derive the Original of their Astronomy and letters forty three thousand years before the Monarchy of *Alexander* the Great: now the years whereby they computed antiquity of their letters, being as *Xenophon* interprets to be accounted Lunary: the compute will arise unto the time of *Adam*. For forty three thousand Lunary years make about three thousand six hundred thirty four years, which answereth the Chronology of time from the beginning of the world unto the raign of *Alexander*, as *Annius* of *Viterbo* computeth in his Comment upon *Berosus*.

The second space or interval of time is accounted from the flood unto the first Olympiad, that is, the year of the world 3174, which extendeth unto the days of *Isaiah* the Prophet, and some twenty years before the foundation of *Rome*; this they term *Mythicon* or fabulous, because the account thereof, especially of the first part, is fabulously or imperfectly delivered. Hereof some things have been briefly related by the Authors above mentioned: more particularly by *Dares Phrygius, Dictys Cretensis, Herodotus, Diodorus Siculus*, and *Trogus Pompeius*; the most famous *Greek* Poets lived also in this interval, as *Orpheus, Linus, Musæus, Homer, Hesiod*; and herein are comprehended the grounds and first inventions of Poetical fables, which were also taken up by historical Writers, perturbing the *Chaldean* and *Ægyptian* Records with fabulous additions; and confounding their names and stories, with their own inventions.

The third time succeeding until their present ages, they term *Historicon*, that is, such wherein matters have been more truly historified, and may therefore be believed. Of these times also have written *Herodotus, Thucydides, Xenophon, Diodorus*; and both of these and the other preceding such as have delivered universal Histories or Chronologies; as (to omit *Philo*, whose Narrations concern the *Hebrews*) *Eusebius, Julius Africanus, Orosius, Ado* of *Vienna, Marianus Scotus, Historia tripartita, Urpsergensis, Carion, Pineda, Salian*, and with us Sir *Walter Raleigh*.

Now from the first hereof that most concerneth us, we have little or no assistance, the fragments and broken records hereof inforcing not at all our purpose. And although some things not usually observed, may be from thence collected, yet do they not advantage our discourse, nor any way make evident the point in hand. For the second, though it directly concerns us not, yet in regard of our last medium and some illustrations therein, we shall be constrained to make some use thereof. As for the last it concerns us not at all; for treating of times far below us, it can no way advantage us. And though diverse in this last Age have also written of the first, as all that have delivered the general accounts of time, yet are their Tractates little auxiliary unto ours, nor afford us any light to detenebrate and cleare this Truth.

As for holy Scripture and divine relation, there may also seem therein but slender information, there being only left a brief narration hereof by *Moses*, and such as affords no positive determination. For the Text delivereth but two genealogies, that is, of *Cain* and *Seth*; in the line of *Seth* there are only ten descents, in that of *Cain* but seven, and those in a right line with mention of father and son; excepting that of *Lamech*, where is also mention of wives, sons, and a daughter. Notwithstanding if we seriously consider what is delivered therein, and what is also deducible, it will be probably declared what is by us intended, that is, the populous and ample habitation of the earth before the flood. Which we shall labour to induce not from postulates and entreated Maxims, but undeniable Principles declared in holy Scripture; that is, the length of mens lives before the flood, and the large extent of time from Creation thereunto.

We shall only first crave notice, that although in the relation of *Moses* there be very few persons mentioned, yet are there many more to be presumed; nor when the Scripture in the line of *Seth* nominates but ten persons, are they to be conceived all that were of this generation; The Scripture singly delivering the holy line, wherein the world was to be preserved, first in *Noah*, and afterward in our Saviour. For in this line it is manifest there were many more born than are named; for it is said of them all, that they begat sons and daughters. And whereas it is very late before it is said they begat those persons which are named in the Scripture, the soonest at 65, it must be understood that they had none before; but not any in whom it pleased God the holy line should be continued. And although the expression that they begat sons and daughters be not determined to be before or after the mention

446

of these, yet must it be before in some; for before it is said that *Adam* begat *Seth* at the 130 year, it is plainly affirmed that *Cain* knew his wife, and had a son; which must be one of the daughters of *Adam*, one of those whereof it is after said, he begat sons and daughters. And so for ought can be disproved there might be more persons upon earth then are commonly supposed, when *Cain* slew *Abel*; nor the fact so hainously to be aggravated in the circumstance of the fourth person living. And whereas it is said upon the nativity of *Seth*, God hath appointed me another seed instead of *Abel*, it doth not imply he had no other all this while; but not any of that expectation, or appointed (as his name implies) to make a progression in the holy line; in whom the world was to be saved, and from whom he should be born, that was mystically slain in *Abel*.

Now our first ground to induce the numerosity of people before the flood, is the long duration of their lives beyond 7, 8, and 9 hundred years. Which how it conduceth unto populosity we shall make but little doubt, if we consider there are two main causes of numerosity in any kind or species, that is, a frequent and multiparous way of breeding, whereby they fill the world with others, though they exist not long themselves; or a long duration and subsistence, whereby they do not only replenish the world with a new annumeration of others, but also maintain the former account in themselves. From the first cause we may observe examples in creatures oviparous, as Birds and Fishes; in vermiparous, as Flies, Locusts, and Gnats; in animals also viviparous, as Swine and Conies. Of the first there is a great example in the herd of Swine in *Galilee*, although an unclean beast, and forbidden unto the *Jews*. Of the other a remarkable one in *Atheneus*, in the Isle *Astipalea*, one of the Cyclades now called *Stampalia*, wherein from two that were imported, the number so increased, that the Inhabitants were constrained to have recourse unto the Oracle of *Delphos*, for an invention how to destroy them.

Others there are which make good the paucity of their breed with the length and duration of their daies, whereof there want not examples in animals uniparous: First, in bisulcous or cloven-hooft, as Camels, and Beeves, whereof there is above a million annually slain in *England*. It is said of *Job*, that he had a thousand yoak of Oxen, and six thousand Camels; and of the children of *Israel* passing into the land of *Canaan*, that they tooke from *Midianites* threescore and ten thousand Beeves; and of the Army of *Semiramis*, that there were therein one hundred thousand Camels. For Solipeds or firm-hoofed animals, as Horses, Asses, Mules, &c. they are also in mighty numbers, so is it delivered that *Job* had a thousand she Asses: that the *Midianites* lost sixty one thousand Asses. For horses it is affirmed by *Diodorus*, that *Ninus* brought against the *Bactrians* two hundred eighty thousand Horses; after him *Semiramis* five hundred thousand Horses, and Chariots one hundred thousand. Even in creatures steril and such as do not generate, the length of life conduceth much unto the multiplicity of the species; for the number of Mules which live far longer then their Dams or Sires, in Countries where they are bred, is very remarkable, and farre more common then Horses.

For animals multifidous, or such as are digitated or have several divisions in their feet; there are but two that are uniparous, that is, Men and Elephants; who though their productions be but single, are notwithstanding very numerous. The Elephant (as *Aristotle* affirmeth) carrieth the young two years, and conceiveth not again (as *Edvardus Lopez* affirmeth) in many after. yet doth their age requite this disadvantage; they living commonly one hundred, sometime two hundred years. Now although they be rare with us in *Europe*, and altogether unknown unto *America*, yet in the two other parts of the world they are in great abundance, as appears by the relation of *Garcias ab Horto*, Physitian to the Viceroy at *Goa*; who relates that at one venation the King of *Siam* tooke four thousand; and is of opinion they are in other parts in greater number then heards of Beeves in *Europe*. And though this delivered from a *Spaniard* unacquainted with our Northern droves, may seem very far to exceed; yet must we conceive them very numerous, if we consider the number of teeth transported from one Country to another: they having only two great teeth, and those not falling or renewing.

As for man, the disadvantage in his single issue is the same with these, and in the lateness of his generation somewhat greater then any; yet in the continual and not interrupted time thereof, and the extent of his days, he becomes at present, if not then any other species, at least more numerous then these before mentioned. Now being thus numerous at present, and in the measure of threescore, fourscore, or an hundred years, if their dayes extended unto six, seven, or eight hundred, their generations would be proportionably multiplied; their times of generation being not only multiplied, but their subsistence continued. For though the great Grand-child went on, the *Petrucius* and first

Original would subsist and make one of the world; though he outlived all the terms of consanguinity, and became a stranger unto his proper progeny. So by compute of Scripture *Adam* lived unto the ninth generation, unto the days of *Lamech* the father of *Noah*; *Methuselah* unto the year of the flood; and *Noah* was contemporary unto all from *Enoch* unto *Abraham*. So that although some died, the father beholding so many descents, the number of Survivers must still be very great; for if half the men were now alive, which lived in the last Century, the earth would scarce contain their number. Whereas in our abridged and septuagesimal Ages, it is very rare, and deserves a Distick to behold the fourth generation. *Xerxes* complaint still remaining; and what he lamented in his Army, being almost deplorable in the whole world, men seldom arriving unto those years whereby *Methuselah* exceeded nine hundred, and what *Adam* came short of a thousand, was defined long ago to be the age of man.

Now although the length of days conduceth mainly unto the numerosity of mankind, and it be manifest from Scripture they lived very long, yet is not the period of their lives determinable, and some might be longer livers, then we account that any were. For (to omit that conceit of some, that *Adam* was the oldest man, in as much as he is conceived to be created in the maturity of mankinde, that is, at 60 (for in that age it is set down they begat children) so that adding this number unto his 930, he was 21 years older then any of his posterity) that even *Methuselah* was the longest liver of all the children of *Adam*, we need not grant; nor is it definitively set down by *Moses*. Indeed of those ten mentioned in Scripture, with their several ages it must be true; but whether those seven of the line of *Cain* and their progeny, or any of the sons or daughters posterity after them out-lived those, is not expressed in holy Scripture; and it will seem more probable, that of the line of *Cain*, some were longer livers than any of *Seth*; if we concede that seven generations of the one lived as long as nine of the other. As for what is commonly alledged, that God would not permit the life of any unto a thousand, because (alluding unto that of *David*) no man should live one day in the sight of the Lord; although it be urged by divers, yet is it methinks an inference somewhat Rabbinicall; and not of power to perswade a serious examinator.

Having thus declared how powerfully the length of lives conduced unto populosity of those times, it will yet be easier acknowledged if we descend to particularities, and consider how many in seven hundred years might descend from one man; wherein considering the length of their dayes, we may conceive the greatest number to have been alive together. And this that no reasonable spirit may contradict, we will declare with manifest disadvantage; for whereas the duration of the world unto the flood was above 1600 years, we will make our compute in less then half that time. Nor will we begin with the first man, but allow the earth to be provided of women fit for marriage the second or third first Centuries; and will only take as granted, that they might beget children at sixty, and at an hundred years have twenty, allowing for that number forty years. Nor will we herein single out *Methuselah*, or account from the longest livers, but make choice of the shortest of any we find recorded in the Text, excepting *Enoch*; who after he had lived as many years as there be days in the year, was translated at 365. And thus from one stock of seven hundred years, multiplying still by twenty, we shall find the product to be one thousand, three hundred forty seven millions, three hundred sixty eight thousand, four hundred and twenty.

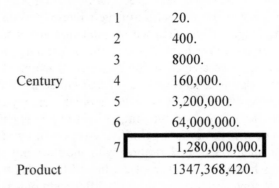

	1	20.
	2	400.
	3	8000.
Century	4	160,000.
	5	3,200,000.
	6	64,000,000.
	7	1,280,000,000.
Product		1347,368,420.

Now if this account of the learned *Petavius* will be allowed, it will make an unexpected encrease, and a larger number than may be found in *Asia, Africa* and Europe; especially if in *Constantinople* the greatest City thereof, there be no more then *Botero* accounteth, seven hundred thousand soules. Which duly considered, we shall rather admire how the earth contained its inhabitants, then doubt its inhabitation; and might conceive the Deluge not simply penall, but in some way also necessary, as many have conceived of translations, if *Adam* had not sinned, and the race of man had remained upon earth immortal.

450

Now whereas some to make good their longevity, have imagined that the years of their compute were Lunary; unto these we must reply: That if by a Lunary year they understand twelve revolutions of the Moon, that is, 354 days, eleven fewer then in the Solary year; there will be no great difference; at least not sufficient to convince or extenuate the question. But if by a Lunary year they mean one revolution of the Moon, that is, a moneth; they first introduce a year never used by the Hebrews, in their Civil accompts; and what is delivered before of the Chaldean years (as *Xenophon* gives a caution) was only received in the Chronology of their Arts. Secondly, they contradict the Scripture, which makes a plain enumeration of many moneths in the account of the Deluge; for so it is expressed in the Text. In the tenth moneth, in the first day of the moneth were the tops of the mountains seen: Concordant whereunto is the relation of humane Authors, *Inundationes plures fuere, prima novimestris inundatio terrarum sub prisco Ogyge. Meminisse hoc loco par est post primum diluvius Ogygi temporibus notatum, cum novem et amplius mensibus diem continua nox inumbrasset, Delon ante omnes terras radiis solis illuminatam sortitamque ex eo nomen.* And lastly, they fall upon an absurdity, for they make *Enoch* to beget children about six years of age. For whereas it is said he begat *Methuselah* at 65, if we shall account every moneth a year, he was at that time some sixe years and an half, for so many moneths are contained in that space of time.

Having thus declared how much the length of mens lives conduced unto the populosity of their kind, our second foundation must be the large extent of time, from the Creation unto the Deluge, that is (according unto received computes about 1655 years) almost as long a time as hath passed since the nativity of our Saviour: and this we cannot but conceive sufficient for a very large increase, if we do but affirm what reasonable enquirers will not deny: That the earth might be as populous in that number of years before the flood, as we can manifest it was in the same number after. And whereas there may be conceived some disadvantage, in regard that at the Creation the original of mankind was in two persons, but after the flood their propagation issued at least from six; against this we might very well set the length of their lives before the flood, which were abbreviated after, and in half this space contracted into hundreds and threescores. Notwithstanding to equalize accounts, we will allow three hundred years, and so long a time as we can manifest from the Scripture, There were four men at least that begat children, *Adam*, *Cain*, *Seth*, and

Enos; So shall we fairly and favourably proceed, if we affirm the world to have been as populous in sixteen hundred and fifty years before the flood, as it was in thirteen hundred after. Now how populous and largely inhabited it was within this period of time, we shall declare from probabilities, and several testimonies of Scripture and humane Authors.

And first, To manifest the same neer those parts of the Earth where the Ark is presumed to have rested, we have the relation of holy Scripture concerning the genealogy of *Japhet*, *Cham* and *Sem*, and in this last, four descents unto the division of the earth in the dayes of *Peleg*, which time although it were not upon common compute much above an hundred years, yet were men at this time mightily increased. Nor can we well conceive it otherwise, if we consider they began already to wander from their first habitation, and were able to attempt so might a work as the building of a City and a Tower, whose top should reach unto the heavens. Whereunto there was required no slender number of persons, if we consider the magnitude thereof, expressed by some, and conceived to be *Turris Beli* in Herodotus; and the multitudes of people recorded at the erecting of the like or inferiour structures: for at the building of *Solomons* Temple there were threescore and ten thousand that carried burdens, and fourscore thousand hewers in the mountains, beside the chief of his officers three thousand and three hundred; and at the erecting of the Piramids in the reigne of King *Cheops*, as *Herodotus* reports, there were *decem myriades*, that is an hundred thousand men. And though it be said of the *Egyptians*, *Porrum & cæpe nefas violare & fragere morsu*; yet did the summes expended in Garlick and Onyons amount unto no less then one thousand six hundred Talents.

The first Monarchy or Kingdom of *Babylon* is mentioned in Scripture under the foundation of *Nimrod*, which is also recorded in humane history; as beside *Berosus*, in *Diodorus* and *Justine*, for *Nimrod* of the Scriptures is *Belus* of the Gentiles, and *Assur* the same with *Ninus* his successour. There is also mention of divers Cities, particularly of *Ninivy* and *Resen* expressed emphatically in the Text to be a great City.

That other Countries round about were also peopled, appears by the Wars of the Monarchs of *Assyria* with the *Bactrians*, *Indians*, *Scythians*, *Ethiopians*, *Armenians*, *Hyrcanians*, *Parthians*, *Persians*,

Susians: they vanquishing (as *Diodorus* relateth) *Egypt*, *Syria*, and all *Asia* minor, even from *Bosphorus* unto *Tanais*. And it is said, that *Semiramis* in her expedition against the *Indians* brought along with her the King of *Arabia*. About the same time of the *Assyrian* Monarchy, do Authors place that of the *Sycionians* in *Greece*, and soon after that of the *Argives*, and not very long after, that of the *Athenians* under *Cecrops*; and within our period assumed are historified many memorable actions of the Greeks, as the expedition of the *Argonautes*, with the most famous Wars of *Thebes* and *Troy*.

That *Canaan* also and *Egypt* were well peopled far within this period, besides their plantation by *Canaan* and *Misraim*, appeareth from the history of *Abraham*, who in less then 400 years after the Flood, journied from *Mesopotamia* unto *Canaan* and *Egypt*, both which he found well peopled and policied into Kingdoms: wherein also in 430 years, from threescore and ten persons which came with *Jacob* into *Egypt*, he became a mighty Nation; for it is said, at their departure, there journeyed from *Rhamesis* to *Succoth* about six hundred thousand on foot, that were men, besides children. Now how populous the land from whence they came was, may be collected not only from their ability in commanding such subjections and mighty powers under them, but from the several accounts of that Kingdom delivered by *Herodotus*. And how soon it was peopled, is evidenced from the pillar of their King *Osyris*, with this inscription in *Diodorus*; *Mihi pater est Saturnus deorum junior, sum vero Osyris rex qui totum peragravi orbem usq; ad Indorum fines, ad eos quoq; sum profectus qui septentrioni subjacent usq; ad Istri fontes, & alias partes usq; ad Oceanum.* Now according unto the best determinations *Osyris* was *Misraim*, and *Saturnus Egyptius* the same with *Cham*; after whose name *Egypt* is not only called in Scripture the land of *Ham*, but thus much is also testified by *Plutarch*: for in his Treatise *de Osyride*, he delivereth that Egypt was called *Chamia a Chamo Noe filio*, that is from *Cham* the son of *Noah*. And if according to the consent of the ancient Fathers, *Adam* was buried in the same place where Christ was crucified, that is Mount *Calvary*, the first man ranged far before the Flood, and laid his bones many miles from that place, where its presumed he received them. And this migration was the greater, if as the text expresseth, he was cast out of the East-side of Paradise to till the ground: and as the Position of the Cherubines implieth, who were placed at the east end of the garden to keep him from the tree of life.

That the remoter parts of the earth were in this time inhabited is also induceable from the like testimonies; for (omitting the numeration of *Josephus*, and the genealogies of the Sons of *Noah*) that *Italy* was inhabited, appeareth from the Records of *Livie* and *Dionysius Halicarnassius*, the story of *Æneas*, *Evander* and *Janus*, whom *Annius* of *Viterbo*, and the Chorographers of *Italy*, do make to be the same with *Noah*. That *Sicily* was also peopled, is made out from the frequent mention thereof in *Homer*, the Records of *Diodorus* and others; but especially from a remarkable passage touched by *Aretius* and *Ranzanus* Bishop of *Lucerium*, but fully explained by *Thomas Fazelli* in his accurate History of *Sicily*; that is, from an ancient inscription in a stone at *Panormo*, expressed by him in its proper characters, and by a *Syrian* thus translated, *Non est alius Deus præter unum Deum, non est alius potens præter eundem Deum, neq; est alius victor præter eundem quem colimus Deum: Hujus turris præfectus est* Saphu *filius* Eliphat, *filii* Esau, *fratris* Jacob *filii* Isaac, *filii* Abraham; *& turri quidem ipsi nomen est* Baych, *sed turri huic proxime nomen est* Pharath. The antiquity of the inhabitation of *Spain* is also confirmable, not only from *Berosus* in the plantation of *Tubal*, and a City continuing yet in his name; but the story of *Gerion*, the travels of *Hercules* and his pillars; and especially a passage in *Strabo*, which advanceth unto the time of *Ninus*, thus delivered in his fourth book. The *Spaniards* (saith he) affirm that they have had Laws and Letters above six thousand years. Now the *Spaniards* or *Iberians* observing (as *Xenophon* hath delivered) *Annum quadrimestrem*, foure moneths unto a year, this compute will make up 2000 solary years, which is about the space of time from *Strabo*, who lived in the days of *Augustus*, unto the reign of *Ninus*.

That *Mauritania* and the coast of *Africa* were peopled very soon, is the conjecture of many wise men, and that by the *Phœnicians*, who left their Country upon the invasion of *Canaan* by the *Israelites*. For beside the conformity of the *Punick* or *Carthaginian* language with that of *Phœnicia*, there is a pregnant and very remarkable testimony hereof in *Procopius*, who in his second *de bello vandalico*, recordeth, that in a town of *Mauritania Tingitana*, there was to be seen upon two white Columns in the *Phœnician* language these ensuing words; *Nos Maurici sumus qui fugimus a facie Jehoschuæ filii Nunis prædatoris*. The fortunate Islands or *Canaries* were not unknown; for so doth *Strabo* interpret that speech in *Homer* of *Proteus* unto *Menalaus*,

Sed te qua terræ postremus terminus extat,
Elysium in Campum cœlestia numina ducunt.

The like might we affirm from credible histories both of *France* and *Germany*, and perhaps also of our own Country. For omitting the fabulous and *Trojan* original delivered by *Jeofrey* of *Monmouth*, and the express text of Scripture; that the race of *Japhet* did people the Isles of the *Gentiles*; the *Brittish* Original was so obscure in *Cæsars* time, that he affirmeth the Inland inhabitants were *Aborigines*, that is, such as reported, that they had their beginning in the Island. That *Ireland* our neighbour Island was not long time without Inhabitants, may be made probable by sundry accounts; although we abate the Traditions of *Bartholanus* the *Scythian*, who arrived there three hundred years after the Flood, or the relation of *Giraldus*; that *Cæsaria* the daughter of *Noah* dwelt there before.

Now should we call in the learned account of *Bochartus*, deducing the ancient names of Countries from *Phœnicians*, who by their plantations, discoveries, and sea negotiations, have left unto very many Countries, *Phœnician* denominations; the enquiry would be much shorter, and if *Spain* in the *Phœnician* Original, be but the region of *Conies*, *Lusitania*, or *Portugal* the Countrey of Almonds, if *Brittanica* were at first *Baratanaca*, or the land of Tin, and *Ibernia* or *Ireland*, were but *Ibernae*, or the farthest habitation; and these names imposed and dispersed by *Phœnician* Colonies in their several navigations; the Antiquity of habitations might be more clearly advanced.

Thus though we have declared how largely the world was inhabited within the space of 1300 years, yet must it be conceived more populous then can be clearly evinced; for a greater part of the Earth hath ever been peopled, then hath been known or described by Geographers, as will appear by the discoveries of all Ages. For neither in *Herodotus* or *Thucydides* do we find any mention of *Rome*, nor in *Ptolomy* of many parts of *Europe*, *Asia*, or *Africa*. And because many places we have declared of long plantation, of whose populosity notwithstanding or memorable actions we have no ancient story; if we may conjecture of these by what we find related of others, we shall not need many words, nor assume the half of 1300 years. And this we might illustrate from the mighty acts of the *Assyrians* performed not long after the flood; recorded by *Justine* and *Diodorus*; who makes relation of expeditions by Armies more numerous then have been ever since. For *Ninus* King of *Assyria* brought against the *Bactrians* 700000 foot, 200000 horse, 10600 Chariots. *Semiramis* his successor led against the *Indians* 1300000 foot, 500000 horse, 100000 Chariots, and as many upon Camels: And it is said, *Staurobates* the *Indian* King, met her with greater forces then she brought against him. All which was performed less then four hundred years after the flood.

Now if any imagine the unity of their language did hinder their dispersion before the flood, we confess it some hindrance at first, but not much afterward. For though it might restrain their dispersion, it could not their populosity; which necessarily requireth transmigration and emission of Colonies; as we read of *Romans, Greeks, Phœniceans* in ages past, and have beheld examples thereof in our days. We may also observe that after the flood before the confusion of tongues, men began to disperse; for it is said, they journyed towards the East: and the Scripture it self expresseth a necessity conceived of their dispersion, for the intent of erecting the Tower is so delivered in the text, Lest we be scattered abroad upon the face of the earth.

Again, If any apprehend the plantation of the earth more easie in regard of Navigation and shipping discovered since the flood, whereby the Islands and divided parts of the earth are now inhabited; he must consider, that whether there were Islands or no before the flood, is not yet determined, and is with probability denied by very learned Authors.

Lastly, If we shall fall into apprehension that it was less inhabited, because it is said in the sixt of *Genesis* about 120 years before the flood, and it came to pass that when men began to multiply upon the face of the earth. Beside that this may be only meant of the race of *Cain*, it will not import they were not multiplied before, but that they were at that time plentifully encreased; for so is the same word used in other parts of Scripture. And so is it afterward in the 9 Chapter said, that *Noah* began to be an husbandman, that is, he was so, or earnestly performed the Acts thereof: so it is said of our Saviour, that he began to cast them out that bought and sold in the Temple; that is, he actually cast them out, or with alacrity effected it.

Thus have I declared with some private and probable conceptions in the enquiry of this truth; but the certainty hereof let the

456

Arithmetick of the last day determine; and therefore expect no further belief than probability and reason induce. Only desire men would not swallow dubiosities for certainties, and receive as Principles points mainly controvertible; for we are to adhere unto things doubtful in a dubious and opinative way. It being reasonable for every man to vary his opinion according to the variance of his reason, and to affirm one day what he denied another. Wherein although at last we miss of truth; we die notwithstanding in inoffensive errors; because we adhere unto that, whereunto the examen of our reasons, and honest enquiries induce us

CHAPTER VII

Of East, and West

The next shall be of East and West; that is, the proprieties and conditions ascribed unto Regions respectively unto those situations; which hath been the obvious conception of Philosophers and Geographers, magnifying the condition of *India*, and the Eastern Countries, above the setting and occidental Climates, some ascribing hereto the generation of gold, precious stones, and spices, others the civility and natural endowments of men; conceiving the bodies of this situation to receive a special impression from the first salutes of the Sun, and some appropriate influence from his ascendent and oriental radiations. But these proprieties affixed unto bodies, upon considerations deduced from East, West, or those observable points of the sphere, how specious and plausible so ever, will not upon enquiry be justified from such foundations.

For, to speak strictly, there is no East and West in nature, nor are those absolute and invariable, but respective and mutable points, according unto different longitudes, or distant parts of habitation, whereby they suffer many and considerable variations. For first, unto some, the same part will be East or West in respect of one another, that is, unto such as inhabit the same parallel, or differently dwell from East to West. Thus as unto *Spain*, *Italy* lyeth East, unto *Italy Greece*, unto *Greece Persia*, and unto *Persia China*; so again unto the Country of *China*, *Persia* lyeth West, unto *Persia Greece*, unto *Greece Italy*, and unto *Italy Spain*. So that the same Countrey is sometimes East and sometimes West; and *Persia* though East unto *Greece*, yet is it West unto *China*.

Unto other habitations the same point will be both East and West; as unto those that are *Antipodes* or seated in points of the Globe diametrically opposed. So the *Americans* are Antipodal unto the *Indians*, and some part of *India* is both East and West unto *America*, according as it shall be regarded from one side or the other, to the right or to the left; and setting out from any middle point, either by East or West, the distance unto the place intended is equal, and in the same space of time in nature also performable.

To a third that have the Poles for their vertex, or dwell in the position of a parallel sphere, there will be neither East nor West, at least the greatest part of the year. For if (as the name *Oriental* implyeth) they shall account that part to be East where ever the Sun ariseth, or that West where the Sun is occidental or setteth: almost half the year they have neither the one nor the other. For half the year it is below their Horizon, and the other half it is continually above it, and circling round about them intersecteth not the Horizon, nor leaveth any part for this compute. And if (which will seem very reasonable) that part should be termed the Eastern point, where the Sun at the Æquinox, and but once in the year ariseth, yet will this also disturb the cardinal accounts, nor will it with propriety admit that appellation. For that surely cannot be accounted East which hath the South on both sides; which notwithstanding this position must have. For if unto such as live under the Pole, that be only North which is above them, that must be Southerly which is below them, which is all the other portion of the Globe, beside that part possessed by them. And thus these points of East and West being not absolute in any, respective in some, and not at all relating unto others; we cannot hereon establish so general considerations, nor reasonably erect such immutable assertions, upon so unstable foundations.

Now the ground that begat or promoted this conceit, was first a mistake in the apprehension of East and West, considering thereof as of the North and South, and computing by these as invariably as the other; but herein, upon second thoughts there is a great disparity. For the North and Southern Pole, are the invariable terms of that Axis whereon the heavens do move; and are therefore incommunicable and fixed points; whereof the one is not apprehensible in the other. But with East and West it is quite otherwise; for the revolution of the Orbs being made upon the Poles of North and South, all other points about the Axis are mutable; and wheresoever therein the East point be determined; by succession of parts in one revolution every point becometh East. And so if where the Sun ariseth, that part be termed East, every habitation differing in longitude, will have this point also different; in as much as the Sun successively ariseth unto every one.

The second ground, although it depend upon the former, approacheth nearer the effect; and that is the efficacy of the Sun, set out and divided according to priority of ascent; whereby his influence is conceived more favourable unto one Countrey than another, and to felicitate *India* more then any after. But hereby we cannot avoid absurdities, and such as infer effects controulable by our senses: For first, by the same reason that we affirm the *Indian* richer than the *American*, the *American* will also be more plentiful than the *Indian*, and *England* or *Spain* more fruitful then *Hispaniola* or golden Castle; in as much as the Sun ariseth unto the one sooner than the other; and so accountably unto any Nation subjected unto the same parallel, or with a considerable diversity of longitude from each other.

Secondly, An unsufferable absurdity will ensue: for thereby a Country may be more fruitful than it self: For *India* is more fertile then *Spain*, because more East, and that the Sun ariseth first unto it; *Spain* likewise by the same reason more fruitful than *America*, and *America* than *India*: so that *Spain* is less fruitful than that Countrey, which a less fertile Country than it self excelleth.

Lastly, If we conceive the Sun hath any advantage by priority of ascent, or makes thereby one Country more happy than another, we introduce injustifiable determinations, and impose a natural partiality on that Luminary, which being equidistant from the earth, and equally removed in the East as in the West, his Power and Efficacy in both places must be equal, as *Boetius* hath taken notice, and *Scaliger* graphically declared. Some have therefore forsaken this refuge of the Sun, and to salve the effect have recurred unto the influence of the Stars, making their activities National, and appropriating their Powers unto particular regions. So *Cardan* conceiveth the tail of *Ursa Major* peculiarly respecteth *Europ*: whereas indeed once in 24 hours it also absolveth its course over *Asia* and *America*. And therefore it will not be easie to apprehend those stars peculiarly glance on us, who must of necessity carry a common eye and regard unto all Countries, unto whom their revolution and verticity is also common.

The effects therefore or different productions in several Countries, which we impute unto the action of the Sun, must surely have nearer and more immediate causes than that Luminary. And these if we place in the propriety of clime, or condition of soil wherein they are produced, we shall more reasonably proceed, than they who ascribe them unto the activity of the Sun. Whose revolution being regular, it hath no power nor efficacy peculiar from its orientality, but equally disperseth his beams, unto all which equally, and in the same restriction, receive his lustre. And being an universal and indefinite agent, the effects or productions we behold, receive not their circle from his causality, but are determined by the principles of the place, or qualities of that region which admits them. And this is evident not only in gemms, minerals, and metals, but observable in plants and animals; whereof some are common unto many Countries, some peculiar unto one, some not communicable unto another. For the hand of God that first created the earth, hath with variety disposed the principles of all things; wisely contriving them in their proper seminaries, and where they best maintain the intention of their species; whereof if they have not a concurrence, and be not lodged in a convenient matrix, they are not excited by the efficacy of the Sun; or failing in particular causes, receive a relief or sufficient promotion from the universal. For although superiour powers co-operate with inferiour activities, and may (as some conceive) carry a stroke in the plastick and formative draught of all things, yet do their determinations belong unto particular agents, and are defined from their proper principles. Thus the Sun which with us is fruitful in the generation of Frogs, Toads and Serpents, to this effect proves impotent in our neighbour Island; wherein as in all other carrying a common aspect, it concurreth but unto predisposed effects; and only suscitates those forms, whose determinations are seminal, and proceedeth from the *Idea* of themselves.

Now whereas there be many observations concerning East, and divers considerations of Art which seeme to extol the quality of that point, if rightly understood they do not really promote it. That the Astrologer takes account of nativities from the Ascendent, that is, the first house of the heavens, whose beginning is toward the East, it doth not advantage the conceit. For, he establisheth not his Judgment upon the orientality thereof, but considereth therein his first ascent above the Horizon: at which time its efficacy becomes observable, and is conceived to have the signification of life, and to respect the condition of all things, which at the same time arise from their causes, and ascend to their Horizon with it. Now this ascension indeed falls out respectively in the East: but as we have delivered before, in some positions there is no Eastern point from whence to compute these ascensions. So is it in a parallel sphere: for unto them six houses are continually depressed, and six never elevated: and the planets themselves, whose revolutions are of more speed, and influences of higher consideration, must find in that place a very imperfect regard; for half their period they absolve above, and half beneath the Horizon. And so for six years, no man can have the happiness to be born under *Jupiter*: and for fifteen together all must escape the ascendent domination of *Saturn*.

That *Aristotle* in his Politicks, commends the situation of a City which is open towards the East, and admitteth the raies of the rising Sun, thereby is implied no more particular efficacy than in the West: But that position is commended, in regard the damps and vaporous exhalations ingendred in the absence of the Sun, are by his returning raies the sooner dispelled, and men thereby more early enjoy a clear and healthy habitation. Upon the like considerations it is, that *Marcus Varro* commendeth the same situation, and exposeth his farm unto the equinoxial ascent of the Sun, and that *Palladius* adviseth the front of his edifice should so respect the South, that in the first angle it receive the rising raies of the Winter Sun, and decline a little from the Winter setting thereof. And concordant hereunto is the instruction of *Columella De positione villæ*: which he contriveth into Summer and Winter habitations, ordering that the Winter lodgings regard the Winter ascent of the Sun, that is, South-East; and the rooms of repast at supper, the Æquinoxial setting thereof, that is the West: that the Summer lodgings regard the Æquinoxial Meridian: but the rooms of cænation in the Summer, he obverts unto the Winter ascent, that is, South-East; and the Balnearies or bathing places, that they may remain under the Sun until evening, he exposeth unto the Summer setting, that is, North-West, in all which, although the Cardinal points be introduced, yet is the consideration Solary, and only determined unto the aspect or visible reception of the Sun.

Jews and *Mahometans* in these and our neighbour parts are observed to use some gestures towards the East, as at their benediction, and the killing of their meat. And though many ignorant spectators, and not a few of the Actors conceive some Magick or Mysterie therein, yet is the Ceremony only Topical, and in a memorial relation unto a place they honour. So the *Jews* do carry a respect and cast an eye upon *Jerusalem*: for which practice they are not without the example of their fore-fathers, and the encouragement of their wise King: For so it is said that *Daniel* went into his house, and his windows being opened towards *Jerusalem*, he kneeled upon his knees three times a day, and prayed. So is it expressed in the prayer of *Solomon*, what prayer or supplication soever be made by any man, which shall spread forth his hands towards this house: if thy people go out to battle, and shall pray unto the Lord towards the City which thou has chosen, and towards the house which I have chosen to build for thy Name, then hear thou in heaven their prayer and their supplication, and maintain their cause. Now the observation hereof, unto the Jews that are dispersed Westward, and such as most converse with us, directeth their regard unto the East: But the words of *Solomon* are appliable unto all quarters of Heaven: and by the Jews of the East and South must be regarded in a contrary position. So *Daniel* in *Babylon* looking toward *Jerusalem* had his face toward the West. So the Jews in their own Land looked upon it from all quarters. For the Tribe of *Judah* beheld it to the North: *Manasses*, *Zabulon*, and *Napthali* unto the South; *Reuben and* Gad unto the West; only the tribe of *Dan* regarded it direct or to the due East. So when it is said, when you see a cloud rise out of the West, you say there cometh a shower, and so it is: the observation was respective unto *Judea*: nor is this a reasonable illation in all other Nations whatsoever: For the Sea lay West unto that Country, and the winds brought rain from that quarter; but this consideration cannot be transferred unto *India* or *China*, which have a vast Sea Eastward: and a vaster Continent toward the West. So likewise when it is said in the vulgar Translation, Gold cometh out of the North; it is no reasonable inducement unto us and many other Countries, from some particular mines septentrional unto his situation, to search after that metal in cold and Northern regions, which we most plentifully discover in hot and Southern habitations.

For the *Mahometans*, as they partake with all Religions in something, so they imitate the *Jew* in this. For in their observed gestures, they hold a regard unto *Mecha* and *Medina Talnabi*, two Cities in *Arabia fælix*; where their Prophet was born and buried; whither they perform their pilgrimages: and from whence they expect he should return again. And therefore they direct their faces unto these parts, which unto the *Mahometans* of *Barbary* and *Egypt* lie East, and are in some point thereof unto many other parts of *Turkie*. Wherein notwithstanding there is no Oriental respect; for with the same devotion on the other side they regard these parts toward the West, and so with variety wheresoever they are seated, conforming unto the ground of their conception.

Fourthly, Whereas in the ordering of the Camp of *Israel*, the East quarter is appointed unto the noblest Tribe, that is the Tribe of *Judah*, according to the command of God, in the East-side toward the rising of the Sun shall the Standard of the Tribe of Judah *pitch*: it doth not peculiarly extol that point. For herein the East is not to be taken strictly, but as it signifieth or implieth the foremost place; for *Judah* had the Van, and many Countries through which they passed were seated Easterly unto them. Thus much is implied by the Original, and expressed by Translations which strictly conform thereto: So *Tremellius, Castra habentium ab anteriore parte Orientem versus, vexillum esto castrorum Judæ*; so hath *R. Solomon Jarchi* expounded it, the foremost or before, is the East quarter, and the West is called behind. And upon this interpretation may all be salved that is alleageable against it. For if the Tribe of *Judah* were to pitch before the Tabernacle at the East, and yet to march first, as is commanded,*Numb.* 10. there must ensue a disorder in the Camp, nor could they conveniently observe the execution thereof: For when they set out from *Mount Sinai* where the Command was delivered, they made Northward unto *Rithmah*: from *Rissah* unto *Eziongaber* about fourteen stations they marched South: From *Almon Diblathaim* through the mountains of *Yabarim* and plains of *Moab* towards *Jordan* the face of their march was West: So that if *Judah* were strictly to pitch in the East of the Tabernacle, every night he encamped in the Rear: and if (as some conceive) the whole Camp could not be less than twelve miles long, it had been preposterous for him to have marched foremost; or set out first who was most remote from the place to be approached.

Fifthly, That Learning, Civility and Arts had their beginning in the East, it is not imputable either to the action of the Sun, or its Orientality, but the first plantation of Man in those parts; which unto *Europe* do carry the respect of East. For on the mountains of *Ararat*, that is part of the hill *Taurus*, between the *East-Indies* and *Scythia*, as Sir *W. Raleigh* accounts it, the Ark of *Noah* rested; from the East they travelled that built the Tower of *Babel*: from thence they were dispersed and successively enlarged, and Learning, good Arts, and all Civility communicated. The progression whereof was very sensible; and if we consider the distance of time between the confusion of *Babel*, and the

Civility of many parts now eminent therein, it travelled late and slowly into our quarters. For notwithstanding the learning of *Bardes* and *Druides* of elder times, he that shall peruse that worke of *Tacitus de moribus Germanorum*, may easily discern how little Civility two thousand years had wrought upon that Nation: the like he may observe concerning our selves, from the same Author in the life of *Agricola*, and more directly from Strabo; who to the dishonour of our Predecessors, and the disparagement of those that glory in the Antiquity of their Ancestors, affirmeth the *Britains* were so simple, that though they abounded in Milk, they had not the Artifice of Cheese.

Lastly, That the Globe it self is by Cosmographers divided into East and West, accounting from the first Meridian, it doth not establish this conceit. For that division is not naturally founded, but artificially set down, and by agreement; as the aptest terms to define or commensurate the longitude of places. Thus the ancient Cosmographers do place the division of the East and Western Hemisphere, that is the first term of longitude in the Canary or fortunate Islands; conceiving these parts the extreamest habitations Westward: But the Moderns have altered that term, and translated it unto the Azores or Islands of St. *Michael*; and that upon a plausible conceit of the small or insensible variation of the Compass in those parts, wherein nevertheless, though upon second invention, they proceed upon a common and no appropriate foundation; for even in that Meridian farther North or South the Compass observably varieth; and there are also other places wherein it varieth not, as *Alphonso* and *Rodoriges de Lago* will have it about *Capo de las Agullas* in *Africa*; as *Maurolycus* affirmeth in the shore of *Peloponesus* in *Europe*: and as *Gilbertus* averreth, in the midst of great regions, in most parts of the earth.

CHAPTER VIII

Of the River Nilus

Hereof uncontrolably and under general consent many opinions are passant, which notwithstanding upon due examination, do admit of doubt or restriction. It is generally esteemed, and by most unto our days received, that the River of *Nilus* hath seven ostiaries; that is, by seven Channels disburdeneth it self into the Sea. Wherein notwithstanding, beside that we find no concurrent determination of ages past, and a positive and undeniable refute of these present; the affirmative is mutable, and must not be received without all limitation.

For some, from whom we receive the greatest illustrations of Antiquity, have made no mention hereof: So *Homer* hath given no number of its Channels, nor so much as the name thereof in use with all Historians. *Eratosthenes* in his description of *Egypt* hath likewise passed them over. *Aristotle* is so indistinct in their names and numbers, that in the first of *Meteors* he plainly affirmeth the Region of *Egypt* (which we esteem the ancientest Nation in the world) was a meer gained ground, and that by the setling of mud and limous matter brought down by the River *Nilus*, that which was at first a continued Sea, was raised at last into a firm and habitable Country. The like opinion he held of *Mæotis Palus*, that by the floods of *Tanais* and earth brought down thereby, it grew observably shallower in his days, and would in process of time become a firm land. And though his conjecture be not as yet fulfilled, yet is the like observable in the River *Gihon*, a branch of *Euphrates* and River of Paradise; which having in former Ages discharged it self into the *Persian* Sea, doth at present fall short; being lost in the lakes of *Chaldea*, and hath left between the Sea, a large and considerable part of dry land.

Others expresly treating hereof have diversly delivered themselves; *Herodotus* in his Euterpe makes mention of seven; but carelesly of two thereof; that is, *Bolbitinum*, and *Bucolicum*; for these, saith he, were not the natural currents, but made by Art for some occasional convenience. *Strabo* in his Geography naming but two, *Pelusiacum* and *Canopicum*, plainly affirmeth there were many more then seven; *Inter hæc alia quinque*, &c. There are (saith he) many remarkable towns within the currents of Nile, especially such which have given the names unto the ostiaries thereof, not unto all, for they are eleven, and four besides, but unto seven and most considerable; that is, *Canopicum, Bolbitinum, Sebenneticum, Phatniticum, Mendesium, Taniticum*, and *Pelusium*: wherein to make up the number, one of the artificial channels of *Herodotus* is accounted. *Ptolomy* an *Egyptian*, and born at the *Pelusian* mouth of *Nile*, in his Geography maketh nine: and in the third Map of *Africa*, hath unto their mouths prefixed their several names; *Heracleoticum, Bolbitinum, Sebenniticum, Pineptum, Diolcos, Pathmeticum, Mendesium, Taniticum, Peleusiacum*: wherein notwithstanding there are no less then three different names from those delivered by *Pliny*. All which considered, we may easily discern that Authors accord not either in name or number; and must needs confirm the Judgement of *Maginus, de Ostiorum Nili numero & nominibus, valde antiqui scriptores discordant.*

Modern Geographers and travellers do much abate of this number; for as *Maginus* and others observe, there are now but three or foure mouths thereof; as *Gulielmus Tyrius* long ago, and *Bellonius* since, both ocular enquirers with others have attested. For below *Cairo*, the River divides it self into four branches, whereof two make the chief and navigable streams, the one running to *Pelusium* of the Ancients, and now *Damiata*; the other unto *Canopium*, and now *Roscetta*; the other two, saith Mr. *Sandys*, do run between these; but poor in water. Of those seven mentioned by *Herodotus*, and those nine by *Ptolomy*, these are all I could either see, or hear of Which much confirmeth the testimony of the Bishop of *Tyre* a diligent and ocular Enquirer; who in his holy war doth thus deliver himself. We wonder much at the Ancients, who assigned seven mouths unto *Nilus*: which we can no otherwise salve, then that by process of time, the face of places is altered, and the river hath lost his chanels; or that our forefathers did never obtain a true account thereof.

And therefore when it is said in holy Scripture, The Lord shall utterly destroy the tongue of the *Egyptian* Sea, and with his mighty wind he shall shake his hand over the river, and shall smite it in the seven streams, and make men go over dry-shod. If this expression concerneth the river *Nilus*, it must only respect the seven principal streams. But the place is very obscure, and whether thereby be not meant the river *Euphrates*, is not without some controversie; as is collectible from the subsequent words; And there shall be an high way for the remnant of his people, that shall be left from *Assyria*; and also from the bare name *River*, emphatically signifying *Euphrates*, and thereby the division of the *Assyrian* Empire into many fractions, which might facilitate their return: as *Grotius* hath observed; and is more plainly made out, if the *Apocrypha* of *Esdras*, and that of the *Apocalyps* have any relation hereto.

Lastly, Whatever was or is their number, the contrivers of Cards and Maps afford us no assurance or constant description therein. For whereas *Ptolomy* hath set forth nine, *Hondius* in his Map of *Africa*, makes but eight, and in that of *Europe* ten. *Ortelius* in the Map of the *Turkish* Empire, setteth down eight, in that of *Egypt* eleven; and *Maginus* in his Map of that Country hath observed the same number. And if we enquire farther, we shall find the same diversity and discord in divers others.

Thus may we perceive that this account was differently related by the Ancients, that it is undeniably rejected by the Moderns, and must be warily received by any. For if we receive them all into account, they were more then seven, If only the natural sluces, they were fewer; and however we receive them, there is no agreeable and constant description thereof. And therefore how reasonable it is to draw continual and durable deductions from alterable and uncertain foundations; let them consider who make the gates of *Thebes*, and the mouths of this River a constant and continued periphrasis for this number, and in their Poetical expressions do give the River that Epithet unto this day.

The same River is also accounted the greatest of the earth, called therefore *Fluviorum pater*, and *totius Orbis maximus*, by *Ortelius*: If this be true, many Maps must be corrected, or the relations of divers good Authors renounced.

For first, In the deliniations of many Maps of *Africa*, the River *Niger* exceedeth it about ten degrees in length, that is, no less then six hundred miles. For arising beyond the Æquator it maketh Northward almost 15 degrees, and deflecting after Westward, without Meanders, continueth a strait course about 40 degrees; and at length with many great currents disburdeneth it self into the Occidental Ocean. Again, if we credit the descriptions of the good Authors, other Rivers excell it in length, or breadth, or both. *Arrianus* in his history of *Alexander*, assigneth the first place unto the River *Ganges*; which truly according unto later relations, if not in length, yet in breadth and depth may be granted to excell it. For the magnitude of *Nilus* consisteth in the dimension of longitude, and is inconsiderable in the other; what stream it maintaineth beyond *Syene* or *Asna*, and so forward unto its original, relations are very imperfect; but below these places, and farther removed from the head, the current is but narrow, and we read in the history of the *Turks*, the *Tartar* horsemen of *Selimus*, swam over the *Nile* from *Cairo*, to meet the forces of *Tonumbeus*. *Baptista Scortia* expresly treating hereof, preferreth the River of *Plate* in *America*; for that as *Maffeus* hath delivered, falleth into the Ocean in the latitude of forty leagues; and with that source and plenty that men at Sea doe tast fresh water, before they approach so near as to discover the land. So is it exceeded by that which by *Cardan* is termed the greatest in the world, that is the River *Oregliana* in the same continent; which as *Maginus* delivereth, hath been navigated 6000 miles; and opens in a chanel of ninety leagues broad; so that, as *Acosta*, an ocular witnesse recordeth, they that sail in the middle, can make no land of either side.

Now the ground of this assertion was surely the magnifying esteem of the Ancients, arising from the indiscovery of its head. For as things unknown seem greater then they are, and are usually received with amplifications above their nature; so might it also be with this River, whose head being unknown and drawn to a proverbial obscurity, the opinion thereof became without bounds; and men must needs conceit a large extent of that to which the discovery of no man had set a period. And this an usual way to give the superlative unto things of eminency in any kind; and when a thing is very great, presently to define it to be the greatest of all. Whereas indeed Superlatives are difficult; whereof there being but one in every kind, their determinations are dangerous, and must not be made without great circumspections. So the City of *Rome* is magnified by the *Latins* to be the greatest of the earth; but time and Geography inform us, that *Cairo* is bigger, and *Quinsay* in *China* far exceedeth both. So is *Olympus* extolled by the *Greeks*, as an hill attaining unto heaven; but the enlarged Geography of aftertimes, makes slight account hereof, when they discourse of *Andes* in *Peru*, or *Teneriffa* in the *Canaries*. And we understand by a person who hath lately had a fair opportunity to behold the magnified mount *Olympus*, that it is exceeded by some peakes of the *Alpes*. So have all Ages conceived, and most are still ready to swear, the Wren is the least of Birds; yet the discoveries of *America*, and even of our own Plantations have shewed us one far less, that is, the Humbird, not much exceeding a Beetle. And truly, for the least and greatest, the highest and lowest of every kind, as it is very difficult to define them in visible things; so is it to understand in things invisible. Thus is it no easie lesson to comprehend the first matter, and the affections of that which is next neighbour unto nothing, but impossible truly to comprehend God, who indeed is all in all. For things as they arise unto perfection, and approach unto God, or descend to imperfection, and draw neerer unto nothing, fall both imperfectly into our apprehensions; the one being too weak for our conceptions, our conceptions too weak for the other.

Thirdly, Divers conceptions there are concerning its increment or inundation. The first unwarily opinions, that this encrease or annual overflowing is proper unto *Nile*, and not agreeable unto any other River; which notwithstanding is common unto many Currents of *Africa*. For about the same time the River *Niger* and *Zaire* do overflow; and so do the Rivers beyond the mountains of the Moon, as *Suama*, and *Spirito Santo*. And not only these in *Africa*, but some also in *Europe* and *Asia*; for it is reported of *Menan* in *India*, and so doth *Botero* report of *Duina* in *Livonia*; and the same is also observable in the River *Jordan* in *Judea*; for so it is delivered, that *Jordan* overfloweth all his banks in the time of harvest.

The effect indeed is wonderful in all, and the causes surely best resolvable from observations made in the Countries themselves, the parts through which they pass, or whence they take their Original. That of *Nilus* hath been attempted by Many, and by some to that despair of resolution, that they have only referred it unto the Providence of God, and his secret manuduction of all things unto their ends. But divers have attained the truth, and the cause alledged by *Diodorus*, *Seneca*, *Strabo*, and others, is allowable; that the inundation of *Nilus* in *Egypt* proceeded from the rains in *Æthiopia*, and the mighty source of

470

waters falling towards the fountains thereof. For this inundation unto the *Egyptians* happeneth when it is winter unto the *Æthiopians*; which habitations, although they have no cold Winter (the Sun being no farther removed from them in Cancer, then unto us in Taurus) yet is the fervour of the air so well remitted, as it admits a sufficient generation of vapours, and plenty of showers ensuing thereupon. This Theory of the Ancients is since confirmed by experience of the Moderns; by *Franciscus Alvarez*, who lived long in those parts, and left a description of *Æthiopia*; affirming that from the middle of June unto September, there fell in his time continual rains. As also *Antonius Ferdinandus*, who in an Epistle written from thence, and noted by *Codignus*, affirmeth, that during the winter, in those Countries there passed no day without rain.

Now this is also usual, to translate a remarkable quality into a propriety, and where we admire an effect in one, to opinion there is not the like in any other. With these conceits do common apprehensions entertaine the antidotal and wondrous condition of *Ireland*; conceiving only in that Land an immunity from venemous creatures: but unto him that shall further enquire, the same will be affirmed of *Creta*, memorable in ancient stories, even unto fabulous causes, and benediction from the birth of *Jupiter*. The same is also found in *Ebusus* or *Evisa*, an Island near *Majorca* upon the coast of Spain. With these apprehensions do the eyes of neighbour Spectators behold *Ætna*, the flaming mountain in *Sicilia*; but Navigators tell us there is a burning mountain in Island: a more remarkable one in *Teneriffa* of the *Canaries*, and many Vulcano's or fiery Hils elsewhere. Thus Crocodiles were thought to be peculiar unto *Nile*, and the opinion so possessed *Alexander*, that when he had discovered some in *Ganges*, he fell upon a conceit he had found the head of *Nilus*; but later discoveries affirm they are not only in *Asia* and *Africa*, but very frequent in some rivers of *America*.

Another opinion confineth its Inundation, and positively affirmeth, it constantly encreaseth the seventeenth day of June; wherein perhaps a larger form of speech were safer, then that which punctually prefixeth a constant day thereto. For this expression is different from that of the Ancients, as *Herodotus, Diodorus, Seneca, &c.* delivering only that it happeneth about the entrance of the Sun into Cancer; wherein they warily deliver themselves, and reserve a reasonable latitude. So when *Hippocrates* saith, *Sub Cane & ante Canem difficiles sunt purgationes*; There is a latitude of days comprised therein; for

471

under the Dog-star he containeth not only the day of its ascent, but many following, and some ten days preceding. So *Aristotle* delivers the affections of animals: with the wary terms of *Circa*, & *magna ex parte*: and when *Theodorus* translateth that part of his, *Coeunt Thunni & Scombri mense Februario post Idus, pariunt Junio ante Nonas*: *Scaliger* for *ante Nonas*, renders it *Junii initio*; because that exposition affordeth the latitude of divers days: For affirming it happeneth before the Nones, he alloweth but one day, that is the Calends; for in the *Roman* account, the second day is the fourth of the Nones of June.

Again, Were the day definitive, it had prevented the delusion of the devil, nor could he have gained applause by its prediction; who notwithstanding (as *Athanasius* in the life of *Anthony* relateth) to magnifie his knowledge in things to come, when he perceived the rains to fall in *Æthiopia*, would presage unto the *Egyptians* the day of its inundation. And this would also make useless that natural experiment observed in earth or sand about the River; by the weight whereof (as good Authors report) they have unto this day a knowledge of its increase.

Lastly, It is not reasonable from variable and unstable causes, to derive a fixed and constant effect, and such are the causes of this inundation, which cannot indeed be regular, and therefore their effects not prognosticable like Eclipses. For depending upon the clouds and descent of showers in *Æthiopia*, which have their generation from vaporous exhalations, they must submit their existence unto contingencies, and endure anticipation and recession from the movable condition of their causes. And therefore some years there hath been no encrease at all, as some conceive in the years of Famin under *Pharaoh*, as *Seneca*, and divers relate of the eleventh year of *Cleopatra*; nor nine years together, as is testified by *Calisthenes*. Some years it hath also retarded, and came far later then usually it was expected, as according to *Sozomen* and *Nicephorus* it happened in the days of *Theodosius*; whereat the people were ready to mutiny, because they might not sacrifice unto the River, according to the custom of their Predecessors.

Now this is also an usual way of mistake, and many are deceived who too strictly construe the temporal considerations of things. Thus books will tell us, and we are made to believe that the fourteenth year males are seminifical and pubescent; but he that shall enquire into the generality, will rather adhere unto the cautelous assertion of *Aris-*

totle, that is, *bis septem annis exactis*, and then but *magna ex parte*. That Whelps are blind nine days, and then begin to see, is generally believed, but as we have elsewhere declared, it is exceeding rare, nor do their eye-lids usually open until the twelfth, and sometimes not before the fourteenth day. And to speak strictly, an hazardable determination it is unto fluctuating and indifferent effects, to affix a positive Type or Period. For in effects of far more regular causalities, difficulties do often arise, and even in time it self, which measureth all things, we use allowance in its commensuration. Thus while we conceive we have the account of a year in 365 days, exact enquirers and Computists will tell us, that we escape 6 hours, that is a quarter of a day. And so in a day which every one accounts 24 hours, or one revolution of the Sun; in strict account we must allow the addition of such a part as the Sun doth make in his proper motion, from West to East, whereby in one day he describeth not a perfect Circle.

Fourthly, It is affirmed by many, and received by most, that it never raineth in *Egypt*, the river supplying that defect, and bountifully requiting it in its inundation: but this must also be received in a qualified sense, that is, that it rains but seldom at any time in the Summer, and very rarely in the Winter. But that great showers do sometimes fall upon that Region, beside the Assertion of many Writers, we can confirm that honourable and ocular testimony, and that not many years past, it rained in Grand Cairo divers days together.

The same is also attested concerning other parts of *Egypt*, by *Prosper Alpinus*, who lived long in that Country, and hath left an accurate Treaty of the medical practise thereof. *Cayri raro decidunt pluviæ, Alexandriæ, Pelusiique & in omnibus locis mari adjacentibus, pluit largissime & sæpe*; that is, it raineth seldom at *Cairo*, but at *Alexandria*, *Damiata*, and places near the Sea, it raineth plentifully and often. Whereto we might adde the latter testimony of Learned Mr. *Greaves*, in his accurate description of the *Pyramids*.

Beside, Men hereby forget the relation of holy Scripture. *Behold I will cause it to rain a very great hail, such as hath not been in* Egypt *since the foundation thereof, even untill now*. Wherein God threatning such a rain as had not happened, it must be presumed they had been acquainted with some before, and were not ignorant of the substance, the menace being made in the circumstance. The same concerning hail is inferrible from *Prosper Alpinus*. *Rarissime nix, grando,* it seldom snoweth or haileth. Whereby we must concede that snow and hail do sometimes fall, because they happen seldom.

Now this mistake ariseth from a misapplication of the bounds or limits of time, and an undue transition from one unto another; which to avoid, we must observe the punctual differences of time, and so distinguish thereof, as not to confound or lose the one in the other. For things may come to pass, *Semper, Plerumq;, Sæpe aut Numquam, Aliquando, Raro*; that is, Always, or Never, For the most part, or Sometimes, Ofttimes, or Seldom. Now the deception is usual which is made by the mis-application of these; men presently concluding that to happen often, which happeneth but sometimes: that never, which happeneth but seldom; and that alway, which happeneth for the most part. So is it said, the Sun shines every day in Rhodes, because for the most part it faileth not. So we say and believe that a Camelion never eateth, but liveth only upon air, whereas indeed it is seen to eat very seldom, but many there are who have beheld it to feed on Flyes. And so it is said, that children born in the eighth moneth live not, that is, for the most part, but not to be concluded alwaies: nor it seems in former ages in all places: for it is otherwise recorded by I concerning the births of *Egypt*.

Lastly, It is commonly conceived that divers Princes have attempted to cut the Isthmus or tract of land which parteth the *Arabian* and *Mediterranean* Sea: but upon enquiry I find some difficulty concerning the place attempted; many with good authority affirming, that the intent was not immediately to unite these Seas, but to make a navigable chanel betweene the Red Sea and the Nile, the marks whereof are extant to this day, it was first attempted by *Sesostris*, after by *Darius*, and in a fear to drown the Country, deserted by them both; but was long after re-attempted and in some manner effected by *Philadelphus*. And so the grand Signior who is Lord of the Country, conveyeth his Gallies into the Red Sea by the Nile; for he bringeth them down to Grand *Cairo* where they are taken in pieces, carried upon Camels backs, and rejoyned together at Sues, his port and Naval station for that Sea; whereby in effect he acts the design of *Cleopatra*, who after the battle of *Actium* in a different way would have conveyed her Gallies into the Red Sea.

And therefore that proverb to cut an Isthmus, that is, to take great pains, and effect nothing, alludeth not unto this attempt; but is by

Erasmus applyed unto several other, as that undertaking of the Cnidians to cut their Isthmus, but especially that of *Corinth* so
unsuccessfully attempted by many Emperours. The Cnidians were deterred by the peremptory disswasion of *Apollo*, plainly commanding
them to desist; for if God had thought it fit, he would have made that
Country an Island at first. But this perhaps will not be thought a reasonable discouragement unto the activity of those spirits which
endeavour to advantage nature by Art, and upon good grounds to promote any part of the universe; nor will the ill success of some be made
a sufficient determent unto others; who know that many learned men
affirm, that Islands were not from the beginning: that may have been
made since by Art, that some Isthmus have been eat through by the
Sea, and others cut by the spade: And if policy would permit, that of
Panama in *America* were most worthy the attempt: it being but few
miles over, and would open a shorter cut unto the East Indies and
China.

CHAPTER IX

Of the Red Sea

Contrary apprehensions are made of the Erythræan or Red Sea; most apprehending a material redness therein, from whence they derive its common denomination; and some so lightly conceiving hereof, as if it had no redness at all, are fain to recur unto other originals of its appellation. Wherein to deliver a distinct account, we first observe that without consideration of colour it is named the *Arabian Gulph*: The Hebrews who had best reason to remember it; do call it *Zuph*, or the weedy Sea, because it was full of sedge, or they found it so in their passage; the *Mahometans* who are now Lords thereof do know it by no other name then the *Gulph* of *Mecha* a City of *Arabia*.

The stream of Antiquity deriveth its name from King *Erythrus*; so slightly conceiving of the nominal deduction from Redness, that they plainly deny there is any such accident in it. The words of *Curtius* are plain beyond Evasion, *Ab Erythro rege inditum est nomen, propter quod ignari rubere aquas credunt*: Of no more obscurity are the words of *Philostratus*, and of later times, *Sabellicus*; *Stulte persuasum est vulgo rubras alicubi esse maris aquas, quin ab Erythro rege nomen pelago inditum*. Of this opinion was *Andræas Corsalius*, *Pliny, Solinus, Dio Cassius*, who although they denied not all redness, yet did they rely upon the original from King *Erythrus*.

Others have fallen upon the like, or perhaps the same conceit under another appellation; deducing its name not from King *Erythrus*, but *Esau* or *Edom*, whose habitation was upon the coasts thereof. Now *Edom* is as much as *Erythrus*, and the red Sea no more then the *Idumean*; from whence the posterity of *Edom* removing towards the

Mediterranean coast: according to their former nomination by the Greeks were called *Phœnicians* or red men: and from a plantation and colony of theirs, an Island near Spain, was by the Greek describers termed *Erithra*, as is declared by *Strabo* and *Solinus*.

Very many omitting the nominal derivation, do rest in the gross and literal conception thereof, apprehending a real redness and constant colour of parts. Of which opinion are also they which hold the Sea receiveth a red and minious tincture from springs, wells, and currents that fall into it; and of the same belief are probably many Christians, who conceiving the passage of the *Israelites* through this Sea to have been the type of Baptism, according to that of the Apostle, All were baptised unto *Moses* in the cloud, and in the Sea: for the better resemblance of the blood of Christ, they willingly received it in the apprehension of redness, and a colour agreeable unto its mystery: according unto that of *Austin, Significat mare illud rubrum Baptismum Christi; unde nobis Baptismus Christi nisi sanguine Christi consecratus?*

But divers Moderns not considering these conceptions: and appealing unto the Testimony of sense, have at last determined the point: concluding a redness herein, but not in the sense received. Sir *Walter Raleigh* from his own and *Portugal* observations, doth place the redness of the Sea, in the reflexion from red Islands, and the redness of the earth at the bottom: wherein Coral grows very plentifully, and from whence in great abundance it is transported into *Europe*. The observations of *Albuquerque*, and *Stephanus de Gama* (as from *Johannes de Barros, Fernandius de Cordova* relateth) derive this redness from the colour of the sand and argillous earth at the bottom; for being a shallow Sea, while it rowleth too and fro, there appeareth a redness upon the water; which is most discernable in sunny and windy weather. But that this is no more then a seeming redness, he confirmeth by an experiment; for in the reddest part taking up a vessel of water, it differed not from the complexion of other Seas. Nor is this colour discoverable in every place of that Sea, for as he also observeth, in some places it is very green, in others white and yellow, according to the colour of the earth or sand at the bottom. And so may *Philostratus* be made out, when he saith, this Sea is blew; or *Bellonius* denying this redness, because he beheld not that colour about Sues; or when *Corsalius* at the mouth thereof could not discover the same.

Now although we have enquired the ground of redness in this Sea, yet are we not fully satisfied: for what is forgot by many, and known by few, there is another Red Sea whose name we pretend not to make out from these principles; that is, the *Persian* Gulph or Bay, which divideth the *Arabian* and *Persian* shore, as *Pliny* hath described it, *Mare rubrum in duos dividitur sinus, is qui ab Oriente est Persicus appellatur*; or as *Solinus* expresseth it, *Qui ab Oriente est Persicus appellatur, ex adverso unde Arabia est, Arabicus*; whereto assenteth *Suidas, Ortelius*, and many more. And therefore there is no absurdity in *Strabo* when he delivereth that *Tigris* and *Euphrates* do fall into the Red Sea, and *Fernandius de Cordova*, justly defendeth his Country-man *Seneca* in that expression;

> *Et qui renatum prorsus excipiens diem*
> *Tepidum Rubenti Tigrin immiscet freto.*

Nor hath only the *Persian* Sea received the same name with the *Arabian*, but what is strange, and much confounds the distinction, the name thereof is also derived from King *Erythrus*; who was conceived to be buried in an Island of this Sea, as *Dionysius Afer, Curtius* and *Suidas* do deliver. Which were of no less probability than the other, if (as with the same authors *Strabo* affirmeth) he was buried neer *Caramania* bordering upon the *Persian* Gulph. And if his Tomb was seen by *Nearchus*, it was not so likely to be in the *Arabian* Gulph; for we read that from the River *Indus* he came unto *Alexander* at *Babylon*, some few days before his death. Now *Babylon* was seated upon the River *Euphrates*, which runs into the *Persian* Gulph. And therefore however the Latin expresseth it in *Strabo*, that *Nearchus* suffered much in the *Arabian Sinus*, yet is the original κόλπος πέρσικος, that is the Gulf of *Persia*.

That therefore the Red Sea or *Arabian* Gulph received its name from personal derivation, though probable, is but uncertain; that both the Seas of one name should have one common denominator, less probable; that there is a gross and material redness in either, not to be affirmed: that there is an emphatical or appearing redness in one, not well to be denied. And this is sufficient to make good the Allegory of the Christians: and in this distinction may we justifie the name of the Black Sea, given unto *Pontus Euxinus*: the name of *Xanthus*, or the yellow River of *Phrygia*: and the name of *Mar Vermeio*, or the Red Sea in *America*.

CHAPTER X

Of the Blackness of Negroes

It is evident not only in the general frame of Nature, that things most manifest unto sense, have proved obscure unto the understanding: But even in proper and appropriate Objects, wherein we affirm the sense cannot err, the faculties of reason most often fail us. Thus of colours in general, under whose gloss and vernish all things are seen, few or none have yet beheld the true nature; or positively set down their incontroulable causes. Which while some ascribe unto the mixture of the Elements, others to the graduality of Opacity and Light; they have left our endeavours to grope them out by twi-light, and by darkness almost to discover that whose existence is evidenced by Light. The *Chymists* have laudably reduced their causes unto Sal, Sulphur, and Mercury; and had they made it out so well in this, as in the objects of smell and tast, their endeavours had been more acceptable: For whereas they refer Sapor unto Salt, and Odor unto Sulphur, they vary much concerning colour; some reducing it unto Mercury, some to Sulphur; others unto Salt. Wherein indeed the last conceit doth not oppress the former; and though Sulphur seem to carry the master-stroak, yet Salt may have a strong co-operation. For beside the fixed and terrestrious Salt, there is in natural bodies a *Sal niter* referring unto Sulphur; there is also a volatile or Armoniack Salt, retaining unto Mercury; by which Salts the colours of bodies are sensibly qualified, and receive degrees of lustre or obscurity, superficiality or profundity, fixation or volatility.

Their general or first Natures being thus obscure, there will be greater difficulties in their particular discoveries; for being farther removed from their simplicities, they fall into more complexed considerations; and so require a subtiler act of reason to distinguish and call forth their natures. Thus although a man understood the general nature of colours, yet were it no easie Problem to resolve, Why Grass is green? Why Garlick, Molyes, and Porrets have white roots, deep green leaves, and black seeds? Why several docks and sorts of Rhubarb with yellow roots, send forth purple flowers? Why also from Lactary or milky plants which have a white and lacteous juyce dispersed through every part, there arise flowers blew and yellow? Moreover, beside the specifical and first digressions ordained from the Creation, which might be urged to salve the variety in every species; Why shall the marvail of *Peru* produce its flowers of different colours, and that not once, or constantly, but every day, and variously? Why Tulips of one colour produce some of another, and running through almost all, should still escape a blew? And lastly, Why some men, yea and they a mighty and considerable part of mankind, should first acquire and still retain the gloss and tincture of blackness? Which whoever strictly enquires, shall finde no lesse of darkness in the cause, than in the effect it self; there arising unto examination no such satisfactory and unquarrelable reasons, as may confirm the causes generally received; which are but two in number. The heat and scorch of the Sun; or the curse of God on *Cham* and his Posterity.

The first was generally received by the Ancients, who in obscurities had no higher recourse than unto Nature, as may appear by a Discourse concerning this point in *Strabo*. By *Aristotle* it seems to be implied in those Problems which enquire why the Sun makes men black, and not the fire? Why it whitens wax, yet blacks the skin? By the word *Æthiops* it self, applied to the memorablest Nations of *Negroes*, that is of a burnt and torrid countenance. The fancy of the Fable infers also the Antiquity of the opinion; which deriveth this complexion from the deviation of the Sun, and the conflagration of all things under *Phaeton*. But this opinion though generally embraced, was I perceive rejected by *Aristobulus* a very ancient Geographer; as is discovered by *Strabo*. It hath been doubted by several modern Writers, particularly by *Ortelius*; but amply and satisfactorily discussed as we know by no man. We shall therefore endeavour a full delivery hereof, declaring the grounds of doubt, and reasons of denial, which rightly understood, may, if not overthrow, yet shrewdly shake the security of this Assertion.

And first, Many which countenance the opinion in this reason, do tacitly and upon consequence overthrow it in another. For whilst they make the River *Senaga* to divide and bound the *Moors*, so that on the South-side they are black, on the other only tawny; they implie a secret causality herein from the air, place or river; and seem not to derive it from the Sun. The effects of whose activity are not precipitously abrupted, but gradually proceed to their cessations.

Secondly, If we affirm that this effect proceeded, or as we will not be backward to concede, it may be advanced and fomented from the fervour of the Sun; yet do we not hereby discover a principle sufficient to decide the question concerning other animals; nor doth he that affirmeth that heat makes man black, afford a reason why other animals in the same habitations maintain a constant and agreeable hue unto those in other parts, as Lions, Elephants, Camels, Swans, Tigers, Estriges. Which though in *Æthiopia*, in the disadvantage of two Summers, and perpendicular Rayes of the Sun, do yet make good the complexion of their species, and hold a colourable correspondence unto those in milder regions. Now did this complexion proceed from heat in man, the same would be communicated unto other animals which equally participate the Influence of the common Agent. For thus it is in the effects of cold, in Regions far removed from the Sun; for therein men are not only of faire complexions, gray-eyed, and of light hair; but many creatures exposed to the air, deflect in extremity from their natural colours; from brown, russet and black, receiving the complexion of Winter, and turning perfect White. Thus *Olaus Magnus* relates, that after the Autumnal Æquinox, Foxes begin to grow white; thus *Michovius* reporteth, and we want not ocular confirmation, that Hares and Partridges turn white in the Winter; and thus a white Crow, a proverbial rarity with us, is none unto them; but that inseparable accident of *Porphyrie* is separated in many hundreds.

Thirdly, If the fervour of the Sun, or intemperate heat of clime did solely occasion this complexion, surely a migration or change thereof might cause a sensible, if not a total mutation; which notwithstanding experience will not admit. For *Negroes* transplanted, although into cold and flegmatick habitations, continue their hue both in themselves, and also their generations; except they mix with different complexions; whereby notwithstanding there only succeeds a remission of their tinctures; there remaining unto many descents a strong shadow of their Originals; and if they preserve their copulations entire, they still maintain their complexions. As is very remarkable in the dominions of the Grand Signior, and most observable in the *Moors* in *Brasilia*, which transplanted about an hundred years past, continue the tinctures of their fathers unto this day. And so likewise fair or white people translated into hotter Countries receive not impressions amounting to this complexion, as hath been observed in many *Europeans* who have lived in the land of *Negroes*: and as *Edvardus Lopes* testifieth of the *Spanish* plantations, that they retained their native complexions unto his days.

Fourthly, If the fervour of the Sun were the sole cause hereof in *Ethiopia* or any land of *Negroes*; it were also reasonable that Inhabitants of the same latitude, subjected unto the same vicinity of the Sun, the same diurnal arch, and direction of its rayes, should also partake of the same hue and complexion, which notwithstanding they do not. For the Inhabitants of the same latitude in *Asia* are of a different complexion, as are the Inhabitants of *Cambogia* and *Java*, insomuch that some conceive the *Negro* is properly a native of *Africa*, and that those places in *Asia* inhabited now by *Moors*, are but the intrusions of *Negroes* arriving first from *Africa*, as we generally conceive of *Madagascar*, and the adjoyning Islands, who retain the same complexion unto this day. But this defect is more remarkable in *America*; which although subjected unto both the Tropicks, yet are not the Inhabitants black between, or near, or under either: neither to the South-ward in *Brasilia*, *Chili*, or *Peru*; nor yet to the Northward in *Hispaniola*, *Castilia del Oro*, or *Nicaragua*. And although in many parts thereof there be at present swarms of *Negroes* serving under the *Spaniard*, yet were they all transported from *Africa*, since the discovery of *Columbus*; and are not indigenous or proper natives of *America*.

Fifthly, We cannot conclude this complexion in Nations from the vicinity or habitude they hold unto the Sun; for even in *Africa* they be Negroes under the Southern Tropick, but are not all of this hue either under or near the Northern. So the people of *Gualata*, *Agades*, *Garamantes*, and of *Goaga*, all within the Northern Tropicks are not *Negroes*; but on the other side about *Capo Negro*, *Cefala*, and *Madagascar*, they are of a jetty black.

Now if to salve this Anomaly we say the heat of the Sun is more powerful in the Southern Tropick, because in the sign of Capricorne fals out the Perigeum or lowest place of the Sun in his

482

Excentrick, whereby he becomes nearer unto them than unto the other in Cancer, we shall not absolve the doubt. And if any insist upon such niceties, and will presume a different effect of the Sun, from such a difference of place or vicinity; we shall ballance the same with the concernment of its motion, and time of revolution, and say he is more powerful in the Northern Hemisphere, and in the Apogeum; for therein his motion is slower, and so his heat respectively unto those habitations, as of duration, so also of more effect. For, though he absolve his revolution in 365 days, odd hours and minutes, yet by reason of Excentricity, his motion is unequal, and his course far longer in the Northern Semicircle, than in the Southern; for the latter he passeth in 178 days, but the other takes him 187, that is, eleven days more. So is his presence more continued unto the Northern Inhabitants; and the longest day in Cancer is longer unto us, than that in Capricorn unto the Southern Habitator. Beside, hereby we only infer an inequality of heat in different Tropicks, but not an equality of effects in other parts subjected to the same. For, in the same degree, and as near the earth he makes his revolution unto the *American*, whose Inhabitants notwithstanding partake not of the same effect. And if herein we seek a relief from the Dog-star, we shall introduce an effect proper unto a few, from a cause common unto many; for upon the same grounds that Star should have as forcible a power upon *America* and *Asia*, and although it be not vertical unto any part of *Asia*, but only passeth by *Beach, in terra incognita*; yet is it so unto *America*, and vertically passeth over the habitations of *Peru* and *Brasilia*.

Sixthly, And which is very considerable, there are *Negroes* in *Africa* beyond the Southerne Tropick, and some are so far removed from it, as Geographically the clime is not intemperate, that is, near the cape of good Hope, in 36 of Southern Latitude. Whereas in the same elevation Northward, the Inhabitants of *America* are fair; and they of *Europe* in *Candy, Sicily*, and some parts of *Spain*, deserve not properly so low a name as *Tawny*.

Lastly, Whereas the *Africans* are conceived to be more peculiarly scorched and torrified from the Sun, by addition of driness from the soil, from want and defect of water; it will not excuse the doubt. For the parts which the *Negroes* possess, are not so void of Rivers and moisture, as is presumed; for on the other side the mountains of the Moon, in that great tract called *Zanzibar*, there are the mighty Rivers of *Suama*, and *Spirito Sancto*; on this side, the great River *Zaire*, the

483

mighty *Nile* and *Niger*; which do not only moisten and contemperate the air by their exhalations, but refresh and humectate the earth by their annual Inundations. Beside, in that part of *Africa*, which with all disadvantage is most dry, that is, in situation between the Tropicks, defect of Rivers and inundations, as also abundance of Sands, the people are not esteemed *Negroes*; and that is *Lybia*, which with the *Greeks* carries the name of all *Africa*. A region so desert, dry and sandy, that Travellers (as *Leo* reports) are fain to carry water on their Camels; whereof they find not a drop sometime in six or seven days. Yet is this Country accounted by Geographers no part of *terra Nigritarum*, and *Ptolomy* placeth herein the *Leuco Æthiops,*or pale and Tawny Moors.

Now the ground of this opinion might be the visible quality of Blackness observably produced by heat, fire, and smoak; but especially with the Ancients the violent esteem they held of the heat of the Sun, in the hot or torrid Zone; conceiving that part unhabitable, and therefore that people in the vicinities or frontiers thereof, could not escape without this change of their complexions. But how far they were mistaken in this apprehension, modern Geography hath discovered: And as we have declared, there are many within this Zone whose complexions descend not so low as unto blackness. And if we should strictly insist hereon, the possibility might fall into question; that is, whether the heat of the Sun, whose fervour may swart a living part, and even black a dead or dissolving flesh; can yet in animals, whose parts are successive and in continual flux, produce this deep and perfect gloss of Blackness.

Thus having evinced, at least made dubious, the Sun is not the Author of this blackness, how and when this tincture first began is yet a Riddle, and positively to determine it surpasseth my presumption. Seeing therefore we cannot discover what did effect it, it may afford some piece of satisfaction to know what might procure it. It may be therefore considered, whether the inward use of certain waters or fountains of peculiar operations, might not at first produce the effect in question. For, of the like we have records in *Aristotle*, *Strabo*, and *Pliny*, who hath made a collection hereof, as of two fountains in Bœotia, the one making Sheep white, the other black; of the water of *Siberis* which made Oxen black, and the like effect it had also upon men, dying not only the skin, but making their hairs black and curled. This was the conceit of *Aristobulus*, who received so little satisfaction

484

from the other, or that it might be caused by heat, or any kind of fire, that he conceived it as reasonable to impute the effect unto water.

Secondly, It may be perpended whether it might not fall out the same way that *Jacobs* cattle became speckled, spotted and ringstraked, that is, by the Power and Efficacy of Imagination; which produceth effects in the conception correspondent unto the phancy of the Agents in generation; and sometimes assimilates the Idea of the Generator into a realty in the thing ingendred. For, hereof there pass for currant many indisputed examples; so in *Hippocrates* we read of one, that from an intent view of a Picture conceived a Negro. And in this History of *Heliodore* of a Moorish Queen, who upon aspection of the Picture of *Andromeda*, conceived and brought forth a fair one. And thus perhaps might some say was the beginning of this complexion: induced first by Imagination, which having once impregnated the seed, found afterward concurrent co-operations, wh^{ch} were continued by Climes, whose constitution advantaged the first impression. Thus *Plotinus* conceiveth white Peacocks first came in. Thus many opinion that from aspection of the Snow, wh^{ch} lyeth long in Northern Regions, and high mountains, Hawks, Kites, Beares, and other creatures become white; and by this way *Austin* conceiveth the devil provided, they never wanted a white spotted Ox in *Egypt*; for such an one they worshipped, and called *Apis*.

Thirdly, It is not indisputable whether it might not proceed from such a cause and the like foundation of Tincture, as doth the black Jaundice, which meeting with congenerous causes might settle durable inquinations, and advance their generations unto that hue, which were naturally before but a degree or two below it. And this transmission we shall the easier admit in colour, if we remember the like hath beene effected in organical parts and figures; the Symmetry whereof being casually or purposely perverted; their morbosites have vigorously descended to their posterities, and that in durable deformities. This was the beginning of *Macrocephali*, or people with long heads, whereof *Hippocrates* hath clearly delivered himself: *Cum primum editus est Infans, caput ejus temellum manibus effingunt, & in longitudine adolescere cogunt; hoc institutum primum hujusmodi, naturæ dedit vitium, successu vero temporis in naturam abiit, ut proinde instituto nihil amplius opus esset; semen enim genitale ex omnibus corporis partibus provenit, ex sanis quidem sanum, ex morbosis morbosum. Si igitur ex caluis calvi, ex cæciis cæcii, & ex distortis, ut plurimum, distorti gignuntur, eademque in cæteris formis valet ratio, quid prohibet cur non ex macrocephalis macrocephali gignantur?* Thus as *Aristotle* observeth, the Deers of *Arginusa* had their ears divided; occasioned at first by slitting the ears of Deer. Thus have the *Chineses* little feet, most *Negroes* great Lips and flat Noses; And thus many *Spaniards*, and *Mediterranean* Inhabitants, which are of the race of *Barbary Moors* (although after frequent commixture) have not worne out the *Camoys* Nose unto this day.

Artificial *Negroes*, or *Gypsies* acquire their complexion by anointing their bodies with Bacon and fat substances, and so exposing them to the Sun. In *Guiny Moors* and others, it hath been observed, that they frequently moisten their skins with fat and oyly materials, to temper the irksom drines thereof from the parching rayes of the Sun. Whether this practise at first had not some efficacy toward this complexion, may also be considered.

Lastly, If we still be urged to particularities, and such as declare how, and when the seed of *Adam* did first receive this tincture; we may say that men became black in the same manner that some Foxes, Squirrels, Lions, first turned of this complexion, whereof there are a constant sort in divers Countries; that some Chaughs came to have red Legs and Bils, that Crows became pyed: All which mutations however they began, depend on durable foundations; and such as may continue for ever. And if as yet we must farther define the cause and manner of this mutation, we must confess, in matters of Antiquity, and such as are decided by History, if their Originals and first beginnings escape a due relation, they fall into great obscurities, and such as future Ages seldom reduce unto a resolution. Thus if you deduct the administration of Angels, and that they dispersed the creatures into all parts after the flood, as they had congregated them into *Noahs* Ark before; it will be no easie question to resolve, how several sorts of animals were first dispersed into Islands, and almost how any into *America*: How the venereal Contagion began in that part of the earth, since history is silent, is not easily resolved by Philosophy. For whereas it is imputed unto Anthropophagy, or the eating of mans flesh; that cause hath been common unto many other Countries, and there have beene Canibals or men eaters in the three other parts of the world, if we credit the relations of *Ptolomy*, *Strabo* and *Pliny*. And thus if the favourable pen of *Moses* had not revealed the confusion of tongues, and positively declared their division at *Babel*; our disputes concerning their beginning had been without end; and I fear we must have left the hopes of that decision unto *Elias*.

And if any will yet insist, and urge the question farther still upon me, I shall be enforced unto divers of the like nature, wherein perhaps I shall receive no greater satisfaction. I shall demand how the Camels of *Bactria* came to have two bunches on their backs, whereas the Camels of *Arabia* in all relations have but one? How Oxen in some Countries began and continue gibbous or bunch-back'd? what way those many different shapes, colours, hairs, and natures of Dogs came in? how they of some Countries became depilous, and without any hair at all, whereas some sorts in excess abound therewith? How the Indian Hare came to have a long tail, whereas that part in others attains no higher then a scut? How the hogs of *Illyria* which *Aristotle* speaks of, became solipedes or whole-hoofed, whereas in other parts they are bisulcous, and described cloven-hoofed by God himself? All which with many others must needs seem strange unto those that hold there were but two of the unclean sort in the ark; and are forced to reduce these varieties to unknown originals.

However therefore this complexion was first acquired, it is evidently maintained by generation, and by the tincture of the skin as a spermatical part traduced from father unto Son; so that they which are strangers contract it not, and the Natives which transmigrate, omit it not without commixture, and that after divers generations. And this affection (if the story were true) might wonderfully be confirmed, by what *Maginus* and others relate of the Emperour of *Æthiopia*, or *Prester John*, who derived from *Solomon* is, not yet descended into the hue of his Country, but remains a *Mulatto*, that is, of a Mongril complexion unto this day. Now although we conceive this blackness to be seminal, yet are we not of *Herodotus* conceit, that their seed is black. An opinion long ago rejected by *Aristotle*, and since by sense and enquiry. His assertion against the Historian was probable, that all seed was white; that is, without great controversy in viviparous Animals, and such as have Testicles, or preparing vessels wherein it receives a manifest dealbation. And not only in them but (for ought I know) in Fishes not abating the seed of Plants, whereof at least in most though the skin and covering be black, yet is the seed and fructifying part not so: and may be observed in the seeds of *Onyons*, *Pyonie*, and *Basil*. Most controvertible it seems, in the spawn of Frogs, and Lobsters, whereof notwithstanding at the very first the spawn is white, contracting by degrees a blackness, answerable in the one unto the colour of the shell, in the other unto the Porwigle or Tadpole; that is that Animall which first proceedeth from it. And thus may it also be in the generation and sperm of Negroes; that being first and in its naturals white, but upon separation of parts, accidents before invisible become apparent; there arising a shadow or dark efflorescence in the out-side; whereby not only their legitimate and timely births, but their abortions are also dusky, before they have felt the scorch and fervor of the Sun.

CHAPTER XI

Of the same

A second opinion there is, that this complexion was first a curse of God derived unto them from *Cham*, upon whom it was inflicted for discovering the nakedness of Noah. Which notwithstanding is sooner affirmed then proved, and carrieth with it sundry improbabilities. For first, if we derive the curse on *Cham*, or in general upon his posterity, we shall denigrate a greater part of the earth then was ever so conceived; and not onely paint the Æthiopians and reputed sons of *Cush*, but the people also of *Egypt, Arabia, Assyria*, and *Chaldea*; for by his race were these Countries also peopled. And if concordantly unto *Berosus*, the fragment of *Cato de Originibus*, some things of *Halicarnasseus, Macrobius*, and out of them of *Leandro* and *Annius*, we shall conceive of the travels of *Camese* or *Cham*; we may introduce a generation of *Negroes* as high as *Italy*; which part was never culpable of deformity, but hath produced the magnified examples of beauty.

Secondly, The curse mentioned in Scripture was not denounced upon *Cham*, but *Canaan* his youngest son, and the reasons thereof are divers. The first, from the Jewish Tradition, whereby it is conceived, that *Canaan* made the discovery of the nakedness of *Noah*, and notified it unto *Cham*. Secondly, to have cursed *Cham* had been to curse all his posterity, whereof but one was guilty of the fact. And lastly, he spared *Cham*, because he had blessed him before. Now if we confine this curse unto *Canaan*, and think the same fulfilled in his posterity; then do we induce this complexion on the Sidonians, then was the promised land a tract of Negroes; For from Canaan were descended the *Canaanites*, *Jebusites*, *Amorites*, *Gergazites*, and *Hivites*, which were possessed of that land.

Thirdly, Although we should place the original of this curse upon one of the sons of *Cham*, yet were it not known from which of them to derive it. For the particularity of their descents is imperfectly set down by accountants, nor is it distinctly determinable from whom thereof the *Æthiopians* are proceeded. For, whereas these of *Africa* are generally esteemed to be the Issue of *Chus*, the elder son of *Cham*, it is not so easily made out. For the land of *Chus*, which the Septuagint translates *Æthiopia*, makes no part of *Africa*, nor is it the habitation of Blackmores, but the Country of *Arabia*, especially the Happy and Stony, possessions and Colonies of all the sons of *Chus*, excepting *Nimrod*, and *Havilah*: possessed and planted wholly by the children of *Chus*, that is, by *Sabtah* and *Raamah*, *Sabtacha*, and the sons of *Raamah*, *Dedan*, and *Sheba*, according unto whose names the Nations of those parts have received their denominations, as may be collected from *Pliny* and *Ptolomy*; and as we are informed by credible Authors, they hold a fair Analogy in their names, even unto our days. So the wife of *Moses* translated in Scripture an *Æthiopian*, and so confirmed by the fabulous relation of *Josephus*, was none of the daughters of *Africa*, nor any Negroe of *Æthiopia*, but the daughter of *Jethro*, Prince and Priest of *Madian*, which was a part of *Arabia* the stony, bordering upon the Red Sea. So the Queen of *Sheba* came not unto *Solomon* out of *Æthiopia*, but from *Arabia*, and that part thereof which bore the name of the first planter, the son of *Chus*. So whether the Eunuch which *Philip* the Deacon baptised, were servant unto *Candace* Queen of the *African Æthiopia* (although *Damianus à Goes*, *Codignus*, and the Æthiopick relations averr) is yet by many, and with strong suspicions doubted. So that Army of a million, which *Zerah* King of *Æthiopia* is said to bring against *Asa*, was drawn out of *Arabia*, and the plantations of *Chus*, not out of *Æthiopia*, and the remote habitations of the Moors. For it is said that *Asa* pursuing his victory, tooke from him the city of *Gerar*; now *Gerar* was no City in or near *Æthiopia*, but a place between *Cadesh* and *Zur*, where *Abraham* formerly sojourned. Since therefore these *African Æthiopians* are not convinced by the common acception to be the sons of *Chus*, whether they be not the posterity of *Phut*, or *Mizraim*, or both, it is not assuredly determined. For *Mizraim*, he possessed *Egypt*, and the East parts of *Africa*. From *Lubym* his son came the *Lybians*, and perhaps from them the *Æthiopians*. *Phut* possessed *Mauritania*, and the Western parts of *Af-*

rica and from these perhaps descended the Moors of the West, of *Mandinga*, *Meleguette* and *Guinie*. But from *Canaan*, upon whom the curse was pronounced, none of these had their original; for he was restrained unto *Canaan* and *Syria*; although in after Ages many Colonies dispersed, and some thereof upon the coasts of *Africa*, and prepossessions of his elder brothers.

Fourthly, To take away all doubt or any probable divarication, the curse is plainly specified in the Text, nor need we dispute it, like the mark of *Cain*; *Servus servorum erit fratribus suis*, Cursed be *Canaan*, a servant of servants shall he be unto his brethren; which was after fulfilled in the conquest of *Canaan*, subdued by the *Israelites*, the posterity of *Sem*. Which Prophecy *Abraham* well understanding, took an oath of his servant not to take a wife for his son *Isaac* out of the daughters of the *Canaanites*; and the like was performed by *Isaac* in the behalf of his Son *Jacob*. As for *Cham* and his other sons this curse attained them not; for *Nimrod* the son of *Chus* set up his kingdom in *Babylon*, and erected the first great Empire; *Mizraim* and his posterity grew mighty Monarchs in *Elgypt*; and the Empire of the *Æthiopians* hath been as large as either. Nor did the curse descend in generall upon the posterity of *Canaan*: for the *Sidonians*, *Arkites*, *Hamathites*, *Sinites*, *Arvadites*, and *Zemarites* seem exempted. But why there being eleven Sons, five only were condemned and six escaped the malediction, is a secret beyond discovery.

Lastly, Whereas men affirm this colour was a Curse, I cannot make out the propriety of that name, it neither seeming so to them, nor reasonably unto us; for they take so much content therein, that they esteem deformity by other colours, describing the Devil, and terrible objects, white. And if we seriously consult the definitions of beauty, and exactly perpend what wise men determine thereof, we shall not apprehend a curse, or any deformity therein. For first, some place the essence thereof in the proportion of parts, conceiving it to consist in a comely commensurability of the whole unto the parts, and the parts between themselves: which is the determination of the best and learned Writers. Now hereby the Moors are not excluded from beauty: there being in this description no consideration of colours, but an apt connexion and frame of parts and the whole. Others there be, and those most in number, which place it not only in proportion of parts, but also in grace of colour. But to make Colour essential unto Beauty, there will arise no slender difficulty: For *Aristotle* in two definitions of pulchritude, and *Galen* in one, have made no mention of colour. Neither will it agree unto the Beauty of Animals: wherein notwithstanding there is an approved pulchritude. Thus horses are handsome under any colour, and the symmetry of parts obscures the consideration of complexions. Thus in concolour animals and such as are confined unto one colour we measure not their Beauty thereby; for if a Crow or Blackbird grow white, we generally account it more pretty: And in almost a monstrosity descend not to opinion of deformity. By this way likewise the Moors escape the curse of deformity: there concurring no stationary colour, and sometimes not any unto Beauty.

The Platonick contemplators reject both these descriptions founded upon parts and colours, or either: as *M. Leo* the Jew hath excellently discoursed in his Genealogy of Love, defining beauty a formal grace, which delights and moves them to love which comprehend it. This grace say they, discoverable outwardly, is the resplendor and Ray of some interiour and invisible Beauty, and proceedeth from the forms of compositions amiable. Whose faculties if they can aptly contrive their matter, they beget in the subject an agreeable and pleasing beauty; if over-ruled thereby, they evidence not their perfections, but run into deformity. For seeing that out of the same materials, *Thersites* and *Paris*, Beauty and monstrosity may be contrived; the forms and operative faculties introduce and determine their perfections. Which in natural bodies receive exactness in every kind, according to the first *Idea* of the Creator, and in contrived bodies the phancy of the Artificer. And by this consideration of Beauty, the Moors also are not excluded, but hold a common share therein with all mankind.

Lastly, In whatsoever its *Theory* consisteth, or if in the general, we allow the common conceit of symmetry and of colour, yet to descend unto singularities, or determine in what symmetry or colour it consisted, were a slippery designation. For Beauty is determined by opinion, and seems to have no essence that holds one notion with all; that seeming beauteous unto one, which hath no favour with another; and that unto every one, according as custome hath made it natural, or sympathy and conformity of minds shall make it seem agreeable. Thus flat noses seem comely unto the Moor, an Aquiline or hawked one unto the *Persian*, a large and prominent nose unto the Romane; but none of all these are acceptable in our opinion. Thus some think it most ornamental to weare their Bracelets on their Wrests, others say it is better to have them about their Ancles; some think it most comely to wear their Rings and Jewels in the Ear, others will have them about their Privities; a third will not think they are compleat except they hang them in their lips, cheeks, or noses. Thus *Homer* to set off *Minerva* calleth her γλαυκoπις, that is gray or light-blew eyed: now this unto us seems far less amiable then the black. Thus we that are of contrary complexions accuse the blackness of the Moors as ugly: But the Spouse in the *Canticles* excuseth this conceit, in that description of hers, I am black, but comely. And howsoever *Cerberus*, and the furies of hell be described by the Poets under this complexion, yet in the beauty of our Saviour blackness is commended, when it is said, his locks are bushie and black as a Raven. So that to inferr this as a curse, or to reason it as a deformity, is no way reasonable; the two foundations of beauty, Symmetry and complexion, receiving such various apprehensions; that no deviation will be expounded so high as a curse or undeniable deformity, without a manifest and confessed degree of monstrosity.

Lastly, It is a very injurious method unto Philosophy, and a perpetual promotion of Ignorance, in points of obscurity, nor open unto easie considerations, to fall upon a present refuge unto Miracles; or recurr unto immediate contrivance, from the insearchable hands of God. Thus in the conceit of the evil odor of the Jews, Christians without a farther research into the verity of the thing, or inquiry into the cause, draw up a judgement upon them from the passion of their Saviour. Thus in the wondrous effects of the clime of *Ireland*, and the freedom from all venemous creatures, the credulity of common conceit imputes this immunity unto the benediction of S. *Patrick*, as *Beda* and *Gyraldus* have left recorded. Thus the Ass having a peculiar mark of a cross made by a black list down his back, and another athwart, or at right angles down his shoulders; common opinion ascribes this figure unto a peculiar signation; since that beast had the honour to bear our Saviour on his back. Certainly this is a course more desperate then Antipathies, Sympathies, or occult qualities; wherein by a final and satisfactive discernment of faith, we lay the last and particular effects upon the first and general cause of all things; whereas in the other, we do but palliate our determinations; until our advanced endeavours do totally reject, or partially salve their evasions.

CHAPTER XII

A Digression concerning Blackness

There being therefore two opinions repugnant unto each other, it may not be presumptive or skeptical to doubt of both. And because we remain imperfect in the general Theory of colours, we shall deliver at present a short discovery of blackness; wherein although perhaps we afford no greater satisfaction then others, yet shall we Emperically and sensibly discourse hereof; deducing the causes of Blackness from such Originals in nature, as we do generally observe things are denigrated by Art. And herein I hope our progression will not be thought unreasonable, for Art being the imitation of Nature, or Nature at the second hand: it is but a sensible expression of effects dependant on the same, though more removed causes: and therefore the works of the one may serve to discover the other. And though colours of bodies may arise according to the receptions, refraction, or modification of Light; yet are there certain materialls which may dispose them unto such qualities.

And first, Things become black by a sootish and fuliginous matter proceeding from the Sulphur of bodies torrified; not taking *fuligo* strictly, but in opposition unto ἀτμίς, that is any kind of vaporous or madefying excretion; and comprehending ἀναθυμίασις, that is as *Aristotle* defines it, a separation of moist and dry parts made by the action of heat or fire, and colouring bodies objected. Hereof in his Meteors, from the qualities of the subject he raiseth three kinds; the exhalations from ligneous and lean bodies, as bones, hair, and the like he calleth κάπνος, *fumus*, from fat bodies, and such as have not their fatness conspicuous or separated he termeth λίγνυς, *fuligo*, as wax, rosin, pitch, or turpentine; that from unctuous bodies, and such whose oyliness is evident, he nameth κνίσσα or *nidor*. Now every one of these do black bodies objected unto them, and are to be conceived in the sooty and fuliginous matter expressed.

I say, proceeding from the sulphur of bodies torrified, that is the oylie, fat, and unctuous parts wherein consist the principles of flammability. Not pure and refined sulphur, as in the Spirits of wine often rectified; but containing terrestrious parts, and carrying with it the volatile salt of the body, and such as is distinguishable by taste in soot; nor vulgar and usual sulphur, for that leaves none or very little blackness, except a metalline body receive the exhalation.

I say, torrified, sindged, or suffering some impression from fire; thus are bodies casually or artificially denigrated, which in their naturals are of another complexion; thus are Charcoals made black by an infection of their own suffitus, so is it true what is affirmed of combustible bodies. *Adusta nigra, perusta alba*; black at first from the fuliginous tincture, which being exhaled they become white, as is perceptible in ashes. And so doth fire cleanse and purifie bodies, which will never be mundified by water. Thus Camphire of a white substance, by its *fuligo* affordeth a deep black. So is pitch black, although it proceed from the same tree with Rosin, the one distilling forth, the other forced by fire. So of the suffitus of a torch, do Painters make a velvet black: so is lamp-black made: so of burnt Harts-horn a sable; so is Bacon denigrated in chimnies: so in Feavers and hot distempers from choler adust is caused a blackness in our tongues, teeth and excretions: so are ustilago, brant corn and trees black by blasting; so parts cauterized, gangrenated, siderated and mortified, become black, the radical moisture, or vital sulphur suffering an extinction, and smothered in the part affected. So not only actual but potential fire: not burning fire, but also corroding water will induce a blackness. So are Chimnies and Furnaces generally black, except they receive a clear and manifest sulphur: for the smoak of sulphur will not black a paper, and is commonly used by women to whiten Tiffanies, which it performeth by an acide vitriolous, and penetrating spirit ascending from it, by reason whereof it is not apt to kindle any thing nor will it easily light a Candle, untill that spirit be spent, and the flame approacheth the match. This is that acide and piercing spirit which with such activity and compunction invadeth the brains and nostrils of those that receive it. And thus when *Bellonius* affirmeth that Charcoals made out of the wood of Oxycedar are white, Dr. *Jordan* in his judicious Discourse of mineral waters yeeldeth the reason, because their vapours are rather sulphureous then of any other combustible substance. So we see that *Tinby* coals will not black linnen being hanged in the smoak thereof, but rather whiten it, by reason of the drying and penetrating quality of sulphur, which will make red Roses white. And therefore to conceive a general blackness in Hell, and yet therein the pure and refined flames of sulphur, is no Philosophical conception, nor will it well consist with the real effects of its nature.

These are the advenient and artificial wayes of denigration, answerably whereto may be the natural progress. These are the wayes wherby culinary and common fires do operate, and correspondent hereunto may be the effects of fire elemental. So may Bitumen, Coals, Jet, Black-lead, and divers mineral earths become black; being either fuliginous concretions in the earth, or suffering a scorch from denigrating Principles in their formation. So men and other animals receive different tinctures from constitution and complexional efflorescences, and descend still lower, as they partake of the fuliginous and denigrating humor. And so may the *Æthiopians* or *Negroes* become coalblack, from fuliginous efflorescences and complexional tinctures arising from such probabilities, as we have declared before.

The second way whereby bodies become black, is an Atramentous condition or mixture, that is a vitriolate or copperose quality conjoyning with a terrestrious and astringent humidity; for so is *Atramentum Scriptorium*, or writing Ink commonly made by copperose cast upon a decoction or infusion of galls. I say a vitriolous or copperous quality; for vitriol is the active or chief ingredient in Ink, and no other salt that I know will strike the colour with galls; neither Alom, Sal-gem, Nitre, nor Armoniack. Now artificial copperose, and such as we commonly use, is a rough and acrimonious kind of salt drawn out of ferreous and eruginous earths, partaking chiefly of Iron and Copper; the blew of copper, the green most of Iron: Nor is it unusual to dissolve fragments of Iron in the liquor thereof, for advantage in the concretion. I say, a terrestrious or astringent humidity; for without this there will ensue no tincture; for Copperose in a decoction of Lettuce or Mallows affords no black, which with an astringent mixture it will do, although it be made up with oyl, as in printing and painting Ink. But whereas in this composition we use only Nut-gals, that is an excrescence from the Oak, therein we follow and beat upon the old receit; for any plant of austere and stiptick parts will suffice, as I have experimented in *Bistorte, Myrobolans, Myrtus Brabantica, Balaustium*, and

Red-roses. And indeed, most decoctions of astringent plants, of what colour soever, do leave in the Liquor a deep and Muscadine red: which by addition of vitriol descends into a black: and so *Dioscorides* in his receit of Ink, leaves out gall, and with copperose makes use of soot.

Now if we inquire in what part of vitriol this Atramental and denigrating condition lodgeth, it will seem especially to lie in the more fixed salt thereof; For the phlegm or aqueous evaporation will not denigrate; nor yet spirits of vitriol, which carry with them volatile and nimbler Salt: For if upon a decoction of Copperose and gall, be poured the spirits or oyl of vitriol, the liquor will relinquish his blackness; the gall and parts of the copperose precipitate unto the bottom, and the Ink grow clear again; which it will not so easily do in common Ink, because that gum is dissolved therein, which hindereth the separation. But Colcothar or vitriol burnt, though unto a redness containing the fixed salt, will make good Ink, and so will the Lixivium, or Lye made thereof with warm water; but the Terra or Insipid earth remaining, affords no black at all, but serves in many things for a gross and useful red. And though Spirits of vitriol, projected upon a decoction of gals, will not raise a black, yet if these spirits be any way fixed, or return into vitriol again, the same will act their former parts and denigrate as before.

And if we yet make a more exact enquiry, by what this salt of vitriol more peculiarly gives this colour, we shall find it to be from a metalline condition, and especially an Iron Property or ferreous participation. For blew Copperose which deeply partakes of the copper will do it but weakly; Verdigrise which is made of Copper will not do it at all, But the filings of Iron infused in vinegar, will with a decoction of gals make good Ink, without any copperose at all; and so will infusion of Load-stone; which is of affinity with Iron. And though more conspicuously in Iron, yet such a Calcanthous or Atramentous quality, we will not wholly reject in other metals; whereby we often observe black tinctures in their solutions. Thus a Lemmon, Quince or sharp Apple cut with a knife becomes immediatly black: And from the like cause, Artichokes; so sublimate beat up with whites of Eggs, if touched with a knife, becomes immediately black. So *Aqua fortis*, whose ingredient is vitriol, will make white bodies black. So leather dressed with the bark of Oak, is easily made black by a bare solution of Copperose. So divers Mineral waters and such as participate of Iron, upon an infusion of gals, become of a dark colour, and entering upon black. So steel infused, makes not only the liquor duskie, but in bodies wherein it concurs with proportionable tinctures makes also the excretions black. And so also from this vitriolous quality *Mercurius dulcis*, and vitriol vomitive occasion black ejections. But whether this denigrating quality in Copperose proceedeth from an Iron participation, or rather in Iron from a vitriolous communication; or whether black tinctures from metallical bodies be not from vitriolous parts contained in their sulphur, since common sulphur containeth also much vitriol, may admit consideration. However in this way of tincture, it seemeth plain, that Iron and Vitriol are the powerful Denigrators.

Such a condition there is naturally in some living creatures. Thus that black humor by *Aristotle* named θολός, , and commonly translated *Atramentum*, may be occasioned in the Cuttle-fish. Such a condition there is naturally in some Plants, as Black-berries, Walnut-rinds, Black-cherries; whereby they extinguish inflamations, corroborate the stomack, and are esteemed specifical in the Epilepsie. Such an atramentous condition there is to be found sometime in the blood, when that which some call *Acetum*, others *Vitriolum*, concurs with parts prepared for this tincture. And so from these conditions the Moors might possibly become Negroes, receiving Atramentous impressions in some of these wayes, whose possibility is by us declared.

Nor is it strange that we affirm there are vitriolous parts, qualities, and even at some distance Vitriol it self in living bodies; for there is a sower stiptick salt diffused through the Earth, which passing a concoction in plants, becometh milder and more agreeable unto the sence, and this is that vegitable vitriol, whereby divers plants contain a gratefull sharpness, as Lemmons, Pomegranats, Cherries, or an austere and inconcocted roughness, as Sloes, Medlars and Quinces. And that not only vitriol is a cause of blackness, but that the salts of natural bodies do carry a powerful stroke in the tincture and vernish of all things, we shall not deny, if we contradict not experience, and the visible art of Dyars; who advance and graduate their colours with Salts. For the decoctions of simples which bear the visible colours of bodies decocted, are dead and evanid, without the commixture of Alum, Argol, and the like. And this is also apparent in Chymical preparations. So Cinaber becomes red by the acide exhalation of sulphur, which otherwise presents a pure and niveous white. So spirits of Salt upon a blew paper make an orient red. So Tartar or vitriol upon an infusion of violets affords a delightfull crimson. Thus it is wonderful what variety of colours the spirits of Saltpeter, and especially, if they be kept in a glass while they pierce the sides thereof; I say, what Orient greens they will project: from the like spirits in the earth the plants thereof perhaps acquire their verdure. And from such salary irradiations may those wondrous varieties arise, which are observable in Animals, as Mallards heads, and Peacoks feathers, receiving intention or alteration according as they are presented unto the light. Thus Saltpeter, Ammoniack and Mineral Spirits emit delectable and various colours; and common *Aqua fortis* will in some green and narrow mouthed glasses, about the verges thereof, send forth a deep and Gentianella blew.

Thus have we at last drawn our conjectures unto a period; wherein if our contemplations afford no satisfaction unto others, I hope our attempts will bring no condemnation in our selves (for besides that adventures in knowledge are laudable, and the assayes of weaker heads afford oftentimes improveable hints unto better), although in this long journey we miss the intended end; yet are there many things of truth disclosed by the way: and the collaterall verity, may unto reasonable speculations some what requite the capital indiscovery.

CHAPTER XIII

Of Gypsies

Great wonder it is not we are to seek in the original of *Æthiopians* and natural Negroes, being also at a loss concerning the Original of Gypsies and counterfeit Moors, observable in many parts of *Europe*, *Asia*, and *Africa*.

Common opinion deriveth them from *Egypt*, and from thence they derive themselves, according to their own account hereof, as *Munster* discovered in the letters and pass which they obtained from *Sigismund* the Emperour; that they first came out of lesser *Egypt*, that having defected from the Christian rule, and relapsed unto Pagan rites, some of every family were enjoyned this penance to wander about the world; or as *Aventinus* delivereth, they pretend for this vagabond course, a judgement of God upon their forefathers, who refused to entertain the Virgin *Mary* and Iesus, when she fled into their Countrey.

Which account notwithstanding is of little probability: for the generall stream of writers, who enquire into their originall, insist not upon this; and are so little satisfied in their descent from *Egypt*, that they deduce them from severall other nations: *Polydore Virgil* accounting them originally *Syrians*, *Philippus Bergomas* fetcheth them from *Chaldæa*, *Æneas Sylvius* from some part of *Tartary*, *Bellonius* no further then *Wallachia* and *Bulgaria*, nor *Aventinus* then the confines of *Hungaria*.

That they are no *Egyptians Bellonius* maketh evident: who met great droves of Gypsies in *Egypt*, about Gran Cairo, Matærea, and the villages on the banks of *Nilus*: who notwithstanding were accounted strangers unto that Nation, and wanderers from foreign parts, even as they are esteemed with us.

That they came not out of *Egypt* is also probable, because their first appearance was in *Germany*, since the year 1400. nor were they observed before in other parts of *Europe*, as is deducible from *Munster*, *Genebrard*, *Crantsius* and *Ortelius*.

But that they first set out not far from *Germany*, is also probable from their language, which was the Sclavonian tongue; and when they wandered afterward into *France*, they were commonly called *Bohemians*, which name is still retained for Gypsies. And therefore when *Crantsius* delivereth, they first appeared about the Baltick Sea, when *Bellonius* deriveth them from *Bulgaria* and *Wallachia*, and others from about *Hungaria*, they speak not repugnantly hereto: for the language of those Nations was Sclavonian, at least some dialect thereof.

But of what nation soever they were at first, they are now almost of all; associating unto them some of every country where they wander: when they will be lost, or whether at all again, is not without some doubt: for unsetled nations have out-lasted others of fixed habitations: and though Gypsies have been banished by most Christian Princes, yet have they found some countenance from the great Turk, who suffereth them to live and maintain publick Stews near the Imperial city in *Pera*, of whom he often maketh a politick advantage, imploying them as spies into other nations, under which title they were banished by *Charles* the fift.

CHAPTER XIV

Of some others

We commonly accuse the phancies of elder times in the improper figures of heaven assigned unto Constellations, which do not seem to answer them, either in Greek or Barbarick Spheres: yet equall incongruities have been commonly committed by Geographers and Historians, in the figurall resemblances of severall regions on earth; While by *Livy* and *Julius Rusticus* the Island of *Britain* is made to resemble a long dish or two-edged ax; *Italy* by *Numatianus* to be like an Oak-leaf: and *Spain* an Ox-hide; while the phancy of *Strabo* makes the habitated earth like a cloak, and *Dionysius Afer* will have it like a sling: with many others observable in good writers, yet not made out from the letter or signification; acquitting Astronomy in their figures of the Zodiack: wherein they are not justified unto strict resemblances, but rather made out from the effects of Sun or Moon in these several portions of heaven, or from peculiar influences of those constellations, which some way make good their names.

Which notwithstanding being now authentick by prescription, may be retained in their naked acceptions, and names translated from substances known on earth. And therefore the learned *Hevelius* in his accurate Selenography, or description of the Moon, hath well translated the known appellations of Regions, Seas and Mountains, unto the parts of that Luminary: and rather then use invented names or humane denominations, with witty congruity hath placed *Mount Sinai*, *Taurus*, *Mæotis Palus*, the Mediterranean Sea, *Mauritania*, *Sicily*, and *Asia* Minor in the Moon.

More hardly can we finde the Hebrew letters in the heavens, made out of the greater and lesser Stars which put together do make up words, wherein Cabalisticall Speculators conceive they read the events of future things; and how from the Stars in the head of *Medusa*, to make out the word *Charab*; and thereby desolation presignified unto *Greece* or *Javan*, numerally characterized in that word, requireth no rigid reader.

It is not easie to reconcile the different accounts of longitude, while in modern tables the hundred and eighty degree, is more then thirty degrees beyond that part, where *Ptolomy* placeth an 180. Nor will the wider and more Western term of Longitude, from whence the Moderns begin their commensuration, sufficiently salve the difference. The ancients began the measure of Longitude from the fortunate Islands or Canaries, the Moderns from the Azores or Islands of S. *Michael*; but since the Azores are but fifteen degrees more West, why the Moderns should reckon 180. where *Ptolomy* accounteth above 220. or though they take in 15 degrees at the West, they should reckon 30 at the East, beyond the same measure, is yet to be determined; nor would it be much advantaged, if we should conceive that the compute of *Ptolomy* were not so agreeable unto the Canaries, as the Hesperides or Islands of *Cabo Verde*.

Whether the compute of moneths from the first appearance of the Moon, which divers nations have followed, be not a more perturbed way, then that which accounts from the conjunction, may seem of reasonable doubt; not only from the uncertainty of its appearance in foul and cloudy weather, but unequal time in any; that is sooner or later, according as the Moon shall be in the signs of long descention, as *Pisces*, *Aries*, *Taurus*, in the Perigeum or swiftest motion, and in the Northern Latitude: whereby sometimes it may be seen the very day of the change, as will observably happen in 1654. in the moneths of April and May? or whether also the compute of the day be exactly made, from the visible arising or setting of the Sun, because the Sun is sometimes naturally set, and under the Horizon, when visibly it is above it; from the causes of refraction, and such as make us behold a piece of silver in a basin, when water is put upon it, which we could not discover before, as under the verge thereof.

Whether the globe of the earth be but a point, in respect of the Stars and Firmament, or how if the rayes thereof do fall upon a point, they are received in such variety of Angles, appearing greater or lesser from differences of refraction?

Whether if the motion of the Heavens should cease a while, all things would instantly perish? and whether this assertion doth not make the frame of sublunary things, to hold too loose a dependency upon the first and conserving cause? at least impute too much unto the motion of the heavens, whose eminent activities are by heat, light and influence, the motion it self being barren, or chiefly serving for the due application of celestial virtues unto sublunary bodies, as *Cabeus* hath learnedly observed?

Whether Comets or blazing Stars be generally of such terrible effects, as elder times have conceived them; for since it is found that many, from whence these predictions are drawn, have been above the Moon; why they may not be qualified from their positions, and aspects which they hold with stars of favourable natures; or why since they may be conceived to arise from the effluviums of other Stars, they may not retain the benignity of their Originals; or since the natures of the fixed Stars, are astrologically differenced by the Planets, and are esteemed Martial or Jovial, according to the colours whereby they answer these Planets; why although the red Comets do carry the portensions of Mars, the brightly-white should not be of the Influence of Jupiter or Venus, answerably unto *Cor Scorpii* and Arcturus; is not absurd to doubt.

End of Book VI

THE SEVENTH
BOOK:

Concerning many Historical Tenents generally received, and some deduced from the history of holy Scripture.

CHAPTER I

Of the Forbidden Fruit

That the Forbidden Fruit of Paradise was an Apple, is commonly believed, confirmed by Tradition, perpetuated by Writings, Verses, Pictures; and some have been so bad *Prosodians*, as from thence to derive the Latine word *malum*, because that fruit was the first occasion of evil; wherein notwithstanding determinations are presumptuous, and many I perceive are of another belief. For some have conceived it a Vine; in the mystery of whose fruit lay the expiation of the Transgression: *Goropius Becanus* reviving the conceit of *Barcephas*, peremptorily concludeth it to be the *Indian* Fig-tree; and by a witty Allegory labours to confirm the same. Again, some fruits pass under the name of *Adams* apples, which in common acception admit not that appellation; the one described by *Mathiolus* under the name of *Pomum Adami*, a very fair fruit, and not unlike a Citron, but somewhat rougher, chopt and cranied, vulgarly conceived the marks of *Adams* teeth. Another, the fruit of that plant which *Serapion* termeth *Musa*, but the Eastern Christians commonly the Apples of *Paradise*; not resembling an apple in figure, and in taste a Melon or Cowcumber. Which fruits although they have received appellations suitable unto the tradition, yet can we not from thence infer they were this fruit in question: No more then *Arbor vitæ*, so commonly called, to obtain its name from the tree of life in Paradise, or *arbor Iudæ*, to be the same which supplied the gibbet unto *Judas*.

Again, There is no determination in the Text; wherein is only particulared that it was the fruit of a tree good for food, and pleasant unto the eye, in which regards many excell the Apple; and therefore learned men do wisely conceive it inexplicable; and *Philo* puts determination unto despair, when he affirmeth the same kind of fruit was never produced since. Surely were it not requisite to have been concealed, it had not passed unspecified; nor the tree revealed which concealed their nakedness, and that concealed which revealed it; for in the same chapter mention is made of fig-leaves. And the like particulars, although they seem uncircumstantial, are oft set down in holy Scripture; so is it specified that *Elias* sat under a juniper tree, *Absolon* hanged by an Oak, and *Zacheus* got up into a Sycomore.

And although to condemn such Indeterminables unto him that demanded on what hand *Venus* was wounded, the Philosopher thought it a sufficient resolution to re-inquire upon what leg King *Philip* halted; and the *Jews* not undoubtedly resolved of the Sciatica-side of Jacob, do catelously in their diet abstain from the sinews of both: yet are there many nice particulars which may be authentically determined. That *Peter* cut off the right ear of *Malchus*, is beyond all doubt. That our *Saviour* eat the Passover in an upper room, we may determine from the Text. And some we may concede which the Scripture plainly defines not. That the Dyal of *Ahaz* was placed upon the West side of the Temple, we will not deny, or contradict the description of *Adricomius*. That *Abrahams* servant put his hand under his right thigh, we shall not question; and that the Thief on the right hand was saved, and the other on the left reprobated, to make good the Method of the last judicial dismission, we are ready to admit. But surely in vain we enquire of what wood was *Moses* rod, or the tree that sweetned the waters. Or though tradition or humane History might afford some light, whether the Crown of thorns was made of Paliurus; Whether the cross of Christ were made of those four woods in the Distick of *Durantes*, or only of Oak, according unto *Lipsius* and *Goropius*, we labour not to determine. For though hereof prudent Symbols and pious Allegories be made by wiser Conceivers; yet common heads will flie unto superstitious applications, and hardly avoid miraculous or magical expectations.

Now the ground or reason that occasioned this expression by an Apple, might be the community of this fruit, and which is often taken for any other. So the Goddess of Gardens is termed *Pomona*; so the Proverb expresseth it to give Apples unto *Alcinous*; so the fruit which *Paris* decided was called an Apple; so in the garden of *Hesperides* (which many conceive a fiction drawn from Paradise) we read of golden Apples guarded by the Dragon. And to speak strictly in this appellation, they placed it more safely then any other; for beside the great variety of Apples, the word in Greek comprehendeth Orenges, Lemmons, Citrons, Quinces; and as *Ruellius* defineth, such fruits as have no stone within, and a soft covering without; excepting the Pomegranate. And will extend much farther in the acception of *Spigelius*, who comprehendeth all round fruits under the names of apples, not excluding Nuts and Plumbs.

It hath been promoted in some constructions from a passage in the *Canticles*, as it runnes in the vulgar translation, *Sub arbore malo suscitavi te, ibi corrupta est mater tua, ibi violata est genetrix tua*; Which words notwithstanding parabolically intended, admit no literal inference, and are of little force in our translation, I raised thee under an Apple-tree, there thy mother brought thee forth, there she brought thee forth that bare thee. So when from a basket of summer fruits or Apples, as the vulgar rendreth them, God by *Amos* foretold the destruction of his people; we cannot say they had any reference unto the fruit of Paradise, which was the destruction of man; but thereby was declared the propinquity of their desolation, and that their tranquility was of no longer duration then those horary and soon decaying fruits of Summer. Nor when it is said in the same translation, *Poma desiderii animæ tuæ discesserunt à te*, the apples that thy soul lusted after are departed from thee, is there any allusion therein unto the fruit of Paradise. But thereby is threatned unto *Babylon*, that the pleasures and delights of their Palate should forsake them. And we read in *Pierius*, that an Apple was the Hieroglyphick of Love, and that the Statua of *Venus* was made with one in her hand. So the little Cupids in the figures of *Philostratus* do play with apples in a garden; and there want not some who have symbolized the Apple of Paradise unto such constructions.

Since therefore after this fruit, curiosity fruitlessly enquireth, and confidence blindly determineth, we shall surcease our Inquisition; rather troubled that it was tasted, then troubling our selves in its decision; this only we observe, when things are left uncertain, men will assure them by determination. Which is not only verified concerning the fruit, but the Serpent that perswaded; many defining the kind or species thereof. So *Bonaventure* and *Comestor* affirm it was a Dragon, *Eugubinus* a Basilisk, *Delrio* a Viper, and others a common snake. Wherein men still continue the delusion of the Serpent, who having deceived *Eve* in the main, sets her posterity on work to mistake in the circumstance, and endeavours to propagate errors at any hand. And those he surely most desireth which concern either God or himself; for they dishonour God who is absolute truth and goodness; but for himself, who is extreamly evil, and the worst we can conceive, by aberration of conceit they may extenuate his depravity, and ascribe some goodnesse unto him.

CHAPTER II

That a Man hath one rib less then a woman

That a Man hath one Rib less then a Woman, is a common conceit derived from the History of *Genesis*, wherein it stands delivered, that *Eve* was framed out of a Rib of *Adam*; whence 'tis concluded the sex of man still wants that rib our Father lost in *Eve*. And this is not only passant with the many, but was urged against *Columbus* in an Anatomy of his at *Pisa*, where having prepared the Sceleton of a woman that chanced to have thirteen ribs on one side, there arose a party that cried him down, and even unto oaths affirmed, this was the rib wherein a woman exceeded. Were this true, it would ocularly silence that dispute out of which side *Eve* was framed; it would determine the opinion of *Oleaster*, that she was made out of the ribs of both sides, or such as from the expression of the Text maintain there was a plurality of ribs required; and might indeed decry the parabolical exposition of *Origen*, *Cajetan*, and such as fearing to concede a monstrosity, or mutilate the integrity of *Adam*, preventively conceive the creation of thirteen ribs.

But this will not consist with reason or inspection. For if we survey the Sceleton of both sexes, and therein the compage of bones, we shall readily discover that men and women have four and twenty ribs, that is, twelve on each side, seven greater annexed unto the Sternon, and five lesser which come short thereof. Wherein if it sometimes happen that either sex exceed, the conformation is irregular, deflecting from the common rate or number, and no more inferrible upon mankind, then the monstrosity of the son of *Rapha*, or the vitious excess in the number of fingers and toes. And although some difference there be in figure, and the female *os inominatum* be somewhat more protuberant, to make a fairer cavity for the Infant; the coccyx sometime more reflected to give the easier delivery, and the ribs themselves seeme a little flatter, yet are they equal in number. And therefore while *Aristotle* doubteth the relations made of Nations, which had but seven ribs on a side, and yet delivereth, that men have generally no more then eight; as he rejecteth their history, so can we not accept of his Anatomy.

Again, Although we concede there wanted one rib in the Sceleton of *Adam*, yet were it repugnant unto reason and common observation that his posterity should want the same. For we observe that mutilations are not transmitted from father unto son; the blind begetting such as can see, men with one eye children with two, and cripples mutilate in their own persons do come out perfect in their generations. For the seed conveyeth with it not only the extract and single Idea of every part, whereby it transmits their perfections or infirmities; but double and over again; whereby sometimes it multipliciously delineates the same, as in Twins, in mixed and numerous generations. Parts of the seed do seem to contain the Idea and power of the whole; so parents deprived of hands, beget manual issues, and the defect of those parts is supplied by the Idea of others. So in one grain of corn appearing similary and insufficient for a plural germination, there lyeth dormant the virtuality of many other; and from thence sometimes proceed above an hundred ears. And thus may be made out the cause of multiparous productions; for though the seminal materials disperse and separate in the matrix, the formative operator will not delineate a part, but endeavour the formation of the whole; effecting the same as far as the matter will permit, and from dividing materials attempt entire formations. And therefore, though wondrous strange, it may not be impossible what is confirmed at *Lausdun* concerning the Countess of *Holland*, nor what *Albertus* reports of the birth of an hundred and fifty. And if we consider the magnalities of generation in some things, we shall not controvert its possibilities in others: nor easily question that great work, whose wonders are only second unto those of the Creation, and a close apprehension of the one, might perhaps afford a glimmering light, and crepusculous glance of the other

CHAPTER III

Of Methuselah

What hath been every where opinioned by all men, and in all times, is more then paradoxical to dispute; and so that *Methuselah* was the longest liver of all the posterity of *Adam*, we quietly believe: but that he must needs be so, is perhaps below paralogy to deny. For hereof there is no determination from the Text; wherein it is only particulared he was the longest Liver of all the Patriarchs whose age is there expressed; but that he outlived all others, we cannot well conclude. For of those nine whose death is mentioned before the flood, the Text expresseth that *Enoch* was the shortest Liver; who saw but three hundred sixty five years. But to affirm from hence, none of the rest, whose age is not expressed, did die before that time, is surely an illation whereto we cannot assent.

Again, Many persons there were in those days of longevity, of whose age notwithstanding there is no account in Scripture; as of the race of *Cain*, the wives of the nine Patriarchs, with all the sons and daughters that every one begat: whereof perhaps some persons might out-live *Methuselah*; the Text intending only the masculine line of *Seth*, conduceable unto the Genealogy of our Saviour, and the antediluvian Chronology. And therefore we must not contract the lives of those which are left in silence by *Moses*; for neither is the age of *Abel* expressed in the Scripture, yet is he conceived far elder then commonly opinioned; and if we allow the conclusion of his Epitaph as made by *Adam*, and so set down by *Salian*, *Posuit mærens pater, cui à filio justius positum foret, Anno ab ortu rerum* 130. *Ab Abele nato* 129. we shall not need to doubt. Which notwithstanding *Cajetan* and others confirm, nor is it improbable, if we conceive that *Abel* was born in the second year of *Adam*, and *Seth* a year after the death of *Abel*: for so it being said, that *Adam* was an hundred and thirty years old when he begat *Seth*, *Abel* must perish the year before, which was one hundred twenty nine.

And if the account of *Cain* extend unto the Deluge, it may not be improbable that some thereof exceeded any of *Seth*. Nor is it unlikely in life, riches, power and temporal blessings, they might surpass them in this world, whose lives related unto the next. For so when the seed of *Jacob* was under affliction and captivity, that of *Ismael* and *Esau* flourished and grew mighty, there proceeding from the one twelve Princes, from the other no less then foureteen Dukes and eight Kings. And whereas the age of *Cain* and his posterity is not delivered in the Text, some do salve it from the secret method of Scripture, which sometimes wholly omits, but seldom or never delivers the entire duration of wicked and faithless persons, as is observable in the history of *Esau*, and the Kings of *Israel* and *Judah*. And therefore when mention is made that *Ismael* lived 137 years, some conceive he adhered unto the faith of *Abraham*; for so did others who were not descended from *Jacob*; for *Job* is thought to be an *Idumean*, and of the seed of *Esau*.

Lastly (although we rely not thereon) we will not omit that conceit urged by learned men, that *Adam* was elder then *Methuselah*; inasmuch as he was created in the perfect age of man, which was in those days 50 or 60 years, for about that time we read that they begat children; so that if unto 930 we add 60 years, he will exceed *Methuselah*. And therefore if not in length of days, at least in old age he surpassed others; he was older then all, who was never so young as any. For though he knew old age, he was never acquainted with puberty, youth, or Infancy; and so in a strict account he begat children at one year old. And if the usual compute will hold, that men are of the same age which are born within compass of the same year; *Eve* was as old as her husband and parent *Adam*, and *Cain* their son coetaneous unto both.

Now that conception, that no man did ever attain unto a thousand years, because none should ever be one day old in the sight of the Lord, unto whom according to that of *David*, A thousand years are but as one day; doth not advantage *Methuselah*. And being deduced from a popular expression, which will not stand a *Metaphysical* and strict examination, is not of force to divert a serious enquirer. For unto God a

514

thousand years are no more then one moment, and in his sight *Methu-selah* lived no nearer one day then *Abel*, for all parts of time are alike unto him, unto whom none are referrible; and all things present, unto whom nothing is past or to come. And therefore, although we be measured by the Zone of time, and the flowing and continued instants thereof, do weave at last a line and circle about the eldest: yet can we not thus commensurate the sphere of *Trismegistus*, or sum up the unsuccessive and stable duration of God.

CHAPTER IV

That there was no Rainbow before the Flood

That there shall be no Rainbow appear forty years before the end of the world, and that the preceding drought unto that great flame shall exhaust the materials of this Meteor, was an assertion grounded upon no solid reason: but that there was not any in sixteen hundred years, that is, before the flood, seems deduceable from holy Scripture, *Gen.* 9. I do set my bow in the clouds, and it shall be for a token of a Covenant betweene me and the earth. From whence notwithstanding we cannot conclude the nonexistence of the Rainbow; nor is that Chronology naturally established, which computeth the antiquity of effects arising from physical and settled causes, by additional impositions from voluntary determinators. Now by the decree of reason and Philosophy, the Rainbow hath its ground in Nature, as caused by the rays of the Sun, falling upon a roride and opposite cloud: whereof some reflected, others refracted, beget that semi-circular variety we generally call the Rainbow; which must succeed upon concurrence of causes and subjects aptly predisposed. And therefore, to conceive there was no Rainbow before, because God chose this out as a token of the Covenant, is to conclude the existence of things from their signalities, or of what is objected unto the sense, a coexistence with that which is internally presented unto the understanding. With equall reason we may infer there was no water before the institution of Baptism, nor bread and wine before the holy Eucharist.

Again, while men deny the antiquity of one Rainbow, they anciently concede another. For, beside the solary Iris which God shewed unto *Noah*, there is another Lunary, whose efficient is the Moon, visible only in the night, most commonly at full Moon, and some degrees above the Horizon. Now the existence hereof men do not controvert, although effected by a different Luminary in the same way with the other. And probably appeared later, as being of rare appearance and rare observation, and many there are which think there is no such thing in Nature. And therefore by casual spectators they are lookt upon like prodigies, and significations made, not signified by their natures.

Lastly, We shall not need to conceive God made the Rainbow at this time, if we consider that in its created and predisposed nature, it was more proper for this signification then any other Meteor or celestial appearency whatsoever. Thunder and lightning had too much terrour to have beene tokens of mercy; Comets or blazing Stars appear too seldom to put us in mind of a Covenant to be remembered often: and might rather signifie the world should be once destroyed by fire, then never again by water. The Galaxia or milky Circle had been more probable; for (beside that unto the latitude of thirty, it becomes their Horizon twice in four and twenty hours, and unto such as live under the Æquator, in that space the whole Circle appeareth) part thereof is visible unto any situation; but being only discoverable in the night, and when the ayr is clear, it becomes of unfrequent and comfortless signification. A fixed Star had not been visible unto all the Globe, and so of too narrow a signality in a Covenant concerning all. But Rainbows are seen unto all the world, and every position of sphere. Unto our own elevation they may appear in the morning, while the Sun hath attained about forty five degrees above the Horizon (which is conceived the largest semidiameter of any Iris) and so in the afternoon when it hath declined unto that altitude again; which height the Sun not attaining in winter, rain-bows may happen with us at noon or any time. Unto a right position of sphere they may appear three hours after the rising of the Sun, and three before its setting; for the Sun ascending fifteen degrees an hour, in three attaineth forty five of altitude. Even unto a parallel sphere, and such as live under the pole, for half a year some segments may appear at any time and under any quarter, the Sun not setting, but walking round about them.

But the propriety of its Election most properly appeareth in the natural signification and prognostick of it self; as containing a mixt signality of rain and fair weather. For being in a roride cloud and ready to drop, it declareth a pluvious disposure in the air; but because when it appears the Sun must also shine, there can be no universal showrs, and consequently no Deluge. Thus when the windows of the great deep were open, in vain men lookt for the Rainbow: for at that time it could not be seen, which after appeared unto *Noah*. It might be therefore existent before the flood, and had in Nature some ground of its addition. Unto that of nature God superadded an assurance of his Promise, that is, never to hinder its appearance, or so to replenish the heavens again, as that we should behold it no more. And thus without disparaging the promise, it might rain at the same time when God shewed it unto *Noah*; thus was there more therein then the heathens understood, when they called it the *Nuncia* of the gods, and the laugh of weeping heaven; and thus may it be elegantly said; I put my bow, not my arrow in the clouds, that is, in the menace of rain the mercy of fair weather.

Cabalistical heads, who from that expression in *Esay*, do make a book of heaven, and read therein the great concernments of earth, do literally play on this, and from its semicircular figure, resembling the Hebrew letter כ Caph, whereby is signified the uncomfortable number of twenty, at which years *Joseph* was sold, which *Jacob* lived under *Laban*, and at which men were to go to war: do note a propriety in its signification; as thereby declaring the dismal Time of the Deluge. And Christian conceits do seem to strain as high, while from the irradiation of the Sun upon a cloud, they apprehend the mystery of the Sun of Righteousness in the obscurity of flesh; by the colours green and red, the two distructions of the world by fire and water; or by the colours of blood and water, the mysteries of Baptism, and the holy Eucharist.

Laudable therefore is the custom of the *Jews*, who upon the appearance of the Rainbow, do magnifie the fidelity of God in the memory of his Covenant; according to that of *Syracides*, look upon the Rainbow, and praise him that made it. And though some pious and Christian pens have only symbolized the same from the mysterie of its colours, yet are there other affections which might admit of Theological allusions. Nor would he find a more improper subject, that should consider that the colours are made by refraction of Light, and the shadows that limit that light; that the Center of the Sun, the Rainbow, and the eye of the Beholder must be in one right line, that the spectator must be between the Sun and the Rainbow; that sometime three appear, sometime one reversed. With many others, considerable in Meteorological Divinity, which would more sensibly make out the Epithite of the Heathens; and the expression of the son of *Syrach*. Very beautiful is the Rainbow, It compasseth the heaven about with a glorious circle, and the hands of the most High have bended it.

518

CHAPTER V

Of Sem, Ham and Iaphet.

Concerning the three sons of *Noah*, *Sem*, *Ham* and *Iaphet*, that the order of their nativity was according to that of numeration, and *Japhet* the youngest son, as most believe, as *Austin* and others account, the sons of *Japhet*, and *Europeans* need not grant: nor will it so well concord unto the letter of the Text, and its readiest Interpretations. For so is it said in our Translation, *Sem* the father of all the sons of *Heber* the brother of *Iaphet* the elder: so by the Septuagint, and so by that of *Tremelius*. And therefore when the Vulgar reads it, *Fratre Iaphet majore*, the mistake as *Iunius* observeth, might be committed by the neglect of the Hebrew accent; which occasioned *Ierom* so to render it, and many after to believe it. Nor is that Argument contemptible which is deduced from their Chronology; for probable it is that *Noah* had none of them before, and begat them from that year when it is said he was five hundred years old and begat *Sem*, *Ham* and *Iaphet*. Again it is said he was six hundred years old at the flood, and that two years after *Sem* was but an hundred, therefore *Sem* must be born when Noah was five hundred and two, and some other before in the year of five hundred and one.

Now whereas the Scripture affordeth the priority of order unto *Sem*, we cannot from thence infer his primogeniture. For in *Sem* the holy line was continued: and therefore however born, his genealogy was most remarkable. So is it not unusuall in holy Scripture to nominate the younger before the elder: so is it said, That *Tarah* begat *Abraham*, *Nachor* and *Haram*: whereas *Haram* was the eldest. So *Rebecca* is termed the mother of *Iacob* and *Esau*. Nor is it strange the younger should be first in nomination, who have commonly had the priority in the blessings of God, and been first in his benediction. So

Abel was accepted before *Cain, Isaac* the younger preferred before *Ishmael* the elder, *Iacob* before *Esau, Ioseph* was the youngest of twelve, and *David* the eleventh son and minor cadet of *Jesse.*

Lastly; though *Japhet* were not elder then *Sem,* yet must we not affirm that he was younger then *Cham,* for it is plainly delivered, that after *Sem* and *Iaphet* had covered *Noah,* he awaked, and knew what his youngest son had done unto him, υιος ho νεοτερος, is the expression of the Septuagint, *Filius minor* of *Ierom,* and *minimus* of *Tremelius.* And upon these grounds perhaps *Josephus* doth vary from the Scripture enumeration, and nameth them *Sem, Japhet* and *Cham*; which is also observed by the *Annian Berosus*; *Noah cum tribus filiis, Semo, Iapeto, Cham.* And therefore although in the priority of *Sem* and *Iaphet,* there may be some difficulty, though *Cyril, Epiphanius* and *Austin* have accounted *Sem* the elder, and *Salian* the Annalist, and *Petavius* the Chronologist contend for the same; yet *Cham* is more plainly and confessedly named the youngest in the Text.

And this is more conformable unto the Pagan history and Gentile account hereof, unto whom *Noah* was *Saturn,* whose symbol was a ship, as relating unto the Ark, and who is said to have divided the world between his three sons. *Ham* is conceived to be *Jupiter,* who was the youngest son; worshipped by the name of *Hamon,* which was the *Egyptian* and *African* name for *Iupiter,* who is said to have cut off the genitals of his father, derived from the history of *Ham,* who beheld the nakedness of his, and by no hard mistake might be confirmed from the Text, as Bochartus hath well observed.

CHAPTER VI

That the Tower of Babel was erected against a second deluge

An opinion there is of some generality, that our fathers after the flood attempted the Tower of *Babel* to secure themselves against a second Deluge. Which however affirmed by *Josephus* and others, hath seemed improbable unto many who have discoursed hereon. For (beside that they could not be ignorant of the Promise of God never to drown the world again, and had the Rain-bow before their eyes to put them in mind thereof) it is improbable from the nature of the Deluge; which being not possibly causable from natural showers above, or watery eruptions below, but requiring a supernatural hand, and such as all acknowledg irresistible; must needs disparage their knowledg and judgment in so successless attempts.

Again, They must probably hear, and some might know, that the waters of the flood ascended fifteen cubits above the highest mountains. Now, if as some define, the perpendicular altitude of the highest mountains be four miles; or as others, but fifteene furlongs, it is not easily conceived how such a structure could be effected. Although we allowed the description of *Herodotus* concerning the Tower of *Belus*; whose lowest story was in height and bredth one furlong, and seven more built upon it; abating that of the Annian *Berosus*, the traditional relation of *Jerom*, and fabulous account of the *Jews*. Probable it is that what they attempted was feasible, otherwise they had been amply fooled in the fruitless success of their labours, nor needed God to have hindered them, saying, Nothing will be restrained from them, which they begin to do.

It was improbable from the place, that is a plain in the land of *Shinar*. And if the situation of *Babylon* were such at first as it was in the days of *Herodotus*; it was rather a seat of amenity and pleasure, than conducing unto this intention. It being in a very great plain, and so improper a place to provide against a general Deluge by Towers and eminent structures, that they were fain to make provisions against particular and annual inundations by ditches and trenches, after the manner of *Egypt*. And therefore Sir *Walter Raleigh*, accordingly objecteth: If the Nations which followed *Nimrod*, still doubted the surprise of a second flood, according to the opinions of the ancient *Hebrews*, it soundeth ill to the ear of Reason, that they would have spent many years in that low and overflown valley of Mesopotamia. And therefore in this situation, they chose a place more likely to have secured them from the worlds destruction by fire, then another Deluge of water: and as *Pierius* observeth, some have conceived that this was their intention.

Lastly, The reason is delivered in the Text. Let us build us a City and a Tower, whose top may reach unto heaven, and let us make us a name, lest we be scattered abroad upon the whole earth, as we have already began to wander over a part. These were the open ends proposed unto the people: but the secret design of *Nimrod*, was to settle unto himself a place of dominion, and rule over his Brethren, as it after succeeded, according to the delivery of the Text, the beginning of the kingdom was *Babel*.

CHAPTER VII

Of the Mandrakes of *Leah*.

We shall not omit the Mandrakes of *Leah*, according to the History of *Genesis*. And *Reuben* went out in the daies of Wheatharvest, and found Mandrakes in the field, and brought them unto his mother *Leah*; then *Rachel* said unto *Leah*, give me, I pray thee, of thy sons Mandrakes: and she said unto her, is it a small matter that thou hast taken my husband, and wouldest thou take my sons Mandrakes also? and *Rachel* said, Therefore he shall lie with thee this night for thy sons Mandrakes. From whence hath arisen a common conceit, that *Rachel* requested these plants as a medicine of fecundation, or whereby she might become fruitfull. Which notwithstanding is very questionable, and of incertain truth.

For first from the comparison of one Text with another, whether the Mandrakes here mentioned, be the same plant which holds that name with us, there is some cause to doubt. The word is used in another place of Scripture, when the Church inviting her beloved into the fields, among the delightfull fruits of Grapes and Pomegranates, it is said, The Mandrakes give a smell, and at our gates are all manner of pleasant fruits. Now instead of a smell of Delight, our Mandrakes afford a papaverous and unpleasant odor, whether in the leaf or apple, as is discoverable in their simplicity or mixture. The same is also dubious from the different interpretations: for though the Septuagint and *Josephus* do render it the Apples of Mandrakes in this Text, yet in the other of the *Canticles*, the *Chaldy* Paraphrase termeth it Balsame. R. *Solomon*, as *Drusius* observeth, conceives it to be that plant the *Arabians* named Iesemin. *Oleaster* and *Georgius Venetus*, the Lilly, and that the word *Dudaim*, may comprehend any plant that hath a good smell, resembleth a womans breast, and flourisheth in wheat harvest. *Tremelius* interprets the same for any amiable flowers of a pleasant and delightfull odour: but the *Geneva* Translators have been more wary then any: for although they retain the word Mandrake in the Text, they in effect retract it in the Margin, wherein is set down the word in the Original is *Dudaim*, which is a kind of fruit or Flower unknown.

Nor shall we wonder at the dissent of exposition, and difficulty of definition concerning this Text, if we perpend how variously the vegetables of Scripture are expounded, and how hard it is in many places to make out the *species* determined. Thus are we at variance concerning the plant that covered *Jonas*; which though the Septuagint doth render Colocynthis, the *Spanish* Calabaca, and ours accordingly a Gourd: yet the vulgar translates it Hedera or Ivy; and, as *Grotius* observeth, *Jerom* thus translated it, not as the same plant, but best apprehended thereby. The Italian of *Diodati*, and that of *Tremelius* have named it *Ricinus*, and so hath ours in the Margin, for *palma Christi* is the same with *Ricinus*. The *Geneva* Translators have herein been also circumspect, for they have retained the Original word *Kikaion*, and ours hath also affixed the same unto the Margin.

Nor are they indeed alwayes the same plants which are delivered under the same name, and appellations commonly received amongst us. So when it is said of *Solomon*, that he writ of plants from the Cedar of Lebanus, unto the Hysop that groweth upon the wall, that is, from the greatest unto the smallest, it cannot be well conceived our common Hysop; for neither is that the least of vegetables, nor observed to grow upon wals; but rather as *Lemnius* well conceiveth, some kind of the capillaries, which are very small plants, and only grow upon wals and stony places. Nor are the four species in the holy oyntment, Cinnamon, Myrrhe, Calamus and Cassia, nor the other in the holy perfume, Frankinsence, Stacte, Onycha and Galbanum, so agreeably expounded unto those in use with us, as not to leave considerable doubts behind them. Nor must that perhaps be taken for a simple unguent, which *Matthew* only termeth a precious oyntment; but rather a composition, as *Mark* and *John* imply by pistick *Nard*, that is faithfully dispensed, and may be that famous composition described by *Dioscorides*, made of oyle of Ben, Malabathrum, Juncus Odoratus, Costus, Amomum, Myrrhe, Balsam and Nard; which *Galen* affirmeth to have been in use with the delicate Dames of *Rome*, and that the best thereof was made at *Laodicea*; from whence by Merchants it was conveyed unto other parts. But how to make out that Translation concerning the Tithe of Mint, Anise and Cumin, we are still to seek; for we finde not a word in the Text that can properly be rendred Anise; the Greek being ανηθόν which the Latines call *Anethum*, and is properly Englished Dill. Lastly, What meteor that was, that fed the *Israelites* so many years, they must rise again to inform us. Nor do they make it out, who will have it the same with our Manna; nor will any one kind thereof, or hardly all kinds we reade of, be able to answer the qualities thereof, delivered in the Scripture; that is, to fall upon the ground, to breed worms, to melt with the Sun, to taste like fresh oyl, to be grounded in Mils, to be like Coriander seed, and of the colour of Bdellium.

Again, It is not deducible from the Text or concurrent sentence of Comments, that *Rachel* had any such intention, and most do rest in the determination of *Austin*, that she desired them for rarity, pulchritude or suavity. Nor is it probable she would have resigned her bed unto *Leah*, when at the same time she had obtained a medicine to fructifie her self. And therefore *Drusius* who hath expressely and favourably treated hereof, is so far from conceding this intention, that he plainly concludeth, *Hoc quo modo illic in mentem venerit conjicere nequeo*; how this conceit fell into mens minds, it cannot fall into mine; for the Scripture delivereth it not, nor can it be clearly deduced from the Text.

Thirdly, If *Rachel* had any such intention, yet had they no such effect, for she conceived not many years after of *Joseph*; whereas in the mean time *Leah* had three children, *Isachar*, *Zebulon*, and *Dinah*.

Lastly, Although at that time they failed of this effect, yet is it mainly questionable whether they had any such vertue either in the opinions of those times, or in their proper nature. That the opinion was popular in the land of *Canaan*, it is improbable, and had *Leah* understood thus much, she would not surely have parted with fruits of such a faculty; especially unto *Rachel*, who was no friend unto her. As for its proper nature, the Ancients have generally esteemed it Narcotick or stupefactive, and it is to be found in the list of poysons, set down by *Dioscorides*, *Galen*, *Ætius*, *Ægineta*, and several Antidotes delivered by them against it. It was I confess from good Antiquity, and in the days of *Theophrastus* accounted a philtre, or plant that conciliates affection; and so delivered by *Dioscorides*. And this intent might seem most probable, had they not been the wives of holy *Jacob*: had *Rachel* presented them unto him, and not requested them for her self.

Now what *Dioscorides* affirmeth in favour of this effect, that the grains of the apples of Mandrakes mundifie the Matrix, and applied with Sulphur, stop the fluxes of women, he overthrows again by qualities destructive unto conception; affirming also that the juice thereof purgeth upward like Hellebore; and applied in pessaries provokes the menstruous flows, and procures abortion. *Petrus Hispanus*, or Pope *John* the twentieth speaks more directly in his *Thesaurus pauperum*: wherein among the receits of fecundation, he experimentally commendeth the wine of Mandrakes given with *Triphera magna*. But the soul of the medicine may lie in *Triphera magna*, an excellent composition, and for this effect commended by *Nicolaus*. And whereas *Levinus Lemnius* that eminent Physitian doth also concede this effect, it is from manifest causes and qualities elemental occasionally producing the same. For he imputeth the same unto the coldness of that simple, and is of opinion that in hot climates, and where the uterine parts exceed in heat, by the coldness hereof they may be reduced into a conceptive constitution, and Crasis accommodable unto generation; whereby indeed we will not deny the due and frequent use may proceed unto some effect, from whence notwithstanding we cannot infer a fertilitating condition or property of fecundation. For in this way all vegetables do make fruitful according unto the complexion of the Matrix; if that excel in heat, plants exceeding in cold do rectifie it; if it be cold, simples that are hot reduce it; if dry moist, if moist dry correct it; in which division all plants are comprehended. But to distinguish thus much is a point of Art, and beyond the Method of *Rachels* or feminine Physick. Again, Whereas it may be thought that *Mandrakes* may fecundate, since *Poppy* hath obtained the Epithite of fruitful, and that fertility was Hieroglyphically described by *Venus* with an head of *Poppy* in her hand; the reason hereof was the multitude of seed within it self, and no such multyplying in human generation. And lastly, whereas they may seem to have this quality, since *Opium* it self is conceived to extimulate unto venery, and for that intent is sometimes used by *Turks*, *Persians*, and most oriental Nations; although *Winclerus* doth seem to favour the conceit, yet *Amatus Lustanus*, and *Rodericus a Castro* are against it; *Garcias ab Horto* refutes it from experiment; and they speak probably who affirm the intent and effect of eating Opium, is not so much to invigorate themselves in coition, as to prolong the Act, and spin out the motions of carnality.

CHAPTER VIII

Of the three Kings of Collein

A common conceit there is of the three Kings of *Collein*, conceived to be the wise men that travelled unto our Saviour by the direction of the Star; Wherein (omitting the large Discourses of *Baronius*, *Pineda*, and *Montacutius*,) that they might be Kings, beside the ancient Tradition and Authority of many Fathers, the Scripture also implieth. The Gentiles, shall come to thy light, and Kings to the brightnesse of thy rising. The Kings of *Tharsis* and the Isles, the Kings of *Arabia* and *Saba* shall offer gifts, which places most Christians and many *Rabbins* interpret of the *Messiah*. Not that they are to be conceived potent Monarchs, or mighty Kings; but Toparks, Kings of Cities or narrow Territories; such as were the Kings of *Sodom* and *Gomorrah*, the Kings of *Jericho* and *Ai*, the one and thirty which *Joshua* subdued, and such as some conceive the Friends of *Job* to have been.

But although we grant they were Kings, yet can we not be assured they were three. For the Scripture maketh no mention of any number; and the numbers of their presents, Gold, Myrrhe and Frankincence, concludeth not the number of their persons; for these were the commodities of their Country, and such as probably the Queen of *Sheba* in one person had brought before unto *Solomon*. So did not the sons of *Jacob* divide the present unto *Joseph*, but are conceived to carry one for them all, according to the expression of their Father: Take of the best fruits of the land in your vessels, and carry down the man a present. And therefore their number being uncertain, what credit is to be given unto their names, *Gaspar*, *Melchior*, *Balthazar*, what to the charm thereof against the falling sickness, or what unto their habits, complexions, and corporal accidents, we must rely on their uncertain story, and received pourtraits of *Collein*.

Lastly, Although we grant them Kings, and three in number, yet could we not conceive that they were Kings of *Collein*. For though *Collein* were the chief City of the *Ubii*, then called *Ubiopolis*, and afterwards *Agrippina*, yet will no History inform us there were three Kings thereof. Beside, these being rulers in their Countries, and returning home, would have probably converted their subjects: but according unto *Munster*, their conversion was not wrought until seventy yeares after by *Maternus* a disciple of *Peter*. And lastly, it is said that the wise men came from the East; but *Collein* is seated West-ward from *Jerusalem*; for *Collein* hath of longitude thirty four degrees, but *Jerusalem* seventy two.

The ground of all was this. These wise men or Kings, were probably of *Arabia*, and descended from *Abraham* by *Keturah*, who apprehending the mystery of this Star, either by the Spirit of God, the prophesie of *Balaam*, the prophesie which *Suetonius* mentions, received and constantly believed through all the East, that out of Jury one should come that should rule the whole world: or the divulged expectation of the *Jews* from the expiring prediction of *Daniel*: were by the same conducted unto *Judea*, returned into their Country, and were after baptized by *Thomas*. From whence about three hundred years after, by *Helena* the Empress their bodies were translated to *Constantinople*. From thence by *Eustatius* unto Millane, and at last by *Renatus* the Bishop unto *Collein*: where they are believed at present to remain, their monuments shewn unto strangers, and having lost their *Arabian* titles, are crowned Kings of *Collein*.

CHAPTER IX

Of the food of John Baptist, Locusts and Wild honey

Concerning the food of *John Baptist* in the wilderness, Locusts and Wild-honey, lest popular opiniatry should arise, we will deliver the chief opinions. The first conceiveth the Locusts here mentioned to be that fruit the Greeks name κεράτιον, mentioned by *Luke* in the diet of the Prodigal son, the Latins *Siliqua*, and some *Panis Sancti Johannis*, included in a broad Cod, and indeed of a taste almost as pleasant as Honey. But this opinion doth not so truly impugn that of the Locusts: and might rather call into controversie the meaning of Wild-honey.

The second affirmeth they were the tops or tender crops of trees; for so *Locusta* also signifieth: which conceit is plausible in Latin, but will not hold in Greek, wherein the word is ακρίς, except for ακρίδες, we read ακρόδρυα, or ακρέμονες, which signifie the extremities of trees, of which belief have divers been: more confidently *Isidore Pelusiota*, who in his Epistles plainly affirmeth they think unlearnedly who are of another belief. And this so wrought upon *Baronius*, that he concludeth in neutrality; *Hæc cum scribat Isidorus definiendum nobis non est, & totum relinquimus lectoris arbitrio; nam constat Græcam dictionem* ακρίδες, *& Locustam, insecti genus, & arborum summitates significare. Sed fallitur*, saith Montacutius, *nam constat contrarium,* ακρίδα *apud nullum authorem claßicum* ακρόδρυα *significare.* But above all *Paracelsus* with most animosity promoteth this opinion, and in his book *de melle*, spareth not his

Friend Erasmus. *Hoc à nonnullis ita explicatur ut dicant Locustas aut cicadas Johanni pro cibo fuisse; sed hi stultitiam dißimulare non possunt, veluti Jeronymus, Erasmus, & alii Prophetæ Neoterici in Latinitate immortui.*

A third affirmeth that they were properly Locusts: that is, a sheath-winged and six-footed insect, such as is our Grashopper. And this opinion seems more probable than the other. For beside the authority of *Origen, Jerom, Chrysostom, Hillary* and *Ambrose* to confirme it; this is the proper signification of the word, thus used in Scripture by the Septuagint, Greek vocabularies thus expound it. *Suidas* on the word ακρίς observes it to be that animal whereon the Baptist fed in the desert; in this sense the word is used by *Aristotle, Dioscorides, Galen,* and several humane Authors. And lastly, there is no absurdity in this interpretation, or any solid reason why we should decline it, it being a food permitted unto the *Jews,* whereof four kinds are reckoned up among clean meats. Beside, not only the *Jews,* but many other Nations long before and since, have made an usual food thereof. That the *Æthiopians, Mauritanians* and *Arabians* did commonly eat them, is testified by *Diodorus, Strabo, Solinus, Ælian* and *Pliny:* that they still feed on them is confirmed by *Leo, Cadamustus* and others. *John* therefore as our Saviour saith, came neither eating nor drinking: that is far from the diet of *Jerusalem* and other Riotous places: but fared coursly and poorly according unto the apparel he wore, that is of Camels hair: the place of his abode, the wilderness; and the doctrin he preached, humiliation and repentance.

CHAPTER X

That John the Evangelist should not die

The conceit of the long-living, or rather not dying of *John* the Evangelist, although it seem inconsiderable, and not much weightier than that of *Joseph* the wandring *Jew*: yet being deduced from Scripture, and abetted by Authors of all times, it shall not escape our enquiry. It is drawn from the speech of our Saviour unto *Peter* after the prediction of his Martyrdom; *Peter* saith unto Jesus, Lord what shall this man do? Jesus saith unto him, If I will that he tarry untill I come, what is that to thee? Follow thou me; then went this saying abroad among the brethren, that this disciple should not die.

Now the belief hath been received either grossly and in the general, that is not distinguishing the manner or particular way of this continuation, in which sense probably the grosser and undiscerning party received it. Or more distinctly apprehending the manner of his immortality; that is, that *John* should never properly die, but be translated into Paradise, there to remain with *Enoch* and *Elias* until about the coming of Christ; and should be slain with them under Antichrist, according to that of the Apocalyps. I will give power unto my two witnesses, and they shall prophesie a thousand two hundred and threescore days cloathed in sack-cloth, and when they shall have finished their Testimony, the beast that ascendeth out of the bottomeless pit, shall make war against them, and shall overcome them, and kill them. Hereof, as *Baronius* observeth, within three hundred years after Christ, *Hippolytus* the Martyr was the first assertor, but hath been maintained by *Metaphrastes*, by *Freculphus*, but especially by *Georgius Trapezuntius*, who hath expresly treated upon this Text, and although he lived but in the last Century, did still affirm that *John* was not yet dead.

The same is also hinted by the learned Italian Poet *Dante*, who in his Poetical survey of Paradise, meeting with the soul of St. *John*, and desiring to see his body; received answer from him that his body was in earth, and there should remain with other bodys, until the number of the blessed were accomplished.

> In terra è terra il mio corpo, & saragli
> Tanto con gli altri, che il numero nostro
> Con l'eterno proposito s'agguagli.

As for the gross opinion that he should not die, it is sufficiently refuted by that which first occasioned it, that is the Scripture it self, and no further off, than the very subsequent verse: Yet Jesus said not unto him, he should not die, but if I will that he tarry till I come, What is that to thee? And this was written by *John* himself, whom the opinion concerned; and as is conceived many years after, when *Peter* had suffered and fulfilled the prophesie of Christ.

For the particular conceit, the foundation is weak, nor can it be made out from the Text alledged in the Apocalyps: for beside that therein two persons are only named, no mention is made of *John*, a third Actor in this Tragedy. The same is also overthrown by History, which recordeth not only the death of *John*, but assigneth the place of his burial, that is *Ephesus*, a City in *Asia* minor, whither after he had been banished into *Patmos* by *Domitian*, he returned in the reign of *Nerva*, there deceased, and was buried in the days of Trajan. And this is testified by *Jerom*, by Tertullian, by *Chrysostom* and *Eusebius*, in whose days his Sepulchre was to be seen; and by a more ancient Testimony alleadged also by him, that is of *Polycrates* Bishop of *Ephesus*, not many successions after *John*; whose words are these in an Epistle unto *Victor* Bishop of *Rome, Johannes ille qui supra pectus Domini recumbebat, Doctor optimus, apud Ephesum dormivit*: many of the like nature are noted by *Baronius, Jansenius, Estius, Lipellous*, and others.

Now the main and primitive ground of this error, was a gross mistake in the words of Christ, and a false apprehension of his meaning; understanding that positively which was but conditionally expressed, or receiving that affirmatively which was but concessively delivered. For the words of our Saviour run in a doubtful strain, rather reprehending than satisfying the curiosity of *Peter*; as though he should have said, Thou hast thine own doom, why enquirest thou after thy Brothers? What relief unto thy affliction, will be the society of another? Why pryest thou into the secrets of Gods will? If he stay until I come, what concerneth it thee, who shalt be sure to suffer before that time? And such an answer probably he returned, because he fore-knew *John* should not suffer a violent death, but go unto his grave in peace. Which had *Peter* assuredly known, it might have cast some water on his flames, and smothered those fires which kindled after unto the honour of his Master.

Now why among all the rest *John* only escaped the death of a Martyr, the reason is given; because all others fled away or withdrew themselves at his death, and he alone of the Twelve beheld his passion on the Cross; Wherein notwithstanding, the affliction that he suffered could not amount unto less then Martyrdom: for if the naked relation, at least the intentive consideration of that Passion, be able still, and at this disadvantage of time, to rend the hearts of pious Contemplators; surely the near and sensible vision thereof must needs occasion Agonies beyond the comprehension of flesh; and the trajections of such an object more sharply pierce the Martyred soul of *John*, than afterward did the nails the crucified body of *Peter*.

Again, They were mistaken in the Emphatical apprehension, placing the consideration upon the words, If I will: whereas it properly lay in these, when I come. Which had they apprehended as some have since, that is, not for his ultimate and last return, but his coming in Judgment and destruction upon the *Jews*; or such a coming, as it might be said, that that generation should not pass before it was fulfilled; they needed not, much less need we suppose such diuturnity. For after the death of *Peter*, *John* lived to behold the same fulfilled by *Vespasian*: nor had he then his *Nunc dimittis*, or went out like unto *Simeon*; but old in accomplisht obscurities, and having seen the expire of *Daniels* prediction, as some conceive, he accomplished his Revelation.

But besides this original and primary foundation, divers others have made impressions according unto different ages and persons by whom they were received. For some established the conceit in the disciples and brethren, which were contemporary unto him, or lived about the same time with him; and this was first the extraordinary affection our Saviour bare unto this disciple, who hath the honour to be called the disciple whom Jesus loved. Now from hence they might be apt to believe their Master would dispence with his death, or suffer him to live to see him return in glory, who was the only Apostle that beheld him to die in dishonour. Another was the belief and opinion of those times, that Christ would suddenly come: for they held not generally the same opinion with their successors, or as descending ages after so many Centuries; but conceived his coming would not be long after his passion, according unto several expressions of our Saviour grossly understood, and as we find the same opinion not long after reprehended by St. *Paul*: and thus conceiving his coming would not be long, they might be induced to believe his favourite should live unto it. Lastly, the long life of *John* might much advantage this opinion; for he survived the other twelve, he was aged 22 years when he was called by Christ, and 25 that is the age of Priesthood at his death, and lived 93 years, that is 68 after his Saviour, and died not before the second year of *Trajan*. Now having outlived all his fellows, the world was confirmed he might live still, and even unto the coming of his Master.

The grounds which promoted it in succeeding ages, were especially two. The first his escape of martyrdom: for whereas all the rest suffered some kind of forcible death, we have no history that he suffered any; and men might think he was not capable thereof: For as History informeth, by the command of *Domitian* he was cast into a Caldron of burning oyl, and came out again unsinged. Now future ages apprehending he suffered no violent death, and finding also the means that tended thereto could take no place, they might be confirmed in their opinion, that death had no power over him, that he might live always who could not be destroyed by fire, and was able to resist the fury of that element which nothing shall resist. The second was a corruption crept into the Latin Text, reading for *Si, Sic eum manere volo*; whereby the answer of our Saviour becometh positive, or that he will have it so; which way of reading was much received in former ages, and is still retained in the vulgar Translation; but in the Greek and original the word is εαν, signifying *Si* or if, which is very different from Ουτως, and cannot be translated for it: and answerable hereunto is the translation of *Junius*, and that also annexed unto the Greek by the authority of *Sixtus Quintus*.

The third confirmed it in ages farther descending, and proved a powerfull argument unto all others following; because in his tomb at

Ephesus there was no corps or relique thereof to be found; whereupon arose divers doubts, and many suspitious conceptions; some believing he was not buried, some that he was buried but risen again, others that he descended alive into his tomb, and from thence departed after. But all these proceeded upon unveritable grounds, as *Baronius* hath observed; who alledgeth a letter of *Celestine* Bishop of *Rome*, unto the Council of *Ephesus*, wherein he declareth the reliques of *John* were highly honoured by that City; and by a passage also of *Chrysostome* in the Homilies of the Apostles, That *John* being dead, did cures in *Ephesus*, as though he were still alive. And so I observe that *Esthius* discussing this point concludeth hereupon, *Quod corpus ejus nunquam reperiatur, hoc non dicerent si veterum scripta diligenter perlustrassent.*

Now that the first ages after Christ, those succeeding, or any other should proceed into opinions so far divided from reason, as to think of Immortality after the fall of *Adam*, or conceit a man in these later times should out-live our fathers in the first; although it seem very strange, yet is it not incredible. For the credulity of men hath been deluded into the like conceits; and as *Ireneus* and *Tertullian* mention, one *Menander* a *Samaritan* obtained belief in this very point; whose doctrin it was, that death should have no power on his disciples, and such as received his baptism should receive Immortality therewith. Twas surely an apprehension very strange; nor usually falling either from the absurdities of Melancholy or vanities of ambition. Some indeed have been so affectedly vain, as to counterfeit Immortality, and have stoln their death, in a hope to be esteemed immortal; and others have conceived themselves dead; but surely few or none have fallen upon so bold an errour, as not to think that they could die at all. The reason of those mighty ones, whose ambition could suffer them to be called gods, would never be flattered into immortality; but the proudest thereof have by the daily dictates of corruption convinced the impropriety of that appellation. And surely, although delusion may run high, and possible it is that for a while a man may forget his nature, yet cannot this be durable. For the inconcealeable imperfections of our selves, or their daily examples in others, will hourly prompt us our corruption, and loudly tell us we are the sons of earth.

CHAPTER XI

More compendiously of some others

Many others there are which we resign unto Divinity, and perhaps deserve not controversie. Whether *David* were punished only for
pride of heart in numbring the people, as most do hold, or whether as
Josephus and many maintain, he suffered also for not performing the
Commandment of God concerning capitation; that when the people
were numbred, for every head they should pay unto God a shekell, we
shall not here contend. Surely, if it were not the occasion of this
plague, we must acknowledge the omission thereof was threatned with
that punishment, according to the words of the Law. When thou takest
the sum of the children of *Israel*, then shall they give every man a ran-
som for his soul unto the Lord, that there be no plague amongst them.
Now how deeply hereby God was defrauded in the time of *David*, and
opulent State of Israel, will easily appear by the sums of former lustrations. For in the first, the silver of them that were numbred was an
hundred Talents, and a thousand seven hundred threescore and fifteen
shekels; a Bekah for every man, that is, half a shekel, after the shekel
of the Sanctuary; for every one from twenty years old and upwards, for
six hundred thousand, and three thousand and five hundred and fifty
men. Answerable whereto we read in *Josephus*, *Vespasian* ordered that
every man of the *Jews* should bring into the Capitol two dragms;
which amounts unto fifteen pence, or a quarter of an ounce of silver
with us: and is equivalent unto a Bekah, or half a shekel of the Sanctuary. For an Attick dragm is seven pence half-peny or a quarter of a
shekel, and a didrachmum or double dragm, is the word used for Tribute money, or half a shekel; and a stater the money found in the fishes
mouth, was two Didrachmums, or an whole shekel, and tribute sufficient for our Saviour and for *Peter*.

We will not question the Metamorphosis of Lots wife, or whether she were transformed into a real statua of Salt: though some conceive that expression Metaphorical, and no more thereby then a lasting and durable column, according to the nature of salt, which admitteth no corruption: in which sense the covenant of God is termed a Covenant of Salt; and it is also said, God gave the Kingdom unto *David* for ever, or by a Covenant of Salt.

That *Absalom* was hanged by the hair of the head, and not caught up by the neck, as *Josephus* conceiveth, and the common argument against long hair affirmeth, we are not ready to deny. Although I confess a great and learned party there are of another opinion; although if he had his Morion or Helmet on, I could not well conceive it; although the Translation of *Ierom* or *Tremelius* do not prove it, and our owne seems rather to overthrow it.

That *Iudas* hanged himself, much more that he perished thereby, we shall not raise a doubt. Although *Iansenius* discoursing the point, produceth the testimony of *Theophylact* and *Euthymius*, that he died not by the Gallows, but under a cart wheel, and *Baronius* also delivereth this was the opinion of the *Greeks*, and derived as high as *Papias*, one of the Disciples of *Iohn*. Although also how hardly the expression of *Matthew* is reconcilable unto that of Peter, and that he plainly hanged himself, with that, that falling headlong he burst asunder in the midst, with many other, the learned *Grotius* plainly doth acknowledge. And lastly, although as he also urgeth, the word ἀπήγξατο in *Matthew*, doth not only signifie suspension, or pendulous illaqueation, as the common picture describeth it, but also suffocation, strangulation or interception of breath, which may arise from grief, dispair, and deep dejection of spirit, in which sense it is used in the history of *Tobit* concerning *Sara*, ελυπήθη σφόδρα Οστε απάγξασθαι, *Ita tristata est ut strangulatione premeretur*, saith *Iunius*; and so might it happen from the horrour of mind unto *Iudas*. So do many of the *Hebrews* affirm, that *Achitophel* was also strangled, that is, not from the rope, but passion. For the Hebrew and Arabick word in the Text, not only signifies suspension, but indignation, as *Grotius* hath also observed.

Many more there are of indifferent truths, whose dubious expositions, worthy Divines and Preachers do often draw into wholesome and sober uses whereof we shall not speak; with industry we decline such Paradoxes, and peaceably submit unto their received acceptions.

CHAPTER XII

Of the Cessation of Oracles

That Oracles ceased or grew mute at the coming of Christ, is best understood in a qualified sense, and not without all latitude, as though precisely there were none after, nor any decay before. For (what we must confess unto relations of Antiquity) some pre-decay is observable from that of *Cicero* urged by *Baronius*; *Cur isto modo jam oracula Delphis non eduntur, non modo nostra aetate, sed jam diu, ut nihil possit esse contemptius.* That during his life they were not altogether dumb, is deduceable from *Suetonius* in the life of *Tiberius*, who attempting to subvert the Oracles adjoyning unto *Rome*, was deterred by the Lots or chances which were delivered at *Preneste*. After his death we meet with many; *Suetonius* reports, that the Oracle of *Antium* forewarned *Caligula* to beware of *Cassius*, who was one that conspired his death. *Plutarch* enquiring why the Oracles of *Greece* ceased, excepteth that of *Lebadia*: and in the same place *Demetrius* affirmeth the Oracles of *Mopsus* and *Amphilochus* were much frequented in his days. In brief, Histories are frequent in examples, and there want not some even to the reign of *Julian*.

What therefore may consist with history, by cessation of Oracles with *Montacutius* we may understand their intercision, not abscission or consummate desolation; their rare delivery, not total dereliction, and yet in regard of divers Oracles, we may speak strictly, and say there was a proper cessation. Thus may we reconcile the accounts of times, and allow those few and broken divinations, whereof we read in story and undeniable Authors. For that they received this blow from Christ, and no other causes alledged by the heathens, from oraculous confession they cannot deny; whereof upon record there are some very remarkable. The first that Oracle of *Delphos* delivered unto *Augustus.*

> *Me puer Hebræus Divos Deus ipse gubernans*
> *Cedere sede jubet, tristemq; redire sub orcum;*
> *Aris ergo dehinc tacitus discedito nostris.*

> An Hebrew child, a God all gods excelling,
> To hell again commands me from this dwelling.
> Our Altars leave in silence, and no more
> A Resolution e're from hence implore.

A second recorded by *Plutarch*, of a voice that was heard to cry unto Mariners at the Sea, Great Pan is dead; which is a relation very remarkable, and may be read in his Defect of Oracles. A third reported by *Eusebius* in the life of his magnified *Constantine*, that about that time *Apollo* mourned, declaring his Oracles were false, and that the righteous upon earth did hinder him from speaking truth. And a fourth related by *Theodoret*, and delivered by *Apollo Daphneus* unto *Julian* upon his *Persian* Expedition, that he should remove the bodies about him before he could return an answer, and not long after his Temple was burnt with lightning.

All which were evident and convincing acknowledgements of that Power which shut his lips, and restrained that delusion which had reigned so many Centuries. But as his malice is vigilant, and the sins of men do still continue a toleration of his mischiefs, he resteth not, nor will he ever cease to circumvent the sons of the first deceived. And therefore expelled from Oracles and solemn Temples of delusion, he runs into corners, exercising minor trumperies, and acting his deceits in Witches, Magicians, Diviners, and such inferiour seducers. And yet (what is deplorable) while we apply our selves thereto, and affirming that God hath left to speak by his Prophets, expect in doubtfull matters a resolution from such spirits; while we say the devil is mute, yet confess that these can speak; while we deny the substance, yet practise the effect and in the denied solemnity maintain the equivalent efficacy; in vain we cry that Oracles are down; *Apollos* Altar still doth smoak; nor is the fire of *Delphos* out unto this day.

Impertinent it is unto our intention to speak in general of Ora-cles, and many have well performed it. The plainest of others was that of *Apollo Delphicus* recorded by *Herodotus*, and delivered unto *Crœsus*; who as a trial of their omniscience sent unto distant Oracles; and so contrived with the Messengers, that though in several places, yet at the same time they should demand what *Crœsus* was then doing. Among all others the Oracle of *Delphos* only hit it, returning answer, he was boyling a Lamb with a Tortoise, in a brazen vessel, with a cover of the same metal. The stile is haughty in Greek, though some-what lower in Latine.

Æquoris est spatium & numerus mihi notus arenœ,
Mutum percipio, fantis nihil audio vocem.
Venit ad hos sensus nidor testudinis acris,
Quœ semel agninâ coquitur cum carne labete,
Aere infra strato, & stratum cui desuper as est.

I know the space of Sea, the number of the sand,
I hear the silent, mute I understand.
A tender Lamb joyned with Tortoise flesh,
Thy Master King of *Lydia* now doth dress.
The scent thereof doth in my nostrils hover
From brazen pot closed with brazen cover.

Hereby indeed he acquired much wealth and more honour, and was reputed by *Crœsus* as a Diety: and yet not long after, by a vulgar fallacy he deceived his favourite and greatest friend of Oracles into an irreparable overthrow by *Cyrus*. And surely the same success are likely all to have that rely or depend upon him. 'Twas the first play he practised on mortality; and as time hath rendred him more perfect in the Art, so hath the inverterateness of his malice more ready in the execution. 'Tis therefore the soveraign degree of folly, and a crime not only against God, but also our own reasons, to expect a favour from the devil; whose mercies are more cruel than those of *Polyphemus*; for he devours his favourites first, and the nearer a man approacheth, the sooner he is scorched by *Moloch*. In brief, his favours are deceitfull and double-headed, he doth apparent good, for real and convincing evil after it; and exalteth us up to the top of the Temple, but to humble us down from it.

CHAPTER XIII

Of the death of Aristotle

That *Aristotle* drowned himself in *Euripus*, as dispairing to resolve the cause of its reciprocation, or ebb and flow seven times a day, with this determination, *Si quidem ego non capio te, tu capies me*, was the assertion of *Procopius, Nazianzen, Justin Martyr*, and is generally believed amongst us. Wherein, because we perceive men have but an imperfect knowledge, some conceiving *Euripus* to be a River, others not knowing where or in what part to place it; we first advertise, it generally signifieth any strait, fret, or channel of the Sea, running betweene two shoars, as *Julius Pollux* hath defined it; as we read of *Euripus Hellespontiacus, Pyrrhæus*, and this whereof we treat, *Euripus Euboicus* or *Chalcidicus*, that is, a narrow passage of Sea dividing *Attica*, and the Island of *Eubœa*, now called *Golfo de Negroponte*, from the name of the Island and chief City thereof; famous in the wars of *Antiochus*, and taken from the *Venetians* by *Mahomet* the Great.

Now that in this *Euripe* or fret of *Negropont*, and upon the occasion mentioned, *Aristotle* drowned himself, as many affirm, and almost all believe, we have some room to doubt. For without any mention of this, we find two ways delivered of his death by *Diogenes Laertius*, who expresly treateth thereof; the one from *Eumolus* and *Phavorinus*, that being accused of impiety for composing an Hymn unto *Hermias* (upon whose Concubine he begat his son *Nichomachus*) he withdrew into *Chalcis*, where drinking poison he died; the Hymn is extant in *Laertius*, and the fifteenth book of *Athenæus*. Another by *Apollodorus*, that he died at *Chalcis* of a natural death and languishment of stomach, in his sixty third, or great Climacterical year; and answerable hereto is the account of *Suidas* and *Censorinus*. And if that were clearly made out, which *Rabbi Ben Joseph* affirmeth, he found in an *Egyptian* book of *Abraham Sapiens Perizol*; that *Aristotle* acknowledged all that was written in the Law of *Moses*, and became at last a Proselyte; it would also make improbable this received way of his death.

Again, Beside the negative of Authority, it is also deniable by reason; nor will it be easie to obtrude such desperate attempts upon *Aristotle*, from unsatisfaction of reason, who so often acknowledged the imbecility thereof. Who in matters of difficulty, and such which were not without abstrusities, conceived it sufficient to deliver conjecturalities. And surely he that could sometimes sit down with high improbabilities, that could content himself, and think to satisfie others, that the variegation of Birds was from their living in the Sun, or erection made by deliberation of the Testicles; would not have been dejected unto death with this. He that was so well acquainted with he Οτι, and πότερον *utrum*, and *An Quia*, as we observe in the Queries of his Problems; with hισως and επί το πολυ, *fortasse* and *plerumque*, as is observable through all his Works: had certainly rested with probabilities, and glancing conjectures in this: Nor would his resolutions have ever run into that mortal Antanaclasis, and desperate piece of Rhetorick, to be compriz'd in that he could not comprehend. Nor is it indeed to be made out that he ever endeavoured the particular of *Euripus*, or so much as to resolve the ebb and flow of the Sea. For, as *Vicomercatus* and others observe, he hath made no mention hereof in his Works, although the occasion present it self in his Meteors, wherein he disputeth the affections of the Sea: nor yet in his Problems, although in the twenty third Section, there be no less than one and forty Queries of the Sea. Some mention there is indeed in a Work of the propriety of Elements, ascribed unto *Aristotle*: which notwithstanding is not reputed genuine, and was perhaps the same whence this was urged by *Plutarch*.

Lastly, the thing it self whereon the opinion dependeth, that is, the variety of the flux and reflux of *Euripus*, or whether the same do ebb and flow seven times a day, is not incontrovertible. For, though *Pomponius Mela*, and after him *Solinus* and *Pliny* hath affirmed it, yet I observe *Thucydides*, who speaketh often of *Eubœa*, hath omitted it. *Pausanias* an ancient Writer, who hath left an exact description of *Greece*, and in as particular a way as *Leandro* of *Italy*, or *Cambden* of

544

great *Britain*, describing not only the Country Towns, and Rivers; but Hills, Springs and Houses, hath left no mention hereof. *Æschines* in *Ctesiphon* only alludeth unto it; and *Strabo* that accurate Geographer speaks warily of it, that is, Ος φασι, and as men commonly reported. And so doth also *Maginus, Velocis ac varii fluctus est mare, ubi quater in die, aut septies, ut alii dicunt, reciprocantur æstus. Botero* more plainly, *Il mar cresce e cala con un impeto mirabile quatro volte il di, ben che communimente si dica sette volte,* &c. This Sea with wondrous impetuosity ebbeth and floweth four times a day, although it be commonly said seven times, and generally opinioned, that *Aristotle* despairing of the reason, drowned himself therein. In which description by four times a day, it exceeds not in number the motion of other Seas, taking the words properly, that is, twice ebbing and twice flowing in four and twenty hours. And is no more than what *Thomaso Porrchacchi* affirmeth in his description of famous Islands, that twice a day it hath such an impetuous flood, as is not without wonder. *Livy* speaks more particularly, *Haud facile infestior classi statio est & fretum ipsum Euripi, non septies die (sicut fama fert) temporibus certis reciprocat, sed temere in modum venti, nunc huc nunc illuc verso mari, velut monte præcipiti devolutus torrens rapitur.* There is hardly a worse harbour, the fret or channel of *Euripus* not certainly ebbing or flowing seven times a day, according to common report: but being uncertainly, and in the manner of a wind carried hither and thither, is whirled away as a torrent down a hill. But the experimental testimony of *Gillius* is most considerable of any: who having beheld the course thereof, and made enquiry of Millers that dwelt upon its shore, received answer, that it ebbed and flowed four times a day, that is, every six hours, according to the Law of the Ocean: but that indeed sometimes it observed not that certain course. And this irregularity, though seldom happening, together with its unruly and tumultuous motion, might afford a beginning unto the common opinion. Thus may the expression in *Ctesiphon* be made out: And by this may *Aristotle* be interpreted, when in his Problems he seems to borrow a Metaphor from *Euripus*: while in the five and twentieth Section he enquireth, why in the upper parts of houses the Air doth Euripize, that is, is whirled hither and thither.

A later and experimental testimony is to be found in the travels of Monsieur *Duloir*; who about twenty years ago, remained sometime at *Negroponte*, or old *Chalcis*, and also passed and repassed this *Euripus*; who thus expresseth himself. I wonder much at the Error concerning the flux and reflux of *Euripus*; and I assure you that opinion is false. I gave a Boat-man a Crown, to set me in a convenient place, where for a whole day I might observe the same. It ebbeth and floweth by six hours, even as it doth at *Venice*, but the course thereof is vehement.

Now that which gave life unto the assertion, might be his death at *Chalcis*, the chief City of *Eubœa*, and seated upon *Euripus*, where tis confessed by all he ended his days. That he emaciated and pined away in the too anxious enquiry of its reciprocations, although not drowned therein, as *Rhodiginus* relateth, some conceived, was a half confession thereof not justifiable from Antiquity. Surely the Philosophy of flux and reflux was very imperfect of old among the Greeks and Latins; nor could they hold a sufficient theory thereof, who onely observed the Mediterranean, which in some places hath no ebb, and not much in any part. Nor can we affirm our knowledg is at the height, who have now the Theory of the Ocean and narrow Seas beside. While we refer it unto the Moon, we give some satisfaction for the Ocean, but no general salve for Creeks, and Seas which know no flood: nor resolve why it flowes three or four foot at *Venice* in the bottom of the Gulf, yet scarce at all at *Ancona*, *Durazzo*, or *Corcyra*, which lie but by the way. And therefore old abstrusities have caused new inventions; and some from the Hypotheses of *Copernicus*, or the Diurnal and annual motion of the earth, endeavour to salve the flows and motions of these Seas, illustrating the same by water in a boal, that rising or falling to either side, according to the motion of the vessel, the conceit is ingenuous, salves some doubts, and is discovered at large by Galileo.

But whether the received principle and undeniable action of the Moon may not be still retained, although in some difference of application, is yet to be perpended; that is, not by a simple operation upon the surphace or superiour parts, but excitation of the nitro-sulphureous spirits, and parts disposed to intumescency at the bottom; not by attenuation of the upper part of the Sea, (whereby ships would draw more water at the flow than at the ebb) but inturgescencies caused first at the bottom, and carrying the upper part before them: subsiding and falling again, according to the Motion of the Moon from the Meridian, and languor of the exciting cause: and therefore Rivers and Lakes who want these fermenting parts at the bottom, are not excited unto æstutations; and therefore some Seas flow higher than others, according to the Plenty of these spirits, in their submarine con-stitutions. And therefore also the periods of flux and reflux are various, nor their increase or decrease equal: according to the temper of the terreous parts at the bottom: who as they are more hardly or easily moved, do variously begin, continue or end their intumescencies.

From the peculiar disposition of the earth at the bottom, wherein quick excitations are made, may arise those Agars and im-petuous flows in some æstuaries and Rivers, as is observable about *Trent* and Humber in *England*; which may also have some effect in the boisterous tides of *Euripus*, not only from ebullitions at the bottom, but also from the sides and lateral parts, driving the streams from ei-ther side, which arise or fall according to the motion in those parts, and the intent or remiss operations of the first exciting causes, which main-tain their activities above and below the Horizon; even as they do in the bodies of plants and animals, and in the commotion of *Catarrhes*.

However therefore *Aristotle* died, what was his end, or upon what occasion, although it be not altogether assured, yet that his mem-ory and worthy name shall live, no man will deny, nor grateful Scholar doubt, and if according to the Elogy of *Solon*, a man may be only said to be happy after he is dead, and ceaseth to be in the visible capacity of beatitude, or if according unto his own Ethicks, sense is not essential unto felicity, but a man may be happy without the apprehension thereof; surely in that sense he is pyramidally happy; nor can he ever perish but in the Euripe of Ignorance, or till the Torrent of Barbarism overwhelm all.

A like conceit there passeth of *Melesigenes, alias Homer,* the Father Poet, that he pined away upon the Riddle of the fishermen. But *Herodotus* who wrote his life hath cleared this point; delivering, that passing from *Samos* unto Athens, he went sick ashore upon the Island *Ios,* where he died, and was solemnly interred upon the Sea side; and so decidingly concludeth, *Ex hac ægritudine extremum diem clausit Homerus in Io, non, ut arbitrantur aliqui, Ænigmatis perplexitate enectus, sed morbo.*

CHAPTER XIV

Of the Wish of Philoxenus

That Relation of *Aristotle*, and conceit generally received concerning *Philoxenus*, who wished the neck of a Crane, that thereby he might take more pleasure in his meat, although it pass without exception, upon enquiry I find not only doubtful in the story, but absurd in the desire or reason alledged for it. For though his Wish were such as is delivered, yet had it not perhaps that end, to delight his gust in eating; but rather to obtain advantage thereby in singing, as is declared by *Mirandula. Aristotle* (saith he) in his Ethicks and Problems, accuseth *Philoxenus* of sensuality, for the greater pleasure of gust desiring the neck of a Crane; which desire of his, assenting unto *Aristotle*, I have formerly condemned: But since I perceive that *Aristotle* for this accusation hath been accused by divers Writers. For *Philoxenus* was an excellent Musician, and desired the neck of a Crane, not for any pleasure at meat; but fancying thereby an advantage in singing or warbling, and dividing the notes in musick. And many Writers there are which mention a Musician of that name, as *Plutarch* in his book against usury, and *Aristotle* himself in the eighth of his Politicks, speaks of one *Philoxenus* a Musician, that went off from the Dorick Dithyrambicks unto the Phrygian Harmony.

Again, Be the story true or false, rightly applied or not, the intention is not reasonable, and that perhaps neither one way nor the other. For if we rightly consider the Organ of tast, we shall find the length of the neck to conduce but little unto it. For the tongue being the instrument of tast, and the tip thereof an exact distinguisher, it will not advantage the gust to have the neck extended; Wherein the Gullet and conveying parts are only seated, which partake not of the nerves of gustation, or appertaining unto sapor, but receive them only from the sixth pair; whereas the nerves of tast descend from the third and fourth propagations, and so diffuse themselves into the tongue. And therefore Cranes, Herns and Swans have no advantage in taste beyond Hawks, Kites, and others of shorter necks.

Nor, if we consider it, had Nature respect unto the taste in the different contrivance of necks, but rather unto the parts contained, the composure of the rest of the body, and the manner whereby they feed. Thus animals of long legs, have generally long necks; that is, for the conveniency of feeding, as having a necessity to apply their mouths unto the earth. So have Horses, Camels, Dromedaries long necks, and all tall animals, except the Elephant, who in defect thereof is furnished with a Trunk, without which he could not attain the ground. So have Cranes, Herns, Storks and Shovelards long necks: and so even in Man, whose figure is erect, the length of the neck followeth the proportion of other parts: and such as have round faces or broad chests and shoulders, have very seldom long necks. For, the length of the face twice exceedeth that of the neck, and the space betwixt the throat pit and the navell, is equall unto the circumference thereof. Again, animals are framed with long necks, according unto the course of their life or feeding; so many with short legs have long necks, because they feed in the water, as Swans, Geese, Pelicans, and other fin-footed animals. But Hawks and birds of prey have short necks and trussed leggs; for that which is long is weak and flexible, and a shorter figure is best accommodated unto that intention. Lastly, the necks of animals do vary, according to the parts that are contained in them, which are the weazon and the gullet. Such as have no weazon and breath not, have scarce any neck, as most sorts of fishes; and some none at all, as all sorts of pectinals, Soals, Thornback, Flounders; and all crustaceous animals, as Crevises, Crabs and Lobsters.

All which considered, the Wish of *Philoxenus* will hardly consist with reason. More excusable had it been to have wished himselfe an Ape, which if common conceit speak true, is exacter in taste then any. Rather some kind of granivorous bird then a Crane, for in this sense they are so exquisite that upon the first peck of their bill, they can distinguish the qualities of hard bodies; which the sense of man discerns not without mastication. Rather some ruminating animal, that he might have eat his meat twice over; or rather, as *Theophilus* observed in *Athenæus*, his desire had been more reasonable, had he wished himself an Elephant, or an Horse; for in these animals the appetite is more vehement, and they receive their viands in large and plenteous manner. And this indeed had been more sutable, if this were the same *Philoxenus* whereof *Plutarch* speaketh, who was so uncivilly greedy, that to engross the mess, he would preventively deliver his nostrils in the dish.

As for the musical advantage, although it seem more reasonable, yet do we not observe that Cranes and birds of long necks have any musical, but harsh and clangous throats. But birds that are canorous, and whose notes we most commend, are of little throats and short necks, as Nightingales, Finches, Linnets, Canary birds and Larks. And truly, although the weazon, throtle and tongue be the instruments of voice, and by their agitations do chiefly concurr unto these delightfull modulations, yet cannot we distinctly and peculiarly assign the cause unto any particular formation; and I perceive the best thereof, the nightingale, hath some disadvantage in the tongue; which is not acuminate and pointed as in the rest, but seemeth as it were cut off, which perhaps might give the hint unto the fable of *Philomela*, and the cutting off her tongue by *Tereus*.

CHAPTER XV

Of the Lake Asphaltites

Concerning the Lake *Asphaltites*, the Lake of *Sodom*, or the dead Sea, that heavy bodies cast therein sink not, but by reason of a salt and bituminous thickness in the water float and swim above, narrations already made are of that variety, we can hardly from thence deduce a satisfactory determination; and that not only in the story it self, but in the cause alledged. As for the story, men deliver it variously; some I fear too largely, as *Pliny*, who affirmeth that bricks will swim therein. *Mandevil* goeth farther, that Iron swimmeth, and feathers sinke. *Munster* in his Cosmography hath another relation, although perhaps derived from the Poem of *Tertullian*, that a candle Burning swimmeth, but if extinguished sinketh. Some more moderately, as *Josephus*, and many others: affirming only that living bodies float, nor peremptorily averring they cannot sink, but that indeed they do not easily descend. Most traditionally, as *Galen*, *Pliny*, *Solinus* and *Strabo*, who seems to mistake the Lake *Serbonis* for it. Few experimentally, most contenting themselves in the experiment of *Vespasian*, by whose command some captives bound were cast therein, and found to float as though they could have swimmed: divers contradictorily, or contrarily, quite overthrowing the point. *Aristotle* in the second of his Meteors speaks lightly there, Οσπερ μυθολογουσι, which word is various rendred, by some as a fabulous account, by some as a common talk. *Biddulphus* divideth the common accounts of *Judea* into three parts, the one saith he are apparent Truths, the second apparent falshoods, the third are dubious or between both; in which form he ranketh the relation of this Lake. But *Andrew Thevet* in his Cosmography doth ocularly overthrow it; for he affirmeth, he saw an Ass with his Saddle cast therein, and drowned. Now of these relations so different or contrary unto each other, the second is most moderate and safest to be embraced, which saith, that living bodies swim therein, that is, they do not easily sink; and this, untill exact experiment further determine, may be allowed, as best consistent with the quality, and the reasons alledged for it.

As for the cause of this effect, common opinion conceives it to be the salt and bituminous thickness of the water. This indeed is probable, and may be admitted as far as the second opinion concedeth. For certain it is that salt water will support a greater burden then fresh; and we see an egg will descend in salt water, which will swim in brine. But that Iron should float therein, from this cause is hardly granted; for heavy bodies will only swim in that liquor, wherein the weight of their bulk exceedeth not the weight of so much water as it occupieth or taketh up. But surely no water is heavy enough to answer the ponderosity of Iron, and therefore that metal will sink in any kind thereof, and it was a perfect miracle which was wrought this way by *Elisha*. Thus we perceive that bodies do swim or sink in different liquors, according unto the tenuity or gravity of those liquors which are to support them. So salt water beareth that weight which will sink in vineger, vineger that which will fall in fresh water, fresh water that which will sink in spirits of Wine, and that will swim in spirits of Wine which will sink in clear oyl; as we made experiment in globes of wax pierced with light sticks to support them. So that although it be conceived an hard matter to sink in oyl, I beleeve a man should find it very difficult, and next to flying, to swim therein. And thus will Gold sink in Quick-silver, wherein Iron and other metals swim; for the bulk of Gold is only heavier then that space of Quick-silver which it containeth: and thus also in a solution of one ounce of Quick-silver in two of *Aqua fortis*, the liquor will bear Amber, Horn, and the softer kinds of stones, as we have made triall in each.

But a private opinion there is which crosseth the common conceit, maintained by some of late, and alleadged of old by *Strabo*, that the floating of bodies in this Lake proceeds not from the thickness of the water, but a bituminous ebullition from the bottom, whereby it wafts up bodies injected, and suffereth them not easily to sink. The verity thereof would be enquired by ocular exploration, for this way is also probable. So we observe, it is hard to wade deep in baths where springs arise; and thus sometime are bals made to play upon a sprouting stream.

And therefore, until judicious and ocular experiment confirm or distinguish the assertion, that bodies do not sink herein at all, we do not yet believe; that they not easily, or with more difficulty descend in this then other water, we shall readily assent. But to conclude an impossibility from a difficulty, or affirm whereas things not easily sink, they do not drown at all; beside the fallacy, is a frequent addition in humane expression, and an amplification not unusual as well in opinions as relations; which oftentimes give indistinct accounts of proximities, and without restraint transcend from one unto another. Thus, forasmuch as the torrid Zone was conceived exceeding hot, and of difficult habitation, the opinions of men so advanced its constitution, as to conceive the same unhabitable, and beyond possibility for man to live therein. Thus, because there are no Wolves in *England*, nor have been observed for divers generations, common people have proceeded into opinions, and some wise men into affirmations, they will not live therein although brought from other Countries. Thus most men affirm, and few here will believe the contrary, that there be no Spiders in *Ireland*; but we have beheld some in that Country; and though but few, some Cob-webs we behold in Irish wood in *England*. Thus the Crocodile from an egg growing up to an exceeding magnitude, common conceit, and divers Writers deliver, it hath no period of encrease, but groweth as long as it liveth. And thus in brief, in most apprehensions the conceits of men extend the considerations of things, and dilate their notions beyond the propriety of their natures.

In the Mapps of the dead Sea or Lake of *Sodom*, we meet with the destroyed Cities, and in divers the City of *Sodom* placed about the middle, or far from the shore of it; but that it could not be far from *Segor*, which was seated under the mountains neer the side of the Lake, seems inferrible from the sudden arrival of *Lot*, who coming from *Sodom* at day break, attained *Segor* at Sun rising; and therefore *Sodom* to be placed not many miles from it, and not in the middle of the Lake, which is accounted about eighteen miles over; and so will leave about nine miles to be passed in too small a space of time.

CHAPTER XVI

Of divers other Relations

1. The relation of *Averroes*, and now common in every mouth, of the woman that conceived in a bath, by attracting the sperm or seminal effluxion of a man admitted to bath in some vicinity unto her, I have scarce faith to believe; and had I been of the Jury, should have hardly thought I had found the father in the person that stood by her. 'Tis a new and unseconded way in History to fornicate at a distance, and much offendeth the rules of Physick, which say, there is no generation without a joynt emission, not only, a virtual but corporal and carnal contaction. And although *Aristotle* and his adherents do cut off the one, who conceive no effectual ejaculation in women, yet in defence of the other they cannot be introduced. For, if as he believeth, the inordinate longitude of the organ, though in its proper recipient, may be a means to improlificate the seed; surely the distance of place, with the commixture of an aqueous body, must prove an effectual impediment, and utterly prevent the success of a conception. And therefore that conceit concerning the daughters of *Lot*, that they were impregnated by their sleeping father, or conceived by seminal pollution received at distance from him, will hardly be admitted. And therefore what is related of devils, and the contrived delusions of spirits, that they steal the seminal emissions of man, and transmit them into their votaries in coition, is much to be suspected; and altogether to be denied, that there ensue conceptions thereupon, however husbanded by Art, and the wisest menagery of that most subtile impostor. And therefore also that our magnified *Merlin*, was thus begotten by the devil, is a groundless conception; and as vain to think from thence to give the reason of his prophetical spirit. For if a generation could succeed, yet should n ot the issue inherit the faculties of the devil, who is

but an auxiliary, and no univocal Actor; Nor will his nature substantially concur to such productions.

And although it seems not impossible, that impregnation may succeed from seminal spirits, and vaporous irradiations containing the active principle, without material and gross immissions; as it happeneth sometimes in imperforated persons, and rare conceptions of some much under pubertie or fourteen. As may be also conjectured in the coition of some insects, wherein the female makes intrusion into the male; and from the continued ovation in Hens, from one single tread of a cock, and little stock laid up near the vent, sufficient for durable prolification. And although also in humane generation the gross and corpulent seminal body may return again, and the great business be acted by what it caryeth with it: yet will not the same suffice to support the story in question, wherein no corpulent immission is acknowledged; answerable unto the fable of the *Talmudists*, in the storie of *Benzira*, begotten in the same manner on the daughter of the Prophet *Jeremie*.

2. The Relation of *Lucillius*, and now become common, concerning *Crassus* the grand-father of *Marcus* the wealthy *Roman*, that he never laughed but once in all his life, and that was at an Ass eating thistles, is something strange. For, if an indifferent and unridiculous object could draw his habitual austereness unto a smile: it will be hard to believe he could with perpetuity resist the proper motives thereof. For the act of Laughter which is evidenced by a sweet contraction of the muscles of the face, and a pleasant agitation of the vocal Organs, is not meerly voluntary, or totally within the jurisdiction of our selves: but as it may be constrained by corporal contaction in any, and hath been enforced in some even in their death, so the new unusual or unexpected jucundities, which present themselves to any man in his life, at some time or other will have activity enough to excite the earthiest soul, and raise a smile from most composed tempers. Certainly the times were dull when these things happened, and the wits of those Ages short of these of ours; when men could maintain such immutable faces, as to remain like statues under the flatteries of wit, and persist unalterable at all efforts of Jocularity. The spirits in hell, and *Pluto* himself, whom *Lucian* makes to laugh at passages upon earth, will plainly condemn these Saturnines, and make ridiculous the magnified *Heraclitus*, who wept preposterously, and made a hell on earth; for

rejecting the consolations of life, he passed his days in tears, and the uncomfortable attendments of hell.

3. The same conceit there passeth concerning our blessed Saviour, and is sometimes urged as an high example of gravity. And this is opinioned, because in holy Scripture it is recorded he sometimes wept, but never that he laughed. Which howsoever granted, it will be hard to conceive how he passed his yonger yeares and childhood without a smile; if as Divinity affirmeth, for the assurance of his humanity unto men, and the concealment of his Divinity from the devil, he passed this age like other children, and so proceeded until he evidenced the same. And surely herein no danger there is to affirm the act or performance of that, whereof we acknowledge the power and essential property; and whereby indeed he most nearly convinced the doubt of his humanity. Nor need we be afraid to ascribe that unto the incarnate Son, which sometimes is attributed unto the uncarnate Father; of whom it is said, He that dwelleth in the heavens shall laugh the wicked to scorn. For a laugh there is of contempt or indignation, as well as mirth and Jocosity; And that our Saviour was not exempted from the ground hereof, that is, the passion of anger, regulated and rightly ordered by reason, the schools do not deny; and besides the experience of the money-changers, and Dove-sellers in the Temple, is testified by St. *John*, when he saith, the speech of *David* was fulfilled in our Saviour.

Now the Alogie of this opinion consisteth in the illation; it being not reasonable to conclude from Scripture negatively in points which are not matters of faith, and pertaining unto salvation. And therefore although in the description of the creation there be no mention of fire, Christian Philosophy did not think it reasonable presently to annihilate that element, or positively to decree there was no such thing at all. Thus whereas in the brief narration of *Moses* there is no record of wine before the flood, we cannot satisfactorily conclude that *Noah* was the first that ever tasted thereof. And thus because the word *Brain* is scarce mentioned once, but Heart above an hundred times in holy Scripture; Physitians that dispute the principality of parts are not from hence induced to bereave the animal Organ of its priority. Wherefore the Scriptures being serious, and commonly omitting such Parergies, it will be unreasonable from hence to condemn all laughter, and from considerations inconsiderable to discipline a man out of his nature. For this is by a rustical severity to banish all urbanity; whose

harmless and confined condition, as it stands commended by morality; so is it consistent with Religion, and doth not offend Divinity.

4. The custom it is of Popes to change their name at their creation; and the Author thereof is commonly said to be *Bocca di porco*, or
swines face; who therefore assumed the stile of *Sergius* the second, as
being ashamed so foul a name should dishonour the chair of *Peter*;
wherein notwithstanding, from *Montacutius* and others I find there
may be some mistake. For *Massonus* who writ the lives of Popes, acknowledgeth he was not the first that changed his name in that Sea;
nor as *Platina* affirmeth, have all his successors precisely continued
that custom; for *Adrian* the sixt, and *Marcellus* the second, did still
retain their Baptismal denominations. Nor is it proved, or probable,
that *Sergius* changed the name of *Bocca di Porco*, for this was his
sirname or gentilitious appellation: nor was it the custom to alter that
with the other; but he commuted his Christian name *Peter* for *Sergius*,
because he would seem to decline the name of *Peter* the second. A
scruple I confess not thought considerable in other Seas, whose Originals and first Patriarchs have been less disputed; nor yet perhaps of
that reality as to prevail in points of the same nature. For the names of
the Apostles, Patriarchs and Prophets have been assumed even to affectation; the name of Jesus hath not been appropriate; but some in
precedent ages have born that name, and many since have not refused
the Christian name of *Emmanuel*. Thus are there few names more frequent then *Moses* and *Abraham* among the *Jews*; The *Turks* without
scruple affect the name of *Mahomet*, and with gladness receive so honourable cognomination.

And truly in humane occurrences there ever have been many
well directed intentions, whose rationalities will never bear a rigid examination, and though in some way they do commend their Authors,
and such as first began them, yet have they proved insufficient to per-
petuate imitation in such as have succeeded them. Thus was it a
worthy resolution of *Godfrey*, and most Christians have applauded it,
That he refused to weare a Crown of Gold where his Saviour had worn
one of thorns. Yet did not his Successors durably inherit that scruple,
but some were anointed, and solemnly accepted the Diadem of regal-
ity. Thus *Julius*, *Augustus* and *Tiberius* with great humility or
popularity refused the name of *Imperator*, but their Successors have
challenged that title, and retain the same even in its titularity. And thus
to come nearer our subject, the humility of *Gregory* the Great, would

557

by no means admit the stile of universal Bishop; but the ambition of *Boniface* made no scruple thereof, nor of more queasie resolutions have been their Successors ever since.

5. That *Tamerlane* was a *Scythian* Shepherd, from Mr. *Knolls* and others, from *Alhazen* a learned *Arabian* who wrote his life, and was Spectator of many of his exploits, we have reasons to deny. Not only from his birth, for he was of the blood of the *Tartarian* Emperours, whose father *Og* had for his possession the Country of *Sagathy*, which was no slender Territory, but comprehended all that tract wherein were contained *Bactriana*, *Sogdiana*, *Margiana*, and the nation of the *Massagetes*, whose capital City was *Samarcand*; a place though now decaid, of great esteem and trade in former ages. But from his regal Inauguration, for it is said, that being about the age of fifteen, his old father resigned the Kingdom, and men of war unto him. And also from his education; for as the storie speaks it, he was instructed in the *Arabian* learning, and afterward exercised himselfe therein. Now *Arabian* learning was in a manner all the liberal Sciences, especially Mathematicks, and natural Philosophy; wherein not many Ages before him there flourished *Avicenna*, *Averrhoes*, *Avenzoar*, *Geber*, *Almanzor* and *Alhazen*, cognominal unto him that wrote his History, whose Chronology indeed, although it be obscure, yet in the opinion of his Commentator, he was contemporary unto *Avicenna*, and hath left sixteen books of Opticks, of great esteem with ages past, and textuary unto our days.

Now the ground of this mistake was surely that which the Turkish Historian declareth. Some, saith he, of our Historians will needs have *Tamerlane* to be the Son of a Shepherd. But this they have said, not knowing at all the custom of their Country; wherein the principal revenews of the King and Nobles consisteth in cattle; who despising gold and silver, abound in all sorts thereof. And this was the occasion that some men call them Shepherds, and also affirm this Prince descended from them. Now, if it be reasonable, that great men whose possessions are chiefly in cattle, should bear the name of Shepherds, and fall upon so low denominations; then may we say that *Abraham* was a Shepherd, although too powerfull for four Kings; that *Job* was of that condition, who beside Camels and Oxen had seven thousand Sheep; and yet is said to be the greatest man in the East. Thus was *Mesha* King of *Moab* a Shepherd, who annually paid unto the Crown of *Israel*, an hundred thousand Lambs, and as many Rams.

558

Surely it is no dishonourable course of life which *Moses* and *Jacob* have made exemplary: 'tis a profession supported upon the natural way of acquisition, and though contemned by the *Egyptians*, much countenanced by the Hebrews, whose sacrifices required plenty of Sheep and Lambs. And certainly they were very numerous; for, at the consecration of the Temple, beside two and twenty thousand Oxen, King *Solomon* sacrificed an hundred and twenty thousand Sheep: and the same is observable from the daily provision of his house: which was ten fat Oxen, twenty Oxen out of the pastures, and an hundred Sheep, beside row Buck, fallow Deer, and fatted Fowls. Wherein notwithstanding (if a punctual relation thereof do rightly inform us) the grand Seignor doth exceed: the daily provision of whose Seraglio in the reigne of *Achmet*, beside Beeves, consumed two hundred Sheep, Lambs and Kids when they were in season one hundred, Calves ten, Geese fifty, Hens two hundred, Chickens one hundred, Pigeons an hundred pair.

And therefore this mistake concerning the noble *Tamerlane*, was like that concerning *Demosthenes*, who is said to be the Son of a Black-smith, according to common conceit, and that handsome expression of *Juvenal*.

> *Quem pater ardentis massæ fuligine lippus,*
> *A carbone & forcipibus, gladiosq; parante*
> *Incude, & luteo Vulcano ad Rhetora misit.*

Thus Englished by Sir Robert Stapleton.

> Whom's Father with the smoaky forg half blind,
> From blows on sooty Vulcans anvil spent
> In ham'ring swords, to study Rhet'rick sent.

But *Plutarch* who writ his life hath cleared this conceit, plainly affirming he was most nobly descended, and that this report was raised, because his father had many slaves that wrought Smiths work, and brought the profit unto him.

CHAPTER XVII

Of some others

1. We are sad when we reade the story of *Belisarius* that worthy Cheiftain of *Justinian*; who, after his Victories over the *Vandals, Goths, Persians*, and his Trophies in three parts of the World, had at last his eyes put out by the Emperour, and was reduced to that distress, that he begged relief on the high-way, in that uncomfortable petition, *Date obolum Belisario*. And this we do not only hear in Discourses, Orations and Themes, but find it also in the leaves of *Petrus Crinitus, Volaterranus* and other worthy Writers.

But, what may somewhat consolate all men that honour vertue, we do not discover the latter Scene of his misery in Authors of Antiquity, or such as have expresly delivered the story of those times. For, *Suidas* is silent herein, *Cedrenus* and *Zonaras*, two grave and punctual Authors, delivering only the confiscation of his goods, omit the History of his mendication. *Paulus Diaconus* goeth farther, not only passing over this act, but affirming his goods and dignities were restored. *Agathius* who lived at the same time, declareth he suffered much from the envy of the Court: but that he descended thus deep into affliction, is not to be gathered from his pen. The same is also omitted by *Procopius* a contemporary and professed enemy unto *Justinian* and *Belisarius*, and who hath left an opprobrius book against them both.

And in this opinion and hopes we are not single, but *Andreas Alciatus* the Civilian in his *Parerga*, and *Franciscus de Cordua* in his *Didascalia*, have both declaratorily confirmed the same, which is also agreeable unto the judgement of *Nicolaus Alemannus*, in his notes upon that bitter History of *Procopius*. Certainey, sad and Tragical stories are seldom drawn within the circle of their verities; but as their Relators do either intend the hatred or pitty of the persons, so are they set forth with additional amplifications. Thus have some suspected it hath happened unto the story of *Oedipus*; and thus do we conceive it hath fared with that of *Judas*, who having sinned beyond aggravation, and committed one villany which cannot be exasperated by all other: is also charged with the murther of his reputed brother, parricide of his father, and Incest with his own mother, as *Florilegus* or *Matthew* of *Westminster* hath at large related. And thus hath it perhaps befallen the noble *Belisarius*; who, upon instigation of the Empress, having contrived the exile, and very hardly treated Pope *Serverius*, Latin pens, as a judgment of God upon this fact, have set forth his future sufferings: and omitting nothing of amplification, they have also delivered this: which notwithstanding *Johannes* the Greek, makes doubtful, as may appear from his Jambicks in *Baronius*, and might be a mistake or misapplication, translating the affliction of one man upon another, for the same befell unto *Johannes Cappadox*, contemporary unto *Belisarius*, and in great favour with *Justinian*; who being afterward banished into *Egypt*, was fain to beg relief on the high-way.

2. That *fluctus Decumanus*, or the tenth wave is greater and more dangerous then any other, some no doubt will be offended if we deny; and hereby we shall seem to contradict Antiquity; for, answerable unto the literal and common acception, the same is averred by many Writers, and plainly described by Ovid.

Qui venit hic fluxtus, fluctus supereminet omnes,
Posterior nono est, undecimoq; prior.

Which notwithstanding is evidently false; nor can it be made out by observation either upon the shore or the Ocean, as we have with diligence explored in both. And surely in vain we expect a regularity in the waves of the Sea, or in the particular motions thereof, as we may in its general reciprocations whose causes are constant, and effects therefore correspondent. Whereas its fluctuations are but motions subservient; which winds, storms, shores, shelves, and every interjacency irregulates. With semblable reason we might expect a regularity in the winds; whereof though some be statary, some anniversary, and the rest do tend to determinate points of heaven, yet do the blasts and undulary breaths thereof maintain no certainty in their course; nor are they numerally feared by Navigators.

561

Of affinity hereto is that conceit of *Ovum Decumanum*, so called, because the tenth egg is bigger then any other, according unto the reason alledged by *Festus, Decumana ova dicuntur, quia ovum decimum majus nascitur*. For the honour we bear unto the Clergy, we cannot but wish this true: but herein will be found no more of verity than in the other: and surely few will assent hereto without an implicite credulity, or Pythagorical submission unto every conception of number.

For, surely the conceit is numeral, and though not in the sense apprehended, relateth unto the number of ten, as *Franciscus Sylvius* hath most probably declared. For, whereas amongst simple numbers or Digits, the number of ten is the greatest: therefore whatsoever was the greatest in every kind, might in some sense be named from this number. Now, because also that which was the greatest, was metaphorically by some at first called *Decumanus*; therefore whatsoever passed under this name, was literally conceived by others to respect and make good this number.

The conceit is also Latin; for the Greeks to express the greatest wave, do use the number of three, that is, the word τρικυμία, which is a concurrence of three waves in one, whence arose the proverb, τρικυμία κακον, or a trifluctuation of evils, which *Erasmus* doth render, *Malorum fluctus Decumanus*. And thus, although the terms be very different, yet are they made to signifie the self-same thing; the number of ten to explain the number of three, and the single number of one wave the collective occurrence of more.

3. The poyson of *Parysatis* reported from *Ctesias* by *Plutarch* in the life of *Artaxerxes*, whereby annointing a knife on the one side, and therewith dividing a bird; with the one half she poysoned *Statira*, and safely fed her self on the other, was certainly a very subtile one, and such as our ignorance is well content it knows not. But surely we had discovered a poyson that would not endure *Pandoras* box, could we be satisfied in that which for its coldness nothing could contain but an Asses hoof, and wherewith some report that *Alexander* the great was poysoned. Had men derived so strange an effect from some occult or hidden qualities, they might have silenced contradiction; but ascribing it unto the manifest and open qualities of cold, they must pardon our belief; who perceive the coldest and most Stygian waters may be

included in glasses; and by *Aristotle* who saith, that glass is the perfectest work of Art, we understand they were not then to be invented.

And though it be said that poyson will break a Venice glass, yet have we not met with any of that nature. Were there a truth herein, it were the best preservative for Princes and persons exalted unto such fears: and surely far better than divers now in use. And though the best of China dishes, and such as the Emperour doth use, be thought by some of infallible vertue unto this effect; yet will they not, I fear, be able to elude the mischief of such intentions. And though also it be true, that God made all things double, and that if we look upon the works of the most High, there are two and two, one against another; that one contrary hath another, and poyson is not without a poyson unto it self; yet hath the curse so far prevailed, or else our industry defected, that poysons are better known than their Antidotes, and some thereof do scarce admit of any. And lastly, although unto every poyson men have delivered many Antidotes, and in every one is promised an equality unto its adversary, yet do we often find they fail in their effects: Moly will not resist a weaker cup then that of Circe; a man may be poysoned in a Lemnian dish; without the miracle of *John*, there is no confidence in the earth of *Paul*; and if it be meant that no poyson could work upon him, we doubt the story, and expect no such success from the diet of *Mithridates*.

4. A story there passeth of an Indian King, that sent unto *Alexander* a fair woman fed with Aconites and other poysons, with this intent, either by converse or copulation complexionally to destroy him. For my part, although the design were true, I should have doubted the success. For, though it be possible that poysons may meet with tempers whereto they may become Aliments, and we observe from fowls that feed on fishes, and others fed with garlick and onyons, that simple aliments are not always concocted beyond their vegetable qualities; and therefore that even after carnall conversion, poysons may yet retain some portion of the natures; yet are they so refracted, cicurated and subdued, as not to make good their first and destructive malignities. And therefore the Stork that eateth Snakes, and the Stare that feedeth upon Hemlock, though no commendable aliments, are not destructive poysons. For, animals that can inoxiously digest these poisons become antidotall unto the poyson digested. And therefore whether their breath be attracted, or their flesh ingested, the poysonous reliques go still along with their Antidote: whose society will not per-

mit their malice to be destructive. And therefore also animals that are not mischieved by poysons which destroy us, may be drawn into Antidote against them; the blood or flesh of Storks against the venom of Serpents, the Quail against Hellebore, and the diet of Starlings against the draught of *Socrates*. Upon like grounds are some parts of Animals Alexipharmacall unto others; and some veins of the earth, and also whole regions, not only destroy the life of venemous creatures, but also prevent their productions. For, though perhaps they containe the seminals of Spiders, and Scorpions, and such as in other earths by suscitation of the Sun may arise unto animation; yet lying under command of their Antidote, without hope of emergency they are poysoned in their matrix by powers easily hindring the advance of their originals, whose confirmed forms they are able to destroy.

5. The story of the wandring Jew is very strange, and will hardly obtain belief; yet is there a formall account thereof set down by *Matthew Paris*, from the report of an Armenian Bishop; who came into this kingdom about four hundred years ago, and had often entertained this wanderer at his Table. That he was then alive, was first called *Cartaphilus*, was keeper of the Judgement Hall, whence thrusting out our Saviour with expostulation pf his stay, was condemned to stay untill his return; was after baptized by *Ananias*, and by the name of *Joseph*; was thirty years old in the dayes of our Saviour, remembred the Saints that arised with him, the making of the Apostles Creed, and their several peregrinations. Surely were this true, he might be an happy arbitrator in many Christian controversies; but must impardonably condemn the obstinacy of the Jews, who can contemn the Rhetorick of such miracles, and blindly behold so living and lasting conversions.

6. Clearer confirmations must be drawn for the history of Pope *Joan*, who succeeded *Leo* the fourth, and preceding *Benedict* the third, then any we yet discover. And since it is delivered with *aiunt* and *ferunt* by many; since the learned *Leo Allatius* hath discovred, that ancient copies of *Martinus Polonus*, who is chiefly urged for it, had not this story in it; since not only the stream of Latine Historians have omitted it, but *Photius* the Patriarch, *Metrophanes Smyrnœus*, and the exasperated Greeks have made no mention of it, but conceded *Benedict* the third to bee Successor unto *Leo* the fourth; he wants not grounds that doubts it.

564

Many things historicall which seem of clear concession, want not affirmations and negations, according to divided pens: as is notoriously observable in the story of *Hildebrand* or *Gregory* the seventh, repugnantly delivered by the Imperiall and Papal party. In such divided records partiality hath much depraved history, wherein if the equity of the reader do not correct the iniquity of the writer, he will be much confounded with repugnancies, and often finde in the same person, *Numa* and *Nero*. In things of this nature moderation must intercede; and so charity may hope, that Roman Readers will construe many passages in *Bolsech, Fayus, Schlusselberg* and *Cochlæus*.

7. Every ear is filled with the story of Frier *Bacon*, that made a brazen head to speak these words, *Time is*. Which though there want not the like relations, is surely too literally received, and was but a mystical fable concerning the Philosophers great work, wherein he eminently laboured: implying no more by the copper head, then the vessel wherein it was wrought; and by the words it spake, then the opportunity to be watched, about the *Tempus ortus*, or birth of the mystical child, or Philosophical King of *Lullius*: the rising of the *Terra foliata* of *Arnoldus*, when the earth sufficiently impregnated with the water, ascendeth white and splendent. Which not observed, the work is irrecoverably lost; according to that of *Petrus Bonus*. *Ibi est operis perfectio aut annihilatio; quoniam ipsa die, immo horâ, oriuntur elementa simplicia depurata, quæ egent statim compositione, antequam volent ab igne.*

Now letting slip this critical opportunity, he missed the intended treasure. Which had he obtained, he might have made out the tradition of making a brazen wall about *England*. That is, the most powerfull defence, and strongest fortification, which Gold could have effected.

8. Who can but pity the vertuous *Epicurus*, who is commonly conceived to have placed his chief felicity in pleasure and sensual delights, and hath therefore left an infamous name behinde him? How true, let them determine who read that he lived seventy years, and wrote more books then any Philosopher but *Chrysippus*, and no less then three hundred, without borrowing from any Author. That he was contented with bread and water, and when he would dine with *Jove*, and pretend unto epulation, he desired no other addition then a piece of *Cytheridian* cheese. That shall consider the words of *Seneca, Non*

dico, quod pleriq; nostrorum, sectam Epicuri flagitiorum magistram esse: sed illud dico, male audit, infamis est, & immerito. Or shall read his life, his Epistles, his Testament in *Laertius*; who plainly names them Calumnies, which are commonly said against them.

The ground hereof seems a mis-apprehension of his opinion, who placed his Felicity not in the pleasures of the body, but the minde, and tranquillity thereof, obtained by wisdom and vertue, as is clearly determined in his Epistle unto *Menæceus*. Now how this opinion was first traduced by the *Stoicks*, how it afterwards became a common belief, and so taken up by Authors of all ages, by *Cicero, Plutarch, Clemens, Ambrose* and others; the learned pen of *Gassendus* hath discovered.

CHAPTER XVIII

More briefly of some others

1. Other relations there are, and those in very good Authors, which though we do not positively deny, yet have they not been unquestioned by some, and at least as improbable truths have been received by others. Unto some it hath seemed incredible what *Herodotus* reporteth of the great Army of *Xerxes*, that drank whole rivers dry. And unto the Author himself it appeared wondrous strange, that they exhausted not the provision of the Countrey, rather then the waters thereof. For as he maketh the account, and *Budeus de Asse* correcting the mis-compute of *Valla*, delivereth it; if every man of the Army had had a chenix of Corn a day, that is, a sextary and half; or about two pints and a quarter, the Army had daily expended ten hundred thousand and forty Medimna's, or measures containing six Bushels. Which rightly considered, the *Abderites* had reason to bless the Heavens, that *Xerxes* eat but one meal a day; and *Pythius* his noble Host, might with less charge and possible provision entertain both him and his Army. And yet may all be salved, if we take it hyperbolically, as wise men receive that expression in *Job*, concerning *Behemoth* or the Elephant; Behold, he drinketh up a River and hasteth not, he trusteth that he can draw up *Jordan* into his mouth.

2. That *Annibal* eat or brake through the Alps with Vinegar, may be too grossly taken, and the Author of his life annexed unto *Plutarch* affirmeth only, he used this artifice upon the tops of some of the highest mountains. For as it is vulgarly understood, that he cut a passage for his Army through those mighty mountains, it may seem incredible, not only in the greatness of the effect, but the quantity of the efficient and such as behold them, may think an Ocean of Vinegar

too little for that effect. 'Twas a work indeed rather to be expected from earthquakes and inundations, then any corrosive waters, and much condemneth the Judgement of *Xerxes*, that wrought through Mount *Athos* with Mattocks.

3. That *Archimedes* burnt the ships of *Marcellus*, with speculums of parabolical figures, at three furlongs, or as some will have it, at the distance of three miles, sounds hard unto reason, and artificial experience: and therefore justly questioned by Kircherus, who after long enquiry could find but one made by *Manfredus Septalius* that fired at fifteen paces. And therefore more probable it is, that the ships were nearer the shore, or about some thirty paces: at which distance notwithstanding the effect was very great. But whereas men conceive the ships were more easily set on flame, by reason of the pitch set about them, it seemeth no advantage. Since burning glasses will melt pitch or make it boyl, not easily set it on fire.

4. The story of the *Fabii*, wherof three hundred and six marching against the *Veientes*, were all slain, and one childe alone to support the family remained; is surely not to be paralleld, nor easie to be conceived, except we can imagine, that of three hundred and six, but one had children below the service of war; that the rest were all unmarried; or the wife but of one impregnated.

5. The received story of *Milo*, who by daily lifting a Calf, attained an ability to carry it being a Bull, is a witty conceit, and handsomly sets forth the efficacy of Assuefaction. But surely the account had been more reasonably placed upon some person not much exceeding in strength, and such a one as without the assistance of custom could never have performed that act; which some may presume that *Milo* without precedent artifice or any other preparative, had strength enough to perform. For as relations declare, he was the most pancratical man of *Greece*, and as *Galen* reporteth, and *Mercurialis* in his Gymnasticks representeth, he was able to persist erect upon an oyled plank, and not to be removed by the force or protrusion of three men. And if that be true with *Atheneus* reporteth, he was little beholding to custom for this abilitie. For in the Olympick games, for the space of a furlong, he carried an Ox of four years upon his shoulders; and the same day he carried it in his belly; for as it is there delivered he eat it up himselfe. Surely he had been a proper guest at *Grandgous-*

iers feast, and might have matcht his throat that eat six pilgrims for a salad.

6. It much disadvantageth the Panegyrick of *Synesius*, and is no small disparagement unto baldness, if it be true what is related by *Ælian* concerning *Æschilus*, whose bald-pate was mistaken for a rock, and so was brained by a Tortoise which an Æagle let fall upon it. Certainly it was a very great mistake in the perspicacity of that Animal. Some men critically disposed, would from hence confute the opinion of *Copernicus*, never conceiving how the motion of the earth below should not wave him from a knock perpendicularly directed from a body in the air above.

7. It crosseth the Proverb, and *Rome* might well be built in a day; if that were true which is traditionally related by *Strabo*; that the great Cities *Anchiale* and *Tarsus*, were built by *Sardanapalus* both in one day, according to the inscription of his monument, *Sardanapalus Anacyndraxis filius, Anchialen & Tarsum una die edficavi, Tu autem hospes Ede, Lude, Bibe, &c.* Which if strictly taken, that is, for the finishing thereof, and not only for the beginning; for an artificial or natural day, and not one of *Daniels* weeks, that is, seven whole years; surely their hands were very heavy that wasted thirteen years in the private house of *Solomon*: It may be wondered how forty years were spent in the erection of the Temple of *Jerusalem*, and no less then an hundred in that famous one of *Ephesus*. Certainly it was the greatest Architecture of one day, since that great one of six; an Art quite lost with our Mechanicks, a work not to be made out, but like the wals of *Thebes*, and such an Artificer as *Amphion*.

8. It had been a sight only second unto the Ark to have beheld the great *Syracusia*, or mighty Ship of *Hiero*, described in *Atheneus*; and some have thought it a very large one, wherein were to be found ten stables for horses, eight Towers, besides Fish-ponds, Gardens, Tricliniums, and many fair rooms paved with Agath, and precious Stones. But nothing was impossible unto *Archimedes*, the learned Contriver thereof; nor shall we question his removing the earth, when he findes an immoveable base to place his Engine upon it.

9. That the *Pamphilian* Sea gave way to *Alexander* in his intended March toward *Persia*, many have been apt to credit, and

Josephus is willing to believe, to countenance the passage of the *Israelites* through the Red Sea. But *Strabo* who writ before him delivereth another account; that the Mountain *Climax* adjoyning to the *Pamphilian* Sea, leaves a narrow passage between the Sea and it, which passage at an ebb and quiet Sea all men take; but *Alexander* coming in the Winter, and eagerly pursuing his affairs, would not wait for the reflux or return of the Sea; and so was fain to pass with his Army in the water, and march up to the navel in it.

10. The relation of *Plutarch* of a youth of *Sparta*, that suffered a Fox concealed under his robe to tear out his bowels, before he would either by voice or countenance betray his theft; and the other of the Spartan Lad, that with the same resolution suffered a coal from the Altar to burn his arm, although defended by the Author that writes his life, is I perceive mistrusted by men of Judgment, and the Author with an *aiunt*, is made to salve himself. Assuredly it was a noble Nation that could afford an hint to such inventions of patience, and upon whom, if not such verities, at least such verisimilities of fortitude were placed. Were the story true, they would have made the only Disciples for *Zeno*, and the *Stoicks*, and might perhaps have been perswaded to laugh in *Phaleris* his Bull.

11. If any man shall content his belief with the speech of *Balaams* Ass, without a belief of that of *Mahomets* Camel, or *Livies* Oxe; if any man make a doubt of Giges ring in Justinus, or conceives he must be a *Jew* that believes the Sabbatical river in *Josephus*. If any man will say he doth not apprehend how the tayl of an *African* Weather out-weigheth the body of a good Calf, that is, an hundred pound, according unto *Leo Africanus*, or desires before belief, to behold such a creature as is the Ruck in *Paulus Venetus*, for my part I shall not be angry with his incredulity.

12. If anyone shall receive as stretcht or fabulous accounts what is delivered of *Cocles*, *Scævola* and *Curtius*, the sphere of *Archimedes*, the story of the *Amazons*, the taking of the City of *Babylon*, not known to some therein in three days after; that the nation was deaf which dwelt at the fall of *Nilus*, the laughing and weeping humour of *Heraclitus* and *Democritus*, with many more, he shall not want some reason and the authority of *Lancelotti*.

13. If any man doubt of the strange Antiquities delivered by Historians, as of the wonderful corps of *Antæus* untombed a thousand years after his death by *Sertorius*. Whether there were no deceipt in those fragments of the Ark so common to be seen in the days of *Berosus*; whether the Pillar which *Josephus* beheld long ago, *Tertullian* long after, and *Bartholomeus de Saligniaco*, and *Borchardus* long since, be the same with that of *Lots* wife; whether this were the hand of *Paul*, or that which is commonly shewn the head of *Peter*, if any doubt, I shall not much dispute with their suspicions. If any men shall not believe the Turpentine Tree, betwixt *Jerusalem* and *Bethlem*, under which the Virgin suckled our Saviour, as she passed between those Cities; or the fig-tree of *Bethany* shewed to this day, whereon *Zacheus* ascended to behold our Saviour; I cannot tell how to enforce his belief, nor do I think it requisite to attempt it. For, as it is no reasonable proceeding to compel a religion, or think to enforce our own belief upon another, who cannot without the concurrence of Gods spirit, have any indubitable evidence of things that are obtruded. So is it also in matters of common belief; whereunto neither can we indubitably assent, without the co-operation of our sense or reason, wherein consist the principles of perswasion. For, as the habit of Faith in Divinity is an Argument of things unseen, and a stable assent unto things inevident, upon authority of the Divine Revealer: So the belief of man which depends upon humane testimony, is but a staggering assent unto the affirmative, not without some fear of the negative. And as there is required the Word of God, or infused inclination unto the one, so must the actual sensation of our senses, at least the non opposition of our reasons procure our assent and acquiescence in the other. So when *Eusebius* an holy Writer affirmeth there grew a strange and unknown plant near the statue of Christ, erected by his Hæmorrhoidal patient in the Gospel, which attaining unto the hem of his vesture, acquired a sudden faculty to cure all diseases. Although he saith he saw the statue in his days, yet hath it not found in many men so much as humane beliefe? Some believing, others opinioning, a third suspective it might be otherwise. For indeed, in matters of belief the understanding assenting unto the relation, either for the authority of the person, or the probability of the object, although there may be a confidence of the one, yet if there be not a satisfaction in the other, there will arise suspensions; nor can we properly believe until some argument of reason, or of our proper sense convince or determine our dubitations.

And thus it is also in matters of certain and experimental truth:

for if unto one that never heard thereof, a man should undertake to perswade the affections of the Load-stone, or that Jet and Amber attracteth straws and light bodies, there would be little Rhetorick in the authority of *Aristotle*, *Pliny*, or any other. Thus, although it be true that the string of a Lute or Viol will stir upon the stroak of an Unison or Diapazon in another of the same kinde; that Alcanna being green, will suddenly infect the nails and other parts with a durable red; that a Candle out of a Musket will pierce through an Inch-board, or an urinal force a naile through a Plank, yet can few or none believe thus much with a visible experiment. Which notwithstanding fals out more happily for knowledge; for these relations leaving unsatisfaction in the Hearers, do stir up ingenuous dubiosities unto experiment, and by an exploration of all, prevent delusion in any.

CHAPTER XIX

Of some Relations whose truth we fear

Lastly, As there are many Relations whereto we cannot assent, and make some doubt thereof, so are there divers others whose verities we fear, and heartily wish there were no truth therein.

1. It is an unsufferable affront unto filiall piety, and a deep discouragement unto the expectation of all aged Parents, who shall but read the story of that barbarous Queen; who after she had beheld her royall Parents ruin, lay yet in the arms of his assassine, and carowsed with him in the skull of her father. For my part, I should have doubted the operation of antimony, where such a potion would not work; 'twas an act me thinks beyond Anthropophagy, and a cup fit to be served up only at the Table of *Atreus*.

2. While we laugh at the story of *Pygmaleon*, and receive as a fable that he fell in love with a statue; we cannot but fear it may be true, what is delivered by *Herodotus* concerning the *Egyptian* Pollinctors, or such as annointed the dead; that some thereof were found in the act of carnality with them. From wits that say 'tis more then incontinency for *Hylas* to sport with *Hecuba*, and youth to flame in the frozen embraces of age, we require a name for this: wherein *Petronius* or *Martial* cannot relieve us. The tyrannie of *Mezentius* did never equall the vitiosity of this *Incubus*, that could embrace corruption, and make a Mistress of the grave; that could not resist the dead provocations of beauty, whose quick invitements scarce excuse submission. Surely, if such depravities there be yet alive, deformity need not despair; nor will the eldest hopes be ever superannuated, since death hath spurs, and carcasses have been courted.

3. I am heartily sorry and wish it were not true, what to the dishonour of Christianity is affirmed of the *Italian*; who after he had

inveighed his enemy to disclaim his faith for the redemption of his life, did presently poyniard him, to prevent repentance, and assure his eternal death. The villany of this Christian exceeded the persecution of Heathens, whose malice was never so Longimanous as to reach the soul of their enemies; or to extend unto the exile of their *Elysiums*. And though the blindness of some ferities have savaged on the bodies of the dead, and been so injurious unto worms, as to disenter the bodies of the deceased; yet had they therefore no design upon the soul: and have been so far from the destruction of that, or desires of a perpetual death, that for the satisfaction of their revenge they wisht them many souls, and were it in their power would have reduced them unto life again. It is a great depravity in our natures, and surely an affection that somewhat savoureth of hell, to desire the society, or comfort our selves in the fellowship of others that suffer with us; but to procure the miseries of others in those extremities, wherein we hold an hope to have no society our selves, is me thinks a strain above *Lucifer*, and a project beyond the primary seduction of hell.

4. I hope it is not true, and some indeed have probably denied, what is recorded of the Monk that poysoned *Henry* the Emperour, in a draught of the holy Eucharist. 'Twas a scandalous wound unto Christian Religion, and I hope all Pagans will forgive it, when they shall read that a Christian was poysoned in a cup of Christ, and received his bane in a draught of his salvation. Had he beleived Transubstantiation, he would have doubted the effect; and surely the sin it self received an aggravation in that opinion. It much commendeth the innocency of our forefathers, and the simplicity of those times, whose Laws could never dream so high a crime as parricide: whereas this at the least may seem to out-reach that fact, and to exceed the regular distinctions of murder. I will not say what sin it was to act it; yet may it seem a kind of martyrdom to suffer by it. For, although unknowingly, he died for Christ his sake, and lost his life in the ordained testimony of his death. Certainly, had they known it, some noble zeales would scarcely have refused it; rather adventuring their own death, then refusing the memorial of his.

Many other accounts like these we meet sometimes in history, scandalous unto Christianity, and even unto humanity; whose verities not only, but whose relations honest minds do deprecate. For of sins heteroclital, and such as want either name or president, there is oft times a sin even in their histories. We desire no records of such enormities; sins should be accounted new, that so they may be esteemed monstrous. They omit of monstrosity as they fall from their rarity; for, men count it veniall to err with their forefathers, and foolishly conceive they divide a sin in its society. The pens of men may sufficiently expatiate without these singularities of villany; For, as they encrease the hatred of vice in some, so do they enlarge the theory of wickedness in all. And this is one thing that may make latter ages worse then were the former; For, the vicious examples of Ages past, poyson the curiosity of these present, affording a hint of sin unto seduceable spirits, and soliciting those unto the imitation of them, whose heads were never so perversly principled as to invent them. In this kind we commend the wisdom and goodness of *Galen*, who would not leave unto the world too subtile a Theory of poysons; unarming thereby the malice of venemous spirits, whose ignorance must be contented with Sublimate and Arsenick. For, surely there are subtiler venenations, such as will invisibly destroy, and like the Basilisks of heaven. In things of this nature silence commendeth history; 'tis the veniable part of things lost; wherein there must never rise a Pancirollus, nor remain any Register but that of hell.

And yet, if as some Stoicks opinion, and *Seneca* himselfe disputeth, these unruly affections that make us sin such prodigies, and even sins themselves be animals; there is an history of *Africa* and story of Snakes in these. And if the transanimation of *Pythagoras* or method thereof were true, that the souls of men transmigrated into species answering their former natures: some men must surely live over many Serpents, and cannot escape that very brood whose sire Satan entered. And though the objection of *Plato* should take place, that bodies subjected unto corruption, must fail at last before the period of all things, and growing fewer in number, must leave some souls apart unto themselves; the spirits of many long before that time will find but naked habitations: and meeting no assimilables wherein to react their natures, must certainly anticipate such natural desolations.

Lactant.

Primus sapientiæ gradus est, falsa intelligere.

F I N I S .

CHAPTER Z

Of Welsh Rabbits

The common opinion of the Welsh Rabbit conceits that it is a species of *Cuniculus* indigenous unto Wales; of which Assertion, if Prescription of time and Numerosity of assertors were a sufficient Demonstration, we might sit down herein as an orthodoxial Truth, nor should there need ulterior Disquisition. *Pliny* discourseth of it under the Head of *De Animalibus Walliæ*. *Seneca* describeth it as an exosseous Animal, or one of the invertebrated or boneless kinde. *Claudian* saith that it delighteth to burrow underground in Coal Holes and Cyder Cellars. *Scaliger* affirmeth it to be like to the Hyæna, incapable of Domitation or taming, for the cause that he never heard of one being domesticated in a Hutch. *Sarenus Sammonicus* determineth it to be like unto the Salamander, moist in the third degre, and to have a mucous Humidity above and under the Epidermis or outer skin, by virtue whereof it endureth the Fire for a time. Nor are such conceits held by Humane authors only, for the holy Fathers of the Church have likewise similarly opinionated. *Austin* declareth it to be an unclean Animal; insomuch that like to the Polecat it is Graveolent, emitting a strong Murine or Micy Effluvium. *Beda* averreth that it is Noctiparent, as the Bat or Owl, and seldom quitteth its Warrene until Midnight, for food; for the reason being that being Coecigneous, or possessing no organs of Vision, it loveth Tenebrosity.

All which notwithstanding, upon strict inquiry, we find the Matter controvertible. *Diodorus,* in his Eleventh Book, affirmeth the Welsh Rabbit to be a creature of Figment, like unto the Sphinx and Snap-Dragon. *Mathiolus,* in his Comment on *Dioscorides,* treateth it not as an Animal, but as a Lark. *Sextius,* a Physitian, sayeth that having well digested the matter, he was compulsed to reject it; whilest *Salmuth* the Commentator of *Pancirollus,* averreth that one *Podocaterus,* a Cyprian, kept one for Months in a Cage, without ever having attained the sight of the remotest Manifestation of Vitality.

Now, besides Authority against it, Experience doth in no way confirm the existence of the Welsh Rabbit as an Animant Entity. But, contrariwise, the principles of Sense and Reason conspire to asseverate it to be, like unto the Myths of Paganism, an Inanimate Body, vivificated by the Ignoration and Superstitiosity of Men. For had they but inquired into the Etymon, or true meaning of the name of the Entity in question, they would have experienced that it was originally merely a Synonyme for a British Dainty, or Cymric Scitamentum; insomuch as it was primitively appellated, The Welsh Tid, or Rare-Bit; which by elision becoming Metamorphosed into Ra'bit, was, from its Homophony, vulgarly supposed to have respect to the *Cuniculus* rather than to the *Scitamentum* of Wales.

Againe, the Doctrine of the Existency of the Welsh Rabbit as a Vivous Entity doth in nowise accord with the three definitive Confirmators and Tests of things dubious: to wit, Experiment, Analysis, and Synthesis. And first by Experiment. For if we send to Wales for one of the Rabbits vernacular to the Princpality, we shall discriminate on the attainment of it, no Difformity in its Organism from that of the Cuniculi vulgar to other Countryes. And if we then proceed to discoriate and exossate the Animal thus attained, or to deprive it of both its Skin and Bones, and after to macerate the residuary Muscular Fibre into a papparious Pulp, we shall experience, upon diffusing the same on an *Offula tosta* or thin slice of toast, that so far from the concoction partaking in the least of the delectable Sapor of the Welsh *Scitamentum,* it will in no way titillate the lingual Papillæ; but, contrariwise, offer inordinate Offence to the Gust.

And, secondly, by Analysis. If, in the stead of sending to Wales, we betake ourselves to any Hostelrie or place of Coenatory Resort, vicine to Covent Garden (whereanent they be celebrious for the concoction of such like Comestibles, for the Deipnophagi or eater of Suppers), and thence provide ourselves with one of the Welsh Rarebits or Scitamenta, whereof we are treating, we shall discriminate upon the Dissolution or Discerption of its Part, that it consisteth not of any Carnal Substance, but simply of a Superstratum of some flavous and adipose Edible, which, to the Sense of Vision, seemeth like unto the Unguent denominated Basilicon, or the Emplastrum appellated Diachylon; whilest to the Sense of Olfaction it beareth an Odour that hath an inviting Caseous or Cheesy Fragor, and fulfilleth all the conditions and Prædicaments of caseous matter or Cheese, which hath undergone the process of Torrefaction; whereof, indeed, if we submit a portion to the Test of Gust, we shall, from the peculiar Sapor appertinent thereto, without Dubitation determine it to consist.

And thirdly and lastly, by Synthesis. If we provide ourselves with about a Selibra or half pound of the Cheese, entitulated *Duplex Glocestrius,* or Double Gloucester; and then go on to cut the intrinsic caseous Matter into tenuous Segments or Laminæ; and, positing such Segments within the coquinary commodity distinguished by Culinarians as the *Furnus Bataviæ* or Dutch Oven, submit the same to the Fire, until by the action of the Caloric they become mollified unto Semiliquidity: whereupon, if we diffuse the caseous fluid on an Offula of Bread, the Superfices whereof hath been previously torrefied, and then Season the same with a slight aspersion of the Sinapine, Piperine, and Saline Condiments, or with Mustard, Pepper, and Salt, we shall find that the Sapor and Fragor thereof differ in no wise from the Gust and Odour of the Edible we had præ-attained from the Covent Garden Coenatorium; and consequentially that the Welsh Rabbit is not, as the Vulgar Pseudodox conceiteth, a species of Cuniculus vernacular to Wales, but as was before predicated, simply a Savoury and Redolent Scitamentum or Rarebit, which is much existimated by the *Cymri* or Welsh people, who, from time prætermemorial, have been cognized as a Philocaseous or Cheese-loving Nation

Also from Benediction Books ...

Wandering Between Two Worlds: Essays on Faith and Art
Anita Mathias
Benediction Books, 2007
152 pages
ISBN: 0955373700

Available from www.amazon.com, www.amazon.co.uk
www.wanderingbetweentwoworlds.com

In these wide-ranging lyrical essays, Anita Mathias writes, in lush, lovely prose, of her naughty Catholic childhood in Jamshedpur, India; her large, eccentric family in Mangalore, a sea-coast town converted by the Portuguese in the sixteenth century; her rebellion and atheism as a teenager in her Himalayan boarding school, run by German missionary nuns, St. Mary's Convent, Nainital; and her abrupt religious conversion after which she entered Mother Teresa's convent in Calcutta as a novice. Later rich, elegant essays explore the dualities of her life as a writer, mother, and Christian in the United States-- Domesticity and Art, Writing and Prayer, and the experience of being "an alien and stranger" as an immigrant in America, sensing the need for roots.

About the Author

Anita Mathias was born in India, has a B.A. and M.A. in English from Somerville College, Oxford University and an M.A. in Creative Writing from the Ohio State University. Her essays have been published in The Washington Post, The London Magazine, The Virginia Quarterly Review, Commonweal, Notre Dame Magazine, America, The Christian Century, Religion Online, The Southwest Review, Contemporary Literary Criticism, New Letters, The Journal, and two of HarperSanFrancisco's The Best Spiritual Writing anthologies. Her non-fiction has won fellowships from The National Endowment for the Arts; The Minnesota State Arts Board; The Jerome Foundation, The Vermont Studio Center; The Virginia Centre for the Creative Arts, and the First Prize for the Best General Interest Article from the Catholic Press Association of the United States and Canada. Anita has taught Creative Writing at the College of William and Mary, and now lives and writes in Oxford, England.

"Yesterday's Treasures for Today's Readers"
Titles by Benediction Classics available from Amazon.co.uk

Religio Medici, Hydriotaphia, Letter to a Friend, Thomas Browne

Pseudodoxia Epidemica: Or, Enquiries into Commonly Presumed Truths, Thomas Browne

Urne Buriall and The Garden of Cyrus, Thomas Browne

The Maid's Tragedy, Beaumont and Fletcher

The Custom of the Country, Beaumont and Fletcher

Philaster Or Love Lies a Bleeding, Beaumont and Fletcher

A Treatise of Fishing with an Angle,   Dame Juliana Berners.

Pamphilia to Amphilanthus, Lady Mary Wroth

The Compleat Angler, Izaak Walton

The Magnetic Lady, Ben Jonson

Every Man Out of His Humour, Ben Jonson

The Masque of Blacknesse. The Masque of Beauty,. Ben Jonson

The Life of St. Thomas More, William Roper

Pendennis, William Makepeace Thackeray

Salmacis and Hermaphroditus attributed to Francis Beaumont

Friar Bacon and Friar Bungay Robert Greene

Holy Wisdom, Augustine Baker

The Jew of Malta and the Massacre at Paris, Christopher Marlowe

Tamburlaine the Great, Parts 1 & 2 AND Massacre at Paris, Christopher Marlowe

All Ovids Elegies, Lucans First Booke, Dido Queene of Carthage, Hero and Leander, Christopher Marlowe

The Titan, Theodore Dreiser

Scapegoats of the Empire: The true story of the Bushveldt Carbineers, George Witton

The Place of The Lion, Charles Williams

The Greater Trumps, Charles Williams

My Apprenticeship: Volumes I and II, Beatrice Webb

Last and First Men / Star Maker, Olaf Stapledon

Last and First Men, Olaf Stapledon

Darkness and the Light, Olaf Stapledon

The Worst Journey in the World, Apsley Cherry-Garrard

The Schoole of Abuse, Containing a Pleasaunt Invective Against Poets, Pipers, Plaiers, Iesters and Such Like Catepillers of the Commonwelth, Stephen Gosson

Russia in the Shadows, H. G. Wells

Wild Swans at Coole, W. B. Yeats

Five hundreth good pointes of husbandrie, Thomas Tusser

The Collected Works of Nathanael West: "The Day of the Locust", "The Dream Life of Balso Snell", "Miss Lonelyhearts", "A Cool Million", Nathanael West

Miss Lonelyhearts & The Day of the Locust, Nathaniel West

The Worst Journey in the World, Apsley Cherry-Garrard

Scott's Last Expedition, V1, R. F. Scott

The Dream of Gerontius, John Henry Newman

The Brother of Daphne, Dornford Yates

The Downfall of Robert Earl of Huntington, Anthony Munday

Clayhanger, Arnold Bennett

The Regent, A Five Towns Story Of Adventure In London , Arnold Bennett

The Card, A Story Of Adventure In The Five Towns , Arnold Bennett

South: The Story of Shackleton's Last Expedition 1914-1917, Sir Ernest Shackketon

Greene's Groatsworth of Wit: Bought With a Million of Repentance, Robert Greene

Beau Sabreur, Percival Christopher Wren

The Hekatompathia, or Passionate Centurie of Love, Thomas Watson

Chamber Music, James Joyce

Blurt, Master Constable, Thomas Middleton, Thomas Dekker

Since Yesterday, Frederick Lewis Allen

The Scholemaster: Or, Plaine and Perfite Way of Teachyng Children the Latin Tong , Roger Ascham

The Wonderful Year, 1603, Thomas Dekker

Waverley, Sir Walter Scott

Guy Mannering, Sir Walter Scott

Old Mortality, Sir Walter Scott

The Knight of Malta, John Fletcher

The Double Marriage, John Fletcher and Philip Massinger

Space Prison, Tom Godwin

The Home of the Blizzard Being the Story of the Australasian Antarctic Expedition, 1911-1914, Douglas Mawson

Wild-goose Chase , John Fletcher

If You Know Not Me, You Know Nobody. Part I and Part II, Thomas Heywood

The Ragged Trousered Philanthropists, Robert Tressell

The Island of Sheep, John Buchan

Eyes of the Woods, Joseph Altsheler

The Club of Queer Trades, G. K. Chesterton

The Financier, Theodore Dreiser

Something of Myself, Rudyard Kipling

Law of Freedom in a Platform, or True Magistracy Restored, Gerrard Winstanley

Damon and Pithias, Richard Edwards

Dido Queen of Carthage: And, The Massacre at Paris, Christopher Marlowe

Cocoa and Chocolate: Their History from Plantation to Consumer, Arthur Knapp

Lady of Pleasure, James Shirley

The South Pole: An account of the Norwegian Antarctic expedition in the "Fram," 1910-12. Volume 1 and Volume 2, Roald Amundsen

A Yorkshire Tragedy, Thomas Middleton (attrib.)

The Tragedy of Soliman and Perseda, Thomas Kyd

The Rape of Lucrece. Thomas Heywood

Myths and Legends of Ancient Greece and Rome, E. M. Berens

In the Forbidden Land, Henry Savage Arnold Landor

Across Unknown South America, by Arnold Henry Savage Landor

Illustrated History of Furniture: From the Earliest to the Present Time, Frederick Litchfield

A Narrative of Some of the Lord's Dealings with George Müller Written by Himself (Parts I-IV, 1805-1856), George Müller

The Towneley Cycle Of The Mystery Plays (Or The Wakefield Cycle): Thirty-Two Pageants, Anonymous

The Insatiate Countesse, John Marston.

Spontaneous Activity in Education, Maria Montessori.

On the Art of Writing, Sir Arthur Quiller-Couch

The Well of the Saints, J. M. Synge

Bacon's Advancement Of Learning And The New Atlantis, Francis Bacon.

Catholic Tales And Christian Songs, Dorothy Sayers.

Two Little Savages: Being the Adventures of Two Boys who Lived as Indians and What they Learned, Ernest Thompson Seton

The Sadness of Christ, Thomas More

The Family of Love, Thomas Middleton

The Passing of the Aborigines: A Lifetime Spent Among the Natives of Australia, Daisy Bates

The Children, Edith Wharton

A Record of European Armour and Arms through Seven Centuries., (Volumes I, II, III, IV and V) Francis Laking

The Book of the Farm: - Detailing The Labours Of The Farmer, Steward, Plowman, Hedger, Cattle-Man, Shepherd, Field-Worker, and Dairymaid. (Volume I), Henry Stephens

The Book of the Farm: - Detailing The Labours Of The Farmer, Steward, Plowman, Hedger, Cattle-Man, Shepherd, Field-Worker, and Dairymaid. (Volume II), Henry Stephens

The Book of the Farm: - Detailing The Labours Of The Farmer, Steward, Plowman, Hedger, Cattle-Man, Shepherd, Field-Worker, and Dairymaid. (Volume III). by Henry Stephens

The Naturalist On The River Amazons, by Henry Walter Bates.

Antarctic Penguins: A Study of their Social Habits, Dr. George Murray Levick

The Dragon's Secret, Augusta Huiell Seaman.

The Nonsense Books: A Complete Collection of the Nonsense Books of Edward Lear, Edward Lear

The Cestus of Aglaia and The Queen of the Air With Other Papers and Lecture on Art and Literature, 1860-1870, John Ruskin.

and many others…

Tell us what you would love to see in print again, at affordable prices!
Email: **benedictionbooks@btinternet.com**

CPSIA information can be obtained
at www.ICGtesting.com
Printed in the USA
LVHW111653250219
608674LV00024B/1214/P

9 781849 029377